TOP
MBA
PROGRAMS

Finding the Best Business School for You

David Petersam
Founder of AdmissionsConsultants

Top MBA Programs

Finding the Best Business School for You

© 2010 by David Petersam

Published by JIST Works, an imprint of JIST Publishing
7321 Shadeland Station, Suite 200
Indianapolis, IN 46256-3923

Phone: 800-648-JIST   Fax: 877-454-7839
E-mail: info@jist.com   Web site: www.jist.com

Quantity discounts are available for JIST products. Please call our Sales Department at 800-648-JIST for a free catalog and more information.

Visit www.jist.com for information on JIST, tables of contents, sample pages, and online ordering.

Acquisitions Editor: Susan Pines
Copy Editors: Stephanie Koutek, Chuck Hutchinson, Kelly Henthorne
Cover Designer: Amy Adams
Interior Designer and Layout: Toi Davis
Proofreaders: Paula Lowell, Jeanne Clark
Indexer: Cheryl Lenser

Printed in the United States of America

14 13 12 11 10 09   9 8 7 6 5 4 3 2 1

Library of Congress Cataloging-in-Publication Data

Petersam, David, 1970-
  Top MBA programs : finding the best business school for you / David Petersam.
    p. cm.
  Includes index.
  ISBN 978-1-59357-673-8 (includes cd-rom : alk. paper)
 1. Master of business administration degree. 2. Business schools. 3.
Business education. I. Title.
  HF1111.P48 2010
  658.0071'1--dc22

                              2009035468

We have been careful to provide accurate information throughout this book, but it is possible that errors and omissions have been introduced. Please consider this in making any career plans or other important decisions. Trust your own judgment above all else and in all things.

ISBN 978-1-59357-673-8

ABOUT THIS BOOK AND CD-ROM

If you are trying to decide where to go for dinner, would you make your decision based solely on my advice or the advice of another person or entity? Of course not. You realize the subjectivity of something like choosing a restaurant.

Think of the top 5 to 10 business schools as five-star restaurants and the remainder as four-star restaurants. In other words, the chances are very high that you will have a pleasant experience at any of those schools. However, given a choice between a good experience and a life-altering experience, which would you choose? Because few people ever experience a life-altering job, earning your Master of Business Administration very well may be your best chance for career-related nirvana.

Now consider that an MBA will cost a huge multiple of a five-star restaurant bill and that it will constitute one to two years of your life—again a huge multiple of the few hours tops you will spend dining on any particular meal.

No single source of information can tell you how to decide where to apply for your MBA. Hearsay from friends and colleagues is a matter of opinion and may not match you because their experiences are subjective. Ask graduates from the top business schools profiled in this guide, and they will tell you how the graduate business school experience has changed and enriched their lives. Press them for more details, and they will undoubtedly tell you about the analytical frameworks that changed the way they view the world and that are highly powerful tools for helping them strengthen their employers' competitive standing and, in turn, their own career trajectories.

A key purpose of this book is to serve as a useful tool for your career mapping. Not only do you maximize your admission chances by accurately selecting your best-fit schools, but selectivity is the only way you will get the most out of your graduate business education and provide yourself with the best chance to achieve your post-MBA career ambitions. I've included tips to help you navigate the entire process from whether an MBA is the optimal degree for your needs to tips for success after you've started your MBA.

At the back of this book, you will find a CD-ROM that provides access to the AdmissionsConsultants' Web site with thousands of pieces of data about the top schools profiled in this guide. Use this interactive resource to help determine which selection factors are most important to you and then to select the best schools for your needs.

Quite simply, this book has been painstakingly developed to be the next best thing to visiting each of these campuses yourself, which, by the way, is something you

(continued)

(continued)

are encouraged to do—if not before you apply, then certainly before you accept any admission offers.

It really is that simple and straightforward. Welcome to your best-fit business school education.

Is this book right for you?

Before you dive in, make sure that this information is right for you. This book assumes that you are applying to one or more of the 31 top U.S. and international business schools profiled in Part IV. The concept of fit can be applied to any business school (or, for that matter, to any type of educational program, period). However, this guide focuses exclusively on the 31 top business schools worldwide. This book spotlights these schools because they are the ones about which most applicants want detailed information, especially regarding finding their best fit.

ACKNOWLEDGMENTS

This book has been a collaborative effort, and I could not have done it without help.

Thank you to these expert professionals:

Cindy Baquiran, Diane Baraclough, Nancy Bennett, Heather Berk, Doug Braithwaite, Elisa Cottrell, Maria Cvitkovic, Pamela DeLoatch, Ron Dicker, Ann Driscoll, Carol Dunlap, Eric Erikson, Melanie Florence, Cristina Freeman, Kent Harrill, John Heiser, Cheryl Hosmer, Vishal Ingole, Amy Johnson, Amy Kurtz, Jess Landers, Mennette Larkin, Denise Lee, Patrick May, Sheryl McCormick, Gina McDonnell, Paul McGarrity, Johnny Nguyen, Kathryn Owens, Jennifer Petersam, John Petersam, Susan Pines, Kathryn Owens, Ben Rome, Karen Schwartz, Mindy Schwartz, Michie Shaw, Heike Spahn, Cindy Sullivan, Chris Thompson, Elandee Thompson, Yana Try, Lauren Wagner, Sari Warren, Sarah Wheeler, Sara Withee, Matt Whittaker, and Nicole Witt

With the help of AccelerMark, LLC, thousands of surveys from students, alumni, and corporate recruiters were compiled.

In selecting the final MBA programs, these standout programs were also considered:

Babson College, Olin

Brigham Young, Marriott

CEIBS

ESADE

HEC Montreal/HEC Paris

IIM, Indian Institutes of Management

IIT, Indian Institutes of Technology

IMD

Michigan State University, Broad

Ohio State University, Fisher

Purdue, Krannert

Southern Methodist University, Cox

Texas A&M, Mays

University of Arizona, Eller

University of Iowa, Tippie

University of Illinois, Urbana-Champaign

University of Minnesota, Twin Cities, Carlson

University of Rochester, Simon

Washington University in St. Louis, Olin

York University, Schulick

CONTENTS

INTRODUCTION I

PART I: SETTING YOUR FOUNDATION 5

Chapter 1: What Is the Value of the MBA Degree? 6

Measuring Value 6

Beware the Incentivized Endorsement 7

Value of a "Brand" School Degree 8

Other Considerations Related to an MBA's Value 9

Chapter 2: What Fit Is and Why It Matters 11

What Does Fit Mean? 12

Why Fit Matters to Schools—and to You 13

A Study in Fit 15

Chapter 3: What Are the Fit Factors? 18

Tell Me What You Really Want 19

The Role of Rankings 19

Accreditation: What Does It Mean? 20

What Are the Teaching Styles? 21

A School's Profile and What It Means to You 21

Research, Ask, Explore 24

What Schools Want from You 25

PART II: BUILDING YOUR DREAM 27

Chapter 4: What It Means to Position Yourself 28

View Your Candidacy the Same Way as an Admissions Committee Does ... 29

Getting the Timing Right 30

The Dilemma of Return on Investment 31

When Is the Timing Right? 32

The Hurdle of Test Scores 33

Prepare and Review, and Then Act 34

Will Your Undergrad School Affect Your Chance of Admission to a Top MBA Program? 35

Improving Standardized Test Scores 37

Admissions Committee Perspective on Your Transcript 38

Transcripts Not All They Could Be? Try an Alternative 39

Recommenders Are Crucial 40

The Right Number of Recommendations 41

Your Message 41

Chapter 5: What It Means to Manage Your Applications 42

Outlining Your Application Tasks 43

Know Your Due Dates 44

Timeline for What to Do When 45

Wrap It Up 50

Chapter 6: What Is Your Essay Master Plan? 51

How to Strategize and Stay Organized 51

Different Types of Essay Questions 52

How to Approach and Write Your Essays 52

Drafting Your Essays and Creating Your Themes 54

Grammar and Spelling Do Matter! 56

A Holistic Approach 57

Are You Ready to Submit? 58

**Chapter 7: What to Do After You Have Submitted Your
Applications** 59

The Waiting Game 59

What Happens to Your Application After You Submit It 60

An Invitation to Interview: Now What? 62

The Interview 63

Avoiding Common Interview Mistakes 64

Backup Plans and How to Devise Them 65

The Final Decision: Your Wait Is Over 66

**Chapter 8: What It Means to Deal with Acceptance, Waitlists,
and Rejection** 67

How to Anticipate Your Acceptance Letter 68

What to Do When Facing Multiple Acceptance Letters 68

What the Waitlist Process Means to You 70

What a Deferral Means 71

How to Handle Rejection 72

Assess the Values and Strategies of a Reapplication 73

Good "Admit" Etiquette 73

PART III: MOVING IN AND MOVING ON 75

   Chapter 9: What to Do Before You Matriculate 76

      How to Leave Work on Good Terms 76

      How B-School Differs from College or Work 77

      How to Face the Basics—Housing, Transportation, Banking, and More ... 78

      Start Your Career Research Early and Get a Jump on the Competition....... 80

      How to Perfect the Art of Preparing to Perform 81

   Chapter 10: What Is the Business School Balancing Act? 82

      How to Hit the Ground Running and Get the Most from Your Classes 83

      Why Business School Is More Than Your GPA 85

      How to Use Career Services, Networking, and Other Resources
        Effectively 87

      How Alumni Help with Career Placement 87

      Managing Your Emotions 89

   Chapter 11: Putting It All Together 90

PART IV: TOP BUSINESS SCHOOLS 93

   Carnegie Mellon University: David A. Tepper School of Business 95

   Columbia University: Columbia Business School 107

   Cornell University: S.C. Johnson Graduate School of Management 120

   Dartmouth College: Tuck School of Business 132

   Duke University: The Fuqua School of Business 143

   Emory University: Goizueta Business School.. 155

   Georgetown University: Robert E. McDonough School of Business...... 166

   Harvard University: Harvard Business School 178

   Indiana University: Kelley School of Business...................................... 191

   Massachusetts Institute of Technology (MIT): Alfred P. Sloan
     School of Management... 203

   New York University: Leonard N. Stern School of Business 215

   Northwestern University: Kellogg School of Management...................... 228

   Stanford University: Graduate School of Business 243

   University of California, Berkeley: Walter A. Haas School
     of Business... 255

   University of California, Los Angeles (UCLA): Anderson School
     of Management... 267

   The University of Chicago: Booth School of Business.............................. 279

University of Maryland: Robert H. Smith School of Business 292

University of Michigan: Stephen M. Ross School of Business................. 305

University of North Carolina at Chapel Hill: Kenan-Flagler
    Business School 318

University of Pennsylvania: The Wharton School of Business 329

University of Southern California: Marshall School of Business............. 342

University of Texas at Austin: McCombs School of Business 354

University of Virginia: Darden Graduate School of Business
    Administration 367

Vanderbilt University: Owen Graduate School of Management............. 379

Yale University: Yale School of Management 391

Indian School of Business (ISB) 402

INSEAD Business School: Institut Européen d'Administration
    des Affaires 414

London Business School 427

University of Navarra: IESE Business School... 438

University of Toronto: Joseph L. Rotman School of Management.......... 451

University of Western Ontario: Richard Ivey School of Business........... 464

Appendix: About the Accompanying CD-ROM 476

Index 479

INTRODUCTION

Right Fit, Right School, Right Direction

Since her freshman year at Northwestern University, Stacy had her eye on business school. A double major in economics and marketing, Stacy was active in Gamma Phi Delta, a professional business woman's sorority. She also founded and led a marketing club—all while maintaining a 3.8 GPA and graduating with distinction. After graduation, she went to work for Motorola and distinguished herself as a smart, creative, and capable worker. She rose quickly to a departmental management position, introducing innovative marketing concepts while reducing costs. Stacy impressed her supervisors and team members with her quick thinking and solid decision-making skills.

After some discussion with her supervisor, she decided that pursuing an MBA degree was the right course to move her forward on her career track. Stacy celebrated her twenty-sixth birthday by submitting her application to Harvard Business School. In the weeks that followed, she applied to Northwestern's Kellogg School of Management, Columbia Business School, and Michigan's Ross School of Business—schools she selected for their strong marketing programs. She was looking forward to celebrating her twenty-seventh birthday as a first-year MBA student at one of these schools.

Unfortunately, when admissions decisions were released a few months later, she learned that she had been waitlisted (basically put on a waiting list) at Kellogg and Columbia and rejected by Harvard and Michigan Ross. Where had she gone wrong?

Many potential MBAs are like Stacy. Interested candidates often make the too-common mistake of assuming that all MBA programs are alike. In reality, the top schools take different approaches to business education and applicant selection. At Harvard, students analyze densely written case histories in give-and-take classroom sessions. Conversely, students at Michigan Ross develop intuitive connections between theory and practice through experiential learning. The Stanford University MBA experience is based on a tight community setting, which is reinforced through the shared on-campus living. Students at the University of Virginia's Darden School of Business tackle a curriculum that alumni describe only half-jokingly as business boot camp.

With such a broad array of degrees, programs, curricula, and teaching methods, it is easy to see that one particular MBA is not always more valuable than others. What admissions committees look for in particular is called *fit,* where the prospective student's lifestyle, learning methods, career goals, and experiences mesh with the program that best suits him or her to produce a better business leader, innovator, and alum. Finding the right school that fits is a process started by the applicant and finalized by the committee. Qualified students who are successful in communicating their cases are most likely to be accepted to the program that best works for them.

Where School Selectivity and Personal Fit Meet

Successful admission to an MBA program occurs when school selectivity and personal fit connect. Selectivity is school-driven and is all about what the school wants in an applicant. Personal fit is applicant-driven and is all about what you want out of a school's program. The purpose of this book is to help you find the best-fit MBA programs for you and to help you articulate how you are a perfect fit for that program.

MBA applications are on the increase, and this rise breeds fierce competition. The applications are an exhaustive and comprehensive view of who you are. Schools want to know so much about you that you may become convinced you are preparing your autobiography! Extensive preparation is a must for the arduous task of applying to top MBA programs. Although this process could feel invasive, it serves to weed through competing applications on several levels including academic ability, work progression, career vision, need for an MBA, leadership potential, diversity, and of course, fit.

What's in This Book?

Anyone who has applied to business school can tell you that it is a complicated and time-intensive process that includes choosing your schools, researching your schools, visiting your schools, juggling your recommenders, ordering transcripts, studying for and taking the GMAT (or in some cases the GRE), filling out applications, preparing for interviews, and—most time-consuming of all—writing your essays.

It is this book's goal to provide you with the tools to move through this process in an organized, efficient manner that allows your strengths to shine through and arms you with the greatest chances for admission to *your* top-ranked schools.

The first part ("Setting Your Foundation") helps you plan and set your foundation. The chapters help you think about the value of the MBA. Would an MBA add value to your resume and career? Do you really need an MBA to get where you are going? If your answer is yes, then you need to plan your application strategy. Yet how will you know to which schools you should apply? School selection should be taken seriously and not simply left to rankings. There are many considerations when developing your long and short list of school programs. You explore how fit should drive your school selection.

In Part II ("Building Your Dream"), you get detailed suggestions on how to effectively position yourself and manage your application process, especially when applying to several schools. You find critical advice for developing your essay strategy, content, and themes. Essays are the heart of the application, allowing admissions committees to learn more about who you are. Essays are your opportunity to stand out and tell your story in a powerful way. The chapters guide you through the process before, during, and after you complete your application and suggest ways to navigate school offers and rejections successfully.

Further, in Part III ("Moving In and Moving On"), you learn what you should do before you matriculate and how to position yourself to succeed once on campus.

The fourth part ("Top Business Schools") contains in-depth narratives on 31 of the top business schools in the world. These extensive profiles were compiled through a combination of campus visits, interviews, questionnaires, and one-on-one focus group discussions. The focus group discussions with students were used to build the level of trust necessary to help uncover the real scoop and dig deeper than the survey-based methodology allows. These profiles help you tap into a school's personality and assist you as you explain to admissions officers why you are a perfect fit with their program. Although you should never allow anyone else's judgment to substitute for your own, these profiles will aid your school selection process and offer unique views of the schools.

And finally, the CD-ROM contains your AdmissionsConsultants' Web site subscription. This information helps you determine your unique business school rankings based on your values, interests, and needs. In addition, the book's business school profiles are kept up to date on the site. Admissions-Consultants has been helping business school applicants since 1996 and is passionate about assisting clients.

Together, the resources in this book will help you target the right schools and prepare applications that tell admissions committees what they need to know to see you for the perfect-fit applicant that you are.

PART I

SETTING YOUR FOUNDATION

Chapter 1. **What Is the Value of the MBA Degree?** Distinguishing a Golden Goose from a Tinfoil Turkey

Chapter 2. **What Fit Is and Why It Matters.** Forcing Square Pegs into Round Holes

Chapter 3. **What Are the Fit Factors?** Learning How the Little Things Make a Big Difference

WHAT IS THE VALUE OF THE MBA DEGREE?

DISTINGUISHING A GOLDEN GOOSE FROM A TINFOIL TURKEY

Mike believed an MBA would be his ticket to success. It was a way to increase his worth—and his salary. So he was determined to go to business school directly from college. That way he could step onto the fast track rather than waste his time slogging through an entry-level job. Unfortunately for Mike, not every MBA degree is equal its weight in future career benefits.

Although Mike did receive his MBA straight out of college, his projected career track lagged appreciably behind many of his colleagues at his company. He was their same age and possessed a similar background and experience, yet his colleagues had taken the time to research their options and chose to increase their valuable job experience before pursuing an MBA. When Mike entered the workforce, they were leaving it to pursue their degrees and ended up rehired by the company at a much higher level. One of them even became Mike's new supervisor.

Many misconceptions exist about what applicants can and cannot realistically expect from an MBA program. This chapter sets the record straight on what an MBA education's value is, how important where you get your degree from is, and what benefits come from earning the degree.

Measuring Value

The value of an MBA is determined by the individual seeking an MBA, employers and recruiters, and the business world at large. The successful effect of an MBA on your resume depends on how you engage in your career interests during your educational experience, your internships, your networking, and your success with career services. The value of the MBA then takes shape by how you conduct your career and how the business world perceives your achievements.

> ## "WE'RE GOING TO PERMANENTLY CHANGE THE WAY YOU THINK ABOUT THE WORLD AROUND YOU."
>
> These words, or something nearly verbatim, were declared by Robert Hamada, then dean of the University of Chicago Booth School of Business on one of my first days at the b-school. To say that I was skeptical would have been an understatement. I bought into another concept he presented: I was going to be stretched and challenged and would emerge stronger after the two years.
>
> This made sense based on the career progression I had achieved to this point as well as my ability to translate his statement to a weight-resistance metaphor. But change the way I think? No, I wasn't buying it. Yet by the time I graduated I couldn't stop myself from trying to apply the many new analytical frameworks and game theories I had learned at Booth to all kinds of everyday issues, and it wouldn't take long for me to realize how cocky I was when I first matriculated into the school.
>
> The truth is my experience isn't unique. My classmates all felt the same way I did, and I've since spoken to countless MBAs from other top schools who wholeheartedly agree with this transformation. So, when you embark for your MBA, be prepared to have the way you think about the world permanently changed. It's okay if you're skeptical. Just don't say I didn't tell you so!

Top MBA programs provide high-quality, rigorous management education training facilitated by prestigious faculty. The faculty members who conduct the classes have earned their prestige through research and vital contributions in their areas of expertise. In some instances, a faculty member may have written the text you are using. In addition, many top schools boast Nobel laureates among both teaching and retired faculty.

It is common for students to juggle intense classes with hours of group work, reading, and homework. At the same time, they are preparing for internship or job searches and participating in one or more clubs or student activities. The full-time MBA experience offers leadership opportunities, internships, networking, career development, study abroad options, involvement in clubs and extracurricular activities, and real-world learning experiences. Earning your degree is a life-changing experience that bonds you to the institution and to the people with whom you have shared the experience. You will find that you value your MBA because of how drastically it changes your career path. Employers value it because of the proven results that top MBA employees have repeatedly executed.

Beware the Incentivized Endorsement

All kinds of educational institutions earn profits from students' paid tuition. The difference between not-for-profit and for-profit business schools is in how profits are generated. After reading a Web site endorsement, many people pay for a for-profit MBA degree without understanding what they are getting.

Do you know what "online MBA programs rule!" types of ads really represent? For-profit "schools" typically pay $25 or more for each potential student referral generated from their advertisements scattered across a multitude of Web sites. A referral can be as simple as a computer user clicking on the ad and transferring to an online school's information Web site. And each student who signs up for a degree program represents a huge contribution margin to these for-profit schools.

Although these programs are appropriate options for many people and for many reasons, they are very different from a degree through an established university. For-profit degrees have their value. The business world in general values these MBA programs the least, however, and most of the value lies with the individual receiving it, often based on his or her goal in earning it. The drawbacks can include minimal networking, no school involvement, lack of internships, and nonexistent career services. One reason that online programs may earn the least respect is that they generally do not have strict admissions parameters. To obtain the most from an online degree, make sure the associated school is properly accredited and reputable.

Not-for-profit schools no doubt earn a profit in some cases, but they spend significant money on finding the best students for their programs (not just the largest number of prospective students they can attract) and on providing the best faculty and resources. Their "profits" are used to increase their endowment and subsidize the rest of the university's programs. Their students receive a stellar education.

In the United States, one of the most respected accrediting bodies for business schools is the Association to Advance Collegiate Schools of Business International. Many for-profit school students receive an education without the benefit of AACSB oversight. AACSB is discussed in further detail in Chapter 3. Accreditation ensures that your education meets high standards that support excellence in management education. AACSB International accreditation represents one of the highest standards of achievement for business schools worldwide. Institutions that earn accreditation confirm their commitment to quality and continuous improvement through a rigorous and comprehensive peer review.

Value of a "Brand" School Degree

All programs are not created equal. Hundreds of MBA programs exist, but most people have heard only of the top 30 or so. This book provides details on the top 31 programs worldwide. Rankings and perception highly influence the value of an MBA, certainly to the individual earning it, and more importantly to the top employers. Your goal is to find the MBA program that adds the most value to your resume. You need to look closely at your programs of interest to determine whether they can add value. Consider each program's strengths and weaknesses by learning about the school's career services, recruiting results, internships, financial aid, scholarships, faculty, curriculum, teaching style, clubs, extracurricular activities, facilities, resources, networking, prestige, and community environment.

> **YOUR CLASSMATES SHOULDN'T LEAN ON YOU, THEY SHOULD PUSH YOU.**
>
> Business school requires group work, which means lots of collaboration and teamwork. At a lower-tier b-school, you may find you are the big fish in a small pond. If this happens, your classmates will be leaning on you and teaching you very little compared to what you teach them.
>
> Don't think for a second that this will happen at a top-tier school. Your classmates will be so bright, talented, and diverse that you will learn plenty from them. This is a good thing. After all, you will spend more time with them than with your professors.
>
> To put it another way, if you want to improve your athletic skills, you would have a higher ceiling for improvement if you practiced with professionals instead of beginners.

How valuable is attending a top-tier MBA program? For the most part, a top-tier MBA education is exceedingly valuable. The typical student in these schools possesses exceptional motivation, intelligence, and academic excellence and receives more and better opportunities in the work world with his or her degree. In general, a top-school graduate commands a higher salary and has more promotion opportunities than lower-tiered MBAs after graduation. A top-tier school also prompts the most attention from recruiters, has more networking resources, employs the most sought-after faculty, offers the most clubs and activities, and provides more international study experiences.

Mid-tier MBA programs have their unique value as well. There are so many strong programs that simply do not make the top-tier rankings and perception cut. They have a strong curriculum and faculty, but they may not have as many resources, especially in career services. For example, a strong regional school can provide an excellent education coupled with strong recruiting opportunities specific to that region. If you are interested in employment in your region after graduation, the value of a mid-tier can come close to that of an out-of-region, top-tier school. Research has shown that many students attending rigorous MBA programs remain in the geographical area to pursue their next job. Mid-tier programs also tend to offer more scholarship programs, making them very attractive.

Other Considerations Related to an MBA's Value

Selectivity makes a big difference in your application strategies. The part-time MBA program at your local university might well be the best fit for your interests and needs. It teaches management skills well, it has a class schedule that allows you to continue working while you get your degree, its faculty and student body will expand your contacts with the local business community, and your employer may pay part of your tuition. If those things are important to you, you've made a good decision by picking that program. Yet in most cases you probably don't need this book's help to prepare a successful application.

Although this book is for applicants to the top-tier schools, it would be remiss not to address some of the most common reasons students decide not to attend one of the many fine schools that are included in Part IV. One consideration is convenience. Sometimes applicants have family or other obligations that make an out-of-town program unfeasible. Another concern is the high cost of switching jobs. Some applicants don't intend to leave their current employers but need an MBA for advancement. Their employers love them and aren't attached to where they obtain their degree. Further, applicants have personal preferences and may have a strong need to stay in a particular geographic region that has more jobs of interest or wish to be a part of a particular campus. Area friends, the desire to support a sports team, or affinity for a hometown can outweigh broader life experiences or wider career options at a top MBA program.

SHOULD YOU CONSIDER A JOINT OR DUAL DEGREE?

Maybe you are considering a combined degree or two degrees (one of which is your MBA). As an applicant for these programs, you need to be very clear about why you want both degrees. Pursuing an additional degree because it seems "cool" is going to wear thin once you recognize all of the work and money that goes into completing these types of programs.

When you review a school's programs, keep in mind the definitions of a joint degree versus a dual degree. Some applicants may mistakenly believe they are the same thing. A joint degree is awarded by more than one school. You receive one degree in two areas from two different institutions. For example, you may receive an MBA and an MD. For each, you need to apply to the separate schools for acceptance, even if the schools are under the same university umbrella.

A dual degree is pursued in different fields at the same school. To earn both degrees, the curriculum is set up to satisfy the requirements simultaneously. For example, you may receive an MBA followed by a PhD. Requirements for your MBA are applied to your PhD because it is an expansion of information in the same field. Often full-time students in dual-degree programs take courses in the summer to complete the course load in time.

Some applicants may value a distance-learning program. These programs have the benefit of offering the same degree to their distance learner students as to the full-time MBA students. These types of programs are geared toward executives and usually have limited residency requirements combined with virtual learning.

The MBA is thought to be losing its remarkable high standing as an advanced degree, in part because its proven value spawned a general demand for business degrees for more and more company employees. The desirability of the Master of Business Administration designation rose because of the excellent educational advances developed by leading universities. Now this market is being flooded with online and nonaccredited programs, which certainly address the needs of many people. However, top-tier and mid-tier MBAs remain in their own category and maintain a high value in the business world.

Chapter 2

WHAT IS FIT AND WHY IT MATTERS

FORCING SQUARE PEGS INTO ROUND HOLES

Everyone who knew her was shocked. Didn't Maria realize that Harvard was the best, the most prestigious, the hardest-to-get-into business school in the United States? How could she turn down the chance to go there?

In fact, Maria knew exactly what she was doing. She had thought carefully about why she wanted an MBA degree and what she wanted to do with it. She developed her personal ranking of schools that fit her goals. She also had some personal preferences about where she attended school. She preferred small schools to big ones, the Northeast to the West or Midwest, and small towns to big cities.

The decision between Harvard University and Cornell University wasn't easy, but in the end Cornell edged out Harvard in all of the categories that Maria cared about most. The deal maker was that Cornell offered Maria a special opportunity that fulfilled one of her top criteria: She was awarded admission to the Park Leadership Fellow Program that offers a full tuition scholarship for two years to outstanding students who demonstrate leadership. She also preferred the smaller class size and the reputation of faculty availability and the immersion learning method. So she accepted Cornell's offer, received a top-notch MBA education, and had a great time. That choice enabled her to launch her own business within one year of obtaining her degree—a goal she probably would have had to postpone if she had chosen to attend Harvard. With her Cornell fellowship, she graduated without school debt and was able to build her business model and possibly take on debt for her start-up. If she had attended Harvard, years of paying off student loans would have prohibited any financial flexibility.

Maria was able to tap into her values and base her MBA program choice on what mattered most to her. In doing so, she received the MBA that best supported her career goals.

Most unsuccessful MBA applicants aren't dinged on qualifications. They are dinged on fit. Applicants who do best in graduate school are objective in their search and not preoccupied by a school's name or prestige.

Applicants sometimes complain that school selection turns out to be more time-consuming than they thought. That's usually because there are so many factors to consider when deciding which business schools are the best fits. But the difference that careful school selection can make to application outcomes makes it well worth the time and trouble. This is all the more reason why it is smart to get started on this step of the application process early—at least three months before the deadline.

Regardless of the economy or the MBA job market, the one truth in business school admissions year after year is that the vast majority of applicants to the top MBA programs are turned down. Harvard, for example, receives approximately 10 applications for every seat in its MBA program. The Wharton School, Stanford, and Kellogg have similarly high application volumes. Acceptance rates at the more accommodating of the top schools seldom rise above 20 percent. Statistically, any applicant's chances of winning admission to a top MBA program are usually no better than one in five. This book was written to help you understand a simple and powerful concept that can improve those odds in your favor: the concept of your business school fit.

Most unsuccessful applicants are not declined acceptance based on qualification. In fact, admissions committees know that most MBA applicants meet or exceed the minimum expectations for work experience, GMAT (or GRE) performance, and undergraduate GPA. Where most applications fall short is more complex and subtle: They fail to provide one or more key pieces of information that would make an admissions committee feel confident about welcoming the applicant into its program. Much of the time, this missing information is related to the issue of fit.

What Does Fit Mean?

At first glance, the concept of fit may seem like a superficial quality. People tend to think of it in social contexts, as in whether someone fits in with a certain clique or group. And most of us don't like to say that someone doesn't fit in. It sounds elitist, exclusionist, or just plain mean.

But fit has a different meaning in organizations. It has to do with how well an individual's abilities, ambitions, and values complement those of the organization. When individuals and organizations are in sync, both benefit. The organization receives productive workers, committed members, or enthusiastic students. The individual receives a supportive and appreciative home for his or her efforts and growth.

Imagine yourself as a hiring manager who has interviewed two job candidates with identical qualifications. One candidate gave you the impression that she was applying for this job simply because she needed a job and was qualified for this one. You suspect that she sent the same résumé and cover letter to a lot of other companies, too. The other candidate wrote a cover letter that indicated she had researched your company and learned something about its history and operations. In the interview, she told you three specific things about this particular opening that appealed to her and fit into her long-term career goals. She told you why she thought her work experience and skills would complement the position you have open as well as the company's work culture.

Which candidate would you hire? If you're like most people, your answer is candidate two. Why? Because she showed an interest in your company and understood the position you were trying to fill. She demonstrated that she had work experience and abilities of specific value to your company, and she persuaded you that she would gain more from the job than just the paycheck. That's an employer-employee match you can get excited about. That's fit.

Why Fit Matters to Schools—and to You

MBA admissions committees feel much the same way about accepting students as employers do about hiring staff. They don't want students who are mediocre. They want students who are great. They look for candidates who are genuinely drawn to their school and who seem likely to thrive in its academic and social environment. They want students who will connect with faculty, bond with classmates, and contribute to the alumni network. In short, they want students with fit.

Fit should be an important consideration on your side of the admissions process, too. You will maximize your chances of winning admission to an MBA program if you target the schools that best fit your interests, needs, and values. Moreover, you'll get the most out of your MBA investment by getting your degree at one of your best-fit schools.

So what are your best-fit schools? That's a question only you can answer. The answer is not in the rankings or in the experience of someone you know. It is with you and your talents and aspirations. Many grad school applicants may think they want to go to Harvard and only Harvard or Wharton and only Wharton, but often this is simply not true. If a student is accepted into a program and finds the experience to be miserable and grueling, he chose the wrong program. What is miserable and grueling at school will carry over into the jobs he is offered and the career he will build.

This book and the accompanying CD-ROM provide access to data and analytical tools that you can use to identify which of the 31 highly selective U.S. and international business schools best match your career goals, educational needs, and personal preferences.

The first step in identifying your best-fit business schools is to abandon any idea you might have that all of the top schools are alike. There are certainly many similarities among them: They all prepare students for general management careers, they all offer extensive career placement services, and they all look good on a résumé. But more differences than similarities exist among the schools, especially from a student's perspective.

Take, for example, the simple question of class size. How large was your high school graduating class? How did you feel about being a member of a group that size? Did you like being one of a class of 250 seniors because it was small enough that you were able to know everyone's name? Or did you thrive on the energy and diversity that came with 1,000 peers?

Now take a look at this table, which compares first-year MBA enrollment:

Schools by MBA Program Size (Class of 2010)

University of Maryland, Smith (Maryland)	133
University of Western Ontario, Ivey (Ontario, Canada)	144
Emory University, Goizueta (Georgia)	158
Vanderbilt University, Owen (Tennessee)	176
Yale School of Management (Connecticut)	193

(continued)

(continued)

Carnegie-Mellon University, Tepper (Pennsylvania)	210
IESE (Barcelona, Spain)	215
University of Southern California, Marshall (California)	219
Indiana University, Kelley (Indiana)	227
Dartmouth College, Tuck (New Hampshire)	240
University of California Berkeley, Hass (California)	240
Georgetown University, McDonough (Washington, D.C.)	256
University of Toronto, Rotman (Toronto, Canada)	262
University of Texas Austin, McCombs (Texas)	264
Cornell University, Johnson (New York)	272
University of North Carolina, Kenan-Flagler (North Carolina)	279
London Business School (London)	320
University of Virginia, Darden (Virginia)	333
Massachusetts Institute of Technology, Sloan (Massachusetts)	350
University of California Los Angeles, Anderson (California)	360
Stanford Graduate School of Business (California)	370
New York University, Stern (New York)	410
Duke University, Fuqua (North Carolina)	434
University of Michigan, Ross (Michigan)	434
INSEAD (France and Singapore)	457
Northwestern University, Kellogg (Illinois)	485
Columbia Business School (New York)	539
University of Chicago, Booth (Illinois)	550
Indian School of Business (India)	569
University of Pennsylvania, Wharton (Pennsylvania)	800
Harvard Business School (Massachusetts)	900

At which school do you think you would feel most at home?

Of course, class size is only one of many factors that will influence how comfortable you would be in different programs. You may feel that it's not an important factor in school selection at all. Or you may feel that it's a significant factor but that you'd be willing to trade off on class size to gain another benefit. For example, someone might like the idea of being in a program with just a few hundred classmates but would still be thrilled to go to Wharton or Harvard because that's where her ideal employers recruit most heavily. Besides, Harvard and Wharton, like many other schools, assign first-year students to smaller *cohorts* (also called sections or teams) so you could be sure that, on a day-to-day basis, you would interact with a more manageable number of people.

School fit covers other, more complex aspects of school selection and admissions, too. To explore some of these issues, look at a hypothetical case based on the experiences of some typical MBA applicants.

A Study in Fit

Jin is a financial analyst with a top brokerage firm. He maintained a 4.0 GPA as an undergrad at a prestigious college and has a near-perfect GMAT score. His participation and leadership in several extracurricular activities and charity work kept him busy during his undergraduate studies. He wants an MBA to advance his career in the financial services industry. Jin believes in quality. His lifelong philosophy has been to aim high and accept nothing less than the best. His ideal career track reflects this philosophy, and he determined that his graduate education should reflect that as well. So, he chose to apply to three schools that he had always seen rise to the top of the various business school rankings: Harvard, Stanford, and Wharton.

Jin examined the school data provided by the rankings closely and decided that he was a qualified candidate for any of the three schools. In fact, he was very confident about his chances of being admitted. His work experience, undergrad GPA, and GMAT score were all significantly better than the median figures the rankings gave for previously admitted students. If those people got in, Jin thought, I certainly can.

The Failure to Fit

Although he spent a lot of time and energy on his applications, Jin had already made a crucial mistake in his graduate school plan. He completed his applications and essays carefully. He had always heard that first-round MBA applicants had a better chance of being accepted than applicants in later rounds, so he made sure to finish everything in time to submit his application packets by the first set of deadlines. (Learn more about rounds later in the book.) Then he sat back, confident that he would start the new year with the pleasant dilemma of having to decide which of the three schools to attend.

Every school turned him down without an interview. Jin was stunned. He couldn't understand what he had done wrong. Jin had misunderstood the crucial issue of fit. He thought this meant that an MBA applicant needed to match the statistical profile of current and past students. Fit is much more complex than that.

URBAN LEGEND: TRUE OR FALSE? MBA ADMISSIONS COMMITTEES PREFER BLUE-CHIP EXPERIENCE.

One persistent myth is that you can't get into a top business school unless you have worked at a blue-chip firm. Don't try to apply to Wharton or Harvard or Chicago, the advice goes, unless your resume shows employment at a Fortune 500 or similarly prestigious company. And, by logical extension, anyone who is interested in eventually going to business school should make employment at a blue-chip company an absolute top priority.

(continued)

(continued)

Nothing could be further from the truth. When it comes to b-school applications, the crucial thing isn't where you worked but what you did. Business schools don't accept or reject applicants on the basis of their employer's prestige. They decide based on how much promise you show as a graduate business student and future business leader.

Actually, working for a smaller company has its advantages. It will give you more opportunities to see how an entire enterprise works, to understand different operations, to try things, to take chances, to goof up and take responsibility for it—and to learn from the experience. You make yourself a more attractive MBA applicant when you show that you've been a leader—and when you have opportunities to distinguish your candidacy from the other highly qualified applicants.

So the next time you hear this blue-chip urban legend, smile politely and change the subject before you have to endure any other bad advice. Although many business school students have worked at the likes of Goldman Sachs and McKinsey, the fact is that big companies employ a large percentage of ambitious people, and of those, a fair number are Ivy League MBA applicants. By the same token, you'll find a lot of Fortune 500 veterans in MBA programs. But because so many applicants come from these same employers, these numbers alone don't mean anything in terms of admissions.

Jin knew that the Harvard Business School produces many of the world's corporate leaders. He therefore thought it best to highlight his corporate experience and credentials in his Harvard application. What he didn't understand is that Harvard wants leaders. He submitted good, substantive, well-written essays, but they lacked any evidence of leadership qualities or vision. As a result, his application made Jin seem more like an exceptionally intelligent and competent foot soldier than a commander or a mentor. The Harvard admissions committee thought he was a fine candidate for business school—somewhere else. The committee rejected his application.

Jin knew that Stanford is a prestigious business school. He took care to highlight his business experience and contacts in his application. What Jin didn't understand, however, is how much Stanford prizes its reputation for intellectual leadership in the business community. It wants students who show intellectual curiosity and original thinking and who will contribute actively to class discussions. Jin gave the Stanford admissions committee no reason to doubt that he was smart enough for their MBA program; after all, he had the GPA and GMAT scores to prove he was. But his application provided nothing that portrayed Jin as more than a bright but conventional thinker. The Stanford admissions committee first low-ranked his application and then moved it to a rejection.

Jin knew that Wharton is widely regarded as the school for finance and banking, and so he wrote his Wharton application to highlight his extensive financial experience and play up his interest in continuing his career in financial services. What he didn't understand is that Wharton values well-rounded students who want to study management beyond a narrow financial perspective. The admissions committee looked through Jin's application in vain for evidence that he was interested in moving beyond the realm of finance. Finding none, it rejected his application.

Jin Finds His Fit

Had Jin understood fit better, he could have written more effective applications the first year he applied to business schools. He also might have made different school selections. Stanford was, in fact, a poor fit for Jin's intellect and learning style, as he learned when he visited the campus as part of his reapplication effort. Jin sat in on two classes during his campus visit. He was surprised to find how quickly he grew impatient with the class discussion. It was a little too big picture for his practical tastes.

Jin was also taken aback to learn how many first-year MBA students lived on campus in the same residence hall. They told him that being in such close contact was an integral part of the Stanford experience. He couldn't see himself doing that. The more Jin saw of Stanford, the harder he found it to picture himself spending two years there.

On the plane back to New York, Jin decided to scrap his Stanford application and look at other business schools. On the strength of discussions with alumni and school visits, he added Chicago, Columbia, Darden, and Stern School of Business to his list of target schools, alongside Harvard and Wharton.

Jin was accepted at four of the six schools. To his surprise, Darden wound up being his top pick. The finance class he sat in on when he visited Charlottesville, Virginia, was fascinating. He enjoyed seeing the case method in action. He knew he could learn this way. He liked the idea of learning through case studies, as students did at Harvard, but in a more intimate and sociable setting. Darden's rigorous curriculum was another attraction. Jin knew he would learn a lot and be proud of having done well. The one issue about which he was hesitant was Darden's relative disadvantage in attracting corporate recruiters because of its geographic location. However, Jin decided he had strong enough ties in New York to offset that. The more he thought about his choices, the more he realized that Darden was the right school for him.

Jin's experience describes what admissions consultants have seen many business school applicants go through. Understanding the issue of fit and using that knowledge will maximize your MBA admissions chances and enrich your educational experience.

If, however, you hope to get a Harvard, Kellogg, or Stanford MBA, you need all the help you can get. Even the best-qualified applicants face an uphill battle in winning admission to these schools. It's not that the schools set impossible standards—it's that there's far more demand for a top MBA education than these schools can meet. If you're still determined to pursue admission to the school of your dreams in the face of those odds, then you're the kind of reader who is perfect for this book. Let's move on to the task of identifying your best-fit schools.

Chapter 3

WHAT ARE THE FIT FACTORS?

LEARNING HOW THE LITTLE
THINGS MAKE A BIG DIFFERENCE

Maria had always impressed those who knew her well with her ability to conform, which is certainly critical for success in the business sector—while maintaining her strikingly independent views and thought processes. She personally felt that this was her most important method for bolstering her creative marketing skills. So it came as no surprise to Maria or her close friends when she took a slightly different approach to the business school selection process than most other applicants. For one thing, Maria cared about rankings only to the extent that she wanted a b-school with a strong brand name, which meant that she had about 30 or so schools from which to select. While she voraciously read everything she could find about these schools, she steadfastly remained centered with the realization that she was reading others' opinions and couldn't entrust them with what was the biggest personal investment she would likely ever make.

And she realized that their primary research was her secondary research. She also realized that if she read about a "beautiful and quiet rural setting," the description was inadequate. Did that mean lots of trees and forests, or did that mean lots of golf courses or farmland? Even still, beautiful and quiet are subjective. So, while she had to use her secondary research to narrow down her list, she visited her top five schools and talked to as many students and recent alumni from those schools as she could track down.

Let's face it: Your challenge is to gain admission into the most reputable, dynamic, and powerful MBA program possible that matches your character and aspirations well. An MBA program's challenge is to find the brightest, most diverse contributors and potential leaders possible. Before you begin filling out applications, you must select the schools to which you will apply. Yet while you're sifting through possible schools, the schools have the daunting task of sifting through thousands of applications. You will experience a greater chance of acceptance to the schools that clearly see your fit with their program. Keep in mind, fit goes both ways: It involves fulfilling your needs in a program and it addresses what the schools want from you.

Tell Me What You Really Want

First look at what factors are important for you to consider when selecting an MBA program. This will be different for everyone, but this chapter will cover some of the most common factors affecting people's choices when looking at programs. You will get a comprehensive feel for a program by looking at its brand name, class size, location, faculty, teaching styles, quality of education, curriculum strengths, international opportunities, extracurricular opportunities, school resources, career services, alumni base, and class profile. One of the biggest mistakes an MBA applicant can make is to assume that all business schools and all MBA programs are alike.

MY PRIORITIES ARE NOT YOUR PRIORITIES.

People view their experience in relation to themselves—what they need, what they value, what feels comfortable to them. Finding the best-fit MBA program is no different. Certainly, you conduct your own research. Probably you listen to others' opinions. Possibly you solicit advice from experts. Yet the only one who knows which school is right for you is you.

Say, for example, you love winter and are seeking a business program to complement your winter sports enthusiasm. Your snow-loving friend may have visited the Tuck School of Business at Dartmouth and exclaimed how beautiful it is, nestled in the hills of New Hampshire. Another snow-loving friend may have visited the Ivey School of Business at University of Western Ontario and exclaimed how beautiful it is, settled among the forested expanses of southern Canada. Both of these schools have lots of snow. Would you have the same experience at both? No.

Remember, there is a difference between subjectivity and objectivity. Keep your objectivity and let your decision be your own.

You should apply to multiple schools but not to any program that you wouldn't attend. "This year I am only going to apply to Harvard Business School and Stanford Graduate School of Business" is not a good strategy. If you are not accepted, you will have lost a year. Of course, there are exceptions to this high-risk strategy. For instance, if your spouse has an established career or if moving the household will cause major domestic disruption, applying to faraway schools is a bad move. Or for applicants who are considering an MBA only if they can attend certain schools because only those programs will benefit their careers, looking elsewhere is irrelevant. But for the average MBA applicant, the more time you spend discovering your fit, the better chance you will have a successful admittance and educational experience.

The Role of Rankings

Most likely rankings will play a role in your school selection process. They are a great place to start your search for the perfect MBA program fit, because they compare aspects of the schools. The overall ranking shows you the top schools based on various survey data. What you need to find, however, is how your possible schools rank on categories you care about. And that knowledge can serve as a starting point for further exploration. Rankings are only the beginning of the process, not the end.

A school's reputation is important, of course, but your personal success is your first priority. Pursuing a degree based on the ability to flout your alma mater may not serve you during your long work life. You will be well served by approaching "best" rankings with a healthy skepticism. Consider that many rankings use methodology that ends up skewing results. Some data collection methods are flawed or inaccurate, relying on subjective or incomplete data that creates biased results. Many MBA programs are not included in rankings solely because of their small size, regardless of the strength of their program, even if they are AACSB accredited. So while you should consider rankings, your search must go much deeper.

Although rankings may play a role in your initial research, the real work in selecting your schools begins with knowing yourself—why you want an MBA and what you want to achieve in your career. Do you want to live in a big city or a small town? Are you are interested in a specific geographic region? Do you want to study internationally? What academic setting do you prefer? How do various teaching styles affect your ability to learn? Do you work well in teams or better on your own? These and others are important considerations.

Accreditation: What Does It Mean?

Institutional accreditation is different from *specialized accreditation*. Most countries require institutional accreditation before a school has the authority to grant degrees or—in the United States—receive federal funding. The entire school must meet minimum criteria for its curriculum, instruction, financial resources, and physical facilities, as well as quality of students, faculty, and administration.

What separates one school from another is specialized accreditation, which goes one step farther. Specialized accreditation demonstrates the highest quality and an ongoing commitment to excellence within professional programs. To be recognized as a top business school, AACSB is one of the most important designations to have. In 2009, 567 business schools worldwide achieved AACSB accreditation for management education. See other details about AACSB in Chapter 1.

What this means to you as a student is that each MBA program must maintain an exceptional level of education and a commitment to continuous improvement. These requirements are reviewed through rigorous school-based evaluations as well as peer reviews. If you are pursuing a top-tier education, you have the AACSB distinction to confirm you are attending a top-tier school. With the exceptions of Western Ontario Ivey (EQUIS), IESE (in process), and Indian School of Business (in process), all schools profiled in this guide are AACSB accredited.

EQUIS (European Quality Improvement System), run by the European Foundation for Management Development, and AMBA (Association of MBAs) are two other accreditation agencies of particular importance to non-U.S. schools.

What Are the Teaching Styles?

When you are considering your top choices for graduate programs, be sure to investigate how each school will present information to you. Most schools have a combination of teaching methods, and some use one type more than others.

Case study involves taking a hypothetical business with a specific problem faced by working managers. You are given background information on the organization and required to identify the specific issues. You evaluate options for a solution, make reasonable assumptions, and recommend a feasible action plan. Case study is the primary teaching method for Harvard, IESE, Darden, and Western Ontario Ivey, among others.

Lecture style involves professors addressing the class as well as guest speakers presenting their expertise. Both groups reinforce the fundamentals of your management education. Proponents contend that the lecture method best provides you with the broad theories and concepts that otherwise are not discussed in business practices. Lecture is a prominent style at Vanderbilt University Owen, University of California Los Angeles Anderson, and University of Toronto Rotman, among others.

The *team project* approach tests your collaborative learning and classmate interaction skills. Teams are often comprised of members with disparate backgrounds. Projects also may incorporate complicated parameters to facilitate higher interaction. Stern School of Business students can look forward to a third of their instruction based on the team project method.

The *business simulation* method relies on the business savvy of you and your classmates to run a virtual company on computers. Teams from different MBA programs often compete to demonstrate their winning real-world strategies. Simulations cross into global business issues and take on product branding, leadership performance, and financial growth to test your evolving skills. Carnegie-Mellon Tepper, Indiana University Kelley, and Dartmouth Tuck are a few examples of schools that champion this teaching method.

A School's Profile and What It Means to You

A school's profile is composed of characteristics such as class size, geographic location, faculty, teaching styles, quality of education, curriculum strengths, international opportunities, school resources, extracurricular opportunities, career services, and alumni base. These factors can be found on a school program's Web site, in the program brochures, or at numerous Internet locations concerned with providing this information.

You may have a definite feel for the size program in which you would excel. Top MBA programs range in incoming class size as well as the size of their cohort groups, as well as how many students are in specific classes. So while some programs are so small that each student receives generous faculty attention and each incoming class develops a close-knit family atmosphere such as at Cornell and Dartmouth, larger programs tend to develop the close-knit feeling by splitting classes up into cohorts, thereby supporting a cohesion to build solid relationships with your classmates. There are benefits to both approaches, and you need to weigh which you prefer.

You may care where your top MBA program is located. You will be able to find top schools in big cities, mid-size cities, college towns, and fairly secluded settings. You can find top schools in all regions of the United States and all over the world. If you have definite ideas about living in a big city, you want to rule out early those programs in less-populated areas. A significant other's career considerations often affect this issue.

BIG-CITY SCHOOLS

Columbia Business School (New York, New York)

Emory University, Goizueta (Atlanta, Georgia)

Georgetown University, McDonough (Washington, DC)

Harvard Business School (Cambridge/Boston, Massachusetts)

INSEAD (Singapore)

Indian School of Business (Hyderabad, Andhra Pradesh, India)

London Business School (London)

Massachusetts Institute of Technology, Sloan (Cambridge/Boston, Massachusetts)

New York University, Stern (New York, New York)

University of Chicago, Booth (Chicago, Illinois)

University of California Los Angeles, Anderson (Los Angeles, California)

University of Pennsylvania, Wharton (Philadelphia, Pennsylvania)

University of Southern California, Marshall (Los Angeles, California)

University of Toronto, Rotman (Toronto, Ontario, Canada)

MID-SIZE CITY SCHOOLS

Carnegie-Mellon University, Tepper (Pittsburgh, Pennsylvania)

Duke University, Fuqua (Durham, North Carolina)

IESE (Barcelona, Spain)

Stanford Graduate School of Business (Palo Alto, California)

University of Texas Austin, McCombs (Austin, Texas)

Vanderbilt University, Owen (Nashville, Tennessee)

Yale School of Management (New Haven, Connecticut)

TOWN SCHOOLS

Indiana University, Kelley (Bloomington, Indiana)

Northwestern University, Kellogg (Evanston, Illinois)

University of California Berkeley, Haas (Berkeley, California)

University of Michigan, Ross (Ann Arbor, Michigan)

University of Maryland, Smith (College Park, Maryland)

University of North Carolina, Kenan-Flagler (Chapel Hill, North Carolina)

University of Virginia, Darden (Charlottesville, Virginia)

University of Western Ontario, Ivey (London, Ontario, Canada)

OUT-OF-THE-WAY SCHOOLS

Cornell University, Johnson (Ithaca, New York)

Dartmouth College, Tuck (Hanover, New Hampshire)

INSEAD (Fontainebleau, France)

A school with deep knowledge and experience in your area of interest is vital to your education. Research a school's faculty, predominant teaching style, and quality of education. You will have an advantage if you know which faculty and classes will have direct relevance for your career goals. With this information, you can narrow your research to specific faculty members and what they teach. Many schools boast Nobel laureates on staff, a good sign that the school is on the cutting edge of business research and innovative thinking. Most schools use a combination of teaching styles, using some lecture, case study, experiential learning, team projects, and simulations. The top schools can range dramatically in what percentage of each teaching method they use. For example, virtually every top business school uses case study, but the percentage of how much case study is used varies from 25 percent, such as at Chicago Booth, to 80 percent, such as at Harvard.

Next, examine the curriculum closely. If you are like many MBA seekers, you cannot wholly articulate your career vision. However, you will be building on your current career progression or you want to change careers altogether. If you are a career changer, you will need to have ideas of where you are headed to narrow your search. Curriculums range from set to extremely flexible. They also vary greatly in the number of core classes required, electives offered, and concentrations. Each business school excels in a variety of areas and has unique classes and programs that stand out in those areas. Identifying the schools with exceptional focus in your area of interest is a good way to narrow down your school selection.

Extracurricular activities are an essential part of any top program. Actively research each school's clubs, student groups, activities, sports, networking events, lecture series, study abroad programs, community relations, and leadership opportunities. You need to consider your interests and your

---

preferred level of involvement. For some, a program that provides their spouses or families with opportunities for involvement is a must, whereas for others it is irrelevant. You may want a program heavy in international experiences, whereas others have no interest in international exposure. You may be interested in specific clubs that will provide leadership opportunities; others might lean toward heavy community involvement.

Career services are an integral part of any MBA program. Look at internship placement statistics and job placement statistics at graduation and identify which schools have successfully placed students in your area of interest. Find out the top recruiting companies and what you can expect in salary offers. Also, consider the strength and size of the alumni base. This will enhance career services and your networking opportunities.

Reading student profiles is a good way to see with whom you will be studying, networking, forging lifelong relationships, perhaps even building businesses, and in some cases marrying! Identify whether the school has a competitive feel or a collaborative feel, and know what fits your style best. Teamwork is an essential part of the learning process, as is class discussion. It stands to reason that the people with whom you share this experience are a fundamental consideration.

Research, Ask, Explore

How do you go about getting the inside scoop on business schools? Research the schools' Web sites, blogs, and brochures. Speak to members of the school community through appointments, open houses, information sessions, student events, and alumni contacts. Read books on the subject like this one, and most important, if at all possible, visit those schools! All of these activities have a direct impact on your enthusiasm for the program, which tends to shine through in your essays and interviews, not to mention impresses the admissions committee by showing your genuine interest, affecting how the committee views your all-important fit with its program.

When selecting an MBA program, think about the school's history as well as how it envisions its future. Programs change over time. The MBA program your uncle attended is not the one you will attend. And if the school hasn't changed, that is not a good sign. Business programs began more than 100 years ago as one-dimensional vocational training programs that offered no practical experience with curriculums unable to keep up with the economic developments. Turbulent economic times after World War II necessitated dramatic changes in the scope and dissemination of quality business education. Many business programs took off by emulating a few top MBA programs that addressed the business issues of the day, as well as implementing internships to provide firsthand training.

By researching each school's mission and vision, you will be able to identify how it approaches current pressing business matters. Through the years, issues such as technology, international business, business ethics, and entrepreneurship have evolved. Most recently, social responsibility and environmental stewardship are coming to the fore. In addition, when economic crisis hits as hard as it did in 2008, you should see reaction from the best business schools through their research and their curriculum development.

WHAT SHOULD INFLUENCE YOU AND WHAT SHOULDN'T.

Some factors are vital to your school decision, yet some of your perceptions can influence you adversely. For example, when you are visiting a campus, you may find the weather is uncomfortable. Perhaps some people you met were less than gracious. Maybe you had to wait longer than you anticipated to meet with administrators. These kinds of factors may color your overall opinion of the school. Be careful. Make sure you are weighing the school's program and your fit. Incidental encounters may seem significant at the time; however, recognize them for what they are—incidental.

What Schools Want from You

Now consider what schools are looking for in terms of fit. Consider that you must surmount two hurdles to be accepted. The first has to do with your ability to handle the coursework and the rigorous program. Schools use your academic record in conjunction with the standardized test score from the GMAT (or now in some cases the GRE) to determine this information. If you have a solid GPA and a good GMAT or GRE score, you clear that hurdle and the committee is on to assess the next one. If you do not clear that hurdle then the admissions committee will conclude that you will be unable to handle the curriculum, and the committee will have no choice but to reject your candidacy. More than 80 percent of applicants clear the academic hurdle. So the second hurdle plays an incredibly important role in determining fit. This second hurdle encompasses the rest of the information in your application, including your resume, essays, letters of recommendation, and an interview (if extended).

KNOW YOUR ENGLISH LANGUAGE PROFICIENCY TESTS.

When reviewing requirements for admission, you will notice a number of acronyms referring to standardized tests for applicants whose first language is not English. Be sure you understand what is required by the school before you complete your application.

IELTS (International English Language Testing System): IELTS assesses ability to listen, read, write, and speak English. The scores are based on a nine-band scale from the lowest (non user) to the highest (expert user).

TOEFL (Test of English as a Foreign Language): The TOEFL specifically tests North American English (not British English). There are two versions of this test, paper and computer. The computer version has four sections: listening, structure, reading, and writing.

TOEIC (Test of English for International Communication): The original TOEIC assesses listening and reading and is divided into seven parts—four for listening and three for reading.

(continued)

(continued)

TOEIC is a multiple-choice test on paper. Scores are based on correct answers from 1 to 100 in each section. The new TOEIC is a computer-based addition that accesses speaking and writing.

Other standardized tests and terms include

- MFT (Major Field Tests)
- TMA (Tutor Marked Assessments)
- TSE (Test of Spoken English)
- TWE (Test of Written English)

You have considerable control in putting together the rest of your application. You must take advantage of this control and submit the strongest, most powerful application possible. Admissions committee members will specifically evaluate your career progression, career goals, why you need an MBA, why you are interested in their school, and why now is the right time for your MBA education. They will evaluate your leadership potential and your level of involvement with your community, your interests, values, integrity, maturity, initiative, and curiosity. They want to know what you can contribute to their program, and they look for people who thrive in analytical environments. They will find evidence of these points in your resume, essays, recommendations, and interview. By examining your motivations and by learning about you, they attempt to identify a strong fit with their program's community, values, and goals. If you can clear both hurdles, you are closer to an offer of admission.

PART II

BUILDING YOUR DREAM

Chapter 4. **What It Means to Position Yourself.** Determining Who, What, and When for Your Applications

Chapter 5. **What It Means to Manage Your Applications.** Choosing Wisely and Making It to the Finish Line on Time

Chapter 6. **What Is Your Essay Master Plan?** Using a Holistic Approach to Make Each Essay Powerful

Chapter 7. **What to Do After You Have Submitted Your Applications.** Navigating Beyond Stress and Uncertainty

Chapter 8. **What It Means to Deal with Acceptance, Waitlists, and Rejection.** Taking the Offer and Running

Chapter 4

WHAT IT MEANS TO POSITION YOURSELF

DETERMINING WHO, WHAT, AND WHEN FOR YOUR APPLICATIONS

Nancy made a great impression on Doug, a business school admissions consultant. She was clearly a smart, active, and motivated young woman. Her college transcripts and GMAT score showed she could handle graduate school. Her work history and volunteer activities portrayed an up-and-comer with a manager's vision and a leader's touch. Based on his previous experience as an admissions officer at a top U.S. business school, Doug was certain that Nancy would prove an attractive candidate for any highly selective MBA program. He had only one question: Why had Nancy not been accepted at the schools where she applied the year before?

When he read the applications Nancy had submitted to those schools, he saw the problem immediately. The applications didn't sound remotely like the woman he had spoken with on the phone. Nothing in the résumé Nancy prepared suggested she had ever had a life outside of the office. Her essays painted a picture of someone who was reserved, dutiful, and dull. The overall impression he gained from her essays was of a deskbound workaholic.

Doug asked Nancy why she hadn't mentioned her sports activities in her application. In their conversations, Nancy's athletic background had come up whenever he asked her for examples of teamwork, personal growth, or leadership. She had been captain of her college basketball team and currently volunteered with a nonprofit that helped children develop social and leadership skills through sports. More recently, she had persuaded her boss to enter the company softball team in an annual charity tournament—a move that, with the help of Nancy's athletic skills on the field and her organizational skills behind the scenes, won the company much publicity and good will in the community. Doug reminded Nancy that she had told him these stories and explained that her essays would be much better if she included them.

Nancy replied with a question of her own. "Won't I sound like a dumb jock if I write about sports?" she asked. "I mean, women are a minority in MBA programs anyway. I thought I should write about things that show I'm a serious person." Doug sighed. On the one hand, he was impressed that Nancy had thought about this aspect of her business school applications. At least she wasn't one of the many applicants who treat applications as little more than cover sheets for GMAT scores. Yet Nancy had made a terrible mistake. No one on a business school admissions committee would have dismissed her as lowbrow for talking about how her sports involvement had shaped her life. To the contrary, Nancy had sabotaged her application by holding this information back.

View Your Candidacy the Same Way as an Admissions Committee Does

Applicants have a better grasp of the admissions process when they see their strengths and weaknesses the way an admissions committee will. First, delve into the question, Who am I? By looking at your application from the viewpoint of an admissions officer, you can better understand how to communicate your story effectively and strike the right chord to bring about that acceptance letter. The key attribute in any application is to stand out in the crowd and capture the committee's attention through your uniqueness.

My company, AdmissionsConsultants, has combined the analyses of many experts to determine how you can best demonstrate fit. For instance, by using examples from dinged applications and looking at what particular points (or lack thereof) caused a rejection, we understand and appreciate what it takes to create a successful application. What is important is that you know your own character. No matter who you are, you are one of a kind. Successful applicants show this. Rejected applicants often share an anonymous similarity.

Athletics were clearly a vital part of Nancy's life experience and personal growth. She often used sports metaphors and experiences in explaining her values and why she was the person she was. When she withheld that information from her application, she withheld characteristic information about herself that could have persuaded an admissions committee member that she belonged in the school's MBA program.

Nancy's admissions consultant, Doug, complimented her for thinking about how her application would make her look to an MBA admissions committee. He explained, however, that she had misunderstood the culture of the schools to which she had applied. Her sports experience belonged in her applications. Doug told Nancy that recently he had read an article by a Harvard Business School faculty member on women's participation in sports and their development as leaders. Nancy could rest assured that an essay drawing on her sports background would be well received. Harvard wanted leaders for its MBA program, and Nancy's athletic accomplishments showed she was a leader.

Why did Nancy write her essay the way she did? She had preconceived ideas about what the top-tier schools wanted. Instead of matching her skills and accomplishments to the MBA program that would value her strengths, she sent her applications to schools ranked highly in books and journals. It is important that while you have an eye on what a particular school is looking for, you do not create an application geared toward what the admissions committee wants. Instead of the question, What do they want?, answer, What do I want in my MBA program? Tell your own story and use that viewpoint as a guide as you fill out your application.

Getting the Timing Right

When is the right time for your MBA? These days, the average full-time MBA student has between four and five years of professional work experience. Is that too much? Too little? Just right? Some believe that entering graduate business school right after college—or within a year or two of college graduation—has benefits for MBA students. Young, aspiring candidates earn their degrees at a more convenient point in their lives without having to make the larger financial and family sacrifices needed to return to school in their late twenties or early thirties. Others argue that the best age to earn an MBA depends on personal factors. In fact, both views are correct depending on the applicant's circumstances. However, only you can determine when your timing is right.

Your best age to enter an MBA program may not apply to that very young fellow who came out of the admissions interview just before you. Instead, your acceptance depends on what you have accomplished academically and professionally so far and, once you have your MBA diploma, the kind of profession you hope to enter. If you had some trouble in your academic performance as an undergrad, by the time five to seven years have passed, admissions committees will be less concerned with that aspect of your application. This is particularly true if you have performed well professionally and shown potential through a strong GMAT. However, if you performed only at an average level as an undergrad and are applying for an MBA within five years, this aspect will weigh much heavier. Most students in the top MBA programs have a combination of high GPAs and GMATs compared to their undergraduate classmates. What is important to remember is that top schools offer MBA programs for well-rounded, qualified students regardless of age.

The more significant factor is career. In some cases, youth and brevity in the workplace will earn points. For example, certain areas within investment banking prefer younger applicants; employers are looking mainly for very smart people who they can mold to work well in their corporate environment. The same is true with many management rotational programs in which you work for two years each in a variety of areas to determine what field is best for you. Fields where age and career experience are an advantage are management consulting and consumer marketing. Admissions officers reviewing MBA applicants for these fields look for solid experience. "Days are long gone when a 23-year-old MBA can step into an executive's office and tell her how to manage her business. It just doesn't cut it these days," states senior admissions consultant Kent Harrill.

Nothing is cast in stone about age, work experience, and MBA admissions. Thirty years ago, the practice of going directly from college to business school was more common. Yet while a handful of grad schools (for example, Harvard Business School) accepts a small number of applicants directly from college, the average amount of work experience held by the class of 2009 first-year students was four years. The same class also includes a student with thirteen years of work experience. College seniors and those with a year or two of work experience will want to weigh several factors when they ask themselves whether now, rather than later, is the best time to invest two years in an MBA education.

There are clearly some valid points to consider when deciding whether to pursue an MBA immediately after college. For example, if you go early, you remain in an academic environment and the lifestyle that goes with it. You will probably have fewer obligations—outside of academic performance—than you might have in a few years' time. Upon graduation, you will be far more competitive in the hiring arena than you would be without an MBA. Yet, your lack of work experience may limit your business school choices, and you might settle for a less-prestigious program. The values and insights you can gain from a few years of full-time employment can enhance your competitiveness for admission to the top business schools where admissions officers prefer to admit a diverse array of applicants. Schools know that much of your MBA education does not come from passive learning but from group discussions and collaborative projects. They know that students with impressive career trajectories have much to share with their peers.

Scant work experience could mean that you may not absorb everything you should in your classes. MBA coursework is designed for people who have some firsthand experience of how businesses and organizations work. That experience provides a crucial context for the theories and tools you learn in class. You will be at a disadvantage without it.

Another bonus of earning substantial work experience before entering an MBA program is that it will help you narrow down your range of career interests. By knowing the day-to-day realities of one or more jobs or industries, you have a good idea of what you do and don't want to do with the rest of your life. Without that knowledge, you will have to double your research to assure that you choose a concentration and internship that put you on the right track.

The Dilemma of Return on Investment

If you are too young and inexperienced when you graduate with your MBA, you may end up shortening the shelf life of your degree. Shelf life can be defined as the period of time your MBA remains relevant to employers. To put it another way, your valuation by prospective employers will depend heavily on the "what have you done for me lately?" factor. If you earn an MBA too soon and your work results do not impress your first post-MBA employer, then your career will stagnate or even decline and the aura of your MBA degree will be quickly dissipated (see chart on next page). However, if you had gained more work experience prior to b-school, you may have been better able to handle the expectations of your post-MBA employer. That means that, for example, six years from now, you would be better off with four years of work experience capped off with an MBA versus earning your MBA now before entering the workforce.

One other argument, with holes, against enrolling in an MBA while you are a freshly minted college graduate is that you will undercut your monetary business school return on investment (ROI). However, the differences are not great enough to matter in the end. In fact, in 2007, graduates from Kellogg had an average salary of $103,500 for one to two years of experience versus $112,250 for 10 to 15 years of work experience.

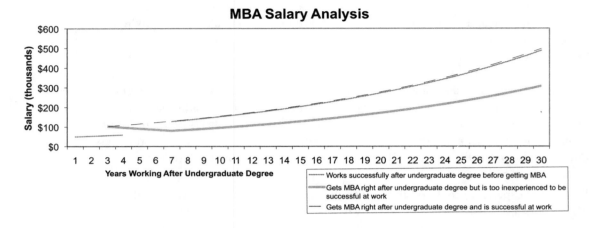

Bigger differences in starting salaries can be found in the types of industries and jobs people enter after they complete their MBAs. Beyond that, an MBA from a top-tier school will provide an excellent ROI no matter how little or how much work experience the graduate had when he enrolled.

A KEY TO SUCCESS: ONE GOOD DEGREE.

While an MBA provides a lifetime of value, most of it is consumed in landing that critical first job out of business school that hopefully jump-starts your career. The same can be argued of the undergraduate degree. Imagine someone who completed high school at 14 and started his post-undergrad career at 18 compared to someone who followed the more traditional path of completing undergrad around the age of 22. How would their career prospects differ? Chances are good that the 22-year-old possesses a lot of additional maturity and poise and, consequently, better prospects.

The same could be true of older versus younger b-school applicants. So be sure you are going to be competitive for your chosen field to ensure you get the most out of your MBA investment and understand this is a one-shot deal. You will not be eligible for another MBA if you don't fully make use of this first one.

When Is the Timing Right?

You may have the grades, GMAT scores, and extracurricular accomplishments required for admission to a top MBA program. If you are determined to launch your graduate business education now instead of later, there are ample reasons to do so, especially if you plan to enter a profession where your absence of work experience will be viewed more as a clean slate than a deficit. Yet, older applicants will find no substitute for the synergy created by combining professional experience with graduate business education.

The bottom line on business school timing is that you should go for your degree when the timing is right for you. Your MBA education is one of the largest investments you will make in your life. I want you to maximize the return you receive for your time, efforts, and money. A realistic appraisal of your undergraduate record, GMAT score, career progression, long-term goals, and your school choices are the best guideposts for deciding whether to further your education now or wait until you are work seasoned.

The Hurdle of Test Scores

A common misperception is that test scores and grades—two pieces of the academic qualifications hurdle—are interchangeable. In other words, a high GPA will easily compensate for a low GMAT or GRE and vice versa. The truth is the GPA is used more as an indicator of your academic work ethic, and the GMAT and GRE are used more as gauges of your analytical skills and aptitude. Understanding this fine difference is one key to successfully positioning your candidacy.

The GMAT and GRE are addressed in detail in many books. So briefly, here are some strategic concerns related to the admissions process. Most reputable programs will require that you sit for the GMAT, although the trend is growing for GRE acceptance. Take the GMAT unless you are highly confident you will perform much better on the GRE. The GMAT gives you a wider selection of schools to which you can apply. Taking the GMAT also shows you are serious about pursuing graduate business studies rather than hedging your chances in case you aren't admitted to a good graduate business program. Regardless of which test you choose to take, the advice in this chapter is the same for both. So feel free to substitute GRE for GMAT, if that is the test you select. It is important for you to understand that admissions officers largely view standardized testing as a necessary evil to level the playing field, given the vast array of undergrad institutions and degree curriculums represented in the applicant pool.

The first thing you must do when you decide to sit for the GMAT is to perform a self-diagnostic. Because of the quality difference between the official test and most commercial GMAT practice questions, you will help yourself immensely by downloading the free GMAT test preparation software at mba.com. The link for this test changes from time to time, so visit www.admissionsconsultants.com/mbabooks/gmatbooks.asp for the most current link on the Graduate Management Admission Council–run Web site. After you have taken the test, look at your score to see whether and where you need improvement. Should you happen to do well in some of the five sections, you will know to focus most of your preparation on the areas of weakness.

Your next step should be to review more practice questions and see whether you understand the explanations and, more specifically, why you missed the questions that you did.

> ## Self-study versus classroom courses or tutors for GMAT test preparation.
>
> Here are some rules to help you determine the best course of action for GMAT test preparation, according to gmatallies.com:
>
> Many people report bad experiences with their test preparation efforts. Sometimes, it is because they do not have an organized or disciplined approach. Other times, they rush to sign up for a course without first understanding their specific needs.
>
> If the explanations to the preliminary practice questions make sense, you should be able to adequately self-study for the test.
>
> If you feel you would benefit from a social support network of like-minded individuals with GMAT concerns in a structured setting, and you feel like you need help with all sections of the test, then a prep course may be your best option. Beware that some prep courses receive much better reviews than others, so do your research carefully.
>
> If you feel that you need help only with certain sections of the GMAT, that you require one-on-one attention, or that perhaps you want someone to identify and evaluate any trends in your test results (for example, maybe you do well on fraction math problems but poorly on exponential math problems), then a competent tutor may be your best option.

Prepare and Review, and Then Act

Unless you quickly hit a score that puts you in the top range for your schools of interest, your best strategy for success is to practice the GMAT until you plateau at a certain score before taking the actual test. This way, you can be reasonably sure that you will achieve your strongest possible score. While most schools accept the highest GMAT score (and they are supposed to ignore the other scores), they do see how many times you've taken it over the last five years and what scores you received. Schools are more impressed if you've taken the GMAT only once and earned a solid score. If at all possible, prepare for the test so that you will be taking it only once. The test is both costly and time consuming. If you have planned it out well, you will show your highest potential the first time around.

Now reverse the situation and assume that you are an admissions officer. You have two applicants who are identical in every way except that one took the GMAT once and the other needed several attempts to achieve the same score as the first applicant. Which would you choose? Admissions committees commonly see more than one score, but multiple scores generally affect your application negatively if you have taken the test more than three times.

After you have decided when to apply and you have selected the schools to which you will apply, preparation moves into high gear for positioning yourself. By now, you have thoroughly researched your school selections, and you have extensive knowledge about these programs as well as about yourself. You should be very confident at this point that you are a solid fit with these schools. Now you need to take this information to maximize your chances of acceptance into your programs of choice.

You need to start by turning a critical eye on your strengths and weaknesses. In your application, you will need to demonstrate your strengths while mitigating potential weaknesses. In some cases, there may be no obscuring a weakness, such as a low GMAT score. In that case, you need to make sure that the rest of the application is working overtime.

Review your academic record. Top MBA programs post student profiles, including average GPAs and average GMAT scores. By using these averages as a guide, you can assess your academic strength. If you are at or above the averages, this is an area of strength for you. You have cleared that all-important first hurdle and you can move on to assess the rest of your application. However, if you fall below the averages in one or both of these areas, then evaluate whether you can strengthen this area and how you can go about doing that. Your GMAT or GRE score is one small piece of your application, but schools need to know that you can handle the rigorous academic materials and pace. If you come up short here, the rest of your application efforts will not pay off.

Doug was delighted with the revised application that Nancy sent him a few days later. Her resume now included her volunteer coaching and her participation in her company's softball team. More important, she had drafted an entirely new essay about the lessons she had learned as captain of her sometimes-winning, sometimes-losing college basketball team.

Nancy wasn't finished working on her application yet. The essays needed more reflection and revision, and the overall package needed polishing. However, the revised application represented a quantum leap in Nancy's understanding of the task before her. This was a good start toward an application that projected Nancy's personality and confidence. That was the kind of application she needed to prevail in one of the fiercest competitions of her life: the struggle for admission to a top-ranked MBA program.

Will Your Undergrad School Affect Your Chance of Admission to a Top MBA Program?

Without exception, the top U.S. b-schools are associated with the country's top universities: Wharton with the University of Pennsylvania, Sloan with MIT, Kellogg with Northwestern, Harvard with Harvard, Stanford with Stanford, and Columbia with Columbia.

Some MBA applicants wonder whether this means that holding an undergraduate degree from a less-celebrated college or university could lessen their chances of winning admission to a top U.S. business school. The truth is that it may, but not by much, and not in any way that couldn't be offset by following an appropriate application strategy.

The Ivy League Advantage

Applicants who hold degrees from Ivy League and peer institutions have an edge in graduate and professional school admissions. The *Wall Street Journal* conducted a survey several years ago of the top U.S. feeder schools for the top-ranked business, law, and medical schools in the country. The three schools that came out at the top of that list were Harvard, Yale, and Princeton.

Different factors play into that trend. Harvard, Yale, Princeton, and their peers are highly selective schools to begin with. They attract exceptionally ambitious and accomplished students. Not surprisingly, those students apply to grad schools in greater-than-average numbers and succeed at grad school admissions at a higher-than-average rate. Many of these individuals would be successful no matter what undergraduate institution they attended because they are extremely gifted.

Another factor that works in the favor of elite university grads is that companies go to more trouble to recruit students from schools such as Harvard and Princeton than they do to recruit students from their local commuter schools. That can give an Ivy League graduate entry-level opportunities that someone coming out of a lesser-known school can only dream about. Those entry-level opportunities, in turn, help position a young professional to be a competitive candidate to the top MBA programs a few years down the road.

In addition, there's no denying that graduates from the Ivy League and other national universities benefit simply from the name value of their undergraduate institutions. When an admissions committee member sees a BA from Harvard or Yale on an applicant's record, he or she assumes the applicant has something going for himself or herself. And in most cases that's not an unreasonable assumption. The students who make it through the admissions gauntlet into the top-tier schools are typically exceptionally bright, disciplined, and energetic.

. . . And Ivy League's Limits

That doesn't mean, however, that a bachelor's from the right college or university is all you need to secure admission to a top MBA program. A Princeton alum's application may get a second look by admissions officers because of the name on his diploma, but they won't decide whether to admit or deny him on that basis alone. They'll hold an Ivy League graduate to the same standards that they hold all other applicants. If this hypothetical Princetonian doesn't have the required GMAT score, work experience, recommendations, or essays, he won't get in.

The top business schools select MBA students from a wide range of educational and career backgrounds. The schools with three or more alumni in Dartmouth Tuck's class of 2008 include the University of Oklahoma, University of Texas Austin, and UCLA. Graduates of more than 260 colleges and universities around the world are represented in Kellogg's class of 2008. The students who enrolled at the Stanford Graduate School of Business in fall of 2006 hold degrees from more than 160 different colleges and universities worldwide, including 84 U.S. institutions.

The bottom line on undergrad institutions and MBA admissions is that having a degree from a top national university garners you extra attention. If you don't have that going for you, you'll have to package your applications in such a way that your attention-getters (your wow factors) are highlighted. This changes a possible disadvantage into an opportunity for you to stand out from the crowd.

The Bottom Line

Business schools are very democratic when it comes to admissions decisions. They don't care as much about the name of an applicant's undergraduate college or the prestige of her previous employer as they do about what the applicant achieved there. They're looking for talent, and they know that it can come from anywhere.

Don't let doubts about the name recognition of your undergraduate institution hold you back from pursuing your dream of getting an MBA. It's what you've done with your education, not where you got it that will make the difference in your business school application outcomes. If you recognize your strengths and present them in the right way, you may well find yourself beating out applicants from better-known schools in the competition for the limited number of seats at the top business schools.

Regardless of whether you went to an Ivy League or a non-flagship state university, all applicants have to be able to answer these two questions: Why was the undergraduate institution selected? How did they make the most of the experience?

As senior admissions consultant Cristina Freeman summarizes, "The MBA admissions process isn't about weeding out people who don't have the best perceived pedigree. It's about identifying people who have stood out from their peers, taken on leadership roles, and made the most of every opportunity."

Improving Standardized Test Scores

If your GPA is fine but your GMAT is low, is it realistic that you can raise your GMAT score? If you prepared well for the GMAT and you feel that you did everything possible to get your very best score, it may not be feasible to improve the score by much. If however, you feel you can improve your score by studying on your own, taking a prep class, or hiring a tutor, you may want to put the time and effort into earning a better test score. The rule of thumb is to only retake the GMAT if you are confident you can boost your score by at least 30 points. If you cannot improve your score, consider taking a few classes and earning high marks, preferably As. This is also a great way to overcome a low undergraduate GPA.

The GPA is a little trickier for the purposes of positioning yourself because schools look at a few factors in relation to your undergraduate record. Many schools evaluate the strength of the program you attended and your overall GPA score, and then they often break it down by semester. So for example, if your freshman GPA is lower, but you increased your GPA each year, and your last year had a much stronger GPA, then this helps your case. But if it went down each year, you have some explaining to do. Also, if your GPA is low and your GMAT is solid, you want to consider how old your GPA is.

If you graduated more than five years ago and you have had a successful career and a strong GMAT score, your GPA will lose some relevance. If, however, you recently graduated and have less experience, it takes on more importance. If you have a low GPA and low GMAT score and there is no way to raise your GMAT score, you may need to reevaluate the schools to which you plan to apply. If you don't sail over the academic hurdle, it is incredibly difficult to gain admission to a top program.

Admissions Committee Perspective on Your Transcript

Remember that class your freshman year, the one at 8 a.m. that you kept missing because you overslept, your first "D" on a report card? And what about the term that everything in your life seemed to fall apart at once—your personal life, a death in the family, and lack of finances—so your grades took a steep tumble?

Chances are you've spent the last few years forgetting about such blemishes on your undergraduate record, especially if you had no immediate plans to go to graduate school. But when you apply to business school, the first thing the admissions committee will consider is your undergraduate record. All those missteps can come back to haunt you.

Some applicants think that all the admissions committees care about is your GPA. But actually, they look at every course you took. They look for trends. Did your grades improve as you went along? They look for anomalies. Was one term worse than the others? Do you have Cs or Ds on your transcript? They look for clues about academic trouble. Did you take far fewer courses one term only to make up the credits in the summer? Did you graduate in more than four years? They also look for evidence that you are well-rounded. Did you take many classes outside your major? If you studied business as an undergrad, did you take electives in the social sciences and the humanities? And they look for awards. Were you on the Dean's List? Were you elected to Phi Beta Kappa or Beta Gamma Sigma?

Further, admissions officers know all the tricks of particular schools—such as universities that omit Fs from transcripts, as if a student had never signed up for an additional course. But admissions officers can easily spot that term with the lighter load, followed by a summer school course or a heavy load the next term, and ascertain that a student had failed a course. They also know that your senior class ranking means more or less depending on the school you attended. By reviewing thousands of transcripts each year, they know how to interpret your grades.

So, before you submit your first application, make sure that you review your transcript thoroughly and be prepared to explain anything unusual. Be honest, be straightforward, and be professional. If you don't offer an explanation and simply hope for the best, you may be setting yourself up for a big disappointment.

Transcripts Not All They Could Be? Try an Alternative

If you're looking for ways to get started on your applications, here's a suggestion: Contact your undergraduate school (or schools) and request copies of your transcripts for your own use.

You might want to sit down before you look at the printouts your college sends you. It can be a shock when you see the results of four or more years of classes laid out on a sheet of paper. Even if you graduated with a respectable overall GPA, you may find yourself suddenly and rudely reminded of an academic misstep that had faded to a vague blip in your memory. What's worse is that on paper a single sub-par grade can cast a shadow over your entire academic record. That can be a real problem, because that piece of paper is what the admissions committees will use to size up your undergraduate achievements. Of course, there's nothing you can do to change your transcripts now. All you can do is assess how much of a problem you might be dealing with and take steps to mitigate that weakness in other parts of your application.

If your problem is a single poor grade in a subject that you can otherwise show you have mastered—for example, if you failed a quant-intensive course in college but have since demonstrated your quant skills at work and got a high score on the quant section of the GMAT—you may not need to do anything more than to explain the circumstances behind the poor grade in an optional essay.

But if your problem is broader than that—say, if you never achieved a grade higher than a B-minus in a quant-intensive course and your GMAT quant score is only average—you'll have to work harder to mitigate the damage. One option is to create what's called an *alternative transcript* of additional courses. You can build an alternative transcript by taking classes at a local college or university, either on a credit or noncredit basis. A good quality online course might be another option.

"An alternative transcript is a good way to offer proof to an admissions committee to support your claim that an undergrad grade, or your GMAT score, is not truly indicative of your quantitative abilities. Without such substantiation, why should they believe your claim?" asks senior admissions consultant Nicole Witt. "The fact that you've gone to the effort to build an alternative transcript also communicates to an admissions committee that you're truly committed to pursuing your MBA," she adds. "It shows dedication, determination, and perseverance—all of which are qualities that can only help to boost your candidacy."

Ask yourself some questions when choosing classes for an alternative transcript:

Is this class at the right level to mitigate my application weakness? For example, if your weakness lies in your perceived quant skills, it probably won't do you much good to take an introductory-level mathematics course. You'll need to show the admissions committees that you can handle quant work at the graduate level.

Will this class look credible on my alternative transcript? It won't do you any good to ace a class unless the admissions committee believes it was a credible program. Ask yourself what you would be able to say if asked to give specifics about what material the class covered and what the teacher's qualifications and standards were.

Will this class be useful to me apart from providing an item on my alternative transcript? You'll be committing a significant amount of money and time to the class or classes you take to build an alternative transcript. You may as well get the most back from that investment. Ask yourself whether the material you'll learn will be useful in your work or future studies.

Whatever class you decide to take for an alternative transcript, make sure you commit yourself to doing your best in it. A good grade will not only show that you can master the material in question, but also that you have the motivation and discipline to perform well in a class setting.

Let's assume you are academically strong. Now you need to develop a strong positioning statement on why you need an MBA and why this point in your career is the right time for it. A school must be convinced that you need an MBA to go where you are planning to go. No school wants to give a seat to someone who does not need it. Articulate clearly how critical an MBA is for your career. There must be no question that the degree is crucial to your future success.

Recommenders Are Crucial

Choosing your recommenders is another area in which you have a great deal of control, so you need to choose wisely. Your recommenders have a great opportunity to enhance your application. Most top MBA programs want to hear from a direct supervisor for one of your letters. Next, choose someone who knows you very well and can provide anecdotal evidence of your strengths. You need people who can speak to many different aspects of your character, work ethic, leadership potential, intellect, and teamwork skills through examples and personal experience with you.

While letters of reference are often on a critical time path, wait whenever possible until your essays are at least in good draft form before reaching out to your recommenders. This is because the references present a great opportunity to tie the overall application together. For instance, if a significant accomplishment essay reads as if it is too good to be true, a letter of recommendation can be used to substantiate it. Likewise, if you are not completely happy with how strong your leadership skills come across as hard as you tried, you could coach a recommender to cite your strong leadership skills.

In some cases, you will not be able to obtain a recommendation from your current supervisor. Should you find yourself in this position, do not fret. It happens much more often than many realize. Not every applicant is coming from a background such as investment banking or the military where you are expected to leave. Instead, many jobs such as public accounting are "up or out" (advance up the ranks or leave), and applicants from those fields often find themselves in a position where they cannot get a recommendation from a current supervisor. For circumstances like this, you will need to explain why you did not get a recommendation from your supervisor and substantiate that you are a valuable employee. Most applicants are best advised to use the optional essay to explain why they did not obtain a recommendation from their supervisor and include performance evaluations or seek an alternate recommendation from a client or peer. Just be sure to follow the schools' guidelines. MIT Sloan, for example, does not accept peer recommendations.

The Right Number of Recommendations

A few top programs require three letters, in which case you can diversify and ask someone from other areas of your life for the third, such as someone who directs you in a volunteer organization or someone who sits on a board with you. Other schools allow the option of a third letter, which may be helpful but should be used with caution.

When positioning yourself, consider how you want to present yourself outside of work. Which of your interests, extracurricular activities, or community contributions do you want to showcase? The more you are able to show aspects of yourself, the clearer will be the picture you provide to admissions officers.

Your Message

Positioning yourself can be as easy as knowing your message and knowing your audience. Your message is your life story, which is unique to you. Your audience is that top MBA program, which you have thoroughly researched and which you are passionate about attending.

HOW MUCH DO YOU LOVE THIS SCHOOL?

Senior admissions consultant Mennette Larkin states, "Your admissions essays should be like love letters. Any school that receives one should feel like it is the one and only—a perfect match with the applicant. When I was reading applications at Chicago and I would sense that an applicant would be a better fit at Kellogg or would prefer Wharton, for example, I would drill in and scrutinize other aspects of the application more carefully."

You need to convince the admissions committee that its program is your number one choice and that you are a perfect fit with the school's program. You need to show how you fit while offering unique characteristics that will enhance the overall incoming class. Clearly identify all the ways in which the school's approach will help you achieve your goals as well as how you enhance the program as a participant.

Chapter 5

WHAT IT MEANS TO MANAGE YOUR APPLICATIONS

CHOOSING WISELY AND MAKING IT TO THE FINISH LINE ON TIME

Jack was applying to six business schools. He was astounded at how much work it turned out to be. The overall process was as complex as anything he had to manage for his company's clients. The Round 1 deadlines at Harvard and Stanford were less than a month away. Were his applications ready to send in?

Jack decided to rush through his application to meet the Round 1 deadline because he heard from several friends that Harvard and Stanford filled up nearly all of their classes with early applicants. Though he was uncomfortable with doing such a rush job, he submitted his application on the deadline date. Unfortunately, he was not accepted to either school and now had to wait to reapply.

Jack did himself a disservice by rushing. He would have been better served to apply in the second round with more powerful applications. Proper time management in the application process is an oft-overlooked but essential part of a successful application. Knowing what to send in and when is just as important as the body of the application itself. While the timeline for b-school applications is fairly similar across the board, often knowing the ins and outs of the schedules of the schools being applied to can alleviate a lot of the stress inherent to the process. Highly competitive schools, such as Harvard and Stanford, see a large volume of applicants for Round 1 but do not by any means fill up their entire class with those applicants.

Knowing which schools to apply to and understanding their individual deadlines is important because good time management can space out deadlines and workload. For maximum effectiveness, each application needs to be tailored to the individual school, so this is a crucial part of the application process—even more so if you are considering more than two or three programs to which to apply.

Outlining Your Application Tasks

It is never too early to start mapping your strategy for applying to business school. This chapter gives you a step-by-step timeline. Also see the timeline at www.admissionsconsultants.com/mba/timeline. asp, which includes suggestions for the GMAT, school selection, academics, extracurricular activities, strategic positioning, and, of course, applications.

There are those ultra-prepared individuals who have always known that they would eventually attend a graduate business school. After graduating, they enter the workforce with the desire to make an impact, develop their business skills, and take full advantage of opportunities to lead projects and people, produce innovative ideas, and influence others. Outside of work they pursue their passions through activities and community involvement. They create relationships, build networks, and secure a mentor who provides career guidance. That type of planning sets a great foundation for the application process. However, many individuals may realize their need for an MBA right before they decide to apply. Hopefully they have been building a solid resume.

A KEY TO SUCCESS: MANAGEMENT MATERIAL.

B-schools look for applicants who are senior management material. Creating relationships, building networks, securing mentors, and developing business skills are all good things to do even if you don't apply to b-school. These skills are valuable later in your career. Remember that the more successful you become, the more resourceful your competition is becoming as well. If you want to get ahead, start playing the game now. Even if you never attend b-school, you'll still be glad you took the time to develop and continually strengthen these invaluable skills.

Ideally, if you can plan your MBA application strategy 8 to 18 months before your application deadlines, you can achieve optimal results with less stress. Your goal is to submit your strongest application possible, and this does not happen overnight.

Although Jack was denied admission to Harvard and Stanford, he now had 8 months to meticulously prepare and plan to reapply. He was going to use the time to visit the schools and find out every detail he could about the programs. He was going to use this information to identify exactly why he was a perfect fit for these programs and articulate what he had to offer. Although he had a solid GMAT score, he chose to retake it because his background in investment banking was more competitive than others from more obscure fields. He took advantage of leadership opportunities at work and received a promotion.

Jack continued his involvement in the community and strengthened his relationships there. He developed a more comprehensive positioning statement, met with his recommenders early in the process to review his interest in business school, and helped them understand how critical an MBA was to his career vision. He provided them with a thorough outline of his accomplishments, responsibilities, and strengths. His applications were in pristine condition a few days before the deadline.

MAKE CERTAIN YOU REALLY WANT AN MBA.

While researching this book, the AdmissionsConsultants staff and I observed that most students who dropped out of b-school did so for nonacademic reasons. The two most common reasons were a true interest in a non-MBA field (think medicine, engineering, and law) and family pressures. Generally these individuals leave after their first year with a lot of debt and one year of their professional lives "wasted" on an endeavor that brought them no closer to attaining their career goals.

Know Your Due Dates

Obviously it's important to know when applications for full-time MBA programs are due. Here are the approximate deadlines:

- Round 1—fall
- Round 2—winter
- Round 3—spring

Each school has specific deadlines, which may not be posted until the early summer before they are relevant, but you can use the previous year's deadlines as a guide.

THE BEST ROUND IN WHICH TO SUBMIT YOUR APPLICATIONS IS...

...the one when you're sure your application is ready and reflects 100 percent of your best effort. A Round 3 application may be worth a try as long as "why Round 3?" is addressed in the application.

Keep in mind that some schools have early-decision rounds, rolling admissions, or four or more rounds, so it is important to research your specific deadline dates. Early-decision rounds are beneficial if you know which school is your clear first choice and are willing to forego other programs' offers of admission. If admitted in early decision, you are generally required to submit a hefty deposit and a signed agreement that you will attend the program. Rolling admission generally has one main final deadline. You may apply anytime during the application period and will generally receive a decision within 10 to 12 weeks. It is important to note that deadlines may differ for international students.

The applications typically are not available until the August before the deadlines, so you can loosely work from the prior year. The essays may change from year to year, so you cannot complete your essays until the new essays come out, but you can develop some solid positioning and at least have a working draft of your goals and your fit with your specific schools.

Timeline for What to Do When

There are two types of MBA school candidates: those who have planned for years to attend a business school, and those for which the idea of further education is a recent consideration. If you are in the latter category, you may find yourself in need of information quickly. You may want to rush forward with your school program research and submit your applications as soon as possible. You may feel the future of your career depends on attending grad school this year. Even if all of these factors apply to you, throwing yourself into the process is a bad idea.

A successful candidate for a top MBA school program has the wherewithal to present a strong application. You have the academic experience, motivation, and vision to see yourself as a leader in your field. Unless you are in that first category of candidates, what you don't have is a plan.

Don't start your essays too early.

Every year, generally from winter through late spring, eager applicants contact Admissions-Consultants to get started on the coming fall's application essays. These MBA hopefuls are usually aware that their essays could change, and many times they are still willing to pay for editing help. Although the company's consultants enjoy working with these applicants, they should use their time in more productive activities unless their schedules won't allow them to work on their essays in the fall.

It's important to think of the application process as a marathon race. It's critical that you pace yourself accordingly so you don't experience burnout part of the way through and can cross the finish line with a strong push. For example, there's no need to start your essays months before the deadline. Some better experience could occur to you between now and then that you may want to discuss instead.

Here is good timeline:

8 to 18 Months Before Applying

- Research and select schools.
- Prepare for and take appropriate standardized test(s): GMAT/GRE and/or TOEFL.
- Start a filing system.
- Look at the school's current application to get an idea of what is involved.
- Decide whether you need to take some relevant courses to compensate for a low undergraduate GPA or to fulfill some school requirement.
- Create a financial plan and research financial options to cover tuition and other expenses.

Research and select schools. Consider giving ample time to school selection. Researching the schools and deciding which schools you fit best takes time. The CD-ROM included with this book is a great place to start. You also need to talk to people, visit the schools, and research their Web sites. These time-consuming activities are critical in choosing the right program for you.

Prepare for and take standardized tests. Giving yourself plenty of time to prepare for and take your standardized tests is a very good idea. Squeezing hours of study time into a hectic schedule can be challenging. You may want to take the test far enough in advance that you have time to retake the test if needed. If English is your second language, find out whether you are required to take the TOEFL in addition to the GMAT or GRE. Prepare for and take the GMAT or GRE depending on which test is appropriate for your schools.

Start a filing system. It is a good idea at the beginning of this process to develop a file system to keep your application strategy organized. Outline your own timeline, including deadline dates and to-do lists. Create a reasonable timeline for finishing various application components.

FINISH WHAT YOU START.

Because the unexpected can and does occur, you need to work all the way through one application before starting the next. Nothing is worse than watching a deadline pass with four applications that are each 50 percent complete when two of the applications could have been 100 percent complete.

Review school application contents. To understand what is involved in the application process, look at the school's application. When you look at the application this far in advance, keep in mind that it may change a little for the next season of applications. But you can get a sense of what is involved in the process as well as how much time it will take to prepare. You can find out how many letters of recommendation you need (usually need two or three), details about the application fee, what information is needed, and when it is needed.

Take additional classes. If you need to compensate for a low undergraduate GPA, now is the time to enroll in a class or two. It is critical that you earn a high grade, preferably an A. Take a relevant course such as calculus, statistics, or microeconomics. Additionally, some programs require these basic classes. If your selected programs have this prerequisite, then it is a good time to get it out of the way.

Plan your finances. As with any academic endeavor, you must consider the financial implications. You need to consider how you will pay for your education. Each school's Web site has a link to financial aid, where you will get a good idea of your options for that school. You can look up scholarship information as well as loan information. In many cases, lower-tiered schools have more generous scholarships.

If you anticipate securing loans to fund your business education, obtain a copy of your credit report well in advance. The sooner you receive your credit report, the sooner you can clean up credit problems and ensure you qualify for the best loan rates. Credit reports often contain inaccurate information, and by getting a copy of your report now, you should have plenty of time to correct mistakes. A great place to request a free credit report every 12 months is www.annualcreditreport.com.

Typically, applicants begin the financial aid application process in January or February because they want to have their tax information to complete the Free Application for Federal Student Aid (FAFSA). Even if you don't plan to ask for financial aid, the FAFSA is used to determine your eligibility for federal loans. Most MBA students use a combination of federal, institutional, and private loans to pay for their education.

THE FAFSA WEB SITE IS FREE TO ALL.

The FAFSA is available at the official Web site, www.fafsa.ed.gov. The FAFSA Web site should not be confused with commercial Web sites that use similar URLs and charge a fee for you to complete financial aid documentation. The official FAFSA Web site and application are free to all users.

Federal loans are administered through American business schools, with each school deciding how much money an applicant is eligible to borrow. The amounts for which you qualify vary from school to school. Federal loans are attractive to students because they carry lower interest rates than private loans. However, the amount of money that can be borrowed under federal loan programs is often not enough to cover full tuition and living expenses at a top b-school.

For 2009, most U.S. students should be eligible to borrow a maximum of $20,500 in subsidized and unsubsidized federal Stafford and Ford loans. Probably the best federal loan for graduate students is the Perkins loan. The interest is paid by the U.S. government during the school year and for a nine-month period after you graduate. The rate is 5 percent, and the loan can be repaid over 10 years. Many business school students take out private educational loans (also known as alternative education loans) from banks and other lenders to cover the gap.

6 to 8 Months Before Applying

- Decide on recommenders. Start talking to them about your plans.
- Develop positioning statements, goals, and reasons to apply to each of your selected schools.
- Start visiting schools the spring before you apply (or the fall of the year you apply).

Decide on recommenders. Choose your recommenders wisely and if possible, discuss your plans to attend an MBA program and your career goals early in the process. At this point, it is necessary only to begin the discussion. Think about your recommenders and solidify relationships now before you need them in a few months. Recommenders should not start writing the recommendations until the application comes out and ideally after your story themes and wow factors have been developed and your essays are at least in good draft form.

Develop positioning statements, goals, and reasons. You may not get the exact essay questions until a few months before applications are due, but some main questions are fairly standard, although worded differently in each application. There is usually a "goals" question, a "why MBA" question, and a "why this school and why now" question. While you do not have to write the whole essay, you can get together a detailed outline answering each of these typical questions. This process serves to prepare you for writing your essays, as well as gives you a clear idea on why you are doing this in the first place.

Start visiting schools. If possible, visit the schools to which you are applying. You may do this as a way to decide on which schools to apply to, or you may do this once you have selected your schools. Visits help you learn more about the program and give you a good sense of how you fit in the environment. They also give you plenty to discuss in your essays, and your enthusiasm usually shows through quite naturally when you have firsthand experiences on campus. Admissions committees look favorably on applicants who have visited their school. But keep in mind that schools understand that not everyone can visit, and it is not held against you if you do not visit.

3 to 6 Months Before Applying

- Request transcripts.
- Open an online account with each school when the applications become available.
- Start writing your essays.
- Work with your recommenders and give them detailed instructions and deadlines.
- Schedule interviews with schools that require one (as opposed to invitation-only schools).

Request transcripts. You will need to send transcripts from all academic institutions you have attended. If the program asks you to submit a transcript with your application, check the transcript after you scan and upload it. As a general rule, if you can't read it, the admissions staff can't read it. If your university provided A/B/C/D/F grades, calculate your grade point average on a four-point scale (A = 4, A- = 3.7, B+ = 3.3, B = 3, C = 2, D = 1). Do this even if your university did not calculate the grade point average. If you completed your undergraduate degree outside of the United States, make sure you follow all the instructions for international applicants, including obtaining official and translated copies of transcripts, providing TOEFL scores, and requesting waivers.

Open an online account. As soon as your schools have posted their applications for the year in which you will be applying, get into their online application system. The online application gives you access to the essay questions, the letters of recommendation information, and the data fields that each school requires. Until you click Submit, you can save your work, make revisions, and return to your application as often as you like. Much of the basic information required, such as a description of extracurricular activities, employment history, and resume, can be modified for the different schools. Some schools give applicants seemingly unlimited space to describe their experiences. Others have very strict character limits. But the basic format is generally the same, so coming up with a good set of descriptions for your various activities and jobs will stand you in good stead. And your one-page resume can be uploaded to all the schools.

Since these sections invariably take longer to complete than most people expect, it is a good idea to start working on them as soon as possible. Make sure you double-check your work and follow all the directions. Many smart people make the mistake of entering their first (given) name where their last (family) name is requested. In the employment history, you must supply a specific reason for leaving, not just acceptance of a new job. Once you've been accepted, the schools often verify your employment at each company, so you want to be as accurate as possible. When calculating your months of work experience, include only post-college work and provide the months (not the years) through matriculation of the year in which you plan to enroll (not as of the date you're applying). You need to explain gaps in your employment and any significant period when you were underemployed or unemployed. Because so many people were laid off in 2008 and 2009, schools are accustomed to seeing gaps. But you must acknowledge the gap and explain what you were doing in between jobs.

All the schools want to know what you do and have done outside of work and school. This gives them a sense of who you are, what you do for fun, and how you've shown leadership and teamwork skills. And even if a school, such as Wharton, gives you unlimited room to describe your activities, be concise. You don't want to either bore or exhaust your admissions reader before he or she has a chance to read your essays. Some schools request that you list activities in order of importance to you or give you a maximum number of activities to list. Use your best judgment because you are being evaluated on your choice of activities to include as well as the quality of your involvement.

Start writing your essays. Essay writing is covered in the next chapter. Just keep in mind to leave yourself plenty of writing time for these essays. Essays will take up evenings and weekends for many weeks and months depending on how many schools you target.

Work with your recommenders. Give your recommenders the information they need to provide an accurate and strong letter of recommendation. Give them the instructions and deadline dates. This is especially critical when you need them to write several letters for several schools. Usually you input the recommender's information into the school's application system, and the school directly e-mails your recommender the forms or directions. If possible, sit down with your recommenders or have a phone discussion to outline your motivations for getting an MBA and your goals. Give them a current resume and an outline of your major accomplishments so they have the information readily available when they start to write the letter. You should always try to get a recommendation from your current supervisor or director. If you can't get a recommendation from your current supervisor, provide a brief explanation (one or two sentences) in the additional information section of the online application.

If the school requests a peer reference, please make sure the person you pick is indeed a peer (an equal). Though few people like hierarchy, our supervisors are not our peers. Even if your supervisor is your friend, he or she by definition is not your peer. While many peers are friends, remember that not all friends are good choices for recommendations.

Schedule interviews. For those schools that require an interview, contact them and arrange for an interview. Many schools interview by invitation only, in which case you will need to wait and see whether you receive an invitation.

0 to 3 Months Before Applying

- Check with recommenders to ensure that they get their letters in on time.
- Edit your essays by having someone review them for errors and give you feedback on content. Be sure the person you choose is appropriately qualified.
- Review your application. Edit remaining errors or typos. Submit the application.

Check in with recommenders. You should be able to see when your recommenders' letters are submitted and received by the school on the online application account. If they are not submitted close to the deadline, get in touch with the recommenders to remind them of the looming deadline. Submit your application only after your recommenders have submitted your letters of reference. It is a good idea to send your recommenders a thank-you note after they have submitted the letter.

Edit your essays. If you are working with a consultant on your applications, you already have someone reviewing your essays and making sure that they are in pristine condition from a content and grammatical perspective. Otherwise, have trusted people read your essays for grammatical errors and typos. Remember to triple check whether you have the correct school name in your essays before sending.

Review your application. Before you click that submit button, review the entire application and if possible have someone else review it for glaring typos or omissions. Don't forget to send the application fee. After you submit your application, the waiting begins.

If you are offered an invitation to interview from those schools that are invitation-only, be sure to thoroughly prepare for the interview with just as much preparation as you devoted to your application process. Developing your message and practicing the interview is key. Read more about interviews in Chapter 7.

Wrap It Up

If you have taken the time to prepare your applications thoroughly, you will be submitting the most powerful and thoughtful representation of your candidacy. While there is a huge part of this process that you have no control over, this part of the process is in your complete control. You need to do everything you can to submit a convincing and compelling case for your admission.

Chapter 6

WHAT IS YOUR ESSAY MASTER PLAN?

USING A HOLISTIC APPROACH TO MAKE EACH ESSAY POWERFUL

More background on Jack: He had already completed his applications for Wharton, Chicago Booth, and Kellogg. He was almost done with MIT Sloan because he had a friend who was in his first year who had been encouraging him to apply since August. But now he was exhausted and a huge project had just landed on his desk. The Round 1 deadline at Harvard was less than a week away. Because Harvard was his first choice, he had felt a little intimidated about starting the application. Now he had no choice but to finish it quickly or not at all. The following week he'd be out of town on business, so he knew he'd be too busy to work on his essays. He'd barely have time to finish his MIT application and then get started on Stanford before they were both due.

How to Strategize and Stay Organized

Once you have decided where you want to apply, the next step is deciding which school's application to focus on first. Depending on when you start the process, you can start with the school that has the earliest deadline, the school that you think will be the most difficult, or the school that you most want to attend. If you plan to apply in the first round and you can start your applications in August, then you will have plenty of time to write and refine your essays. If you are starting later, perhaps a month before the first school's deadline, then you should look at the questions of the schools with the two nearest deadlines and decide which one you want to tackle first. If you have cut it closer than two weeks, then you should first consider applying to a later round. If that isn't feasible, then you need to be prepared to really focus on your essays and spend late nights and entire weekends writing, revising, and refining.

Applicants to Harvard and Wharton often start with Wharton because the essays allow more words and offer a good opportunity to refine the story of your career progress and goals. Harvard's essays are more focused and concise. On the other hand, if you can say what you need to say in a few words for Harvard, you can often expand on those themes for other schools. Some applicants prefer to look at all the essay questions for all the schools they are applying to and then figure out which school will be first.

Because staring at a blank computer screen for hours is never a good way to start, perhaps your best strategy is to begin with the essay questions that inspire you the most. But keep in mind that those deadlines are set in stone, so give yourself plenty of time to do your best work.

Different Types of Essay Questions

Common themes appear throughout most business school applications—career progress and goals, leadership roles, teamwork, and substantial accomplishments. Strong MBA candidates truly shine in these areas. Some types of questions you might encounter include the following: What are your most substantial accomplishments and why do you consider them such? What matters most to you and why? How have you inspired and motivated others? How do you define leadership and how do you still need to develop as a leader? What have you learned from a failure or mistake? How have you worked with a team and how have you dealt with a difficult team member? What pivotal choices have you made in your life? How have you handled cross-cultural challenges? How have you contributed to your community? Discuss a piece of constructive criticism you received, how you handled it, and what you learned from it. What are your career goals and why? All the schools will ask why you want an MBA and why you want to attend their school. This requires considerable thought about why an MBA is necessary to achieve your goals and considerable knowledge about a specific program and what appeals most to you about it.

How to Approach and Write Your Essays

Essays are your opportunity to tell your own story in your own way. One school refers to the essays as conversations on paper, and that is a good way to think about them. The admissions committee wants to understand who you are, what motivates you, and where you are headed. Committees want to know how you will contribute to their MBA program and whether you are a good fit for the school. Before you start writing, it's a good idea to get your thoughts in order. Spend time thinking about the common themes—leadership, teamwork, accomplishments, personal background, contributions to the community, career progression, and goals. Perhaps make notes on each topic with specific examples, primarily from your professional experience. Then decide what you most want to convey to the admissions committee. What are your three top strengths? What is most important to you? Do you have any unique characteristics, something that will make you stand out from others with similar educational and professional backgrounds?

SAMPLE ESSAYS: FRIEND OR FOE?

Often, sample essays are likely to stifle creativity rather than spur it. Whether applicants realize it or not, they end up "borrowing" ideas from essays they have seen elsewhere. Perhaps more important, many admissions officers have voiced concern about the lack of originality in essays.

One admissions official noted that in one year, multiple versions of the same lacrosse stick story arrived at his business school's admissions office. The story revolved around how the applicant gazed at his old lacrosse stick across the room, which spurred him to reflect on the value of teams, and how his grand memories of his lacrosse games helped him crystallize his MBA aspirations. No doubt someone did experience such an entertaining epiphany, but too many other applicants borrowed the story or adapted it to their own circumstances.

If you are tempted to scour the Internet for essay ideas, you may need a primer on the purpose of business school essays. Your personal essays are essential statements of who you are, and it's your vehicle for transmitting the image to admissions committee members. An original, effective essay helps you stand out in committee members' minds. Your essay shows readers that you are an original, intelligent, and diligent human being and convince decision makers that you are worthy of their full consideration.

Unfortunately, people who borrow ideas from others risk doing the exact opposite. They make themselves sound like a clone of a hundred other applicants in the admissions pool.

You should also spend a great deal of time reading through the school's Web site and learning about the individual program. For example, is the school looking for someone with a global perspective? Do you have that? How can you demonstrate it? Does the school Web site spend a great deal of space on the activities, courses taught, and achievements of its faculty? If so, what professors and courses most interest you? Are they in your primary field of interest? What information indicates the school's emphasis on teamwork and a collaborative environment or a more competitive environment? How can you show you are a team player or have exceptional intellectual curiosity? What are the school's main teaching methods and how do they relate to you? How have you been creative at work? Are you a leader? Then think about what it means to be a good leader and different ways to demonstrate that trait. What do the students talk about in their blogs and profiles? What does the school value? Most importantly, read through all the information on admissions. What are their criteria for admission? How can you show that you meet those? The essays should be filled with specific examples to illustrate your points and focus on the why and the how and not just the what.

URBAN LEGEND: TRUE OR FALSE? USE HUMOR TO PERSUADE THE ADMISSIONS COMMITTEE TO LIKE YOU.

Admissions officials often are concerned about applicants' use of humor. So, to avoid misinterpretation, follow this simple advice: Exercise caution if you are contemplating a comedic approach. Remember that your goal is to prove to the reader that you are going to make a great senior manager, not a great comedian. Humor is individual in taste and if miscalculated, you risk offending the reader or worrying him or her that you will not represent the school well.

Drafting Your Essays and Creating Your Themes

When you are ready to start writing, the most important piece of advice is to answer the actual questions and each component of each question. Beware of cutting and pasting! Develop your essays for each school separately. Even if you are answering a similar question for more than one school, you should tailor your answers for only the program to which you are sending your application package. There are common themes certainly, but each school has a slightly different approach.

The admissions officers spend a great deal of time each summer thinking about their application questions and making changes, some minor, some major, for the following year. The schools all know that you are applying to more than one school, but they will quickly deny anyone who makes the mistake of substituting another school's answer, or, worse, referring to another school in an essay.

DOUBLE-CHECK THE SCHOOL NAME IN YOUR ESSAY.

Double-checking the school's name in your essay may sound like a no-brainer, but rest assured about 5 to 10 percent of essays read along the lines of, "And that's why I really want to attend [name of a different school]." There is no reason to torpedo your chances by making such a careless error and giving the school any reason to suspect you may embarrass it by committing a similar mistake in front of school recruiters.

Also be careful to follow all the instructions. Most schools have page or word limits. Some specify single line spacing; others specify double spacing. Many require 12-point font for readability in a typeface such as Times New Roman. If in doubt, call or send an e-mail to the admissions staff to ask for their preferences for the format. If you neglect to follow the directions and submit a two-page essay when the school has requested a two- or three-paragraph essay, you will likely be denied admission, regardless of your other qualifications. Similarly, if a question has many different parts and you forget to include an answer to one part, the readers will be ready to move on to the next applicant. Be particularly careful to note any additional instructions, such as including experiences from only the past three years or discussing the outcome and responses to a particular situation instead of a general one.

Before you write your essays, consider your life themes. What key factors and highlights in your life do you want to impart to the admissions committee? Additionally, what do you have in your experience that defines who you are? It may be helpful for you to reverse your thought processes and review the obstacles in your history that you have had to overcome. Often, how you surmounted various setbacks is as important as how you have excelled and achieved. When admissions committees look for the wow factor, they are looking for superlatives. At Wharton, wow means walk on water—in other words, the best of the best. Wow factors certainly include academic, extracurricular, and community success. But remember, they also mean most courageous, most prepared, most dedicated, or most improved despite life's circumstances.

For his first three applications, Jack had been very organized. He had spent a lot of time thinking about his answers to all the questions before he started writing. He had a spreadsheet with the questions listed for each school, the word or page limits, and the deadlines. He had prepared bullet points on a variety of topics with specific examples from his professional experience and personal background. He tackled one application at a time, and he had a good idea of what he would be able to include in each subsequent application. When it came time to write Harvard's essays, he realized he hadn't thought about what made this program's questions different from other schools. He knew he had written a strong essay for Wharton about his career progress, so he decided to use what he could to fit Harvard's 400-word limit for the career vision essay. He suspected Harvard might be expecting something different, but he didn't have time to think about it. With the demands on him at work, he was lucky to be able to cut and paste at this point.

When he returned form his business trip, he put the finishing touches on his Sloan application and started thinking about Stanford. What really mattered to him? At this point, sleep! But he couldn't write about his love of sleep. Or could he? Would that catch their attention? No, they would probably think he was being silly. Unfortunately, since he actually was sleep-deprived, he couldn't think of anything original. He wrote about his family and sports. Both were important to him, but the essay seemed a little dull. Maybe he was just tired. Maybe it was better than he thought. He also decided to talk about the organization he led in college since he knew it was a great example of his leadership style. He only had time for one draft of each essay, but since it was his final application he hoped that he didn't need more. Jack had also meant to have his mother, an English teacher for many years, read over his essays to Harvard and Stanford before he submitted them, just as he had done with his other essays. But he ran out of time.

On his Stanford application, Jack forgot to discuss his responses and used examples from college (more than three years earlier), so the admission committee eliminated him quickly from the competition. You might think these are trick questions or excuses for readers to deny your application, but in fact they are concerned with your attention to detail.

Grammar and Spelling Do Matter!

It is so much easier to write today than it was in the days of typewriters and white-out. Computers allow you to write and rewrite, cut and paste, save and delete. Software programs check spelling and grammar as you type. But you would be making a mistake if you relied too heavily on your software. You need to read and reread what you've written to make sure that you haven't accidentally typed a word that is a real word but not the one you meant to say. Your computer won't tell you whether you've left out a word or if what you've written makes no sense. If you are uncertain of your knowledge of grammar, punctuation, and spelling, ask someone who is strong in those areas to read your essays before you submit them. You should proofread your resume and the data sections of your application. If you are sloppy on your applications, then you probably aren't the candidate the schools are seeking. You should also make sure that your writing style is consistent throughout, not chatty and conversational in one essay and formal in another. Your essays should flow as a complete package. This is another reason why it is essential to give yourself enough time to do your best. If you are rushing to finish your essays the day they are due, chances are you will make mistakes—easily avoidable ones.

---

10 ISSUES THAT A SPELL CHECKER WON'T CATCH.

Before clicking the submit key on the application Web site, be sure to proofread your work. That means printing your application and having it checked for errors by eye rather than trusting a spell checker to do the job for you. In case you're wondering why, here are some examples of mistakes that most spell checkers will not catch.

1. Homonyms (words that sound the same but have different meanings depending on their spelling and use): Spell checkers won't pick up that you intended to write "pair" instead of "pare" or "pear," or "there" instead of "their."

2. Incorrectly divided compound words: Spell checkers won't alert you that "can not" should be spelled "cannot" or that "Inter net" should be "Internet."

3. Incorrect pronouns: Spell checkers won't mark that you typed "his" or—worse—"its" when you should have typed "hers," or "she" when it should have been "he." Checks won't catch such phrases as "people that" instead of "people who."

4. Usage errors: Spell checkers probably won't alert you to typos involving "its" or "it's."

5. Missing words: Spell checkers probably won't catch the missing word in a phrase such as "I attended the University Michigan."

6. Wrong words: Spell checkers won't highlight a gaffe such as "My supervisory experience sensitized me to the martial difficulties that married employees can encounter when pressed to work overtime."

7. Wrong dates: Spell checkers won't question a statement such as "Entering the workforce in the late 1790s, I learned..."

8. Misspelled names: Spell checkers won't find mistakes with people's names or with most place names.

---

9. Incorrect verb tenses: Spell checkers won't warn that you mixed up past and present verb tenses.

10. Repetition: Spell checkers will alert you if you've typed the same word twice in a row, but they won't catch other kinds of repetition, like typing the same phrase or sentence twice in a row—or saying the same thing twice in different words.

Spell checkers are a handy tool for screening out many small mistakes everyone makes when writing drafts. They can't catch every mistake, however, and they are not able to catch the really big mistakes, which can only be recognized and corrected by careful editing. Use a spell checker as a first step in proofing your application, but don't count on it to do the entire job for you.

A Holistic Approach

When you read your essays all together, they should give a complete picture of who you are and what you have to offer a particular MBA program. If you feel that the essay questions the school has asked don't present all that you wish the program knew about you, there is usually an optional essay. This essay can be used to address your personal or family background, your travels, or some other aspect of your character or experience. It can address anomalies in your academic background that haven't been addressed in the data section. These anomalies are referred to as extenuating circumstances. But don't feel compelled to use the optional essay. If you have included a lot of information and have made all of your key points—highlighted your strongest attributes—then you are done. You don't want to bore your reader just when he or she had formed a favorable impression of you. And you don't want to repeat information that you have discussed elsewhere. Most importantly, if you decide to use an essay that you wrote for another school as your optional essay, make sure it doesn't read that way. Tailor it to the particular school.

A KEY TO SUCCESS: WRITE IT RIGHT AND SHORT.

You aspire to accelerate your career and perhaps become a senior manager. Not coincidentally, admissions committees are seeking this prime characteristic in their applicants. However, the more responsibility you take on, the more important timely, well-written communication becomes. Since business writing is concise, you need to master the skill.

Jack had been very pleased with all his essays for Wharton. He felt they presented him very well in all the areas he thought Wharton was most interested in, and he liked the balance he achieved between his career mapping, extracurriculars, and personal introspections. He knew Wharton was interested in a global perspective, so he had written about his experience on his college study abroad program. His individual essays read well by themselves, and together they really did give the admissions committee the overall picture he knew they would like. Since the application wasn't due for another three weeks, he decided to let it sit and work on his other applications.

Although he was originally thrown for a loop about what to choose for his Chicago PowerPoint presentation, once he chose his themes he had a lot of fun. As he was writing his Kellogg essay about his background, he realized he had a lot more to say about his international experience and what he had learned from his various travels. In fact, he was so pleased with his Kellogg essay that he decided to see whether he could use it to rework his final Wharton essay. When he reread all the Wharton essays together, he thought he now had a much stronger story to tell. He was glad he had left himself plenty of time to revisit his essays.

Are You Ready to Submit?

After you have completed your application, let it sit for a few days. Then go back and reread it. Make sure it presents you at your best and that you have double-checked everything, including all the data forms and your resume. You gain nothing by submitting early (except at schools with rolling admissions), so submitting the day of or the day before the deadline is fine. You should make sure you follow each school's requirements about when to submit your application, especially concerning letters of recommendation. Some schools, such as Stanford, don't want you to submit until after your recommenders have submitted their letters. Other schools, such as Chicago, will allow you to submit before your letters arrive (but you should let the school know if the letters will be delayed). But once you are sure you have answered all the questions in a coherent, meaningful fashion, resist the temptation to endlessly tweak. The admissions committees are looking at the overall picture rather than the minutiae of word choice. Have you told the story you wanted to tell? Have you covered all your key points? Have you answered the actual questions that are asked? Have you proofread and followed all the instructions? Then you are ready to submit. Best of luck.

Chapter 7

WHAT TO DO AFTER YOU HAVE SUBMITTED YOUR APPLICATIONS

NAVIGATING BEYOND STRESS AND UNCERTAINTY

Sanjay had spent all of his free time for the past half year on his business school applications. For six months he was thinking about which schools to apply to, researching and visiting schools, talking to alumni and current students, contacting and following up with recommenders, and then writing and revising innumerable essays. After he had submitted his applications, it seemed strange not to have any more essays to revise. It seemed a bit wrong, too. Sanjay had a hard time ignoring a nagging sense that he should be doing more to position himself for business school. For instance, should he be talking to more alumni? He wondered, too, how he could be sure that the schools had received his recommendation letters and transcripts. When would his applications be complete? When would they start reviewing his applications? Would it be appropriate to call the admissions offices to check?

Luis had waited for weeks and finally received his e-mail invitations to interview from both Smith and McCombs. Since he wanted to visit both schools and sit in on classes, he decided to schedule on-campus interviews. He had attended Smith as an undergrad, but since he had majored in history he didn't know very much about the business school. Fortunately, he had a number of friends in Baltimore who had attended Smith either as undergrads or as MBA students, so he felt prepared. He didn't know as much about McCombs, but his brother had gone to the University of Texas at Austin for college and was now working for a computer company in Austin. He really wanted to move to Austin to be near his brother. What should he be doing once he scheduled his interview? And how long would it be before he heard whether he had been admitted?

The Waiting Game

If you have done everything right, there is almost nothing for you to do for a few weeks after you click "submit" but wait. First, you are waiting to hear whether you have an interview. Then you are waiting to hear whether you have been admitted. Some schools release almost, if not all, of their invitations on one day during each round. Or they have a mid-decision date, by which time you will either have been invited to interview or won't be. This information should be on their Web sites, especially in their admissions blogs. Other schools release their invitations seemingly one by one for weeks or months. Most MBA hopefuls are waiting to hear about interviews, and then waiting to hear about admissions. For most schools, though, the timing of your interview invitation has nothing to do with the perceived quality of your application. You were simply invited—or not—when your file was reviewed, regardless of what your last name begins with, where you live, where you went to school, or where you work. Everyone waits his or her turn.

Many people want to know what they should do while they are waiting. Should they submit additional letters of recommendation? Should they alert the committee to a new project with increased responsibility or a new job? What else can they do? Keep in mind that hundreds of people are asking the same questions. If you make a nuisance of yourself by bombarding the admissions office with updates and additional information, you are likely to wind up with a note in your file describing you in uncomplimentary terms. In general, admissions committees do not want to read additional letters of recommendation. That makes more work for them and could give the committee the impression that you believe you deserve special treatment. Some schools, however, will welcome brief letters of support from alumni. It is wise to find out first, though, before contacting your dad's golfing buddy or your mother's employer and asking for help at their alma mater. Each school has its own policies, so it's best to follow them.

What Happens to Your Application After You Submit It

It is a good idea to track and monitor your applications after they have been submitted. Following up on your application and knowing what comes next in the application process are essential steps in managing your anxiety. The improper approach can cause you to oversubmit addendums that might hurt your chances rather than improve them. Since most applications are submitted online, it is easy to check the current status of your application on a regular basis. The first thing you will learn is that your file is submitted. That means you made the deadline! The next thing you will learn is that your file is complete. Once the admissions staff has confirmed that it has received all the required information—letters of recommendation, GMAT scores, TOEFL or IELTS scores, and transcripts—your file status will change. Unless you are concerned about the arrival of an international transcript or a similar unusual circumstance, there is no point in calling the office to check since the school may have hundreds or even thousands of files to sort through before they get to yours. If you learn that some item from your file is missing, you should contact the office right away so that you can resolve the issue. Usually you will receive an e-mail alerting you, but checking your online status is a proactive approach. If your file remains incomplete and you know that it is close to the middle of the admissions round, then sending an e-mail to the admissions staff to check your status is a good idea.

Once your application is complete, the file is ready for review by an admissions committee member. Regardless of when you submit your application, your file won't be reviewed until the submission deadline has passed. Schools that have rolling admissions, however, will review your file after it is complete. The date when your file is reviewed is random because files are put in batches and distributed to the individual readers. (Many schools still print out application materials, so a literal paper file is distributed.) The general process is that the first reader makes a recommendation before passing it on for a second read. If the decisions of the two readers match, then a mid-decision is reached. If they don't agree, the dean or director of admissions has the final say. At that point, the applicant is either invited to interview or given a final decision (deny or waitlist without interview). If no interview has been offered, the applicant generally won't receive the news until the final decision date. Some schools, such as Indiana Kelley and Dartmouth Tuck, strongly suggest that all applicants interview before applying, but the schools will grant some interviews to selected candidates after submission. However, Kellogg requires all candidates to interview (except in the rare cases of a waiver), so it mostly uses alumni interviewers throughout the world.

Schools usually send e-mails alerting candidates that they are being invited to interview, but sometimes e-mails go astray. As one distressed candidate discovered, if you don't respond quickly to an e-mail invitation, the school may assume you aren't interested and decide to deny you. Fortunately, with a great deal of persistence, the candidate was able to convince the director of admissions to let her interview long after the final decision. If she had checked her online status every week, she would have discovered two weeks earlier that her status had changed to "Held for Interview" and saved herself a great deal of anxiety and frustration. Another candidate went out of the country on vacation after submitting his applications and was unable to check his e-mail in a remote location. Fortunately, when he returned he was able to explain why he hadn't responded to his e-mails for two weeks and promptly scheduled an interview. Although he didn't anticipate being invited to interview so soon after he submitted his application, he could have sent a brief e-mail to the staff members, alerting them that he was going to be unavailable for two weeks.

Sanjay had already heard from London Business School, but he started getting nervous that he hadn't heard anything about an interview at MIT Sloan or Columbia, even though several of his friends and colleagues had. Was something wrong with his applications? He reread both of them, looking for flaws. He even asked his colleague who had received an interview invitation from MIT Sloan to send him a copy of his essays.

Sanjay wondered whether he should call the admissions office. He searched online blogs for clues on whether the schools were still sending invitations. His friends told him to relax, but he was having a hard time doing that. Finally, he decided to visit his sister for the weekend and think nothing about business school (if that was possible). At a minimum, he would be occupied with the daily concerns of his sister, his brother-in-law, and their kids for a couple of days. He would try to remember what it felt like to be a normal person again. He decided not to check his e-mail from Friday night until Monday morning, no matter how tempted he was.

When he returned to work on Monday, he felt more relaxed than he had been in months. It had been a crazy weekend filled with activities, but it was good to get away from his anxiety. On Tuesday morning, he received an e-mail from Columbia inviting him to interview. And on Wednesday, he received one from MIT Sloan. Now to prepare!

An Invitation to Interview: Now What?

If you are invited to interview, you have already made the second cut. Depending on the school and the applicant pool that year, it means that you are among the top 50 percent or the top 25 to 30 percent of all the applicants from around the world. Generally you are given the opportunity to sign up for an interview with an alum in your area or come to campus for an interview with an admissions officer or second-year student. Some admissions officers also do interviews in hub cities, on campus, or by phone. Regardless of with whom you interview, the interviews are standardized and are weighted the same. Although schools would love for you to come to campus, meet with current students, and sit in on classes, they realize that not everyone has the time or the means to do so.

Superior interviewees remain undaunted and answer all questions concisely while providing examples and background to illustrate their responses. It is important to impress your interviewer by setting yourself apart and highlighting your unique qualities. This takes a lot of thoughtfulness and practice.

Practicing the interview repeatedly is a good idea, and being able to conduct a mock interview with a professional admissions consultant who can provide you with constructive feedback is highly recommended. The mock interview can help you highlight your strengths and address areas of concern. Interviews with admissions officers and alumni are sometimes different, so your preparation will depend on who is interviewing you. For example, an alum interviewer tends to be protective of his or her alma mater and really wants to see evidence of critical thinking and leadership that is found in an MBA. What this means is that you will want to construct your answers for an alum interview by using detailed critical thought, especially when speaking about your goals and career progression. However, when interviewing with an admissions committee member, emphasize the ways you have met your potential because he or she wants evidence that you can achieve your career goals.

PREPARE FOR THE STRESS INTERVIEW SOMETIMES CONDUCTED BY ALUMNI.

Despite the best intentions of the business schools, sometimes their alumni conduct stress interviews. Hence, if your interview is to be held with an alum, you should be prepared for this possibility. A stress interview is very easy to identify. Your interviewer will try to make you feel uncomfortable. As long as you maintain your cool, you will pass this test. Please be advised that admissions officers do not conduct this style of interview. They are fully aware that most applicants put enough stress on themselves already.

To navigate an interview successfully, you need to master three tiers. The first tier is the ability to express why you are pursuing an MBA, why now, and why at this specific school. The second tier is presenting yourself well through appropriate attire, poise, good articulation, eye contact with the person sitting across from you, and insightful answers. The third tier is conveying to the interviewer how you approach decision making through progressive and critical thinking. Excelling at all three tiers lead to your objective—a letter of acceptance.

The Interview

Your best opportunity to position yourself comes with the interview. This is when you bring your application to life and express what motivates you and how passionate you are about your goals. You want your interviewer to leave the interview thinking that he or she would be proud to have you join the program. Prepare by knowing your resume inside and out and remain consistent with the message you conveyed in your application. Clearly articulate your career progression and how that relates to your career vision. Give a complete view of who you are and why you are a perfect fit for the school's program.

Interviews, often squeezed into a 30 to 45 minute block of time, expose your ability to articulate ideas clearly and concisely. Top MBA programs attempt to assess a lot about the applicant in this one interview, so they focus on evidence of strong communication skills, intellectual curiosity, social skills, self-confidence, teamwork success, work ethic, independence, and adaptability. Senior admissions consultant Cindy Sullivan notes, "When I conducted interviews for University of Chicago's Booth School of Business, it became clear that the most prepared applicants came across as professional, personable, and interesting."

You must demonstrate these qualities as well as clear and effective thinking. Are you able to take a hypothetical problem and identify the key issues that need to be addressed? Can you determine what resources you need to tackle each issue? Can you define possible obstacles to success? How about dealing with the unexpected? These and other questions may be put to you so the interviewer understands your critical-thinking process.

THE BEST WAY TO WOW YOUR INTERVIEWER.

While you must follow your interviewer's lead, be sure you are prepared with the points you need to make. In addition to the points that highlight your strengths and mitigate weaknesses, be sure to work in some other relevant and key points not found in the application. If you are successful at this step, you will wow the interviewer and give him or her the accurate impression that you are much more than what you could cram into the application!

Most schools do *blind interviews,* meaning that the interviewer has not read your file and has only your resume for reference. A few schools, such as Harvard and MIT Sloan, have *informed interviews* and use them to get into more depth about elements of your application. If it isn't clear in the interview invitation, be sure to ask the admissions office whether the interviewer will have read your file. If you are being interviewed by an alum, the interview should be blind, so be sure to let the admissions office know if the interviewer asks you directly to send a copy of your application. That is usually a sign of an inexperienced interviewer, so the office will want to follow up with the interviewer for additional training before you have your interview. If you want to include new information on your resume, this is the time to update it and send it to both the admissions office and the interviewer.

Interviews are another opportunity to discuss your background, your interests, and your plans. Often the interviews are treated by the school as conversations lasting 30 minutes or more to assess your communication skills. Once you have thought out your answers and know how you intend to answer them, be sure not to over-rehearse your answers, because you want to be relaxed and make sure you are listening to the actual questions asked.

Questions are straightforward and cover topics such as why you seek an MBA, why you feel you are a good fit for the school (and vice versa), what your career goals are, how you spend your spare time, what you value, what you are passionate about, and so on. Most schools will not ask you to analyze a case study or demonstrate your ability to speak on particular subjects. Questions may center on specific examples or detailed descriptions of events, projects, or experiences that demonstrate how situations you've faced in the past have been handled and what you learned from them. Behavioral interviewing assumes that past performance predicts future behavior. Probably the best way to prepare is by rereading your essays for all the schools you've applied to so that you have specific examples in your mind. For most schools the two most important questions are "Why do you want an MBA?" and "Why do you want to attend this program?" Further, the interview is your best chance to demonstrate your fit with the school and what you will contribute as a student and as an alum. So, before your interview, talk to as many current students and alumni as you can and thoroughly review the school's Web site so that you can speak intelligently about particular programs that interest you and ask informed questions of the interviewer. Finally, be enthusiastic, be genuine, be thoughtful, and be honest.

Luis was excited to get an interview at McCombs. He hadn't seen his brother since the summer, so he decided to use his frequent flyer miles and book a flight from Baltimore to Austin. He called the school and set up an interview for the following Friday. His brother was equally excited and told him about a band that was playing at his favorite club on Friday night. They made more plans for the weekend, and Luis decided to do some research on Austin since he had been there only twice. He already pictured himself living there, going to school during the week, and hanging out with his brother and his friends on weekends.

Luis had planned to prepare for his interview on Wednesday and Thursday nights, but it turned out he needed to complete a huge project and worked very late Wednesday since he was taking off Thursday afternoon and Friday. He decided he would make some notes and look them over on the plane flight to Texas. Unfortunately, he was tired on the flight and couldn't really focus. When he arrived Thursday night, his brother picked him up at the airport, and they went out for a late dinner and drinks.

The next morning he headed to McCombs for an information session and tour, followed by his interview and class visit. He found out a lot about the school during the morning, but halfway through the interview he realized he hadn't thought through his reasons for attending McCombs other than its proximity to his brother. Even to him his answer to "why McCombs?" sounded weak. He hoped the rest of his answers were more impressive.

Avoiding Common Interview Mistakes

The most common mistake applicants make is not taking advantage of the opportunity to tell the interviewer their strengths, how their work experience has shaped them, and how they will contribute to the program. But more than that, they are confronted with an inability to clearly articulate why they need an MBA. During an economic recession, some people are looking for a place to hide for two years. Business schools don't want to admit those people. Instead, they want students who want an MBA regardless of the economy and who are prepared to participate fully in every aspect of the program. That's the only way someone will get the full value of the MBA program. In interviews, some applicants make the mistake of saying that they hate their jobs and see the MBA as a means to a better job. That may be a reason, but it shouldn't be the main reason. And it probably shouldn't be the one you reveal to the interviewer. You need to know how the MBA is going to move you forward to where you want to go, even if you don't end up doing precisely what you imagine after you graduate. But you need to be able to hit the ground running so that you can start to network and interview not long after you begin classes.

You should also be prepared to talk about your current status if you've been laid off—whether it happened before, during, or after you submitted your application. Because so many companies downsized in 2008 and 2009, there is no shame in having been laid off. Divisions and even entire companies have disappeared all over the world, and your interviewer knows that as well as you do. Instead, focus on what you have been doing since you were laid off and what steps you have taken to improve your circumstances. If the setback has changed your initial goals, discuss that as well. If you have a new job, even if it isn't comparable to your previous position, be prepared to discuss what you are learning from it. Again, be thoughtful and be honest.

Backup Plans and How to Devise Them

As the final decisions draw near, many candidates become nervous. What happens if they are not admitted anywhere? Is there still time to apply in a later round? Would they have a chance in a later round, or will all the spots other than a handful be filled? Will their supervisors think less of them for not being admitted? Has the company been making plans for their departure so that staying after all would be awkward? During the interview, some schools ask applicants what they will do if they are not admitted. They want to know—if you are unable to get into your top choice this year—whether you would settle for your second-choice school or reapply next year.

At some point during the application process, you should think through your alternatives. Some candidates are interested only in certain schools; they figure the opportunity cost is too high for them to attend more than a handful of schools. Reapplying would be the obvious choice. For others, adding a school or two in a later round can increase their chances, especially if one of the schools has a strong regional reputation but may not be as competitive nationally and globally. As long as you are happy with the school's program and career opportunities, a second-tier school could be a good alternative. If you have already applied to five or more schools, it makes sense to wait to see how things turn out after the interviews. If no offers are forthcoming, then keeping your job for another year and trying different ways to reposition yourself may be the best option. Many reapplicants are able to improve their chances significantly the following year by gaining more work experience with increased responsibilities, taking classes, retaking the GMAT, or adding to their community involvement. As long as you have a plan in mind, you should be able to manage your anxiety while you wait.

The Final Decision: Your Wait Is Over

After the interview is completed, the file is reviewed for a third time with the addition of the interview feedback. Usually an admissions officer who has not read the file previously will review the file. He or she makes a decision to admit, send the file to committee, or deny the applicant. If all decisions match, a final decision is made. If the file goes to committee, a group of admissions officers debate the file and make a recommendation to accept, waitlist, or deny the applicant. For schools such as Kellogg that require all applicants to interview, the final admissions decision can come at any time before or on the decision date. The final determination is always reviewed by the director or dean of admission. If you are denied admission or waitlisted, be assured that you've been reviewed by three or four people who have made that decision. If you're admitted, you've been reviewed by more than four people who have been your advocates along the way and who are looking forward to meeting you at an admitted students event—either at a reception in a major city or on campus at a weekend full of events designed to introduce you to current students and alumni and show you the MBA program at its best.

UPDATE YOUR DESTINATION, INTERNATIONAL STUDENTS.

If you are an international admit to a U.S. school, be sure that you list the school you will be attending on the I-20 when you apply for your visa. If the embassy or consulate later sees a different school's name—perhaps because you changed your mind on where you would like to attend—it may become suspicious in this post-9/11 world, and that can delay or cancel your visa application.

Chapter 8

WHAT IT MEANS TO DEAL WITH ACCEPTANCE, WAITLISTS, AND REJECTION

TAKING THE OFFER AND RUNNING

Luis received word that he had been accepted to Smith. But his happiness quickly turned to anxiety. He knew that he hadn't been accepted into McCombs. He had one pressing question on his mind: Could he get into McCombs if he reapplied the following year? Would it be possible for him to reposition himself? Should he reconsider McCombs or should he accept Smith's offer now? His boss was encouraging him to start business school this year. But after visiting McCombs, he was still excited about the possibility of going to Texas.

Sanjay was disappointed when he found out he was on the waitlist to his top-choice program at MIT Sloan, even though he had been accepted at London Business School and Columbia. Should he decide between his two acceptances or wait out his time on the MIT Sloan waitlist? Could he do anything to tip the decision into his favor at MIT Sloan? As for London Business School, he had friends who were considering the school and he had family in London. However, he was living in New York, so attending Columbia would be an easy transition. But MIT Sloan still seemed like the ideal school for him. What should he do to help him decide?

So what do those responses you receive from schools mean—waitlist, acceptance, and rejection? And how do you go about handling multiple admission offers, waitlist decisions, and updates? Does reapplying to a school that rejected you have value?

Understanding the possible responses from your target schools is important, because it helps set the stage for the next possible step. You need to take a hard look at which program is the most important; if you are waitlisted at your dream school but accepted at another, what choice will you make?

Knowing the pros and cons of reapplying to a b-school is also important. While you have the chance to rethink and tweak your rejected application, you also need to be aware of pitfalls that might arise during the reapplication process.

How to Anticipate Your Acceptance Letter

Months ago you decided which schools to apply to and you probably ranked your choices, but since then you have probably visited several if not all of the schools, met and talked to alumni and current students, and heard lots of feedback from friends and relatives. Now you may not be so sure that your first choice is still your first choice. One technique is to list the pros and cons of each school. For some people, location or cost is a big factor; for others it's the alumni network and brand of the school. If you visited a school, were impressed with the students, and felt at home there, then you might decide that it is the right school for you regardless of where it is ranked or what your friends think. But first you have to get accepted.

Because schools release their decisions at different times, it is difficult in many cases to anticipate when you will hear from them. For schools such as Harvard, Wharton, or Chicago that have a mid-decision, it is easy to guess that if you didn't get an invitation to interview you are likely to be denied. And some schools release those decisions at the midpoint as well. But Harvard releases names of accepted candidates in waves as applications are reviewed. Many people become anxious as the class fills up and hope to be one of the lucky ones who get a late interview invitation. Many schools put candidates on waitlists, even without an interview, on the decision date. Other schools seem to be on no particular schedule. Invites go out throughout the cycle, and decisions are only guaranteed no later than a certain date. Kellogg interviews everyone, so it sends out final decisions at different points during the round. UCLA, McCombs, and Vanderbilt, among others, send out decisions as they are made. For many people, the first news they get is negative.

What to Do When Facing Multiple Acceptance Letters

Most candidates, if they have done their homework properly, will be happy to go to any school that admits them. Those who are lucky enough to be admitted to multiple schools face a more complicated choice. A candidate who has attracted the notice of four admissions committees discovers with each acceptance letter a mixture of relief, jubilation, and uncertainty. If this happens to you, once the first school says yes, you will probably be thrilled. But now you are looking at four great choices. If any school offers you a sizeable scholarship, your choice is even harder. Not everyone has those choices, of course, but many successful applicants have to decide between at least two choices.

If you can't eliminate any of your choices immediately, you should attend the events for admitted students and get as many of your questions answered through the admitted students' portal on the Web site. Most schools have weekend events where you can meet students, alumni, faculty, and the admissions officers who admitted you. If you live in another country or far from campus, many schools hold admitted student receptions in major cities. These are all great opportunities to get to know the school better. This time they are trying their best to impress you—rather than you trying to impress them.

The best choice for you is your main consideration. Unless you are married or have a significant other who will be moving with you, this should be your decision. And although no business school is inexpensive, factors such as tuition and moving costs vary widely from school to school. A scholarship may tip the scales for candidates who have families or who know they plan to go into a less lucrative field after graduation, such as a nonprofit, a nongovernment organization (NGO), or the public sector. Some schools have loan forgiveness programs for those who enter these fields. For international students, especially, the ability to get visas and loans taken care of before entry is a definite consideration.

Once you are admitted, you should take the time to reconsider what matters most to you—your experience during school or your career options and alumni network once you graduate. In some cases, applicants discover their preferences have changed because of the additional research and introspection they have undertaken. Although rankings go up and down and vary from publication to publication (and no one remembers the ranking in five years), a school's brand can equal credibility. Since employers in the most competitive fields such as investment banking and consulting like to fill their ranks with graduates from the top MBA programs, you might consider that. Graduates from certain schools may be able to land better, higher-paying jobs with more opportunities for growth. If you have the opportunity to attend one of those schools, you may have the opportunity to connect with people who will one day be in positions of great power. This can open up an entirely new world for you. On the other hand, your goals may be more modest. You may be looking for increased knowledge and credibility in your field or in your region. You may find that you need to stay close to home or at a school known for a particular area of study. Everyone's needs are different, so don't get distracted by others' opinions—or by rankings.

Sanjay agonized over his decision. He had been dreaming of attending MIT Sloan for years. He had visited friends who attended the school and met lots of alumni. His family was no help. They told him to make a decision and get on with his life. But it was his life he was trying to decide about! Cambridge, London, and New York are very different cities, and each school was likely to head him in a different direction. How serious was he about an international business career? Sure, he had written about that in his essays, but did he mean it? He decided his first step was to attend the admit weekend events for London Business School and Columbia. Although Columbia was practically down the street, he wanted to know who his classmates would be and get a true feel for the school. And London Business School? Well, he had originally applied there because of its reputation for a collaborative atmosphere and for a chance to become truly global in his perspective. He was impressed that more than 60 nationalities were usually represented in each entering class. If he chose London Business, he knew he was much more likely to launch his post-MBA career outside the United States. He decided he had better book a flight to London for a visit.

Even if you have visited the school once, twice, or three times before, if you are seriously considering attending an MBA program you should plan to attend its admit weekend. This is your best chance to not only meet current students, other admitted students, alumni, faculty, and staff, but it is a great chance to have all your questions answered. After you are admitted you will have access to the admitted students' section of the Web site, and there you will have a chance to find many answers. But being in the same room with candidates just like you who have been through the same process and who will be your potential classmates for the next two years is an opportunity not to be missed.

Each school schedules a variety of activities that will keep you—and your significant other—busy for two or more days. You will have a chance to congregate informally over drinks, lunches, and dinners attended by other admits and current students. You may be assigned to a study group and then attend a class immersion experience together. You and your fellow admits may work together to analyze a business problem from a case study. You will hear from faculty about what changes might be happening in the curriculum and learn what to expect from the different departments and programs within the MBA program. You will hear about housing options, and if there are on-campus options, such as at Stanford, you will be taken on a tour of the various buildings. You will learn about career services and specialty programs, receive specific information about industries and job functions, and hear current students talk about their full-time and internship job searches. You will get to know the larger university and surrounding area on excursions hosted by current students. Most schools run concurrent programs for significant others, so while you are getting to know your fellow admits, significant others meet other partners and learn about job search strategies and housing options. At the end of the final day of meeting and greeting and questions and answers, you will likely have a much stronger feel for the school and a clear idea of whether it's the right school for you.

What the Waitlist Process Means to You

For some applicants, discovering that they have been waitlisted is almost worse than being denied. Instead of the decision signifying the end of a long wait, the wait continues for an indefinite time. But the good news is that the committee saw many strengths in your application and definitely wants you in its entering class if there is room.

The main purpose of a waitlist is to control *yield.* That means that an MBA program doesn't want to admit more applicants than necessary to fill an exact number of spots. The dean or director of admissions has to determine how many offers of admission to make to match that number, based on past yields. Since admissions isn't an exact science, waitlists allow a modicum of control. If one applicant turns down an offer, then a waitlisted applicant can be admitted. Because every school wants a well-rounded class professionally, geographically, and personally, the waitlist helps it build a heterogeneous class by allowing it to choose another candidate who complements the class. And as you wait patiently to hear your fate, the admissions committee has launched into full recruiting mode and is waiting to hear back from their admitted applicants and receive deposits.

Most schools do not rank waitlisted candidates, and they continually review their files as space becomes available. There is no set number of candidates on a school's waitlist; the number varies from year to year and from round to round. Some schools decide to waitlist candidates who have been interviewed, and the committee wants to delay the final decision until more applications have been reviewed. Other applicants are waitlisted without an interview, although they may be asked to interview later. Some candidates are reviewed with the next batch of applicants during a later round and receive favorable news quickly. Others wait to hear their fate until the late summer. Just because it is June and you haven't heard doesn't mean you won't get in, but your plans have to be very flexible to be able to wait until sometime in August to set plans for September. Of course, it is possible to set a timetable for yourself. If you don't hear by a certain date, you should remove your name from the waitlist and attend another school.

If you are offered a spot on a school's waitlist, the first thing you should do is follow the school's specific directions. If, like Columbia, the school says not to send additional information, then simply confirm that you wish to be on the waitlist with an enthusiastic, well-written e-mail reiterating your strong commitment to the school. Consider mentioning the names of current students or alumni whom you know well who have recommended the school to you. But whatever you do, don't go overboard. You don't want to wind up decreasing your chances. If the school says, "Please do not send in additional materials," then don't.

If, like many schools (MIT Sloan, Stern, or Washington University Olin, for example), they ask for additional information, then start by expressing your continued interest and then consider weaknesses in your application that you can address. Is there an area that you can improve at this point? If your GMAT is on the lower end of their admitted-applicant range and you believe you can improve it with additional studying, then consider retaking it. If so, send an e-mail letting the school know your intention and your scheduled exam date, and the school will add this information to your file. If you feel your quantitative background is weak, then perhaps a class in microeconomics, accounting, or statistics would be a good idea. If you don't feel you can address any particular weakness, then a well-written letter describing any changes at your job and why the program remains your top choice is fine.

Some schools but not all welcome endorsements from students and alumni. A quick call to the admissions office or your assigned waitlist manager can confirm that. You can ask whether endorsements are welcome. Senior admissions consultant Susan Shaffer says, "Being on a waitlist causes anxiety, but try to be patient. The school obviously saw strengths in your application, and it needs time to reevaluate it. Schools always accept people from the waitlist later in the process, and you are still in the game."

Sanjay had already sent in an updated resume to MIT Sloan listing his new position and increased responsibilities, but still no news came. The school had given him a choice of June 1, July 1, August 1, or September 1 to stay on the waitlist, and he had chosen June 1 because he promised himself that he wouldn't wait until the summer to hear whether he got in. If it were just between Sloan and Columbia, he could wait until September since he wouldn't have to move. But after his visit to London Business School with one friend from London and another friend from New York—both of whom were planning to attend the school—he knew that the program was also a very good fit, and he was excited about the possibility of working in Europe. As much as he liked Columbia, he realized it was time for him to leave his New York experience and reestablish himself back home in the United Kingdom. If he heard from Sloan before the date that the London Business School deposit was due, then he would figure out what he wanted to do. Otherwise, he decided to send in his deposit to London Business School to reserve his spot and make plans to move back to London.

What a Deferral Means

MBA programs offer two basic deferrals. One is a deferral from one round to the next. Some schools use this type in the first round when they are most uncertain about what the rest of the applicant pool looks like. Instead of being placed on a waitlist, you are thrown into the pool again with the next round of applicants and reconsidered.

The other type of deferral is generally reserved for candidates with little or no post-university work experience—a common practice in the past. Schools admit college seniors with the contingency that they work for two years before starting the MBA program. Although this deferral is less common now, in the last few years Harvard has reinstituted its 2+2 program—two years of work experience followed by two years of immersion in the MBA program. Other schools have instituted similar offerings. Although many schools admit some candidates with exceptional leadership potential straight after college, other schools ask those with little full-time work experience to defer admission for one or two years. If the MBA program that offers this option is your first choice school, then your decision is simple—although finding a job after having made plans to return to school may be harder. If you think you would benefit more from going to school next fall, then you have no need to wait.

REJECTION WITH ENCOURAGEMENT.

A rejection with encouragement is similar to the deferral. The applicant is not admitted in the current admission cycle but is strongly encouraged to reapply (generally after two years) with some additional work experience, and then his or her candidacy will be reevaluated. This type of rejection is similar to a deferral because in every case AdmissionsConsultants has seen since 1996, the applicant was ultimately admitted to the school.

Another type of deferral is initiated by the admitted candidate. MBA programs are very cautious about allowing candidates to defer their admissions. For example, serious medical reasons or an unexpected military deployment are acceptable. Each request is reviewed on a case-by-case basis. If you think you will be unable to attend school next year due to family or personal matters, then you should delay applying to any program for a year or more. If a school turns down your request for a deferral, then you risk having to start the application process all over again next year.

How to Handle Rejection

Rejection is hard to bear. It is especially hard to handle when you're rejected for something that you have been planning and dreaming of for months if not years. If you apply to a range of schools—the reach schools, the strong possibilities, and the safety schools—then your chances are better that you will be admitted to at least one school. But if you applied late in the cycle or only to your dream schools, then you may not receive the news you were hoping to hear. And to a certain extent, there is the luck of the draw. The overall quality of applicants to the top 30 MBA programs is extremely high. The majority would do well in the programs academically if they were admitted. So, what it boils down to is the intangible notion of fit discussed throughout this book. Three or four members of the admissions committee read your file and judge it in comparison to the other files they have read in that round. They remember particulars of many files that are judged to be best-fit applicants, but others go by in a blur. If your file is deemed "okay, not great," then you will be denied. Waitlisted candidates are often marked "admit if there's room." But if you didn't take the care you needed to on the essays and the rest of the application, the comments may be "weak essays" or "nothing compelling." There will be many other comments as well, but those two comments are telling.

Luis spent a number of sleepless nights thinking about his decision. Additionally, his employer was eager for him to attend Smith since he had earned his own MBA there and knew it had a great alumni network on the East Coast. On the other hand, Luis's mother and girlfriend wanted him to stay in the area. But he knew this might be the only time in his life when he could move to another part of the country for two years. He wouldn't have to stay in Texas when he graduated, but it could be a great experience for him. Since his brother lived in Austin, he wouldn't be headed completely into the unknown; he knew the area. He could spend time on the weekends with his brother when he wasn't studying. Plus he had been really impressed with the students he met, and he loved the class he visited. He could see himself at McCombs.

But what if he turned down Smith this year and didn't get into McCombs next year? Would he lose the chance to attend business school if he didn't go this year? Finally, he decided that he would not reapply to McCombs. Although he knew that McCombs was a great school, he knew he wanted his long-term career to be in the Washington, D.C., area. His employers were telling him that if he promised to work for them after he got his MBA at Smith, they would pay a substantial portion of his tuition. Austin would have to wait. Now that he had made up his mind, he felt much better. And he was able to focus on his job and the rest of his life again.

Assess the Values and Strategies of a Reapplication

If you want to reapply next year, either because you didn't get into the school you most wanted to attend or because you know you didn't put your best effort into your applications, then you should first see whether the school offers feedback to denied applicants. Some schools have online chats during the summer. Others will respond to written requests for individual feedback. The admissions staff will let you know the school's policy if you can't find it easily on the Web site. But even individual feedback may not tell you what you need to know.

If the letters of recommendation are what sunk you, you will not be told this. But you might be told nicely that your essays or your leadership skills could have been stronger or that your quantitative skills could use some work. It may be useful to seek the help of a qualified consultant who can evaluate your submitted applications, transcripts, and scores and give you an honest assessment of where you went wrong and whether and how you can bolster your chances as a reapplicant.

Good "Admit" Etiquette

The main rule of etiquette for admitted applicants is that once you decide that you definitely don't want to attend a particular school, immediately let that school know. It may not be your first choice, but it is certainly someone else's first choice, and that person is waiting to hear good news. So, just give the school a call. Someone somewhere will be silently thanking you.

PART III

MOVING IN AND MOVING ON

Chapter 9. **What to Do Before You Matriculate.** Transitioning to Student Life

Chapter 10. **What Is the Business School Balancing Act?** Hitting the Ground Running Without Tripping

Chapter 11. **Putting It All Together**

WHAT TO DO BEFORE YOU MATRICULATE

Transitioning to Student Life

Nancy was excited and happy at the end of Stanford's Admit Weekend. She no longer had any doubt whether her b-school investment would pay off. As soon as she got home, she mailed her deposit and turned to the to-do list she had started over the weekend. Her list was daunting, but she had to take care of as many tasks as possible before reporting to campus. However, she was not sure how to balance preparing for the fall semester and her final weeks at work.

The transition from work to business school can be traumatic if not understood or prepared for properly. What should you expect once classes start? What should you take care of before the term begins? Of special consideration for those applicants who have been in the workplace for many years: How do you handle a sudden shift from a solid career back to school again?

How to Leave Work on Good Terms

Some aspiring MBAs work until the last moment in an attempt to save as much money as possible before quitting their jobs. Others prefer to take time off to travel, visit friends and family, or move to get settled at their new school. Some schools offer special trips toward the end of the summer to help MBA candidates make the transition. And most programs start with an orientation program.

TAKE THIS TIME TO TRAVEL, RELAX, AND MAKE THE TRANSITION.

You'll make so much money after you graduate that now is the time to enjoy your leisure while your leisure time is relatively inexpensive. If you had a life adventure during or after college (backpacking in Europe, for example), take what might now be your last opportunity and do it again. If you missed out on this event as an undergrad, don't let this opportunity get away. By

---

the time you have another opportunity to travel for extended periods, more than likely you will be much older and not willing to do so on the budget that you have right now.

Spend time with your family or explore by yourself or with your pals. Need more encouragement? In the next chapter, you'll realize how much work you will be doing when you get to school. If you come in relaxed and refreshed, you will be giving yourself an important leg up.

Whatever you decide to do, give yourself enough time to switch from work to school as smoothly as possible. Additionally, this allows you and your employer enough time to plan for your departure.

If one or more of your managers wrote your letters of recommendation, the fact that you will be leaving soon for business school won't be a surprise. You should still give your manager plenty of warning about when you plan to leave. If you want to leave on the best terms, two or three months will give your department a chance to find a replacement or shift job responsibilities. If your company hires a replacement, the extra time will allow the new person a chance to join the company and train while you are available for questions. Tell employers that they should feel free to call you at school. They probably won't take you up on it, but it's nice to make the offer. Besides, if your employer does need you, he or she would try calling you at school regardless. Consider documenting the knowledge you carry in your head so that the next person doesn't have to reinvent the job. Remember, too, that your current employer will be your most recent reference when you are searching for an internship.

KEEP YOUR WORK OPTIONS OPEN.

Once you have completed your first year in school, you will start your summer internship. You may want the option of returning to your former employer for three months. You want to keep that door open so you also can talk about returning to the firm full-time after graduation. And the contacts you've made at work now may come in handy to find your next position, either at your current company or another in the same industry. So keeping the lines of communication open is a very good idea, especially in a tough economy.

How B-School Differs from College or Work

Returning to life as a student after having a substantial income for a number of years can be a real shock. On the one hand, you probably won't have to get up early and fight rush-hour traffic, sit through innumerable meetings, and deal with the demands of clients and managers. Your schedule will be much more flexible, but you will quickly find ways to fill all that free time. Along with classes, there will be group projects, study sessions, club meetings and events, and job searches and networking. For the minority of those who have come from extremely fast-paced, highly demanding careers, the pace of business school may seem more leisurely. For those whose jobs were not so intense and who had flexible schedules, the competing demands of classes, projects, new friends, clubs, and careers may seem overwhelming. The key is to prioritize the competing demands and manage your time.

Besides time, another issue is likely to be money, specifically the loss of an income. Because you will probably be taking out loans to pay for tuition and school expenses, you have to think carefully about how you spend your money. Even if you have been living on your own for a number of years, you might consider finding one or more roommates to share a house or large apartment. Because you and your classmates have all been in the workforce for a number of years, you needn't fear rowdy roommates and huge parties, but you may have to give up some privacy in exchange for study partners and companionship. You will probably be eating at home more. Fortunately, when you do go out to eat, you'll find an abundance of inexpensive restaurants and cafes on campus or near most universities. But learning to cook and befriending those who like to cook is a good idea.

Some unexpected expenses of business school are a couple of good suits and the accompanying dry-cleaning bills. Dress codes have remained constant at business schools, so when you look around the classroom on any given day, any number of your classmates will be wearing suits. Men: If you've been in a field where a pair of khakis is considered dressy, you may have to buy another suit, a few shirts, and new ties. For women, you also need suits, and depending on the field or industry you plan to interview for, pants may not be acceptable and panty hose may be expected.

Of course, weather is another, perhaps new, consideration. If you are moving from a warmer climate to a colder one, you will need a winter coat, gloves, and probably boots. Mail order and Internet companies such as Land's End and L.L. Bean have good quality products for reasonable prices. It's a good idea to order these clothes in advance so that you don't wake up one morning and discover a snow drift outside your door and not have anything warmer than a rain coat. Because you will likely be interviewing in the winter, it is a good idea to have a presentable coat that can be worn over a suit rather than a parka or ski jacket. If you are moving to a warmer climate, you should have a wardrobe that anticipates rain and heat. Find out what you can about the area where you will be headed and plan accordingly.

How to Face the Basics—Housing, Transportation, Banking, and More

Before you start school, take time to research the community where you'll live. Unless you choose to attend a program in your local area, you will be relocating, maybe to a different state or even a different country. Talk to current students to find out where they live, where they bank, and where they shop. Some programs, such as Harvard and Stanford, encourage students to live on campus at least for their first year, because the camaraderie of fellow students is part of the experience. Other schools, such as Indiana Kelley and Michigan Ross, are located in neighborhoods or towns that appeal to students. If you want to live near other business school students, find out what neighborhoods and what apartment buildings they favor. For those late-night study groups in the dead of winter, you don't want to be driving around merely to join your group. Although living with friends or relatives may save rent money, think twice about the opportunity cost of being far from your classmates and school. A rush-hour commute isn't much fun for a professional, and it isn't much fun for a b-school student. One of the many pleasures of business school life is bonding with classmates in the evenings and on weekends. If you live within walking distance of your classmates, you'll see them more often and get to know them better.

Think also about what to do with the stuff you have accumulated over the years of professional life. Do you need to take it with you to business school? Maybe it makes sense to sell it or store it for one or two years. Most universities have a huge number of students coming and going each year, so it's relatively easy to find the furniture you need. That antique dresser from Aunt Mary might be something you'll want to hang on to, but shipping it across the country will cost a lot. Again, talk to current students and find out what they have done. If possible, get in touch with students in the spring when they are still at school since it is much harder to track them down in the summer. Sometimes you will discover that a group of second-year students is moving out of a great apartment filled with serviceable furniture, and you can arrange to take over their lease. Admit weekends are a great time to meet potential roommates. And admitted student blogs and discussion forums are other ways to find out who might be looking to share an apartment or house.

If you have a spouse or partner, most MBA programs have clubs for partners. Club members are good resources for where to live and what to expect. If you have young children, you may need help finding day care, babysitters, or preschool. Since these services are always popular, often you need to have them arranged long before you start the MBA program. If you need to register older children for school, learn the local requirements and choose your neighborhood carefully. But, again, try to find a neighborhood close to campus, or you will miss out on many activities.

If you are going to live on campus, consider whether you need a car. At NYU Stern or Columbia, having a car is more trouble than it's worth. If you need a car on the weekend, you can rent one. At Chicago Booth, some students have cars and some don't. If you have a car, you have to worry about finding parking on crowded streets and learning superb parallel-parking skills. You have to avoid tickets on street-sweeping days and deal with digging your car out of the snow. If you don't have a car, public transportation is fairly reliable, or you can combine trips with classmates who have cars. Conversely, if you go to school in California, you will need a car. Even if you use public transportation to get yourself to and from school at Berkeley, Stanford, UCLA, or USC, it will take a lot of planning and patience. And you'll still need a car for the evenings and weekends when public transportation is less reliable. For other schools in big cities, find out how reliable the public transportation is and how difficult or expensive parking is and plan accordingly. With some schools, either a bus pass or a bike is enough to give you a measure of freedom. If you absolutely don't want to have a car, make sure you live near campus and near a grocery store.

Just as you would do when you move to any new area, you will quickly need to figure out the best places to shop, where to bank, the best dry cleaner and shoe repair shop, and the best places to eat and drink. Exploring a new neighborhood can be a lot of fun, and no doubt you will find plenty of classmates to accompany you.

Also make sure you are technologically prepared. Some essentials include a laptop for in class and studying, Blackberry, cell phone, and an iPod for downloading lectures. Find out which electronics the school provides and what the rules are for using them in the classroom or sharing them with classmates.

Start Your Career Research Early and Get a Jump on the Competition

After competing with a group of extremely talented business school applicants for the opportunity to earn an MBA from a top program, you will next be tasked with competing with the crème-de-la-crème of that group for the true crown jewel: the venerable first job out of school. Even at Harvard and Stanford, there aren't enough top-level jobs to go around. Just as the person in the workforce who puts in the extra time gets ahead, the same is true of b-school. The people who spend the extra time are the people who gain the career advantage.

You have heard over and over that business schools want you to hit the ground running. What exactly does that mean? It means that if you want to transition into a new career, you should already know quite a bit about it and be prepared to start networking and interviewing for jobs not long after you arrive on campus. You already have an updated resume, at least one dating from when you last submitted an application. But while you are still at work, it is a good idea to think about all those additional accomplishments and quantifiable results. If you were laid off and found a new job or did extensive volunteer work before you started the program, be sure to add that to your resume. The career services staff will review your resume and give you some pointers, but having a solid resume to start with will save a lot of time and energy.

Recruiting will be a major part of your business school experience, perhaps even more so than you would like. Nonetheless, you may want to strengthen your interviewing skills if you think you may otherwise be at even a slight disadvantage to many of your peers. You do not want to wait until after the first wave of prestigious recruiters has come through your campus with summer internships to realize your skills are lagging. A number of excellent books on interviewing can help you understand the employer's perspective, focus on your strengths and what you'll contribute to a company, prepare for behavioral interviews, and identify and deflect illegal questions.

If you wish to enter popular fields such as management consulting, investment banking, or venture capital, good books cover those careers. If you want to target a specific company that you know recruits on campus, company and industry leader profiles are available. Since different industries have different cultures and jargon, the more you know before those crucial first interviews, the better off you will be. Books can help you prepare for the interview questions you will face in a particular field. The research you did before you applied to business school is a good start, but it is not nearly enough when it comes to applying for jobs. For some specific titles, check www.admissionsconsultants.com/mbabooks/career.asp.

DO YOU NEED A HEAD START TO GAIN AN ADVANTAGE?

If you have an idea for a new club or project, get an early start on it before classes begin. The spring and summer before matriculation are an excellent time to contact graduating students and network with the people who can best help you make your new club or project a successful reality. In addition, you could make a great first impression on campus and have a leg up if you decide to run for a student officer position.

How to Perfect the Art of Preparing to Perform

When students ask how they should prepare for their MBA enrollments, quite frequently they are most concerned about the quantitative workload of the programs, and they fear their quant skills have diminished since they were undergrads. In general, if you are able to get accepted, then you are smart enough to handle the work. However, MBA courses are taught at a higher level than undergraduate courses and advance more quickly, so some review is probably a good idea. Depending on your background and the number of years since you've been in school, consider reading an introductory statistics book. If you come from a nontraditional background, such as not-for-profit management, the public sector, or the arts, you may want to gain an overview of accounting concepts or microeconomics to feel more confident in first-year courses. If you are bound for Harvard, Darden, or another case-intensive school, consider reviewing an elementary book on accounting. If your statistics skills are rusty, seriously consider brushing up on this quantitative skills subset because you will encounter it in many classes. Schools such as Berkeley Haas have quantitative methods workshops prior to orientation in the summer and require attendance for those they think will benefit the most.

Finally, if you don't spend your days on the computer and aren't well-versed in Microsoft Word, Excel, or PowerPoint, spend some time prior to your matriculation becoming familiar with these software products. You can expect to write many papers, produce many spreadsheet models, and make many PowerPoint presentations in graduate business school.

Chapter 10

WHAT IS THE BUSINESS SCHOOL BALANCING ACT?

Hitting the Ground Running Without Tripping

Luis strikes people as a remarkably organized and productive person. At his job, people commented on how neat his desk was and how easy it was for him to find everything that his colleagues needed. He felt on top of things at work. He knew the people who could offer help when he needed it, he knew the best ways to get things done, and he was confident that he would be successful. Yet he confides to friends that he felt overwhelmed for much of his first year as an MBA student at Smith. "Everything came at me so quickly," he reveals. "I wish I could go back and redo my first term, knowing the things that I learned later on."

Jack originally entered the MBA program at Wharton looking forward to studying finance in preparation for furthering his career goals. Yet after a management class in technology strategy that he really enjoyed, he questioned his original decision. Was he missing his calling in the blossoming business technology field? Would he derail his education by switching focus now?

These two stories are not unusual. Most MBA graduates appreciate their educational experiences, but many wish they had been a bit more savvy about the practicalities of business school options before beginning their programs.

One aspect of attaining an MBA degree is the ability to answer the question "What happens next?" after your acceptance is in hand. How you make the most of your degree during and after your education is a critical component to your future career success. Knowing what courses to take and what paths and opportunities might lay ahead at the school of your choice is as critical as knowing what kind of environment and teaching models the school uses. Keeping your focus on "whatever will get me into the program" is shortsighted and can hamper your long-term career path. By utilizing all of the school's offered tools in the short term, you can make sure that your educational experience will help your long-term career, not simply help you obtain your next full-time job.

How to Hit the Ground Running and Get the Most from Your Classes

Depending on what school you choose, you may have already attended a workshop or series of classes to give you a jumpstart on the core courses, such as statistics, financial accounting, corporate finance, and managerial econ. You will also have the opportunity to waive out of some core courses and move to the next level at most schools. Since classes move at a rapid pace, though, you need to be ready to absorb huge amounts of information very quickly.

In the sixth week of classes, Luis sent an e-mail to his best friend from work describing how he was falling behind. Luis had attended to a family emergency at home over the weekend and was attempting to catch up on his readings by getting even less sleep than usual. A good night's sleep was six hours, but lately it had dropped to four. He had long ago realized that his idea of attending McCombs and hanging out with his brother on the weekends was a pipe dream, and he confessed, "I've been dropping everything coming at me this week and have hit an all-time low. I passed on a cold call in one class and totally messed up my answer on another cold call. I've got to find a way to hide when I'm not prepared." Plus, the learning curve was getting steeper at a time when resumes were due, alumni networking was in full swing, and recruiting was about to begin. "Let's just hope I don't get the flu, particularly while I'm dealing with this sleep deficit."

The good news is that your classmates know exactly what you are going through, because they are going through the same thing. The reality, though, is that some people are better able to cope than others. For example, the notorious *cold call* is a method professors use to test the level of your understanding of current concepts. First-year students sitting in an 8 a.m. class after having studied the material until after midnight the night before have diverse reactions to the cold call. The classmate on your left may be preparing her answer in frenzied anticipation of the professor's next question. The classmate on your right may be hiding behind his laptop screen trying to follow the conversation as best he can while praying that he will not be singled out to answer. Tomorrow morning, their reactions may be reversed, and so may your own.

Organizing your school life is also an adjustment. If you are used to the semester system in college, switching to a quarter system in b-school will take some getting used to. Conversely, semester-long courses often mean more courses to keep track of at once. Although taking four or five courses may not sound like a lot, it is when you add social activities, clubs, alumni networking, and recruiting. You may also want to maintain a personal life outside of school with family and friends.

If you are interested in a career in investment banking or consulting, your grades are important because competition is fierce in those fields, and professors often recommend top students to employers. Even if your priority in business school is not academics, if you let academics slide you'll never catch up. So, try your best to keep up with readings and assignments. If you need help, seek it. Some schools have tutoring programs where second-years tutor first-years. Members of your study group should also be of help. Chances are, unless you were a business or econ major, a lot of the course material will be unfamiliar to you. Even if you did study business or economics and waived some basic courses, the classes will take off at an accelerated pace. Therefore, strong time management skills are a must, plus you'll need a good way to keep track of conflicting priorities—whether it be through a Blackberry, iPhone, or another type of PDA.

TECHNOLOGY IN THE CLASSROOM.

You have your financial calculator. You have your Blackberry. And, of course, you have your loaded laptop ready to fire up. Modern-day business schools require tech-savvy students. Most b-school buildings are wired or have wireless networks.

As wonderful as all this techno-learning can be, no doubt the rules of what is and isn't allowed have changed. There have been cheating scandals involving MBAs in recent years. One rule is constant, though: Anyone caught cheating can be expelled and be eliminated from receiving an MBA from a top program. So, before you bring your cell phone out of your pocket during an exam, make sure you know whether it will be immediately confiscated. Professors don't want to worry whether a student is photographing answers or texting questions to classmates, so check your program's policy before you make a mistake. Darden has a centuries-old honor code that is so embedded in the culture of the school that students can take exams at home. But different schools have different rules and expectations.

Even the simple matters of courtesy and professionalism may vary from school to school—do phones need to be turned to vibrate during class? Is photographing a white board during a discussion allowed? Will texting during class disturb the professor? For those who are used to being in constant electronic contact, business school may require some adjustments.

Oh, yeah, and iPods. Missed lectures can be downloaded. And you gotta have music to keep you sane.

It is not uncommon to be on campus from 8 in the morning until 6 at night with almost no breaks; go home to grab something to eat and maybe change clothes; attend an alumni networking, club, or social event from 7 to 10; return home to study until 2 or 3 in the morning—and then repeat the routine the next day. It simply isn't possible to do everything you would like to do, so being able to prioritize is key. Even though many clubs sound interesting in theory, they demand time, so think carefully about which ones to sign up for. And think about which ones will get you where you want to go in terms of networking, speaker series, and leadership roles. Three clubs, plus one or two major events to coordinate or participate in (such as a talent show or conference or business plan competition), plus one or two other activities are probably more than enough to keep most students busy. So don't sign up for too many things the first term until you know how much you can handle at once.

Here are tips from students who have already survived their first year. First, a good calendaring system is essential. Find a quiet place to study on campus, away from all the distractions of the business school. If there aren't assigned seating charts and you want to avoid being cold-called, try to figure out the spot where you are least likely to be called on. If you can't make it to class (if you are sick or it's a religious holiday), then find out whether the class has been recorded and can be downloaded. That's much more reliable than asking for someone's notes. Ask for help when you don't understand something or feel yourself falling behind. Invest in caffeine—coffee, strong tea, chocolate—to keep you awake and alert for class and late-night studying. And don't forget incentives for studying hard and surviving finals.

At most schools you will encounter a combination of lectures, case studies, and plenty of opportunities for experiential learning. You will probably spend a lot of time meeting with your study group or learning team—most likely one you are assigned to by the school so that each member has a different background. (Remember all that talk about diversity? They meant different industries, different job functions, and different parts of the country and the world, as well as diverse personal backgrounds.) The challenge is taking diverse knowledge, values, and motivations for attending business school and fashioning a productive and supportive team. At most schools, though, collaboration is the name of the game, so your fellow students will soon be your biggest supporters and biggest source of help when preparing deliverables and learning new concepts. You will also be assigned group projects, so all those questions about teamwork in the applications have an impact.

YOUR MBA EXPERIENCE WILL BE PERVASIVE.

So you feel ready for the long hours that will be devoted to coursework, job searching, and networking, and you are comfortable with that. It's not 24/7 after all, and there will be some fun activities at any of the profiled schools given their work hard, play hard philosophies. But do you realize that the MBA experience will infiltrate these experiences, too?

Here are a few examples. At Chicago Booth, new students often take trips—typically abroad—before school begins to network with their fellow classmates. These trips, called Random Walks, are named after the theory that stock market prices cannot be accurately predicted. At Berkeley Haas, the Consumption Function is a monthly social activity students share with their classmates. It's also the name of an economic theory first introduced by John Maynard Keynes. Kellogg has the Joint Ventures group for significant others of MBA students. Joint ventures, of course, are also common in business.

And, finally, if a classmate quips he will be having a side of CAPM with his dinner, just take it in stride. CAPM is the Capital Asset Pricing Model. You'll learn all about that, too, before you complete your MBA.

Why Business School Is More Than Your GPA

Club events, conferences, and competitions are great opportunities to increase your exposure to different industries, get real-world experience, and boost your leadership skills. Most MBA programs encourage students to start new clubs or competitions, such as business plan or social venture competitions. Whether it's the Sales Club at MIT Sloan, the Education Club at Berkeley Haas, or anything else that you are passionate about, you can probably find a sizeable group of like-minded students

---

who will encourage you to explore a new field. Starting a club, organizing a conference, or participating in a competition are also great ways to get noticed by employers, who actively seek out those who show initiative. It can also give you experience in a field where you have none or simply provide a great social outlet. Clubs usually meet at lunch, so you'll always be busy in the middle of the day. And team competitions and professional conferences require months of planning, so they will keep you busy for a long time. But students find them all to be a vital and rewarding part of their MBA experience.

Another way to showcase your talents to employers and broaden your knowledge of the global economy is getting involved on a global level. That doesn't necessarily mean going on an international exchange program your second year, but it does mean jumping at opportunities that are offered. Some schools, such as Stanford, require a global component for all students. Others, such as Wharton, Berkeley Haas, and MIT Sloan, offer global consulting projects to selected students. Many offer career treks to other countries over breaks. Either studying or finding a summer internship abroad can be a valuable way to make contacts and land a full-time job in another country. But if you want to participate in on-campus recruiting, spending the fall term of your second year at another school could hinder your job search.

STUDY ABROAD

First the good news: If you want to study abroad, it should be pretty feasible. Generally, the school will allow as many of its students to study at a foreign partner school as that school has students to reciprocate. If you are at one of the top schools profiled in this book, you shouldn't have a problem studying anywhere you want due to that positive selectivity differential. However, the downside is that students can hurt their job searches because they can't conduct in-person interviews on their campuses. So, as long as you are willing to keep in mind there is a chance your internship search or full-time job search may be extended a bit longer than you would like, don't let the opportunity to go abroad stop you. As Chicago Booth alum Matt Whitaker stated about his study abroad experience in Korea, "I was living in another culture. I learned about that part of the world. It probably cost me less than living in Chicago. I loved every minute of it."

If you want to change careers, take every opportunity to attend club meetings, workshops, speaker series, conferences, and networking events related to your proposed career.

To test out his new interest, Jack decided to attend a lunchtime EIS (employer information session) on career opportunities in technology management. There were presenters from a number of technology companies, two of them with MBAs from Wharton. Besides the free pizza, Jack thought he received a good sense of his options. That evening he attended an alumni networking event. He found himself in an intense discussion with an alumnus who worked for a company that he decided he was not interested in. That meant he missed his chance to talk to other alums from other companies. And he had skipped the Finance Club event to attend it. But he still felt he was making progress and the free food was great. He decided the next day to attend the EIS sponsored by a private equity firm, one that was still hiring, to test his interest in that direction.

How to Use Career Services, Networking, and Other Resources Effectively

In a recession like the one occurring as this book was written, an MBA degree retains its value, but MBA students have to make more of an effort to get the jobs they want after they graduate. The number of recruiters for both full-time and internship candidates interviewing on campus decreased by 25 percent at many schools during 2008–2009, and those numbers will likely continue to be affected for several more seasons. Directors of career services offices hope that the decline is temporary and that the numbers will begin to turn around in 2010–2011. In previous down cycles, it usually ·takes two years before numbers start to improve. Career success also depends on timing: Get the right job when the right job is available.

Regardless of the economy, it is a good idea to be proactive in your job search since competition for jobs is always strong, especially in investment banking, consulting, and venture capital. Recruiters search all over the country for the top MBA candidates to hire, so your competition is not just your fellow classmates but MBAs from other schools. Take advantage of one-on-one coaching and workshops offered by career services on resume writing, interview skills, and specific industries. If you want to go into consulting, you should seek help from career services and consulting club members to practice case interviews. In general, once recruiting season begins your overall workload will increase. On-campus recruiting typically begins six or seven weeks after school starts, so you'll need to have your resume polished and a plan in place before then. If you really did your homework when you were applying to business school, you will have a long-term plan and some ideas about short-term approaches that will get you there. Think carefully about what you will be successful doing and truly enjoy doing. Think carefully about the long-term prospects for certain sectors of the economy. It may be years before the consumer products and retail sectors recover, but health care, energy, and technology are growing. Your summer internship is very important because it will define your career and provide you with contacts in the field. And your first job out of school should launch the next stage of your career.

How Alumni Help with Career Placement

Searching for your next job starts at the same time as your MBA program. You are simultaneously a student and a networker. Eventually, you will become a workplace participant again—either for an established company or for your own startup. The time to meet your future is now. Here are some pointers:

Build your network. One main reason that people apply to business schools is to increase their professional network. Your fellow students, professors, and even the staff are great sources of information to help you land your next job or start your next venture. But a huge resource is the connection to thousands of alumni all over the world. Alumni come on campus to help with panel discussions, resume reviews, and interview skills workshops. They serve as advisors, mentors, and competition judges. They can be available as virtual contacts through sites such as LinkedIn and Facebook. Since LinkedIn members update their own profiles, it is likely to be more up-to-date than a school's alumni database, so a student looking for a job with McKinsey in New York could search those keywords along with the b-school's name and get a list of contacts. MBAs join groups on LinkedIn, so these groups can be a good way to connect and find out about job opportunities.

Choose your conversations. When attending networking events on campus, target specific alumni from specific companies that interest you. Your goal is not to return home with everyone's business cards. Research the people and the companies beforehand. Otherwise, you'll wind up like Jack, spending an hour talking to someone from a company where you soon realize you'd never be happy. Spend time talking with each person, assessing his or her capacity and willingness to become part of your network. Set goals that work for you. Remember that it's better to reach out to a handful of people each day than nobody at all. This isn't an all-or-nothing competition. Someone else may be glad-handing dozens of people a day, but it's far better to focus on the quality of your connections than the quantity.

Rehearse your points. If you're shy, you are likely to be detail-oriented. Use this to your advantage by customizing your pitch to your networking contacts because they will have different ways they may be able to help. You may need to work on your body language. This means learning how to use good posture to your advantage; how to maintain a comfortable, natural level of eye contact; and how to smile at the right time. Work with a friend to get feedback on your body language and consult with the staff at the career services office. Listening is a key aspect to successful networking. People appreciate the individual who remembers their details. If you are a good listener, you possess a valuable attribute.

Manage your network. Your network will fail you if it is not properly managed. Too many people (not only MBA students) commit the error of mistaking quantity for quality; they walk into a networking event, smile, shake hands left and right, repeatedly give their elevator pitch, and grab as many business cards as they possibly can. Inevitably, they join the legions who utter the word "networking" with sheer cynicism. A network is an extremely powerful tool only if it is properly managed. With the advent of online tools such as LinkedIn, managing a network is easier than ever.

Prioritize your contacts. Ask yourself the following questions: Who can best help me? Who is most willing to help me? With whom do I have the closest ties? What groups can I join or have I already joined whose members can help me? You should target these people first. Here's one hint: If others offer to mentor you, take them up on it and make them a high priority.

Offer to help others. Reciprocation can grow your network exponentially. But you are an unemployed student, you say? So what? If someone is passionate about a particular volunteer group, this can be a great way to reciprocate—and simultaneously grow your network through your interaction with new acquaintances. If someone needs a hand, perhaps you can offer to look over a proposal or do a bit of research. This is also a great way to showcase your skills. You can offer to introduce someone to a member of your network. Since most people come to business school hoping to change careers, your fellow students are a great source of contacts in different industries, so be prepared to share your own network as well.

Design and implement a schedule. It doesn't have to be perfect, but once you have figured out your priorities, determine how often you want to contact each individual. Some may be twice a month and others may be once a year. If you don't keep track of your contacts, you will lose touch with members as quickly as you add new ones.

Become memorable by remembering others. Remembering birthdays is one good way to stay in contact. Sending Thanksgiving cards is another, especially since it is in the midst of recruiting season. Remembering the names of family members and a few pertinent details is appreciated. Take notes when you meet someone, file them where you can easily find them, and refer to your notes the next time you contact the person. Everyone appreciates being remembered.

Managing Your Emotions

Remember, it's okay to be uncomfortable reaching out to strangers. Most people are flattered if someone approaches them in the right way. One day a very enterprising young woman called me and even though I was very busy, she convinced me to go to lunch with her. For lunch, this woman arrived dressed for a job interview, making me feel that she valued the time I took with her. I found her to be smart and resourceful. Had I known of a job, I certainly would have passed the news along to her. A few months later, her photo in the newspaper's business section accompanied an announcement of her great new job. Who knows how many rejections she encountered or how much time she spent being uncomfortable? In the end, it paid off.

Finally, be patient. Be prepared to spend a lot of time developing your network. It's not realistic to believe that you're going to receive enough valuable job leads from a single or even a few networking sessions. Don't expect new acquaintances to give you recommendations to their trusted peers if they have just met you. It takes time to build trust. The effort you put into meeting new people and learning what they do and how they got there will help you in many ways as you launch your new career. And that's one of the many values of an MBA.

Chapter 11

PUTTING IT ALL TOGETHER

Writing this book, visiting the campuses, and talking to so many students, alumni, and recruiters has been an exhilarating experience. It's helped remind me of just how blessed I am that I was able to have two years at a top MBA program (Chicago Booth in my case) to sharpen my analytical skills, explore my career options, learn from faculty engaged in cutting-edge research, and join a network filled with amazingly talented individuals. As a former b-school applicant, I understand firsthand the anxiety you are experiencing. However, I can assure you that if you have sound reasons for wanting an MBA, and you select the programs where you represent the best fits, you will be assured of receiving a truly life-altering experience for your substantial investment of time and money as opposed to just a good experience that any of the profiled schools can provide. And the benefits of your sheepskin will continue to accrue to you for many years thereafter.

Jin went to school at Darden after finding out that other programs were not for him. He had a life-changing experience because Darden was a perfect fit. Of course, he may have had a good experience at Harvard or Stanford or Wharton as well. Yet after he was rejected by these schools, he made the right decision the next year when he reapplied to Darden. After graduation he started his consulting career with Bain and Company. Three years after graduation, he had developed his client niche consulting financial services companies on merger and acquisition deals and received significant bonuses.

Nancy, after a year delay in her plans because of faulty admissions strategy, ended up being admitted to and attending Stanford. She had a great experience. She credited her acceptance to Stanford to her better understanding of the admissions process. After graduation, Nancy joined Proctor and Gamble. Because of her successful MBA experience, she felt more confident about combining her business skills with her history in athletics. In fact, she became proficient at using sports-based analogies when she communicated with her co-workers. Six years later, she had advanced from analyst to become one of the youngest vice presidents in the P&G marketing group.

Mike did not land the best job right out of school, and within two years of graduation ended up reporting to other MBAs with more experience. Clearly, he underestimated his MBA's shelf life and the importance of securing a good first job and performing well there. As a result, he had irreparably harmed the long career ahead of him. Although he understood in principle how important his MBA was in gaining that critical first job, later he realized that not all MBA degrees are equal. If he had it to do over again, he would have accrued more work experience, conducted better career path research, and applied to higher-tiered programs. Four years after gradua-tion, he had not realized his projected career advancement.

Sanjay attended the London Business School for the right reasons. The school was a good fit. Although Columbia had a strong finance program and placed graduates in Europe, one of Sanjay's goals was to stay with his friends in the United Kingdom. He was already comfortable with the European lifestyle. After graduation, he went to work at the London office of Goldman Sachs. He developed and maintained many contacts through his classmates at other finance companies.

After Luis's late start, he was accepted at Smith. Looking back, he was sure he made the optimal choice because of his personal and career goals. He had a tremendous experience and excelled in his job when he returned full time to work. He assumed a higher position as soon as he rejoined his company and received a promotion a year later.

Maria met her career goal of starting her own business, in part by accepting the Park Fellowship at Cornell and graduating debt free. Now her friends see the wisdom of her decision. Networking is her forté, and Maria knew that bigger wasn't better for her. She fit in well with her classmates, and Cornell's program fit with her. She became president of her alumni chapter and spoke with many potential applicants about her success.

Jack wondered why he had not taken more time and attention with his applications to Harvard and Stanford. Among the other four schools to which he applied in Round 2, he was admitted to Booth, Kellogg, and Wharton. He was waitlisted at MIT Sloan. He regretted not having the option of attending Harvard or Stanford and figured it was likely due to his lack of attention with their essays. His regret for these rejections was temporary after he chose to go to Wharton. From the moment he attended admit weekend, he was hooked. He received an excellent education that combined his original interest in finance with his newfound one in management and went on to establish his own private equity firm. Today his company recruits heavily from Wharton, and he could not be more proud of his graduate education decision.

PART IV

TOP BUSINESS SCHOOLS

TOP U.S. BUSINESS SCHOOLS

Carnegie Mellon University: David A. Tepper School of Business

Columbia University: Columbia Business School

Cornell University: S.C. Johnson Graduate School of Management

Dartmouth College: Tuck School of Business

Duke University: The Fuqua School of Business

Emory University: Goizueta Business School

Georgetown University: Robert E. McDonough School of Business

Harvard University: Harvard Business School

Indiana University: Kelley School of Business

Massachusetts Institute of Technology (MIT): Alfred P. Sloan School of Management

New York University: Leonard N. Stern School of Business

Northwestern University: Kellogg School of Management

Stanford University: Graduate School of Business

University of California, Berkeley: Walter A. Haas School of Business

University of California, Los Angeles (UCLA): Anderson School of Management

The University of Chicago: Booth School of Business

University of Maryland: Robert H. Smith School of Business

University of Michigan: Stephen M. Ross School of Business

University of North Carolina at Chapel Hill: Kenan-Flagler Business School

University of Pennsylvania: The Wharton School of Business

University of Southern California: Marshall School of Business

University of Texas at Austin: McCombs School of Business

University of Virginia: Darden Graduate School of Business Administration

Vanderbilt University: Owen Graduate School of Management

Yale University: Yale School of Management

TOP INTERNATIONAL BUSINESS SCHOOLS

Indian School of Business (ISB)

INSEAD Business School: Institut Européen d'Administration des Affaires

London Business School

University of Navarra: IESE Business School

University of Toronto: Joseph L. Rotman School of Management

University of Western Ontario: Richard Ivey School of Business

Carnegie Mellon University
David A. Tepper School of Business

5000 Forbes Avenue
Pittsburgh, PA 15213

Phone: 412.268.2268
E-mail: mba-admissions@andrew.cmu.edu
Web site: http://tepper.cmu.edu

Dean: Kenneth B. Dunn
Deputy Dean: Ilker Baybars
Associate Dean: Richard Green
Associate Dean: Robert Dammon

"How is it that one of the smallest b-schools stands out among the academic giants? Our alumni and students will recognize the 'secret' as equal parts unconventionality, serious rigor, and a love for extraordinary discoveries. Our faculty is at the heart of what makes us great, and our reputation as a global academic and research concourse is reflected each day, in each classroom and within each Tepper student." —Dean Dunn

Quick Facts

MBA PROGRAMS

Full-time MBA
Flex-time MBA (evening program)
Flex-mode MBA (distance program)

FULL-TIME MBA SNAPSHOT

Total enrollment: 392
Class of 2010: 210
Length of program: 21 months or 16 months (early graduation option)
Campus: Pittsburgh, PA
Program commences in August
Pre-term orientation attendance required

APPLICATION NOTES

Requirements: Professional experience not required but highly recommended, four-year bachelor's degree or equivalent, completed application, resume, GRE not accepted
Letters of recommendation: 2

(continued)

(continued)

Interview: By invitation only
Number of applicants: 1,523
Admittance rate: 27%

CLASS OF 2010 PROFILE

Male 79%, Female 21%
Minority Americans: 9%
International: 23%
Average age: 28
Married or Partnered, Single: 26%, 64%
Combined average years of work experience: 4 years
GMAT average score: 714
GMAT score range (20th–80th percentile): 640–760
GPA average: 3.35

ACADEMIC BACKGROUND OF INCOMING STUDENTS

Business: 22%
Economics: 11%
Liberal Arts/Social Sciences: 10%
Science and Engineering: 57%

Carnegie Mellon University: Made from Steel

In 1900, steel magnate Andrew Carnegie founded the Carnegie Technical Schools in Pittsburgh. The name changed to the Carnegie Institute of Technology in 1912 when the school began granting four-year degrees. In 1949, William Larimer Mellon donated $6 million to found a school of industrial administration. The school quickly became known for its ability to educate world-class managers for the business world. Carnegie Mellon University, as it is known today, was formed in 1967 when the Carnegie Institute of Technology merged with the Mellon Institute of Industrial Research. CMU is home to seven schools and colleges within the greater university, including the Tepper School of Business.

Pittsburgh has more trees per square mile than any other city of its size or larger in the nation. In the Cultural District and elsewhere, there are more theaters, museums, and performing arts groups than in many cities twice its size. Students in Pittsburgh are able to attend performances for discounts and visit many museums for free. First-time visitors to Pittsburgh often realize that their assumptions and stereotypes of Pittsburgh are completely wrong. Pittsburgh's history as a polluted steel town is just that—history. The city has spent the past few decades reinventing its image and has been immensely successful. In a place with so much to offer, it's an added benefit that Pittsburgh has a low cost of living.

Scenes from Tepper.

Situated on the main downtown campus, CMU's School of Business was founded in 1949. The first dean, George Bach, combined the disciplines of economics, business management, and organizational behavior to create the "management science" approach. Management science emphasizes decisions based on quantitative models and analytic problem solving. This model continues to play a prominent role and has been replicated by other business schools around the world. As a result of a $55 million donation from alumnus David A. Tepper and his wife Marlene, the business school was renamed in 2004. David Tepper graduated from CMU in 1982 and went on to apply his analytical abilities on Wall Street. He founded Appaloosa Management, a hedge fund investment firm, using business principles he attributes to his graduate education.

Why Tepper?

"I would argue [that] we are advocates of change," declares James Frick, director of Admissions Operations and Recruiting. Frick remarks, "I've seen four or five revisions of the curriculum" during the 10 years that he has been a member of Tepper's administration because Tepper has an exceptional ability to change. Frick adds, "We're a program that's going to ask more of a student than anyone else." And the reason that expectations are so high for MBA candidates? "First and foremost, they're incredibly adept at solving problems."

Tepper has distinguished itself in part by emphasizing the management science approach but has been careful to involve other modes of learning, such as the case study method and simulation. A successful example is the Management Game, the MBA program's second-year capstone course, which was pioneered in 1958. In the Management Game, student teams run a simulated business and make decisions affecting the businesses operations, finance, marketing, and human resources. Teams compete against other top business schools around the world. Adding a level of realism to the game is the fact that each team is assigned a real-life board of directors made up of local business leaders. Teams also practice contract negotiations with local labor leaders and consult with third-year law students at the University of Pittsburgh.

"I think that the students have a unique experience," opines Frick. "Sometimes people underestimate the value of a small school. There's a leadership opportunity for everyone." Tepper's classes are small, with 210 students in the class of 2010. The student community is tight-knit, supported by a variety of student clubs and activities, case competitions, and team projects in classes. One effective way to apply what you learn in the classroom is through participation in numerous groups and social activities. That involvement will help define you and your classmates for years of your worklife to come. "It's a program where we really look for active involvement," Frick says. "It's a unique campus. There's not a lot of boundaries. Departments work together [and] it gives students the freedom to explore."

Programs and research at Tepper have been so successful that two other colleges at CMU—the School of Computer Science and the Heinz School of Public Policy and Management—were spun off by business school faculty.

RESEARCH CENTERS

Carnegie Bosch Institute for Applied Studies in International Management

The Carnegie Mellon Electricity Industry Center

Center for Analytical Research in Technology

Center for Behavioral Decision Research

Center for Business Communication

Center for Business Solutions

Center for e-Business Innovation

Center for Financial Markets

Center for Interdisciplinary Research on Teams

Center for International Corporate Responsibility

Center for the Management of Technology

Center for Organizational Learning, Innovation, and Performance

Donald H. Jones Center for Entrepreneurship

The Gailliot Center for Public Policy

Green Design Institute

Teaching Innovation Center

Global Excursions

CMU has developed partnerships with educational institutions and industries around the world to provide international study opportunities in a plethora of disciplines. While full-time Tepper students cannot complete an entire MBA program away from the Pittsburgh campus, a number of programs have been developed to augment training received there. For instance, the Global Treks program provides MBA students with the opportunity to visit businesses in other countries to learn about international trends and practice. The treks are two-week programs occurring between the fall and spring semesters. Current treks include China, India, and South Africa.

An option for the student who yearns for a longer international experience is the study-abroad program in Germany. At the partner school, Tepper students study the history, politics, and economy of the European Union (EU) and then study business areas such as finance, marketing, and entrepreneurship within the context of the EU. Students travel to various cities in Germany throughout the semester.

One example of Tepper's increasingly international involvement is Panel Day, held in the spring of 2009. MBA candidates visited Doha and Dubai to acquaint themselves with the culture and business environment of the Gulf Region. The group met with regional business leaders and toured several local organizations. Panel discussions in Doha included entrepreneurship, an introduction to business in the Middle East, economic perspectives, the growth of the economy in Doha and Qatar, and components of the financial community. Also discussed were the Islamic finance and the sukuk market, as well as key challenges for establishing the financial framework in the future.

FUN FACTS

- With the exception of Venice, Italy, Pittsburgh has more bridges than any other city in the world—720 within the city limits.
- The world's only B.A. program in bag piping is taught at Carnegie Mellon University by James McIntosh.
- Tepper was the first business school to create a wireless computing environment and is rated by Yahoo! as the nation's most wired campus. It was also the first business school to use computers for research and teaching (1955) and the first school on Carnegie Mellon's campus to house a computer.

Course Offerings

From the application process to graduation preparations, it is evident that Tepper's roots are quantitative in nature. The school prides itself on its graduates' capability for solving problems based on analytical methods rather than on history or experience. The belief in quantitative and analytic methods is evident through a recently created dual degree. The master's in Computational Finance (MSCF) is ideal for students interested in the financial services industry and requires only one additional semester beyond the MBA program. It combines broad analytical skills with comprehensive, quantitative finance study.

The prestige of Tepper's program should lead you to assume a very rigorous academic experience. The goal in the first year is to prepare you for enviable and useful summer internships. Thus, courses during the first year cover the basics necessary for solid business management. During the second year, the program allows you to take advantage of the mini-semester format and the 120 electives to mold your program with your concentrations or tracks. Apart from the required capstone course, the

Management Game, the second year does not require any specific courses. Electives are required within various fields, but the program can be shaped however best serves your career interests and goals.

Tepper was one of the first business schools to diverge from the semester format for class scheduling. Each semester is split in half, creating two mini-semesters and giving you the opportunity to take eight to 10 courses each semester. Half of these are core courses and the other half are electives. This setup allows you to study a wide variety of topics, thereby exposing you to subjects that may not have attracted you for a full-semester course. Following the mini-semester model, students have the opportunity to take more than 32 different courses during their program; only half of these are required core courses.

The main MBA program offered is the General Management Track, with optional concentrations such as finance, entrepreneurship, strategy, and others. While this system does not differentiate Tepper from other top schools, the option to follow a variety of other MBA tracks does.

The concept of MBA tracks stems from Tepper's belief in cross-campus collaboration. An MBA track involves an integrated sequence of eight to 10 courses, many of those taken within other CMU schools. For example, the Integrated Product Development Track exposes students to courses in design and engineering in addition to business. The Biotechnology Track is an intersection of science, engineering, robotics, computer science, business management, and biomedical engineering. Other tracks available are Analytical Marketing Strategy, Entrepreneurship in Organizations, Global Enterprise Management, Management of Innovation and Product Development, and Technology Leadership.

CONCENTRATIONS AND SPECIALIZATIONS OFFERED IN FULL-TIME MBA PROGRAM

- Accounting
- Biotechnology
- Communications
- Consulting
- Ecommerce
- Economics
- Entrepreneurship
- Finance
- Information Systems
- International Management
- Macroeconomics Business Government
- Management Information Systems
- Marketing
- Operations Management
- Organizational Behavior
- Product Operation Management
- Quantitative Analysis
- Statistics and Operations Research
- Strategy

JOINT DEGREES AND DUAL DEGREES

- MBA/JD
- MBA/Civil and Environmental Engineering
- MBA/Computational Finance
- MBA/Healthcare Policy and Management
- MBA/Public Policy and Management
- MBA/Software Engineering

What Admissions Is All About

Applicants today do a great deal of online research. This is good in general because they know what Tepper offers, but it also can be detrimental because they can find incorrect information or can misjudge their fit with the overall culture. Admissions officers at Tepper place equal emphasis on all portions of the application. Thus, the admissions team works hard to understand the uniqueness of each individual applicant. Apart from a formal interview, campus visits are strongly encouraged, and structured tours give prospective students an opportunity to meet current students, visit a class, and talk with faculty members. In addition, attending information sessions and asking a lot of questions of as many people as possible are the best ways to make an accurate determination about fit.

Executive Director of Masters Admissions Laurie Stewart relates that officers concentrate on finding applicants with strong academic potential that will translate into a strong professional career after graduation. Among the 30 percent or so admitted students every year, less than 10 percent have only a few months to a year of work experience. Additionally, although some schools are considering allowing their own undergraduates to enter the MBA program straight out of college, Tepper is not. All applicants must demonstrate their readiness to take on the rigors of the graduate coursework as well as show how their professional accomplishments add to their knowledge base. Tepper's program is quite competitive and many applicants have more than four years of work experience.

Taking this information into account, it is crucial that your essay and interview allow admissions officers to form a unique picture of you. Thus, their advice is to really reflect on where you see yourself going in your career and impart that in your application essays and in person.

Full-time MBAs receiving financial aid through school: 74%

Institutional (merit-based) scholarships: 70

Assistantships: varies

Full-tuition scholarships school awarded for academic year: 58

Financially Aided

Financial aid officers at CMU provide candid information regarding aid at Tepper. "Our awards are pretty straightforward; all awards are merit-based and determined by a small committee made up of financial services staff and some faculty," said one officer. "None of our awards have teaching requirements; MBAs do not work as TAs at CMU. A small percentage of our full-time students are fully sponsored by their companies, with the understanding that they will continue working for the company for usually three years after graduation. More than half of our part-time students are sponsored fully or in part by their companies with a commitment to continue working for two years after graduation. Of course, the specific requirements can vary widely, but this is what we have seen to be the case."

With a large population of international students at Tepper, the financial services office anticipates questions about financial aid forms. "We have a lot of experience working with international students to fill out requisite visa and financial aid forms. It's a confusing process and we are happy to help the students through it," notes Stewart.

FULL-TIME MBA PROGRAM (TOTAL DIRECT COSTS)

- In-state: $93,840
- Out-of-state: $93,840
- International: $93,840
- Flex time/flex mode: fee per credit hour

What Tepper Professors Teach

The Tepper faculty is world-renowned for research spanning all areas of business. Research is equal to teaching in importance to the school's mission. In fact, six Nobel Prize winners have taught at Tepper throughout its history. Only University of Chicago's Booth School can match that record. With a 1 to 5 faculty-to-student ratio, students enjoy close access to these successful academicians.

All six of the school's Nobel laureates were awarded the distinction because of their work in economics. Robert Lucas was awarded the prize for his pioneering work on rational expectations theory and how it applies to federal macroeconomic and regulatory policies. Merton Miller's and Franco Modigliani's insights into corporate finance are now taught in every business school in the country. Herb Simon developed the idea of bounded rationality in economics and the idea of focusing on human behavior in addition to markets. The work of Finn Kydland and Edward Prescott advanced the study of dynamic macroeconomics and transformed economic research. Today, Tepper faculty members continue to pursue cutting-edge research, which often guides their academic peers.

One example of the many outstanding professors at Tepper is Jack Thorne, who began as a student and ended up as a national standard-bearer of entrepreneurship. Born in 1926, he was a Pittsburgh native who graduated with the first class of Carnegie Mellon's Graduate School of Industrial Administration, pursued a professional career in California, and returned to CMU in 1972 to teach a course in entrepreneurship. By the end of his academic career, he had played a major role in establishing the Donald H. Jones Center for Entrepreneurship, the Morgenthaler Chair in Entrepreneurship, the McGinnis Chair in Entrepreneurship, and the McGinnis Venture Competition.

FACULTY FACTS

Full-time faculty employed by the b-school: 98

Adjunct or visiting faculty: 40

Permanent/tenured professors: 46

Tenured faculty who are women: 4

Tenured faculty who are underrepresented minorities: 2

SAMPLING OF NOTABLE PROFESSORS

- Marvin Goodfriend: Expert in monetary policy
- Rick Green: Renowned as the president of the American Finance Association and the editor of the *Journal of Finance*
- Lester Lave: Protagonist of environmental stewardship, director of the Carnegie Mellon Green Design Initiative, and co-founder of the Carnegie Mellon Electricity Industry Center
- Allan Meltzer: Internationally regarded among the world's foremost economists and the country's historian on the Federal Reserve, first recipient of the Irving Kristol Award for achievement in economics
- Laurie Weingart: Authority on organizational behavior and theory, co-founder with four other scholars of Interdisciplinary Network for Group Research (INGroup)

What Tepper Students Know

Class of 2009 student Jamie Strutz says, "The administration knows that the students will be working hard for two years, so they try to provide a lot of extra activities that are fun. Even with the tours and speakers, they try to make it more casual and fun." She says that the school focuses on the career search from the very beginning of the MBA program. "CMU gets the students to think about their career from the beginning of the program and continues to help us until we find and accept a good job. As a student, it's always understood that the primary reason that we're here is to find a great job. Recruiters come to the school a lot, mostly during the fall. At that time, there is a very competitive spirit in the air. So many good companies come to campus and the best jobs are sought by a large number of students."

When asked whether Tepper meets her expectations, she expounds on the program and the city. "From the very beginning of my search for schools, CMU came across as the one with the biggest quantitative focus. They aren't weak in the other areas, they just emphasize the quantitative subjects and a quantitative approach to problem-solving. [About Pittsburgh,] I didn't think very highly of the city before moving here; I thought it was a dingy steel town. I've discovered that it is so much more. I love it here."

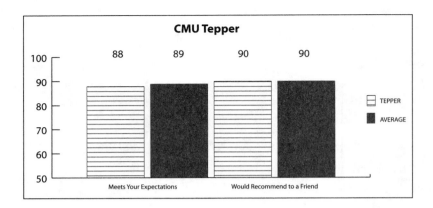

Connecting Tepper to the greater campus and to the city, Laurie Stewart adds, "In the past year, construction for the Gates Center for Computer Science was started. Also, Google started some operations in Pittsburgh. So the buzz around campus has made us all at CMU feel more connected to the big players in the business world."

What's Next? Your Career

The Career Opportunities Center (COC) at Tepper is an integral part of students' time in the MBA program. As one administrator notes, "We work with students to find summer internships starting after the first mini-semester. For permanent employment, students are encouraged to take part in corporate presentations and networking opportunities beginning in the spring of their first year and with a much stronger focus in the very beginning of the second year. [Also,] we send students to conferences throughout the year, usually helping with travel costs in some way. Some recent conferences have been dedicated to females, African Americans, students interested in finance, and international students."

Over the years, the COC has worked with area employers to provide ample opportunities for students. "In Pittsburgh, a degree from CMU is very valuable. We have used the school's reputation to build a strong suite of employers that recruit at Tepper. In recent years, we have expanded our efforts to strengthen our career services for students wishing to work in other parts of the country and of the world. The school does not participate in career fairs very often; we have had so much success with companies recruiting directly at Tepper," adds a career counselor. Because Tepper students learn using rapidly changing real-world situations, companies find that the graduates that they recruit don't require a lot of postgraduate training. Students realize they are all competing, but it serves no one to do it at each other's expense. So instead, classmates help each other out, even during interviews for the same company. It's the idea that you are a part of something bigger.

CAREER CHECK: TEPPER MBA EMPLOYMENT BY JOB FUNCTION

- Finance/Accounting: 38%
- Consulting: 22%
- General Management: 17%

- Marketing/Sales: 17%
- Information Systems: 2%
- Operations/Production: 2%

Tepper alumni are known for the generous help that they provide when students are looking for a job or an internship, deciding on their career path, or looking for a friendly face when traveling. The Career Opportunities Center (COC) relies on the resources of alumni when serving the students. Tepper students have access to a networking database with relevant information about alumni. Laurie Stewart comments, "Most of the incoming MBA students are looking for a job that fits their needs and experience while providing financial freedom. Also, they are usually willing to work anywhere in the country, often anywhere in the world, to meet their goals."

Tepper relies on its alumni for recruiting and brand building. Regarding his experiences with CMU's alumni outreach, Joe Muscari feels positive. "CMU keeps contact with its alumni in the Pittsburgh area very well. There are a lot of speaking engagements and social functions that we are invited to." Rahul Kapish, an alum from India, reflects on his preparation for the business world once he graduated from Tepper. "At CMU, I learned about things besides academics. I learned about networking, interviewing, asking for a raise, and other good job skills. I felt like CMU did a good job of teaching me the people skills necessary to succeed in the business world. My employer has remarked on my ability to solve problems when there isn't a precedent or the problem hasn't really occurred before. I credit that ability in part to CMU."

In addition to appreciating help *from* alumni, Tepper provides resources *to* alumni. A variety of programs allow alumni to connect through networking and fundraising events, reunions, online career resources, lifelong learning programs, and more. Active alumni groups exist around the world. Alumni and students are encouraged to connect with alumni when traveling or relocating. Current alumni cite a "strong feeling of camaraderie" among Tepper alumni that provides a real connection for the rest of their lives.

ALUMNI ACTUALS

MBA alumni worldwide: 7,500+

Business school alumni networking site: www.tepper.cmu.edu/alumni

Current MBA students have access to the alumni database.

Match Made in Heaven: Is the Tepper School of Business Right for You?

You are an ideal student if you

- Enjoy an interdisciplinary environment that prepares leaders for emerging technological business on a global scale.
- Are particularly interested in a career path of management science using analytical decision making.
- Work well with cross-campus collaboration with courses across disciplines.
- Value and want to develop personal competencies such as communication, interpersonal skills, teamwork, and leadership skills.

Columbia University
Columbia Business School

3022 Broadway
Uris Hall
New York, NY 10027

Phone: 212.854.5553
E-mail: mba@columbia.edu
Web site: www.gsb.columbia.edu/mba

Dean: R. Glenn Hubbard
Vice Dean: Amir Ziv

"Financial crisis or not, the most successful MBA programs blend the study of traditional business topics such as finance, accounting, and operations with contemporary courses that help leaders take into account personal integrity, governance and the role of business in society." —Dean Hubbard

Quick Facts

MBA PROGRAMS

Full-time MBA
Executive MBA

FULL-TIME MBA SNAPSHOT

Total enrollment: 1,234
Class of 2010: 721
Length of program: 21 months
Campus location: New York City
Program commences in August or January for first-year students
Pre-term orientation attendance required

APPLICATION NOTES

Requirements: Demonstration of professional accomplishments, superior intellectual ability, bachelor's degree or equivalent, GMAT, essays, recommendations; GRE not accepted
Letters of recommendation: 2
Interview: By invitation only
Number of applicants: 5,999
Admittance rate: 15%

(continued)

(continued)

CLASS OF 2010 PROFILE

Male 68%, Female 32%
Minority Americans: 26%
International: 33%
Average age: 28
Married or Partnered, Single: 16%, 84%
Combined average years of work experience: 4.8 years
Average GMAT score: 710
GMAT score range (20th–80th percentile): 660–760
Average GPA: 3.4

ACADEMIC BACKGROUND OF INCOMING STUDENTS

Accounting/Finance: 36%
Consulting: 8%
Education: 3%
Electronics/Hardware: 4%
Entertainment: 2%
Healthcare: 5%
Investment Banking: 11%
Information Technology and Telecom: 7%
Insurance: 2%
Internet/Media/Communications: 4%
Marketing: 4%
Non-profit/Government: 2%
Real Estate: 2%
Other: 10%

A Program to Bank On

In 1916, A. Barton Hepburn, then president of Chase Manhattan Bank, fulfilled a dream to train budding entrepreneurs and financiers at the highest level. He founded Columbia Business School at Columbia University. A tiny faculty of 11 and student body of 61 (graced by an unheard-of eight women) mushroomed to 420 by 1920.

In 1945, the upper-Manhattan school launched its Master of Business program, which became a worldwide model for producing future CEOs, industrialists, and economic pioneers. How appropriate that the school would soon adopt Hermes, the Greek god aligned with business, commerce, and communication, as its symbol. Columbia quickly ascended the ranks of the business-educating elite. In 1952, Columbia admitted its final undergraduate class and began to focus on graduate students.

Columbia is located in upper Manhattan.

Columbia Business School's symbiotic relationship with nearby Wall Street proved a boon for both the business world and the school. Thirteen Columbia-affiliated scholars have won the Nobel Prize in Economics, and the school's faculty has won four in the last 12 years. Those who teach at the Morningside Heights campus comprise a Who's Who of economic theory, including 2001 winner and former World Bank chief economist Joseph E. Stiglitz and 2006 Nobel Prize winner Edmund S. Phelps. Its graduates include investor Warren Buffett, dubbed the world's richest man in 2008 by Forbes. He now stops in from time to time to lecture.

Why Columbia?

Those seeking to learn business through stodgy textbooks need not apply. Columbia Business School wants big thinkers who want to make the big decisions. It wants self-starters who will lead by reason and guts, not dogma. Through innovative case method study, master classes taught by business leaders, and revamped core electives that address your specific interests, Columbia Business School provides you with the tools for future success.

New York City, with its multicultural population, multinational commerce, stock market hubs, and bigger-than-life hum, gives you an unbeatable "real world" experience. Columbia Business School also teaches you how to shepherd great ideas to fruition by diplomacy. Its Program on Social Intelligence helps you improve your interpersonal skills in a variety of areas.

Columbia prides itself on bridging the classroom to the boardroom so that research now can become practice later. A Columbia MBA program nurtures critical thinking and hones quantitative skills. If you are a busy professional already at the top of your game—or wish to get there—you can enhance your credentials with an Executive MBA. CBS offers you intellectual might and heavily connected alumni in banking, real estate, stocks, and small and big business, giving you access to experts and jobs.

Worldwide, Worldwise

As the business world grows smaller, a Columbia MBA looms larger. Its curriculum sees the big picture, with global case studies that students go overseas to solve. The program covers all facets of competing across time zones, from leadership and cultural awareness to foreign language. It details what business strategies work at home and abroad. The international focus is a natural outcrop of the student body, whose members hail from more than 60 countries and speak more than 40 languages. All of the business school faculty members, most of whom have lived or worked overseas, incorporate a global perspective. Hundreds of students shift their classroom from upper Manhattan to 24 affiliated business schools across the world as part of Columbia's exchange program. As an exchange student, you also learn to talk the talk in one of Columbia's Chazen language immersion programs, which can come in handy: Fifty percent of recent graduates took jobs with international employers.

Choices for a CBS Executive MBA are many. You can participate in the EMBA program in New York City, the Berkeley-Columbia EMBA, the EMBA-Global Asia, or the EMBA-Global Europe and Americas. Over the course of 20 months, you can immerse yourself in the unique CBS curriculum that includes the Individual, Business, and Society focus.

FUN FACTS

Columbia's Morningside Heights neighborhood is rich in higher learning, with Barnard College, Jewish Theological Seminary, Bank Street College of Education, Union Theological Seminary, and the Manhattan School of Music.

Columbia was the site of the Revolutionary War's Battle of Harlem Heights. On Sept. 16, 1776, at 119th and Broadway, the Yankees repelled the British but later had to abandon the area.

Koronet Pizza, a nearby institution for starving students, probably makes the biggest slice of pizza in New York City. The price has climbed to the $3 range, but it's still a bargain. One student called it a yield sign with dough, sauce, and cheese.

Course Offerings

First-year students are grouped into clusters of 60 to 65 fellow MBA candidates to build camaraderie and spark ideas. Demonstrating flexibility, Columbia redesigned its curriculum in 2008 and divided courses into essential core and flexible core. Essential classes include accounting, corporate finance, leadership, marketing, operations, statistics, and strategy. The flexible core offers students one course from categories of Organizations, Performance, and Markets. These courses address organizational change, using social networks, game theory, components of risk management, and macro- or micro-economics. The second term opens up the menu for Columbia's expanded electives.

Also new is the corporate governance module that students delve into during first-year orientation and conclude as a capstone session in the last term. Graduates will go on to become business managers who take into consideration the larger role corporate governance plays in their careers, the economy, and society as a whole—concepts that have been somewhat left to chance in many b-school classrooms.

Perhaps the most popular new option is the master class series, which focuses on a specific industry through real-time project work and practitioner involvement. Budding entrepreneurs are flocking to Launching New Ventures, which teaches planning and acquiring capital, among other subjects. The managerial negotiations course applies behavioral science and game theory. There are nuts-and-bolts labs on management turnaround as well. Classes at Columbia's other graduate schools are also available to students. That means MBA candidates can choose from more than 4,000 courses campus-wide.

COLUMBIA PARTNER SCHOOLS

Asian Institute of Management, Philippines

Chinese University of Hong Kong, Hong Kong University of Science and Technology, China

Ecole des Hautes Etudes Commerciales, Université de Lausanne, Switzerland

Escola de Administração de Empresas de Sao Paulo/Fundação Getulio Vargas, Brazil

HEC School of Management, Paris, France

Helsinki School of Economics, Finland

IESE—International Graduate School of Management, Universidad de Navarra, Barcelona, Spain

Indian Institute of Management, Ahmedabad, India

Keio University, Graduate School of Business, Japan

Leon Recanati Graduate School of Business Administration, Tel Aviv University, Israel

London Business School, England

Melbourne Business School, University of Melbourne, Australia

National University of Singapore, Singapore

Rotterdam School of Management, Erasmus Universiteit Rotterdam, The Netherlands

Scuola di Direzione Aziendale, Bocconi, Italy

Stockholm School of Economics, Sweden

Universidad de San Andrés, Argentina

University of Cape Town, South Africa

University of California Berkeley, Haas School of Business, Berkeley, California

University of St. Gallen for Business Administration, Economics, Law and Social Sciences, St. Gallen, Switzerland

WHU Koblenz, Otto-Beisheim Graduate School of Management, LMU—Ludwig Maximilians Universität, Germany

Wirtschaftsuniversität Wien, University of Vienna, Austria

RESEARCH CENTERS

Arthur J. Samburg Institute for Teaching Excellence

Behavioral Research Lab

Center for Excellence in Accounting and Security Analysis

Center for Excellence in E-Business

Center on Global Brand Leadership

Center on Japanese Economy and Business

Deming Center for Quality, Productivity, and Competitiveness

Eugene Lang Entrepreneurship Center

Financial Markets Laboratory

Heilbrunn Center for Graham & Dodd Investing

Jerome A. Chazen Institute of International Business

Institute for Tele-Information

Paul Milstein Center for Real Estate

Sanford C. Bernstein & Co. Center for Leadership and Ethics

What Columbia Professors Teach

Columbia Business School's faculty teaches students to identify an opportunity and capitalize on it. Charles Jones, professor of economics and finance, declares, "We're trying to train future business leaders." Instructors pride themselves on linking theory and practice. It is the connection that drives any business school intent on producing innovators.

Columbia's New York City location makes it a lot easier to apply what is learned in the classroom to practices in the boardroom. Adjunct professors and master class lecturers fresh from a day off Wall Street trading or shepherding a new medicine onto the market imbue students with the know-how and the know-when. Case studies based in reality demand legitimate solutions. "It's in our DNA here" to set the learning experience in the real world, Jones says. "Our faculty is at the cutting edge of research and grounded in what's happening on the street."

Columbia teachers want students to think for themselves. Theory will change; textbooks will grow obsolete. Jones recently tore up his syllabus because a challenging economy has the entire financial community rethinking what it assumed to be true. The school has sharpened its focus on general management and marketing to adapt to the times as well. Jones believes graduates climb into top positions sooner than they did 10 years ago, so they need to be prepared.

These educators don't rest on their credentials, either. Vice Dean Amir Ziv says he observes so many classes that he jokes the school should charge him MBA tuition. Jones attends seminars with faculty members from other elite institutions to trade ideas on classroom content and delivery. Both Ziv and Jones teach core courses. The basics count, they emphasize, as long as those basics provide the tools for their charges to map their own professional destiny. Says Ziv, "We want to give them the ability to lock in on a problem and formulate a game plan to solve it."

FACULTY FACTS

Full-time faculty employed by the b-school: 136

Adjunct or visiting faculty: 119

Permanent/tenured professors: 72

Tenured faculty who are women: 7

Tenured faculty who are underrepresented minorities: 14

Tenured faculty who are international: 37

SAMPLING OF NOTABLE PROFESSORS

- E. Ralph Biggadike: Expert on strategy formation; organization alignment; and the roles, tasks, and skills of general managers, among many other topics; teaches the core course Strategic Management of the Enterprise and the elective Top Management Processes

- Amarnath Bhidé: Author of numerous articles on entrepreneurship, strategy, contracting, and firm governance and the books *The Origin and Evolution of New Business* and *The Venturesome Economy: How Innovation Sustains Prosperity in a More Connected World*

- Bruce Greenwald: Considered an expert on more than 70 subjects; highly recognized as an outstanding teacher in finance and management; teaches such classes as Value Investing, Economics of Strategic Behavior, Globalization of Markets, and Strategic Management of Media

- Kathryn Harrigan: Specialist in corporate strategy, industry and competitor analysis, diversification strategy, joint ventures, mergers and acquisitions, turnarounds, industry restructurings, and competitive problems of mature and declining-demand businesses

- Frank Lichtenburg: Core course professor; researcher at the National Bureau of Economic Research; researches subjects such as the effects of the productivity of companies, industries, and nations; the effect of computers on productivity in business and government organizations; and the consequences of takeovers and LBOs for efficiency and employment

CONCENTRATIONS AND SPECIALIZATIONS OFFERED TO FULL-TIME MBA STUDENTS

Accounting

Decision, Risk, and Operations

Entrepreneurship

Finance and Economics

Healthcare and Pharmaceutical Management

International Business

Management/Leadership

Marketing

Media

Private Equity

Real Estate

Social Enterprise

Value Investing

(continued)

(continued)

<table>
<tr><td colspan="2" align="center">JOINT DEGREES AND DUAL DEGREES</td></tr>
<tr><td>MBA/DDS (Dental and Oral Surgery)</td><td>Engineering and Applied Science</td></tr>
<tr><td>MBA/JD</td><td>Journalism</td></tr>
<tr><td>MBA/MD</td><td>Nursing</td></tr>
<tr><td>MBA/MS</td><td>Social Work</td></tr>
<tr><td></td><td>Urban Planning</td></tr>
</table>

What Admissions Is All About

No matter what your qualifications—entrepreneurial success, a dazzling grade point average, or soaring GMAT scores—the admissions process for Columbia Business School can generate the urge to impress. However, Linda Meehan, assistant dean for admissions cautions applicants to resist that urge. "It's more important for the applicants to take the time of applying as a self-assessment—who they are, what they want. It's not a sales job."

Once your application is submitted with the proper documentation, at least two admissions officers review the application, asking the basic questions: Can the candidate make it through the rigorous program? Where does the candidate rank in the pool of applicants? And what makes the candidate unique?

Then the admissions office may send out an interview invitation. Prospective students should note that there is no timetable for the interviews, and they are not required for entry into the school. Interviews are usually with an alum in your community. After the interviewer files a report, admissions officials convene again to make a final decision to admit, deny, or wait-list.

The entrance guidelines can be flexible. A student can compensate for a lower-end GMAT score with dynamic business experience or a sparkling undergraduate record. What attracts many hopefuls to Columbia Business School might also scare some off. As an MBA program located in the hustle-bustle of New York City, the financial and business center of the world, it has its perks . . . and difficulties. "If they're intimidated, it's probably not the place for them," Meehan says. "It's not a place to hold your hand and walk you through the program."

Meehan encourages candidates to apply with confidence and says it's important for students to strive outside of their comfort zone. Often admittance is a matter of fit—what's right for the school and for the applicant. Continues Meehan, "This is a holistic evaluation of all the pieces that bring together all aspects of the applicant's life."

Full-time MBAs receiving financial aid: 40%

Institutional (merit-based and need-based) scholarships: Varies

Assistantships: Varies

Full-tuition scholarships school awarded for academic year: 40

Financially Aided

Those vying to be among the Columbia Business School students who receive financial assistance should prioritize application deadlines, clean up any marginal credit history, and leave no option untried. "I encourage students to apply so they don't lose out on opportunities," says Marilena Botoulas, director of financial aid. Columbia offers 34 fellowships.

Receiving monetary help requires timing and sometimes persistence. Students should first apply for Columbia's internal merit-based grants because the deadline is in January, Botoulas recommends. The admissions application acts as the application for fellowships, of which there are dozens. Note that international students are eligible for the same performance-based awards. Candidates apply for Columbia's need-based scholarships separately after admittance, and they must prove financial hardship.

Then students should seek external funds, the director advises, through organizations and businesses that award grants based on ethnicity, nationality, academic excellence, or other criteria. Among the Web resources to consult for thousands of scholarships are findtuition.com and finaid.com.

After exhausting all avenues for free money, it's time for students to pursue relatively low-interest federal Stafford and federal graduate PLUS loans.

FULL-TIME MBA PROGRAM (TOTAL DIRECT COSTS)

In-state: $74,820

Out-of-state: $74,820

International: $74,820

Executive program cost: $144,000

What Columbia Students Know

Alejandra Barbosa got what she paid for: a top-notch business education from an Ivy League giant, access to a powerful alumni network, the buzz of New York City—and a job. Barbosa, from Los Angeles, wrapped up her MBA in May 2009 but not before she was introduced to her future employer at one of Columbia's hosted recruiter visits. The school's location in Manhattan, the global bull's-eye for commerce and industry, made it convenient.

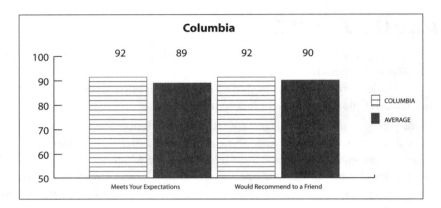

"We have so many opportunities near us here on the career side, the recruiting side," she says. "You could meet with companies easily." She was to begin working as a consultant for a Dallas energy firm after graduation. After attending Princeton as an undergraduate and working briefly in corporate finance and a family startup, Barbosa sought a general academic background in business to guide her on the path to policy-making in the energy industry. Her first term delved into theory and academics. "The second was more practical and applied," she says.

Barbosa's experience went by in an enjoyable, challenging blur. She did not go the internship route. As a career fellow on an accelerated track, she finished her MBA in 16 months. She still managed to accrue other assets: "What I didn't anticipate was the friendships and relationships with my classmates," she says. "New York City attracts the curious."

Her fond memories extend back to orientation. The vibe was welcoming and set the right tone, she recalls. It was such a positive experience that Barbosa became a peer advisor to help initiate others upon their arrival at Columbia.

Fellow peer advisor Don Baxter, from Oxford, United Kingdom, had plenty to advertise about the school's virtues as well. He came to Columbia because of its reputation for preparing leaders in high finance. An alum of Cambridge College and former consultant for Cap Gemini, he planned to parlay a Columbia MBA into "driving strategic change" for a large organization with a social bent, perhaps one mired in bankruptcy. "The world-class training you're getting helps you capture opportunities," he says, adding that the school hones "attitude and aptitude."

The accessibility of Wall Street made it easy for Baxter to link theory and practice. "No learning from dry textbooks," he says. He called the school's lineup of guest lecturers and adjunct professors "jaw-dropping." He, too, was drawn to the hubbub of New York City. It made a fine second class-room, and its multicultural spectrum mirrored the student body. "Diversity stretches you," he says.

Baxter spent more time with fellow students than most because a 45-minute commute made him take greater advantage of the library and the on-campus socials three to five days a week. A typical day involved a few lectures, meeting with his team to work out case theory, writing his part of the case study, and perhaps attending a student government meeting. Along the way, he says, he developed critical rapport with faculty mentors, whom he would meet with one-on-one at least once a month. "I came in with a focus on technical skills," he says. "I'm leaving with much more of an appreciation for relationship skills. What a difference they make."

CAREER CHECK: COLUMBIA MBA EMPLOYMENT BY JOB FUNCTION

- Finance/Accounting: 55%
- Consulting: 23%
- Marketing/Sales: 8%
- General Management: 2%
- Operations/Production: 1%
- Other: 11%

What's Next? Your Career

Imagine walking out your front door to meet with recruiters from the most important companies in the world. It's routine for students at Columbia Business School. The school's New York City location "really gives students access," explains Regina Resnick, the Assistant Dean and Managing Director of the school's Career Management Center. "We're up the street, so to speak."

The proximity to big business makes the Career Management Center's job easier, but it's still up to the students to take advantage of their opportunities. "They are the ones who close the deal," she says. Companies from every imaginable field visit Columbia, as do their top executives and leaders. Students return the favor, visiting local firms through center-sponsored trips. For example, those striving for a career in media management recently met with Time-Warner, Resnick says. The arrangement is so convenient that it can sometimes feel overwhelming for students because prospective companies often expect students to come to them, the managing director adds.

That is not to say that MBA candidates don't go farther afield to secure their professional futures. Technology-minded MBA candidates recently visited Silicon Valley on a center-sponsored trip to check out the industry and meet with recruiters. The world also comes to Columbia. A number of Asian and European companies recruit on campus. Columbia Business School graduates have a reputation among companies for being technically proficient, down-to-earth, nimble, and ready to hit the ground running, Resnick says.

Students can also utilize Columbia's renowned—and, in many cases, local—alumni network. The center has alumni practitioners acting as career coaches five to 10 hours a week, and there are informal meetings as well. During the recent economic downturn, the center was also preparing students for more protracted employment seeking.

Resnick likes to point out that the center's mission extends far beyond an executive search vehicle. Note the word "management" in the center's title. "It's not just about that first job," she notes. "It's taking a longer view of your career." As Dean Hubbard has been quoted as saying, we live in "one of the most dynamic periods of our economy's history, when the chapters of the next steps are still being written. Business schools—their faculty, research and graduates—have a chance to be part of the solution. They can promote policy and advance ideals and people who will shape regulation, reform, and behavior in the years to come."

ALUMNI ACTUALS

MBA alumni worldwide: 36,000+

Business school alumni networking site: http://www.gsb.columbia.edu/alumni

Current MBA students have access to the alumni database.

They attended Columbia Business School nearly 30 years apart, but Nikos Kotalakidis (class of 2006) and Harold Cohen (class of 1977) have found timeless value in their MBAs. "It presented opportunities and jobs I otherwise wouldn't have obtained," Cohen says. "It gave me a brand name and access," Kotalakidis says. Kotalakidis kept a mental scorecard of how the graduate school influenced his prospects. Call it a victory for Columbia.

Before graduate school, Kotalakidis was well into a consulting career when he approached six top international firms. All of them rejected him on the spot, he said, telling him he lacked "business fundamentals." Thus he applied and was accepted to Columbia Business School. After his first year at Columbia, he made overtures to the same six companies. All six invited him for an interview. Five requested a follow-up. Four made an offer. "This speaks for itself," he says.

Kotalakidis chose the place where he interned between his first and second year, the global management outfit Booz Allen Hamilton. He serves as an engagement manager and senior associate. The position has offered many challenges, he says. He never expected that his MBA would also boost his frequent flyer miles: He has attended weddings of seven former classmates around the world. Although their time together at Columbia was a mere 20 months or so, "Most of our long-term friendships have been formed there," he says.

Harold Cohen holds the position of vice president with Boston Technology Corp. He recalls how Columbia taught him how to manage commerce and capitalism. Three decades later, his MBA still carries weight. "It shows that I'm smart and well trained," he says.

Todd Sternberg, class of 2007, found his biggest Columbia resource was not the degree, but "the network itself." When Sternberg runs into a problem as associate brand manager for Kraft Foods, he consults an e-networking forum of former classmates to help solve it. "I have a lot of experts to turn to," he says. Sternberg also created his own legacy at Columbia. The school had never forged a job-search partnership with Kraft before he went there. But with the help of another Columbia Business School grad at Kraft who recruited Sternberg, the food giant now makes regular campus visits. That's a positive development for any generation.

Match Made in Heaven: Is the Columbia Business School Right for You?

You are an ideal student if you

- Are looking for a program that emphasizes education in capital markets, entrepreneurship, and global business.
- Seek to develop an entrepreneurial approach to business that requires a deep understanding of the vital factors in a successful, evolving marketplace.
- Want a curriculum that merges cutting-edge theory with current and future industry practices.
- Expect a multitude of networking opportunities in New York City and around the world with like-minded business innovators.

Cornell University S.C. Johnson Graduate School of Management

111 Sage Hall
Ithaca, NY 14853

Phone: 607.255.8006
E-mail: mba@cornell.edu
Web site: www.johnson.cornell.edu

Dean: L. Joseph Thomas
Associate Dean, MBA Programs: Douglas M. Stayman

"With the valuable contributions of time, thought, and financial resources from our stakeholders, we can make sure that the Johnson School remains one of the top business schools in the world, and ensure another decade of excellence in graduate business education at Cornell." —Dean Thomas

Quick Facts

MBA Programs

Two-Year MBA
Cornell Executive MBA (evening program, weekend program)
Cornell-Queen's Executive MBA (weekend program)
Accelerated MBA

Two-Year MBA Snapshot

Total enrollment: 589
Class of 2010: 274
Length of program: 21 months
Campus location: Ithaca, New York
Program commences in August
Pre-term orientation attendance required

Application Notes

Requirements: Bachelor's degree; resume; GMAT score; TOEFL or IELTS if applicable; essays; GRE not accepted
Letters of recommendation: 2
Interview: By invitation only

Number of applicants: 2,452

Admittance rate: 22%

CLASS OF 2010 PROFILE

Male 64%, Female 36%

Minority Americans: 22%

International: 27%

Average age: 27

Married or Partnered, Single: 20%, 80%

Average years of work experience: 5 years

GMAT score range (20th–80th percentile): 640–750

GMAT score average: 699

GPA average: 3.3

ACADEMIC BACKGROUND OF INCOMING STUDENTS

Business: 33%

Economics: 11%

Engineering: 27%

Humanities: 8%

Math/Sciences: 13%

Social Sciences (other): 8%

Local Roots, Global Mindset

The S.C. Johnson Graduate School of Management is located in Sage Hall, at Cornell University's main campus, in Ithaca, New York. This has been its home since 1998. The Johnson School is one of only six Ivy League business schools, making it a prestigious choice for any aspiring business school applicant. The Johnson School was founded in 1946. At the time, it was referred to as the Graduate School of Business and Public Administration. It was renamed in 1984 to honor the generosity and philanthropy of the S.C. Johnson family.

Named for a Greek island, Ithaca sits on the southern shore of Cayuga Lake in central New York. The city itself is charmingly small, prized for its many waterfalls and deep gorges lined by rock formations that are more than 400 million years old and crowned by rolling hills. Ithaca, though far from being metropolitan, fairly explodes with a youthful vitality thanks to its Cornell and Ithaca College campuses. The combination of charm and beauty inspire many to fall in love and make Ithaca their home.

Scenes from Cornell.

Because of the global nature of today's economy, business leaders need to possess a full understanding of multinational organizations and offshore businesses and the cultural context of those organizations. The Johnson School's Program for International Business Education provides all students with that knowledge, regardless of whether their specialization is in international business.

Although Johnson's program is moderate, it provides more international business learning opportunities than most business schools of much larger size. The school combines several approaches to achieve this. To begin with, the Program for International Business Education offers a wide variety of international business courses, including many highly specialized options not offered at other, much larger schools of business. Johnson also invites outside speakers and creates other extracurricular learning experiences. Finally, the school uses the international resources and language learning resources available at Cornell University.

Johnson offers students performance-learning opportunities that bridge theory and practice to provide real-world insight and experience. Students manage the Cayuga MBA Hedge Fund and the Cayuga Venture Fund, work with startups through BR Incubator and BR Micro Capital, and work on real-world consulting projects in a semester-long immersion program. Johnson's Center for Sustainable Global Enterprise sponsors courses, projects, and an immersion centered on global sustainability.

In addition to the school's diverse course offerings, all students have opportunities to learn about international business through extracurricular experiences. Events are scheduled at many different times so that at least some of them will fit into every student's schedule. Guest speakers may speak at breakfast or lunch, and small-group meetings with visitors are scheduled all day long. Events can also be scheduled during the "coffee break" on weekdays, "Sage Socials" in the evenings, or even on the weekends. If there is particularly strong interest in a topic, special lectures are scheduled in the evening or on the weekend so that more students can attend them. The eight international student clubs hold events so that students can learn about another country or language.

Apart from course offerings and international business events, the Johnson School also weaves a great deal of international business content into the fabric of its other courses, including examination of international businesses, use of guest speakers, and presentations by the students themselves. In today's market, management in any company—whether international or domestic—must have a good understanding of international business issues.

While the opportunities to learn about international business within Johnson are extensive by themselves, they are enhanced by the international learning resources available at Cornell University. Not far from Sage Hall, the base of the Johnson School, is the Mario Einaudi Center for International Studies, which is an excellent center for international research and study. Many other schools at the university also offer international speakers and courses. Performances, art exhibits, and many other events hosted by various parts of the university system also add opportunities for international learning. In addition, students can take advantage of dual-degree programs, international exchange programs, and language programs offered at Cornell to improve their own understanding of international business and culture.

This diversified approach to international business education, emphasizing both the issues surrounding international business and the cultures where many of these businesses originated, gives students at Johnson School the perspective they will need no matter what area of business they specialize in.

Why Johnson?

One of the most important things that differentiates the Johnson School from other MBA programs is its Immersion Learning program, an intense, hands-on semester of integrated coursework and field work in a specific industry or career. The immersion experience combines coursework, faculty lectures, coaching by leading business practitioners, and problem solving in actual business conditions. During this program, everything that the student does or experiences—including classes, professors, speakers, and field trips—is directly related to whatever aspect of business the student has chosen. Students can choose to immerse themselves in investment banking, sustainable global enterprise, capital markets, and more. In addition, the Johnson School has a very strong brand program. Every year top companies come to Johnson to recruit brand students. In some years, every single brand student has received offers from multiple companies.

The other thing that distinguishes the program at Johnson School is its emphasis on teamwork and diversity. While some things are done individually, more often than not students will find themselves working on a team. The team they work on will consist of students with different specializations, not just a group of investment bankers or accountants all working together. This encourages multiple points of view to address a hypothetical problem, improves the students' skills in working with others, and allows students to see business as a team process rather than different specialized cogs working in isolation. In addition, students experience diversity from the international students and an unusually high number of female students—36 percent, whereas most similar programs have about 25 percent. The emphasis on teamwork at the Johnson School means that the students are not strangers to each other—most students know about 90 percent of their classmates, an exceptionally high figure that few, if any, other schools can boast.

Johnson has much to offer in terms of breadth, depth, and real impact. Johnson maintains its incoming class size, allowing students a broad scope of Cornell resources and alumni. The status of a top graduate school makes a degree from Johnson immediately valuable to graduates and gives them advantages over their counterparts in the business world. The goal of the MBA program is to train and foster business leaders, not mere experts in their field. To that end, leadership development begins the first day and continues through a myriad of practical, hands-on real-world experiences. Graduates are found in nearly every industry, and their contributions are tremendous.

FUN FACTS

- Four state parks are located within 10 miles of Cornell's campus. Students and residents alike have access to biking, hiking, sailing, wind surfing, swimming, golfing, and skiing. Money magazine named Ithaca as one of its "Best Places to Vacation." The city is a five-hour drive from New York City, Philadelphia, and Toronto. The area is served by an airport in Ithaca, but three more exist within 90 minutes of the city.
- Cornell has its own chapter of Amnesty International and many other service groups, all of which are active in the city and beyond. Ithaca's AIDS "Ride for Life" involves hundreds in an annual fund-raising bicycle ride around Cayuga Lake.
- Ithaca is also the site of many festivals, including the Ithaca Festival, Grassroots, Musefest, Apple Harvest Festival, Chili Cook-Off and Winterfest, and Light in Winter, all of which are immensely popular and draw thousands to the city throughout the year.
- Ithaca has a strong sense of community and has developed its own currency, "Ithaca hours," to help stimulate the local economy.

Course Offerings

The MBA program furnishes students with a solid foundation of knowledge in all key areas of business. The program sharpens students' ability to analyze situations critically, think and act outside the box, work with others, make sound decisions quickly, and lead and work effectively on teams. With the help of a rigorous and well-planned curriculum, students build on their knowledge and put theory to practice.

In addition to core courses, which provide foundational knowledge, students also have access to coursework in specialized areas, including consulting, entrepreneurship, sustainable global enterprise, finance, leadership, ethics, and international business. Johnson is small and highly selective. This allows the school to maintain a community that is smart, intense, and warmly collaborative. At Johnson, students work closely with each other, the faculty, alumni, and other individuals and emerge from the program ready to hit the ground running. Johnson grads not only possess sound knowledge and skills, but they are unusually strong in their ability to work with others.

What Johnson Professors Teach

Johnson is dedicated to providing a quality education for its students. Courses are rigorous and based on both management theory and practice. All course content is designed to be applicable to the realities of today's business world. Instruction is designed to build on students' foundational knowledge and to encourage them to explore and determine how that knowledge is expressed in the current business environment. Students are encouraged to seek out and soak up as much as they can from the Johnson experience. Robert Jarrow, professor of investment management, believes that knowledge is what students need in order to excel in their careers. He says that students should take courses in unfamiliar topics in order to broaden their knowledge, and when they run across a topic they are interested in, they should pursue it to its fullest while they are at the Johnson School.

Johnson faculty members are serious about being good teachers. Course evaluations on multiple teaching and curricular measures are published for the benefit of students and to provide feedback for faculty. And excellent teaching is recognized each year when students select winners of teaching awards in each MBA program.

FACULTY FACTS

Full-time faculty employed by the b-school: 57

Adjunct or visiting faculty: 22

Permanent/tenured professors: 38

Tenured faculty who are women: 7

Tenured faculty who are underrepresented minorities: 9

SAMPLING OF NOTABLE PROFESSORS

- Robert Jarrow: Mathematician and leading expert on risk management, specializing in applied mathematics to create quantitative models that are widely used in the business community to price financial securities and manage risk
- Robert H. Frank: Monthly contributor to the *New York Times'* "Economic Scenes" column and author of several notable books, including *Luxury Fever* and *Principles of Economics,* co-authored with Ben Bernanke
- Mark W. Nelson: Valued teacher and mentor; received the Stephen Russell Distinguished Teaching Award in 2008; serves on a variety of distinguished boards and committees, one being the Financial Accounting Standards Advisory Council
- Vithala R. Rao: Noted scholar and author; recipient of the Charles Coolidge Parlin Marketing Award in 2008 for innovation in new market research methods and analyses
- Maureen O'Hara: Leading authority on market microstructure theory; her recent work focuses on liquidity and valuation in uncertain times; the first person to serve as president of each of the top three professional organizations in finance

---

CONCENTRATIONS AND SPECIALIZATIONS OFFERED IN FULL-TIME MBA PROGRAM

Accounting	Global Business
Communications	Management and Organizations
Economics	Marketing
Entrepreneurship	Operations Management
Finance	Technology

JOINT DEGREES AND DUAL DEGREES

MBA/JD	MBA/MILR (Industrial Labor Relations)
MBA/MD	MBA/MPS (Real Estate)
MBA/MEng (Engineering)	

What Admissions Is All About

Johnson's admissions process is designed to find individuals who will best fit the program's atmosphere and vision—those who are likely to succeed in the MBA degree program and will positively affect the organizations they join and the wider world. Strong academics and proven leadership skills are a must. Admissions officers want to see a candidate's track record demonstrate success in all areas of his or her life—professional, academic, and personal. Other fundamental requirements include a clear desire to learn and grow; willingness and ability to collaborate with others; and openness to the many cultures, ideas, and perspectives that make up today's global community.

A new undertaking over the next few years, an admissions representative reveals, is that Johnson will allow more students to enroll in the graduate program directly after college. The majority of Johnson students will continue to have full-time work experience, and those coming directly out of an undergraduate institution (particularly Cornell) will have demonstrated a strong record of leadership and substantial internship experience.

Every application for the program is reviewed by the admissions committee, which includes department members, representatives from the administration, and students. To move past this initial review, applications must contain some fundamental requirements for admission: academic achievement, appropriate coursework, successful work experience, and evidence of leadership (whether at work or in the community).

After the initial review, committee members then look at each applicant's essays and letters of recommendation. One admissions officer cautions applicants to follow the instructions for the essays carefully. The last step in deciding on best-fit candidates involves Johnson interviewing applicants either on campus or at meetings with staff and alumni in various locations around the world. These interviews allow the committee to view you in a larger context: who you are, how you think, what you believe in, what ethical values you hold, how you communicate, and what you want in your future career. Admissions offers then are extended to candidates who successfully pass this last test.

According to Admissions Director Randall Sawyer, every student is part of the fabric of the community. Therefore, Johnson looks for students who will get deeply involved in the assignments. Beyond that, the school seeks individuals who work well in teams, spend time in the building outside of class, form study groups, and strive to know everyone else in their classes. Sawyer believes that the team-based atmosphere at the school is a major part of the learning experience.

There is no preset formula for selection to the Johnson School. Its guiding principle is a strong belief in a diversity of individuals contributing to a dynamic environment. The school views diversity as an educational necessity that stretches students' cultural appreciation. It also leads to new perspectives and approaches, which is why Johnson seeks applicants who have a strong character, leadership skills, and openness to others' ideas.

> Full-time MBAs receiving financial aid through school: 84%
>
> Institutional (merit-based) scholarships: 82
>
> Assistantships: 0
>
> Full-tuition scholarships school awarded for academic year: 25

Financially Aided

As with any MBA program, earning an MBA at the Johnson School requires financial and lifestyle adjustments in order to cover the cost of school and the decrease in income that results in not working full time. Income from work and personal savings are both important sources of funding, but scholarships and loans can help those who would not otherwise be able to afford the costs of the program. The Financial Aid Office works with you to find the best mix of available funding options so that you can meet your educational goals.

Johnson is well known for its Park Leadership Fellowships; up to 25 are available in each Two-Year MBA class. These fellowships include full tuition and a stipend and offer specialized leadership training. Park Fellows are required to complete a service project that gives back to Johnson or Ithaca. Selection is based on leadership, community service, and academic achievement. The Park Leadership Fellowships are available to U.S. citizens.

There are no teaching or research assistantships that help pay for tuition. Although some students do work in this capacity, they are paid hourly wages. Naturally, you can expect to use the Internet and other resources to track down other scholarships for which you may qualify. Some merit-based scholarships are awarded to new and returning U.S. and international students. Others are awarded based on ethnicity, religion, and other specifics. It is always important to apply early to have the best chance of receiving any scholarship.

Most students need student loans in addition to scholarship funds or personal income in order to pay for graduate education. Students who are interested in the Accelerated MBA program must apply separately for summer financial aid. International students may be able to obtain student loans through a U.S. bank, but may need a co-borrower who is a legal citizen or permanent resident of the country.

FULL-TIME MBA PROGRAM (TOTAL DIRECT COSTS)

In-state: $68,994 per year

Out-of-state: $68,994 per year

International: $44,950 (tuition only)

What Johnson Students Know

While most, if not all, of the top business schools endeavor to provide applied learning experiences, the Johnson School strives to deepen this with its "performance learning" approach. This teaching method requires students to perform in a real business setting. While doing this, students learn theory, apply those theoretical frameworks to real-world situations, and receive feedback from experts in the field. Students in all four Cornell MBA programs are exposed to countless performance learning experiences throughout their Johnson School experiences. As with all other areas of the curriculum, the performance learning experiences are tailored to the backgrounds and the career goals of the students within the program, making for a dynamic program.

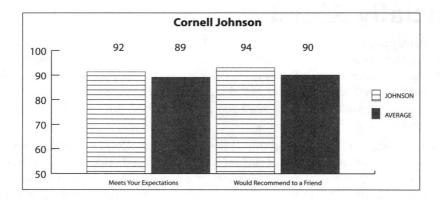

At Johnson, students and faculty form close-knit bonds that last a lifetime. An intense collaborative community of scholars, Johnson retains a small class size by choice. This allows all students and faculty to work closely together. Amy Bruno, class of 2010, is a Johnson Park Fellow and confirms how well the characteristics of the school fit with her career interests. Cornell's location, she decided, makes the atmosphere at the Johnson School far more intimate than would be possible at a school in a large city. Most MBA graduates will spend their careers dealing with crowded cities and the bureaucracies of large corporations. She considers Ithaca to be a good place to be away from all of that, at least for a time. Bruno also notes that even after leaving the Johnson School, members of its community continue looking after one another. The alumni and faculty serve as a community of colleagues, mentors, and friends long after graduation.

Family members and partners are included in this tight community. Johnson has an active partner organization for students and their significant others, for career seekers as well as families. Joint Ventures, as it is called, offers a support network for members with children. More than 40 percent of organization members have at least one child and share in family-oriented activities.

Despite being incredibly busy and challenged in their coursework, Johnson students still manage to have a life outside of academics. Johnson firmly believes in cultivating the whole person and strives to provide valuable personal experiences. Even with their heavy workloads, students at the Johnson school have the opportunity to take part in numerous activities in three different communities: Cornell University, the Johnson School, and the city of Ithaca. Either on or off campus, whether it is skiing or dance or international affairs or entrepreneurship, there is bound to be an activity, a club, or an organization that will allow you to learn and share, make friends, and have fun. Participation in the various school clubs provides networking opportunities and leadership experiences. The clubs are a major part of Johnson's cultural fabric.

CAREER CHECK: JOHNSON MBA EMPLOYMENT BY JOB FUNCTION

- Finance/Accounting: 46%
- Consulting: 20%
- Marketing/Sales: 17%
- General Management: 9%
- Other: 8%

What's Next? Your Career

The Johnson School has a Career Management Center (CMC) which assists students in developing a career plan that matches the students' interests and values; conducting effective job searches; and networking with peers, mentors, and potential employers so that students can get the support, advice, and opportunities they need. CMC helps to place students in internships and assists students in job placement, which is more important than ever in times of economic upheaval.

The CMC prepares students for career success through the Passport Program, which includes career programming, career work groups and clubs, management library research support, and faculty support. The focus is on finding the right career, enhancing communication skills, and building networking savvy.

The CMC makes students available to recruiters through events such as the Just About Jobs interviewing events on the east and west coasts, videoconferencing, and career treks to cities around the world. The school is doing everything it can to help students connect with employers in today's challenging job market. CMC works directly with recruiters from interested companies to evaluate resumes and schedule interviews with MBA graduates. These efforts ensure that students from the Johnson School are given a competitive edge in today's difficult economic climate.

ALUMNI ACTUALS

MBA alumni worldwide: 12,000+

Business school alumni networking site: https://admin.johnson.cornell.edu/alumni/

Current MBA students have access to the alumni database.

At Johnson, membership doesn't end with graduation. Once a Cornellian, always a Cornellian, and your participation is welcomed. Each Johnson graduate becomes a member of a powerful network of fellow business leaders. Johnson School alumni and graduates of other Cornell University schools and colleges are active partners in the education and careers of other Johnson students. Johnson alumni give back to their alma mater in many ways. They often return to campus to give guest lectures, help students prepare cases, and conduct mock interviews in preparation for the real thing. They also eagerly recruit Johnson graduates, not only out of alumni loyalty, but also because of the demonstrated excellence that Johnson students and graduates alike exhibit every day to meet the challenges they encounter in every aspect of their careers.

The Cornell alumni network is composed of more than 300,000 fellow Cornellians. As members of that network, Johnson alumni have access to the Cornell alumni directory, allowing them to connect with fellow alumni worldwide. There are active alumni chapters across North America and around the world, and they serve as vital lifetime resources for recent grads as well as those of years past. Career Services provides several programs designed to help alumni find that perfect career or change careers. One of these is the Cornell Entrepreneur Network. And of course, alumni have unlimited access to a host of Cornell resources, including several online databases and libraries.

Being an alum offers many benefits. For instance, ask graduate Melissa Moore, class of 2005, who feels that her time at Johnson helped her to improve both her business management and nonprofit operations skills. She did this by first consulting for, and later heading, the Community Consulting Group. This is a group of student consultants who work on projects for nonprofits located in or near Ithaca. During her summer internship, she worked at the President's office at the International Fund for Animal Welfare. She was involved in a knowledge management project and conducted research involving risk management for the organization. After earning her degree, Moore became director of institute operations at the Atlanta Institute for Teach for America. Two years later, she became part of the national operations team. Her job is to develop efficient systems and efficient processes for both the finance and technology components of their preparation program for teachers. Moore's story is not uncommon—Johnson School alumni comprise an elite group of leaders and world changers who positively influence any industry of which they are a part.

Making the choice to call Cornell's S.C. Johnson Gradute School of Management your alma mater is one that will pay dividends for a lifetime. The benefits are countless, and the experience is incredible. Director of Admissions Randall Sawyer says team players with an eye for diversity are most preferable. Each year they are on the lookout for around 270 students who have a desire to be at Johnson and who accept that they will be working with people of diverse backgrounds and specialties. A student in investment banking is not going to be working in a group of investment bankers—there will be students studying different areas of business, such as accounting, consulting, and sustainable enterprise. Sawyer believes that this allows each team to look at the problem at hand from multiple viewpoints and with different objectives, leading students to a better understanding of all aspects of business. This is part of the team-based approach to learning, which is the core of the Johnson School experience.

Match Made in Heaven: Is the Johnson School of Business Right for You?

You are an ideal fit for Johnson if you

- Want to be part of a diverse and close-knit community, the members of which will stay with you for a lifetime as both colleagues and friends.
- Consider both teamwork and leadership to be essential and want to improve your skills in both areas.
- Learn well using applied learning experiences, especially using Johnson's "performance learning" approach, which requires performance in actual business settings.
- Want to build your curriculum according to your own needs, including entrepreneurship programs that combine academics, experiential learning, and commercialization interests.

Dartmouth College
Tuck School of Business

100 Tuck Hall
Hanover, NH 03755

Phone: 603.646.0041
E-mail: tuck.admissions@dartmouth.edu
Web site: www.tuck.dartmouth.edu

Dean: Paul Danos
Associate Dean: Matthew Slaughter

"Tuck has been one of the world's most successful MBA programs for 109 years. What's the key? Access to a leading faculty of tough leaders in personal, small-scale venues to fellow students on a fully residential and learning-friendly campus . . . to an amazingly successful alumni group who respond to Tuckies whenever called upon." —Dean Danos

Quick Facts

MBA Programs

Full-time MBA

Full-time MBA Snapshot

Total enrollment: 506
Class of 2010: 240
Length of program: 21 months
Campus: location: Hanover, NH
Program commences in August
Pre-term orientation: attendance optional

Application Notes

Requirements: Transcripts; GMAT; essays; recommendations; interview; written application (prefers online submittal); GRE not accepted
Letters of recommendation: 2 Confidential Statements of Qualifications (CSQ)
Interview: Open-interview policy, student initiated
Number of applicants: 2,898
Admittance rate: 16%

2010 Class Profile

Male 67%, Female 33%
Minority Americans: 17%
International: 31%
Average age at matriculation: 28
Married or Partnered, Single: 30%, 70%
Combined average years of work experience: 5 years
GMAT score range: 590–780
GMAT score average: 712
Average GPA: 3.4

Academic Background of Incoming Students

Business/Finance: 27%
Economics: 16%
Engineering/Computer Science: 18%
Humanities: 29%
Math/Science: 8%
Other: 2%

The World's First Graduate School of Management

Tuck lies nestled in the historic region of Hanover and the surrounding New Hampshire and Vermont area known as the Upper Connecticut River Valley, or as the locals call it, the Upper Valley. The region, settled by Norwegians, is home to the world's first graduate school of management, founded in 1900 by Dartmouth College President William Jewett Tucker and his former undergrad roommate, Edward Tuck. Tuck, a wealthy banker and philanthropist, donated $300,000 in Minnesota railroad company shares to open the Amos Tuck School of Administration and Finance, named after his father, an alum of Dartmouth. He later donated approximately $600,000 more.

The first management class was composed of fewer than 10 students, with graduates earning Master of Commercial Science degrees. Tuck's curriculum became a standard followed by other emerging business schools when the school established the "Tuck Pattern" of combining liberal arts with economics and finance, yet maintaining focus on general business management principles. A decade later, the Scientific Management movement was born in 1911 when Tuck hosted a conference on the subject on its campus.

In 1953, the Master of Commercial Science degree became the Master of Business Administration, and the school shifted from recruiting mainly Dartmouth undergraduates to establishing a national

---

program with a more diverse set of applicants. Throughout the 1960s, the focus included instruction in the emerging disciplines of quantitative and behavioral sciences. In addition, Tuck developed one of the first business and society courses and a business policy course and established the field of organizational behavior.

Tuck students on campus.

Over at Dartmouth, John George Kemeny and Thomas Eugene Kurtz started an educational revolution by creating BASIC (Beginner's All-purpose Symbolic Instruction Code) computer language. Dartmouth became a pioneer for computer use on campus; computer use at Dartmouth became as fundamental as reading is to higher education institutions. In 1974, Tuck introduced its Tycoon simulation game, the first of its kind. Pioneered by Professor James Brian Quinn, Tycoon began as a week-long simulation experience for second-year students to implement knowledge accumulated during two years in the classroom. Quinn and then dean Colin Blaydon took the concept to the next level and worked with Tuck students to found Executive Perspectives (EP) in 1983. Today, EP works with companies worldwide to strategize for growth.

Tuck is one of three professional schools at Dartmouth. The Amos Tuck School of Business is now known as the Tuck School of Business, and the students are called "Tuckies." The Tuck Pattern still stands, only now it is combined with the global and green initiatives that propel the world of business.

Why Tuck?

Tuck's reputation, excellent faculty, curriculum, placement record, deeply involved alumni, and sense of community bring new breadths of learning and living to the lives of Tuck students. Dean Danos points out that Tuck has the unique ability to maximize each student's educational experience because of the school's small class size. In fact, Tuck is adding even more faculty members so they are able to lecture in small-scale seminars. For those who pursue their MBAs, good fit with the Tuck program is crucial for success, because every student has such an effect on everyone else, including the professors.

The accessibility of Tuck's faculty is unsurpassed, both in and out of the classroom, which is one of the hallmarks of the Tuck appeal. The dynamic and complex world of business demands leaders with solid industry backgrounds and foresight to keep up with the evolving business problems and issues that affect our global economies in a world that can be connected within milliseconds. Tuck's community of students, faculty, and alumni have a drive to succeed, but not at the expense of someone else—no cutthroat tactics, no laughing when someone messes up—not here. Students watch out for each other. In the two years you are at Tuck, you are networking with the best and most valued names in business. The school's alumni are respected for their business acumen and their ability to collaborate and to lead; that is why recruiters and students consistently turn to Tuck.

Tuck's "green" energy-efficient buildings are important in a snowy-white, cold New England climate, but now Tuck is even greener! The Achtmeyer and Pineau-Valencienne Halls—Tuck's new three-building learning and living complex—opened in January 2009 and houses 85 first-year business graduate students and executives. The complex has 15 study rooms, three classrooms, many social areas, a conference room, and a leadership library. Adhering to high environmental-impact standards, the building's heating and cooling system runs air over the cold and hot water pipes, and dual-flush toilets allow users to choose between small and full flushes. Master light switches are in each room, although the building was designed for maximum use of natural light. Built-in recycling stations, low-emission paint, natural resource-friendly and organic furniture and carpeting all were chosen as part of a "green" philosophy.

Environmental sustainability, social responsibility, and integrated profitability are the elements that define the "triple bottom line," notes David Adams, class of 2008. These concepts, in turn, define the overall program. Adams co-chaired Tuck's annual student-run Business and Society Conference in January 2009. The conference brings together a diversity of participants from Fortune 500 companies to locally focused nonprofits. Typical of the caliber of the conference, John Brock, president and CEO of Coca-Cola Enterprises, and Matthew R. Simmons, chair of Simmons and Company International, delivered keynote speeches. Panel presentations covered a range of topics from fiscal risk inherent in climate change to investing in clean technologies.

FUN FACTS

- Beer Pong was invented at Dartmouth around 1979. The game involves two-player teams throwing a ping-pong ball across a table to fall into one of several cups of beer on the other end, at which point the defending team drinks that cup of beer.

- The lowest temperature ever recorded in New Hampshire was −47 degrees F on Mount Washington on January 29, 1934. Conveniently, the U.S. Army Corps of Engineers Cold Region Research Lab operates near campus in case anyone wants to learn about the local climate firsthand.

- The Dartmouth College Outing Club held the nation's first modern downhill ski race on March 8, 1927, at Mount Moosilauke. Now, Tuck's Winter Carnival draws in more than 300 skiers from 20 of the top U.S. business schools for a weekend of competition and revelry.

- 1939's *Winter Carnival,* starring Ann Sheridan, was filmed at Dartmouth.

Course Offerings

Tuck distinguishes itself from other MBA programs in that it offers just *one* MBA program: the residential MBA. Through this one program, however, there are several joint MBA degrees, international study, and research initiatives.

As has been its legacy, Tuck's curriculum continually evolves as professors, business professionals, and accomplished alumni integrate new global ideas into the program. It is purposely flexible, allowing students to choose electives according to their interests and career map. Student-chosen electives create well-rounded students who delve deeper through independent investigation, group projects, and international field study. Course offerings prepare Tuck graduates for the fluidity of today's real world of business.

First-year students attend a 32-week core curriculum in general management. Certainly, it is longer than other MBA schools, but its flexibility allows the students to focus on what areas interest them as they develop more effective analysis, communication, and strategic thinking skills.

"It's a lot of work the first year," admits MBA student, Nick Riolo, class of 2009, who was impressed with Tuck from year one's weeklong optional orientation. "You aren't just lectured on the do's and don'ts of Tuck. It's all hands-on from the first day when you meet your study group and work together serving others, to the team-building exercise in the woods where you learn 'the ropes' and learn to trust your team high up in the treetops, to canoeing and orienteering and discussions on ethics."

Riolo was pleasantly surprised that each student received a loaded laptop at the beginning of the program. "All students purchase a laptop through the school that has everything you need for your MBA."

Grace-Anne Wood, class of 2009, acknowledges that all the schools she looked at had "a rigorous first-year curriculum, and they all had the same top finance firms recruit on campus for summer internships, but Tuck was the only school that I visited where I felt I had access to everyone and everything in the program." She continues, "Since the campus is so enclosed and located two hours away from the closest major city, the students really get to know each other and form relationships to help develop that all-important business school network." Says Wood, "I use the study rooms on a daily basis. Ever since the new dorm opened, there has been a lot of room available for studying on campus. This is helpful because it enables us to meet easily as groups to work on assignments together."

For an even broader educational experience, second-year students may spend a term at one of the many MBA exchange programs in Australia, France, Japan, South Africa, Germany, Spain, England, Chile, Switzerland, or Italy.

What Tuck Professors Teach

Tuck has shaped the face of business for more than 100 years. Tuck faculty scholars continually hone their skills by pursuing academic inquiry and maintaining corporate connections. A prime example is the intensity of the annual MBA Stock Pitch Competition. Teams of finance students pitch their buy, sell, or hold recommendations and then defend their positions to win. A first-year MBA team from

Tuck walked away with honors and a prize at the seventh annual competition, held in November 2008, at the Parker Center for Investment Research at Cornell University's Johnson School of Management.

"As the curriculum has evolved from training managers to training business leaders, we try to apply the same rigor to softer skills like ethical decision making and social enterprise that students encounter in courses like finance and accounting," explains adjunct Professor of Business Administration John Vogel. "Co-curricular activities, such as serving on local nonprofit boards, provide students with experiences that reinforce this goal."

Tuck has one of the lowest student-to-faculty ratios of any graduate school of business in the nation, which gives professors the opportunity to know students as individuals. Need to talk? Take your professor to dinner or out to coffee. Their boundaries of inspiration and knowledge far surpass the boundaries of a curriculum.

Tuck faculty also direct the five Tuck research centers. Each center focuses on cross-disciplinary issues that drive today's economy. Tuck professors are not in the habit of teaching you simply how to delve into disparate issues. They are in the business of creating tomorrow's leaders and consummate global problem solvers.

CENTERS FOR RESEARCH

Achtmeyer Center for Global Leadership

Center for Corporate Governance

Center for International Business

Center for Private Equity and Entrepreneurship

Glassmeyer/McNamee Center for Digital Strategies

FACULTY FACTS

Full-time faculty employed by the b-school: 43

Adjunct or visiting faculty: 25

Permanent/tenured professors: 36

Tenured faculty who are women: 4

Tenured faculty who are underrepresented minorities: 5

SAMPLING OF NOTABLE PROFESSORS

- Ella L. J. Edmondson Bell: Leading expert in organizational change and the management of race, gender, and class in organizational life; has appeared on CNN's *Democracy in America* as a nationally recognized expert on race relations in the workplace

- M. Eric Johnson: Director of Tuck's Center for Digital Strategies and toy-industry expert; researches and ranks the yearly list of Top Tech Toys

- Kevin Lane Keller: One of the international leaders in the study of brands, branding, and strategic brand management; served as a consultant and advisor to marketers for some of

(continued)

(continued)

the world's most successful brands; academic trustee for the Marketing Science Institute; and co-author with Philip Kotler of the all-time best selling introductory marketing textbook, *Marketing Management*

- Stephen Powell: Co-author, with Robert Batt, of *Modeling for Insight*, covering innovative methods for building effective models to solve ill-structured problems; that is, problems in which the goals are unclear and little data is available
- Vijay Govindarajan: Leading expert on strategy and innovation; widely recognized top thought leader in the field of strategy; works with CEOs and top management teams in Fortune 1000 corporations to discuss, challenge, and escalate their thinking about strategy; co-author of the best-selling book *Ten Rules for Strategic Innovators: From Idea to Execution*

CONCENTRATIONS AND SPECIALIZATIONS OFFERED IN FULL-TIME MBA PROGRAM

Finance	New Ventures
Global Business	Strategy and Marketing
Healthcare	Nonprofit and Sustainability Management
Marketing	

JOINT DEGREES AND DUAL DEGREES

MBA/MD	MBA/MALD (Law and Diplomacy)
MBA/MEM (Engineering, Manufacturing Management)	MBA/MELP (Environmental Law)
MBA/MPH (Public Health Management)	MBA/MPA (Public Administration)
MBA/MA (Advanced International Studies)	Customized dual degree

What Admissions Is All About

After you submit your online application, the review process is the same for all applicants regardless of test scores, work experience, or any other quantifiable metric. Every file is read at least twice by members of the admissions committee; many are read three or more times. They evaluate the entire application, not just your grades, GMAT scores, or the result of the student-initiated interview. Tuck's commitment to performing a holistic review process for applications ensures that each candidate is considered on his or her own merit. It is after this thorough review process that the admission decision is made.

The director of admissions sees every file. If a file is reviewed several times and a decision has yet to be reached, the file goes to the admissions committee. Tuck's admissions committee is small, assuring that each committee member has a strong understanding of the applicant pool. They will discuss the applicant's strengths and weaknesses, keeping in mind the demographics of the applicants already chosen for offers of admission.

Senior Associate Director of Marketing and Communications Nancy Granada explains, "Tuck offers an open interview policy, which is rare among the top business schools. Any applicant who wishes to be interviewed has the opportunity to schedule a campus visit and interview. All applicant-initiated interviews take place on campus. While the interview is not required, we strongly recommend that applicants take advantage of the opportunity to come to Tuck to tell us their story, one-on-one."

And, introduced in the fall of 2008, the newest tool that prospective students have is a direct line of contact through Tuck's admissions blog spot. As the site explains, it "gives you the chance to perceive the Tuck experience through the eyes of students and partners. Bloggers come from a variety of professional, geographic, and life experience backgrounds. Furthermore, an admissions officer (and occasional guest bloggers) shares thoughts and advice on applying to b-school."

> Full-time MBAs receiving financial aid through school: 80%
>
> Institutional (merit-based and need-based) scholarships: 103
>
> Full-tuition scholarships school awarded for academic year: 41

Financially Aided

Although Tuck operates on a need-blind admissions policy, each year the majority of the student body receives financial assistance in the form of scholarships or loans. Tuck Director of Financial Aid Diane Bonin explains that there is one cost, which is the same for all students. "This includes all expenses, such as tuition, room and board, health, books and supplies, and living expenses." A number of loan programs are available to all accepted students. Tuck offers scholarships, institutional scholarships, and federal loans.

Some of the loans are need-based, and financial need is determined by the financial aid office using needs-analysis and federal methodology. Some loans, such as the DELC loan, require positive U.S. credit history or a guarantor. Applicants are expected to take fiscal responsibility for the financial aspects of earning their MBA to reduce future debt burden and must apply for scholarship and financial aid by the published deadlines.

FULL-TIME MBA PROGRAM (TOTAL DIRECT COSTS)

In-state: $72,700 (1st year), $74,700 (2nd year)

Out-of-state: $72,700–$74,700

International: $72,700–$74,700

What Tuck Students Know

When Grace-Anne Wood considered Tuck among other grad schools, she found that the main difference between Tuck and the other schools she looked at was Tuck's sense of community. "I believe that is a function of both the school's size and also its supportive, congenial culture—which is evident not only among Tuck's current students but among its alumni as well."

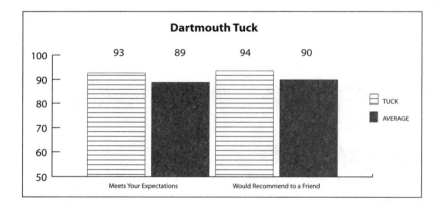

Wood lived in New York before coming to Tuck. "I knew that I wanted to move away from the distractions in New York City so I could really focus on my development as a student. Tuck has been the perfect place for me to do just that. Tuck has, arguably, the prettiest school campus among the top business schools. The scenery at Tuck and its remote location are conducive to self-reflection and development." Not to mention keeping visiting executives close at hand. "When executives come to visit Tuck, the remote location enables students to have closer access to them because the executives have nowhere else to go! They eat their meals with Tuck students and have more time for closer contact because there are fewer distractions in Hanover than in other school locations."

Nick Riolo felt the most welcome at Tuck and that the best thing to do when choosing a school is to visit. "Interview the staff, administrators, professors, take in some classes. Get to know if you are a good fit for Tuck *and* if Tuck is a good fit for you." He maintains that personal attention is the hallmark of Tuck. "They were the only school that took me to lunch!" he laughs. Then seriously, he remarks, "No one slips through the cracks at Tuck. It's a personal experience that feels like family."

As an aside, another Tuckie says, "There are tons of Tuckie marriages. I have been to more classmate weddings than many of my friends who attended larger schools."

There are also a lot of Tuckies taking to the ice for intramural hockey. Everyone who attends the school is familiar with the Tuck Hockey Club, one of the oldest on campus. From an all-male, skate-on-an-iced-lawn beginning, Tuck Puck now has two men's teams, a women's team, and the Tuck Tripods for you newbies who don't know the meaning of "offsides." Of course, you can join many clubs besides this one. Career-related, event-focused, or cultural affinity clubs, Tuckies are involved, from specifically focused MBA subjects to volunteering in community outreach.

Current student Aisha, class of 2009, comments, "I believe that I am cultivating some of the most meaningful relationships of my life; however, it takes energy to cultivate new friendships. Seems as though Tuck makes that energy worth the effort."

CAREER CHECK: TUCK MBA EMPLOYMENT BY JOB FUNCTION

- Financial Services: 35%
- Consulting: 34%
- Technology: 8%
- Consumer Goods: 5%
- Healthcare/Pharma/Biotech: 4%
- Real Estate: 4%
- Retail: 2%
- Other Manufacturing/Services: 8%

What's Next? Your Career

Recruiters are loyal to Tuck and return to the school year after year to hire the talented graduates. Exposure to the highest levels of strategic decision-making is just one reason why nearly a third of Tuck graduates join the ranks of consultants each year. The profession is also an effective springboard to a multitude of post-consulting career choices. Tuck's consulting alumni are never far removed from industry, a proximity that benefits both Tuck and its students.

Tuck graduates do not wait in the wings for their first big break. Right from the start of their MBA program, they have access to top recruiters from companies offering high-level jobs. Many receive tuition reimbursement and/or relocation expenses. In addition, all 2009 students who sought internships received and accepted summer internships in industries such as financial services, consulting, consumer and retail goods, and real estate. They were placed in various finance, strategy, marketing, and business development functions, mostly in the New England/Northeast geographical area of the United States, although some internships were scattered over the continental United States and abroad.

Tuck alumni rise to the top of their organizations—more than 70 percent attain titles of CEO, CFO, partner, founder, or president within 20 years. "The alumni are helpful," explains class of 2009's Nick Riolo. "It doesn't matter if they've been out for a couple of years or are senior executives, they are happy to help with a call, an e-mail, or to pass along your resume."

Mentoring is a key way Tuck alumni keep their hands in the future leadership of the business world through The Tuck Alumni Admissions Program, Tuck Connections, the Tuck Career Advisor Program, the Tuck Diversity Conference, and the Tuck Women in Business Conference.

Alumni keep in touch with each other and their alma mater with Dartmouth's intranet system, Vox, through Alumni Network online. Events, reunions, a job database, and alumni profiles are many ways to stay involved with Tuck's next leaders of the business world. Once a Tuckie, always a Tuckie.

Match Made in Heaven: Is the Tuck School of Business Right for You?

You are an ideal student if you

- Are a true team player as well as an effective, assertive leader and have a track record of successfully working with and leading your peers.
- Thrive when pushed to the limit academically.
- Want to learn how to problem solve, adjust plans quickly with changing economic circumstances, and think on your feet no matter the situation.
- Realize that once you graduate you will be able to do anything.

Duke University
The Fuqua School of Business

1 Towerview Drive
Box 90120
Durham, NC 27708-0120

Phone: 919.660.7705
E-mail: admissions-info@fuqua.duke.edu
Web site: www.fuqua.duke.edu/programs/

Dean: Blair Sheppard
Deputy Dean: William Boulding

"We will build the world's first legitimately global business school." —Dean Sheppard

Quick Facts

MBA Programs

The Duke MBA—Daytime
The Duke MBA—Cross Continent
The Duke MBA—Global Executive
The Duke MBA—Weekend Executive

Daytime MBA Snapshot

Total enrollment: 878
Class of 2010: 434
Length of program: 22 months
Campus location: Durham, North Carolina
Program commences in August
Pre-term orientation attendance required

Application Notes

Application requirements: Bachelor's degree or equivalent; professional experience not required but highly recommended; application; GMAT; resume; recommendations
Letters of recommendation: 2
Interview: By invitation only, except during open interview session
Number of applicants: 2,944
Admittance rate: 30%

(continued)

(continued)

CLASS OF 2010 PROFILE

Male: 61%; Female: 39%
Minority Americans: 19%
International: 40%
Average age: 29
Married or Partnered, Single: 27%, 73%
Combined average years of work experience: 5.4 years
GMAT score average: 696
GMAT range (20th–80th percentile): 640–750
GPA average: 3.4

ACADEMIC BACKGROUND OF INCOMING STUDENTS

Business and Accounting: 32%
Economics: 12%
Engineering/Natural Sciences: 36%
Liberal Arts: 13%
Other: 7%

From Humble Beginnings to Business Legacy

Looking at the impressive modern-design building that is home to the Fuqua School of Business, it's hard to imagine that it traces its start to a tobacco farm in Virginia where J.B. (John Brooks) Fuqua lived with his grandparents. Duke University was founded in 1924 by the wealthy family of Washington Duke, and the business school accepted its first students in 1969, making it one of the youngest top-tier business schools in the country.

J.B. Fuqua (pronounced "few-kwa"), for whom the school is named, was born into the tobacco trade in Virginia. Although he never went to college, he had a thirst for knowledge. As a teenager, he borrowed books by mail from the Duke University library and engineered his own advanced education. He used that knowledge to gain business success, including founding Fuqua Industries, Inc., a Fortune 500 company. To show his appreciation for the institution that spurred his learning, Fuqua gave generously to Duke, with donations totaling more than $40 million. His business career spanned more than 60 years, and he built companies worth billions of dollars. In 1998, Fuqua recalled, "I never paid my [Duke library] book dues. They accumulated until I was over 50 years old. And you know about this compound interest—it got to be a big amount!" However, all was forgiven, and he remains one of Duke University's largest individual benefactors.

Scenes from the Fuqua School of Business.

The Fuqua School of Business started with a class of fewer than two dozen students. Although it is one of the younger business schools, the school has quickly proven its worth and is regularly named one of the top business schools in the country. With a schoolwide enrollment of more than 1,300 students and a variety of courses offered, facilities for the MBA program have also greatly expanded. Since its initial move to Duke University's West Campus in 1983, the school has added several new buildings. The Fox Student Center, Breeden Hall, and the Wesley Alexander Magat Academic Center offer classrooms, auditoriums, offices, and team rooms. Breeden Hall is also the site of the Ford Library. Additional facilities include the R. David Thomas Center, a full-service conference facility.

Why Fuqua?

Perhaps it is the history that is embedded in the school—the sense of connectivity, whether it is with fellow students or studying global business issues—that makes Fuqua different. The school emphasizes a global perspective on commerce, an appreciation for and understanding of different cultures, teamwork, and technological proficiency. However, the prevailing asset mentioned by the "Fuqua family" is its people. Fuqua attracts a unique sort of student, who is intellectually aware and at the same time "real." The faculty, staff, and students embrace a culture of teamwork that creates a challenging, dynamic, and supportive environment.

The Daytime (full-time) MBA program provides additional structure to increase the international perspective, and the first term of school includes the Global Experience, a three-course program that is designed to help students get a jump-start on a worldview of business. Fuqua leaders believe that the perspective gained from the international focus has an impact on all areas of the school and helps students prepare to be not just business leaders, but to be world leaders. Globalization is a buzzword in the business world. Companies are aware of the impact of business and economic decisions worldwide and how international events, trends, and cultures affect work environments elsewhere.

Fuqua recently announced an exciting plan to develop new business school programs in strategic locations including St. Petersburg, Russia; New Delhi, India; London, England; Shanghai, China;

and Dubai, United Arab Emirates. Students attending one of these international programs develop a firsthand, intimate understanding of each country, its culture, and its impact on the world. Students have a unique opportunity to participate in emerging and developed markets, while connecting with business leaders worldwide.

If you wish to remain in the United States, Fuqua provides a truly global perspective, even from the heart of North Carolina. Part of that is inherent—more than one-third of the Fuqua students come from more than 50 different countries, creating an international culture and perspective that enriches every interaction. The International Center at Fuqua helps internationalize the MBA experience for students and helps international students become acclimated to the MBA program in the United States. The Language Institute provides comprehensive language support for international students throughout their years at Fuqua. Through exchange programs (ingoing and outgoing), foreign language study, and cultural events, Fuqua actively seeks to bring the world to its door.

Another important aspect of the Fuqua experience is the emphasis on bringing the real world of business into the classroom. The school has developed strong relations with corporate leaders in the community and worldwide to provide varying views on business issues. Through the Distinguished Speaker Series, students benefit from high-profile leaders who share insights and strategies. At the same time, the school strengthens its relationship with world-class corporations. Recent speakers for the series include Irene Rosenfeld, chairman and CEO of Kraft Foods, Inc.; Jamie Dimon, chairman and CEO of J.P. Morgan; and Pietra Rivoli, Georgetown University professor and author of *The Travels of a T-Shirt in a Global Economy*.

New students at Fuqua are sometimes surprised at the camaraderie they find at the school. Although students are competitive, the school emphasizes the kind of teamwork that graduates find in the working world. Many assignments are designed to be completed by working together through teams, and the facilities support that approach with the many small team rooms. If you are starting to suspect a lack of Southern pace in this top business school, you may be right. However, when you become a member of "Team Fuqua," you are entitled to all the privileges and diversions therein. To name of few of these, there is the Fuqua Prom, generally held toward the end of the first year to allow students and their partners a chance to relax before finals. The wildly popular Fuqua Vision is a series of pretaped "Saturday Night Live"–type skits put together by Fuqua students and shown at the end of every term. The traditional Fuqua Friday is a happy hour event for students, partners, faculty, and staff to kick back and relax. Fuqua's nearly 50 student clubs cover a wide range of topics: art and music, culinary skills, entrepreneurship, finance, golf, health, marketing, real estate, and even wine.

Another principle emphasized at Fuqua is integrity. Fuqua has a detailed honor code that clearly sets expectations for behavior of students and faculty. Violations of the honor code are addressed immediately. Ethics—whether in the classroom or, eventually, in the boardroom—are emphasized.

Even when schedules don't allow much free time, it's nice to be in North Carolina. With colorful autumns, mild winters, and early springs, it is an easy place to live. Although Durham is a thriving metropolitan city with shopping, sports, and art, the business school is located on Duke's West Campus, a slightly quieter end of campus. Students can enjoy a college campus environment, which means access to some of the top college sports, culture, and activities; the quieter, more business-like atmosphere of Fuqua; or the faster-paced environment of Durham and Raleigh.

FUN FACTS

- Under the acclaimed direction of Coach Krzyzewski, the Duke Blue Devils basketball team has won at least 30 games in eight of the past 18 seasons. Coach K is one of the only college basketball coaches to guide a team to the Final Four for five consecutive years.
- Fuqua is host to the World MBA Rugby Championships and fields a team with members from any Duke University school. Fuqua also hosts the MBA Games held each spring for teams of students from MBA programs across the nation.
- Fuqua students are proud to note that since they began hosting the Duke MBA Games in 1989, they have helped raise $1.7 million for Special Olympics.
- At the MBA Poker Championship in 2009, the Duke team won the Beer Pong event.

Course Offerings

As with other top schools, the more prepared you are when you start your first term, the more you will be able to absorb from the teaching, not to mention lower your panic response! Finance courses are some of the toughest in the first year. Accounting and statistics are right up there as well. If these were classes you skimmed in college, take a serious pre-MBA class before you begin your first year. You can do this through distance-learning courses. Pre-term Math Camp is also a good way to sharpen your skills.

All students attend an intense four-week program with The Global Institute called the Global Experience. Introduced in 2007, the curriculum is dynamic, and the content is revised every year based on the feedback from students. Currently, it is composed of three classes: Leadership, Ethics, and Organizations; Global Institutions and Environments; and the first Integrative Leadership Experience. You learn managerial effectiveness and institutions such as laws, conventions, and organizations with a global perspective. When the Global Experience has been completed, you will begin the fall semester with core business classes.

The Fuqua MBA gives you an excellent education in business management through a variety of approaches including lectures, case studies, discussion, presentations, and research. Incoming first-year students become immersed in the Fuqua experience in their first weeks at school. In the second year, Fuqua offers you the opportunity to focus on a particular area of study. Students may select one or two concentrations. Second-year students also have the option of attending a GATE: Global Academic Travel Experience. GATE courses are electives in international business so that you can study the business, culture, economy, and politics of a country or region. You begin your study on campus for six weeks and then you travel, typically for 12 to 14 days. Some of what you do during that time is to visit multinational corporations, local businesses, and governmental agencies. Locations include Cuba, Southeast Asia, India, South America, and Eastern Europe.

CONCENTRATIONS OFFERED TO FULL-TIME MBA STUDENTS

Accounting

Corporate Social Responsibility

Decision Sciences

Energy and Environment

Entrepreneurship and Innovation

Finance (Corporate or Investment)

Financial Analysis

Health Sector Management

Leadership and Ethics

Management

Marketing (Product Management or Market Analysis and Strategy)

Operations Management

Social Entrepreneurship

Strategy

JOINT DEGREES AND DUAL DEGREES

MBA/JD

MBA/MD

MBA/MEM (Environmental Management)

MBA/MF (Forestry)

MBA/MPP (Public Policy)

MBA/MSN (Nursing)

RESEARCH CENTERS

Center for the Advancement of Social Entrepreneurship (CASE)

Center for International Business Education and Leadership (CIBER)

Center of Entrepreneurship and Innovation (CEI)

Center of Finance

Corporate Sustainabilty Initiative (CSI)

Fuqua/Coach K Center of Leadership and Ethics (COLE)

Global Capital Markets Center (GCMC)

Heath Sector Management

What Fuqua Professors Teach

Rated as one of the finest business schools for research, Fuqua also has faculty who are leading authorities in finance, management, accounting, marketing, and strategy. Whether it is researching the psychology of marketing or using decision science to determine the best path for corporate advancement, professors at Fuqua research solutions to issues as well as teach. This quest for knowledge is passed on to students, who reap the benefits of the research.

Fuqua provides the skills that students need at all stages in their careers. Deputy Dean Bill Boulding explains, "We produce a special kind of student by providing depth of analytical skills, plus a breadth of general management skills." He praised the students for their ability to be good leaders as well as good team members. "People think it's either/or. I think our students are both."

FACULTY FACTS

Full-time faculty employed by the b-school: 101

Adjunct or visiting faculty: 30

Permanent/tenured professors: 66

Tenured faculty who are women: 12

Tenured international faculty: 22

SAMPLING OF NOTABLE PROFESSORS

- Dan Ariely: Accomplished behavioral economist and author of the ground-breaking book *Predictably Irrational: The Hidden Forces that Shape Our Decisions*

- J. Gregory Dees: Founding faculty director of the Center for the Advancement of Social Entrepreneurship; received the 2007 Faculty Pioneer Award

- Campbell Harvey: Internationally recognized expert in portfolio management, asset allocation, the cost of capital, and global risk management; editor of the *Journal of Finance*

- Will Mitchell: Leading scholar of business dynamics and business change; co-editor of the *Strategic Management Journal*

- Manju Puri: Leading authority on finance, editor of the *Journal of Financial Intermediation*, and associate editor of several journals, including the *Journal of Finance*

- Katherine Schipper: Former member of the Financial Accounting Standards Board; widely recognized for outstanding teaching, scholarship, and contributions to the field of accounting

What Admissions Is All About

In keeping with technology, the application process is done completely online. Fuqua has four rounds of application spanning from mid-October to mid-March. Students who are not immediately accepted are added to a waitlist in case openings become available.

One admissions officer at Fuqua mentioned that a highly sought-after aspect of the Fuqua MBA is the ability to customize learning. Because of the different types of MBA programs offered, applicants at different stages of experience can find the program that will benefit them most. Although previous work experience is not required, it is the norm and definitely an asset to the Fuqua experience. Says Sheryle Dirks, associate dean for Career Management, "It is quite rare that students enter Fuqua without any previous work history, and those who do must have extraordinary perspective and skills that can serve as a meaningful substitute for prior experience."

A working professional who is ready to take a leap in development may decide to stop working and dedicate time to participating in the Daytime MBA. On the other hand, a more senior executive may decide to continue on the job while pursuing an MBA degree through the Executive MBA program.

Beyond choices of programs, students can customize their focus of study through concentrations. Although not required, concentrations allow students to take more classes in core areas that particularly interest them.

"Fuqua has a more personal touch than some schools," one admissions officer comments. The faculty and staff genuinely care about the students and will work with the students to give them support when needed. Fuqua also has support for student spouses through networking and other social activities. The school actively pursues and supports diversity through collaboration with programs such as the Forte Foundation, National Black MBA Association, and National Society of Hispanic MBAs, among others.

Financially Aided

The majority of students at Fuqua receive some type of financial aid, whether it is in the form of scholarships or loans. About three-fourths of students receive loans. Students may receive independent funding from another source, such as from an employer while on leave to pursue a degree. Fee structures do not vary by student. Because Fuqua is a private school, in-state and out-of-state fees are the same. First-year tuition is higher than second-year tuition, however, because of some one-time fees.

The Financial Aid Office provides guidance and counseling to help find financial resources. The office also assists international students applying for loans, and the Duke International Office provides support for the visa application process.

One of Fuqua's newest scholarships was introduced in 2008. The Center for the Advancement of Social Entrepreneurship (CASE) awarded scholarships to two students entering the MBA program. The scholarship recognizes students for their commitment to pursuing a career in the social sector.

FULL-TIME MBA PROGRAM (TOTAL DIRECT COSTS)

In-state: $95,000

Out-of-state: $95,000

Full-time MBAs receiving some form of financial aid: 81%

Full-time MBAs receiving loans: 75%

Full-time MBAs receiving institutional (merit-based) scholarships or grants: 43%

What Fuqua Students Know

Students come to Fuqua from all regions of the world and with every conceivable pre-MBA experience. They are drawn to Fuqua, which is known for its strong marketing program, because they want to develop leadership skills that they can use in a global marketplace. Be prepared! You may be surprised at the workload the first year. Anticipate being busy.

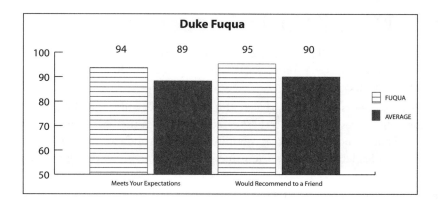

Another surprise is the degree of teamwork necessary for success. Students are assigned to cross-functional teams for their first year core courses. Throughout the year, students become proficient in teamwork, leadership, and communication skills. One first-year MBA candidate mentioned that Fuqua students have numerous opportunities to receive feedback on their communication and performance, all in an effort to help them become stronger managers. Your team will be put to the test while working on cases, for example. Most often, more than one solution is possible, and your team's task is to perform a good analysis, make assumptions if the information is insufficient, state what assumptions you made, and defend your conclusions with class-taught concepts.

Sanjay Mellacheruvu, class of 2009, speaks about the opportunity to work with team members from different areas as he completes his Cross Continent MBA degree: "You have to learn to work in virtual teams, and I had a lot of opportunities to do that at Duke. The fact that they make sure that not all the teammates are in the same geographic vicinity forces every team to experience that." Students feel the environment at Fuqua is deeply supportive, whether the help comes from fellow classmates, faculty, or staff. "When I visited Fuqua, I saw that the students and the faculty really lived the ideals that were in the marketing material," says Vincent Rights, class of 2009. "The people I met, from students to the dean, seemed to embody these ideals. Anyone who has visited Fuqua knows exactly what I am talking about. 'Team Fuqua' has a way of capturing your heart and mind and makes you want to be part of this amazing family."

Students also know that they are part of an inclusive community. Partners of students are also welcomed into the fold and participate in activities with the students as well as in separate activities designed for them.

One area where everyone agrees is that upon graduating from Fuqua, students are prepared to take leadership roles in an increasingly fast-paced, global environment, using sound business skills.

What's Next? Your Career

Fuqua describes its alumni as "leaders of consequence." Companies come to recruit at Fuqua because they are looking for prospective employees with a strong foundation of business knowledge and principles with a global perspective.

Fuqua provides its students with skills that will last their career lifetime, including the specific functional knowledge necessary early in their careers, as well as the broad general management skills needed as they advance. Fuqua students have unique qualities such as innovative thinking and a drive to succeed, as well as leadership and decision-making skills that are particularly attractive to recruiters.

The Career Management Center (CMC) focuses on marketing the school and partnering with company recruiters in a variety of ways, including participation in career fairs and national conferences. The CMC works with students to identify their interests in order to develop good matches. In addition, you can track your activities through Career Compass, the Web-based program that you will use for career management. You can send cover letters, bid for interviews, and learn about recruiters that come to campus, among other things.

"We also work within Fuqua and Duke to develop corporate relationships within the broader institution, which leads to deeper and more strategic relationships that benefit the company, the school, and our students," Associate Dean of Career Management Sheryle Dirks explains.

In the summer following their first year, most students participate in internships, which are an essential part of the Daytime MBA program. The business world experience gives students an opportunity to apply their first year of learning in a real-world situation. Students can test an area of interest and determine whether that is the direction they want to pursue after graduation. Internships also give businesses an opportunity to get to know the Fuqua students and see how they would fit into their organizations in the future. At least one-third of Fuqua graduates are hired by the companies at which they complete their internships.

CAREER CHECK: FUQUA MBA EMPLOYMENT BY JOB FUNCTION

- Finance/Accounting: 32%
- Consulting: 30%
- Marketing/Sales: 23%
- General Management: 10%
- Operations/Production: 2%
- Information Technology: 1%
- Other: 2%

The names "Duke" and "Fuqua" open doors for alumni. To companies looking to hire MBAs, the Fuqua brand denotes a well-rounded graduate with a deep understanding of the global marketplace. With the quality education and the expansive experiences the Fuqua students receive, graduates handily live up to those expectations and are prepared to succeed. The best advice one recent alum received as a student was "choose your functional area and choose your industry," and he means "the sooner the better, like your first few weeks into the term." Set a target for your career, "then take time on a weekly basis to study news reports, journal articles, and experts' online conversations." If you find yourself straying off to other thoughts, reconsider whether you are following your life's passion. If you are, hunt up whatever you can find and immerse yourself in the field because your future job will depend on it. The lure of becoming involved in too many directions may dilute your focus for why you are attending Fuqua in the first place—to land your first job and excel in it.

For Fuqua alum Spurgeon James, class of 1989, some of the skills he learned in business school have been put to use not just in his career, but also in his daily life. "The rigor of thinking through things is what I appreciate," he says. "You learn problem-solving skills and how you make tradeoff choices given constraints."

Recent alum Karen Wang, who holds a degree in media management, recalls an unexpected bonus during her time at Fuqua. "The quantitative emphasis surprised me and challenged me but ended up appealing to the scientist in me." Her advice to incoming students? "Never let up. Don't stop working hard and taking advantage of every single opportunity put before you in the academic program and within the student organization." Insights she learned in the program include "the need for thoroughness and clear communications, and realities of competitiveness," which have translated into a work-world advantage and higher job success.

Fuqua students agree that the exposure the school offers is one of its most valuable aspects. From listening to speakers to joining clubs or working on projects, students have a chance to learn and interact with others in a way that is always eye opening.

Employers value the business skills and forward thinking that Fuqua grads bring into the corporate world. Because the majority of alumni have had pre-MBA work experience, they are able to apply their learning immediately to the business environment.

Even after Fuqua grads begin their careers, Fuqua still offers support. Alumni can participate in additional activities such as the Distinguished Speaker Series, alumni networking, and career management. Being a member of Team Fuqua is a lifelong proposition.

ALUMNI ACTUALS

MBA alumni worldwide: 14,400+

Business school alumni networking site: www.fuqua.duke.edu/alumni/

Current MBA students have access to the alumni database.

Match Made in Heaven: Is the Fuqua School of Business Right for You?

You are an ideal student if you

- Work well in a collaborative team environment and as an integral part of a global community.
- Expect to master crucial business skills such as time management, intense listening, problem solving, and stress management.
- Want to be taught by professors who are thought leaders in health care, protecting the environment, and addressing socioeconomic inequity.
- Aim to be a leader of consequence and able to deal with complex business matters as well as the complicated needs of your colleagues and clients.

Emory University Goizueta Business School

1300 Clifton Road NE
Atlanta, GA 30322

Phone: 404.727.6311
E-mail: admissions@bus.emory.edu
Web site: www.goizueta.emory.edu

Dean: Larry Benveniste
Vice Dean: Maryam Alavi
Associate Dean, Full-time MBA Program: J.B. Kurish
Associate Dean, Director of Evening MBA Program: Susan Gilbert
Associate Dean, Executive MBA Program: Edgar Leonard

"Roberto Goizueta expected the business school to produce great leaders [like himself]. It is our responsibility to meet his expectations." —Dean Benveniste

Quick Facts

MBA Programs

Full-time MBA
Part-time MBA (evening program)
Executive MBA (weekend program, modular program)
Accelerated MBA

Full-Time MBA Snapshot

Total enrollment: 373
Class of 2010: 158
Length of program: 21 months
Campus location: Atlanta, GA
Program commences in August
Pre-term orientation attendance required

Application Notes

Requirements: Four-year bachelor's degree; work experience; TOEFL or IELTS if applicable; references, four essays; GRE not accepted
Letters of recommendation: 2

(continued)

(continued)

Interview: Scheduled by applicant
Number of applicants: 1,216
Admittance rate: 29%

CLASS OF 2010 PROFILE

Male 61%, Female 39%
Minority Americans: 15%
International: 42%
Average age: 28
Married or Partnered, Single: 29%, 71%
Average years of work experience: 5 years
GMAT score average: 680
GMAT score range (20th–80th percentile): 620–750
GPA average: 3.4

ACADEMIC BACKGROUND OF INCOMING STUDENTS

Computer Science: 5%
Economics: 12%
Engineering: 25%
Math/Sciences: 6%
Social Sciences (other): 6%
Other: 6%

History in the Forging

The old elite of business schools often tout their past. Emory University's Goizueta Business School looks beyond the horizon first. It holds a crystallized plan for the future: more emphasis on leadership and more attention to fair play. If you have read the news lately, neither has been in great abundance in worldwide commerce. For Emory, "change" isn't just talk. The school recently overhauled its curriculum to suit the times.

Emory seeks to forge a new path from which tomorrow's business pioneers can begin their unique journeys. With forward thinking comes the gift of vigor. That's why Goizueta (pronounced "goy-swet-uh") can regard itself as 90 or so years young. The South's crown jewel for preparing business pioneers is officially one of the nation's best MBA programs. It consistently earns top rankings, reinforcing Goizueta's goal to provide global perspective in a down-home environment.

On campus at Goizueta.

The history is there, too. The Atlanta, Georgia, school was founded in 1919 as the Emory University School of Economics and Business Administration. Emory founded its MBA program in 1954 and earned major accreditation in 1961. By the 1980s, Emory had established itself among the leading business institutions. In 1994, it became the Goizueta Business School, named for Roberto C. Goizueta, the chairman and chief executive officer of the Coca-Cola Company from 1981 to 1997. It was a perfect fit: a school reaching for greatness and a brand that embodies success on an incomparable scale. "Business schools today cannot just reflect business the way it is," Roberto Goizueta once said. "They must teach business the way it will be." Goizueta was hailed for his ethical and visionary leadership. Those attributes have bolstered the school's motto to produce "principled leaders for global enterprise." In 2005, the opening of the Goizueta Foundation Center for Research and Doctoral Education doubled the school's space. That's the kind of initiative that keeps a school looking ahead, no matter how many decades of excellence roll by.

Why Goizueta?

Goizueta wants its students to be brave and fair, embracing innovation and ethics for the new economy. Few big-time business schools promote good karma as part of their strategy to build future business leaders. Few big-time schools have reacted so vigorously to globalization and the changing needs of its student body. Goizueta revamped its curriculum in 2008 to meet the growing demand for MBAs to hit the ground running in their future jobs.

The school has accelerated the art of analyzing cold hard numbers for flesh-and-blood commerce. It also has reached out to more women with aggressive recruitment plus more convenient residencies for working mothers in its Executive MBA program. The drive for greater diversity on all fronts will continue, Dean Larry Benveniste pledges. Sharp minds from all walks of life are nurtured, not bullied. Thus, a humanist approach thrives. Students are encouraged to volunteer in the community. They learn the basics and beyond in a cozy environment. The school boasts a nearly 1 to 4 faculty-to-student ratio. Students do not have to fight to be heard—or to listen. Dean Benveniste points out that being a leader requires practice. At Goizueta, students are given the opportunity to lead on a daily basis.

The school's location five miles outside the city of Atlanta reinforces its priorities to link theory and practice and to never lose sight of the world at large. Atlanta, a tight-knit metropolis of 4.8 million people, helps drive the economy across continents. Only two U.S. cities have more Fortune 500 headquarters. Atlanta is home to a vibrant technology corridor and multinational giants such as UPS, Home Depot, and, of course, Coca-Cola. The soft-drink titan forged a bond with the university at its inception. Emory's founder, Bishop Warren A. Candler, was the brother of Asa Griggs Candler, the former owner of the Coca-Cola Company. The endowment presents students with a staggering amount of resources.

Beyond campus, Atlanta's airport, said to be the country's busiest, keeps the rest of the world's business movers, shakers, and recruiters at the school's doorstep. On campus, Goizueta students share an institution teeming with intellectual energy. The U.S. Centers for Disease Control and Prevention (CDC) and the American Cancer Society are housed there. Former President Jimmy Carter, the 14th Dalai Lama of Tibet, and Bishop Desmond Tutu are among its 3,000 visiting and permanent professors.

Goizueta's academic muscle starts at the top. Dean Benveniste left the University of Minnesota's well-regarded Carlson School of Management in 2005 to assume the helm at Goizueta. The former Federal Reserve economist said he was intrigued by Emory's quick ascent to prominence and vowed to stoke the momentum. He has kept his word.

FUN FACTS

- Goizueta's alumni group members spend time at the school engaged in cooking classes, economic forums, and speed-networking events.
- Atlanta's zoo has an unusual animal: the East African Naked Mole Rat! This is a must-see when you are visiting.
- The Largest: Atlanta is home to the Peachtree Road Race, the largest 10K race in the world, with more than 45,000 participants each year, and Perimeter Center in Atlanta is the largest suburban office park in the world.

Course Offerings

Goizueta's intensified curriculum focuses on … focus. Students complete nearly all their core courses in the first semester and then take their own specialty path for the next three semesters. A dizzying array of electives and programs await. A home or abroad "real-world" internship between the first and second year puts the practicum into practice. Students can also construct their own emphasis, called Directed Study.

Goizueta isn't skimping on the fundamentals. Its carefully planned five- and six-week blocks in the first term lay a critical foundation for business leadership. Classes such as Leading Organizations and Strategy, Data and Decision Analytics, and Economics challenge and inspire. Students will be nourished on the basics, yet are ready for more.

Then it's on to the electives that will define students' post-Goizueta professional journey. Twenty-three concentrations are packed into Finance, Marketing, Organizations and Management, Information Systems and Operations Management, Accounting, and Management Communication. The concentrations range from the traditional, such as Product and Brand Management, to the emerging, such as Sports, Media, and Entertainment. The menu includes hundreds of courses through Emory's other academic and professional branches. Have a different passion altogether? The Directed Study program allows students to propose their own unique emphasis, and a faculty member helps them put it into action.

Goizueta also offers a one-year MBA, in which students accelerate through core requirements such as Finance Statistics in a summer and then take electives for the next two semesters. (The school assures that its compressed degree gets equal respect.) Two-year students get a first-hand chance to apply what they've absorbed in coursework during a summer internship. The Career Management Center, MBA office, and Emory's network of corporate partners work with students to place them in jobs in just about any field, just about anywhere.

But the first steps begin in the classroom.

What Goizueta Professors Teach

Rick Gilkey, professor in the practice of organization and management at Goizueta, likes to think of business leadership as an art. Perhaps that's why he paraphrases the French artist Edgar Degas: "It's not what you can see. It's what you can help others see." Gilkey says leadership percolates at the core of what he and his colleagues teach at Goizueta. Without leadership, a boss is no more effective than a football coach schooled in X's and O's but clueless in motivating players. Professor, author, and consultant, Gilkey recalls a class of 110 students in which he gave the highest grade to a practicing executive who wrote a "full game plan" detailing how he was going to develop each of his employees. Gilkey immediately concluded, "This guy gets it."

In another example of the kinds of intangibles Gilkey seeks to hone, one day he was walking the halls of Goizueta when he saw a student who looked like Joe College greet a well-regarded professor and physician. The student used the Sanskrit "Namaste," meaning, "I bow to you." Gilkey observes, "That's an A in the making."

Business is so much more than seizing the reins, Gilkey continues. Goizueta sets a premium on casting enterprises as more collaborative and team oriented, he says. Entrepreneurs, financiers, and captains of industry do not get ahead by undermining others. Challenging economies require more leadership because the "impulse is to act on the worst," he says.

So, how do you teach leadership the right way? "You can learn leadership if you can have a platform for it because it's tricky, it requires more effort," relates Peter Topping, a GBS associate professor of organization and management. "In order to get at the leadership side requires more effort than taking Topping's spring elective class." He explains that GBS's mandate is to teach movers and shakers how to tap into their particular leadership strengths and adapt them to any situation students might face.

GBS students learn through improvisation, one-on-one coaching, case studies, dissection of theory, psychology, hands-on experience through internships, and other tools. Topping keeps his own continuing education within the "real world," working as a consultant and executive coach.

For his part in the real world, Gilkey likes to explore the minds of decision makers. Also a professor of psychiatry, Gilkey conducts neuroscans of executives to dissect the biology of business. MRIs measure the metabolic activity of subjects facing dilemmas, such as, "What do I do with this inside information?" Gilkey says he and other GBS instructors intend to change practices and reconstruct the new entrepreneur as one who imparts wisdom, not just gives orders.

Goizueta's comprehensive approach extends from the inside out. For leaders to take care of others, they must take care of themselves first. They must learn to manage stress. The program puts a fine point on "personal resilience," Gilkey comments. Such a characteristic is developed through activities such as sky diving—yes, sky diving—to expand your limits and face your fears. Ultimately, GBS aims to produce MBAs grounded in the fundamentals and imbued with forward thinking, so you can take a step further. Refined toughness can serve as fuel for your entire professional and life journey. There are many definitions of leadership to pursue in a classroom, Gilkey says, but one of his favorites is "A leader is a person who makes everyone reach their potential."

FACULTY FACTS

Full-time faculty employed by the b-school: 84

Adjunct or visiting faculty: 20

Permanent/tenured professors: 38

Tenured faculty who are women: 8

Tenured faculty who are underrepresented minorities: 10

SAMPLING OF NOTABLE PROFESSORS

- Robert K. Kazanjian: Noted authority on organization and management; edited and written numerous outstanding works; co-edited with Edward Hess *The Search for Organic Growth*

- Jeffrey A. Rosensweig: Widely recognized expert in the sectors of international business and finance; served as senior international economist at the Federal Reserve Bank of Atlanta

- Jay Shanken: Widely published author; advisory editor for the *Journal of Financial Economics*; associate editor of the *Review of Quantitative Finance and Accounting*

- Ashish Sood: Recognized for teaching excellence and research productivity on such topics as innovation, technology, management, and financial analysis; quoted for *Wall Street Journal* and *New York Times* articles

- Kristy Towry: Highly regarded researcher; bestowed with the Best Early Career Researcher Award from the American Institute of Certified Public Accountants

---

CONCENTRATIONS AND SPECIALIZATIONS OFFERED IN FULL-TIME MBA PROGRAM

Business Development	Global Management
Business Process Consulting	Leadership
Business Technology Management	Management Communication
Capital Markets	Management Consulting
Corporate Finance	Marketing Consulting
Decision Analysis	Marketing Leadership
Entrepreneurship	Operations Management
Finance	Organization and Management Strategy
Financial Analysis	Product and Brand Management
Global Financial Reporting and Analysis	Real Estate

JOINT DEGREES AND DUAL DEGREES

MBA/JD	MBA/DPT (Physical Therapy)
MBA/MD	MBA/MPH (Public Health)
MBA/MDiv (Divinity)	MBA/RN (Nursing)

What Admissions Is All About

Emory's Goizueta Business School has always been keen on admitting potential leaders. It's just that GBS has gotten better at promoting it, says Julie Barefoot, the associate dean of admissions. So it is more important than ever that GBS applicants highlight their leadership attributes in a tasteful way. From application to interview, students bear the responsibility of presenting themselves as a solid fit for Goizueta's mission to train innovators who operate profitably and fairly—who command and live for the greater good.

"If they have not been involved in volunteer work, that can be very damaging for them," Barefoot says. "High-level executives who have been consumed by managing a business might not have time for extracurricular activities, so they better have been involved in college," Barefoot cautions. The mix of undergraduate grades, GMAT scores, and proven business acumen can vary within acceptable limits. Interpersonal skills can also pull attention away from a weakness but not perform miracles, according to Barefoot. As for the nuts and bolts of applying, Barefoot recommends applicants lay the groundwork early. Visit and interview early at one of GBS's three "Super Saturday" on-campus recruiting sessions in the fall, or at the one in January. Note that Goizueta hosts three annual recruiting events in New York City as well.

Candidates should try to meet the February 1 deadline to be eligible for all GBS scholarships. Be sure to write the correct school in the application's essay portion (an assembly-line mentality or rush

---

job might cause one to leave in the name of another school). Have someone proofread the essay. Use spellcheck. The application's letters of recommendation need to be just that: laudatory statements that address the applicants' values and ability to meet rigorous academic demands. Choose endorsers carefully. You would be surprised how many letters the Admissions Office receives that are short of flattering, Barefoot says. Or they are from inappropriate sources such as a parent's business partner or a manager who has known the applicant for too brief a period.

When it comes time for the interview, a delicate balance of "I" and "we" when recounting business accomplishments is imperative, Barefoot relates. "Goizueta wants to know you are a leader with initiative, but that you're also a team player." You should bone up on the program, even if you haven't visited the campus. A lack of awareness or falsely imparting a sense of awareness (Barefoot says antennae are up for that) will produce a clunky encounter. It also raises a red flag that you might falsely represent yourself to recruiters from such vital Goizueta partners as Coca-Cola and Kraft. "We can't have that," Barefoot says.

Most among Goizueta's pool of interviewers will want a few examples of what you contributed on the job, what you want to do with your MBA, and why you are a good match for that particular job. "Answer concisely," Barefoot urges. Imagine having to convince a board of directors to grant you more R&D funds when you sound instead like you're delivering a filibuster.

"Confidence is attractive," Barefoot says. Bluster can be a deal-killer. So can inappropriate gifts. If you're sending anything, it should be a thank-you note. In conclusion, there is no magic formula for gaining admittance into Goizueta Business School, Barefoot advises. Have "solid to strong" quantitative skills, quality work experience, interpersonal skills, and demonstrated leadership with community involvement. The bottom line: Admissions officials must see that you can handle the work. Clarifies Barefoot, "We're pretty straightforward in what we're looking for."

Full-time MBAs receiving financial aid through school: 86%

Institutional (merit-based) scholarships: 107

Assistantships: 0

Full-tuition scholarships school awarded for academic year: 46

Financially Aided

Goizueta is a program that offers three types of full-tuition scholarships: merit-based Robert W. Woodruff Fellowships for the crème de la crème of academic achievers; Goizueta Fellowships, also for the crème de la crème and equal in honor to the Woodruff awards; and merit-based Dean's Scholarships for exceptional MBA candidates. For need-based financial support—in other words, almost everybody—the school's financial aid officers can explain the federal loans options, availability of private loans, and how much you will need to spend to get through your education and afford late-night coffee and pizza as well.

FULL-TIME MBA PROGRAM (TOTAL DIRECT COSTS)

In-state: $82,856

Out-of-state: $82,856

International: $82,856

Part-time program cost: $22,500 per year (tuition only)

EMBA program cost: $78,000 per year (tuition only)

What Goizueta Students Know

Aaron Kuney, class of 2009, needed big city culture, a prominent real estate market, and a cozy environment in which to link his classroom experience to the real world. He found it all at Emory's Goizueta Business School in Atlanta. "From the moment I set foot on campus I was really struck by the strength of the community at Goizueta," says Kuney, "I knew that Goizueta was a place that I wanted to devote myself to over the next two years of my life and beyond." Kuney's journey to a post-MBA career in real estate and/or finance began at the March orientation. It eased his worries, introduced him to his future classmates, and helped him gain a basic understanding of his surroundings, he says. Another series of preparatory events before the first semester in September served as reinforcement.

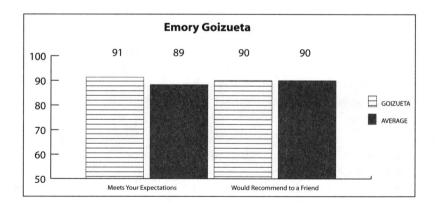

However, for all the items he had on his MBA-search checklist, Kuney (who also serves as his class's vice president of alumni relations) says his experience so far had been defined by his instructors and administrators. "I have developed relationships with a number of my professors which have stretched outside the bounds of simply a teacher/student relationship and more in the realm of friend, confidant, advisor, and mentor," he says. "I have found this to be the case with people throughout the school; from the MBA Program Office and Alumni/Development Office, to the Dean's Office and the teaching faculty across multiple departments. [My experience] has really validated one of the important reasons that I chose Emory to begin with."

Parul Lahoti, class of 2010, lauds the program's core values of integrity, collaboration, and teamwork. All emerge throughout his typical day: class in the mornings, meetings with team members and faculty, lunch in the commons with friends, reading catch-up in the afternoon, and more classes. Evenings are filled with company presentations, club events, and a Thursday mixer. Lahoti is planning a career as a human resources manager and has already met with several recruiters. Conferences, company visits on campus, networking events, and fact-finding treks to Atlanta-area businesses such as Coca-Cola and AT&T already created ample opportunities. A summer internship at Procter & Gamble in Cincinnati was already in the planning stages. Says Lahoti, "As a first-year student, I have felt welcomed to Goizueta since day one, and have truly benefited from the collaborative and nurturing environment."

What's Next? Your Career

Associate Dean and Executive Director Wendy Tsung wants students to embrace the long-term benefits of Goizueta's MBA Career Services. The office has your back in the short term, too. "This is the only time in their lives that companies will come to them," explains Tsung. "You don't want to rely on that. They need to learn skills in their careers going forward." Tsung emphasizes that Career Services should be a partner in the job search, not a placement center. The partnership is a powerful one. Students receive one-on-one counseling from both a Career Services coach and a second-year peer counselor throughout the program. There are mock interviews, resume workshops, and other brainstorming functions. Goizueta's fine-tuned internship and work experience program places high percentages of students in all the major disciplines, Tsung says.

When it comes time to seal the deal for employment after graduation, students can rest assured that Goizueta has the done the legwork in making it easier for recruiters to meet them. "We focus on the personal touch with companies," she says. The school has a reputation for ensuring that recruiters will interview only quality candidates so they don't have to pore through 500 resumes to find the five they need, Tsung explains.

Goizueta also rallies around its own in a way that some of the business school giants can't. When GBS Dean Larry Benveniste made a direct appeal to all branches of the business school to redouble their efforts to secure jobs for its students, Tsung says alumni and outside companies responded in force. Some knew of openings from colleagues. Others had their own needs to fill. "Our community sets us apart," Tsung declares.

CAREER CHECK: GOIZUETA MBA EMPLOYMENT BY JOB FUNCTION

- Marketing/Sales: 30%
- Consulting: 27%
- Finance/Accounting: 22%
- General Management: 14%
- Human Resources: 1%
- Operations/Logistics: 1%
- Other: 5%

ALUMNI ACTUALS

MBA alumni worldwide: 7,400+

Business school alumni networking site: www.goizueta.emory.edu/alumni/index.asp

Current MBA students have access to the alumni database.

Goizueta students fulfill their end by just being who the top businesses expect them to be. "A common theme is that students here are team players and hard working," the executive director says. "They're well-prepared, smart people who can hit the ground running." The statistics bear that out. Seventy-one percent of GBS students secured employment before graduation. Three months after graduation, 94 percent of students have received offers and 86 percent have accepted them.

If Career Services has its way, its relationship with GBS graduates will thrive well after that. The school's unique "6 Degrees" electronic conferencing enables graduates to tap into a vast network of alumni for problem solving, tips, and contacts. That can be a big help at any time in a career.

Match Made in Heaven: Is the Goizueta Business School Right for You?

You are an ideal student if you

- Want to stretch your character in new ways, including taking calculated risks you never before considered.
- Learn best in an environment where the emphasis is on expounding analytical skills to address problem solving and decision making in business.
- Like the convenience of a close-by city and the atmosphere of a sprawling campus.
- Seek a holistic education that provides an environment connecting theory and practice and teaching those concepts through extensive immersion in real-world work experience.

Georgetown University Robert E. McDonough School of Business

37th and O Streets NW
Washington, DC 20057

Phone: 202.687.4200
E-mail: mba@georgetown.edu
Web site: http://mba.georgetown.edu

Dean: George G. Daly
Deputy Dean: Ricardo Ernst

"Our faculty, staff, and student leaders work extremely hard to deliver the highest-quality MBA program possible. Affective experiences are shared experiences. [For an individual] who has the ability and drive to earn an MBA at Georgetown, students have the advantage of all that a prestigious degree bestows: skills, understanding, and a network that lasts a lifetime." —Dean Daly

Quick Facts

MBA PROGRAMS

Full-time MBA
Part-time MBA (evening program)
Executive MBA (Georgetown-ESADE)

FULL-TIME MBA SNAPSHOT

Total enrollment: 521
Class of 2010: 256
Length of program: 21 months
Campus location: Washington, DC
Program commences in August
Pre-term orientation attendance required

APPLICATION NOTES

Application requirements: Professional experience not required but highly recommended; a 4-year bachelor's degree or equivalent; GMAT scores; transcript; four essays mandatory; GRE not accepted
Letters of recommendation: 2
Interview: By invitation only

Number of applicants: 1,883
Admittance rate: 30%

CLASS OF 2010 PROFILE

Male 70%, Female 30%
Minority Americans: 46%
International: 24%
Average age: 28
Married or Partnered, Single: 25%, 75%
Average years of work experience: 5 years
GMAT average: 678
GMAT range (20th–80th percentile): 640–730
GPA average: 3.35

ACADEMIC BACKGROUND OF INCOMING STUDENTS

Business: 36%
Computer Science: 4%
Economics: 16%
Engineering: 15%
Humanities: 9%
Natural Sciences: 4%
Social Sciences: 9%
Other: 7%

Birth of a Nation and an Institution

Having traveled to Maryland to preach to and convert the local Native Americans, in 1640 Father Ferdinand Poulton received official permission from the English Provincial of the Jesuits to establish the first American Catholic college. Despite the laws of the time, which constricted Catholic education, the Jesuits established a school in Cecil County, Maryland. Among the school's students was John Carroll, soon to be founder of his own school.

In 1784, the Pope selected Father John Carroll as Superior of the Missions in the Thirteen United States of America. Later Father Carroll was appointed Prefect Apostolic, Bishop, and finally Archbishop—the first in the United States. Among his many contributions to education was the founding of Georgetown College in January 1789 at its current site.

Scenes from Georgetown.

The School of Business, established in 1957, was named for Robert Emmett McDonough in 1998 after he donated $30 million. The McDonough Business School used to be housed in the first of Georgetown University's structures, the Old North Building—followed by the Georgetown Car Barn. Now it is in the campus's newest building. The 172,000-square foot, five-story structure is located in the center of campus and features state-of-the-art classrooms, conference rooms, meeting offices, a 400-seat auditorium, and expansive open spaces for students.

Students themselves are wandering scholars on campus. Along with the choice of taking electives at other Georgetown schools (such as the School of Public Policy, Law Center, or School of Medicine), students have a choice of numerous dual degrees.

Why McDonough?

Devin Kalman, class of 2009, characterizes the McDonough philosophy as "competitive yet collaborative. I would sum it up as 'I am because we are.' That's a South African philosophy, actually."

MBA courses build skills in all functional areas and integrate these skills to address crucial business issues. Students are required to participate in an international consulting project. Elective courses are meant to bolster your chosen career track. MBA students may also pursue joint-degree programs with Georgetown University's Law Center, the School of Foreign Service, Graduate Public Policy Program, Medical Center, and graduate physics department. On-campus classes consist of a series of lectures and case studies about the country's economy, business system, polity, and culture that include readings and written or oral graded work and supervision of team projects by faculty members with weekly meetings and deliverables. For those students coming to D.C. to immerse themselves in the public policy field, Georgetown University's main library houses more than two million volumes, and the business library has an exceptional collection of government documents. This is in addition to the Library of Congress in downtown Washington, home of a mind-boggling array of political history resources.

Attending graduate school in the nation's capital is just the beginning. The McDonough School of Business is committed to furthering global commerce education. The MBA is unique in many areas, one of which is student access to the Georgetown School of Foreign Service as well as the broad range of local businesses. If you want a career at a development bank, developmental consulting firm, think tank, or government consulting firm or with lobbying and policy groups, you are at the right school. McDonough has the networking access to high-level professionals and well-connected professors in these fields.

Exposure to this wide world is accomplished through "residencies"—four integrative courses that complement regular course instruction. The first year you will participate in residencies in the fundamentals of global business and innovation, the second year in leadership and globalization. The Globalization Residency is the capstone of your experience at Georgetown. You will team with a group of classmates to undertake a consulting project for a foreign organization or Fortune 500 company with operations overseas. All students participate in this 16-month immersion program in eight geographic areas, including the McDonough/Walsh School of Foreign Services in Washington, D.C.

Teams have traveled to Brazil, China, the Czech Republic, United Arab Emirates, South Africa, and Vietnam. The Globalization Residency consists of activities such as speakers from local business and government, joint sessions with local business school faculty and students, factory visits, and top management briefings. If this isn't enough, you also participate in corporate responsibility or community service events, cultural events around the country, and fieldwork to support your team's project. Your team's recommendations are presented to the client company's senior leadership after you have finalized your results.

Because it is a crucial part of your MBA, the outcome of the Globalization Residency is designed to expand your ability to conduct international business with comfort and confidence in a foreign culture as well as take on whatever task is needed to produce results for the client. As a result, you will come away with improved problem-solving ability, analytical ability, communication skills, and knowledge integration of all you have learned during the MBA program.

As one student explains, "No matter where we are from, we applied certain business notions to our plans that simply did not hold water in the economies we were visiting and researching. And that was the beauty of the assignment—to learn the necessity of flexibility, of shaping what we learn, and fitting it to environments or situations entirely new to us."

Course Offerings

McDonough's curriculum is organized into intensive team-based experiences, courses that integrate various functional areas and elective courses that offer choice. It gives you the tools and skills you need to anticipate, analyze, and solve increasingly interrelated and complex business challenges. Throughout the curriculum, you practice international management strategies and ethical decision making, as well as strong interpersonal, teamwork, and presentation skills. The focus is global—where business is now and in the future. In your first year, you begin with a weeklong opening residency to introduce you to business cases and working in teams. The first year's core curriculum provides a general management framework in accounting, decision sciences, economics, finance, marketing, and management.

Devin Kalman describes a day in the life of a Georgetown grad student. "There is no such thing as a typical day." However, he does have a routine. "I wake at 8 A.M. every day and have my first class at 10 A.M. I'm done by 11:30. I eat lunch while reading for my afternoon class. I chat with friends (and sometimes I don't finish reading). I go to my second class at 1:30 P.M. and finish at 3 P.M. I have my group meeting from 3:30 to 4:30 (while eating a snack). Then it's homework from 5 P.M. to 8 P.M., or I have more group meetings. After that, dinner, gym, and to bed by 11 P.M."

An addition to the curriculum in 2008 was the Career Track residency, a weeklong, immersion experience working on a partner company's current case within one of three functional areas (marketing, finance, or consulting). Through this residency, students working in teams are able to implement classroom learning immediately from the core curriculum into a real-world setting and have their outcomes judged by working professionals in a case competition.

RESEARCH CENTERS

Capital Markets Research Center	GU Business Ethics Institute
Center for Business and Public Policy	GU Women's Leadership Initiative
Credit Research Center	

What McDonough Professors Teach

Professor of Finance Reena Aggarwal believes in the future of the MBA. She relates, "The McDonough MBA will continue to be a truly global program that will be at the forefront of leading issues facing the world." As a participant in this vision, Aggawal explores real-world events in the classes she teaches. "The courses that I have taught include Investment Banking, Alternative Investments, and Global Residency. Each of these courses is very practical where students have to work on 'live' cases. Students are also exposed to a number of speakers that have a global perspective." She adds, "The last decade has clearly shown the need for responsible global leaders who are of integrity and moral values. At Georgetown's McDonough School of Business, in addition to training students in the business disciplines, we also immerse them in understanding responsible leadership. This educational principle is not only seen in the courses but also in the types of activities our students are engaged in outside the classroom. It is also evident in the speakers who come on campus and the questions our students ask."

Teaching in Washington, D.C., has its own rewards. Stanley Nollen, professor and researcher in International Business shares, "We have all the resources close at hand—international organizations, corporate offices, public policy makers, industry associations, embassies. We are located next to the decision makers, and we have access to them. The city is an attractive living environment with good services and institutions and an internationally oriented population, and the East Coast location embraces sophistication."

As Sherry El-Gawly, class of 2009, expounds about McDonough's professors. "They are one of the highlights of my experience. We had an all-star line-up our first year—from Professor Almeida for Strategy to Nollen for Macroeconomics to Macher for Microeconomics to Holtom for Organizational Behavior. I really feel privileged to have had such passionate, seasoned academics as my teachers. Not only were they excellent at their respective subjects, but they really got to know us as students. As a second-year, I feel no different. Most of the professors I have had have been top notch. Professor Romanelli taught us strategy via the case method in one of the best classes I've had in business school. Professor Blemaster's M&A class is one of the best I've had, and Professor Blemaster has become a friend I have coffee with from time to time. Jett Pihakis is someone I always love seeing around, and who I turn to for advice. Overall, I hope to maintain the relationships I formed with some of these amazing people."

From a professor's prospective, Nollen explains the workings of his teaching. "We treat international business as something that is always present and integral to all that we do; it is not something special or elective. We have had this approach for many years; it is not recently adopted. For example, all of our MBA students in all of our programs take our Global Residency course that includes on-campus instruction, a week-long foreign residency in one country, and intensive engagement with companies operating abroad via consulting projects conducted by five-person teams of our MBA students. This course is not elective, and it is not academic tourism." In addition, Nollen expects students to show professionalism in their conduct and to communicate skillfully in all situations.

FACULTY FACTS

Full-time faculty employed by the
  b-school: 74

Adjunct or visiting faculty: 46

Permanent/tenured professors: 48

Tenured faculty who are women: 8

Tenured faculty who are underrepresented
  minorities: 9

SAMPLING OF NOTABLE PROFESSORS

- Paul Almeida: Five-time winner of the Best Professor Award for the International Executive MBA program, recipient of the Joseph LeMoine Award for Graduate and Undergraduate Teaching Excellence
- Alan R. Andreasen: Successful author and contributor to a variety of disciplines including strategic planning, consumer behavior, and marketing regulations; serves as a Honorary Editor for the *International Journal of Non-Profit Marketing*
- Robert J. Bies: Distinguished professor and co-author of *Getting Even: The Truth About Workplace Revenge—And How to Stop It*
- Michael R. Czinkota: Acclaimed expert on international business and trade; served as an advisor to the U.S. government, United Nations, and World Trade Organization, recipient of the Lifetime Contribution Award in Global Marketing from the American Marketing Association

(continued)

(continued)

> • Jeffrey T. Macher: Highly regarded specialist in strategy and economics; serves on the editorial board of the *Strategic Management Journal* and the *International Journal of Strategic Change Management*

CONCENTRATIONS OFFERED TO FULL-TIME MBA STUDENTS

Accounting and Business Law	Management
Operations and Information Management	Marketing
Economics	Public Policy
Ethics	Strategy
Finance	

JOINT DEGREES AND DUAL DEGREES

MBA/JD	MBA/MSFS (Foreign Service)
MBA/MD	MBA/MS (Physics)
MBA/MPP (Public Policy)	

What Admissions Is All About

Assistant Dean of Full-Time MBA Admissions Kelly R. Wilson describes ideal candidates for the program as well rounded, smart, and motivated to succeed in a diverse environment. "You need to have demonstrated leadership ability as well as strong interpersonal and communication skills. In addition, you need to have a clear idea of how the MBA degree will help to connect the dots between your experience and goals for the future. Finally, keep in mind that how you present yourself professionally in person has major import for admissions consideration," she states.

Hilary Puskar, assistant director of full-time admissions, tells prospective students, "You will get the greatest return on investment when you go into business school with a clear career focus. As the classes, club activities, and recruiting activities begin almost the moment you step on campus, business school is not a place to 'figure it out.'" Puskar continues, "Because we are a general management program, we have students that go into a variety of fields. While many pursue more traditional tracks such as finance, consulting, and marketing, many students go to non-profit companies or government positions, or less traditional jobs."

Mira Lutova, assistant director of full-time admissions, describes McDonough. "The atmosphere in classes is very team oriented and collaborative. The method of teaching is a mixture of case-based and lecture-based approaches. Also, you can take electives at other schools within Georgetown, which broadens your education experience."

Wilson notes, "We strongly suggest that all applicants read the instructions as a starting point. The instructions outline all required components of the application and provide specific details to inform the candidate of exactly what to submit. By following these instructions, candidates can ensure that they put together a polished, professional application for review by the admissions committee." Continues Wilson, "We encourage candidates to take advantage of the opportunities available to get to know the community. Through on- and off-campus recruiting activities, a candidate can enhance his or her understanding of how he/she might fit into our community. Gather as much information as you can to make a well-informed decision." Finally, Wilson explains, "The approach Georgetown's MBA Admissions takes is a holistic one and assesses the overall strength of an applicant. We do not zero in on one area of the application more than another. That said, if a candidate has a sub-standard GMAT or academic record, we would look for the application to balance that weakness in some way. The admissions process is competitive, meaning the admissions committee considers the candidates admissibility as well as how competitive one application is compared to the rest of the pool."

Financially Aided

Students have opportunities for need-based and merit-based assistance from the school through scholarships, assistantships, or loans. McDonough's MBA Scholars Program is based on academic merit and leadership potential and provides both full- and partial-tuition scholarships. You are not required to request financial aid or scholarship consideration because all students who apply in the first or second application rounds are considered. Tuition assistance is given in the form of credits/reimbursement to a student's financial account.

If you are awarded an MBA scholarship, you will be working with faculty on topical business research projects that teach you research methodology. For faculty, working with scholars provides fresh insights and creativity not often found with traditional research assistants.

Two principal sources of funding are available to MBA candidates of Georgetown University's McDonough School of Business: scholarships and loans. After an admitted candidate submits the deposit, he/she should begin the process of applying for loans. Grants are not available for graduate students.

Opportunities for funding an MBA education are available from sources outside the university. Approximately one-third of the class receives scholarships. The amount varies per academic year from covering partial to full cost of tuition. Kelly Wilson comments, "We do understand that the process for financial aid can be daunting. The MBA Admissions Office can provide a candidate with general information on the financial aid process. However, we encourage candidates to review thoroughly the Web site of the Office of Student Financial Services. For questions that remain after a candidate reads through our Web site, the University's Office of Student Financial Services has staff on hand to provide guidance on this process to newly admitted and continuing students. Contact information is listed on their Web site through the same link."

For international students, "The financial aid process is the same as for U.S. citizens and U.S. permanent residents. Candidates are considered for scholarships as an automatic step in the admissions process," Wilson confirms. "All candidates who apply by the round-two application deadline will automatically be considered for merit-based scholarships. Notification of scholarship award will be included within the admissions letter."

All eligible students are encouraged to apply for the Free Application for Federal Student Aid (FAFSA), as well as other loan programs including the Federal Entitlement Program. In addition, U.S. citizens have the option of acquiring private loans, and international students need to have loans in place before arriving on campus.

FULL-TIME MBA PROGRAM (TOTAL DIRECT COSTS)

In-state: $83,868

Out-of-state: $83,868

International: $83,868

Part-time: $1,166 per credit

IEMBA 15: $53,994

IEMBA 17: $70,929

GEMBA: $130,000

Full-time MBAs receiving financial aid: 75%

Institutional (merit-based) scholarships: 64

Assistantships: 25

Full-tuition scholarships school awarded for academic year: 10

What McDonough Students Know

Sherry El-Gawly found that "pre-term orientation was informative and data-packed in terms of the program." El-Gawly decided to attend McDonough because, besides its international reputation, "Washington D.C. Georgetown has the brand name." The location of the school also was a key factor for her: "D.C was a big draw for me, as was the Georgetown area itself. I love the culture, politics, and shopping of the city—everything from musicals at the Kennedy Center to biking on the Potomac [River trail], the history of the monuments, and the gorgeous art of the Smithsonian Museums." El-Gawly would have welcomed more time being introduced to the city. Newcomers are often amazed at the grid-system setup of D.C. streets and insiders' knowledge of how to get around to the sites and activities from one side of town to the other.

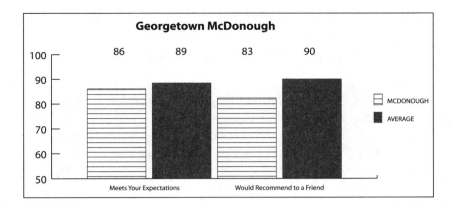

Networking is, as most students know, crucial for future success, and it starts the first week on campus. One piece of advice McDonough imparts to students is to be nice to other people. This seems obvious, yet many very focused and driven students forget to take the extra time to hear other people's stories. Networking is a two-way street, and often the best way to position yourself is to help someone else get ahead.

Involvement in clubs is an integral part of the experience, and most students belong to three or four. Wherever your core interest lies, an organization exists that brings you together with other like-minded students. One of the newest of these is the Energy Club.

CAREER CHECK: McDONOUGH MBA EMPLOYMENT BY JOB FUNCTION

- Finance/Accounting: 43%
- Consulting: 20%
- Marketing/Sales: 17%
- General Management: 14%
- Operations/Logistics: 4%
- Other: 2%

What's Next? Your Career

Georgetown attracts students who already have a global mindset. The rigorous curriculum trains students to reach for excellence in the real world. Because McDonough's grading system is considered transparent, students can see how they are held accountable for their coursework.

Some of the newer industries are hiring McDonough MBAs, including the gaming industry. Strong student interest exists in the health-care and marketing clubs lately, and Career Services invites companies in these fields to meet with candidates. Career counselors spend a bit more effort to bring businesses that are particularly popular with students to campus each year.

Jeannette Frett, assistant dean and director of MBA Career Management, relates the many ways students and recruiters are introduced to each other. McDonough students attract recruiters because they embody the "four basic concepts that define Georgetown's McDonough School of Business." She imparts that students are part of "a community of achievement in one of the world's great universities [which has] a long-standing global mindset that teaches students to thrive in international organizations, a focus on leadership, and a location at the center of world politics and business in Washington, D.C." Recruiters come to McDonough for the same reasons as other school community members— the "high level of talent that attracts students and faculty, as well as the valuable career enhancement [the school] provides." Forty-five percent of recruiters hire their summer interns. And of the 114 companies that listed open positions on the Career Services site for the class of 2008–2009, 51 posted internships. Within three months of graduation, 99 percent of students seeking employment had job offers, and 98 percent had accepted offers.

Kalman describes his experience with recruiters on campus. "Interaction with recruiters varies depending on your career path. For me and others seeking investment banking positions, interaction begins in early October of the first year. The Finance Club organizes a trip to New York to visit with a dozen or so organizations. The companies host panels for us and explain their organizations. Often these sessions are followed by a more social cocktail hour. These sessions are coordinated by company recruiters, but the bankers themselves host the sessions (and cocktail hours). So, our interaction is mostly with the bankers. After our weeklong trip to New York, each student individually reaches out to many of the bankers he or she met. The students coordinate follow-up meetings throughout the months of October, November, and early December. These meetings are informal interviews. In January, the bankers at each firm coordinate internally to discuss the students with whom they have met. Then each firm decides which students they wish to formally interview in early to mid-January. That's pretty much the process."

For those who are pursuing other careers besides banking, the recruiting process is much longer. Recruiters come to campus in January and select students whom they wish to interview based on resume submission.

Frett shares, "The best way to encourage employers to recruit our students is by providing numerous opportunities for students and potential employers to interact. Competition to hire Georgetown MBA students is intense. The most successful organizations develop a plan to raise their visibility and reach out to students early and regularly." She adds, "The McDonough Career Management staff helps companies customize their branding strategy on campus through participation in events."

Through additional career forums, she says, "Georgetown students have some of the best attendance rates among MBA programs at national and regional conferences." Frett names some of the amazing array of opportunities that students have come to appreciate: Careers Xtravaganza (CX), Corporate Treks, Functional Days, Global Diversity Day, Ultimate 4, Non-Profit Auction, Corporate Affiliates Program, and Monday morning coffee and Thursday evening socials.

Working with student organizations gives recruiters direct contact with students. Corporate contacts interact with students through speaker presentations, career education sessions, and outside consulting projects. Moreover, to prepare for recruiter meetings, during the year, Georgetown alumni at recruiting firms help current students practice behavioral and case interview skills. Conducted individually or as part of practice days, APIs are a great way for former Georgetown students to be involved in the recruiting process.

ALUMNI ACTUALS

MBA alumni worldwide: 4,770+

Business school alumni networking site: http://msb.georgetown.edu.alumni

Current MBA students have access to the alumni database.

Match Made in Heaven: Is the McDonough School of Business Right for You?

You are an ideal student if you

- Learn best using theories and models with real-world data to solve practical problems, as well as think critically.
- Have an international outlook and want to be part of the growing global business community.
- Seek to develop capability and comfort operating as a manager in a range of cultures and environments.
- Expect a teaching environment that incorporates the geo-politically vibrant D.C. surroundings to engage locally while developing a broad-focus business flexibility.

Harvard University
Harvard Business School

Soldiers Field
Boston, MA 02163

Phone: 617.495.6000
E-mail: admissions@hbs.edu
Web site: www.hbs.edu/mba

Dean: Jay O. Light
Senior Associate Dean and Chair of the MBA Program: Joseph Badaracco

"The mission of Harvard Business School is to educate leaders who make a difference in the world."
—Harvard Business School's mission statement

Quick Facts

MBA Programs

Full-time MBA
Executive Education

Full-Time MBA Snapshot

Total enrollment: 1,801
Class of 2010: 900
Length of program: 18 months
Campus: Boston, MA
Program commences in August
Pre-term orientation attendance required

Application Notes

Requirements: resume; recommendations; essays; work and academic history; GMAT or GRE
score; GRE accepted
Letters of recommendation: 3
Interview: By invitation only
Number of applicants: 8,661
Admittance rate: 12%

CLASS OF 2010 PROFILE

Male 62%, Female 38%
Minority Americans: 27%
International: 33%
Average age: 26
Combined average years of work experience: 4 years
GMAT average score: 720
GMAT score range (20th–80th percentile): 690–750
GPA average GPA: 3.66

ACADEMIC BACKGROUND OF INCOMING STUDENTS

Business: 23%
Engineering and Natural Sciences: 32%
Humanities and Social Sciences: 42%
Other: 4%

Historic Foundations and Modern Transformations

Harvard Business School was founded in 1908 with 80 students. It was originally located in Harvard Yard on the Cambridge, Massachusetts, side of the scenic Charles River. In 1926, it moved to its present location in Allston, which is part of Boston, across the Charles River from the main Harvard campus in Cambridge. This campus, with its stately Georgian buildings, was dedicated in June 1927. Women were first admitted to the school's two-year MBA program with the Class of 1965. The firm of well-known landscape architect Frederick Law Olmsted, who designed New York City's Central Park, also designed the landscaping for Harvard Business School. Today, HBS's 33 buildings sit on 40 acres, and a series of underground tunnels connects the basements of nearly every building on campus, with the exception of several student housing facilities.

Cambridge and Boston represent two of the most historic sites in all of the United States. When not studying, you can find every ethnic cuisine imaginable in Central Square, journey along the Freedom Trail and down Beacon Hill's cobblestone lanes to view how Boston looked during the Revolutionary War, and explore Newbury Street's fashionable shops. From Harvard Square to the city's bustling downtown district, you can find a wide variety of neighborhoods to explore, as well as some of the country's most well-known institutions, including the Boston Symphony, the Boston Pops, Fenway Park, and the Museum of Fine Arts. Not too far away are the beaches of Cape Cod, the quiet beauty of New Hampshire and Vermont, and many scenic New England coastal towns.

Harvard's historic campus.

Why Harvard?

Harvard Business School is known for its emphasis on case teaching, or the Socratic method, whereby students prepare cases and discuss them extensively in class with a professor as the moderator and facilitator. By graduation, you can expect to have examined more than 500 cases. Each case addresses a particular topic and provides an example of how the topic can be applied in the real world. New cases are produced continually by various professors, and second-year students are often given the opportunity to assist in the case-writing process. In fact, producing cases has become such an integral part of the Harvard Business School experience that many other business schools purchase case studies from HBS.

"The people who do best don't just come in like a sponge," says Doug Braithwaite, senior admissions consultant, HBS alumnus, and a former director of Harvard MBA Admissions. "People who are really proactive are going to get more out of the program. I think it is an incredible opportunity to rub shoulders with these people. It's a wonderful experience."

Incoming HBS classes are comprised of approximately 900 students who are divided into sections of 90, with each section taking classes together for the first year of study. This practice facilitates forming lasting social and academic bonds that carry beyond graduation. During the first year, you are assigned to a learning team with six students each. Teams meet each day to prepare daily class assignments.

Backgrounds of HBS students are purposefully diverse; your section may include attorneys, teachers, investment bankers, physicians, consultants, brand managers, professional athletes, military officers, and entrepreneurs. During classroom discussions, students draw on their own experiences, creating a dynamic atmosphere supplemented by the faculty's insights and perspectives. One alum who attended HBS in the 1990s declares, "The quality of my fellow students was much higher than I expected. In my section alone, we had an Olympian, a former professional athlete, an early member of Microsoft, and many other notable businesspeople."

Because most MBA students at Harvard Business School have been at the top of their classes in high school and in undergraduate school, the environment at HBS is understandably more competitive than perhaps at other business schools. At the same time, the relationships among students are not as cutthroat as is sometimes rumored, and, in fact, the learning environment is friendly and collaborative. The graduation rate at HBS is an impressive 98 percent.

HBS is well known for its in-depth "immersion programs" that supplement in-class academic experiences. These popular programs enable first- and second-year students to immerse themselves in academic, cultural, and organizational fieldwork during an intensive 5- to 12-day period between the end of the first term and the beginning of the second. Students collaborate with faculty to explore regional economies or topical economic issues in locations throughout the world. These trips combine travel with an intense learning experience that introduces you to prominent individuals who are leaders in emerging markets, to new technologies, and to innovative business practices.

In recent years, immersion programs have included the China Immersion, under the guidance of HBS professors Richard Vietor and David Collis and Harvard University Chinese scholar and professor William Kirby. Students met with business leaders and governmental officials in Beijing, Hangzhou, Sanya, Hong Kong, Shanghai, and Shenzhen. The New Orleans Immersion sent HBS students, faculty, and staff to New Orleans to contribute time and talent to a variety of post-Hurricane Katrina rebuilding efforts, Habitat for Humanity home-building projects, and career support efforts for Dillard University undergraduates. Locally, for the Healthcare Immersion, students took advantage of Boston's premiere medical centers and studied medical specialties by visiting local labs, companies, and hospitals. Leading physicians, including renowned cancer researcher Judah Folkman and medical ethicist Jerry Avorn, led discussions on topics including surgical techniques and pharmaceutical research.

Throughout the year, all students are invited to presentations by more than 300 speakers and nearly 20 conferences, in addition to the multitude of activities that are held by the on-campus clubs. One of the largest clubs on campus is the HBS Finance Club, which promotes activities and careers related to the finance field by sponsoring events such as the annual finance conference and the Days on Wall Street Trek. Another popular student organization is the Social Enterprise Club, reflecting the importance of this topic.

Baker Library/Bloomberg Center is the iconic image of the HBS campus. Named after New York banker George F. Baker, it contains collections that span seven centuries. The library serves the research needs of not only HBS faculty, students, and staff, but also the larger Harvard communities.

The Spangler Center, designed by architect Robert A.M. Stern, is the heart of campus life at HBS. Students gather there to enjoy a snack or a meal, meet with their learning teams, and sit by the fireplace on cold winter evenings.

Want to work out or have some fun? Shad Hall contains a state-of-the-art health club and an indoor elevated walking/jogging track; racquetball, squash, and tennis courts; three basketball courts; table-tennis courts; an indoor golf net; aerobics studios; a fitness equipment area; and whirlpool, steam, and sauna rooms. Shad Hall also has a top-notch team of personal trainers and other professionals who offer counseling on nutrition, fitness, and stress management. Golf swing clinics and ballroom dance lessons are also available.

FUN FACTS

- Harvard University has the second largest library in the country with more than 15 million volumes. Only the Library of Congress in Washington, D.C., has a greater number of volumes. The Boston Public Library is third with more than 14 million volumes.
- The school owns Harvard Business Publishing, which publishes business books, online management tools, teaching cases, and the monthly *Harvard Business Review*.
- Kwame Jackson (class of 2000) became famous as a contestant on the NBC television program *The Apprentice*. He went on to create Legacy LLC, a holding company, with the goal of supporting African-American entrepreneurship.
- Harvard Business School was the first school to offer the MBA degree in 1910.

Course Offerings

Harvard Business School's full-time MBA program consists of one year of required courses and a second year of elective courses. The first semester focuses mainly on the internal workings of a company and includes such courses as Technology and Operations Management; Marketing; Financial Reporting and Control; Leadership and Organizational Behavior; and Finance. During the second semester, students study the external operations of a company. Courses include Strategy; The Entrepreneurial Manager; Negotiation; and Leadership and Corporate Accountability. There is also a semester-long macroeconomics course called Business, Government, and the International Economy. Working through the required courses helps students develop strong analytic and quantitative skills while forging lasting relationships with their fellow students. The second-year elective courses run the gambit from Doing Business in China to Managing Medicine to The Moral Leader. You can choose from among 96 different courses or, in lieu of a class, you can complete a field study or an independent research project. Independent study enables you to work closely with faculty members and research a real-world issue, develop a new business, or launch a new product. Often, students have the opportunity to create projects that align with their personal and professional interests.

During the second year of study, you can cross-register for one or two classes at the Sloan School of Business at MIT, Fletcher School of Law and Diplomacy at Tufts University, or at any of the other Harvard University graduate programs. Second-year students may also select to cross-register for an enrichment course in an area, including studying a language.

In April 2007, Harvard Business School and Harvard's Kennedy School of Government introduced a joint degree program in business and government. This degree opens opportunities in business, government, and nonprofit organizations that address key issues such as health care, the environment, economic development, and government regulation. The program takes three years to complete, and students earn degrees from both schools upon graduation.

RESEARCH CENTERS

Asia-Pacific Research Center (Hong Kong)

Arthur Rock Center for Entrepreneurship

California Research Center (Menlo Park)

Computer Lab for Experimental Research

Europe Research Center (Paris)

Japan Research Center (Tokyo)

Latin America Research Center (Buenos Aires)

India Research Center (Mumbai)

What HBS Professors Teach

Harvard Business School's faculty is divided into 10 academic units. These are Accounting and Management; Business, Government and the International Economy; Entrepreneurial Management; Finance; General Management; Marketing; Negotiation, Organizations, and Markets; Organizational Behavior; Strategy; and Technology and Operations Management. You get to know professors in most of these units, and here is just a sample.

Robert Simons, a member of the Accounting and Management Unit, has spent the last 25 years teaching accounting, management control, and strategy implementation courses. In 2009, he completed development of a second-year course called "Driving Corporate Performance," which is held for executives in finance as well as general managers.

David. E. Bell, a professor of Business Administration, leads courses on managerial economics, risk management, marketing and retailing, and agribusiness. He chairs the annual global Agribusiness seminar where hundreds of food industry executives meet to discuss industry trends. Following six years as head of the school's marketing department, he is now Senior Associate Dean with responsibilities including faculty recruiting.

A member of the Entrepreneurial Management Unit, Associate Professor Mary Tripsas teaches several popular courses on leading innovative ventures, entrepreneurial management, and technology's role in competitive strategy. She also participates in executive education. Before coming to Harvard, she taught at the Wharton School, which has a different approach to business education. Through her experience, she exposes students in her classes to both educational concepts.

Brian J. Hall is a professor of Business Administration and head of the Negotiation, Organization, and Markets Unit. He is also a faculty affiliate of the Rock Center for Entrepreneurship. He teaches and researches organizational strategy and focuses on performance management and incentive systems. Among the courses he has led are organizational strategy, incentives, and negotiations. Bell's class participants explore topics such as how managers negotiate and organize to drive organizational value and performance.

John Deighton, a professor in the Marketing Unit, delves into how to use digital marketing tools, interactive marketing (using the Customer Equity Test), and additional marketing management and consumer behavior topics. Deighton researches, teaches, and writes cases, which become part of many MBA programs' curriculum.

Strategy Unit Professor Bharat Anand focuses on corporate strategy. His research in applied and empirical industrial organizations, corporate strategy, and competition in information goods markets (such as media and entertainment) informs classroom discussions. State-of-the-art research drives Harvard MBA education as quickly as the business world changes.

Lee Fleming, a professor of Business Administration in the Technology and Operations Management Unit, integrates business, science, and engineering for his courses' commercialization projects. Additionally, you may explore cases in technology and operations management, innovation, product development, green businesses, executive education courses in innovation and product development, and intellectual property. Fleming's students also use applied statistical methods.

FACULTY FACTS

Full-time faculty employed by the
b-school: 263

Adjunct or visiting faculty: 37

Permanent/tenured professors: 90

Tenured faculty who are women: 15

Tenured international faculty: 28

SAMPLING OF NOTABLE PROFESSORS

- Rawi E. Abdelal: Globally recognized authority on the international political economy; wrote *National Purpose in the World Economy,* which won the Shulman Prize for its tremendous contribution to the field of international relations

- Amy C. Edmondson: Lauded professor of leadership, team decision making, and organizational learning; earned (among other recognitions) the Cummings Award from the Academy of Management's Organizational Behavior Division and produced 20 teaching cases used at the school

- Rosabeth M. Kanter: World-renowned researcher and professor; served as editor of the *Harvard Business Review,* named by the *Times* of London as one of the "50 most powerful women in the world," and authored many highly regarded books, including *Confidence: How Winning Streaks & Losing Streaks Begin & End*

- Krishna G. Palepu: Lead authority on strategy and governance; co-authored, with Paul M. Healy and Victor L Bernard, *Business Analysis and Valuation,* which received both the Wildman Award and the Notable Contribution to Accounting Literature Award

- Michael E. Porter: Provided ground-breaking analysis in modern strategy, management, competitiveness of nations and regions, and health care; highly regarded prolific researcher; author of *Competitive Strategy: Techniques for Analyzing Industries and Competitors*

- Toby E. Stuart: Esteemed author and contributor to business development, including entrepreneurship and corporate strategy; recipient of the Kauffman Prize Medal for Distinguished Research in Entrepreneurship; co-wrote "Aging, Obsolescence, and Organizational Innovation" with Jesper B. Sørensen, which earned the *Administrative Science Quarterly*'s Scholarly Contribution Award

---

CONCENTRATIONS AND SPECIALIZATIONS OFFERED IN FULL-TIME MBA PROGRAM

Harvard's focus is on general management and it does not offer any formal concentrations. However, students are free to choose any electives in their second year.

JOINT DEGREES AND DUAL DEGREES

MBA-DMD

MBA/JD

MBA/MD

MBA/MPA-ID (Public Administration/ International Development)

MBA/MPP (Public Policy)

What Admissions Is All About

Admissions officers narrow the field of applicants after reading the applications, test scores, and recommendations for each student. "The rest of the decisions are made on judgment." Choosing who will be interviewed is a weighty responsibility, relates Doug Braithwaite. "Probably 70 percent of the people who apply could do the work if they got in. However, the job of the admissions committee at any of these schools is to admit the very best class." How is that determined? Admissions officers have criteria that may differ from year to year depending on business needs as HBS grows and changes. "Harvard isn't the best school for everyone. You have to know your learning style. I believe the beauty of the case method is that in addition to its being complex, ambiguous, etc., the student/ protagonist must make a decision and defend it even though he or she could do better with more complete data. Just like in the real world, one must decide and can't ever wait for complete information or perfect circumstances."

The Admissions Office is particularly looking for a habit of leadership, a capacity for intellectual growth, and engaged community citizenship. The majority of admissions officers are HBS alumni who want to maintain the high quality in incoming students. They advise you to consider these questions when preparing for an interview: Why are you one of the best? How does your resume differentiate you from other applicants who are equally qualified? Explain what is unique about you. During your interview, you should expect several follow-ups on a single question. Make sure you illustrate your competitive advantage through a detailed explanation of your answer rather than just a factual answer. Admissions board members are often skilled in counseling, training, and communications, so you need to impress them with your communication skills.

According to an internal memo from Dean Jay Light in February 2009, the school is considering increasing its class size by 5 percent. The memo was sent to HBS alumni informing them that the school is cutting its budget by about 5 percent and planning for another 5 percent cut if needed. HBS is going to increase class size "slightly" for the upcoming class. Dean Light reported that applications are up and the quality is very high.

HBS receives 7,000 to 10,000 applications for each incoming class. Interview invitations are extended on a rolling basis throughout the course of each application round. Interviewers seek applicants who exhibit a wide range of skills and achievements that have clearly shown leadership potential and the ability to thrive in a demanding and fast-paced academic environment. This is especially true for international applicants. HBS requires the IELTS or the Internet-based TOEFL (iBT) and strongly encourages a TWE score as well. Of primary interest is a high total score. For instance, HBS requires 110 or above on a scale of 0 to 120 for the TOEFL.

Although applicants must demonstrate the ability to master analytical and quantitative concepts, HBS's case-based method of learning requires that admitted students actively participate in class discussions. They assess, analyze, and act on complex information, often within ambiguous contexts. Because of this, Braithwaite discloses that even the best-prepared students will—at some point during their two years in the program—flub an answer, offer a misguided solution, or otherwise misstep in front of their classmates. What happens then depends on your resiliency. Such a situation is not the end of the world, and those who are able to pick themselves up and get through the embarrassment are the students who will gain the most from their overall education. Consequently, your resiliency most definitely is tested if you are invited for an admission interview.

Visiting in person has no direct effect on an applicant's admission. Starting in October of each year, HBS applicants can arrange class visits through the Admissions office, and current students are available to eat lunch with visitors and provide tours in the afternoons. However, if an applicant finds it easier to tour the campus during the summertime, members of the HBS Admission Board will be on hand to conduct information sessions, and the school now features an iPod walking tour of the campus that applicants can take on their own. Applicants can also get a good idea of what the case method is all about by going to the HBS Web site and viewing the video "Inside the Case Method."

In 2008, the school started its novel 2 + 2 program for college juniors. Participants complete their two years of undergraduate study, obtain two years of work experience, and then matriculate into HBS. The program is designed to attract applicants from non-business backgrounds, and Harvard maintains relationships with a number of employers who seek to hire these special admits. Whereas estimated deferred admits to HBS fluctuated between roughly 20 and 50 per year prior to the inception of this program, 106 applicants were admitted through the 2 + 2 program the year this book went to press. Consequently, and barring any significant class size increase, future applicants will be competing for fewer spots in the incoming class.

One alum offers this advice for applicants: "Really hone in on what is truly meaningfully differentiated in your background. It doesn't have to be business-related, but HBS sees lots of candidates . . . you have to be unique."

Full-time MBAs receiving financial aid through school: 74%

Institutional (need-based) scholarships: 500

Assistantships: varies

Full-tuition scholarships school awarded for academic year: varies

Financially Aided

HBS is strongly committed to making its MBA program accessible to students who demonstrate financial need. Students are encouraged to draw on their own personal resources wherever possible, although a majority of students receive some sort of financial assistance, which is composed of a combination of fellowships and loans. Need-based funding includes general scholarships provided through the Financial Aid office to about 400 students every year. The Committee on General Scholarships administers the process.

Specific to HBS students are the Zuckerman Fellows Program and the Catherine B. Reynolds Foundation Fellowship in Social Enterprise. For those pursuing joint degrees with the Kennedy School, funding opportunities include George Family Foundation Fellowships and the Rubenstein Fellowship Program.

Loan repayment assistance may be granted to students who accept private sector or social enterprise positions that traditionally pay less than high-profile corporate jobs. The basic types of loans available to HBS students are the Federal Direct Stafford/Ford loan, Federal Perkins loan, Federal Direct Graduate PLUS loans, and private loans. HBS also participates in the Yellow Ribbon Program for veterans of the U.S. Armed Forces who are 100 percent elegible for the new G.I. Bill.

FULL-TIME MBA PROGRAM (TOTAL DIRECT COSTS)

In-state: $76,600

Out-of-state: $76,600

International: $76,600

What HBS Students Know

What is leadership? Most students arrive at HBS with an idea of what it means. Rakhi Mehra, class of 2009, worked for CARE in India and understood the complexities of management in a large organization. What she found as an MBA candidate was a new definition for leadership: working together to achieve managed expectations. HBS provides across-the-board skills for graduates to transition successfully into the global world of business. Yet, the school is known for and excels at the case method. Case discussions allow the interchange of ideas during the process of investigating different scenarios. Students possess strong judgments, hidden biases, and knowledge gaps that are weeded out through group exchange. You become open to others' opinions. You value the talents your classmates bring to the conversation. You find yourself seeking solutions drawn from their diverse experiences. Your thinking changes, and it is transformational. Leadership is not an individual endeavor. At HBS, everyone has a role.

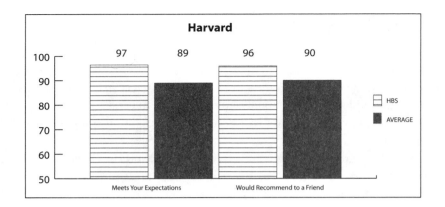

Perceptions are based on experience. Orkun Kilic grew up in Istanbul, Turkey, and equated leadership with dictatorship. Leaders as he understood them were decision makers in control. However, after he participated in his class's Subarctic Survival Situation, he found that leadership comes in many forms. The Subarctic Survival Situation is a re-enactment of the aftermath of a plane crash in the wilderness. The life-and-death decisions the students make determine the fate of the group. Kilic knew he was good at crisis management, but a classmate with 15 years of military experience was better. Kilic's best decision was to step back and give leadership to the other student. Dictators would never have thought to do that.

The intellectual stimulation that Jaime Mendez experienced in his classes was unique. Mendez received his MBA in 2009. A native of Pico Rivera, California, he previously worked at Goldman Sachs in prime brokerage. When he returned to California after his first semester at HBS, he told his family that he had a completely different sense of himself as a leader. The fact that his classes contained classmates with diverse cultures, interests, and backgrounds advanced his understanding (and management) of people and ideas. The case method was a great fit to prepare him for participation in global business.

What's Next? Your Career

In April 2009, Harvard Business School MBA Career Services and the Europe Research Center invited its European recruiting partners to an event in Paris to discuss HBS and the international marketplace. The specific goal of the event was to better understand the European recruiting environment and to collaborate with global firms on ways to connect with HBS students. In return, global firms got the opportunity to learn more about HBS and about recruiting HBS students.

In June 2009, a similar program was held in Shanghai. HBS Career Services hosted a conference that focused on understanding the Asian recruiting environment; HBS Career Services professionals engaged Asian recruiters and alumni in a discussion about HBS, its students, and the global marketplace.

In order to hire HBS students for internships, companies are encouraged to visit the HBS campus during "Company Information Days." In 2008, these were held in November as the kick-off to first-year recruiting. During "Industry Weeks," HBS first-year students establish a better understanding of various industries and how to successfully conduct a job search. Through helpful sessions with Career Services staff, coaches, alumni, and company representatives, HBS students are able to make better educated decisions about potential career paths. More than 40 trained career coaches are available to work one-on-one with HBS students from the time they arrive on campus to the time they decide to conduct their search for a permanent position. They can help students write resumes and cover letters, create and execute a job search strategy, prepare for interviews, negotiate salaries, and improve networking techniques.

A senior recruiter for a consulting firm who has hired MBAs from many of the top b-schools says, "Our firm has a very collegial culture. It's a bit of a stereotype, but generally we try to spend a bit more energy indoctrinating our HBS hires and, thus far, we have been very happy with the results."

Harvard Business School posts job opportunities by local region for members of the 116 HBS alumni clubs that exist throughout the world. The school's "Alumni Navigator" enables alumni to use cutting-edge technology to network and stay in touch with alums based on characteristics including industry, company, location, undergraduate college, degree, state, and home country. Upon graduation, you discover that you are part of one of the most exclusive networks in postsecondary education. You will have this noted affiliation for the rest of your career.

CAREER CHECK: HARVARD BUSINESS SCHOOL
MBA EMPLOYMENT BY JOB FUNCTION

- General Management: 52%
- Finance/Accounting: 16%
- Consulting: 11%
- High Technology: 7%
- Health and Human Services/Nonprofit: 6%
- Other: 8%

ALUMNI ACTUALS

MBA alumni worldwide: 70,000+

Business school alumni networking site: www.alumni.hbs.edu/

Current MBA students have access to the alumni database

Match Made in Heaven: Is Harvard Business School Right for You?

You are an ideal student if you

- Learn best through the case study method and the team approach it requires.
- Seek a diversified student body comprised of individuals from many backgrounds and nationalities.
- Can engage in intense short-term and topic-centric long-tern experience by immersion.
- Expect an excellent education from a first-rate business school education located in a city environment.

Indiana University Kelley School of Business

1275 E. Tenth Street
Bloomington, IN 47405

Phone: 812.855.8600
E-mail: mbaoffice@indiana.edu
Web site: www.kelley.iu.edu/mba/

Dean: Daniel C. Smith
Chairperson, MBA Program: Philip T. Powell

"What sets the Kelley School apart from other business schools? It's not only what you will learn or the incredible career opportunities we provide. We will dramatically change what you believe is possible." —Dean Smith

Quick Facts

MBA PROGRAMS

Full-time MBA
Part-time MBA
Distance Learning (Online) MBA
Global EMBA

FULL-TIME MBA SNAPSHOT

Total enrollment: 473
Class of 2010: 227
Length of program: 21 months
Campus: Bloomington, IN
Program commences in August
Pre-term orientation attendance required

APPLICATION NOTES

Requirements: U.S. bachelor's degree or equivalent (traditional business background not required); work experience and leadership abilities; GMAT; essays; GRE not accepted
Letters of recommendation: 2
Interview: By request (prior to submission of application), by invitation only (after application submitted)

(continued)

(continued)

Number of applicants: 1,381
Admittance rate: 34%

CLASS OF 2010 PROFILE

Male 74%, Female 26%
Minority Americans: 17%
International: 37%
Average age: 28
Married or Partnered, Single: 25%, 75%
Average years of work experience: 5 years
GMAT score range (20th–80th percentile): 580–730
GMAT score average: 663
GPA average: 3.35

ACADEMIC BACKGROUND OF INCOMING STUDENTS

Business: 37%
Humanities/Social Sciences: 26%
Science/Engineering: 35%
Other: 2%

Foundation of Excellence

In the 1820s, what was to become Indiana University's Kelley School of Business was just a humble seminary of 10 students. In 1920 it was established as the School of Commerce and Finance. Today it is one of the world's most respected business schools, with top-rated faculty and more than 14,000 successful alumni all over the globe.

The educational institution that would become Indiana University defined Bloomington from the beginning. Bloomington became a settlement around 1816. After Indiana became a state in 1816, President James Monroe settled on Bloomington as the site for a seminary, endowing it with an academic aspect. That has set the town apart ever since. Indiana Seminary opened with 12 students and one teacher in 1825 and grew steadily from the get-go. By 1829, it was a college, and by 1848, the college had become a full-fledged 50-student university.

Disastrous fires in the 1880s moved the school from the town center to a new campus in nearby Dunn's Woods. There, the university's enrollment continued to grow. Even World War I and the Great Depression could not bring it down. By the mid-1920s, Indiana University was bringing in $1 million each year, helping it to expand while other towns collapsed. Civic pride continued to swell as

Bloomington constructed more and more buildings, many of which still stand today as a testament to Indiana University's strength.

The Kelley School of Business.

Of course, one of the best testaments to IU Kelley's strength is its alumni. One particularly impressive alumnus, E. W. "Ed" Kelley graduated from the business administration program in 1939. Kelley was active in numerous campus organizations, founding the school's Accounting Club and becoming student body president of the School of Business. After graduation, Kelley went on to head the Bird's Eye division of General Foods and then served as president of Fairmont Foods, where he helped to pioneer such U.S. brands as Tang, Cool Whip, Lean Cuisine, Klondike, and Grey Poupon. Later in his career, Kelley founded Kelley and Partners Ltd., turned Steak 'n' Shake into a multimillion-dollar chain, and became a frequent speaker at the Columbia Business School.

Kelley also became a generous donor to his alma mater, providing IU Kokomo with a scholarship fund and three buildings. At IU Bloomington, he lent his name to establish the E. W. Kelley Chair in Business Administration and provided support to IU Bloomington's Virgil T. DeVault Alumni Center, Mellencamp Pavilion, Alva Prickett Chair in Accounting, and Jacobs School of Music. In 1997, a $23 million gift from Kelley initiated the Kelley Scholars Program, which provides four years of full tuition, room, board, and living expenses to undergraduate business students who show exceptional promise. Later that year IU's business school was renamed in Kelley's honor, and today the Kelley School of Business carries on his legacy of innovative leadership through its faculty, students, and alumni.

Why Kelley?

As the number six college sports town in the United States, as designated by *Sports Illustrated on Campus*, and deemed one of the top 10 places for campus culture by *USA Today*, Bloomington is a cultural mecca, boasting a wealth of musical and artistic offerings each week. The town has a variety of exotic restaurants within minutes from campus and, of course, the time-honored Hoosier tradition of IU basketball.

But location is just the beginning. Exceptional faculty, hands-on experience, and access to some of the leading firms and top executives in the world are what truly make Kelley one of the country's best business schools. Major corporations approach Kelley each year with opportunities for real-world, real-time learning. Students confront these challenges in the classroom (through the Kelley Academies) and within student organizations and collaboratively develop unique solutions. The result is win-win: The companies gain fresh perspective and insight into a new generation of business strategy, and you gain invaluable hands-on knowledge of the world you are about to enter—and, most important of all, the confidence and creativity that are keys to success.

An example of Kelley's real-world approach is Bloomington Brands (B2), the brand management team for Osmocote® Plant Food, a best-selling brand for the Scotts Miracle-Gro Company. This team is composed of Kelley MBA students. First-year students interview for positions on the team and, if selected, work on the brand for two semesters. Scotts owns the trademark and provides key support, but all marketing functions including brand strategy, pricing, promotions, and consumer communications are handled by the students. This program has paid off tremendously: B2 alumni routinely move on to top positions at companies such as Scotts, Kellogg, Kraft, Nestle, and General Mills.

Kelley MBA students also gain meaningful experience through programs such as its Investment Banking Network, Kelley Consulting Network, and MBA Academies. All these programs emphasize collaboration among classmates, in much the same way as it happens in the workplace. And MBA graduates are ready to do business on a global scale, thanks to Kelley's emphasis on international study through its Certificate of Global Business Achievement program, GLOBASE global social entrepreneurship program, and the Kelley International Perspectives (KIP) program, which allows you to design your own global study experience. KIP locations include Australia, Brazil, Chile, China, Cuba, Czech Republic, India, Ireland, Japan, Poland, South Africa, and Peru. For some students, Student Treks are a highlight of their hands-on experience. You and your classmates travel to various cities and regions of the country and meet with corporate leaders. Based on your understanding of each company's culture and market goals, you may apply to spend your summer internship at a particular company. Furthermore, you may develop your new contacts and pursue your passions through a post-graduate position with a company you have come to know during your MBA days.

For those who enjoy especially intense learning, Kelley offers local immersion opportunities as well. One is a week-long immersion program in the Washington Campus Program in Washington, D.C., where you meet with policy specialists, business leaders, and power brokers. You will have first-hand insight on the workings of both national government and international business. Speaking of immersion, Bloomington has the advantage of a small-town atmosphere. As such, students and professors run into each other often outside class. Professors are encouraged to live close to campus and therefore travel the same paths as students in their everyday lives. While some MBA candidates see little of their scholastic leaders outside instruction hours, you may find yourself chatting with your professors almost anywhere.

FUN FACTS

- Bloomington, Indiana, has one of only 16 Tibetan restaurants in the nation. His Holiness, the 14th Dalai Lama of Tibet, is a regular visitor to Bloomington and often stops by Anyetsang's Little Tibet restaurant.
- The city of Bloomington was possibly named after an early settler, William Bloom. Another legend relates that a group of early settlers were impressed with the rich flora in the area and thus decided on the name of Bloomington.
- Little 500, the largest collegiate bike race in the United States, takes place each year at IU Bloomington. Modeled after the Indianapolis 500 and featured in the 1979 Academy Award–winning film *Breaking Away*, the race now is celebrated with a weeklong festival; notable guests have included Lance Armstrong and President Barack Obama.
- In his book *The Campus as a Work of Art*, Thomas Gaines named IU Bloomington as one of the five most beautiful college campuses.

Course Offerings

Central to Kelley's approach to learning is its Integrated Core program, which differs from traditional coursework at other top MBA programs. Co-taught by eight faculty who teach class sessions in teams, the integrated core combines into one 15-week course the essentials of business principles, including Economic Foundations, Critical Thinking and Ethics, Corporate Finance, Marketing, Operations Strategy, and Strategic Management. You learn alongside the same group of classmates during your core semester, working in culturally diverse teams of three to five students from a wide variety of industries, beginning from their first semester.

When asked about his best experience in Kelley's MBA program, Rocco Scandizzo, Senior Manager for New Business at Sierra Entertainment, replies, "Definitely the core courses. They were rigorous and challenging, and I learned so much that I use every day." Scandizzo notes the concepts he learned in Michael Metzger's critical thinking class and Wayne Winston's advanced decision models class were particularly helpful to him. Alongside the Integrated Core program in their first semester, students take Leadership, Professional, and Career Development. Topics covered include job search skills, networking, and diversity in the workplace.

Another integral part of the Kelley MBA approach is Kelley Academies. In this unique program, students choose a career concentration for their studies; then the selected Academy pairs the student with an academy director—a professor who is an expert in the student's chosen field. This professor becomes a mentor who not only offers counsel, but helps to facilitate real-world projects and networking contacts for the student in that particular sphere of business. Kelley Academies include the Business Marketing Academy; Consulting Academy; Consumer Marketing Academy; Corporate Finance Academy, Entrepreneurial Management Academy, Venture Development, Corporate Innovation, and Emerging Life Sciences; Investment Banking Academy; Investment Management Academy; and the Supply Chain and Global Management Academy. The newest academy is PLUS Life Sciences, based at the Center for the Business of Life Sciences (CBLS). Sixteen students participated in the first program. In 2008, there were 29 first-year students, 27 second-year students, and 10 dual-program students.

Case competitions, which pit students against students—first their own classmates, and then MBAs from other schools—are a key component of being an MBA candidate at Kelley. The competitions are based on real challenges that real businesses are facing. Kelley students do very well in regional and national case competitions. Among others, they won the Cornell Marketing Case Competition in 2007, the DuPont Case Competition in 2008, and the Big 10 Case Competition in 2008.

Kelley also has excellent resources for those interested in entrepreneurship and innovation. While many executives are assessing their companies' futures in the global marketplace, more MBA candidates are choosing entrepreneurship as an attractive career direction. Because faculty in Kelley's Department of Management and Entrepreneurship produced the highest number of published articles on entrepreneurial research, the Kelley school achieved first place in 2009 in the World Rankings for Entrepreneurship Productivity. This achievement is based on articles appearing in the *Journal of Business Venturing*, *Entrepreneurship Theory and Practice*, and *Strategic Entrepreneurship*—the three leading industry journals. As a student, you are the recipient of the best and brightest ideas in the field.

CENTERS AND INSTITUTES

Benecki Center for Real Estate Studies (BCRES)

Center for Brand Leadership (CBL)

Center for Econometric Model Research (CEMR)

Center for Education and Research in Retailing (CERR)

Center for Global Sales Leadership (CGSL)

Center for International Business Education and Research (CIBER)

Center for the Business of Life Sciences (CBLS)

Indiana Business Research Center (IBRC)

Information Management Affiliates (IMA)

Institute for Corporate Governance (ICG)

Johnson Center for Entrepreneurship and Innovation (JCEI)

Tobias Center for Leadership Excellence

What Kelley Professors Teach

Kelley's faculty represents some of the leading minds in the business world. Contributors to the top publications in their fields, their discoveries and insight are highly sought after and respected across industries. Consistently ranked in the top 20 internationally for research, Kelley faculty are renowned authors, top consultants, and corporate board members—but above all, they're teachers, dedicated to making Kelley graduates the best-prepared professionals there are.

"A professor has never turned me down when I have asked for assistance," says Matt Callahan, class of 2010. "Not only that, but I have had the privilege of spending time with various professors for social occasions." Professor of Strategic Management Idie Kesner is one of Callahan's favorites. "Her engaging, interactive classes are always fun." Another 2010 student with concentrations in Finance and Strategy relates that Financial Accounting Professor Jamie Pratt is one of his best professors. "The way he makes accounting classes interactive and interesting for students is his best attribute."

"One of the best experiences I've had at Kelley is learning from Professor Jim Wahlen," says Zandi Zungu, another MBA Finance student. "He facilitated class discussions that incorporated elements of accounting, finance, and strategy. The deliverables we had in his class helped me gain the confidence to study accounting. And the forecast model we learned in class added significant value to my project."

Another student says that Professor of Finance Andrew Ellul creates a "great classroom environment, challenging course work, and thought-provoking discussions—even in derivatives!"

Obviously, students find great value in their classroom experience. In a further example, Professor of Economics Philip Powell is "energetic, passionate, and dedicated to helping students understand the material and real-world relevance," exclaims a 2010 MBA candidate in Management and Marketing.

FACULTY FACTS

Full-time faculty employed by the b-school: 197

Adjunct or visiting faculty: 29

Permanent/tenured professors: 78

Tenured faculty who are women: 14

Tenured faculty who are underrepresented minorities: 7

Tenured international faculty: 10

SAMPLING OF NOTABLE PROFESSORS

- Jonlee Andrews: Recipient of the MBA Teaching Excellence Award; Associate Chair of the MBA Program and Director of the Center for Brand Leadership
- Utpal Bhattacharya: Global lecturer and notable author currently serving as the associate editor of the *Journal of Financial Markets*
- Donald F. Kuratko: Celebrated scholar and expert on the topic of entrepreneurship; author of the book *Entrepreneurship: Theory, Process, and Practice*, which received the 2007 Australian Award for Excellence in Education Publishing
- Alan M. Rugman: Widely published author; consultant to many private and intergovernmental agencies, including two Canadian Prime Ministers
- Rosann L. Spiro: Distinguished researcher and co-author, with William Stanton and Gregg Rich, of *Management of a Sales Force* and recipient of the Lifetime Achievement Award from the American Marketing Association

---

MAJORS OFFERED IN FULL-TIME MBA PROGRAM

Entrepreneurship and Corporate Innovation

Finance

Management

Marketing

Strategic Analysis of Accounting
  Information

Supply Chain and Operations

JOINT DEGREES AND DUAL DEGREES

JD/MBA Program

MBA/MA Program

MBA/Telecom Program

What Admissions Is All About

Director of Admissions and Financial Aid James Holmen describes what the admissions committee members would like to see in applicants. "Ideal Kelley MBA candidates have a demonstrated record of academic and professional success. They have made a positive impact on the organizations, companies, and communities in which they've worked. They have well-developed short- and long-term career goals and are interested in working within a team-based, collaborative learning environment. Ideal MBA candidates want to get involved and enhance their leadership skills as they take an active role in the program and within the Kelley community."

Holmen knows that many applicants are anxious about their GMAT scores when considering applying to Kelley. He says, "A strong academic record can compensate for a lower GMAT score. A strong GMAT score can also balance a less successful academic record. If a candidate's GMAT and academic record are both marginal, he or she should consider taking a few rigorous post-baccalaureate courses to both prepare for the MBA experience and to demonstrate current academic potential. Given the highly quantitative nature of the MBA program, demonstrating the potential to successfully handle quantitative course work is especially helpful."

Full-time MBAs receiving financial aid through school: 95%

Institutional (merit-based) scholarships: 120

Assistantships: varies

Full-tuition scholarships school awarded for academic year: 67

Financially Aided

James Holmen assures MBA candidates, "At the Kelley School, the financial aid process is not daunting. The Kelley MBA program has a dedicated financial aid professional who manages both need-based and merit-based financial aid programs and provides valuable counsel and advice to current and prospective MBA students. All students offered admission to the MBA program are automatically considered for merit-based financial aid; there is no additional application to complete. While some awards are in the form of scholarships and fellowships, others are in the form of graduate assistantships. The school considers many factors when making merit-based awards. The school also offers prestigious Dean's Fellowships that provide a full tuition scholarship as well as Forté Foundation Fellowships that provide full or half tuition scholarships. For need-based financial aid consideration, students should simply complete the Free Application for Federal Student Aid forms, which starts the process for securing student loans."

Most students receive financial aid, and more than half receive merit-based aid, with awards ranging from $5,000 to full tuition. All financial aid, including assistantships, is awarded through the admissions department.

FULL-TIME MBA PROGRAM (TOTAL DIRECT COSTS)

In-state: $47,994

Out-of-state $83,454

International: $83,454

What Kelley Students Know

Matt Callahan, a major in Finance with minors in Accounting and Entrepreneurship, is a great fit with Kelley's program. "I love Kelley!" he says. "The strategy focus at Kelley fosters well-rounded students that upon graduation will enter the workforce and be able to see how their division's work affects the organization's vision as a whole."

Are there any aspects Callahan didn't like? Actually, he wishes he had realized from the beginning "how important networking is," and now that he is at this point in his studies, he finds frustration in "not being able to take advantage of all the possible offerings. I would like more days in the week." And after Kelley? "Upon graduation I plan to enter the strategy division of a Life Science company," he says.

Other students are going in a different direction. One plans to "switch industries and specialize further in marketing." Another says he'd like to "switch careers from finance and management consulting to technology" and use his MBA to jumpstart his career in an industry "where I see myself 10 years into the future," and a third plans to "reach positions in firms where I can add significant value through financial or strategic management roles."

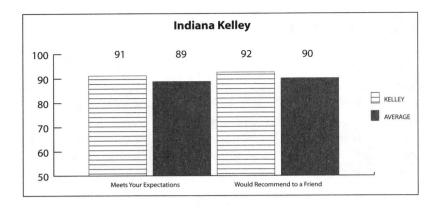

Like several other top programs, Kelley has a business chapter of Net Impact—an organization of 10,000 MBA students and professionals whose goal is to promote corporate social responsibility. In 2008, Kelley focused on its own leadership and ethics goals to enhance the future impact of graduates in society. Kelley offers one of the best programs in the country, says Jessica Kapadia. "It's an excellent education. They offer an amazing classroom experience, and the professors are so excited to be there."

CAREER CHECK: KELLEY MBA EMPLOYMENT BY JOB FUNCTION

- Marketing/Sales: 36%
- Finance/Accounting: 32%
- Consulting: 15%
- General Management: 5%
- Operations/Logistics: 3%
- Other: 9%

What's Next? Your Career

Graduate Career Services (GCS) prides itself on its team of seasoned career services professionals. Throughout your time at Kelley, GCS provides personalized attention and customized career coaching to help develop you and your capabilities, whether your dream company is one that recruits on campus or your firm of choice is in a niche industry or targeted geographic region.

Nina Camfield, associate director at GCS, relates, "We provide online resume books through our own web site and MBAFocus, implementing Career Nights, Networking Nights, and presentation opportunities." Employers meet with students, "facilitating interactions in the classroom and through Kelley Academies." Recruiters often express how Kelley graduates exhibit the unique attributes they seek when hiring. Camfield continues, "Employers comment on the work ethic of Kelley graduates, their willingness to do whatever is needed to get the job done. They are team-oriented. Their analytical and problem-solving skills rate high, as do leadership skills, creativity, and strategic thinking."

Kelley takes a strategic approach in the delivery of professional and career development content. You take a career and personality assessment test before you even arrive as a student so that GCS will know best how to help. The GCS team will then guide you through everything from your first networking activity to the negotiations process when you land your full-time job in your second year. GCS is unique in the amount of one-on-one time spent with each student. Career counselors also provide a vast number of workshops, such as Résumé and Interviewing Bootcamp, Networking 101, Advanced Networking, and Internship 501. Students have additional resources through online tools, such as podcasts, Vault Gold, Interview Stream, and CQ Interactive. These supplements to workshops and events provide around-the-clock access to career and job search information.

The career services office is attuned to individual student needs by working closely with a number of student groups, such as the GCS Advisory Council, the MBA Association Professional Development Committee, and the International Student Task Force, and with the Office of International Services to keep abreast of current visa issues.

To complement your Kelley experience, you are encouraged to pursue an internship between your first and second years. In fact, more than 80 companies actively recruit Kelley students on campus to fill internships each year. Camfield explains, "The most common internships available for students at Kelley are in brand management, corporate finance, investment banking, investment management, strategy, business-to-business marketing, market research, consulting, supply chain, and logistics. Of the companies that recruit at Kelly, 98 percent hire for internships." GCS can also guide you in the search for internships abroad through connections with international universities and multinational companies. You could become one of the many students whose internship results in a full-time job offer.

ALUMNI ACTUALS

MBA alumni worldwide: 14,000+

Business school alumni networking site: https://kelleynetwork.affinitycircles.com/kelley/auth/login

Current MBA students have access to the alumni database.

"Every employer wants employees who are driven to continuously improve both their technical and leadership skills," says Christine Nevill, class of 2005, who now is employed in Columbus, Ohio, as a risk officer. "Earning an MBA from a school like Kelley does just that, not only by sharpening the skills but also by strengthening the foundation for long-term success." In her current role with J. P. Morgan, Nevill works with managers to identify, assess, and mitigate risks. A typical day might include meeting with a manager to conduct a review; researching a regulatory, legal, or tax requirement; reviewing requirements for a new system; or researching solutions to client questions or requests.

When Goldman Sachs representatives came to Kelley, Andrew Baldwin, class of 2007, was well prepared to land a job. A member of Kelley's Investment Banking and Capital Markets Workshop, Baldwin used the vast alumni network to gain tips on what the company looked for in potential candidates. Not surprisingly, this paid off. Baldwin landed a summer internship with the company and is now in a full-time position with Goldman as a financial analyst. Although Baldwin had set his sights on Goldman as a student, his main concern once he started working there was whether the company would be a good fit for him, personally and professionally. "I love the group culture there," he says. "I was never afraid to ask a question. It is an excellent fit." And Baldwin certainly stood out from the crowd for Goldman because of his successes and experiences as a student. Baldwin, a Kelley Scholar and student ambassador, epitomizes the multidimensional graduate for which Kelley is known. "When someone asks me, 'Why Kelley,' it's always an easy answer. All the majors and programs are exceptional."

Match Made in Heaven: Is the Kelley School for Business Right for You?

You are an ideal student if you

- Thrive on experiential learning through team projects, case competitions, leadership development, and Kelley's unique Bloomington Brands and Student Treks programs.
- Seek a cooperative atmosphere that emphasizes individual intellectual exploration as well as group problem solving.
- Embrace the evolving business atmosphere of corporate social responsibility.
- Possess a passion for innovative solutions and "thinking outside the box" while experiencing an integrated curriculum with a goal of global business participation.

Massachusetts Institute of Technology (MIT)
Alfred P. Sloan School of Management

50 Memorial Drive
Cambridge, MA 02142

Phone: 617.253.2659
E-mail: mbaadmissions@sloan.mit.edu
Web site: www.mitsloan.mit.edu

Dean: David Schmittlein
Deputy Deans: Steven D. Eppinger, Robert M. Freund, Joanne Yates, Alan F. White, Donna Behmer

"MIT Sloan's mission is to develop principled, innovative leaders who improve the world." —Dean Schmittlein

Quick Facts

MBA PROGRAMS

Full-time MBA
Sloan Fellows Program in Innovation and Global Leadership
Accelerated MBA

FULL-TIME MBA SNAPSHOT

Total enrollment: 780
Class of 2010: 350
Length of program: 21 months
Campus: Boston, MA
Program commences in September
Pre-term orientation attendance required

APPLICATION NOTES

Requirements: Four-year bachelor's degree or equivalent; professional work experience strongly recommended; GRE accepted
Letters of recommendation: 2
Interview: by invitation only
Number of applicants: 3,896
Admittance rate: 10%

(continued)

(continued)

CLASS OF 2010 PROFILE

Male 65%, Female 35%
Minority Americans: 22%
International: 36%
Average age: 28
Average years of work experience: 5 years
GMAT score range (20th–80th percentile): 650–760
GMAT score average: 710
Average GPA: 3.56

ACADEMIC BACKGROUND OF INCOMING STUDENTS

Arts, Humanities, and Social Sciences: 27.5%
Business and Commerce: 19.5%
Computer Science: 8.5%
Engineering: 37%
Math/Sciences: 7%

A Need for Engineers, Innovators, and Managers

Founded by William Barton Rogers, the Massachusetts Institute of Technology (MIT) began teaching its first engineering and science courses in Boston in 1865. Its goal was to provide practical research to improve industry.

MIT added its first engineering administration courses in 1914, two years before relocating across the Charles River to Cambridge. Although the engineering administration program grew steadily, the major push came in 1930, when Alfred P. Sloan Jr., an 1895 MIT graduate and head of General Motors, called MIT Professor Erwin H. Schell and said his engineers needed more management training. Schell suggested starting a new type of sponsored program to help promising engineers develop these skills. Funded by Sloan's personal foundation, the one-year Sloan Fellowship Program began at MIT in 1938 with five candidates. This program marked a new day in higher education: the world's first executive management training program.

Later in life, Sloan wanted to do more. After building General Motors into the number one U.S. automaker by decentralizing it into divisions, he knew business was going to need stronger managers. In 1950, Sloan gave his alma mater more than $5 million to establish the School of Industrial Management on MIT's Cambridge campus. The school was renamed for him in 1964.

In the four decades since, Sloan has expanded far beyond a school for engineer managers. Its research in marketing, finance, health, and public affairs has shaped corporations and policies around the world. Faculty and students have constructed solutions that increase productivity, defy the limits, and truly excite with possibilities, and MIT remains known for its technical business expertise. Today its curriculum includes a diverse selection of electives and requires 144 units to graduate.

Why Sloan?

Sloan stays ahead of the curve by always digging deeper until it reaches great breakthroughs, such as Professor Jay Forrester's first computer RAM memory in the 1960s or alumni Robert Metcalfe's Ethernet in the 1970s. Each generation of graduates who learn under these legacies leaves the next one hungrier for their turn. "There's a whole ecosystem around entrepreneurship we've built up at MIT, including mentoring and venturing plans and activities and clubs for students. . . . You really don't feel that same kind of entrepreneurial spirit at other types of business schools," Deputy Dean Steven D. Eppinger explains.

In May 2009, Sloan hosted a new conference: BIG (Business in Gaming). Most of the growth in this industry is in online media, and the conference explored current needs and trends. One observation that came out of the meeting is especially appropriate for MBA students interested in entrepreneurship. In the gaming industry, if you follow an established business model, you are already behind the curve. Gaming is a business sector that draws on all your class-based expertise to innovate and simulate for results.

Sloan has also been a leader in global relations, starting in the 1980s by establishing alliances with Chinese universities shortly after the Communist nation began welcoming outsiders. The latest foray into international collaboration took place in February 2009 when MIT teamed with the Moscow School of Management SKOLKOVO to teach a series of programs through project-based learning. The two schools expect to form a long-term relationship for education and research. MIT's Russian ties go back to the 1960s when professors worked with the Institute of Systems Studies teaching management principles. Back on the technology front, Sloan began teaching e-commerce well before its heyday in the 1990s—and the list goes on. "We don't teach our students best practices," says Rod Garcia, director of MBA admissions. "Instead, we stay ahead of best practices, by teaching them subjects that will be relevant not just to them, but in the business world several years from now."

These days, the other big draw is the William A. Porter Center for Management Education, scheduled to open in 2010. Porter, founder of eTrade and the International Securities Exchange, is the major donor behind the center, which will house all faculty offices, executive education programs, and most MBA classes under the same roof for the first time.

The Porter Management Center towers six stories high over a 425-car underground garage on the eastern edge of MIT's 168-acre campus. Ultimately, it will connect to the Alfred P. Sloan Building and the Arthur D. Little Building—former headquarters for the world's first management consulting company. When it is completed in 2010, the new building will be the greenest building on campus with environmentally friendly features such as daylighting, chilled beams, and radiant ceiling panes.

MIT Sloan students on campus.

FUN FACTS

- George Eastman, inventor of the world's first commercial film, donated the funds to move the MIT campus to Cambridge back in 1916. MIT legend says it's good luck to stop and rub a plaque honoring Eastman on Building 6.
- MIT's buildings have names, but they're better known by numbers. Some have both letters and numbers. For example, the letter E or W before the building number means the building is on the east or west side of campus. Building E51 is where MIT graduate Richard S. Morse's National Research Corp. used vacuum processes to extend the life of blood plasma—and create frozen orange juice in the 1940s. The latter invention launched the Minute Maid brand.
- Randall D. Pinkett, winner of season 4 on NBC's *The Apprentice*, graduated from MIT Sloan's Leaders for Manufacturing program.
- MIT's motto is *Mens et Manus,* Latin for "Mind and Hand."

Course Offerings

Sloan students commit full time to its MBA program. The school does not offer an EMBA or part-time program. Similar to other business schools, first-semester students are assigned to a team of five or six students who all take the same classes and work on group projects together.

You choose your own classes starting in the second semester, and Sloan has two optional tracks to help focus learning: Entrepreneurship and Innovation, and Finance. The entrepreneurship program has quickly become a favorite, accounting for about 25 percent of students in the couple of years since it began. Each year includes a Sloan Innovation Period, a week of learning and career exploration sandwiched in between two six-week semesters. This week is about informal learning through guest lectures, special viewings of faculty work, and team problem-solving activities.

You can also spend a semester in the E-Lab, working with students from other disciplines to solve a real-world problem challenging a local CEO. The E-Lab expands on the work of the MIT Entrepreneurship Center and the $100 MIT Entrepreneurship Competition, a 19-year tradition that has created 85 companies, including Akamai Technologies.

The MIT Sloan Fellows Program in Innovation and Global Leadership is the result of a merger in 2004 of the MIT Sloan Fellows Program and the MIT Management in Technology Program. The current iteration offers a 12-month intensive or a 24-month extended option (the latter for Massachusetts residents only). At London Business School, the Sloan Fellows Program can be completed in 11 months, and at Stanford GSB, it can be completed in 10 months.

Sloan introduced two one-year master's degree programs in 2008: a Master of Science in Management for international MBA students and a Master of Finance degree. The two programs are the school's first new curriculum additions in 20 years. Sloan also offers several joint programs. The Biomedical Enterprise Program takes advantage of Sloan's unique location near Cambridge's biotech hub to teach students about bringing new drugs and medical products to market. Notable professors include Richard Cohen, founder of Cambridge Heart, which makes non-invasive technologies that identify patients at risk for sudden cardiac attack.

Leaders for Manufacturing is an example of a two-year dual program in which students seek an MBA and a Master of Engineering degree from Sloan and the MIT School of Engineering. The SM (Master of Science) is an advanced professional degree combining an MBA degree with a dissertation. The program has strong internship and partnership programs with Amazon.com, Boeing, General Motors, Genzyme, Intel, and Motorola. The System Design and Management program began in 1996 to encourage a systems-thinking approach for engineers throughout product development and lifecycle. Sloan has opened this program up for distance learning—a first for any Sloan MBA program, though it does require some on-campus time. Sloan's joint program with Harvard's Kennedy School of Government allows students to earn an MBA and MPA in three years. Sloan students have until the end of their first semester to join.

Reaching Around the World

International education is a major focus of Sloan's curriculum. Having reached out to China business schools, Russian business schools, and more, Sloan has deeper international ties than many American business schools. The ties were formalized in the mid-1990s, when Sloan began the MIT-China Management Education Project to help establish MBA programs in the previously closed country.

Faculty from schools such as Shanghai's Fudan University and Beijing's Tsinghua University traveled to Cambridge to study under Sloan faculty. Sloan professors also taught occasional short courses overseas. The goal was to create MBA programs in English for Chinese business people and add an international perspective.

The next phase started in fall 2009 by bringing foreign MBA students to Sloan's home campus for a year to better understand international business and further develop research ties. Sloan opened its new Master of Science in Management Studies program to students at four international schools—Fudan University in Shanghai, Tsinghua University in Beijing, HEC Paris in France, and SKK

Graduate School of Business at Korea's Sungkunkway—after they complete their MBA programs. Talks are underway about starting a separate semester exchange program between Sloan and the international students, according to Paul Denning, director of media relations for Sloan.

Sloan students currently gain most of their international business experience through the Global Entrepreneurship Lab (G-Lab), which began in 2000. Students begin the course in September and are divided into teams of four charged with solving a real-life problem at an international company. Come January break, the teams are dispatched around the world to work with companies on-site and make recommendations. In recent years, students have traveled to Brazil, China, New Zealand, Australia, Russia, Uruguay, and Portugal to study problems at a wide range of companies—from ESPN in Brazil to restaurants looking to enter the U.S. market to software and distribution companies.

The goal is for students to exercise their entrepreneurial skills in a new culture with other possible challenges such as technology limits or different environmental conditions. Students say it's also great networking. "During school I met tons of people from all over the world," proclaims Nathan Williams, class of 2008, who now works in sales for Microsoft in the Redmond, Washington, area. "I have good friends in Brazil. I know people in Japan. Everywhere I go in the world, I know people there. I have a network there of entrepreneurs."

FACULTY FACTS

Full-time faculty employed by the b-school: 93

Adjunct or visiting faculty: 16

Permanent/tenured professors: 62

Tenured faculty who are women: 13

Tenured faculty who are underrepresented minorities: 5

Tenured international faculty: 6

What Sloan Professors Teach

Once known mostly for starting large Massachusetts companies such as Teradyne and Meditech, the Sloan professors of today are involved with businesses all over the globe. "Our school has a group of faculty that is really strongly grounded in business practice," Deputy Dean Steven D. Eppinger remarks. "We study business. We look at business. We consult with businesses. So we're able to bring that perspective into our classrooms."

Sloan makes teaching leadership, business ethics, clean energy practices, and analysis priorities in its curriculum. Although leadership and analysis are standard business school lessons, Eppinger says the students have made it clear they want to help the environment, and Sloan wants to prepare students for ethical challenges ahead. "We have some pretty tough decisions we have to work through in business," he said.

Sloan also focuses on teaching teamwork throughout its curriculum. Eppinger teaches an interdisciplinary product development course at Sloan that includes art, business, and engineering students. Students learn first-hand what other disciplines offer to the process—important knowledge in today's competitive marketplace, where there's increasing pressure to develop products faster than ever. "Why is their perspective not just different from my mine, but why is it important?" Eppinger asks. "And why can it contribute something of value that I can't? And usually it's because it's different that they can contribute something that I can't. They get a concrete lesson in terms of appreciating differences."

SAMPLING OF NOTABLE PROFESSORS

- Dan Ariely: Leading expert on behavioral economics, head of Sloan's eRationality research lab, and author of the recent book, *Predictably Irrational: The Hidden Forces That Shape Our Decisioins*
- John Carrington Cox: One of the world's experts on options theory and an inventor of the Cox-Ross-Rubinstein model for option pricing and the Cox-Ingersoll-Ross model for interest rate dynamics
- Kristin J. Forbes: Youngest-ever member of the President's Council of Economic Advisors, serving from 2003 to 2005; former Deputy Secretary at the U.S. Treasury, researcher on global economic issues at Sloan
- John Richard Harrington: Head of the Marketing Group and co-founder of the Marketing Science field
- Peter Sange: *Fortune* magazine's top management expert and author of the classic *The Fifth Discipline*
- Jack Welch: Former chair and CEO of General Electric and *Fortune* magazine's "Manager of the Century" in 2000

CONCENTRATIONS AND SPECIALIZATIONS OFFERED IN FULL-TIME MBA PROGRAM

Entrepreneurship and Innovation   Finance

JOINT DEGREES AND DUAL DEGREES

MBA/BEP (Biomedical Enterprise Program)

MBA/LFM (Leaders for Manufacturing)

MBA/MPA/MPP (International Management, Economic Development)

MBA/SDM (System Design and Management)

What Admissions Is All About

Although the admissions committee wants to hear about your past three years of work life and specific examples of how you performed compared to professional colleagues, Sloan's admission process is all about demonstrating how you are willing to step outside your comfort zone and show leadership.

Admissions rest entirely with a 12-person professional committee. Unlike other schools, alumni do not interview candidates, declares Rod Garcia, director of MBA admissions. "Professional readers are easier to train and are more consistent," Garcia comments. Keeping the process small allows the committee to meet regularly to compare candidates and make sure all undergo the same review, Garcia says. He adds, "The committee wants recommendation letters showing strong job performance. We do ask for very specific attributes or skills seen in a professional setting, which is why [Sloan] students are not good recommenders, because if they have seen [candidates], it is on a peer basis." Additionally, "Academic recommendations are probably not as good as professional recommendations because they talk about academic preparation."

After reviewing applications, the admissions staff invites candidates to interview over the phone or in one of the major U.S. or international cities to which they travel each year. Prepare a brief summary of your resume as well as explain why you want to attend Sloan and why you want an MBA at this point in your career. You also need to be ready for questions about workplace conflicts, such as times when you may have addressed a co-worker who was not carrying his weight, you had to defend your position on a controversial issue, or you persuaded others to change their views.

Sloan's admissions committee fills half of the class seats in each period but usually receives more applications in the second round. The school doesn't limit admissions by study interest or program. Many still view it as a school strictly for engineering managers, but less than half its students have undergraduate engineering degrees, and MIT undergraduates account for a small number of the admitted students.

Full-time MBAs receiving financial aid through school: 71%

Institutional (merit-based and need-based) scholarships: 15

Assistantships: 150

Full-tuition scholarships school awarded for academic year: 1

Financially Aided

Sloan makes many efforts to help you reduce your debt. The majority of students receive some form of merit or need-based scholarships through the school. The school offers a variety of fellowships and scholarships to encourage a worldwide incoming class every year. The Trust Scholarship provides a first-year MBA student with tuition based on need. The Peter Englander fund underwrites a student from the United Kingdom. The McKinsey Award is given to four students based on exceptional academic achievement, demonstrated leadership, professional accomplishment, and involvement in community and campus activities. The Thomas and Lorraine Williams scholarship is in place to aid a Georgia Institute of Technology graduate who has been accepted into the Sloan program.

The Leaders for Manufacturing program provides benefits that include students paying 25 percent of their tuition while a company picks up the rest. Students are under no obligation to work for their sponsor company after graduation but must make a good faith effort.

Other scholarships include the Class of 2004 Diversity scholarship. This is based on class donations from 2004 and was established to aid applicants with nontraditional work experience, those with unique educational paths, and underrepresented minorities. Philosophically, Sloan relies on a broad range of individual experiences to enhance the educational experience for everyone.

FULL-TIME MBA PROGRAM (TOTAL DIRECT COSTS)

In-state: $77,224

Out-of-state: $77,224

International: $77,224

What Sloan Students Know

Students say club participation is as important as internships and classes at Sloan. The school offers dozens of clubs for everything from foreign business to real estate, and students are free to start new groups. Nathan Williams, class of 2009, comments that he joined a first-year group, the Sales Club, seeking sales experience to help him start his own business someday. The problem was corporate recruiters did not want to come to a business school campus to recruit salespeople. But as Sales Club president, Williams organized the first Sales Competition, bringing several other U.S. business schools to campus to give short presentations—enough to persuade corporate recruiters from large companies such as Hewlett Packard, Microsoft, Google, and Novell among others to make the trip. "At which point, Microsoft said, 'This guy, he has potential. He ran one of the largest clubs at school'," notes Williams, who now works in sales for the computer giant.

Because of the purposeful diversity of students Sloan admits, many students come with spouses, partners, or families. Boston is a big place, and although the actual site of MIT Sloan is the small town of Cambridge, you are surrounded by the pros and cons of city life. MIT FamilyNet is an online site with the mission of acclimating and supporting those who have newly arrived. Besides practical advice, such as where to buy groceries and how to get there, the site connects members to other members through groups, forums, education, job opportunities, and various support areas. In addition, the Significant Others of Sloan (SOS) Club allows you to concentrate on your studies while your loved ones are involved in the area's social activities and personal growth opportunities.

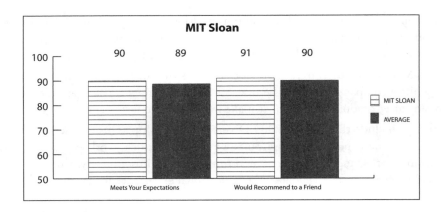

CAREER CHECK: SLOAN MBA EMPLOYMENT BY JOB FUNCTION

Finance: 34%

Consulting: 30%

Business Development 11%

Marketing/Sales: 11%

Operations/Logistics: 3%

Other: 11%

What's Next? Your Career

Sloan boasts a strong connection between school-facilitated activities and students finding a job, with internships, job postings, and related efforts helping 77 percent of the class of 2008 land positions. Most found the right match by graduation or shortly afterward. Students start working with the Career Development Office in their first semester in a weekly class. Faculty speakers and staff help students assess their skills, rewrite resumes, and prepare for interviews with an immediate focus on finding the all-important summer internship.

Sloan puts a strong emphasis on real-life work experience. Students typically roll up their sleeves on projects and internships for at least three companies during their two-year program. They visit many others on "treks" to places such as Silicon Valley and China, which include panel discussions, cocktail receptions, and meetings with alumni working in the field. MIT Sloan graduates are well known all over the world and include Carly Fiorina, former chair and CEO of Hewlett Packard; Benjamin Netanyahu, former Prime Minister of Israel; and Kofi Annan, former U.N. secretary general and Nobel Peace Prize winner.

"It was a great way for me to know how it probably is to work in New York and know what these people are doing in their jobs," says Jacklyn Sing, class of 2009, about her two-day New York City finance trek.

As for campus recruiting, students say it's rare to eat lunch without Google, Microsoft, or other like companies at the table. "There's a strong representation of companies that come to campus to recruit," Sing says. Sing, a citizen of the Philippines, is among the 20 percent of Sloan students who seek jobs outside the United States. She says students in similar situations need to arrange their own interviews in New York City. "There are more niche careers that are harder to come by and also, if you're talking about companies that are outside the U.S., it's much harder to come to campus." Sing clarifies, "so most students have to do their own searches." With a goal of working in finance in Hong Kong, Sing says she had to make her internship count. So she squeezed in two internships during the summer before her second year. Sing returned to classes a week late, but she did so with a job offer.

Pat St. Germain expected alumni to be supportive when she took over as Sloan's director of alumni relations. Yet she was overwhelmed by their support when it came to meeting students during trips on the school's annual Silicon Valley Tech trek. "In some of these regions, the alumni really look forward to it," St. Germain remarks. "I began to get notes in the fall about January visits. They see this as an annual opportunity to connect with rising members of Sloan."

Sloan has 20,000 alumni in 90 countries, with the largest alumni clubs in New York City, Boston, San Francisco, and Silicon Valley. Add that to MIT's 120,000-member alumni network, and students open many doors for themselves, St. Germain says. "For the students who choose to affiliate with the program, it's important for them to look at what they have access to in alumni of MIT as well, which really gives them a diverse resource bank to work with," she remarks.

Nathan Williams claims his MIT "Brass Rat" class ring is recognized far beyond alumni circles. "It's a very respected brand name," he says, "probably one of the most respected brand names there is."

Students have the opportunity to connect with an assigned mentor during their Sloan days. After graduation, they can join a local alumni club for regular professional development and networking. As for career help, Sloan has an alumni resume database on par with most top business schools for major companies and other alumni to browse. The alumni relations office is looking to improve the database and wants to start hosting regular Career Outreach programs in areas served by its U.S. alumni clubs. The initial two-day session was held in New York City in December 2008.

ALUMNI ACTUALS

MBA alumni worldwide: 20,000+

Business school alumni networking site: http://mitsloan.mit.edu/alumni/edu

Current MBA students have access to the alumni database.

Sloan has a strong bond with its Asian partner schools. MBA graduates from Beijing's Tsinghua International, for example, are entered in the alumni database so that graduates from both the U.S. and China campuses can continue to correspond long after finishing their degrees.

Match Made in Heaven: Is the Sloan School of Management Right for You?

You are an ideal student if you

- Are deeply motivated with a talent for academics and achievement.
- Are comfortable learning in a variety of styles such as lecture, case study, team projects, writings, problem sets, presentations, company visits, and guest speakers among others.
- Seek a school that is serious about bringing excellent research into the classroom.
- Want a first-class education in management that can lead you to guide emerging markets and business challenges worldwide.

New York University
Leonard N. Stern School of Business

Henry Kaufman Management Center
44 West 4th Street
New York, NY 10012

Phone: 212.998.0600
E-mail: sternmba@stern.nyu.edu
Web site: www.stern.nyu.edu

Dean: Thomas F. Cooley
Assistant Dean, MBA Admissions: Anika Davis Pratt
Vice Dean, MBA Programs: Kim Corfman
Vice Dean, Executive Programs: Thomas Pugel

"A research mindset brings a powerful focus to business education. It is forward looking rather than backward looking. It moves education away from teaching students a collection of facts to teaching them how to think. It moves them from a stultifying 'best practice' mentality towards developing analytical ability." —Dean Cooley

Quick Facts

MBA PROGRAMS

Full-time MBA
Part-time MBA (Langone: evening, weekend, and in Westchester)
Executive MBA
TRIUM Executive MBA (Stern-HEC Paris-LSE)

FULL-TIME MBA SNAPSHOT

Total enrollment: 841
Class of 2010: 410
Length of program: 21 months
Campus location: New York City
Program commences in September
Pre-term orientation attendance required

APPLICATION NOTES

Requirements: Application; GMAT; transcripts; work history; resume; essays; GRE not
  accepted

(continued)

(continued)

Letters of recommendation: 2
Interview: By request only
Number of applicants: 4,779
Admittance rate: 14%

CLASS OF 2010 PROFILE

Male 59%, Female 41%
Minority Americans: 30%
International: 33%
Average age: 27
Average years of work experience: 4.9 years
GMAT score average: 708
GMAT score range (20th–80th percentile): 660–760
GPA average: 3.4

ACADEMIC BACKGROUND OF INCOMING STUDENTS

Business: 30%
Economics: 18%
Engineering, Math, Sciences: 19%
Humanities, Arts, Other: 15%
Social Sciences: 18%

City Centered, Internationally Focused

Located in downtown New York City's Greenwich Village, New York University's Stern School of Business offers a broad portfolio of academic programs at the graduate and undergraduate levels, as well as Executive Education programs that enable senior executives to lead organizational change at their organizations. Stern also partners with other NYU schools, as well as leading educational institutions around the world, to offer joint degree programs. Stern's community of academic scholars, students, and alumni fosters a collaborative environment of knowledge creation and dissemination, with the school actively leading the dialogue on how business impacts society.

In 1988, following a generous $30 million donation from alumnus Leonard N. Stern, the NYU School of Business was renamed the NYU Stern School of Business. Stern is an entrepreneur who is the son of an entrepreneur. Max Stern built the Hartz Mountain Company, and today the Hartz brand of pet products is nationally known. Leonard Stern learned his father's skills and grew the business as well as began his own. He diversified into several industries including real estate development. Among his other interests, Stern has a continued involvement in the real estate market and currently is on the board of governors for the Real Estate Board of New York, which promotes best public practices in all matters affected by real estate.

New York City has more than eight million people speaking more than 170 languages. Given the business-oriented, leadership-driven, culturally mixed environment, the Stern School of Business naturally created its home there. Located in the edgy, bohemian mecca of Greenwich Village, Stern meshes those creative surroundings with the analytics and theory of business by moving students out of their chairs and into the trenches with NYC's most noted business and community leaders.

Stern is located in New York City.

New York University has been a fixture in the city since 1831. Around the turn of the 20th century, NYC rapidly became a major player in world commerce, and NYU's new School of Commerce, Accounts and Finance attracted Wall Street analysts and brokers in droves to its Washington Square campus. It wasn't long before women joined in an effort to increase the number of women in senior executive positions. By the end of World War II, graduates of the business school came from 36 countries and all 48 states.

Business was going global, and international programs became the norm in the 1960s and 1970s, including study abroad programs. Stern School of Business now has its place as one of the world's leading MBA programs.

Why Stern?

Stern is a melting pot of culture and ideas, close to the world's top financial centers, where access is just a few blocks in any direction and diversity is key to the city. Not only are NYU's "Sternies" at the forefront of tomorrow's leadership, they transcend the linear goals regarding the old ideas of business and finance to become increasingly global in perspective.

"NYU Stern is on the move, defining business education in the world's most dynamic city. Our faculty is among the very best in the nation. The diversity, talent, initiative and drive of our student body truly set us apart," Dean Thomas Cooley explains. Stern recognizes that each MBA student is unique and uniquely suited to the holistic realm of business. When you get right down to it, business isn't all numbers and big decisions; it is about people. The Greenwich Village location and culture are a perfect complement to the hard lines of a global MBA program. The "city that never sleeps" with its 24-hour transportation system allows 24-hour access to opportunity. Students find themselves transported into Stern's classrooms at the state-of-the-art Kaufman Management Center where real-world experience meets the leaders of tomorrow.

The school's rigorous, globally oriented curriculum is taught by leading research faculty. The atmosphere is competitive yet supportive within a very collaborative environment. A Stern MBA student can benefit from unrivaled access to global corporations, institutions, and markets while living among and learning from the leading minds and most influential movers and shakers of the Manhattan business community.

One of the program's notable features is its excellent leadership training. Students lead and manage a vast array of clubs, organizations, and committees and have strong voices regarding the direction of the school. Stern also has the largest part-time MBA program in the country. The same rigorous curriculum is delivered by the same full-time faculty as the full-time MBA program, but it is scheduled to fit the needs of working professionals. Dean Cooley states, "NYU Stern is on the move, defining business education in the world's most dynamic city. Our faculty is among the very best in the nation. The diversity, talent, initiative and drive of our student body truly set us apart."

New in 2009 is the Volatility Institute, created by finance professor and Nobel Laureate Robert F. Engle. The recent worldwide economic crisis prompted a need for a new, independent source of information for the business community so that its members can manage risk effectively. The first conference hosted by the Volatility Institute at Stern was held in April 2009. Its subject was Volatilities and Correlations in Stressed Markets. One innovative component of the Institute is the Volatility Laboratory (Vlab), created to access real-time dynamics in the market. Vlab's forecasts are meant to guide risk managers and regulators by using up-to-the-minute results. Vlab measures markets by running 300 analyses using 84 centralized data sets that produce 1,000 series per day.

FUN FACTS

- Live skits, songs, and videos liven up the joint with the annual and eagerly awaited Stern Follies, a lighthearted look at business school. The follies are written and performed by Stern students and attended by more than 600 people each spring.

- Food Fight! In February 2009, Stern students donated enough cash and food to the Food Bank of New York for 14,238 meals. Food Fight is one of Stern's many community service projects.

- Every Beer Blast event has two security guards present. Beer Blast is held every Thursday night throughout the school year and even in the summer session.

- No starving artists in Greenwich Village: The average listing price for real estate is $1.9 million!

Course Offerings

Stern's MBA program is 60 credits with more than half composed of electives. The key to this innovative program is its flexible core curriculum, so you can customize your own education toward your professional goals. The Stern teaching methodology is divided into team projects, case studies, experiential learning, and lectures, with a smattering of other methods. Each class is divided into six blocks (cohorts) of 60 to 70 students. Study groups averaging five students are assigned to address core coursework. For electives, you choose your own study groups.

The first year combines coursework and the Career Development Program (CDP). The CDP hosts corporate presentations straight away in September, and counselors work closely with you so that you are fully prepared to meet employers. The CDP includes industry panels, resume critiques, networking workshops, and mock interviews.

Financial Accounting and Reporting, Statistics and Data Analysis, Teams and Leaders, and Professional Responsibility are part of every student's program. Additionally, Stern offers what it calls the selective core courses, where you choose five out of seven classes among Competitive Advantage from Operations, Firms and Markets, Foundations of Finance, The Global Economy, Leadership in Organizations, Marketing, and Strategy.

In the second year, you customize the curriculum to meet specific academic and professional goals. You may complete up to three specializations, or instead simply take a breadth of electives and not choose any specialization. Popular electives include courses in economics, entertainment, media and technology, law, public administration, real estate, and statistics and math.

The innovative, experiential programs use New York City as their extended classroom. Students benefit from the exclusive New York City case studies, which immerse them in the challenges facing leading locally based institutions such as the Metropolitan Opera and the Mets baseball franchise. Students can also give back while gaining valuable consulting experience through the Stern Consulting Corps. Through this program, they serve as consultants to New York City nonprofits while being advised by senior consultants from top firms such as Booz Allen Hamilton and Deloitte. For those students interested in making a career switch, Stern offers the Industry Mentoring Initiative, a year-long small group mentoring program conducted onsite at top companies in industries including consulting, entertainment and media, investment banking, luxury and retail, marketing, and sales and trading.

For those wanting the international experience abroad, there are intensive one- or two-week courses called Doing Business in... (DBi). Locations include Italy, China, Argentina, and Central Europe. You not only gain an entirely new perspective on business and insight into a different culture, but also emerge with in-country expertise and key contacts. If you want a longer-term experience and a complete immersion in another culture, Stern's study abroad semester has a selection of more than 40 partner graduate business schools in 26 countries.

RESEARCH CENTERS

Berkley Center for Entrepreneurship and Innovation

Center for Digital Economy Research

Center for Japan-U.S. Business and Economy Studies

Glucksman Institute for Research in Securities Markets

NYU Pollack Center for Law and Business

Salomon Center for the Study of Financial Institutions

Vincent C. Ross Institute of Accounting Research

Volatility Institute

What Stern Professors Teach

The resounding answer to what makes the Stern program different from other MBA programs is … New York! From a professor's standpoint, the city is the counterpoint to his or her teaching. Since there is no enclosed campus, you are thoroughly grounded in reality. Marketing efforts and business practices are on display on every block. As Professor Aswath Damodaran says, "There is immediate feedback from the environment. Look at Canal [Street]—it's the ultimate mercantile experience!" Professors such as Damodaran emphasize that product management is more specific to the field of brand management while most marketing positions involve significant strategic thinking.

Professor Jeff Carr teaches Marketing and serves as the executive director of the Berkley Center for Entrepreneurship. This innovative Center offers real-world, hands-on experience and grant funds through the Social Venture Fund Practicum course and the Entrepreneur Business Plan Competition. The competition also provides hefty cash prizes to launch new businesses. As Carr says, "I try to think of students as 'the product' so coursework is about making that product attractive to the customer, in this case companies that come to recruit and hire the students. So it is about giving students skills and tools to be more valuable employees."

With 25 percent of the Fortune 500 companies located in the tri-state area, the goal of pursuing a top-notch career is fueled by the competition. Big name companies are the top recruiters; they in turn attract and inspire top talent. The imprimatur of an MBA from Stern opens doors both in the corporate world and in the extensive alumni network. However, the diverse faculty members are the ones who teach the students to identify problems, develop a set of alternatives for addressing the problems, and plan a course of action for implementing the solutions. In keeping with that philosophy, Dean Cooley, an economist by training, recently co-authored a book, *Restoring Financial Stability: How to Repair a Failed System,* with a team of 32 academics from Stern. He also has compiled 18 white papers providing specific policy recommendations for restructuring the financial industry.

FACULTY FACTS

Full-time faculty employed by the
b-school: 202

Adjunct or visiting faculty: 74

Permanent/tenured professors: 108

Tenured faculty who are women: 17%

Tenured faculty who are underrepresented
minorities: 19%

SAMPLING OF NOTABLE PROFESSORS

- Edward Altman: Internationally recognized corporate bankruptcy expert
- Adam Brandenburger: Leading game theorist and co-author of *Co-opetition*
- Aswath Damodaran: Foremost expert in valuation of companies
- Robert Engle: Nobel Laureate in Economics
- Scott Galloway: Founder of Red Envelope and director of The New York Times Company
- Nouriel Roubini: Well known in global economics and international business for his work in computational models of risk management and strategy
- Sheila Wellington: Former president of Catalyst, the premier nonprofit supporting women in business leadership

CONCENTRATIONS AND SPECIALIZATIONS OFFERED IN FULL-TIME MBA PROGRAM

Accounting

Banking

Corporate Finance

Data, Models and Decisions

Economics

Entertainment, Media and Technology

Entrepreneurship and Innovation

Finance

Financial Instruments and Markets

Financial Systems and Analytics

Global Business

International Finance

Law and Business

Leadership and Change Management

Management

Management of Technology and Operations

Marketing

Product Management

Quantitative Finance

Social Innovation and Impact

Strategy

Supply Chain Management and Global
Sourcing

(continued)

(continued)

JOINT DEGREES AND DUAL DEGREES

MBA/JD

MBA/MS Mathematics in Finance

MBA/MFA (Fine Arts)

MBA/MA (French Studies or Politics)

MBA/MPA (Public Administration)

MBA/MS (Biology)

MBA/MBA at HEC (one year at NYU Stern, one year at HEC, France)

MBA/MFA (Producing)

What Admissions Is All About

Admissions officers want to ensure that accepted applicants feel that they are the "right fit" personally and professionally with NYU Stern. To that end, the admissions committee focuses on not only academic ability and professional potential, but also the holistic characteristics of each individual.

Stern reviews each application as it arrives. Three deadlines are provided for student convenience; however, it is best to take the time to prepare a competitive application and not rush to meet a certain time frame. Be mindful of scholarship deadlines and financial aid deadlines and plan your application accordingly.

Around 30 percent of all applicants are invited to the highly personalized interview. Each trained admissions officer expertly assesses each applicant after reading his or her application. Most interviews are held at the Greenwich Village campus. Be sure to review your application before coming to the interview. Be prepared to articulate a focused career plan and to let the admissions officers know why Stern is the right fit for you.

Throughout Stern's admissions process, finding the "right fit" is paramount. The application's famous "third essay" encourages a kind of personal expression from applicants, and the school's highly experienced admissions staff interviews every full-time MBA admit, ensuring that each incoming class is in tune with Stern's unique culture and values. Stern consistently admits one of the highest percentages of underrepresented groups and women among top business schools, and approximately one-third of its full-time MBA class hails from outside the U.S.

Another notable fact to consider: Of all the top business schools, Stern maintains a lead in the number of female students enrolled. The entering class for the full-time MBA in 2008 was 41 percent female. Since 2005, there has been an increase of 13 percent in the number of women.

Full-time MBAs receiving financial aid through the school: 71%

Assistantships: varies

Full-tuition scholarships school awarded for academic year: 42

Financially Aided

Stern offers a variety of financial aid programs to assist students in funding their MBA education. NYU Stern directly awards merit-based scholarships to domestic and international students. They are also given by organizations such as the Consortium and the Forté Foundation. Stern scholarships and donor awards are also awarded to second-year students. The Kenshin Oshima Scholarship is awarded to the most promising first-year MBA students who are particularly focused on Asian culture. The Kenshin Oshima Prize Program awards a scholarship to second-year students who hold the most impressive academic achievements. Oshima is a prominent businessman in Japan and a friend and supporter of the NYU Stern School of Business.

New York University itself offers tuition scholarships for graduate students going into social entre-preneurship. The Reynolds Foundation Graduate Fellowship in Social Entrepreneurship is awarded to students who are in any of the school's graduate or professional schools full time.

Other sources of financial assistance for international students include private loans, company spon-sorship, and external aid.

FULL-TIME MBA PROGRAM (TOTAL DIRECT COSTS)

In-state (per year): $68,306

Out-of-state (per year): $68,306

Part-time program cost: $1,470 per credit

EMBA program cost: $137,000

What Stern Students Know

When students are looking for an urban and international experience, geography is a deciding factor in choosing the right school, and Stern's location means that it simply offers a broader palette across the board. In fact, the Stern MBA program is known for bringing New York City into the classroom and making a classroom of the city itself. There is a plethora of innovative programs and network systems that enhance the learning experience and complement the coursework. For example, Stern is great for career switchers. One program is the Industry Mentoring Initiative. This is an immersion for first-year MBA students who want to learn about the industry they plan to enter after earning their degree.

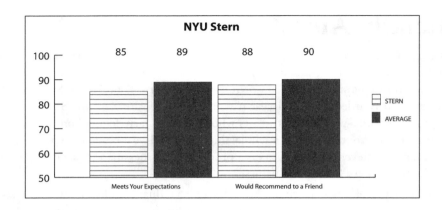

Career switchers are also lucky to have exceptional access to the entertainment industry. Because New York City is the second most popular location for filming (after Los Angeles), it should come as no surprise that Stern has a strong program in Entertainment, Media, and Technology (EMT). Complementing the program is the Media, Entertainment, and Sports Association (MESA) on campus, which holds events to introduce you to industry leaders. Success in entertainment is often about "who you know." MESA helps you develop professional relationships, and EMT alumni help you expand your network throughout the entertainment field.

The Stern Consulting Corps (SCC) is a program that enables Stern MBA students to have consulting engagements with nonprofit organizations in New York City. The SCC gives students practical consulting experience, which relates directly to their future careers and their sense of community involvement. In every aspect of daily life, the school motto, "Downtown, down to earth, down to business," is very much the way students interact with each other. In addition to the merging of skill sets through teamwork where the mutual advantages are evident, there are corporate presentations, student activities, and a host of other community integrations. Furthermore, with classes being held in the evenings, this opens the field to the best of the industry specialists. For example, if a CEO of a major publishing business is teaching at Stern, the only way he can do it is to be based in New York and teach after work.

The flexibility of scheduling is also a key advantage in Stern's MBA program. The coursework is customized, and students take more courses in their specializations, even if they have more than one. For example, a student may take Decision Models and Competitive Strategy, which covers marketing and strategy. On the one hand, the curriculum is flexible, which allows you to meet your specialized needs. On the other hand, you are shouldering most of the responsibility for your future success because you are choosing what you believe you will need to know.

CAREER CHECK: STERN MBA EMPLOYMENT BY JOB FUNCTION

- Finance/Accounting: 58%
- Marketing/Sales: 20%
- Consulting: 14%
- General Management: 4%
- Operations/Production: 2%

What's Next? Your Career

An MBA at Stern places you within reach of your end goal of embarking on an exciting and rewarding career. Stern's location in the heart of downtown Manhattan is ideal for access to the world's top companies, business leaders, and corporate recruiters. Numerous companies recruit Stern students for both domestic and international positions within a wide range of industries, including consulting, entertainment, finance, luxury and retail, marketing, nonprofit, and real estate. Most marketing students are interested in opportunities within the United States. Therefore, while international marketing positions are available to Stern MBAs, the job opportunities presented on campus are primarily domestic. The great majority of all positions are made available via on-campus recruiting, alumni, job postings, and career fairs, as well as Stern resources. Students frequently remark on the success of job placement, noting that major banks start recruiting from the first semester. Stern continues to offer a steady flow of support to all alumni throughout their careers. The Career Center for Working Professionals (CCWP) offers many services, such as individual career counseling appointments with a focus on self-assessment, job search strategy, resume review, networking techniques, interview preparation, and mock interviews. The Career Center also stages professional development workshops. Its online job search resources include updated job postings, research tools, and career development guides, along with the CCWP event calendar.

The Career Development Program, a two-year program required for all full-time students, includes one-on-one counseling with the Career Development Team, interview coaching from professionals, and alumni mentorship. More than 300 companies employed Stern students in the past two years in fields including consulting, consumer products and beauty, entertainment, finance, health care, luxury and retail, and nonprofit. The vast majority of Stern students secure full-time positions through Stern sources, such as on-campus recruiting, alumni, Stern job postings, and onsite career fairs.

ALUMNI ACTUALS

MBA alumni worldwide: 48,000+

Business school alumni networking site: https://alumnionline.stern.nyu.edu/

Current MBA students have access to the alumni database.

With a vast network of Stern alumni in more than 100 countries, you have a great network of contacts, sources for advice, and mentors available. Stern manages several services to link you directly with alumni in your fields of interest. The Stern Worldwide Access Platform (SWAP) is an online directory searchable by company, industry, or location. It also provides networking tools for regular contact with the alumni base such as resume posting, class and regional group Web sites, and e-mail forwarding for life. The Career Advisory Program (CAP) offers guidance on a one-on-one basis. Housed within SWAP, alumni volunteers in CAP serve as mentors for both current students and fellow alumni, as they share their work experiences and insights about organizational cultures via e-mail, phone, or in-person meetings. Alumni from all types and sizes of consulting firms are helpful and great resources.

For marketing students, the Graduate Marketing Association holds knowledge management sessions specifically to prep students for hire in the marketing industry. Another resource is the Luxury and Retail Club, which includes almost two dozen of Stern's board members. They are often on campus and available to advise you on how to pursue opportunities. In addition, the annual Luxury and Retail Conference features CEOs of leading companies. Stern students are currently working to create a retail specialization.

With academic flexibility comes the opportunity to explore additional activities such as networking events and club membership. Among the 40 clubs for MBA students at Stern, the newest is the Government and Business Association (GBA), started in spring 2009. The club is tasked with providing "career, networking and volunteer opportunities to students interested in working at the intersection of business and government, politics or policy."

Students can have consultants as mentors through the Industry Mentoring Initiative program (IMI). This program prepares first-year MBA students making career changes into consulting, entertainment and media, luxury and retail, investment banking, marketing, or sales and trading. A number of former consultants also are currently classmates and provide each other with frank and honest feedback about the field, with their contact information accessible through a database.

Finally, there is the New Venture Mentor Program for advice on entrepreneurial business ventures. This program is housed at the Berkley Center for Entrepreneurial Studies and connects students and alumni to business professionals to help guide the aspiring entrepreneurs who have a business concept but need further refinement in their ideas, planning, and funding efforts. The mentors coach these entrepreneurs and advise them on key issues in their new or emerging business. The Berkley Center is also home to the Stern Incubator, a creative platform that develops and nurtures new ventures partnered by MBA students and alumni. Help comes in the form of supplying office facilities, administrative support, and hands-on coaching.

In keeping with Stern's tradition of work hard, play hard, alumni host numerous events. At the end of each year, many alumni reunite and attend the Annual Stern Alumni Ball at a premier New York City landmark, such as the Museum of Natural History, the Guggenheim, or the Museum of Modern Art (MoMA). New graduates have a joyous opportunity to connect with the devoted new group of peers, to develop their professional network, and celebrate being an ongoing part of the Stern community.

On the world stage, Stern hosts the Global Alumni Conferences where alumni hail from all over the globe for the opportunity to learn from an eminent group of leading speakers on pertinent geopolitical and economic topics. In 2009, the Global Alumni Conference was held in Barcelona, Spain.

Match Made in Heaven: Is the Stern School of Business Right for You?

You are an ideal student if you

- Are self-motivated, energetic, driven, and possess a mind filled with curiosity.
- Are intrigued about the fascinating career possibilities in finance, strategy, marketing, and entrepreneurship.
- Love to learn from your peers and work in a highly collaborative environment.
- Enjoy living in the high-energy environment of New York City and know how to make the most of nonstop exposure to professions and opportunities.

Northwestern University Kellogg School of Management

Donald P. Jacobs Center
2001 Sheridan Road
Evanston, IL 60208

Phone: 847.491.3300
E-mail: MBAadmissions@kellogg.northwestern.edu
Web site: www.kellogg.northwestern.edu

Interim Dean: Sunil Chopra

Quick Facts

MBA PROGRAMS

Full-time MBA
Part-time MBA (evening program, weekend program)
Executive MBA
One-Year MBA

FULL-TIME MBA SNAPSHOT

Total enrollment: 1,200
Class of 2010: 650
Length of program: 22 months
Campus location: Evanston, IL
Program commences in September
Pre-term orientation attendance required

APPLICATION NOTES

Requirements: GMAT score; resume and work experience; essays; recommendations; tran scripts; GRE not accepted
Letters of recommendation: 2
Interview: Must be requested by the applicant
Number of applicants: 5,051
Admittance rate: 19%

CLASS OF **2010** PROFILE

Male 65%, Female 35%
Minority Americans: 24%
International: 35%
Average age: 28
Married or Partnered, Single: 40%, 60%
Combined average years of work experience: 5 years
GMAT score average: 712
GMAT score range (20th–80th percentile): 650–760
GPA average: 3.5

ACADEMIC BACKGROUND OF INCOMING STUDENTS

Business: 27%
Economics: 18%
Engineering/Sciences: 38%
Social Studies/Humanities: 17%

A True University Town

Located along the shores of scenic Lake Michigan in suburban Cook County, Illinois, Evanston is directly north of the city of Chicago, east of Skokie, and south of Wilmette. Evanston was formally incorporated as a town in 1863 but officially became a city in 1892 following the annexation of the village of South Evanston. The 1892 boundaries were similar to those that exist today.

Northwestern University was founded before the city of Evanston even existed. The men who founded Northwestern were seeking the perfect site for a new Methodist-affiliated institution of higher learning. While making plans for the school, the founders also laid plans for the city that would eventually surround it. Thus, Evanston has grown around the university, and has become well known for its architecture and beautiful homes, as well as the successes of the university and its graduates.

On campus at Kellogg.

The Kellogg School of Management marked its one-hundredth anniversary in 2008. Originally, it was founded as Northwestern University's School of Commerce, which was a part-time evening program and one of 16 founding members of the American Assembly of Collegiate Schools of Business, the organization that sets accreditation standards for business schools.

The school's original mission was to educate business leaders with "good moral character." It initiated the group project curriculum that the majority of business schools utilize today and emphasized the importance of teamwork and team leadership in the business world. In 1915, two of the school's leaders started a group called the National Association of Teachers of Advertising, which later became the Chicago-based American Marketing Association.

Today, Kellogg offers full-time, part-time, Ph.D., and executive programs. It boasts a world-class faculty and a curriculum emphasizing intellectual depth, experiential learning, global perspectives, leadership, and social responsibility.

In honor of its centennial, Northwestern University Press published *Wide Awake in the Windy City,* which utilized archival material, first-person narratives, and photographs to trace the century-long ascent of the Kellogg School of Management from 1908 to its development into a worldwide management education leader.

Why Kellogg?

Kellogg is regarded as one of the top business schools in the world. Alumni hold leadership positions in government, for-profit, nonprofit, and academic institutions around the globe. Regardless of what area of study you choose to pursue, you leave with a solid foundation in management. The school also has a strong finance program, and many people put "Kellogg" and "marketing" in the same sentence.

In 1999, Kellogg integrated its joint degree program. Students submit a single application for the JD-MBA and have a single tuition bill. Those who enroll spend the first year in the law school and the second in the business school. During the third year, JD-MBA students return to the law school. This level of integration demonstrates the school's overall philosophy of education.

Leadership development is also a strong focus and is nurtured through team class projects and by participation in many of the clubs, courses, conferences, and lecture series that Kellogg offers. Kellogg's Leadership in Organizations course is one that you take early in your academic career; it emphasizes the importance of teamwork and ethical decision making. Another course, Values and Crisis Decision Making, helps you improve your strategic thinking, team building, and communications skills in high stress work situations.

Peer leadership flourishes through more than 80 professional and special-interest organizations and 13 business conferences. Finance and Consulting Club members assist with interview preparation for corporate finance positions and coordinate programs in all of the finance-related clubs at the Kellogg School of Management. The club Business with a Heart hosts a variety of activities, including blood drives, school tutoring, and volunteering locally at such places as senior centers, childcare centers, the local YMCA, libraries, and schools. Kellogg's Executive Leader in Residence Series brings high-level executives to Kellogg to talk about executive responsibilities and leadership issues, including Michael Moskow, former head of the Federal Reserve Bank of Chicago, who spoke to Kellogg students twice in 2008.

The Kellogg Distinguished Lecture Series, sponsored by the school's Office of the Dean, brings in well-known leaders from various industries. Recent speakers have included Nobel laureate, Princeton University economist, and *New York Times* columnist Paul Krugman; *Newsweek* editor Jon Meacham; and Pulitzer Prize winner and *Wall Street Journal* columnist James B. Stewart.

FUN FACTS

- Evanston has become known as the "Headquarters City," as many for-profit and not-for-profit organizations have established their national headquarters here, including Alpha Phi International women's fraternity, Rotary International, National Lekotek Center, Sigma Alpha Epsilon fraternity, Sigma Chi fraternity, and the Women's Christian Temperance Union.

- Northlands Storytelling Network in nearby McHenry is a community of storytellers and story listeners in the upper Midwest. In addition to its annual spring Storytelling Conference and its annual *Storytelling Journal*, the Network also offers New Voices Conference scholarships to young adults interested in using storytelling in their respective fields.

- The business school (later named Kellogg) played an important role in establishing the Graduate Management Admission Test, the standardized test used to measure the intellectual skills of MBA applicants.

Course Offerings

The Kellogg curriculum offers students more than knowledge of general management principles; it provides you with the opportunity to choose from more than 200 courses to explore your own interests and prepare for your professional future. Students even have the opportunity to travel to countries around the world to complete coursework of their own design and choosing. The full-time MBA includes studies at the Indian Institute of Management, Bangalore, and China Europe International Business School.

Kellogg offers one- and two-year MBA programs with core courses in accounting, management and organizations, marketing, finance, decision sciences, and management and strategy. You can also earn a dual degree through the MMM program, which integrates management, operations, and design.

The Global Lab course that Kellogg offers enables you to come up with innovative strategies for Indian clothing retailers or consult with a Brazilian company on international expansion strategies. The Global Initiatives in Management course provides you with the opportunity to learn a country's business and political climate in depth; the course culminates in a two-week research trip to the particular country that is being studied. Kellogg requires everyone to take at least one course with a global focus. Cross-Cultural Negotiation, Global Marketing, International Business Strategy, and International Finance are other courses containing global elements.

Experiential learning is a big part of the Kellogg School of Management curriculum. For example, you might discuss the recent sub-prime lending crisis and examine how it could have been prevented. You might manage and invest part of the school's endowment, solve a real company's financial problems, or act as a consultant for a local business or nonprofit organization.

RESEARCH CENTERS

Accounting Research Center

Center for Biotechnology Management

Center for Executive Women

Center for Family Enterprises

Center for Financial Institutions and Market Research

Center for Game Theory and Economic Behavior

Center for Health Industry Market Economics

Center for Market Leadership

Center for Mathematical Studies in Economics and Management Science

Center for Nonprofit Management

Center for Operations and Supply Chain Management

Center for Research on Strategic Alliances

Center for Research on Technology and Innovation

Center on the Science of Diversity

Dispute Resolution Research Center

Ford Motor Company Center for Global Citizenship

General Motors Research Center for Strategy in Management

Guthrie Center for Real Estate Research

Heizer Center for Entrepreneurial Studies

International Business Research Center

Larry and Carol Levy Institute for Entrepreneurial Practice

Kellogg Team and Group Research Center

Zell Center for Risk Research

What Kellogg Professors Teach

Kellogg is well known as a premiere—perhaps the best—marketing program in the nation. Professor Philip Kotler has been widely lauded as one of the world's top marketing experts. He teaches international marketing at the Kellogg School of Management and is the author of *Marketing Management: Analysis, Planning, Implementation and Control,* the most widely used marketing book in graduate business schools worldwide. Former Kellogg Dean Dipak Jain is a pioneer is quantitative marketing. Associate Professor of Marketing Kent Grayson teaches the school's core marketing course. Among other topics, he teaches students about marketers and their methods of convincing people to buy products that they don't necessarily need.

An incoming student may find this wealth of knowledge overwhelming. However, the class of 2009's Alex Barth majored in marketing and says his relationships with the faculty have been very supportive. His professors have been "professional but approachable," and they have encompassed a wide range of teaching styles. They have office hours and give out their phone numbers and e-mail addresses. On a typical day in January, he remarks that he had a couple of professors talking about Super Bowl marketing during a lunch discussion. Barth adds that professors also appear as guest speakers at the Kellogg marketing club to which he belongs.

If you are considering another focus besides marketing, you have a depth of professorial knowledge and experience as well since all teaching faculty are also researchers. Are you looking for a professor well versed in Kellogg's teaching principles? Linda Vincent earned her doctorate degree from Kellogg and currently is an associate professor of accounting information and management at the school. Would you like to study management? Professor Adam Galinsky is currently the Morris and Alice Kaplan professor of Ethics and Decision in Management at the Kellogg School of Management. He has published more than 75 scientific articles, chapters, and teaching cases in the fields of management and social psychology. His teaching and research focus on leadership, negotiation, decision-making, and the development of organizational values and culture.

How about finance? Paola Sapienza is an associate professor in the finance department. Prior to joining Kellogg, she worked as an economist in the research department of the Bank of Italy. She is interested in corporate finance and has written articles on banking, state-ownership, social capital, and financial development. She also co-authors the quarterly *Financial Trust Index*.

Want to explore business ethics? Daniel Diermeier is the IBM Distinguished Professor of Regulation and Competitive Practice, a Professor of Managerial Economics and Decision Sciences at Kellogg, the director of the Ford Center, and a Professor of Political Science at the Weinberg College of Arts and Sciences at Northwestern University. His teaching and research focus on political institutions, the interaction of business and politics, crisis leadership, issue and reputation management, non-market strategy, and strategic aspects of corporate social responsibility.

What are your entrepreneurial aspirations? Steven Rogers is the Gordon and Liura Gund Family Distinguished Professor of Entrepreneurship. He teaches Entrepreneurial Finance at Kellogg and is the director of the Larry and Carol Levy Institute for Entrepreneurial Practice. In addition to the regular MBA program, Professor Rogers teaches in many Kellogg executive programs in North America and Hong Kong.

Why is Kellogg's faculty so good at what they do? One reason is the innovative Mini MBA, introduced in 2008 as an orientation for incoming instructors. The two-day course features cross-disciplinary collaboration and conversation with senior professors. It is a comprehensive process to introduce new professors to the Kellogg culture of rigorous performance for teaching and research. Part of the orientation involves observing veteran professors using case studies, mini cases, and quantitative lectures in the classroom, which are among the broad array of teaching techniques employed by faculty.

Alum Paul Earle found his professors to be extraordinary. They knew their individual subjects well, were charismatic, and gave thoroughly engaging lectures. The outstanding professors, Earle pointed out, "went above and beyond to enrich and enliven students' experiences; teaching and learning didn't end when class did." They were especially available to students after classes ended each day.

KELLOGG PARTNER SCHOOLS

Kellogg co-founded the Indian School of Business in Hyderabad, India, and Sasin Graduate Institute of Business Administration of Chulalongkorn University in Thailand. Kellogg also partners with

- ESSEC Business School, Paris
- Guanghua School of Management, Beijing
- Shailesh J. Mehta School of Management, Bangalore
- Recanati Graduate School of Management, Tel Aviv
- School of Business and Management, Hong Kong University of Science and Technology, Hong Kong
- Schulich School of Business at York University, Toronto
- WHU-Otto Beisheim School of Management, Vallendar, Germany

FACULTY FACTS

Full-time faculty employed by the b-school: 164

Adjunct or visiting faculty: 58

Permanent/tenured professors: 157

Tenured faculty who are women: 30

Tenured faculty who are underrepresented minorities: 34

SAMPLING OF NOTABLE PROFESSORS

- Bala Balachandran: One of the top management accountants in the world; pioneer of Activity Based Costing
- Julie Hennessy: Leader in the fields of brand and marketing management, consumer products, marketing strategy planning policy, and new product development
- Philip Kotler: Leading authority on marketing for more than 30 years
- Sergio Rebelo: Renowned economist and finance expert; influential author on subjects such as macroeconomics and derivatives and finance
- Brian Uzzi: Recognized specialist on networks and complex systems in firms and markets; researcher on the dynamics of innovation, diffusion, and change in market-based social networks
- Linda Vincent: Recognized expert, professor, and researcher of business combinations, divisive restructurings, real estate, and financial reporting data; serves on the editorial boards of the *Journal of Accounting* and *Economics and Accounting Horizons*

CONCENTRATIONS AND SPECIALIZATIONS OFFERED IN FULL-TIME MBA PROGRAM

Accounting Information and Management	Management and Organizations
Analytic Finance	Management and Strategy
Analytical Consulting	Managerial Economics
Biotechnology Management	Marketing
Decision Sciences	Marketing Management
Entrepreneurship and Innovation	Media Management
Finance	Operations Management
Health Enterprise Management	Real Estate Management
Health Industry Managment	Social Enterprise at Kellogg
Human Resource Management	Technology Industry Management
International Business	

JOINT DEGREES AND DUAL DEGREES

JD-MBA	The MMM Program

What Admissions Is All About

Assistant Dean and Director of Admissions and Financial Aid Beth Flye explains how an application travels through the admissions office in Evanston. "When a prospective student's file is complete, each application has three evaluative reviews. For many students, the first evaluation is done by a member of the student review admissions committee, then an evaluation is done by one of the admissions officers, then I do a final review of the application. We typically have three application deadlines: in October, January, and March." Flye adds that each application undergoes a "holistic" evaluation process "that takes into account an applicant's intellectual ability, his or her academic and work record, written essays, letters of recommendation, if the student is team-oriented, and [the student's] overall fit with the school."

The Kellogg School of Management does not accept students straight out of undergraduate school without any quality full-time work experience. The average work experience is five years. All qualifying Kellogg applicants are required to request an interview; however, because applicants live throughout the world, not everyone visits the campus to meet with admissions officers. Some prospective students are interviewed by alumni living in close proximity to where applicants reside.

Flye notes that for the past two years, about 20 percent of all applicants have been admitted into the school's full-time programs. On average, around 30 percent of international students who apply are admitted into the full-time MBA program. No type of cap exists when it comes to the number of foreign students admitted to Kellogg. "We try to have a diverse class, and that includes geographic diversity," Flye notes. As for what advice she would give international students applying to Kellogg, Flye says, "Reach out to us, come and visit us in Evanston if you can. Kellogg has more than 80 clubs where you can connect with other students before you come to school."

If you want to know what Kellogg considers an ideal candidate, there isn't one. Rather, Kellogg's MBA candidates are comprised of a wide variety of students from different backgrounds and cultures. "We are not a cookie-cutter type of culture," Beth Flye insists. "We have very diverse types of students. We want to admit a great group of students who want to be a part of Kellogg. We want people to develop holistically, not just perform in the classroom. We want high-impact individuals who want to make the world better, whether it's through a particular idea or product."

Full-time MBAs receiving financial aid through school: 64%

Institutional (merit-based and need-based) scholarships: 355

Assistantships: N/A

Full-tuition scholarships school awarded for academic year: 20+

Financially Aided

Because Kellogg is so strongly committed to enrolling an exceptional and diverse set of students regardless of their financial need, the Office of Admissions and Financial Aid guides students to identify potential financial resources for their MBA. Kellogg's Office of Admissions awards a broad range of merit scholarships to outstanding students who demonstrate excellence in numerous areas of their applications. After applicants are admitted, their eligibility for all merit scholarships is automatically considered; additional application materials are not required.

One scholarship program has been in place for more than 80 years. The F. C. Austin scholarships were instrumental back in 1929 in encouraging Northwestern to expand its graduate program to attract top faculty and students. Now, 20 MBA candidates for each incoming class receive merit-based scholarships that cover half of their tuition. Two other merit-based awards provide full funding: the Peter L. Frechette scholarship and the David F. and Margaret T. Grohne Family scholarship.

For students who will join the global leadership and emerging markets management fields, ArcelorMittal confers scholarships for the one-year, two-year, and MMM programs. Corporate funding is awarded to encourage class diversity as well and is sponsored by well-known financial firms. Incoming MMM candidates have another opportunity to receive financial help through the Wally Hopp scholarship, which partially underwrites tuition and is based on academic merit. The scholarship covers $10,000 of the year's tuition. And for high-achieving women pursuing their education at Kellogg, Forté Foundation funds partial scholarships to encourage exceptional female leaders.

Loans remain an option for full-time students who are U.S. citizens and permanent residents: The Federal Stafford Loan (FSL), Unsubsidized Federal Stafford Loan (UFSL), Perkins Loan, and Grad PLUS are among the choices. The Northwestern International Loan Program is designed to help international students. Additionally, Kellogg awards Donald P. Jacobs international scholarships to incoming foreign-born students.

Full-Time MBA Program (Total Direct Costs)

In-state: $72,539

Out-of-state: $72,539

International: $73,517

One-year program: $95,480

International: $95,672

Part-time program cost (per unit): $4,679

EMBA program cost: $135,000–$142,000

What Kellogg Students Know

Alex Barth decided to attend Kellogg for a variety of reasons. "The school was regarded as a great academic institution, and the students I met were bright, ego-free, and the kind I would be comfortable getting a beer with, very likeable," Barth says. "I had a friend who was at Kellogg, and he entertained me for a weekend and I sat in on some classes. Reputation and brand do matter; but most importantly, I wanted to get into a school that was renowned for its marketing curriculum." Additionally, Kellogg appealed to Barth because of its proximity to downtown Chicago and its being situated in the middle of the country. "I'm from Seattle," Barth notes, "and Kellogg is a convenient jumping off point to get to all points of the country."

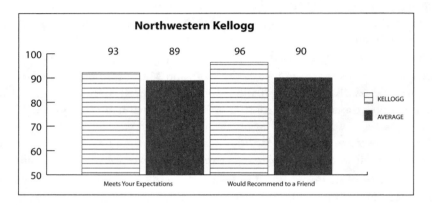

Barth's orientation experience at Kellogg was a positive one. He arrived in Evanston with his fiancée and became active in the Joint Ventures Club—a club on campus that was started in 1982 for spouses, significant others, and family members of Kellogg students. It hosts a variety of activities for incoming students, including happy hours, dinners, cultural and sporting outings, and other events in order to ease the transition into the full-time MBA program at Kellogg. "It was very helpful in getting acclimated to Kellogg," Barth recalls.

Barth also participated in the popular KWEST program before classes started. Entirely student-run and one of the most popular student activities at Kellogg, KWEST (Kellogg Worldwide Experiences and Service Trips) brings admitted Kellogg students and four or five second-year trip leaders together through a variety of outdoor and community service activities. Students visit a locale in the United States or an international destination. In Barth's case, he visited the Dominican Republic for a week and recalls that it was "a great way to form friendships with future classmates."

Barth also spent his 10-week summer internship between his first and second years of school at Kellogg at a packaged goods company in the Midwest. "It was a very positive experience," Barth recalls. "I had never spent any time in a large company, and while interning, I encountered a different type of culture. I learned about how a product gets developed and how it eventually gets placed on a store shelf."

Kellogg has a broad range of summer internships between your first and second years of study to broaden your learning and put what you have learned into practice. You apply for these company positions in areas you would like to pursue after earning your degree. If you are interested in exploring careers in the social enterprise field, you can pursue a summer internship in nonprofit, public, or social entrepreneurial organizations.

Barth finds that he meets regularly with his fellow students for academic support. He often finds himself with four or five other students to study and talk about a particular business case. "There's a lot of collaboration here, and that makes Kellogg unique. Even though students are competitive, I have never encountered at Kellogg any cut-throatness at the expense of other students. And that's definitely something I wanted to avoid when I was evaluating schools."

A typical day, as Barth explains, involves catching up on his e-mail over lunch, networking with students, participating in some of his club activities (he's a co-chair of the marketing club and co-chair of the sports business club), having dinner with his wife, and finishing a few hours' worth of homework until midnight.

In terms of career support, Barth notes that he has had the opportunity to look through the alumni directory and make some phone calls to Kellogg alums to talk about his career goals after graduation. "We've had some great conversations," he says.

Many students participate each year in "Kellogg Cares," a day of local community service that gives them the opportunity to give back to the local Evanston-Skokie community. It is one of the school's largest community service events. In 2008, more than 200 Kellogg students volunteered at nearly 20 philanthropic organizations throughout Evanston and Skokie, including Shore Community Services, the McGaw YMCA, Family Focus, the Child Care Center of Evanston, and the Evanston Ecology Center. Students performed a variety of tasks, from advising nonprofits on marketing tactics to gardening at the Evanston Ecology Center.

CAREER CHECK: KELLOGG MBA EMPLOYMENT BY JOB FUNCTION

- Consulting: 36%
- Finance/Accounting: 29%
- Marketing/Sales: 22%
- General Management: 6%
- Operations/Production: 1%
- Other: 6%

What's Next? Your Career

Practical work experience is crucial for students entering the Kellogg School of Management, according to Roxanne Hori, assistant dean and director of Kellogg's Career Management Center. "Work plays a major role in the classroom as students are better equipped to participate in discussions and group work," Hori explains. "They have a better frame of reference for the business problems they're discussing. Secondly, employers are seeking people with some prior work experience versus applicants with no experience entering business school. Recruiters are looking for the maturity and other experiences beyond academics in candidates for their openings. On average, incoming Kellogg students have five years of work experience."

Recruiters are attracted to Kellogg students because of their collaborative skills; ability to deal with conflict in a positive, constructive way; and their ability to work as part of a team.

How is this impressive result achieved? The Kellogg Career Management Center (CMC) introduces corporations to its talented students through several programs. One of these is alumni outreach. The CMC contacts and encourages Kellogg alumni already established in their fields to mentor or hire Kellogg graduates. On campus, the CMC invites company representatives to events, as well as coordinates outreach to employers in various cities and industries based on student interest.

Kellogg students may attend "Lunch and Learns," which are non-recruiting educational events whereby a company's senior managers discuss important business issues or cases in a Kellogg classroom. Senior managers may then discuss employment opportunities for no longer than five minutes at the end of these events.

The CMC hosts career panels that expose Kellogg students to various careers. These panels involve alumni and are held in the early fall quarter. "Resumania" is another popular service, which involves one-on-one resume reviews with various company representatives. For social networking, the CMC sponsors Kellogg Networking Nights (KNNs) cocktail receptions whereby up to 15 companies from a particular industry or group of industries meet with Kellogg students. In addition, Career Forum is a Kellogg-only career fair that provides networking access to first- and second-year Kellogg students. It accommodates up to 25 companies. Kellogg students attended a November 2008 Kellogg Career Forum event that featured representatives from Aquent, Accenture, and Deloitte. Speakers discussed the various options companies offer employees in order to maintain a positive work-life balance.

For recruiters and students, CMC oversees student treks. Career counselors arrange for small groups of students to visit various companies in different markets. During the treks, students ask questions about the hiring process to be better prepared and more familiar with the company. They are a terrific way to highlight a company's culture and a good opportunity for companies who are unable to visit the Kellogg campus. For example, real estate treks have provided Kellogg students with the opportunity to visit companies in cities such as Chicago, New York, San Francisco, and Los Angeles; learn about various firms; and network with real estate professionals. Over the years, Kellogg students have visited numerous firms including Prudential, Jones Lang LaSalle, Related Midwest, JMB, Mesirow Stein, Walton Street Capital, and others.

ALUMNI ACTUALS

MBA alumni worldwide: 51,000+

Business school alumni networking site: http://alumni.kellogg.northwestern.edu

Current MBA students have access to the alumni database.

Paul Earle is president of River West Brands, a Chicago-based company that acquires and redevelops brand intellectual property. He attended Kellogg on a full-time basis and received his MBA in 1999, with a concentration in Marketing. Right after graduation, he went to work for Kraft Foods, where he had interned between his first and second years at Kellogg.

Earle found the "people experience" the most valuable thing about acquiring an MBA at Kellogg. "I broadened my horizons intellectually, professionally, and in every way, and that was mainly due to the great privilege of working with many extraordinary classmates and professors," Earle says." The overall quality of people throughout the whole experience was just off the charts. In my class alone, we had our share of accountants, bankers, consultants, and marketing types, but we also had a NASA rocket scientist, a handful of doctors, a guy whose company specialized in putting out oil refinery fires, a jet fighter pilot, a cartoonist, a cartoon publisher, a professional tennis player, a vintner, and so on. Behind all of that were equally as interesting personal hobbies. 'You did what?' was frequently overheard when we were all getting to know each other—add to that an extremely high level of intelligence, and at least some ability to and interest in getting along with others and having fun. It was a community of renaissance people. I directly worked with people from Japan, China, Australia, India, Brazil, Argentina, Mexico, Nigeria, Switzerland, Germany, France, Spain, England, Ireland, and Scotland . . . and I'm sure I'm missing a few places."

Laura George also received her MBA from Kellogg in 1999 with a concentration in marketing. "In the 10 years since my graduation, I have found that I value the people I met at Kellogg and subsequently the networking connections I made the most," George says. "My Kellogg education also equipped me with the thinking skills, leadership ability, and strategic vision to succeed in both corporate marketing and as an independent entrepreneur."

George also participated in a variety of other activities while she was at Kellogg, including Special K, Kellogg Outdoor Adventures, Business with a Heart, and her collaboration with other members of her entrepreneurship team. She also took advantage of mentorship opportunities that were available through the Women's Business Association and talked with a number of professors, including Clinical Professor of Entrepreneurship Barry Merkin. Reflecting on how her graduate education experience at Kellogg changed her and how she views the world, George comments that she regards her two years at Kellogg as "the most stimulating, educationally diverse, and enjoyable period of my life." She met and made friends with students from around the world who have enriched her life both personally and professionally.

Match Made in Heaven: Is Kellogg School of Management Right for You?

You are an ideal student if you

- Learn well from a cross-disciplinary approach to key subjects and through collaboration.
- Are able to spend focused time preparing for classes, which is rewarded with a stimulating and engaging classroom experience.
- Expect to broaden your intellectual, experiential, philosophical, and professional opportunities.
- Want to take your experimental learning experience and become a national or international business leader.

Stanford University Graduate School of Business

518 Memorial Way
Stanford, CA 94305

Phone: 650.723.2766
Contact form: www.gsb.stanford.edu/mba/contact/ask_question.html
Web site: www.gsb.stanford.edu/

Dean: Garth Saloner
Associate Dean and Director of the MBA Program: Sharon Hoffman
Senior Associate Director of the MBA Program: Lisa Schwallie

"This new educational model builds on the enormous advantage of our small size to create a high-touch, customized program, with a significant new faculty-student advising and placement component that will challenge every student to his or her fullest capability." —Former Dean Robert L. Joss

Quick Facts

MBA PROGRAMS

Full-time MBA
Accelerated Sloan MBA

FULL-TIME MBA SNAPSHOT

Total enrollment: 739
Class of 2010: 370
Length of program: 20 months
Campus: Palo Alto, CA
Program commences in August
Pre-term orientation attendance: None

APPLICATION NOTES

Requirements: Four-year bachelor's degree or equivalent; transcripts; GMAT; essays; resume; recommendations; TOEFL if applicable; application; work experience not required; GRE accepted
Letters of recommendation: 3
Interview: By invitation only
Number of applicants: 6,575
Admittance rate: 8%

(continued)

2010 CLASS PROFILE

Male 64%, Female 36%
Minority Americans: 24%
International: 34% (includes permanent residents)
Average age: NA
Average years of work experience: 4 years
GMAT average score: 726
GMAT score range (20th–80th percentile): 690–750
GPA average: 3.64

ACADEMIC BACKGROUND OF INCOMING STUDENTS

Business: 19%
Engineering/Math/Natural Sciences: 35%
Humanities/Social Sciences: 46%

Railroads to World Entrepreneurship

California Governor and U.S. Senator Leland Stanford made his money as a railroad entrepreneur. He made history with the completion of the Transcontinental Railroad. He spent multiple millions, however, to build a university and name it for his only son, Leland Jr., who died at 15 of typhoid fever.

"The children of California shall be our children," Leland Stanford told his wife, Jane, in 1884 as they began planning the memorial to their son.

Leland Stanford Junior University opened in 1891 and its first student was future President Herbert Hoover. Stanford's first president, David Starr Jordan, told that initial class that "[we are] hallowed by no traditions ... hampered by none. [Stanford's] fingerposts all point forward."

In 1925, as U.S. Secretary of Commerce, Hoover sought to stop the flight of bright students to East Coast institutions offering business degrees by creating the Stanford Graduate School of Business.

Decades later, the 1990s dot.com era made the Silicon Valley a hotbed of business activity. In 1999, the Center for Electronic Business and Commerce was funded for five years to create a body of knowledge through research and cases about e-commerce and the Internet that could be incorporated broadly into the MBA curriculum.

Scenes from Stanford.

The Center for Entrepreneurial Studies was launched in 1999. Besides its distinct vision of creating knowledge and teaching around entrepreneurship, the school now also supports the Center for Global Business and the Economy; the Center for Leadership Development and Research; and the Center for Social Innovation, which encompasses the School's 39-year-old Public Management Program.

Stanford's Graduate Business School faculty members are world renowned for their cutting-edge research and publications.

The Graduate School of Business, known as the GSB, is building the Knight Management Center. A $350 million campus of eight buildings around three quadrangles, the Center will support a broader array of instruction and learning methods intended to draw people and ideas from across the Stanford campus, which includes seven world-class schools—Humanities and Sciences, Engineering, Medicine, Earth Sciences, Education, and Business—on one contiguous campus. The new campus will include a library, an auditorium, and open community spaces. It will be located on Serra Street, across the street from the Schwab Residential Center, which houses MBAs and executive education participants. The facility was funded in part by a $105 million gift from Nike founder and chairman Philip H. Knight, class of 1962.

Why Stanford?

Stanford is a school of general management with a two-year, full-time residential MBA program dedicated to educating principled leaders. It has a number of joint degree programs, including JD/MBA, MBA/MA Education, MBA/MPP Public Policy, and MBA/MS Environmental Resources. The school also offers non-degree executive education programs for working executives. The school does not have undergrads, an EMBA, or part-time programs. The Sloan Master's Program offers a 10-month program for seasoned executives.

Stanford GSB's student body engages in a network that extends well into their alumni years. The sense of community and collaboration is one of the hallmarks of the school. Stanford always ranks at the top of the MBA programs worldwide and, in addition, is on the cutting edge of "green." The Aspen Institute has twice recognized Stanford as the number one MBA program to incorporate corporate social responsibility and environmental sustainability into its curriculum.

And upon completion in 2010–2011, the new business school campus is expected to achieve the highest-level LEED platinum environmental sustainability certification from the U.S. Green Building Council. The new campus is being built with a new curriculum, introduced in 2007, in mind. Key features of the new curriculum include a required, 16-person "Critical Analytical Thinking" seminar, a global experience requirement, and a menu of classes for core courses that allows students with more experience in areas such as finance or operations to extend their learning through advanced classes. It will have facilities for seminars, leadership exercises in teams of eight, and collaborative multidisciplinary classroom work.

The Center for Leadership Development and Research provides a forum for leadership scholars, students, and practitioners to share experiences and insights on leadership challenges across multiple academic disciplines.

The Center for Entrepreneurship provides students a greater understanding of entrepreneurial companies. The Center provides an environment for entrepreneurs, students, and faculty. Industry players on the faculty make for an intense collaboration between students, faculty, alumni, and local companies.

The Center for Global Business and the Economy states that its goal is to be the leader in the development and dissemination of research, curriculum materials, and conceptual frameworks on global business and economic issues. The Global Center provides academic and experiential learning opportunities for graduates to manage effectively in the global environment.

The Center for Social Innovation was created in response to the Stanford philosophy that business schools "have a responsibility to teach students to be innovative, principled, and insightful leaders who can change the world." The program's multidisciplinary approach to management and leadership education is designed to increase the awareness of social problems. The Center provides a framework for students to engage with the community while studying a curriculum to enhance the leadership and management capacity of graduates committed to creating social and environmental value.

The Public Management Program offers a Certificate in Public Management in government, socially responsible business, or nonprofit management. The Program exposes students to areas of public and nonprofit management, international development, social and environmental entrepreneurship, corporate social responsibility, and environmental sustainability.

Graduates may use the alumni database as well as the Stanford alumni organization Web site. Not only will you be a contributing member ready to give back in a couple of years to the "up-and-comers," but you will garner valuable insight and relationships to last a lifetime.

FUN FACTS

- Stanford's full name is still "Leland Stanford Junior University." Visitors are sometimes bewildered, thinking it is a junior university!
- Vermont legislator Jason Lorber, class of 1995, is also a stand-up comedian.
- Trombonist Gary Tyrrell, class of 1983, made Stanford history by colliding with Cal football's Kevin Moen in the last four seconds of "The Play" during the Big Game on

November 30, 1982. Stanford lost the game when Moen scored the game-winning touchdown by running through confused band members, who had entered the end zone prematurely. Moen knocked Tyrrell and his trombone into oblivion, although Tyrrell got up and began playing again. Most people can laugh about it now, even football great John Elway, class of 1983, who arguably lost the Heisman Trophy because of the game. Tyrrell and Moen have spent the last 25 years talking about it, both coming to terms and having fun with their places in college football history.

Course Offerings

Stanford's new GSB curriculum is designed to accommodate an increasingly diverse group of students coming to business school for managerial leadership and to challenge each one regardless of their past management experience. Senior faculty work closely with students during the first-year "Critical Analytical Thinking" seminar and place them into course selections based on their previous experience and postgraduate objectives. They often encourage students to think of paths they hadn't thought of before. And, because success will depend on how much of the information is ultimately absorbed, everyone is assigned to a study group. As many students learn, in the first-year grad school program, almost everything hinges on study groups. Laptops are required for the MBA program.

First-year students participate in a global study trip, overseas service-learning trip, one of two exchanges to India or China, or an international work project. The GSB offers financial aid for global trip costs for students with demonstrated need.

The GSB offers students approximately 100 electives each year to expand their knowledge into new areas of study and topics of interest. Existing courses are updated often and reflect real changes in the social sector, the business world, or student interests. New courses are offered annually. Some electives are designed to meet requirements toward a certificate in Public Management.

The new curriculum is also purposely global, seeking to broaden each student's view of global management along with current and future issues in the global marketplace. The goal is to reorient the curriculum decisively toward a more personal and more global experience. Foundational courses will still be there: finance, accounting, operations, marketing and strategy, organizational behavior, and economics. But, by keeping the program small and emphasizing leadership, teamwork, moral reasoning, and good management practices from the start, Stanford believes it can continue to stay out in front.

Another unusual offering is the Stanford Sloan program, which celebrated its 50th anniversary in 2008. The program was started by Alfred P. Sloan, the first CEO of General Motors, and exists in only three business schools in the world: MIT Sloan, London Business School, and Stanford GSB. Stanford Sloan Fellows are mid- and senior-level managers who have at least eight years of professional experience. At the end of the 10-month intensive program, students receive a Master of Science in Management degree.

CONCENTRATIONS AND SPECIALIZATIONS OFFERED TO FULL-TIME MBA STUDENTS

Public Management

JOINT DEGREES AND DUAL DEGREES

MBA/JD

MBA/MD

MBA/MA (Education)

MBA/PPA (Public Policy)

MBA/MS (Environment and Resources)

Dual degrees offered with the School of Medicine and other disciplines

Degrees customized with approval

What Stanford Professors Teach

Raj Das, class of 2006, says, "Professors are simply outstanding, some of the best strategy gurus I have encountered in my education and career! Combine that with a very cooperative, team-oriented approach to teaching, and you have a winner in graduate business studies curriculum."

The school's philosophy centers on changing lives, changing organizations, and changing the world. The faculty is committed to challenging individuals to expand their studies and become principled, innovative leaders and problem solvers with a focus on responsible and effective change both in themselves and in their organizations.

Among the faculty members are 3 Nobel laureates, 4 members of the National Academy of Sciences, 17 members of the American Academy of Arts and Sciences, and 2 recipients of the John Bates Clark Medal in Economics. The small seminars allow you to work closely with faculty. Teaching methods vary by course and instructor; they include case studies, discussions, face-to-face feedback, learning labs, problem-solving sessions, role play, simulations, theoretical overviews, and team projects. Incoming class size remains the same from year to year—about 375 students in each class—to allow professors to engage in hands-on learning to bridge theory and real-world practice.

FACULTY FACTS

Full-time faculty employed by the b-school: 167

Adjunct or visiting faculty: 56

Permanent/tenured professors: 67

Tenured faculty who are women: 10

Tenured faculty who are underrepresented minorities: 8

SAMPLING OF NOTABLE PROFESSORS

- Mary Barth: Only U.S. academic seat holder on the International Accounting Standards Board
- Hau Lee and Seungjin Whang: Pioneers in the subject of supply chain management in business schools
- Jeffrey H. Moore: Co-author with Larry R. Weatherford of the textbook *Decision Modeling with Microsoft Excel*
- James Patell: Facilitated the groundbreaking partnership between Stanford and the Light Up the World Foundation, a nonprofit that brings safe, affordable lighting to people in Mexico, India, and China
- Jeffrey Pfeffer: Expert in organizational behavior; author or co-author of 13 books, including his latest book to be published in 2010: *Power: An Organizational Survival Guide*

What Admissions Is All About

Stanford is keen on diversity. Diversity, diversity, diversity. On the surface, this includes lengths of work experience, ethnic backgrounds, geographic regions, male and female, and industry experience. Yet, true diversity is not based on these defined categories. "Breadth of experience" is a term Stanford uses to describe the full measure of the concept. Neil Morganbesser, class of 1990, advises applicants, "Stress what is unique about you. Make your leadership potential clear, make your personality stand out, but make it seem attractive as well. You won't get in if you're just another fill-in-the-blank, like the guy in the next cubicle, and you won't get in if you seem boring, or if you seem like [a jerk]."

"We look for students that will not just survive, but thrive in our rigorous academic program," says Lisa Giannangeli, Director of Marketing for MBA Admissions. "Test scores and transcripts lay the foundation, but your academic attitude is just as important as your aptitude. We value intellectual curiosity, a desire to learn and experience new things, and a willingness to share your knowledge with others." Your MBA from Stanford is a testament to your ability to invite all viewpoints and ways of learning to inform your best decisions.

Of course, the "regular stuff" such as transcripts, letters of recommendation, employment history, essays, and interviews are part of what draws admissions officers to select a prospective student. However, remember that diversity, intellectual vitality, initiative, passion, curiosity, demonstrated leadership potential, character, and integrity are the qualities that have molded you and will support your progress toward a Stanford MBA. Your impact on those around you and the capacity to do ordinary things extraordinarily well are highly valued.

"We evaluate academic performance, standardized scores, employment history, extracurricular activities, recommendations, and essays," says Giannangeli. "There is not one area that is more important than another. Imagine putting together a jigsaw puzzle without having a picture on the box to guide you. To begin, your academic profile forms the border of the puzzle—an important and necessary part of the puzzle—but by itself the picture would be incomplete. What give the puzzle definition and texture are the essays and letters of reference."

Because of Stanford's approach, it is important to note that (unlike most other programs) there is no minimum work experience required for admittance into the MBA program, and college seniors as well as recent graduates are welcome to apply.

The best advice you can follow comes from an admissions committee member who declares, "Stay away from formulas. There is no 'Stanford type' student, except that he or she is someone who does not follow formulas for admission." Stanford today is always looking forward, making certain that the school continually sharpens its curriculum, renews its campus and its extended community, and stays on top of the game as a worldwide player among MBA programs.

Full-time MBAs receiving financial aid through school: 63%

Institutional (need-based only) scholarships: 180

Assistantships: varies

Full-tuition scholarships school awarded for academic year: 23

Financially Aided

Financing your Stanford MBA requires advance planning. No matter what school you attend, MBAs are expensive, and the amount of debt you graduate with can affect your life for years to come. The Financial Aid Office recommends that all students should apply for financial aid. "Many students who think they are not eligible are surprised when they learn that they actually would have been eligible," says Jack Edwards, Director of Financial Aid. "For FY08, 75 percent of the MBA students applied for financial aid at Stanford Graduate School of Business, with 63 percent receiving some form of financial aid. On average, 50 percent of all MBA students are eligible to receive fellowships, and the average award is approximately $21,000. Sixty-four percent of MBA students will borrow student loans. For FY08, the GSB awarded approximately $7.3 million in fellowship funding and $24 million in student loans, both federal and private."

The GSB provides both merit-based and need-based financial aid. All students may qualify for fellowships and loans, including permanent residents and international students. There are no merit-based fellowships. Examples of aid are GSB fellowships, the Charles P. Bonini Partnership for Diversity Fellowship, outside scholarships, and federal and private loans. The Stanford Management Internship Fund provides fellowships to students who work in qualifying nonprofits or the government between the first and second year. The Entrepreneurial Summer Program (ESP) provides credit to students working as summer interns at entrepreneurial companies. In 2008, Stanford partnered with Reliance Dhirubhai India Education Fund. Based on financial need, Stanford GSB awards five Indian students full scholarships to attend the two-year MBA program.

Typically, financial need, determined by your aid application, is met with a quarter to a third in fellowship funds and the rest in loans. Every student, however, is expected to contribute a portion of his or her income and assets, as well as to consider lifestyle changes that will reduce the burden of debt after graduation. To this end, Stanford offers a "CashCourse" Web site that defines and illustrates financial basics such as budgeting, dealing with overspending, setting monetary goals, dealing with credit cards, and handling general financial planning. CashCourse provides useful worksheets and teaches you how to pay for school while living life so that your money doesn't control you. The site hones your personal financial skills.

FULL-TIME MBA PROGRAM (TOTAL DIRECT COSTS)

In-state: $102,642

Out-of-state: $102,642

International: $102,642

What Stanford Students Know

Contrary to one persistent rumor, there is no "typical" GSB student. What makes the Stanford MBA experience unique is as much what you make of it as what is offered to you. Neil Morganbesser relates what he believes his alma mater values that is unlike other schools. "Stanford makes the experience well rounded and fun, not grueling or focused on suffering." Morganbesser reveals the prevailing attitude when he was a student: "If you're not capable of having fun outside of school at Stanford, you were looked down upon. Anyone who focused unduly on the 'school' part of business school was missing out on a key part of experience, and particularly at Stanford. It taught me clearly that success is not just a function of brains or effort, but social interaction as well."

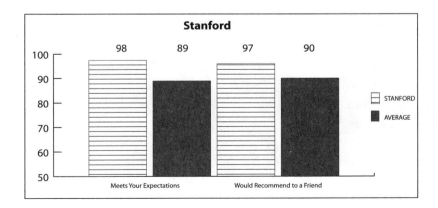

However, Morganbesser might have missed out on this valuable lesson altogether. "I applied to Harvard, Chicago, Wharton, and Stanford. Harvard rejected me. Stanford was my second choice. It should have been my first, but I was an East Coast kid (and Harvard undergrad)." He continues, "What attracted me was the quality of the program and of the student body and professors—but I evaluated these by reading about them in guidebooks and looking at rankings and assessing desirability of getting the brand name." Actually becoming a member of the Stanford GSB's incoming class, Morganbesser notes, was something of a shock. "It surprised me that it was so fun. It was hard work (a lot of work, particularly first year), but it was very team-oriented. The whole team thing was a new approach for me, and it required a new way of dealing with situations ... [and the] class participation thing was different. You were graded on how you spoke up in class—but the content wasn't the key thing. There often wasn't a right answer, and so some classes seemed frustrating because people just talked to hear themselves talk."

Stanford GSB students adhere to an honor code, a requirement that only a minority of other programs have. Whether exams are taken in the classroom or out, they are timed and open book. Because the same rules apply, if you know your stuff, you will make the test deadline. If you don't, no matter where you take the test, it is not going to make much difference! Also take into consideration that study time is at a premium during the first year. For example, before mid-term exams, students have an "extra" class. For a week after the regular schedule when you would expect to be studying for tests, instead you might be cramming in exercises for negotiations. You might be working with your group to position your fictional company. You might be working on your group presentation to the rest of the class after trying hard to reach a solution with the clock ticking. This is one of the methods professors utilize to solidify the guiding principles of business.

CAREER CHECK: STANFORD MBA EMPLOYMENT BY JOB FUNCTION

- Financial Services: 37%
- Consulting: 27%
- Technology: 12%
- Non-Profit: 5%
- Real Estate: 4%
- Consumer Products: 3%
- Media/Entertainment: 3%
- Pharmaceutical/Biotechnology/Healthcare Products: 3%
- Petroleum/Energy: 2%
- Manufacturing: 1%

What's Next? Your Career

There's no pigeonholing of Stanford graduates. There's no mold that can hold such varied talents and interests that graduates bring to their careers. You can lump them under an industry label, but that's as far as it goes. Every consultant brings a new perspective. Every financial services business-person brings a new point of view to the table. As a demonstration, the diversity of industries among Stanford's 30 billionaires include investors Sid Bass, Richard Rainwater (oil futures), Vinod Kohsla, founder Philip Knight (shoe and sportswear manufacturing), Omid Kordestani (high-tech consumer initiatives), and Lorenzo Zambrano Trevino (cement production).

Every GSB student has access to advisors at the Career Management Center who help him or her develop both personal and professional skills and goals that enable each student to make strategic decisions to accelerate achievement of those goals.

The class of 2008 is a prime example. More than 80 percent of graduating students reported a change in both industry and job function from their pre-MBA positions. Nearly 17 percent accepted positions in the Northeastern United States and more than 20 percent accepted positions outside North America. Compensation for Stanford MBA graduates is consistently among the highest of MBA peer schools ($123,171 average base salary for graduates in 2008). But compensation is only one consideration because students report accepting positions primarily for the people, for the opportunity to broaden their careers, or to engage in stimulating intellectual discussions. So throw out the rule book. Stanford GSB graduates know how to weather the hills and valleys of their career paths and pave not only their way but the ways of the future.

"Recruiters have responded very positively to Stanford's all-new MBA curriculum, introduced in 2007," says Celia A. Harms, Senior Associate Director, Recruiting Services & Marketing. "The new curriculum is more personalized with more student advising, more course levels to fit student experience, expanded leadership development, and more global content. An international experience in a country students have not lived or worked in—fulfilled by a study trip, service learning trip, internship, or exchange—is required of all students. The new curriculum allows each student among the incoming class members to take courses that best match their individual backgrounds."

New in 2009 are the Social Innovation Fellowships. This experimental social support program aids graduates who shoulder the research and implementation necessary to address the most entrenched social and environmental problems worldwide. The fellowships are awarded for nonprofit companies that focus on helping marginalized members of societies.

ALUMNI ACTUALS

MBA alumni worldwide: 16,000+

Business school alumni networking site: https://alumni.gsb.stanford.edu

Current MBA students have access to the alumni database.

Stanford alumni are an important part of the GSB experience, actively participating through mentorship, speaking engagements, project resources, and recruiting. These relationships often create lifetime friendships and invaluable networking opportunities. According to the 2007–2008 class surveys, 5 percent of MBA alumni speak four or more languages. Thirteen percent speak three or more. Nearly half speak only one language. Sixty-six percent of alumni outside the United States use a foreign language in business.

Alum Neil Morganbesser reflects, "The point of business school, it seems, is to get a feel for the world of business, get exposed to a wide variety of future business types, make important connections, and get the signaling of the MBA and the brand to let the world know how good you are." Students are also exposed to a wider world. Morganbesser comments he did not anticipate "the exposure to the various disciplines that were not my focus. I knew some finance, I was going into finance, and I took more finance classes, but what I really got out of business school was the benefit of the classes in operations, organizational behavior, accounting, and most of all marketing—all of which were a little alien to me. Stanford also provides a unique exposure to the tech world—the whole Silicon Valley/ entrepreneurship connection. That wasn't for me, but is attractive and enticing, and I'm glad I got familiar with it."

Match Made in Heaven: Is the Stanford Graduate School of Business Right for You?

You are an ideal student if you

- Are open-minded, forward-thinking, and solve problems creatively as well as analytically while working with exceptionally diverse classmates.
- Possess Stanford's values of intellectual vitality, demonstrated leadership potential, and personal makeup of high character so that you will make lasting contributions to society.
- Seek a preponderance of educational subjects as well as exposure to the local high-tech business community.
- Are a nonconformist thinker who looks forward to engaging in new ideas and are genuinely interested in global business.

University of California, Berkeley Walter A. Haas School of Business

S545 Student Services Building, #1900
Berkeley, CA 94720

Phone: 510.642.1405
E-mail: mbaadms@haas.berkeley.edu
Web site: http://mba.haas.berkeley.edu

Dean: Richard K. Lyons

"What differentiates us from other business schools is that Haas embodies innovation, responsible business, and confidence without attitude, all of which contributes to teamwork." —Dean Lyons

Quick Facts

MBA PROGRAMS

Full-time MBA
Part-time MBA (evening and weekend)
Executive MBA, Berkeley-Columbia

FULL-TIME MBA SNAPSHOT

Total enrollment: 500
Class of 2010: 240
Length of program: 21 months
Campus: Berkeley, CA
Program commences in August
Pre-term orientation attendance: None

APPLICATION NOTES

Requirements: Professional experience not required but highly recommended (average work experience is five years); a four-year bachelor's degree or equivalent, with no other MBA; GRE not accepted
Letters of recommendation: 2
Interview: By invitation only
Number of applicants: 3,779
Admittance rate: 12%

(continued)

(continued)

CLASS OF 2010

Male 68%, Female 32%
Minority Americans: 33%
International: 30%
Average age: 28
Combined average years of work experience: 5 years
GMAT average score: 710
GMAT score range (20th–80th percentile): 660–760
GPA average: 3.54

ACADEMIC BACKGROUND OF INCOMING STUDENTS

Business: 22%
Computer Science: 5%
Economics: 23%
Engineering: 26%
Humanities: 7%
Natural Sciences: 4%
Social Sciences: 8%
Other: 3%

The Rise of West Coast Education

Although the business school was not named after him, Arthur Rodgers was the first to envision how the University of California could fulfill its charter by establishing the College of Commerce. Rodgers's original vision was to offer Americans international education as they traveled across the Pacific Ocean to East Asia, studying history, social science, and of course, commerce. Until then, European schools were the primary source of education in commerce. Germany had dozens of commerce education programs, yet not one American university offered a formal degree in the area. All of that changed in 1898 with the launch of the University of California's College of Commerce. San Francisco was the leading economic and financial center of the West Coast, and students were in no short supply as many young men—invigorated by the lure of adventure—flocked to the College of Commerce so they could study abroad in China, Japan, and later Russia.

Enter the Clothing King: The College of Commerce now bears the name of the former chairman and president of the San Francisco–based Levi Strauss & Company. Walter A. Haas, Sr., was an extremely talented businessman. He began working at the company and rose through the ranks to change the struggling business from selling mainly dry goods to focusing on other products. Haas and his two sons, Walter Jr. and Peter, altered the company's business emphasis many times to anticipate the marketplace. The Haas family watched the company grow from a primary distributor of denim jeans to one of the largest clothing manufacturers in the world. Today the business has diversified into a multi-billion-dollar profit maker composed of several strategic business units. The College of Commerce benefited as the Haas family donated the first dollars for the construction of the facilities in 1989 and provided the initial endowment.

Scenes from Haas.

The Haas Business School has educated and developed business leaders for more than 100 years. Known for its diversity and quality of students, faculty, and staff, it has created an innovative academic environment committed to fostering a culture of teamwork, entrepreneurship, and new perspectives.

Although it is the oldest business school at a public university in the United States, the school is influenced heavily by the cutting-edge teaching and research ethos and by its strong connections with business in nearby Silicon Valley. Some of the large industries include technology, biotechnology, venture capital, and private equity companies. On-campus visits by executives—including teaching stints—are regular events at the school, and they create synergy between academics and local commerce. "Think Big" is a common ideology among MBA candidates.

Executive Director of MBA Admissions Peter Johnson explains that Haas provides "a constant emphasis on growth and change." He adds, "People will broaden their ability to think creatively by knowing different approaches.... Our country was founded on doing things differently." Today, "business is changing in the direction [Haas] has always been going. We were one of the early business schools to create a course in corporate and social responsibility [and] if anything, the business world is heading in our direction." Johnson emphasizes, "This isn't just an excellent educational experience, it's a life experience."

Why Haas?

"It's not only about the academic rigor," explains Peter Johnson. "People will broaden their ability to think creatively by knowing different approaches." Yet depth of academic resources is a well-known attribute, and Haas provides students with the opportunity to specialize by industry.

The Management of Technology Program is a response to the all-encompassing impact technology has on business. The program's focus is the management of the activities associated with bringing high-technology products to the global marketplace.

The Lester Center for Entrepreneurship and Innovation allows students to study entrepreneurship and the capitalization of fast-growth and high potential start-ups in the global and domestic markets. The program has business plan forums and hosts a business incubator for MBA students and alumni.

The Fisher Center for Real Estate and Urban Economics is one of the nation's top programs. Students are informed about careers in real estate finance, development, and investment. They can also study housing and the urban economy, which focuses on low-income housing and urban center development.

The Clausen Center for International Business and Policy is home to the International Business Development Program. The program focuses on global management issues and provides students the opportunity to work abroad as consultants to foreign businesses. Students are offered courses on international business and are assigned teams with specific countries of study.

Health-care programs and research are offered through the Certificate in Health Management Program. The program is taught by leading researchers from the U.C. Berkeley health care program. The Healthcare and BioBusiness Club allows students to study the impact of bio-technology on business and work with alumni, industry professionals, and other academic programs at their annual Business of Healthcare Conference.

The Center for Responsible Business reinforces the ethical and social responsibility of business and exposes students to the multifaceted issues surrounding a corporation's role in society. The Center fields one of the country's largest NetImpact Clubs whose aim is to educate and inspire future corporate leaders to promote innovative yet profitable socially responsible business practices to global business community.

The Center for Nonprofit and Public Leadership prepares leaders for the not-for-profit sector in the fundamentals of developing, funding, and marketing of nonprofits and public organizations. The program provides hands-on opportunities, and participants work with hundreds of nonprofit agencies and their leadership structures.

FUN FACTS

- The Berkeley community has been described as the quintessential hippie college town, with eclectic shops, gourmet restaurants, and boutique bookstores scattered throughout the surrounding neighborhood.

- Every month the school has what it calls the Consumption Function, which is typically sponsored by students, but at times is corporate sponsored. One time the students brought in 500 pounds of meat and had a South American festival.

- The Haas MBA is a family-oriented program. As evidence of this, the families in the class of 2008 produced almost two dozen children during their tenure.

Course Offerings

Haas believes that its leading areas of study for full-time MBA students are finance, general management, marketing, and strategy. Along with the many required courses are electives designed to reflect the current trends, ideas, and business thinking. Electives comprise 60 percent of the curriculum, and in addition, students can design courses in conjunction with faculty. Electives with a global perspective are encouraged, such as studies abroad and foreign business three-week internships.

CENTERS AND INSTITUTES

Asia Business Center

Center for Energy and Environmental Innovation

Center for Financial Reporting and Management

Center for Information Technology and Marketplace Transformation

Center for Innovative Financial Technology

Center for Law and Technology

Center for Nonprofit and Public Leadership

Center for Open Innovation

Center for Organization and Human Resources Effectiveness

Center for Responsible Business

Center for Telecommunications and Digital Convergence

Center for Young Entrepreneurs at Haas

Clausen Center for International Business and Policy

Fisher Center for Real Estate and Urban Economics

Fisher Information Technology Center

Intsitute for Business Innovation

Institute for Research on Labor and Employment (IRLE)

Institute for Business and Economics Research (IBER)

Institute of Management, Innovation, and Organization (IMIO)

Lester Center for Entrepreneurship and Innovation

Supply Chain Management Initiative

What Haas Professors Teach

The Haas philosophy of leadership and innovation translates into faculty members who are explorers and discoverers, seeking new ideas and insights of business knowledge. "They have to be good teachers," says Peter Johnson, "and they have to want to teach. That brings a certain type of person." This may explain the school's exceptionally high number of Nobel laureates. "The pressure to be a good teacher is very, very heavy," Johnson continues. As a result, professors approach their students to seek mutual benefit. Johnson explains, "I think they get the benefit from having a group of very talented people who are going to challenge them. They get a lot from the interaction with the students. Having that kind of interaction really adds to the experience for everyone."

In one example, a Haas professor who teaches management technology brings in guest speakers. Afterward he takes his students to a local restaurant where they discuss the lecture—and the professor picks up the tab. "That's exactly the type of professor you would like to have teaching you," Johnson says. "People exit our program with a broad view of what it means to be a leader in the 21st century."

FACULTY FACTS

Full-time faculty employed by the b-school: 84

Adjunct or visiting faculty: 136

Permanent/tenured professors: 76

Tenured faculty who are women: 20

Tenured faculty who are underrepresented minorities: 7

SAMPLING OF NOTABLE PROFESSORS

- Severin Borenstein: Specializes in the fluctuations of the nation's energy markets
- Jennifer Chatman: Leader in the field of organizational culture and post-merger integration
- Teck Ho and John Morgan: Utilize behavioral and experience economics for best strategic decisions
- Michael Katz: Leader in telecommunications strategy and policy
- Hayne Leland and Mark Rubinstein: Two of the world's most knowledgeable experts in the field of securities
- David Teece: Author of numerous books, including *Dynamic Capabilities and the Strategic Management of the Business Enterprises*
- Florian Zettelmeyer: Pioneer in exploring the impact of Internet technology and the effect of massive quantities of consumer data on corporate marketing

CONCENTRATIONS AND SPECIALIZATIONS OFFERED TO FULL-TIME MBA STUDENTS

Accounting	Global Management
Consulting	Health Care Administration
Corporate Social Responsibility	Health Care Management
E-commerce	Human Resource Management
Economics	Industrial Management
Entrepreneurship	International Business
Finance	Leadership

Management Information Systems	Public Administration
Manufacturing and Technology Management	Public Policy
Marketing	Real Estate
Media/Entertainment	Statistics and Operations Research
Operations Management	Strategy
Organizational Behavior	Supply Chain Management
Portfolio Management	Technology
	Transportation

JOINT DEGREES AND DUAL DEGREES

MBA/JD

MBA/MPH (Health Management)

MBA/MIAS (International and Area Studies)

What Admissions Is All About

Admissions officers across all MBA programs agree about one thing: Have you done your homework? Do you know the MBA program well so that you can clearly explain why you are applying? Can you speak with conviction on why your goals and the school's goals complement each other? At Haas, a section of the application inquires about what resources you have used to gather information about the program. This indicates that you have spent some serious thinking time considering the kind of educational experience that awaits you if you are accepted.

What is unique about you? This question may catch you off guard but it is a question that requires some thought and practice. Whether application numbers increase or decrease in any given season, competition is based more on your fit than on competition for available spaces. Peter Johnson cautions that the most important factor for acceptance is always the quality of your particular application. Along with that is demonstrating that you understand how you fit with Haas's overall MBA program. If you have a strong academic track record, progressive and successful work experience, and letters of recommendation that support your assertions, you will make a good MBA candidate, but will you make a good Haas MBA candidate?

Johnson advises that you "know what you want to do professionally and know what aspects of our program are going to get you there." He continues, "One of the things that we see in MBA applicants at large is an exaggerated focus in the applicant pool on the brand identity instead of what they are going to get from a particular school. Take the time you need to do due diligence. You have to come into the program knowing where you are heading so you don't just drift along." Haas looks for people "who want to be actively involved and drive change. It's not only about the academic rigor."

Most top business schools are strong in a number of discipline areas. Additionally, every business school is a member of its geographic community. When considering your career goals, look for a fit that provides networking in the industries that will support your interests. For Haas, the local geography is enhanced by a strong alumni network and full-time career services staff based in New York. Their presence connects West Coast students to East Coast businesses.

What attracts the attention of admissions officers? Scores matter, but what matters more is for you to explain exactly what interests you in your career and why you want to advance it through a Haas MBA. Because Haas offers so many possibilities, after class of 2009 student Swati Reichnuth was accepted, she faced a quandary. "I came to school and I saw there are so many things you can do." As a result, she says, her choice of strategy consulting as her future career "is something that's come about while I've been in school."

Although some schools are very good fits for their students, Haas admissions officers caution that a "perfect" fit may not be a top consideration. Most of the students Admissions has seen over the years would do very well at two or three different schools. The applicant must decide among the slightly different opportunities provided by each. Only you know which one best supports your learning experience and career goals.

Full-time MBAs receiving financial aid: 70%

Institutional (merit- and need-based) scholarships: varies

Assistantships: varies

Full-tuition scholarships school awarded for academic year: 11

Financially Aided

The number of financing options offered by Haas is an encouraging sign of the school's support for its students. First-year, second-year, domestic, and international students qualify for scholarships based on merit or achievement. Haas merit scholarships are awarded in variable amounts, ranging from partial to full tuition and fees for both years of full-time study. Haas achievement awards are given to individuals who have accomplished tremendous success in spite of significant economic, educational, health-related, or other obstacles. As with the merit scholarships, these are awarded at the time of admission and cover partial or full tuition and fees for both years of full-time study. Applicants for Haas Achievement Awards must have answered an optional essay question on the application for admission.

What else, you ask? Lots. Haas is fortunate to have numerous endowed fellowships. The Maxwell Fellows Program is available for entrepreneurial individuals, especially if you have a personal commitment to athletics. This fellowship is a two-year award for those who demonstrate a talent for innovative projects, products, and ideas. The CJ White Grant will interest you if you are planning a career in investment banking. The grant varies from half tuition to full tuition for both years of study. The

Jon Q. Reynolds Real Estate Entrepreneurs Scholarship is given by the faculty of the Fisher Center for Real Estate and Urban Economics to one student in real estate.

The Gap Inc. Scholars in Corporate Social Responsibility (CSR) is a fellowship program providing two-year scholarships to three full-time incoming Haas MBA candidates. You would be selected based on your strong commitment to the field of corporate social responsibility, commitment to ethical business practices on a global scale, and specific plans to integrate the principles of corporate social responsibility into your future career.

The Steve Tirado Scholarship Endowment Fund is for U.S. residents who are also Haas Achievement Award or Merit Scholarship recipients. The Michael Torres Family Fund provides scholarship support to Latino students of good academic standing, as well as future entering students, to reward and foster academic excellence. The Blue Duck Scholarship is awarded to an MBA applicant who has been accepted to Haas after graduating from the University of Oregon. Joint degree students in Public Health pursuing their MBA/MPH degrees may receive an Edgar F. Kaiser Fellowship or a Eugene E. Trefethen Fellowship, both of which underwrite tuition and provide stipends to the recipients.

Naturally, the Haas financial aid office will help you explore any and all federal loans for which you qualify. There are also private and supplement loans that you can consider.

FULL-TIME MBA PROGRAM (TOTAL DIRECT COSTS)

In-state: $66,475

Out-of-state: $84,055

International: $84,055

Part-time MBA costs: $2,049 per unit

What Haas Students Know

"Confidence without attitude" is a prevalent theme around Haas, which Swati Reichnuth has taken to heart. Reichnuth is an evening/weekend student. She works during the day and is taking three years to complete the MBA program. She is also part of the YEAH program—Young Entrepreneurs at Haas—the school's outreach program. "There's a confidence that comes from the academic surroundings and the fact that I'm learning all these things," she remarks. And she is especially happy to be involved in the YEAH program. About 150 students take part each year (undergrad and grad students), serving as mentors to more than 500 sixth to twelfth graders in local public schools. Reichnuth finds that working in the outreach program mirrors her own values: "Number one, it's being able to give back to the community. . . . If I hadn't been able to do the community outreach, I don't think my Haas experience would be complete."

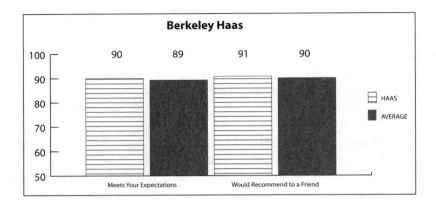

The director of the middle school program at the center, Olive M. Davis, says, "The teaching in the business school is very theory based. What the [YEAH] program gives them is experiential learning.... They learn they have to meet these underserved students where they are before they can take them where they want to be." Among the center's students in eleventh and twelfth grades, 100 percent who take part go on to college. Davis points out that the benefit goes both ways: "I think it's a learning experience for Haas students. I think it makes them better employees."

Because Haas demands an eclectic student mix, an average of 30 percent of incoming classes is international. The school believes it is crucial to pay attention to diversity in student experiences. "They really do mean it when they say they are looking for a diverse student body," Reichnuth affirms. Diversity is important, says Peter Johnson, "because the students are going to find they are leading a diverse work force."

For their part, international students need to understand the importance of extracurricular activities, since many of the strong benefits Haas students gain are through activities that are outside the classroom. Business-planning competitions, student treks, student clubs, and outreach volunteerism: Haas seeks individuals who embrace taking full advantage of all programs, both on and off campus. Olive Davis mentions that one of these opportunities is through YEAH. "International students use YEAH as a training ground."

"I think one of the important things in the business world is to build relationships," Swati Reichnuth comments. At Haas, "Everything is team based.... I wanted to be in an environment where that was the case." Peter Johnson adds that student functions "are very important as networking events. I think we make it pretty clear to students that the community expects it." For example, Haas has a socially responsible fund that students work on. It has about $1.7 million in assets. Community involvement, Johnson notes, "is a chance for them to use the concepts they are exploring while they are here and actually put them into practice."

Reichnuth says choosing Haas for her MBA was "one of the best decisions I've made."

What's Next? Your Career

Haas graduates highly competitive people who have been educated by tremendous faculty. Bart Young, class of 1975, comments that he found he possessed unique skills to be objective and develop criteria for the evaluation of anything. While at Haas, Young reflects, "I was recruited by a Menlo Park [California] firm to conduct a market research program for a new product. The research became my MBA thesis. My counselor, John Myers, told me the best way to evaluate the potential for the product was to segment the market and try to sell the product. 'Get out and show it to people,' he said. 'Document their feedback. Formalize an informal process.' I have used this technique dozens of times in my professional career and my conclusions are never wrong. Grassroots? Yes! Sophisticated? No. But it works every time. Warren Buffet would approve. Berkeley is very strong on practical solutions to real world problems."

As president of a chapter of the Haas Alumni Network, Young imparts that the position "provides me with a wonderful social network that has connected me to many fine people in Southern California. It is much like being active in a church. You make lifelong friends."

Asked how his MBA education has affected him, Young says, "Having attended the business school at Berkeley is the most significant achievement of my life. But the benefits of b-school didn't stop when I graduated. Instead, the confidence and skills I gained at Berkeley have grown inside me over the years. When in doubt, I clock back to those magical debates we had in school and take pleasure in being capable at arriving at a conclusion I can rationalize, articulate, and sell to others. I could not do this without my Berkeley experience. It's like you swallow a compass that guides you wherever you go. It's the Berkeley way finder!"

CAREER CHECK: HAAS MBA EMPLOYMENT BY JOB FUNCTION

- Finance/Accounting: 36%
- Marketing/Sales: 23%
- Consulting: 18%
- General Management: 18%
- Operations/Production: 2%
- Information Systems: 1%
- Other: 2%

ALUMNI ACTUALS

MBA alumni worldwide: 10,800+

Business school alumni networking site: http://haas.berkeley.edu/alumni

Current MBA students have access to the alumni database.

Match Made in Heaven: Is the Haas School of Business Right for You?

You are an ideal student if you

- Want to take advantage of the entire range of the school's available opportunities, such as the business plan competitions and consulting engagements in a diverse, collaborative community.
- Seek an education anchored in the fundamentals of management as well as the latest business theories and best practices.
- Thrive on innovation and unconventional thinking.
- Wish to jump-start your career through the many connections the school offers locally and internationally.

University of California, Los Angeles (UCLA) Anderson School of Management

110 Westwood Plaza
Los Angeles, CA 90095

Phone: 310.825.6944
E-mail: mba.admissions@anderson.ucla.edu
Web site: www.anderson.ucla.edu

Dean: Judy D. Olian
Senior Associate Dean: Alfred E. Armstrong, Jr.
Senior Associate Deans, MBA program: Kevin McCardle and Charles Corbett
Senior Associate Dean, FEMBA and EMBA programs: Carla Hayn

"Schools of management and business are developing the next generations, and I mean plural, the next generations of leaders of institutions around the globe—profit, non-profit, government, and non-government. And I think most schools successfully deliver on that mission—in many diverse forms—and that's part of the strength of our industry." —Dean Olian

Quick Facts

MBA PROGRAMS

Full-time MBA
Part-time MBA (evening program, weekend program)
Executive MBA
Global EMBA (UCLA-NUC)

FULL-TIME MBA SNAPSHOT

Total enrollment: 686
Class of 2010: 360
Length of program: 21 months
Campus location: Los Angeles, CA
Program commences in mid-September
Pre-term orientation attendance not required

(continued)

(continued)

APPLICATION NOTES

Requirements: GMAT score; four-year bachelor's degree or equivalent; essays; resume; recommendations; GRE not accepted

Letters of recommendation: 2

Interview: By invitation only

Number of applicants: 3,693

Admittance rate: 29%

CLASS OF 2010 PROFILE

Male 66%, Female 34%

Minority Americans: 21%

International: 32%

Average age: 28

Married or Partnered, Single: 18%, 82%

Combined average years of work experience: 5 years

GMAT score average: 711

GMAT score range (20th–80th percentile): 660–760

GPA average: 3.55

ACADEMIC BACKGROUND OF INCOMING STUDENTS

Business: 23%

Economics: 19%

Engineering: 24%

Humanities: 7%

Math/Sciences: 9%

Social Sciences (other): 11%

Other: 7%

From Seven Founders, Seven Decades of Education and Growing

The UCLA School of Management was founded in 1935 by seven members of the economics and accounting faculty. At the time these teachers established the College of Business Administration, John Edward Anderson, the school's future namesake, was an 18-year-old high school senior who would graduate valedictorian of his class. After serving in World War II, Anderson went to law school at Loyola in Los Angeles. When UCLA changed the name of its business school in 1955 to the Graduate

School of Business Education, Anderson had already established his own law firm. When the school became the Graduate School of Management in 1971, Anderson had been operating his company called Ace Beverages for 15 years. Then, in 1987, Anderson donated $15 million to the school that now bears his name. At that time, his gift was the largest ever received from an individual to further higher education.

The school occupies its own building on the main campus of the University of California, Los Angeles. The business school emphasizes state-of-the-art, research-based management training in all management functions and disciplines so that both generalists and specialists can meet their career goals. Anderson employs a broad range of teaching methods and maintains a balance between theory and practice and between individual and team approaches.

On campus at UCLA.

Anderson combines first-class teaching and research, a selective admissions process, a track record of success for its graduates, and outstanding facilities to provide an optimal learning environment. Anderson's world-class faculty includes educators and researchers who are experts in many areas of business, including marketing, finance, accounting, operations management, business economics, information systems, and more. The curriculum at Anderson School is driven by the theme of leadership. You have opportunities to develop your leadership skills through team-based management challenges in the Applied Management Research Program and the Global Access Program (GAP). You also can take leadership roles through the student activities and associations the school offers. No matter what you are seeking, as a student at Anderson, you are guaranteed a solid, rigorous business program in a cooperative and friendly student culture. You are provided with easy access to a strong business community and extensive support services both for academic and career advancement.

The Anderson School is home to numerous research centers focusing on various aspects of the business world; a Career Management Center that assists students with networking and employment; and the Marschak Colloquium, which sponsors presentations from leaders in the field and provides a forum for interaction among students, faculty, and visitors to the school.

Why Anderson?

Anderson offers several specialties that few other MBA programs can match, while still leading the pack in the more traditional areas that many of its students value. Anderson's business program consists of a general management curriculum that offers students the flexibility to choose from specializations in 11 different areas—or even create their own. The specializations include Accounting, Finance, Information Systems, Entrepreneurial Studies, Marketing, and Real Estate. For the trailblazing team player, Anderson is a match that can't be beat.

With a reputation as one of the best business schools in the world, Anderson features an award-winning faculty well known for their research and teaching. The members of this premier faculty eagerly share their scholarship and expertise in such fundamental areas as finance, marketing, accounting, business economics, decision sciences, operations and technology management, human resources and organizational behavior, information systems, strategy, and policy. In addition, Anderson alumni are successful in all areas of the business world and give back to their alma mater in numerous ways. For example, Anderson alumni recruit graduates into some of the world's top companies. This isn't just about loyalty; it's about putting the best-trained leaders in the best positions possible. An Anderson grad ensures a great match.

Leadership is the name of the game at Anderson, and this theme is prevalent throughout the curriculum. As an MBA student, you are exposed to such activities as working in teams on real-world management challenges in the Applied Management Research Program and in the Global Access Program. Additionally, many opportunities for leadership exist in the school's many organizations and campus activities.

Anderson's location enables it to have a distinct advantage in the global marketplace because it is situated on both the Pacific Rim and the Latin American Rim. The diversity of cultures and languages in the city of Los Angeles allows students to blend theory with practice, combining local and global viewpoints, experience big business or small entrepreneurial start-ups, and understand what differentiates profit-making organizations from nonprofits. One recent venue for this broad view in education was the 2009 Strategy and the Business Environment Conference. The objective of this annual conference is "to explore the interrelationships between the business strategies of firms and the social, legal, and political environment in which they operate." The location changes every year, with past conferences hosted at Wharton, Stanford, Harvard, Kellogg, and Fuqua. The conference brings together scholars interested in integrating business environment issues and business strategy.

FUN FACTS

- Heather Locklear attended UCLA for a time before choosing acting as her career. Her father, William Locklear, served as UCLA Registrar and Director of the office of Residence Life, among others.
- UCLA coach Tommy Prothro's briefcase sat on the sidelines of every game he coached. People are still wondering whether it even had anything in it!

- Alison Brown, class of 2005, is an award-winning banjo player who recently released her 11th album of bluegrass music.
- UCLA Anderson has added a new twist to one of its essay requirements: It has to be just 250 words and can be audio or text.

Course Offerings

Before you venture into the land of the MBA core, you will complete a five-day, two-unit Leadership Foundations pre-term to introduce you to Anderson's learning culture and the MBA curriculum. It is a valuable week to develop the mindset for your foray into Year One of your coursework. You will also get to know the faculty and classmates.

Year One is the Management Core, 10 courses or 40 units in three quarters of rigorous study. Anderson's scholastic calendar is divided into quarters instead of semesters. Covering the major disciplines of business and the functional areas of business, the first year gives all students a common and solid base to build Year Two, which focuses on the electives that give each MBA its flavor. Seventy-two students comprise each Year One section (known as a cohort at other schools) and gives all students a chance to cultivate relationships within their teams, partnerships that often last into Year Two.

Year Two hinges on customization. You will explore and build through electives to meet your designated career goals. Twelve courses or 46 units comprise your elective year, and most students emphasize certain functional and specialty areas of study. Advanced electives are required for 9 of the 12 elective courses. The final 3 courses are considered "free" electives. Luckily, UCLA has the fifth largest library in the nation, so whatever you choose to explore, you have plenty of resources to research.

The Applied Management Research Project (AMRP) is the final requirement and lasts for two quarters of the second year. Eighty teams of MBA students complete an original AMRP that integrates and expands students' capacity to solve those complex business problems that business leaders face every day. Your team may choose one of three options: Management Field Study, Business Creation, or Special Project.

RESEARCH CENTERS

BIT Global Research Network

Center for International Business Education and Research (CIBER)

Laurence D. and Lori W. Fink Center for Finance and Investments

Entertainment and Media Management Institute (EMMI)

The Harold and Pauline Price Center for Entrepreneurial Studies

Richard S. Ziman Center for Real Estate

UCLA Anderson Forecast

What Anderson Professors Teach

UCLA is widely recognized for its high caliber of intellectual pursuit through teaching and research. Anderson recruits and retains only the highest quality faculty, which is a priority for the school. The diverse and esteemed faculty members publish papers in leading scholarly journals, receive recognition for research excellence, provide leadership in and beyond UCLA, and serve as student mentors. For example, Eric Sussman has advised MBA and FEMBA teams in all things finance and has an unparalleled level of expertise in investment that his students value. Bill Cockrum teaches entrepreneurship, ethics in business, and other subjects. He brings his personal experience into the classroom to demonstrate how the coursework applies to the complicated business world.

Teamwork has always been a central theme of the UCLA Anderson learning model. As such, it is no coincidence that Anderson faculty strive to provide learning experiences that afford students the opportunity to build upon and refine their teamwork skills. After all, successful business men and women must be able to collaborate and communicate well in the work world. Students utilize the latest technology to learn, communicate, and grow, all the while maintaining a collegial, professional environment in which succeeding together is prized.

Part of teamwork is valuing inclusion. Anderson excels at diversity across the board. The Entrepreneurial Bootcamp for Disabled Veterans, for example, is conducted by the Harold and Pauline Price Center for Entrepreneurial Studies and provides more than a year of practical, high-quality training. The program consists of three phases. Through self-study sessions veterans carry on discussions with Anderson faculty before participating in the nine-day, on-campus workshops and seminars. Following this is mentorship and educational support with faculty members.

Regardless of what program you choose, the goal of Anderson educators is to prepare you to think creatively about the important business issues of the day. In addition, leadership skills aren't something people are born knowing, but instead need to be taught and developed. Anderson teaches you the skills you need to make a real impact on the world and its global economy.

FACULTY FACTS

Full-time faculty employed by the b-school: 101

Adjunct or visiting faculty: 16

Permanent/tenured professors: 62

Tenured faculty who are women: 7

Tenured faculty who are underrepresented minorities: 12

Tenured international faculty: 10

SAMPLING OF NOTABLE PROFESSORS

- Anthony Bernardo: Award-winning teacher; associate editor for the *Review of Financial Studies*; author of papers published in journals such as *Journal of Finance*, *Journal of Financial Economics*, *Journal of Political Economy*, *Quarterly Journal of Economics*, and *Review of Financial Studies*

- William Cockrum: One of the top teachers of entrepreneurship in the world
- Charles Corbett: Editor-in-chief of *Foundations and Trends in Technology, Information and Operations Management*; current or former editor of *Management Science, Manufacturing and Service Operations Management, Operations Research*, and *Production and Operations Management*
- Sanford Jacoby: Author of several books, including *The Embedded Corporation: Corporate Governance and Employment Relations in Japan and the United States*; co-editor of *Comparative Labor Law and Policy Journal*; serves on the editorial boards of other journals, including *California Management Review, Enterprise and Society, Industrial Relations, Labor History*, and *Work and Occupations*
- Edward Leamer: Director of UCLA Anderson Forecast; author of *Macroeconomic Patterns and Stories: A Guide for MBAs*

CONCENTRATIONS AND SPECIALIZATIONS OFFERED IN FULL-TIME MBA PROGRAM

International Business

JOINT DEGREES AND DUAL DEGREES

MBA/JD	MBA/MSN (Nursing)
MBA/MD	UCLA-NUS Global Executive MBA
MBA/MCS (Computer Science)	

What Admissions Is All About

To maintain a family-like atmosphere, Anderson limits each entering class to 360 students. This allows close relationships among students and faculty alike. UCLA Anderson's admissions committee selects and admits those students who exemplify excellence in both their academic performance and their overall abilities to enrich the overall educational experience. Admissions officers review biographical and academic background information; GMAT scores and TOEFL scores (for most international applicants); as well as achievements, awards, and honors that you bring. Additionally, employment history, letters of recommendation, and college and community involvement—especially where candidates have served in leadership capacities—are considered.

UCLA Anderson's Director of Admissions Mae Jennifer Shores says she wants applicants "to understand the school's strong belief and commitment to social enterprise. The school's record of social enterprise involvement goes back much further than that of other area business schools." She continues, "The activities available to Anderson students are without parallel at competing schools, including students clubs, student activities, academics, and opportunities for professional experience."

There are four rounds during which an applicant can apply to Anderson. Once an application is received in its entirety, it is sent for review to individual committee members. Application review is holistic in nature, and decisions to interview or deny are based on the strength and merit of the entire application. The initial admissions review can be lengthy; every effort is made to thoroughly review applicants.

The decision to interview is made at this point, and applicants who have successfully survived the first round of reviews are sent invitations. Candidates for admission are interviewed by a panel of faculty, current students, and other individuals. The admissions committee is very diverse, affording the benefit of multiple perspectives during the evaluation process. The committee is composed of seasoned admissions officers who represent formal training and direct experience in business, higher education, and the not-for-profit sectors. The school's varied and deep industry experience allows the committee to collectively craft a similarly rich and diverse class of students.

Once the post-interview evaluations have been completed, the committee has one more formal meeting to give all the files a final review. At this time some decisions may be revised as needed by group consensus. Once done, candidates are issued letters of invitation and acceptance into the prestigious UCLA Anderson MBA program.

Full-time MBAs receiving financial aid through school: 71%

Institutional (merit-based and need-based) scholarships: 255

Full-tuition scholarships school awarded for academic year: 78

Financially Aided

The pursuit of any degree can be costly. However, the financial aid department at UCLA Anderson would rather have students focus on the Anderson experience rather than financial burdens. Hence, UCLA offers merit and need-based fellowships, loans, and non-need-based loans to all students who qualify for assistance, including permanent residents and international students. Just the same, MBA candidates are advised to begin saving far in advance of applying to the program, as all students are expected to contribute some portion of their income toward their Anderson education. Approximately 70 percent of graduate students receive financial aid in the form of scholarships, loans, and assistantships. Stipends and programs dedicated for minority students include first-year minority student fellowships, which pay tuition and fees plus a stipend; second-year students receive a small stipend.

FULL-TIME MBA PROGRAM (TOTAL DIRECT COSTS)

In-state: $66,590

Out-of-state: $77,126

International: $77,126

EMBA program costs: $100,000–$144,000

What Anderson Students Know

Every spring the MBA program's admitted students are treated to Anderson Days (also known as "A Days") where some 200 attending students and more than 100 MBA candidates volunteer. A Days are a chance to show off Anderson's friendly community, fired-up academicians, fierce school loyalty, and fun social activities. Most days for students at UCLA Anderson are dominated by the MBA program from orientation until they earn their degree. However, the MBA experience is not complete without allowing for relaxation to relieve the packed program. For instance, Evelyn Lee, class of 2010, comments how the seemingly normal students at the b-school can get downright crazy given the chance . . . and enough food. During her two weeks of orientation, she "had the types of experiences—spending so much time with your classmates that you have to bond—that make for lasting memories. And it was so much fun."

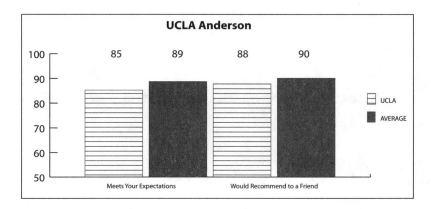

Naturally, you will want to take advantage of a number of student clubs. Anderson has a wide range of more than 30 clubs. Activities allow you to network early and often through events that focus on education, socialization, and recruiting. New in 2008 was the Anderson Automotive Association. And what was the club's first activity? A visit to the showroom of car-of-the-future manufacturer Tesla Motors, which designed the all-electric Roadster.

Part of student bonding is with your classmates, but another part is through helping your community. The largest of Anderson's charitable organizations is Challenge for Charity (C4C), in which volunteers participate in fundraising for LA Works and Special Olympics. Anderson participates in C4C along with eight other business schools on the West Coast. Whichever school team raises the most money is rewarded with the highly prized "Golden Suitcase." As befitting such a team-spirited group, Anderson won the C4C accolade in the 2008–2009 and the 2007–2008 contests by scoring the most volunteer hours served and the most money raised; plus, it received high scores in the accompanying sports events.

What's Next? Your Career

Anderson offers its students stellar opportunities for networking and connecting to career opportunities. More than 300 companies recruit on campus each year. Thanks to a close partnership with the Parker Career Management Center, you can be assured that every effort is taken to ensure your success in your long-term career goals. The Parker Career Management Center (Parker CMC) provides exceptional career services that are delivered professionally, in a timely manner, and with an eye for customer satisfaction. Staff at the Parker CMC helps you identify your career objectives, locate resources, seek out job opportunities, and network. They work on all aspects of the job search experience with you, including coaching you to improve and refine your interviewing skills.

During fall and winter terms, recruiters flock to the school to give presentations to those interested in learning more about the featured company. Employer briefings occur routinely Monday through Thursday. A typical session includes a formal presentation and a question-and-answer session for those in attendance. Likewise, corporate presentations are held Monday through Wednesday and include light refreshments. These events are great opportunities to network, often with excellent results. Once specific requirements have been met, UCLA Anderson second-year full-time MBA students, second-year EMBA students, and third-year FEMBA students may participate in on-campus recruiting.

CAREER CHECK: ANDERSON MBA EMPLOYMENT BY JOB FUNCTION

- Financial Services: 27%
- Technology: 16%
- Consulting: 15%
- Consumer Products: 10%
- Media/Entertainment: 10%
- Real Estate: 7%
- Manufacturing: 3%
- Pharmaceutical/Biotechnology/Healthcare Products: 3%
- Nonprofit: 2%
- Petroleum/Energy: 2%
- Other: 5%

ALUMNI ACTUALS

MBA alumni worldwide: 33,000+

Business school alumni networking site: http://alumni.anderson.ucla.edu

Current MBA students have access to the alumni database.

With Anderson's top-notch faculty, state-of-the-art facilities, and hands-on learning approach, it is no wonder that Anderson grads are successful worldwide. Rebecca Matthews, class of 2006, believes that the Anderson school gave her the "exact experience I needed to make the transition to my career." Anderson had the perfect mix of academics, resources, and a strong culture of mutual support. She found mentors and was able to "build lasting relationships not only with peers, but also the faculty, administrators, alumni, and members of the business community," allowing her to network effectively and gain the resources she needed. Now that she has returned to the business world, she has found herself continuing to work with the same people she met at Anderson because of their continued guidance and support.

Anderson alumni are part of an elite group of more than 35,000 alumni who have graduated from UCLA's business school since its founding in 1935. The alumni association serves the purpose of providing programs, services, and opportunities through a combination of campus activities, alumni communications, and worldwide chapters and clubs. The alumni association also provides access to job postings online and sends e-mails to those who sign up. Alumni Career Services provides professional advice, webinars, and online coaching to help other graduates continue to grow their careers. Part of this includes access to the UC Library and eligibility to enroll family members in the Bruin Woods summer camp.

Dean Olian announced an ambitious $100 million fundraising campaign for the school in 2008, called Accelerate the Campaign for UCLA Anderson, which concludes in 2010. The first half of this sum was reached through private donations and the extraordinary generosity of Anderson's alumni. Their dedication and support spurred the campaign and proved once again that graduates have found lasting value in their education and because of it are able to support their school when called upon. One alum, fundraising co-chair Richard S. Ziman, contributed $1 million. Part of this donation is for the Richard S. Ziman Fellowship that contributes support for MBA students concentrating in real estate. The rest goes into the Richard S. Ziman Center. Jim Easton, UCLA class of 1959 and Board of Visitors member, contributed $2 million in 2008 to create the Jim Easton Global Connection Classroom—a state-of-the-art teaching and media communication facility that provides world-class connectivity. When people comment on Anderson's phenomenal alumni loyalty, this is what they mean!

Match Made in Heaven: Is the UCLA Anderson School of Management Right for You?

You are an ideal student if you

- Value learning in an ethnically, culturally, and otherwise diverse environment, with access to untold resources.
- Value hands-on, fully engaged learning experiences over the traditional lecture or case study approaches.
- Wish to learn in a small, intimate setting with small groups of like-minded, driven individuals.
- Want to succeed in a career path that involves entrepreneurship or wish to make a global impact within the business realm.

The University of Chicago Booth School of Business

5807 South Woodlawn Avenue
Chicago, IL 60637

Phone: 773.702.7369
E-mail: admissions@ChicagoBooth.edu
Web site: www.ChicagoBooth.edu

Dean: Edward A. Snyder
Deputy Dean, Full-Time MBA Program: Stacey Kole
Deputy Dean, Part-Time MBA Programs: Mark Zmijewski

"I think one thing that's peculiar about the job [as dean], especially as it relates to MBAs, is that MBAs come in either every 10 months or 20 months and within about a week of their arrival, they capitalize everything that you've done, so they put enormous pressure on you to improve, which is good." —Dean Snyder

Quick Facts

MBA PROGRAMS

Full-time MBA
Part-time MBA (evening program, weekend program)
Executive MBA (Chicago, London, and Singapore)
International MBA

FULL-TIME MBA SNAPSHOT

Total enrollment: 1,144
Class of 2010: 550
Length of program: 21 months
Campus location: Chicago
Program commences in August
Pre-term orientation attendance is required

APPLICATION NOTES

Requirements: Professional experience not required but highly recommended (average work experience is five years); four-year bachelor's degree or equivalent; GRE accepted
Letters of recommendation: 2
Interview: By invitation only

(continued)

(continued)

Number of applicants: 4,144
Admittance rate: 22%

CLASS OF 2010 PROFILE

Male 65%, Female 35%
Minority Americans: 25%
International: 33%
Average age: 28
Married or Partnered, Single: 22%, 78%
Average years of work experience: 5 years
GMAT score average: 713
GMAT score range (20th–80th percentile): 660–760
GPA average: 3.5

ACADEMIC BACKGROUND OF INCOMING STUDENTS

Business/Finance: 27%
Economics: 25%
Engineering: 24%
Social Sciences/Humanities: 24%

Booth's Researching Roots

At 5 p.m. on the evening of November 6, 2008, Dean Ed Snyder made the announcement at the Harper Center, and it was big news. One man in the audience was openly weeping, and Gene Fama was misty eyed. The University of Chicago Graduate School of Business had just changed its name. By 8 a.m. on Friday morning, the sign in front of the school and the name on the doors said "Chicago Booth"!

The Booth School of Business (previously known as the UC Graduate School of Business through the fall of 2008) is part of the University of Chicago. Booth maintains campuses at the University of Chicago's Hyde Park location and downtown on Chicago's Magnificent Mile. The university was founded in 1892 as a bastion for researchers. Established as the College of Commerce and Politics in 1898, it remained solely an undergraduate program until 1916. The school first offered an MBA degree in 1936. In 1994, it opened the Gleacher Center downtown, and in 2004 the state-of-the-art Charles M. Harper Center opened in Hyde Park.

On campus in Chicago.

Nestled in the neighborhood of Hyde Park, seven miles south of downtown Chicago, the University of Chicago's original campus welcomes visitors and students alike with its quiet, tree-lined streets and Gothic architecture. Left behind are the rumblings of the Windy City's ever-present traffic and daily hustle as students walk to class listening to the simple sounds of the breeze rustling through the leaves and of singing birds—including parrots.

Although the monk parrots' exact genesis is unknown, it is thought that decades ago several escaped after being brought to the area as pets from South America. In 1988, the city planned to remove the birds, but former Mayor Harold Washington wouldn't hear of it. His apartment overlooked a tree that was home to many of the birds' nests, and he was not about to allow his neighbors to be evicted. The parrots built up a solid population until 2004 when the numbers dwindled because the main tree that served as their home fell in a storm. Occasionally, residents can still see the green-feathered members of the monk parrot family on the University of Chicago campus and surrounding areas of Hyde Park. If they choose, students can become involved in charting the birds' migratory courses and helping to document the surviving birds.

Why Chicago Booth?

Chicago Booth enjoys a special place in American economic history as the birthplace of the "Chicago School" of economic thought—the influential theory developed during the 1950s that favors free market economics with minimal government intervention. Theoretical and research work conducted at the school has shaped America's economic policies, which are still followed today.

Chicago Booth is renowned for its academically intense but collegial atmosphere. Students come to Booth to learn from respected leaders in business and economics. All faculty members are required to teach as well as conduct research, so students are exposed to the most advanced theories. Many faculty members serve as consultants to leading businesses and are influential in shaping business and public policy.

Once settled into the school, students will discover that they are not only part of Chicago Booth but also part of the University of Chicago community. The school actively urges students to take advantage of everything the university has to offer from the cafes and restaurants to the college's film series and athletic events. For example, a pub next door to the Harper Center attracts students who relax with friends after a hard day in class or for a quick break during finals' week.

The school also enthusiastically encourages its students to become active in the community and volunteer with groups such as Give Something Back and Net Impact. Participants tutor at local schools, provide consulting services to nonprofit organizations, visit critically ill children at the University of Chicago Hospital, and work with Habitat for Humanity building homes. Volunteering fits closely into the overall Chicago Booth philosophy of enriching the students' career lives and their personal development as well.

"At Chicago Booth, the co-curricular life of the students is seen as an extension of their classroom experience," Associate Dean Ann Harvilla says. "The many activities of the student groups allow students to put theories they learn in their course directly and immediately into practice through their group's management and programming."

Harvilla points out that not all student activities are tied up with business-related events. "The GBC [Graduate Business Council] coordinates a variety of cultural and social activities, both on and off campus, that appeal to a wide range of student interests," she explains. Among them is the Friday Liquidity Preference Function that draws hundreds of students as well as faculty to chat over the beverage of their choice.

FUN FACTS

- Chicago Booth was the first business school to boast a Nobel laureate on its faculty as well as the first to boast a total of six Nobel prize winners.
- Chicago Booth was the first American MBA program with permanent campuses on the continents of North America, Europe, and Asia.
- Jay Berwanger, the winner of the first Heisman Trophy and the first player chosen during the National Football League's inaugural draft, played football at the University of Chicago when the school was a powerhouse in the Big 10 athletic conference. Varsity football was abolished in 1939, and it wasn't until 1969 that the current Division III program was reinstated.
- Chicago's famous deep-dish pizza converts hundreds of Booth students each year who are from regions where the thin-crust variety is more popular.
- Chicago has the most tennis courts per square mile of any city its size.

Cultural Diversity

With business increasingly becoming a global endeavor, Booth has developed the Office of International Programs. Through this department, students can take part in the International MBA (IMBA) degree. The program concentrates on mastering core business disciplines and developing first-rate analytical and problem-solving skills with a foundation in international business concepts and inter-cultural management skills. The program is highly competitive, has a second language prerequisite, and becomes the focus within the student's personally designed MBA program.

Additionally, students can participate in the International Business Exchange Program (IBEP), which hosts courses at 33 partner schools in 21 countries and in a variety of languages. Participating students travel for a few weeks or an entire term to countries as diverse as Austria, Brazil, Chile, China, India, Israel, The Netherlands, Singapore, South Africa, and South Korea.

Associate Director of Admissions and Financial Aid Joanne Legler advises students and potential students that the more involved a student becomes, the richer his or her experience will be. Experience is the component of education that leads students to their ultimate goals: internships and success in the job market.

More than one-third of the students in the on-campus graduate business programs are international, including many from Asia and Latin America. Although students must submit the results of an English proficiency exam as part of their admission process, Chicago Booth assists international students as they acclimate and continue learning English.

"Support for our international students includes mentoring by those who volunteer through the Graduate Business Council, our student government," explains Harvilla. "Professional support is offered by our Office of International Programs, which coordinates and implements the international student orientation prior to the start of autumn programming." Associate Dean for Student Recruitment and Admissions Rose Martinelli adds, "Each incoming class is very diverse—from all parts of the world—and represent all major functions and industries," which is why support is so important.

Chicago Booth has always prided itself in breaking new ground and setting the bar for others to follow. Among other firsts, in 1964, it was the first to offer minority student scholarships at a business school.

Course Offerings

All students have access to other graduate and undergraduate course offerings at the University of Chicago, one of the most widely respected research universities in the world. Students pursuing an Executive MBA may spend the residential period of their program at any one of the worldwide campus locations.

The school's curriculum provides students with essential business fundamentals and then allows them to follow their own interests. There is only one required course, Leadership Effectiveness and Development (LEAD), a 125-hour skill-building course that includes an outdoor adventure team-building experience. The flexible curriculum allows students to get to know a broader cross-section of their classmates because they do not take all their classes with one group. "I chose UC Booth because I liked the flexible curriculum," says Edwin Tan, a 2007 graduate of the school. "Most programs that I looked at required that you spend the first year through a preset schedule." Kelly Fuller, class of 2008 agrees, "It really changed my pace once I began school. I was attracted to this model because it would allow me more freedom when choosing my academic schedule," she explains. "I did not have to take some of the more entry level courses (for example, introductory accounting) that would have been mostly review for me."

In management lab classes, students can work with established corporations on consulting assignments or participate in new venture or small business enterprise labs to assist early-stage companies with market research, strategic development, and consumer and pricing studies.

The one required class, LEAD, simulates real-world situations in a safe and fun environment that allows students to challenge themselves as they prepare for the business world. LEAD is described as a "laboratory class," where participants practice communication skills such as negotiation, team-building, and offering feedback, skills that the school considers critical to success in the MBA program and in business. "LEAD was a great chance for us to break the ice and meet new people," Tan recalls.

As part of the University of Chicago community, MBA students can take up to six general university classes as part of their program. If you want to learn a foreign language to enhance your MBA, the opportunity is only a walk across campus away. Students take 20 classes, in addition to the LEAD course, during their two years at Booth. These courses are grouped as Foundation, Breadth, General Management, and Electives. The school maintains a multidisciplinary approach. Although concentrations are not required, most students develop deeper skills in at least one of the areas offered.

In addition, the school offers an Executive MBA that encompasses an additional edge for the international business world by allowing students to study at Chicago Booth's campuses in London or Singapore, an opportunity not available to the full-time or evening and weekend programs.

What Booth Professors Teach

Successful alumni know that a vibrant, involved faculty lies at the core of a great MBA education, and Chicago Booth is no different. "My favorite part of my two years at school was learning from an elite staff of professors," Tan reveals. "Most of the professors that I had were leaders in their field, and they took the classroom experience very seriously. And in a few situations, my professors went beyond the call of duty in terms of student accessibility."

The professors at Chicago Booth are at the top of their respective fields, many of them world renowned and award winning, including two Nobel Prize winners currently teaching at the Harper Center. Quite often it is the outgoing personality of professors that students cite as one of the favorite aspects of their experience.

Research plays a vital part in keeping any school at the top. Chicago Booth has nine research and learning centers covering areas such as price theory, population economics, and entrepreneurship (one of the most popular with students). Often the most well-liked classes are those with professors who are in the financial or business news and those who actively engage their students to help with their research work. These lab classes fill up quickly, and many students consider them as the most rewarding of the program.

"My favorite class was Managing the Workplace with Canice Prendergast," Fuller says. "It brought up a lot of issues in business that I will potentially have to deal with that I really had not thought about before." Fuller explains that she was so pleased with her experience because, "I felt I was learning practical skills and tools instead of just theoretical issues I might never need in my career." Fuller learned how to deal with real problems that can't be solved with equations. "It was so different than anything I would have normally taken."

The faculty approved changes in the school's curriculum that will add flexibility to an MBA program already known for allowing students wide latitude in course selection. The changes go into effect for students beginning in the summer of 2009.

School officials explained that "although we are giving students more flexibility, this is not a radical departure from our curriculum." In discussions with recent alumni, current students, and corporate recruiters, the existing curriculum consistently received high marks. More than 90 percent of Booth's recent graduates said they were satisfied with the business education they received.

The faculty also voted to add a new academic concentration in analytical management and require all students in the evening MBA program and weekend MBA program to take a leadership development course similar to one required of full-time students. The new course requirement for part-time students was enacted because the faculty felt it is essential that all graduates be exposed to a well-executed leadership program that includes a self-assessment component coupled with opportunities to enhance interpersonal skills.

The flexible Booth curriculum allows teachers such as Prendergast, the W. Allen Wallis Professor of Economics, to work with varied students with assorted interests. According to Ann Harvilla, "Students are free to choose courses according to a professor's teaching style, previous life/work experience, area of interest and relevance to the student's career goals. For these reasons, many professors across multiple areas generate a high demand for their courses year after year. Entrepreneurship, strategy, marketing and, most recently, real estate courses generally experience heavy enrollments."

FACULTY FACTS

Full-time faculty employed by the b-school: 128

Adjunct or visiting faculty: 47

Permanent/tenured professors: 64

Tenured faculty who are women: 3

Tenured faculty who are underrepresented minorities: 0

Tenured international faculty: 19

SAMPLING OF NOTABLE PROFESSORS

- John Cochrane: Present or former editor of the *Journal of Monetary Economics*, the *Journal of Business*, and the *Journal of Economic Dynamics and Control*
- James Schrager: Founding editor of the *Journal of Private Equity*; three-time winner of the Emory Williams Award for Excellence in Teaching
- Mark Zimjewski: Associate editor for *Accounting Review*; received a Hillel J. Einhorn Excellence in Teaching Award from Chicago Booth, an Emory Williams Award for Excellence in Teaching from Chicago Booth, and a Competitive Manuscript Award from the American Accounting Association; author of two books and several academic articles

(continued)

(continued)

- Kevin Murphy: Recipient of the MacArthur Fellow award, John Bates Clark Medalist, and author of two books and several academic articles
- Eugene Fama: Recipient of the Fred Arditti Innovation Award, the Deutsche Bank Prize in Financial Economics, and the Nicholas Molodovsky Award; serves as advisory editor for the *Journal of Financial Economics*

CONCENTRATIONS AND SPECIALIZATIONS OFFERED IN FULL-TIME MBA PROGRAM

Accounting	Human Resource Management
Analytic Finance	International Business
Econometrics and Statistics	Managerial and Organizational Behavior
Economics	Marketing Management
Entrepreneurship	Operations Management
Finance	Strategic Management
General Management	

JOINT DEGREES AND DUAL DEGREES

MBA/JD	MBA/MD
MBA/MA (International Business or Area Studies)	MBA/MPP (Public Policy)
	MBA/MA (Social Services)

What Admissions Is All About

"Every single piece of paper that's in an application gets looked at," says Joanne Legler, Associate Director of Admissions. She explains that Admissions prides itself on following a personal case-by-case process. To Legler and her staff, each applicant is much more than an identification number and a file.

"We would love to see more students coming straight out of college," Legler says. She explains that when Chicago Booth representatives attend recruiting fairs, she encourages all interested individuals to ask questions, no matter what their background. She and her colleagues want to meet with everyone who has an interest in a Chicago Booth MBA.

The industry background of students is extremely diverse. Although there is no stereotypical "Chicago Booth material," the school insists on certain characteristics of its students—qualities that cannot be faked or quickly learned at a summer job. As the application process proceeds, the admissions staff examine applications and letters of recommendation, and as the interview process begins, the true nature of a student's personality starts to emerge.

"People who are lazy aren't going to cut it here," Legler explains as an example. "You're either a hard worker or you're not." However, a serious work ethic isn't always enough. "We seek students who have a demonstrated record of success—professionally, academically, personally," Martinelli says. "Intellectually curious, engaged, and self-directed students thrive in Chicago Booth's flexible curriculum."

Once the admissions staff has received the required information and paperwork, they will select applicants to interview. Every applicant will eventually receive a letter of acceptance or rejection. Legler points out that it is important to the Admissions Office to offer closure for every applicant.

Full-time MBAs receiving financial aid through school: 77%

Institutional (merit-based and need-based) scholarships: 22

Assistantships: 19

Full-tuition scholarships school awarded for academic year: 25

Financially Aided

Before planning your next two years of classes, you need to undertake the often-daunting task of financing your education. Students are automatically considered for scholarships upon admission and can apply for separate fellowships. There are also a limited number of need-based grants available; however, they are offered in the order of processed applications, and prospective students in this category are urged to submit their application information early.

Some of the application requirements and financial aid offerings are a bit different for international students. All international applicants need a college or university degree equivalent to a four-year American baccalaureate degree. In concordance with the Bologna Accord, the school will also accept all three-year international degrees to fulfill the undergraduate prerequisite for application to Chicago Booth.

In general, you are strongly advised to submit your application packets as early as possible to ensure that all your information can be processed. Fuller offers some advice about the daunting task of financial aid. The officers are "awesome at their jobs. I had to change my financial aid needs at the last minute, and it was totally no big deal," she remembers. "The office does a great job laying out exactly what we need to do, step by step, in a very clear and concise manner."

FULL-TIME MBA PROGRAM (TOTAL DIRECT COSTS)

In-state: $81,246

Out-of-state: $81,246

International: $81,246

Part-time program cost: $4,861 per course

EMBA program cost: $95,360 Europe program, $170,000 Singapore program, $134,000 North America program

What Booth Students Know

In addition to the enlightening professors, students have a slate of classes developed to challenge them. Some of the classes become so popular that they reach capacity almost immediately during registration. The most popular courses are the management labs where the class will work as consultants for a company to address a certain project or problem. Often the companies are located overseas, and students will be required to travel to other countries, at the company's expense, to implement the solutions developed in the classroom. One recent class journeyed to China, whereas another found itself in Africa.

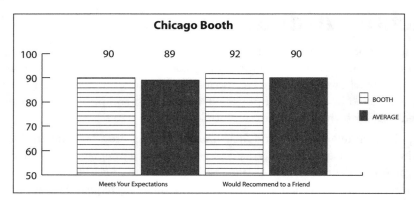

The value of the Booth education is in how well it prepares students for a career in the business world. Chicago Booth believes that if the school helps students build a solid foundation, they can't help but succeed. Manas Das, class of 2005, is now a partner at Das Advisory Services LLC, a business and technology consulting firm. He considers his time at Booth to be transformative. "A good business school teaches you what to think, but a great business school teaches you how. The Booth School of Business nourished my thought process and enabled me to look at any situation from a fresh perspective."

"Students who know how to think are successful no matter the challenges," Martinelli says. "From academic preparation to community support, our graduates know the questions to ask and the people to connect with to frame any future challenge."

Often new students worry about being overwhelmed during their entry into a program, but Legler explains that new students have a large support network. Administrators in the Dean of Students office are actively involved in student life as are teaching assistants and student mentors. Often second-year students help new students become acclimated, Legler claims, "because they remember what it was like to be the new guy."

Teppei Tsutsui, class of 2008, took part in an activity group especially designed for married students and their partners, aptly called the Chicago Partners Group. "Married students and students with children most often seek support from Chicago Partners, a student group that offers informal and formal programming for students, their spouses, and their children." Harvilla explains. "Some activities include get-togethers for spouses, play dates for the children, and outings in Chicago to get to know the city."

Most students belong to at least one career focus group, facilitated by Lunch and Learn sessions with faculty and alumni, trips to other cities worldwide, even a Warren Buffett Group that takes students to meet with the famous investor and "Oracle of Omaha." It would be difficult to exclude oneself from campus activities.

"Students from groups traditionally underrepresented in graduate business education—women, students of color, and gay and lesbian students—almost always take advantage of their respective student group," Ann Harvilla says.

Fuller explains that as a woman in a field historically dominated by men, she found only a small difference in her academic foundation. "My experience at Chicago Booth as a female, in my view, was the same as if I were a male, the only difference being I can be a member of Chicago Women in Business, and we have lots of free dinners and parties," she laughs. Fuller found the culture at Chicago Booth to be very supportive and not competitive at all, a sentiment echoed by Tsutsui and Tan. "In general, the environment is pretty laid back," she says. "I have always found that my classmates are ready and willing to help me out on homework/case write-ups if I ask, and the same is true for me if people ask me for help."

What's Next? Your Career

The Harper Center offers tools for the inevitable internship and job search. Once students visit the Career Services Center, they find that they are not alone in reaching for that next rung on their career ladder. "Career Services was very helpful during my initial internship search," Tan says, remembering his hunt for a place to gain experience. "Investment banking and consulting searches are strengths of the department since they are able to attract top firms that are looking to fill many spots."

In 2008, 84 percent of graduate hires were school facilitated, representing more than 200 companies from around the world. In preparation for these interviews, Career Services has seven career management coaches who work with students both individually and in ongoing workshops. Although much of the work is concentrated on resume preparation and interviewing skills, the school offers other workshops and programs ranging from specific topics to often-overlooked concepts such as networking and dinner etiquette.

"I got a position through Booth's program, Private Equity/Venture Capital Lab," Tsutsui says. He joined the private equity firm Calder Capital Partner's Summer Associate Program, which gave him hands-on experience, including spending time in Japan and Asia helping fund-raise for company investments.

Another component of the job and internship search is The Fisher Career Resource Center, located within the Harper Center, which offers current students and alumni all the information they need before they sit down for that interview. Recruiter reports and profiles on companies, industries, and executives are available in a library setting. If alumni are unable to visit in person, the center has remote access capabilities to download the information you need, whether you are around the corner or across the globe.

Overall, Career Services divides its concentration equally between enhancing the skills of students and continuing and fostering new relationships with companies so that job seekers can make the connections that will chart their life course. Once students walk through the door, the numbers speak for themselves. A number of companies reserve guaranteed positions exclusively for Chicago Booth students, a testament to the school's ongoing level of quality.

"Chicago Booth's philosophy of teaching students how to think is at the core of what we do," Martinelli says. "This begins from our flexible curriculum where students can design their program that complements their background and points them toward their goals. Yes, Chicago Booth has a core curriculum, but we also believe that no two students have the same backgrounds or aspirations for the future. The key to engagement is putting the students in the driver's seat."

CAREER CHECK: BOOTH MBA EMPLOYMENT BY JOB FUNCTION

- Finance/Accounting: 53%
- Consulting: 22%
- General Management: 12%
- Marketing/Sales: 8%
- Operations/Logistics: 2%
- Other: 3%

Chicago Booth is constantly looking to reach out to more companies and introduce them to its students. In the future, the school plans to add to its visibility and corporate marketing while continuing to create a diverse student body. At the core of the Chicago Booth program is one basic idea that will stand the test of time: preparing students for success not only in business but in life. Although the faculty and staff at Chicago Booth have nothing but good things to say about their students and alumni, they are the first to admit that an MBA is only a tool. "As much as a Chicago Booth degree is valuable, the job market is still competitive," Legler explains.

However, students such as Tan are ready to take on the world, armed with their degree and a world-class education that makes them valuable for their skills and not just the theories they learned in class. "I do feel prepared for the business world," Tan says, as he thought about what lay ahead as he stepped into corporate America. "I believe the classes have provided an excellent framework for me to think about everyday business problems. I've also made connections and built a network that I can rely on in the future."

Match Made in Heaven: Is the University of Chicago Booth School of Business Right for You?

You are an ideal student if you

- Question all ideas and want to learn through exploring all possibilities.
- Work well with a flexible, self-driven program surrounded by like-minded individuals.
- Can learn using both collaborative and competitive approaches to problem solving.
- Are curious about how things are yet want to focus on how things can be improved locally, nationally, and internationally.

University of Maryland
Robert H. Smith School of Business

2417 Van Munching Hall
University of Maryland
College Park, MD 20742-1815

Phone: 301.405.2559
E-mail: mba_info@rhsmith.umd.edu
Web site: www.rhsmith.umd.edu

Dean: G. "Anand" Anandalingam
Assistant Dean, MBA and Masters Programs: Michael Marcellino

"Today's business leaders need to lead responsibly with respect to the greater world within a constantly changing business environment. By teaching you how to think creatively, a Smith education will help you meet evolving challenges throughout the life of your career." —Dean Anandalingam

Quick Facts

MBA Programs

Full-time MBA
Part-time MBA (evening and weekend programs)
Executive MBA (College Park and China)

Full-Time MBA Snapshot

Total enrollment: 257
Class of 2010: 130
Length of program: 21 months
Campus location: College Park, Maryland
Program commences in August
Pre-term orientation attendance required

Application Notes

Requirements: Professional experience not required but highly recommended and a 4-year
  bachelor's degree or equivalent; GMAT; essays; resume; recommendations; GRE not accepted
Letters of recommendation: 2
Interview: By invitation only
Number of applicants: 1,204
Admittance rate: 27.8%

CLASS OF 2010 PROFILE

Male 65%, Female 35%
Minority Americans: 19%
International: 34%
Average age: 28
Combined average years of work experience: 5 years
GMAT score range (20th–80th percentile): 610–710
GMAT score average: 660
GPA average: 3.34

ACADEMIC BACKGROUND OF INCOMING STUDENTS

Business: 37%
Computer Science: 8%
Economics: 10%
Engineering: 14%
Humanities: 8%
Math/Sciences: 7%
Social Sciences (other): 14%
Other: 2%

Smith's Earthy Roots

Located outside of Washington, D.C., College Park, Maryland, is home to 25,000 residents. In 1889, College Park was established by John Oliver Johnson and Samuel Curriden as a D.C. suburb. From the 1920s through the mid-1940s, it became the first successful commuter suburb, with transportation available through the Baltimore and Ohio Railroad and the Washington-Baltimore Turnpike in Prince George's County.

College Park's creation was specifically planned to provide middle- and upper-class homes for the nearby Maryland Agricultural College. More than 50 buildings were constructed to meet the needs of the expanding academic community. From privately owned college to boys' preparatory school, Maryland Agricultural College transformed into Maryland State College after the state legislature saved it from bankruptcy in 1916. Subsequent to further merging with several Baltimore professional schools, it became the University of Maryland in 1920.

The Smith campus in Maryland.

Enter Robert H. Smith: From adolescence forward, Robert Smith focused on becoming a builder and land developer. As a student, he found his strengths to be in accounting and finance. He received his master's degree in accounting from University of Maryland's business school in 1950. In 1998 he donated $15 million so that the business school could reach its potential as one of the top 15 in the country.

Smith has a strong MBA program supported with robust technology. The strength of Smith's MBA program is in its focus on socially responsible business leadership and the core drivers of business today—globalization, entrepreneurship, and technology—or "GET." These elements are the prime components of all of Smith's MBA courses. Smith is a leader in management education and research and has been named Number 3 in intellectual capital among universities in the United States.

Smith has an ambitious goal—to be among the world's best universities in 10 years or less.

Why Smith?

One of the distinct advantages of attending Smith is location, location, location. More national and multinational nonprofit organizations are headquartered in Washington and its suburbs than anywhere else in the United States. Downtown D.C. is the epicenter for federal government agencies, and Northern Virginia's high-tech corridor has been referred to as Silicon Valley East. In 2008 the Milken Institute ranked the State of Maryland as second in the country for technology economy preparedness. A state-level initiative will invest $1.1 billion in Maryland's bioscience industry over the next 10 years. Already Maryland is home to a number of leading bioscience and biotech firms. Reflecting the local and campus resources supporting innovation is the school's Dingman Center for Entrepreneurship, a leading national entrepreneurship center that is unique in its experiential approach. The center offers MBA students numerous opportunities to launch and grow businesses while still in school.

Since 1988, Smith has increased its investment in technology to prepare students for participation in the international business market. Over the past few years, the school has spent more than $6 million improving its wireless accessibility and service. Not only does Smith provide BlackBerry handheld devices and service to all full-time MBA students, but students can access MBA program databases and finance applications through the Web.

Van Munching Hall—home to the business school—is one of the most technologically advanced facilities in the world. Teaching theaters, classrooms, and auditoriums are electronically enabled and are the venues for document cameras as well as digitization and recording. With faculty able to network their presentations and teaching materials through a central control room, flexibility is greatly enhanced for lectures and learning experiences.

As a leader in business education, the Smith School plans to launch two centers that speak to the future of the nation and planet. The Center on Financial Policy and Corporate Governance will provide a platform for innovative research in finance that interfaces with public policy and produces dialogue with leading decision makers in Wall Street and policy makers in the federal government and international institutions. The Center for Social Value Creation will bring interdisciplinary and market-based approaches to solving the challenges of modern business while addressing environmental and humanitarian needs.

Collaboration and Hands-On Learning

All MBA programs have their individual styles, and collaboration is a Smith signature.

The Dingman Center for Entrepreneurship is an example of community action and hands-on learning. The West Coast has its Silicon Valley, and the East Coast has students with access to seasoned faculty, experienced entrepreneurs, professional mentors and advisors, and even potential investors. Furthermore, for students looking for start-up expertise, this is the place to be. In September 2008, the Dingman Center expanded its mission of connecting start-up entrepreneurs to potential investors. The Capital Access Network (CAN) added Johns Hopkins Technology Transfer to the network, which already includes more than 32 active, accredited angel investors, and venture capitalists for early-stage capital.

For those who like their finance experience served hot, the Financial Marketing Laboratory allows students to practice fast-paced financial decisions in an environment fashioned after Wall Street's trading floor. Second-year Smith students who prefer longer-term monetary tracking may participate in the Mayer fund. This portfolio is worth more that $1 million and creates an environment to exchange ideas with the top-tier executives who make up the board of directors. The New Markets Venture Partners, an early-stage venture capital firm, was started by, and is housed within, the Smith School. MBA students have the opportunity to work as associates and gain real-world experience in identifying potential investment opportunities and developing financial investment models. Students can also experience hands-on learning in professional consulting and portfolio management.

When Smith students sit down before their computers in the Supply Chain Management Program, they are training on widely used software that allows them immediately to transition from graduate to employee. SAP Business Suite trains students in such areas as forecasting, inventory management and scheduling, among others. This is an example of one technology partnership where solving real-world problems using real-world software leads to real-world workforce advantages.

Global Education, International Diversity

For Smith, global education starts at home. Its Center for Global Business enhances international competencies in both graduate and undergraduate students. Once students are prepped and ready for the wider world, they can choose from eleven graduate semester exchange programs and eight MBA short-term study abroad courses.

For a longer-term international program, Smith partners with the University of International Business and Economics (UIBE) to offer its Executive MBA degree and Executive Education curricula. These are taught in English with courses held in China. Professors from Smith each spend a week with the executives in China, teaching the courses, resulting in an Executive MBA degree in 18 months.

Among the students in the U.S.-based MBA program, 34 percent are international. An increasing number are from India, and many of these students already have earned a master's degree in their homeland.

Other international students have earned the equivalent of the American bachelor's degree before furthering their studies at Smith. Once accepted, students discover that 27 percent of the teaching faculty are themselves born outside the United States.

FUN FACTS

- Local bar and eatery Town Hall is foremost for local residents. Patrons play pool and pinball and eat inexpensive fare. However, the atmosphere of Town Hall attracts a select group of students intrigued by the radical change of culture or lured in from the liquor store next to the bar.

- Some wildlife officials insist that no mountain lions live on the East Coast of the United States. However, in 2008, six legitimate sightings were recorded (in Maryland, Virginia, West Virginia, and Pennsylvania). One mountain lion was spotted in College Park in August 2008.

- University of Maryland's mascot is Testudo the Terrapin (turtle). In 2006, 50 fiberglass sculptures of Testudo were created as a community art project to raise funds for student scholarships. Local artists decorated the sculptures, which were placed all over campus until they were auctioned off.

Course Offerings

For a school with such a deep investment in GET (globalization, entrepreneurship, and technology), continuous improvement is essential to remain comprehensive and competitive. Smith has long been a pioneer in the development of innovative and progressive curriculum. It was one of the first schools to have a focus on business ethics with a required full-time MBA course that included a prison visit to speak with convicted white-collar criminals. This groundbreaking approach has evolved into an annual Ethics Variety Show, where issues such as drugs in the workplace, insider trading, off-shoring, and credit card debt are dramatized and explored by first-year students. In a similar vein, the MBA program's capstone course, the Business Plan Course, uniquely cultivates innovative thinking while integrating knowledge from the MBA program and principles from core courses into one final project. Students form three-person teams to create a business plan to commercialize an innovation and then participate in a competition and judging.

If you are looking for a depth of knowledge in specific concentrations, Smith names several areas of study in which it is especially strong. Full-time MBA candidates should be sure to explore Consulting, Entrepreneurship, Finance, Marketing, and Strategy.

On a broader scale, if you are passionate about socially responsible business practices, global climate change has been in the minds of the university's architects. The Camille Kendall Academic Center at The Universities at Shady Grove opened in November 2007. The center received LEED (Leadership in Energy and Environmental Design), gold-level certification for the green design of its 192,000 square feet and for its sustainable practices. As part of an international business community, corporate responsibility is a matter of ethical stewardship. Net Impact is one of the programs at Smith for graduate students who wish to explore further how business decisions influence our social and environmental futures, and social entrepreneurship is a key element of activities within the Dingman Center and Center for Social Value Creation.

What Smith Professors Teach

What makes the Smith program different from other MBA programs is the combination of academics and hands-on experiences to promote innovation and change. Jeffrey Kudisch teaches and consults in the field of Industrial and Organizational Psychology. "It is critical that real-world experience and coursework feed one another. Several of us in the Management and Organization Department serve as executive coaches to help our students gain the critical insights and skills needed to develop into stronger world-class leaders. For instance, during their year and a half stay, everyone in our EMBA program has an executive coach and participates in a series of assessments (e.g., assessment center-type simulations, psychological tests, 360-degree feedback, and peer feedback from action learning project team members) to better understand their strengths, proficiencies and developmental opportunities. Our faculty is trying to lead research advancements in executive coaching. Many people say they are executive coaches, but if you look at who is doing it, you can see their methods are not necessarily supported by good science. Our leading edge research is extremely important because it includes in-depth evaluations of those processes and tools that are related to effective leadership coaching."

Kudisch continues, "I am blessed to be working with the group I am in, with outstanding educators, staff, and researchers. We are all trying to perform at our highest levels. We look for what we can be doing better, what we can be doing differently. We are innovative, and more than that, we share the same values."

"Leveraging and unleashing the power of diversity is also a key component of successful teaching," explains Kudisch. "The MBA community has changed and I try to adapt my style to address the needs of all my audience members. When I teach negotiations, for instance, I stress that students can use their different strengths to help compensate for potential weaknesses, and I try to facilitate their success by providing them with a lot of specific individualized behavioral feedback to make this happen. To help boost female students' confidence levels I talk about faulty stereotypes that exist (e.g., the belief that women are less effective at negotiating then men), and the importance of challenging such beliefs. As an example, I try to point out to females that often women have greater skills in reading verbal expressions and other unspoken communication than their male counterparts. Explicitly recognizing such strengths helps improve their performance in negotiations. When international students are not as comfortable speaking up, I have to be careful how I enhance their participation while simultaneously preserving their self-esteem. Sometimes I talk to them after class by themselves to make sure I hear their views." Kudisch continues, "Finally, to help increase students' cultural awareness and interpersonal savvy, we strongly encourage students to form diverse teams for class projects. Creating diverse teams also forces students to focus on the "people aspects/challenges" of work teams (e.g., building trust, establishing constructive conflict, achieving commitment to goals, creating accountability), rather than just the task at hand (e.g., researching best company practices or providing consulting solutions). So I guess you can say that one of the competitive advantages of our curriculum is our focus on those "soft skills" requisite for leadership success (e.g., coaching and motivating others, teamwork, interpersonal sensitivity, persuasion and influence)—all of which are critical given that we are training MBAs to be future leaders of organizations and the consultants that serve them.

"We are working on building a stronger community, and we bring that value to both our research and into the classroom. I spend my life teaching and consulting. My professional experience influences the classroom experience. For us it is about teaching and service—building the MBA community—which allows me to heighten the teaching experience by going well beyond the textbooks. Because we have such a productive consulting arm, I can bring my current work experiences back to the classroom. Psychologist Morris Viteles once said, "If it isn't scientific, it's not good practice, and if it's not practical, it's not good science." This scientist-practitioner philosophy continues to guide my academic and professional endeavors, and it is alive and well at the Smith School.

"In addition," Kudisch comments, "Smith ranks in the top five from a research perspective, with much of our research focusing on developing the professional skills that characterize world class leaders and successful entrepreneurs. Thus, I'm able to gain a competitive advantage in the classroom by leveraging my colleagues' research findings and using research to inform practice." Kudisch continues, "Also, our school realizes that the best teachers are not necessarily the best researchers and vice versa. By using a differential staffing philosophy at the Smith School (e.g., recognizing the value of Teaching Fellows in the classroom), we're able to maximize students' learning experiences."

FACULTY FACTS

Full-time faculty employed by the b-school: 138

Adjunct or visiting faculty: 36

Permanent/tenured professors: 35

Tenured faculty who are women: 55

Tenured faculty who are underrepresented minorities: 8

SAMPLING OF NOTABLE PROFESSORS

- Ritu Agarwal: Thought leader in application of information and decision systems in healthcare
- Michael Fu, Lawrence Bodin, Bruce Golden, Saul Gass, Howard Frank, and Michael Ball: Institute for Operations Research and the Management Sciences (INFORMS) Fellows
- Albert "Pete" Kyle: One of the foremost financial theorists in the world
- Peter Morici: Recognized expert on international economic policy, the World Trade Organization, and international commercial agreements
- Roland Rust: Internationally known expert in customer-focused strategy
- Erich Studer-Ellis: Awarded the "Nation's Favorite Business School Professor" in 2006

CONCENTRATIONS AND SPECIALIZATIONS OFFERED TO FULL-TIME MBA STUDENTS

Accounting

Consulting

E-commerce

Entrepreneurship

Finance

Human Resource Management

International Business

Leadership

Management Information Systems

Marketing

Operations Management

Organizational Behavior

Strategy

Supply Chain Management

Technology

JOINT DEGREES AND DUAL DEGREES

MBA/JD

MBA/MS (Science)

MBA/MSN (Nursing)

MBA/MPP (Public Policy)

MBA/MSW (Social Work)

What Admissions Is All About

Smith's MBA is "based on three pillars called the three Cs," explains LeAnne Dagnell, associate director of MBA/MS admissions. "These are curriculum, career, and community. All are equally important."

Recently, the Office of Career Management partnered with Smith's Admissions office for candidate interviewing. Dagnell describes how full-time MBA candidates move through the process. "The submitted application needs to be complete and include work history, previous academics, and a strong GMAT score. These assessments ensure that a candidate is competitive. If an applicant is strong in two out of three of these areas, we often will give that applicant the opportunity to improve through wait-listing. For those who we think can bolster their resumes or academics in a few months, we watch their progress and decide whether to admit them at a later round. This is a benefit of applying earlier rather than later in the process—we offer feedback to applicants."

The Office of Career Services expects candidates to articulate how their strengths complement Smith's program, why they have applied to Smith, and how they can contribute to the class. Although this information is important in all MBA admissions, Smith's program depends on student commitment. "Community volunteerism is highly valued, and the culture of the school requires that students take seriously the time demands of personal involvement both on and off campus," Dagnell notes.

Because each class is composed of a group as diverse as possible, Dagnell emphasizes that students in general do not compete for the same jobs and are able to collaborate and support each other's career goals, which are as varied as finance, biotechnology, IT, international business, and start-up entrepreneurship. The interactive community extends beyond full-time students to include more than 1,000 part-time students who remain part of the work world as they pursue their degrees. The average GMAT for part-time students is 618, and most already have had three to five years of work experience. Full-time, part-time, and executive program participants network and are encouraged to share the deep resources that such a highly connected, multi-talented group contains.

Unique among MBA programs, this accessibility forms a network of business contacts from the moment students begin their degrees through alumni support for years afterward.

Full-time MBAs receiving financial aid: 64%

Institutional (merit-based) scholarships: 58

Assistantships: 25

Full-tuition scholarships school awarded for academic year: 20–30

Financially Aided

Dustin Hodgson, Smith's admissions program manager, points out that students need to be forward thinking in financing their education. "In terms of financing the full-time program, we have fellowships, scholarships, and graduate student assistantships. Assistantships are stipends and direct savings for tuition remission. Also, students are offered a university health plan." Hodgson clarifies, "We designate how many fellowships or scholarships will be offered for each school year. For example, in the 2007–2008 academic year, we awarded 11 fellowships and 17 scholarships. In the 2008–2009 academic year, we awarded 20 fellowships and 10 scholarships. There is no preset amount, and assistance differs depending on the student pool and the goals of the university for the year. All aid is granted during the admissions process and is highly dependent on the competitiveness of the individual student."

Hodgson goes on to say, "For military personnel in the part-time program, there are two merit-based scholarships. For the Executive MBA program that meets on campus, aid is awarded for the three semesters it includes and is merit-based as well. We have an exceptional pool of qualified students in this region."

To fund Smith's expansive vision of its future, the Great Expectations Campaign for Maryland expects to raise $90 million in private donations by 2012. A third of this goes toward scholarships and fellowships for both undergraduate and graduate students.

FULL-TIME MBA PROGRAM (TOTAL DIRECT COSTS)

In-state: $61,242

Out-of-state: $75,034

International: $83,000

Part-time programs costs: fee per credit hour

EMBA program costs: $94,000

What Smith Students Know

Sherika Shaw, class of 2009, says that Smith has a community feel that she noticed even when searching Web sites while deciding on MBA programs to which she planned to apply. Shaw was impressed by how many different groups were available to join and how many student-run organizations are within the MBA program. "I was born and raised in D.C., and a lot of my family is in the region. When I was considering programs, I did research and found out that in 2006, 60 percent of graduates landed jobs in the area where they went to school. I considered other schools, though." As a candidate, she attended Smith events, one of which was called Kaleidoscope and is now called Diversity at Smith. "There, I remember thinking, this is [the school] where I want to go. The day was filled with introductions to key students on campus, officers of career management, and people offering information, such as how to take the GMAT successfully. Smith had a tea with women MBAs; I am president this year. I am a single parent and am in the full-time program. My first year I was introduced to another single parent who is in the master's program, and we have shared our ideas, which has been very helpful."

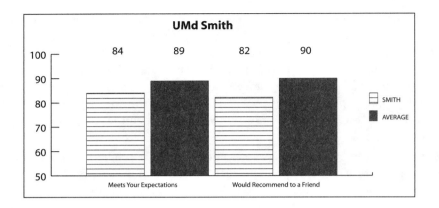

Smith offers two types of orientation for the full-time MBA candidates. "Smith has something called Admitted Students Weekend, which is in April. Students go to Smith and spend the weekend with current students. There is a Clubs Bazaar, bowling, a community fair. Then a week and a half before the term starts in August, on-campus orientation includes academic scheduling, career advice, team building, and a mini-class at Dingman Center for Entrepreneurship. For that, students are put in teams and present a sales pitch in a competition. Also during orientation, club presidents come and talk to students, and there is a happy hour for first and second years. One event I particularly like is the scavenger hunt because it forces Smith students to leave the business school grounds and find out about the activities in the rest of the university."

About the program itself, Smith's school philosophy "often focuses on GET but that is not a complete representation of Smith," Shaw notes. "Everybody must take selectives (not electives) before graduating. These include a variety of subjects, for example entrepreneurship, global business, technology, or leadership."

"The professors are good at keeping their office hours and giving us contact information to reach them. What I have also found is that classmates are willing to help each other. For example, I was struggling in economics and one student with an engineering background helped tutor me and some others. We told him how great he was at explaining the concepts, and with our encouragement, he later became a teaching assistant."

CAREER CHECK: SMITH MBA EMPLOYMENT BY JOB FUNCTION

- Finance/Accounting: 42%
- Marketing/Sales: 23%
- Consulting: 18%
- General Management: 10%
- Operations/Production: 4%
- Information Systems: 3%

What's Next? Your Career

Smith is recognized nationwide for the high post-degree employment rate of its MBAs. In preparation for their careers, students learn practical business through time spent at employers' workplaces. Business-world experience for students while they are in the program is extremely important. Sharon Strange Lewis, Managing Director of the Office of Career Management, notes, "We have found that the internship is a pivotal area in the program. It is a great fit for exploring a new culture or for students who want to try a different field." Sherika Shaw comments, "I thought the internship was going to be easier than it was. It is a heavy time commitment. The companies expect a lot from the MBA students. Students are given problems to solve with minimum of resources because the companies want to see whether you can perform—sink or swim."

Lewis continues, "For a different experience, we have several centers that work with businesses locally, nationally, and internationally, and utilize best practices for their businesses. In the international community, we have a strong program in China. Each year during summer and winter break, students sign up to go abroad with Smith's Study Abroad programs and work on case studies. Smith works with the countries and companies to determine what projects will be done."

"We have a great recruiting program and a wonderful dean who has given us the initiatives of core values, GET, integrity, and accountability in classroom and careers," Lewis continues. "We have students from India, China, Europe, the Middle East, Africa, and South America, and recruiters like our wide diversity of candidates. Because of our small class sizes of no more than 150, professors are able to drill deeper into each subject. This has worked well for us traditionally and we are able to show recruiters we have a unique and well-defined group."

Lewis emphasizes, "Once you walk through the door, you are a Smith student forever. After you have graduated, resources remain available to you as you reenter the work world. The MBA Alumni Mentor Program encourages Smith alumni to share their real-world knowledge and experiences with newly minted MBAs. Mentors act as industry resources, hosts for networking events, and provide job-shadowing opportunities to see day-to-day activities at companies in your field of study. At least once a week we receive a call from an alum to come back to help with mock interviews or to become mentors. Some come to recruit for their companies. They are passionate about making sure MBAs are ready to sit in the chair across from recruiters. By graduation day, two-thirds of our students have already been hired."

ALUMNI ACTUALS

MBA alumni worldwide: 7,800+

Business school alumni networking site: http://alumninetwork.rhsmith.umd.edu

Current MBA students have access to the alumni database.

Lindy Duvall, a 2006 graduate, started her networking even before entering the Smith program. Her father has a local business, and he works with a number of alumni. In addition to using this route to gain first-hand insight, Duvall was also able to network and talk to current colleagues and friends who were current and past students about their education experiences, which bolstered her belief that the Smith MBA was the right program for her. Since then, she says, "I have networked with MBAs and am now in a women's MBA network group, and we meet every other month. A lot of people from Smith stay in the area, both the full-time and part-time students. I was able to expand my knowledge of networking when I was a student and I still use it in my personal and professional life." Duvall now works in the public sector as a consultant for IBM.

While at Smith, Duvall says, "We did a lot of case studies with leadership themes. This raised my confidence in my negotiating skills because we could not pick which of our classmates we would be partnered with. I learned a lot about myself—what my strengths and weaknesses were, my leadership skills, communication skills, and how to work with people with other styles."

Alice Chen, class of 2005, was in the full-time program. "Before going for my MBA I was a family physician. Originally, I went to business school to learn a new set of skills so that I could run a medical practice. What I found was that my Smith MBA, combined with my medical degree, opened up a whole new world of possibilities. I discovered more career choices than I knew existed—ranging from leadership development to executive coaching, medical management, strategic planning, and many others. Since graduation I have been working as a consultant for Kaiser Permanente in a role that allows me to combine both my business and medical training."

Chen continues, "There is such diversity and collaboration among classmates at Smith. Our classmates became our main support network while in school and throughout the job search process, and four years later, we remain connected and close. Networking was a key aspect of our development—with alumni, faculty, industry professionals, as well as with our classmates. The Smith Community is the main reason I chose to attend the school. I definitely made the right choice. Along with providing students with a strong set of business fundamentals, Smith emphasizes interpersonal skills and leadership skills. It is these leadership skills that really give Smith students an advantage in the work world." Duvall adds, "An alum said to me, 'let me give you one piece of advice; when you go through your two years, keep an open mind. Take every class as if it was your primary interest.' There are so many opportunities it is amazing. I met a lot of alumni who were guest speakers and you could choose to call them up and talk to them. Also the professors were great, very approachable. Even now I can call them up and tell them what I am thinking and they offer opinions."

Match Made in Heaven: Is the Smith School of Business Right for You?

You are an ideal student if you

- Want to develop team leadership and organization building skills.
- Have an interest in the public sector and social consciousness for the corporate work world both locally and globally.
- Value access to practical yet scientific research as well as hands-on teaching methods.
- Are a career changer. Seventy-five percent of the full-time MBA students are furthering their education to start a different career after graduation.

University of Michigan
Stephen M. Ross School of Business

701 Tappan Street
Ann Arbor, MI 48109

Phone: 734.764.1817
E-mail: Rossmba@umich.edu
Web site: www.bus.umich.edu/mba

Dean: Robert J. Dolan
Associate Dean for Degree Programs: Valerie Y. Suslow
Associate Dean for Leadership Programming, Executive MBA Program: Sue Ashford

"Here at Ross, we emphasize action-based, collaborative learning that gives students hands-on experience with real challenges facing real businesses." —Dean Dolan

Quick Facts

MBA PROGRAMS

Full-time MBA
Evening MBA
Executive MBA
Global MBA
MAcc (Accounting)
MASM (Supply Chain Management)

FULL-TIME MBA SNAPSHOT

Total enrollment: 861
Class of 2010: 434
Length of program: 20 months
Campus locations: Ann Arbor, Michigan (evening program: Ann Arbor, Dearborn, and South field)
Program commences in September
Pre-term orientation attendance is required

APPLICATION NOTES

Requirements: U.S. bachelor's degree or equivalent; GMAT; resume; transcripts from under graduate and postgraduate education; essays; GRE not accepted
Letters of recommendation: 2

(continued)

(continued)

Interview: By invitation only
Number of applicants: 3,026
Admittance rate: 20%

CLASS OF 2010 PROFILE

Male 66%, Female 34%
Minority Americans: 25%
International: 31%
Average age: 29
Married or Partnered, Single: 16%, 84%
Combined average years of work experience: 5 years
GMAT score average: 706
GMAT score range (20th–80th percentile): 650–760
GPA average: 3.3

ACADEMIC BACKGROUND OF INCOMING STUDENTS

Business: 17%
Computer Science: 7%
Economics: 14%
Engineering: 26%
Humanities/Social Sciences: 19%
Math/Physical Sciences: 9%
Other: 8%

Foundation of Excellence

By the time its School of Business Administration was created in 1924, the University of Michigan itself had gained national recognition and drew prominent lecturers including Mark Twain, Theodore Roosevelt, William Jennings Bryan, and Susan B. Anthony. Dr. Jonas Salk accepted a fellowship at Michigan in the early 1940s where he began research on what would later become the life-saving polio vaccine. During his 1960 presidential campaign, John F. Kennedy gave a speech from the steps of the Michigan student union, proposing the formation of the Peace Corps.

For the first year of the program in 1924, 12 students enrolled. By 1947, 340 students had received their degrees and turned the MBA program into the nation's third largest. Early graduates made their marks throughout U.S. and international business, offering leadership and innovation in some of the world's most influential organizations.

Scenes from Ross.

The school has fine-tuned its focus of providing a practical, hands-on learning experience. Since Robert J. Dolan became dean in 2001, the Ross MBA program has grown in its action-based learning so that students may immerse themselves in real-world situations. "One differentiating factor of the Ross School of Business," says Dean Dolan, "is that we are not a standardized place. Instead, we offer a customized curriculum. At Ross, we stress the importance of you as a student co-creating the curriculum with us. We don't have any one 'cookie-cutter' notion in mind."

In 2004, Stephen Ross, a New York City real estate developer and UM alum (class of 1962), made a historic $100 million donation to the business school—currently the third-largest private donation to a United States business school and the largest amount ever donated to the University of Michigan. Later that fall, the Board of Regents renamed the school the Stephen M. Ross School of Business.

Why Ross?

The Ross School of Business has been a pioneer in the use of action learning, particularly in its Multidisciplinary Action-based Learning Program (MAP). Action learning follows a continuous cycle of observation and analysis, conceptualization and hypothesis forming, and experimentation, bounded by continuous reflection with conclusions being adjusted as new learnings are uncovered. It strives to blend theory and action. The theory makes sense as it is applied to practice, but the practice makes sense only through reflection as enhanced by theory. Action-based learning programs such as MAP develop students with the ability to think independently, function without sufficient data, change their mind in midstream, negotiate, and continually reflect and inquire. Developing this ability for reflective inquiry is a key differentiator between action learning and classroom teaching.

The Ross School of Business is committed to leadership and innovation by means of a unique learning approach. MAP is at the heart of the Ross teaching philosophy and is an integral part of the school's curriculum. The program requires students to look beyond problem solving and apply a combination of analytics, leadership, enthusiasm, and teamwork. In MAP, teams of first-year MBAs are engaged in real business situations in which there are "real stakes" for which they are held accountable. MAP projects are multidisciplinary and can cover a range of business issues from developing a strategic marketing plan for China to working with an AIDS clinic in Papua, New Guinea. They can be domestic, international, corporate, entrepreneurial, or nonprofit projects that have no simple solution.

In January 2009, Ross unveiled a new 270,000-square-foot facility, adjacent to its existing curriculum buildings. According to Ross's Admissions Director Soojin Koh, the new space illustrates the school's placement "at the forefront of a fundamental change in business education—away from lecture-style classes and toward hands-on methods." In form and function, the building speaks to the Ross emphasis on imagination and interaction with fellow students and faculty and the belief that great business innovation is not created in a vacuum.

Breakout rooms for small groups, tiered U-shaped classrooms, and collaborative spaces for informal discussion make up the physical space required to foster action-based learning. State-of-the-art technology includes 20 group study rooms with plasma screens, wireless Internet throughout, classroom media devices for instant data upload from students to mounted screens, all of which maximizes the capacity for information sharing. Additional features include the 500-seat Blau Auditorium, a health and fitness center, the Ross Art Collection, and the Davidson Winter Garden—known as both the figurative and literal center of the Ross collaborative learning community.

FUN FACTS

- The popular retail chain Borders Books has its headquarters in Ann Arbor.
- The city is nicknamed "Tree Town" because of its forests.
- Ann Arbor is proudly known as a nationally important center for learning and opinion.
- Fritz Crisler was the football coach at Michigan when he invented two-platoon football (that is, put your 11 best defensive players on the field when you're playing defense and your 11 best offensive players on the field when playing offense). Up to then, teams played their 11 best the whole game.
- According to legend, Ann Arbor was named by the two founders (who were land speculators) for their wives, Ann and Mary Ann. "Arbor" was added in honor of the huge stands of trees around the settlement.

Course Offerings

Students of the Ross School of Business engage in a curriculum that challenges them with course work, class projects, and experiential learning. In the first year, students take a curriculum in broad-based business subjects, covering all the functional areas of business. In the final seven weeks of this challenging first year, student teams work together on one of the projects selected from the MAP program to put all the knowledge they have acquired to bear on solving a real-world business problem. MAP allows MBA students to work on real-time challenges in addition to classroom case studies.

"Ross strives to provide an educational experience that is not just first-rate, but transformational," asserts Dean Dolan. "We want our graduates to leave with broader aspirations, the tools to achieve them, and the confidence to pursue them."

During the second year of school, there is more flexibility in the schedule, and students can select from among many business electives that interest them. Typical electives are Business Leadership in Changing Times, Valuation, and Advanced Corporate Reporting. In addition, students are encouraged to assume leadership roles in campus clubs and service organizations. This makes for a busy second year, but one that is a lot of fun as well.

What Ross Professors Teach

"Although the idea of teaching leadership is debated," notes Sue Ashford, associate dean for Leadership Development, "Ross knows that it can be taught. Here, student experiences demand leadership of them, which assures they will develop as leaders." As part of this approach, each spring, first-year students devote themselves exclusively to MAP for seven weeks as part of the core curriculum. Jim Walsh, professor of Management and Organizations, explains, "We had the crazy idea to put students out in the field, partnered with faculty, to solve real problems as they're unfolding." To date, Ross students have worked on projects at more than 640 corporate, nonprofit, and entrepreneurial organizations worldwide. Each year, Ross accepts MAP proposals from various companies looking for solutions to their business challenges. You choose from around 100 projects and apply your core business knowledge, innovation, and teamwork toward a solution (or solutions). Each team presents its conclusions to the company representatives for their consideration and implementation.

The MAP program equips students with leadership, problem solving, and communication skills. Maureen Shay, class of 2008, gives an example: "We actually did a business plan for a carpentry facility in Kosovo. We got to travel there, meet with political leaders, and see our plan in action. Overall, it was a great experience."

The Ross philosophy of action-based learning is shared by its faculty. "I have one foot in the business world and one foot in academia," says Christie Nordhielm, professor of Marketing, "and that's exactly where I want to be. And that's exactly what benefits the program here. We're very focused on not just theory, not just practice, but the intersection of both."

Gautaum Kaul, professor of Finance, shares his insight. "Chicago is great at finance, Wharton is good at economics, Northwestern is good at marketing. But those are silos. Those are not what life is all about. No problem in life is about finance alone or marketing alone. Problems in life are about life. And I think the Ross Business School embraces that life."

Dan Weimer, class of 2006, was very impressed with the quality of his instruction. He explains, "The faculty members were like Jedi masters. Their research was outstanding, and whenever I talked to students from other programs, I always felt like I understood the material at a higher level than they did."

FACULTY FACTS

Full-time faculty employed by the b-school: 124

Adjunct or visiting faculty: 39

Permanent/tenured professors: 75

Tenured faculty who are women: 15

Tenured faculty who are underrepresented minorities: 3

SAMPLING OF NOTABLE PROFESSORS

- Guatam Ahuja: Expert in corporate strategy and international business, preeminent researcher on innovation and technology strategy
- Ilia Dichev: Professor and researcher in investment; published in the *American Economic Review*
- Ted London: Leading expert on the role and impact of market-based strategies on poverty alleviation
- Mike Pedler: Leading authority on action learning and a leading academic and consultant on management
- C. K. Prahalad: Known internationally as a consultant to top management of many of the world's foremost companies—a management guru and a brilliant teacher; published works include *The New Age of Innovation: Driving Cocreated Value Through Global Networks*
- Dave Ulrich: One of the world's leading authorities on creating value through human resources

CONCENTRATIONS AND SPECIALIZATIONS OFFERED IN FULL-TIME MBA PROGRAM

Accounting

Business Economics and Public Policy

Business Information Technology

Finance

History and Communication

Law

Management and Organizations

Marketing

Operations and Management Science

Strategy

JOINT DEGREES AND DUAL DEGREES

MBA/JD

MBA/MD

MBA/Asian Studies (Chinese, Japanese, South Asia, or Southeast Asia)

MBA/CE&M (Construction Engineering and Management)

MBA/IOE (Industrial and Operations Engineering)

MBA/MA (Arts)

MBA/MArch (Architecture)

MBA/MEM (Manufacturing Engineering)

MBA/Meng (Engineering, Manufacturing Management)

MBA/MFA (Fine Arts)

MBA/MHSA (Health Services Administration)

MBA/MM (Music)

MBA/MPP (Public Policy)

MBA/MS (Education, Environment, Nursing)

MBA/MSE (Naval Architecture and Marine Engineering)

MBA/MSI (Science Information)

MBA/MSIE (Industrial Engineering)

MBA/MSIM (Information Management)

MBA/MSN (Nursing)

MBA/MSW (Social Work)

MBA/MUP (Urban Planning)

Modern Middle Eastern and North African Studies

Russian and East Europe Studies

INSTITUTES, RESEARCH CENTERS, AND PARTNERSHIPS

American Customer Satisfaction Index (ACSI)

Center for Global Resource Leverage: India

Center for International Business Education (CIBE)

Center for Positive Organizational Scholarship (POS)

Center for Venture Capital and Private Equity Finance

Collaboratory for Research on Electronic Work (CREW)

Domestic Corps

East Asia Management Development Center

Erb Institute for Global Sustainable Enterprise

Graham Environmental Sustainability Institute

Institute of Labor and Industrial Relations

IT Champions

Mitsui Life Financial Research Center

Multidisciplinary Action Project (MAP)

National Quality Research Center (NQRC)

Nonprofit and Public Management Center

Paton Center for Research in Accounting

Samuel Zell and Robert H. Lurie Institute for Entrepreneurial Studies

Tauber Institute for Global Operations

Tax Policy Research Office

Tozzi Electronic Business and Finance Center

William Davidson Institute

Yaffe Center for Persuasive Communication

What Admissions Is All About

Ross wants your application to answer several questions: Can you handle the academic rigor of this MBA program? Do you have the intellectual depth required? Have you had enough work experience to contribute significantly to class discussions and projects? Do you have a set of personal attributes that will complement those of your classmates? Part of what makes Ross unique is its hands-on learning environment. So, much of the program involves teamwork and lively classroom discussions. The best-fit candidates are those who value shared learning and collaboration.

Before you send in your application, be sure to correct some of the common mistakes the Admissions Committee (AdComm) sees in essays. For example, make sure you answer the actual questions that are asked. Read them carefully and understand them fully before preparing your essay. Also, instead of providing an overview of your work history, address your experience expressly for Ross's program. Show AdComm that you are serious about the program and can visualize yourself in it. And finally, personalize your essays. Describe what you have gained from your experience, good or bad, and why your current life ambitions involve a career-enhancing MBA degree from Ross.

AdComm members read and review each application thoroughly when it arrives. For this stage, their task is to sort applicants: You will move to a second read and be invited for an interview, you will move to a second read and be considered for an interview, or you will be taken out of consideration as a candidate. If your application is designated for a second read, it will be passed along to a different AdComm member than whoever read it initially. For those invited to interview, Ross prefers you to come to campus so that you understand the nature of the program and the environment in which you will be learning. Primarily, on-campus interviews are conducted by second-year student members of admissions. After you have interviewed, either on campus or with a Ross alum in your region, the second reader reviews the written interview results and decides whether to extend an invitation to you to attend the program. All AdComm recommendations are reviewed by the admissions director before being sent to the associate dean of each respective degree program for a final review.

Full-time MBAs receiving financial aid through school: 75%

Institutional (merit- and need-based) scholarships: 230

Full-tuition scholarships school awarded for academic year: 48

Financially Aided

Nearly 70 percent of Ross students receive financial aid, usually in a combination of loans and scholarships. To accommodate all students, Ross offers a variety of financial aid options to reduce tuition and fee expenses including merit scholarships (partial and full, for tuition only). Students admitted into the full-time MBA program are considered for scholarships at the time of application and are notified upon admission. No separate application is required. Merit awards are based on academic ability (3.3 GPA and above), professional and personal achievements, and potential to contribute to the Ross community.

In addition to the general merit scholarships, the Tauber Institute for Global Operations and the Erb Institute for Global Sustainable Enterprise offer a number of scholarships to students interested in those areas. No separate application is required for the Tauber and Erb Scholarships (although students must be admitted to these programs).

Ross also offers a limited number of need-based awards for full-time MBA applicants who are U.S. citizens and permanent residents. Award amounts are based on need as estimated in the Free Application for Federal Student Aid (FAFSA). Students are encouraged to search the school Web site for the private scholarship link, which includes a listing of free scholarship search services.

FULL-TIME MBA PROGRAM (TOTAL DIRECT COSTS)

In-state: $80,879

Out-of-state: $90,879

International: $90,879

Part-time program cost: $1,500 for first credit hour, $1,315 per additional credit

EMBA program cost: $120,000 (in-state), $125,000 (out-of-state)

What Ross Students Know

It's snowing in Michigan? What has the weather to do with the school experience? Michigan weather in winter is as challenging as the MBA program. The city is warm and welcoming in September, yet the big challenges lie ahead as the cold settles and students hunker down. You soon understand that winter is here to stay and you need to adapt to overcome it. The cold changes not only how you dress but how you think about the environment. So how does the MBA experience resemble facing the Michigan weather? Because it is about learning to manage a changing environment, an environment that will not be indulgent, an environment that will demand you to think differently, learn quickly, and rise to the challenge it presents. However, you also realize that although the Ross environment might be demanding, it is shaping up to being an awesome experience, like the beautiful snow-covered streets of Ann Arbor.

Further, what makes an MBA program successful? If you add collaborative energy to enthusiasm for courses to personal expectation to be the best, you will have a Ross student. Throw in a dash of fun, and you have the Ross experience. The many state-of-the-art research resources at Ross have enriched Reid Galas's MBA experience. "One of my opportunities at Ross has been the participation in the University's Investment Club and the Maize and Blue Fund, which is a student-run equity fund where we take a piece of the University endowment and manage it." Both programs use the Tozzi Finance Center—a 6,000 square foot facility with a trading floor complete with the same technology found on Wall Street. Galas contends, "The resources we have in terms of fixed income and equity investing are amazing, probably the best in the country."

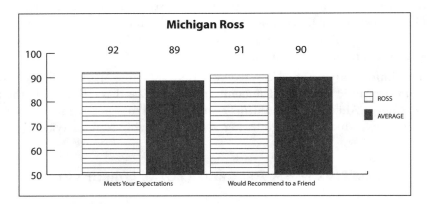

Ross attracts smart, ambitious people. On the one hand, these students are headed for future successful careers. On the other hand, they are comfortable with themselves and value fun and social opportunities. And what do smart, ambitious MBA candidates do to relax? One popular option is a trip to WhirlyBall of Ann Arbor. "WhirlyBall" is a combination of basketball and jai alai played from electric bumper cars with five teams of 10 players each. The team "weapon" is a plastic device for accurate throwing, catching, and shooting. Teammates compete in an enclosed court with a backboard at either end to beat their opponents by scoring more points. There are definite similarities between this kind of entertainment and graduate studies.

CAREER CHECK: ROSS MBA EMPLOYMENT BY JOB FUNCTION

- Consulting: 29%
- Finance/Accounting: 27%
- Marketing/Sales: 25%
- General Management: 10%
- Strategic Planning: 2.5%
- Other: 6.5%

What's Next? Your Career

At Ross, MBA students are encouraged to visualize their ideal career upon matriculation. Al Cotrone, Director of the Office of Career Development, suggests that especially during challenging economic times, students need to "look at what kind of professional you want to be when you graduate." The combination of core curriculum and action-based learning makes Ross students ready to work in real-world situations and, Cotrone adds, "ready to work through messy situations."

In addition to the MAP relationships with actual businesses and their real-world challenges, internships are available with a wide range of companies. For 2008, more than 30 percent of Ross MBA graduates were hired by their internship employer. Angelia Floyd, a recruiter in the information technology and consulting fields, says the main traits she seeks in summer interns are their industry knowledge and interest. Floyd knows that Ross students already have demonstrated a high academic standing. In addition, she adds, "When evaluating MBAs for full-time employment, student success in internships is extremely important."

The Office of Career Development (OCD) provides a variety of services to prepare students for effective, fruitful career searches. Resources include individual counseling, career workshops, recruiting events, and on-campus interviewing. "One of the most important things Ross does is they leverage the connections they have with the university and the surrounding business community," comments Shally Madan, class of 2009.

The OCD helps recruiters develop and benefit from an ongoing relationship with Ross. OCD fulfills two complementary functions: preparing students for a successful career search and managing an extensive on-campus interview process. Recruiters have a variety of resources including online job posting and access to resumes for all MBA and MAcc students. All recruiting events are posted online and throughout campus common areas (plasma TVs and information kiosks) and within student publications.

To help students prepare for the interviewing process, the Ross Marketing Club holds a Super Mock Interview Day when personnel from various companies come to hold "practice" interviews and provide valuable feedback on students' responses to tough interview questions. Mock interviews can be tricky: They are meant to be educational to help students properly prepare, but at the same time, they are not 100 percent mock interviews either. Sometimes job offers come from these mock interviews. Students find themselves doing mock interviews to prepare for the mock interviews to prepare for the real interviews! All this means two things: You can be very, very busy running from one recruiting event to another, and you are wearing a suit a lot of the time.

ALUMNI ACTUALS

MBA alumni worldwide: 25,400+

Ross Alumni Networking site: www.bus.umich.edu/networking/alumnidirectory.asp

Current MBA students have access to the alumni database.

Aaron Spool, class of 2005, earned his degree in finance and accounting and now works in diversified financial services. UM Ross was a perfect fit for him. He values many aspects of his experience and especially liked the school's "culture and collaborative student body." Spool adds, "Getting my MBA at Ross was the single most important and best decision I have made concerning my career." As far as his overall opinion of this school, Spool gives it an excellent rating in meeting his expectations, the quality of teaching, integration of topics, enhancement of the students' analytical skills, and the curriculum's adaptability to a changing business environment, among many others. He sees his MBA's value "as an investment in the real-world relevance [through] your education."

Sanjay Dua, class of 1994, is now a chief marketing officer in Silicon Valley. While at Ross, he specialized in entrepreneurship, and he focused on strategy, economics, and finance. He says that not only would he recommend Ross as an overall school, but he "especially liked the quality of teaching and found the courses to be interesting and challenging." In fact, Dua was pleased with almost every aspect of his educational experience, except for perhaps, "the snow."

The mission of Ross alumni clubs is to provide opportunities for lifelong learning to support the school's mission of "Leading in Thought and Action" and to create a sense of Ross community around the country and around the world. Alumni clubs help to build and maintain relationships with Ross alumni from the moment they graduate. There are more than 20 domestic alumni clubs and nearly 30 international alumni clubs in major cities worldwide including London, Paris, Frankfurt, Zurich, Hong Kong, Singapore, and Mumbai. Ross utilizes a password-protected intranet to access its alumni community. Known as iMpact, this resource allows current students, alumni, faculty, and corporate partners to stay in contact. In addition, alumni are invited to receive MichiganMail, the bimonthly e-newsletter, and *Dividend* magazine.

Within the Ross alumni Web site, a new career service is offered. Ross alumni can immediately market themselves to thousands of potential employers, free of charge via the Ross alumni resume database. Additional resources can be found here, including self-assessment, resume writing, networking skills, and interviewing tips. Alum Scottie Knight recalls, "I knew Ross was a top-five school, and I wanted a degree that would 'travel' throughout the country and my career." Employed as a commercial lender during her part-time MBA program, Knight intended to move on after graduation. Instead, she received an irresistible offer from her employer. "I stayed at the bank and got a huge raise. Once I had that Ross MBA in hand, they knew I could go somewhere else," she says. "I was far more marketable."

"I recall Ross having a big emphasis on having professors who had 'real jobs,'" says alum Ralph Basile. "These people came in not as academics but as real business people. They were leaders in their fields. Many of them had been quite successful in their careers, and they brought us that knowledge." Basile recalls, "The big advantage was that companies—great companies that you were interested in—came to the school to do presentations and interviews," he says. "It seemed like every other day you had employers on campus, looking for you. That felt great."

"I learned so much from my fellow students," remembers Knight. "They made classes interesting and valuable. I would definitely say that I use my Ross MBA every day and it has added value to my life in many ways."

Match Made in Heaven: Is the Ross School of Business Right for You?

You are an ideal student if you

- Want to learn through team collaboration and transfer that style to build innovative organizational cultures.
- Are seeking a transformational experience by applying cutting-edge teaching both in and out of the classroom.
- Consider yourself a "learning entrepreneur."
- Are looking for action-based learning in a real-world environment that involves continuously seeking and connecting to business opportunities.

University of North Carolina at Chapel Hill
Kenan-Flagler Business School

McColl Building, CB 3490
Chapel Hill, NC 27599

Phone: 919.962.3236
E-mail: mba_info@unc.edu
Web site: www.kenan-flagler.unc.edu/programs/mba

Dean: Jim W. Dean, Jr.
Associate Dean, MBA Program: David A. Hofmann

"We can literally be the best school [at leadership] in the entire world" —Dean Dean

Quick Facts

MBA PROGRAMS

Full-time MBA
Part-time MBA (weekend Executive program)
Part-time MBA (evening Executive program)
OneMBA@MBA for Executives

FULL-TIME MBA SNAPSHOT

Total enrollment: 562
Class of 2010: 279
Length of program: 21 months
Campus: Chapel Hill, North Carolina
Program commences early August
Pre-term orientation attendance: mandatory

APPLICATION NOTES

Application requirements: Minimum two years work experience is required but five years experience is recommended; four-year bachelor's degree or equivalent; GRE not accepted
Letters of recommendation: 2
Interview: Highly recommended
Number of applicants: 2,060
Admittance rate: 34%

CLASS OF 2010 PROFILE

Male 78%, Female 32%
Minority Americans: 16%
International: 34%
Average age: 28
Married or Partnered, Single: 31%, 69%
Average years of work experience: 5 years
GMAT score average: 678
GMAT range (20th–80th percentile): 590–750
GPA average: 3.3

ACADEMIC BACKGROUND OF INCOMING STUDENTS

Business: 33%
Economics: 13%
Engineering: 26%
Liberal Arts: 20%
Other: 8%

A Southern Landmark

The University of North Carolina is the oldest state university in the country. The public school is located on a sprawling campus in Chapel Hill, North Carolina, about 40 minutes from the capital city of Raleigh. Established in 1795, the university has weathered some of the most difficult times of this country's history. It was initially a school for men, and was one of the few that managed to stay open during the Civil War. Afterwards, however, it lacked student enrollment and closed briefly during the reconstruction period.

With new support from university trustees, it reopened and grew in number of students and in class offerings. The school expanded to include graduate programs and began admitting women in 1897. A little more than 20 years later, the School of Commerce was established and eventually became the business school. In 1952, the MBA program was created, and in 1991 the school was renamed Kenan-Flagler after philanthropists Mary Lily Kenan Flagler, her husband Henry Morrison Flagler, and another Kenan family member, Frank Hawkins Kenan.

On campus at UNC.

Kenan-Flagler Business School has firmly established its program as one of the best in the country. It is regularly named as one of the top 20 schools and is considered an excellent value for the money.

Dean Jim Dean was selected as head of the business school in mid-2008; but even before that, he had a long history with the school and a vision for its future. In addition to serving as Senior Associate Dean for Academic Affairs, Dean has also been associate dean for both executive development and for the MBA program. His focus is on developing leadership qualities for students by giving them the education and opportunities to acquire real-life skills that will be used in the business world.

Why Kenan-Flagler?

With a strong desire to ensure that UNC MBAs are prepared to immediately take a leadership role, the school has launched a leadership initiative. Students spend part of a semester working on leadership development. Kenan-Flagler also has further leadership opportunities imbedded in all classes. A new Leadership Immersion course provides the opportunity to master core principles. In addition to learning leadership skills, students work in groups for many assignments, therefore building teamwork skills. Communication is another area emphasized, and the school provides many opportunities for practice and feedback.

Even the most experienced managers will have situations that test their knowledge, but knowing what questions to ask and how to make decisions is essential. Through case studies, lectures and experiential learning, simulations, and team projects, students will learn how to approach problems and develop solutions.

As part of a research university, Kenan-Flagler students have the benefit of learning the newest theories, technologies, and practices. Dean Jim Dean has stressed the need to do more than teach theoretical ideas, but to help students learn practical business applications as well.

In addition to being part of cutting-edge research and knowledge, students become skilled in all areas of general management. Depending on their interest, they can also focus on specific areas by taking additional classes in a certain concentration.

Another aspect of the strategic perspective is an understanding of the global nature of business, and it is an essential part of every course. The school offers a range of international experiences, and every student is encouraged to participate in at least one international activity. Twenty-three percent of the faculty and about a third of the MBA students come from outside the U.S., representing at least 40 countries. Today's MBA students are different from students even five years ago. Today's students come with expectations that the technology will meet and exceed their needs. Kenan-Flagler is raising their bar on technology, with increased visual, experiential, and interactive systems. One project the Dean mentioned that is in the works is a 3-D virtual simulation that allows students to feel that they are actually part of a business situation.

A common quote among UNC students, known as Tar Heels, is "God must be a Tar Heel. Why else is the sky Carolina Blue?" Regardless of the reason for the blue sky, it is there in abundance. Chapel Hill's location in North Carolina makes the busy MBA schedule a little easier to take. Climactically, the seasons are mild, and for those rare long weekends, students can easily escape west to the mountains or east to the beach. If you are staying in town, Chapel Hill provides a funky college-town feel with numerous restaurants, bars, and cultural activities. UNC also has a number of collegiate sports from football to basketball that bring out the fan in everyone.

Just a few minutes away is Research Triangle Park, one of the largest high-tech research and development centers in the United States, with numerous research and business opportunities.

FUN FACTS

- On February 12, 1795, Hinton James arrived on the UNC campus to enroll as its first student. More than two weeks passed, they say, until he had the companionship of any other students. By the end of the first term, he was one of 41 students taught by two professors.
- Chapel Hill, North Carolina, has traditional red fire trucks, along with local favorite color Carolina Blue, the color of the Carolina Tar Heels. Engines 31, 32, 33, 34, and 35 show their home state spirit around town.
- New Hope Chapel Hill was the site of a church in the late 1700s. Now shortened to simply Chapel Hill, the church is gone and the Carolina Inn has taken its place.
- In 1950, William Meade Prince wrote a book called *Southern Part of Heaven*, prompting the nickname for Chapel Hill.

Course Offerings

The Kenan-Flagler MBA gives students a thorough preparation for business management using a combination of case studies, experiments, research, lecture, and discussions. Students are assigned to teams for the first year and will work together on class assignments. This approach not only allows a diverse group of students to bring their strengths together to problem solve, but also allows students to develop leadership and team-building skills. Classes are held weekdays during each semester.

Students who want to focus on a particular area of study may select one or two concentrations.

CONCENTRATIONS AND SPECIALTIES OFFERED TO FULL-TIME MBA STUDENTS

Corporate Finance

Customer and Product Management

Entrepreneurship

Global Supply Chain Management

Investment Management

Management Consulting

Real Estate

Sustainable Enterprise

JOINT DEGREES AND DUAL DEGREES

MBA/JD

MBA/ME (Duke University's Nicholas School of the Environment)

MBA/MHA, MBA/MSPH (Public Health)

MBA/MPP (Duke University's Sanford School of Public Policy)

MBA/MRP (UNC Department of City and Regional Planning)

MBA/MSIS (UNC School of Information and Library Science)

UNC encourages students to create customized dual-degree options in consultation with the MBA program office.

RESEARCH CENTERS

The Frank Hawkins Kenan Institute of Private Enterprise, including

- Air Commerce
- Competitive Economies
- Entrepreneurial Studies
- International Business Education and Research

- Logistics and Digital Strategy
- Real Estate Development
- Sustainable Enterprise
- Urban Investment Strategies

Kenan Institute Asia in Bangkok

Institute of Defense and Business

What Kenan-Flagler Professors Teach

It's natural that a research university would have a passion for both the learning and the teaching process. Professors recognize the importance of continuing cutting-edge research while continuing to use those findings in a way that is easily applicable in the daily business world. With more than half of the professors having corporate work experience, they help students make the connection from theoretical to practical.

"Our goal is to graduate students that have outstanding technical skills, and also understand that more than technical skills are required for success. Technical skills must be married with leadership skills and competencies," explains David A. Hofmann, associate dean for the MBA Program, academic director of the Leadership Initiative, and professor of Organizational Behavior/Strategy. "We also would like our students to leave with a broad definition of success—one that includes the broader notion of community," he adds. Whether the focus is on a global or local community, the professors try to model this for the students.

Kenan-Flagler students often comment that the faculty is extremely approachable and responsive. Spencer Hall, class of 2010, appreciates the ease of connecting with faculty. "The professors are tremendous teachers and love to engage with the students," he says. "They are incredibly accessible," he adds, mentioning that the faculty is quick to answer questions outside class via e-mail.

This is an intentional part of the Kenan-Flagler culture. "Kenan-Flagler is a place that really values and rewards our faculty for excellence in both teaching and research," Hofmann imparts. "We also have established and reinforced a culture of accessibility and approachability. In our twice annual student satisfaction [survey], the approachability and accessibility of faculty is consistently one of the top (if not the top) rated item."

FACULTY FACTS

Full-time faculty employed by the b-school: 112

Adjunct or visiting faculty: 22

Permanent/tenured professors: 50

Tenured faculty who are women: 5

Tenured faculty who are underrepresented minorities: 1

Tenured international faculty: 7

SAMPLING OF NOTABLE PROFESSORS

- David A. Hofmann: Forward thinker; well known for his research on organizational behavior and leadership; Fellow for the Society for Industrial and Organizational Psychology

- James H. Johnson: Recently presented with the UNC General Alumni Association's Faculty Service Award for his exceptional service to the university and the alumni association; author of several books including *Prismatic Metropolis: Inequality in Los Angeles*

- Douglas A. Shackelford: Director of the UNC Tax Center; Fellow that includes research with National Bureau of Economic Research

- Jayashankar M. Swaminathan: Prominent contributor to the research fields of global supply-chain management and mass customization; author of *Indian Economic Superpower: Fiction or Future?*

- Valarie Zeithaml: Highly regarded for teaching and research; co-authored with Roland Rust and Katherine Lemon *Driving Customer Equity: How Customer Lifetime Value Is Reshaping Corporate Strategy*, which received the Berry-American Marketing Association Book Prize

---

What Admissions Is All About

The applications process for UNC Kenan-Flagler is completed online. Application material includes GMAT scores, resume, transcript, four required essays (two additional essays are optional), two letters of recommendation, and TOEFL or IELTS results; if appropriate. An early decision deadline is in October for those who are certain that UNC is the school for them. Three other rounds of decisions are made between December and March. Students who are not immediately accepted may be put on a waitlist. In a recent year, nearly 30 percent of those on the waitlist were eventually accepted into that year's program.

One of the best ways for the applicant to know that he or she is a good match for the school is to meet with a school representative for an interview. UNC Kenan-Flagler feels so strongly about this meeting, it makes clear that the interview is not just recommended; it is required.

"Our approach to the application process is very holistic," says Senior Associate Director of MBA Admissions Lisa Beisser. "The various pieces we value equally include: career path and accomplishments, essays, professional recommendations, test scores, and undergraduate performance. In addition, we require a personal interview with every candidate to whom we offer admission. We likely weigh this interview more heavily than some MBA programs, since the UNC culture is so strong and we look for students who we know will be a good cultural fit with the program," she adds.

If in-person interviews are not possible, candidates can have phone interviews, talk with area alumni, or attend admissions events that the school holds throughout the world. The school has recently implemented an invitation-only interview policy. When the applicant submits the application, the admissions office reviews it and determines whether the applicant will be invited to interview.

Students are expected to come into school with strong analytical and quantitative skills. For those needing refreshers in that area, the school recommends taking classes prior to orientation. The school offers a popular Analytic Skills Workshop prior to orientation as well; most students take one ASW session to ease the transition from work to study and to meet fellow students.

Kenan-Flagler admissions officers describe their ideal applicant as someone with drive and motivation, leadership and organizational skills, communication skills and ability to work as part of a team, analytical skills, history of results, and career progression. Beisser adds that having these skills shows that candidates have not only the ability to get things done themselves, but also the ability to make things happen through others.

Admissions requirements for international students are similar to that of U.S. students. TOEFL or IELTS is required for students whose native language is not English, with a few exceptions. The school's Office of International Student and Scholar Services assists students starting the visa application process.

More than one-third of students enrolled at UNC Kenan-Flagler have spouses or partners. The school provides support for that relationship through the MBA Partner's Association, the Kenan Connection. Through a variety of activities and clubs, the Kenan Connection seeks to make the transition smoother for the couple.

FULL-TIME MBA PROGRAM (TOTAL DIRECT COSTS)

In-state: $43,503

Out-of-state: $81,401

Evening MBA: $69,000

Weekend MBA: $84,600

OneMBA: $95,000

Financially Aided

For students interested in applying to Kenan-Flagler, Susan Brooks, assistant director, Office of Scholarships and Student Aid MBA, EMBA, and MAC Programs, strongly suggests you plan expenses in advance. "The most common error I see is students that do not have a realistic understanding of the financial commitment they are entering. They do not have sufficient savings and/or significant outstanding debt. These two factors greatly affect their lifestyle while enrolled." She adds that once you do come to school, you will have a designated financial aid officer so you will always have the same person to contact for assistance.

The majority of students receive some type of financial aid, whether it is in the form of scholarships or loans. Students may receive independent funding from another source, such as from an employer while the student is on leave to pursue the degree.

International students may apply for the North Carolina EXTRA MBA Loan for students who cannot apply for federally funded loans.

Full-time MBAs receiving financial aid: 68%

Institutional (merit-based) scholarships: 70

Assistantships: 0

What Kenan-Flagler Students Know

Students come to UNC Kenan-Flagler from all over the world, although the greatest concentration does come from the southern part of the United States. Students say it is an accepting, multicultural atmosphere. Babar Bilal, class of 2007, adds, "I truly enjoyed the global aspect of the program. I enjoyed the opportunity to learn different business and cultural styles. I enjoyed the teaching style. I enjoyed the international residencies."

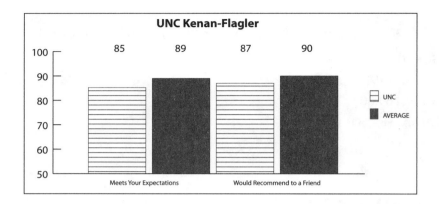

For some, the mild weather played a part in their decision to come here. Others cite the school's focus on leadership and specific concentrations available. In-state tuition fees and team-based learning are also important to students. Once students come to Kenan-Flagler, they are impressed with the opportunities available to them. The chance to lead comes early and often. Whether it is in the assigned teams or elected positions in clubs, students get to put their newly learned skills to work quickly.

Students mention the supportive environment of the school. With a virtual team of classmates, faculty, staff, and alumni, students feel they have lifelines in every direction. "When we say this is a place where people want others to succeed, it really is true," says Megan Godley, class of 2009. "I've been continuously supported by peers, alumni, faculty and staff to be the best possible leader I can be."

Another aspect of Kenan-Flagler that students are particularly proud of is the involvement in the community. Kenan-Flagler students volunteered for Habitat for Humanity and helped build one family's house. Students also provide tutoring for the Durham Scholar's Program. Students mention that Kenan-Flagler demonstrates its core values of excellence, leadership, integrity, community, and teamwork in a tangible way.

"The Kenan-Flagler philosophy is to produce well-rounded business leaders," Godley adds. "Those who seek to advance their personal careers while considering how the skill set they have obtained via school and past experiences can benefit the communities in which they live and serve."

Spencer Hall agrees. "When I visited UNC Kenan-Flagler, I noted that teamwork was a core value, and I could see how that impacts the direction of the school. One of the key questions that influenced our decision was Who do I want to be as a person when I graduate?"

Although the work is demanding, most students believe that with good time management, it's very possible to balance work and life to enjoy the social scene in Chapel Hill. Most students receive internships after their first year. Alumni who are currently in organizations are very helpful to students seeking internships.

What's Next? Your Career

Companies come to UNC Kenan-Flagler because they know students will have strong general management skills and will be ready to contribute immediately. The team learning environment gives new employees the skills and experience to lead and participate in teams in a corporate setting. In 2008, most first-year students were hired in marketing, banking, and finance.

CAREER CHECK: KENAN-FLAGLER MBA EMPLOYMENT BY JOB FUNCTION

- Consulting: 19%
- Investment Banking: 19%
- Marketing: 19%
- Industry Finance: 11%
- Real Estate: 9%
- Strategic Business Development: 7%
- Banking: 4%
- General Management: 4%
- Human Resources: 3%
- Operations/Global Supply Chain Management: 2%
- Other: 3%

The Career Management Center (CMC) at Kenan-Flagler offers a variety of programs to help students get ready to find a job or internship. At the same time, the CMC works diligently to bring corporations into the school to find students. More than 100 companies come to UNC Kenan-Flagler each year to find talented professionals.

"Recruiters hire from UNC Kenan-Flagler because they know they will get top MBAs with the right attitude," says Jennifer Brock, senior associate and director/COO of the MBA Career Management Center. "Kenan-Flagler MBAs are most noted for teamwork and leadership, two qualities that are found in the school's core values. In addition to knowing how to lead and manage people, companies seek out our MBAs for their strong analytical abilities and work ethic," she adds.

An international faculty and involved alumni base help to form a powerful international network with communities, companies, and other organizations that also help bring opportunities to the students. For students, the CMC provides one-on-one counseling and assessments, which include peer counseling for resumes, mock interviews, group training, and workshops. The CMC also helps students focus on the areas where they are most marketable to find jobs in tighter job markets. With the program's small class size, the CMC can help each student pursue individual career goals.

Even before becoming alumni, UNC Kenan-Flagler students have many networking opportunities in addition to faculty, classmates, and guest speakers. Companies come to the school for a variety of events, whether it is to participate in career fairs, career club activities, or other events. With the first-year internship, students have even more opportunities to meet and learn about other companies and jobs.

One career-networking opportunity that is unique to the school is the Student Teams Achieving Results (STAR) program. This program sends student teams on consulting projects for corporations and assists not-for-profits seeking to strengthen their global competitiveness. The STAR program requires an application to try to establish the best fit between clients and students and create teams with well-rounded experience and skills. The project itself is run like a consulting engagement. An engagement letter defines the scope of work, regular status meetings, and deliverables. Students, especially those looking to move into consulting from another field, consider it great training.

Upon graduation, alumni don't stop networking. They network within their new companies and with each other across the country. With Facebook, LinkedIn, and Meetup groups, alumni offer support and friendship in person and through cyberspace.

Maryanne Perrin, partner of Balancing Professionals in Raleigh, earned her Kenan-Flagler MBA more than 15 years ago. "Being an alumnus has proven very beneficial to me for networking," she explains. "[It] facilitates introductions and creates a common link with other business people in the community."

For their part, alumni continue to work with the school mentoring students and providing feedback from the corporate world. UNC Kenan-Flagler continues to offer support to alumni as well. Alumni can continue to use career services for additional job changes; they can also continue their education by attending MBA electives for a nominal fee.

Recruiters give UNC Kenan-Flagler graduates an "A" because they come to the corporate world prepared with the skills and strategies needed to make an immediate impact.

ALUMNI ACTUALS

MBA alumni worldwide: 9,407+

Business school alumni networking site: www.kenan-flagler.unc.edu/alumni/

Current MBA students have access to the alumni database.

Match Made in Heaven: Is UNC Kenan-Flagler Business School Right for You?

You are an ideal student if you

- Embrace the Kenan-Flagler culture of leadership, teamwork, and involvement.
- Work well in a positive, interactive environment.
- Want the benefits of new research as well as wish to learn how to apply theory to a business environment.
- Want to gain the skills and confidence to make an immediate impact in your career.

University of Pennsylvania
The Wharton School of Business

420 Jon M. Huntsman Hall
3730 Walnut Street
Philadelphia, PA 19104-6340

Phone: 215.898.6183
E-mail: mba.admissions@wharton.upenn.edu
Web site: http://mba.wharton.upenn.edu/

Wharton San Francisco (Executive MBA)
101 Howard Street, Suite 500
San Francisco, CA 94105

Phone: 415.777.1000
E-mail: mbaexecwest-admissions@wharton.upenn.edu
Web site: http://west.wharton.upenn.edu/

Dean: Thomas S. Robertson
Vice Dean, Graduate Division: Anjani Jain
Deputy Dean, Chief Academic and Program Officer: Michael R. Gibbons
Deputy Vice Dean of Student Life: Kembrel Jones

"Wharton is all about scale and scope. It's a very large school; it has eleven departments. It has departments that very few schools have, such as insurance and risk management and real estate, or health care management." —Dean Robertson

Quick Facts

MBA Programs

Full-time MBA
Executive MBA
Wharton-Lauder MBA/MA
Accelerated MBA/JD

Full-Time MBA Snapshot

Total program enrollment: 1,651
Class of 2010: 780
Length of program: 20 months
Campus locations: Philadelphia, Pennsylvania, and San Francisco, California
Program commences in August
Pre-term orientation attendance required

(continued)

(continued)

APPLICATION NOTES

Requirements: undergraduate degree from an accredited university; application; GMAT score;
   TOEFL if applicable; four essays; one optional essay; resumes; GRE not accepted
Letters of recommendation: 2
Interview: By invitation only
Number of applicants: 7,328
Admittance rate: 16%

CLASS OF 2010 PROFILE

Male 64%, Female 36%
Minority Americans: 26%
International: 40%
Average age: 28
Married or Partnered, Single: 22%, 78%
Average years of work experience: 6 years
GMAT score average: 715
GMAT score range (20th–80th percentile: 660–760
GPA average: 3.5

ACADEMIC BACKGROUND OF INCOMING STUDENTS

Arts and Sciences/Math: 26%
Business: 23%
Computer Science: 25%
Economics: 22%
Other: 4%

Founding a Liberal Business Education

Joseph Wharton attended several Quaker and private schools in and around Philadelphia until he
was 14 and prepared for college by private tutor until 16. He spent three years with relatives learning farming and studied French and German, and spent two years as an apprentice bookkeeper before
collaborating with his brother in manufacturing at age 21.

As an executive and entrepreneur, he is credited with supplying metals to an industrializing America
in the mid-1880s to the early 1900s. As an education visionary, he helped develop Swarthmore College in 1864 and established the Wharton School of Finance and Commerce in 1881—the latter as
part of the University of Pennsylvania.

The Wharton School was created during the Second Industrial Revolution, a time when technology expanded industries exponentially. Business administrators and finance managers became essential for guiding the growth of large-scale production, especially when the United States experienced a fluctuating economy through 1890s in addition to changing federal laws regulating business. Companies depended on educated, sophisticated management to ensure their survival. From the 1920s, Wharton was known primarily as a finance specialist school.

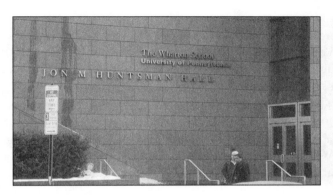 

Wharton is located in Philadelphia.

Philadelphia is the sixth largest city in the United States and has the highest standard of living per dollar of any major city in the Northeast corridor. Both diverse and lively, Philly, as it is called, is a short train ride away to the heart of New York City, Washington, D.C., and Boston, making it the ideal location for a business school such as Wharton. The majority of Wharton students come from outside Philadelphia, creating a wealth of diverse experiences and opportunity. Yet Wharton is small enough to feel like home with its close-knit community and family-like atmosphere. You can get around without a car in Philly and the majority of MBA students do not have a car.

Why Wharton?

Wharton is a powerhouse business school offering 19 majors and more than 200 electives from 11 departments—more than any other business school in the world. You can major in everything from Real Estate to Health Care Management to Technological Innovation to Strategic Management. You may also create your own major that focuses on cross-functional learning paths.

All students attend a required pre-term that levels out the playing field by offering coursework, waiver testing, a Learning Team retreat, and opportunities to explore the Philadelphia area and build relationships that you take into your first year. Members of the Wharton community are quick to emphasize the benefits of learning from students with different professional backgrounds, so the school is extremely interested in your ability to interact in a team-oriented environment. Additionally, Wharton is genuinely interested in knowing what type of person you are outside the professional environment and seeks students who have strong leadership potential.

Within the classroom, all first-year students take a class called Foundations of Teamwork and Leadership. In addition, the administration assigns all incoming students to a learning team composed of five or six students with at least one woman and one international student. Since the learning team must work together on all team assignments in the first-year core curriculum classes, there is plenty of time to develop leadership and teamwork skills. As part of the pre-term session, all first-year students participate in a two-day Learning Team retreat in which team members are introduced and the foundation for success within the team is set.

Outside the classroom, students further develop their leadership and teamwork skills through their participation in student-run clubs, student-organized conferences, and sports teams. Unique to Wharton is Leadership Ventures. More than 400 MBA students participate in 13 leadership ventures each year. The Graduate Leadership Ventures are planned experiential learning opportunities that put you in remote and difficult places to learn from intense experience how to resolve personal conflicts, resolve team problems, and lead teams, as well as follow designated team leaders.

Perhaps no other business school in the United States is as internationally minded as Wharton. International students account for about 40 percent of the student body and represent more than 70 countries. Many students already have vast arrays of international work experience and speak two or more languages. These attributes support Wharton's learning model of viewing business issues in a global context. Wharton values international experience, is very serious about its international mission, and seeks applicants who aid and/or benefit from that mission.

The environment for international students has changed over the past few decades. Partnership with Penn's Lauder Institute of Management and International Studies introduced an even greater international presence at Wharton, and students are currently obligated to spend two months abroad as part of their education. Besides programs offered through Lauder, students can earn premier global dual/joint degrees from the Nitze School of Advanced International Studies at Johns Hopkins University's Washington Campus and the Harvard Kennedy School of Government. Wharton students may also spend seven weeks in France or Singapore through the Wharton/INSEAD Alliance.

FUN FACTS

- For late-night revelers, Little Pete's restaurant is open really, really early.
- Philadelphia was home to the first U.S. stock exchange, and America's first bank opened there in 1791. In addition, Philadelphia was America's largest city for 30 years (1800–1830).
- In 1836, Philadelphia streets were lit by gas instead of oil. America's first gas utility was granted to Philadelphia's United Gas Improvement Company in 1897.
- Public executions were once staged on Logan Square, where the gallows stood until 1823.
- Movies filmed in Philly include *Rocky*, *Rocky II*, *Dressed to Kill*, *Blow Out*, *Birdy*, *Witness*, *Age of Innocence*, *Philadelphia*, *12 Monkeys*, *The Sixth Sense*, and *Fallen*.

Course Offerings

During pre-term, you can take exams to waiver certain first-year classes in which you already have solid knowledge. As an example, CPAs will typically take the waiver exam for the Accounting classes required as part of the core curriculum. Passing these exams will also enable students to forgo the typical first-year finance class and replace it with a more advanced class. Wharton uses its online auction system to manage enrollment in optional pre-term activities, as well as for elective course selection. Students use the pre-term auction as a kind of trial run of the bidding system and report that they appreciate learning bidding strategies before course and interview auctions begin.

Wharton has 19 majors that include accounting, entrepreneurial management, finance, health care management, marketing, operations and information management, real estate, and strategic management. You also have the opportunity to develop an individualized major. The first-year curriculum concentrates on the core courses that provide you with a critical foundation in management, leadership, ethics, and communication. You work on assignments in learning teams, which are central to the learning model. Global Strategic Management, Macroeconomic Analysis, and Public Policy are required first-year courses.

In the second year, for students interested in a more traditional study-abroad experience, Wharton offers exchange programs in 17 countries through 14 partner schools in 153 countries, as well as the Global Immersion Program (GIP) and the Wharton Global Consulting Program (GCP). The optional GIP program runs May and June, and around 135 students yearly participate: five weeks studying a global region such as Africa, China, or Southeast Asia, followed by a four-week study abroad to that region. Students return in time for summer internships.

The GCP program is an elective open to both first- and second-year MBA students, educating them in the issues of international business and consulting. More than 1,000 Wharton students have assisted in the development of market entry strategies for more than 250 companies, adding more than $300 million annual U.S. revenues to their clients. The program currently works with partner schools in Chile, China, Colombia, India, Israel, Peru, and Spain.

RESEARCH CENTERS AND INITIATIVES

Boettner Center for Pensions and Retirement Research

Center for Health Management and Economics

Center for Human Resources

Center for Leadership and Change Management

Council on Employee Relations

Financial Institutions Center

Fishman-Davis Center for Service and Operations Management

Initiative for Global Environmental Leadership

J.H. Baker Retailing Initiative

Leonard Davis Institute of Health Economics

William and Phyllis Mack Center for Technological Innovation

(continued)

(continued)

Pension Research Council

Risk Management and Decision Processes Center

SEI Center for Advanced Studies in Management

Sol C. Snider Entrepreneurial Research Center

Weiss Center for International Financial Research

Wharton Global Family Alliance

Wharton Interactive Media Initiative

Wharton/INSEAD Center for Global Research and Education

Wharton Small Business Development Center

Wharton Sports Business Initiative

Rodney L. White Center for Financial Research

Zell/Lurie Real Estate Center

Carol and Lawrence Zicklin Center for Business Ethics Research

What Wharton Professors Teach

Wharton's more than 250 faculty members are active in business, government, and nonprofits worldwide. They bring a diverse expertise to the table and engage you in real-world, real-time scenarios that allow you to fully invest yourself in your field right from the start.

One student in the class of 2009 shares that, "Managing People at Work (or ManPAW) with Professor Useem is a class you should visit if you are coming to campus. He is amazing and the class is very entertaining. [In particular] learning teams take turns presenting a case by putting on a skit, and those are hilarious."

The word "excellent" is frequently heard from students when commenting on their professors. One of the top teaching departments is Insurance and Risk Management. Neil Doherty, Jean Lemaire, Olivia Mitchell, Kent Smetters—students are amazed by their level of knowledge, teaching abilities, class organization, caring communication … and the list goes on. Of course, Wharton enjoys the expertise of more than 250 faculty members, all of whom are exceptional teachers or researchers, as well as business communicators.

FACULTY FACTS

Full-time faculty employed by the b-school: 232

Adjunct or visiting faculty: 192

Permanent/tenured professors: 141

Tenured faculty who are women: 19

Tenured faculty who are underrepresented minorities: 15

SAMPLING OF NOTABLE PROFESSORS

- Peter Capelli: Founding editor of the Academy of Management Perspectives; research associate at the National Bureau of Economic Research and a fellow of the National Academy of Human Resources; worked at the U.S. Secretary of Labor's Commission on Workforce Quality and Labor Market, as well as the U.S. Department of Education's National Center on the Educational Quality of the Workforce

- Peter Fader: Expert in analysis of behavioral data to understand and forecast customer shopping/purchasing activities; researches using data generated by new information technology to fine-tune business marketing tactics and strategies

- Olivia Mitchell: Expert in pensions and retirement issues; author or co-author of several books including, with Brigitte Madrian and Beth J. Soldo, *Redefining Retirement: How Will Boomers Fare?*

- Jeremy Siegel: "Wizard of Wharton"; teaches a Macroeconomics class that is highly sought-after; gives a 10-minute stock market overview at the beginning of every lecture, often to a standing-room-only audience

- Michael Useem: Expert on leadership; author of many ground-breaking books on leadership and other subjects, including *The Go Point: When It's Time to Decide—Knowing What to Do and When to Do It*

CONCENTRATIONS AND SPECIALIZATIONS OFFERED IN FULL-TIME MBA PROGRAM

Accounting	Insurance and Risk Management
Business and Public Policy	Legal Studies and Business Ethics
Entrepreneurial Management	Managing Electronic Commerce
Environmental and Risk Management	Marketing
Finance	Marketing and Operations Management
Health Care Management	Multinational Management
Human Resource and Organizational Management	Operations and Information Management
Individualized Major	Real Estate
Information: Strategy and Economics	Statistics
	Strategic Management

(continued)

(continued)

JOINT DEGREES AND DUAL DEGREES

MBA/JD	MBA/MPA2 (Public Administration)
MBA/MD	MBA/MPID (Public Administration/
MBA/DMD (Dentistry)	International Development)
MBA/MA (International Management)	MBA/MPP (Public Policy)
MBA/MA (International Studies)	MBA/MSN (Nursing)
MBA/March (Architecture)	MBA/MSW (Social Work)
MBA/MB (Engineering)	MBA/VMD (Veterinary Medicine)

What Admissions Is All About

The Wharton Admissions committee is looking for mature, intelligent people who have demonstrated leadership potential and have a strong sense of themselves and a purpose. Candidates can demonstrate these qualities through their professional experience, involvement in volunteer activities, and through their essays. A former Wharton student looked back on the application process and advises, "Applicants should really think about why they are applying to business school and to the particular program to which they're applying. Applicants then need to clearly communicate this idea in both their essays and their interviews." Wharton students have an average of six years of work experience. Rejected applicants often are told that they could use another year or two of pertinent work experience. That shouldn't dissuade you from applying if your years of experience fall below the Wharton average, but you should be able to answer these questions clearly. Why now? Why Wharton? How will I add value to the classroom? You should especially expect this issue to come up during the interview if you have less than three years of professional experience. If perchance you are not accepted and choose to reapply the following year, the Wharton Admissions Office holds on to your application and, if you request it, offers you feedback on it. This is a valuable service that will give you greater insight on what the school is seeking for its incoming class.

The interview is by invitation only after a thorough review of your application. In most cases, the content of your interview will be consistent with the information in your application. As communication skills are a hallmark of leadership, the interviewer wants to see how you communicate. Will you spend the allotted 30 minutes addressing only the first question? Will you communicate your reasons for your career trajectory? Will you demonstrate your emotional intelligence? Although not the decisive factor in your admissions decision, your interviews provide additional information about your candidacy by helping admissions officers know you better as a person and a professional.

The structure of the interviews is blind, which reduces bias. Your interviewer will have no preconceived ideas of your ability or personality based on your written application. Interviews may include behavioral questions. Questions may center on specific examples or detailed descriptions of events, projects, or experience that demonstrate how situations you've faced in the past have been handled and what you learned from them. Behavioral interviewing assumes that past performance predicts future behavior.

No advance preparation is required. Questions are straightforward and cover topics such as why you seek an MBA, why you feel you are a good fit for Wharton and why Wharton would be a good fit for you, what your career goals are, how you spend your spare time, what you value, about what you are passionate, and so on. You will not be asked to analyze a case study or demonstrate your mastery of particular subjects.

Do not expect the interviewer to give you feedback. Be careful to avoid any interpretation of verbal or nonverbal communication, as both may mislead you. Interviews are not a popularity contest. The interviewer is assessing your fit for the Wharton MBA program, not whether the two of you would make good friends. The key is to relax, be genuine, and enjoy the opportunity to get to know more about the program.

> Full-time MBAs receiving financial aid through school: 30%
>
> Institutional (merit-based or need-based) scholarships: 250
>
> Full-tuition scholarships school awarded for academic year: 11

Financially Aided

The primary resource for funding your MBA is through federal and/or alternative educational loans, fellowships, and grants.

Admittance to Wharton's MBA program is first, and then your admittance packet will guide you through the MBA financing process. For U.S. citizens and other permanent residents, your likely primary source will be through the federal or alternative loan systems. International students are not eligible for federal funds; however, they are eligible for alternative loans and fellowships.

Admitted students must apply for fellowships; consideration is not automatic. Fellowships are awarded based on the strength of your application and are selected by committee. Grants are awarded by need through the separate NeedAccess application and may be taxable as income.

The Global Immersion Program is not included in the Wharton student budget; however, the director submits an official participant list to the financial aid office. Student budgets may be increased, thus making students eligible for more aid.

FULL-TIME MBA PROGRAM (TOTAL DIRECT COSTS)

In-state: $80,000

Out-of-state: $80,000

International: $80,000

EMBA program costs: Philadelphia, $150,870; San Francisco, $159,810

What Wharton Students Know

Work hard, play hard. That's the mantra of students at the University of Pennsylvania, and by extension, Wharton. Wharton students unwind by taking in the nearby downtown Philadelphia nightlife. Because of the nature of Wharton's MBA programs and the work involved, Wharton students are just as likely to enjoy taking on social responsibility projects as they are social get-togethers at restaurants and pubs.

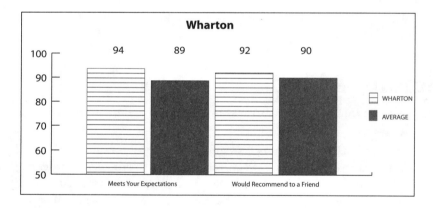

In 2008, Wharton added an administrative position: Deputy Vice Dean of Student Life. Among other duties, newly appointed Kembrel Jones works closely with students, student leaders, clubs, conference organizers, and lecture series organizers to facilitate smooth operations. One result is that the MBA Program Office Advisory Board has been split, with one section focused on academic issues and the other focused on student life. Every year hundreds of students begin classes on campus, and the complexity of issues such a group may encounter is enormous. Jones speaks with students and encourages their feedback so that he can make whatever improvements necessary to ensure an optimal positive experience.

Devin Griffin, class of 2009, relates, "After visiting Wharton for admit weekend, the decision to attend was a slam dunk. I was struck by how down to earth, friendly, and approachable Wharton students and my fellow admits were. I didn't expect this from an elite business school and felt that it

© JIST Works

really fit my style well. Now as I'm about to graduate, I'm happy that my initial impression held true throughout my time here."

Griffin is starting his own company called Seven Rivers and has received significant support at Wharton. "For better or worse, it's easy to pigeonhole Wharton as just a finance school. As an entrepreneur, I have found this to be far from the truth. Wharton provides a lot of academic and administrative support services for launching a business. Beyond formal programming support, I'm lucky to have so many of my classmates helping me work on my venture. I've received so many insights and so much great work from my classmates who are truly the best of the best, including McKinsey consultants, bankers, and venture capital investors. Right now, I have three different teams of students helping me flesh out various aspects of my business plan. There is no way I could have made so much progress so quickly without the strong support of the school and unfettered enthusiasm of my classmates at Wharton."

Rory Conway, class of 2009, relates, "There are 1,600 Type A students here, and there is so much activity with clubs and events. There is an annual boxing event, and we even have fashion shows. These events are student driven and they really reinforce the energy level of the students. Students really do drive and are co-creators of the experience." Conway further comments, "Wharton has kept me very busy throughout my two years. I have a few more weeks to go and then I have the summer off before starting with Microsoft in late August. The whole articulation of the goals essays I did for my applications gave me a game plan that has helped me throughout my time here at Wharton. I have been very involved in the General Management Club and have helped organize many conferences. There are a lot of students here who are passionate about general management and we're actively working to shift the perception that Wharton is purely a finance school."

One recent alum recalls, "Wharton is continually highly ranked and has name recognition as well as an honored reputation. Graduates of Wharton tend to be smart, personable individuals who are interested in the world around them." As a result, "Student life at Wharton is very dynamic and there is always some sort of event happening. One club in which I was very involved was the real estate club. Due to my involvement, I had the opportunity to really know some of my classmates who were also pursuing a career in real estate. Many of these relationships are still strong today."

Erica Henning, class of 2003, relates, "I chose Wharton for three reasons: strength of the program, student-driven environment, and well-rounded business curriculum. Wharton prepared me very well for my career. . . . I learned the fundamental concepts that enabled me to hit the ground running." And yes, true to form for most MBA candidates, she did not believe everything she had heard about the Wharton workload. "Although everyone told me that business school involved a great deal of work, I didn't quite appreciate this until I attended my first few classes. You tend to forget how time intensive classwork can be when you've been out of school for a few years."

What's Next? Your Career

The Wharton Entrepreneurial Program (WEP) is one of the premier influential entrepreneurial centers in the world. Part of the management department at Wharton, the WEP is led by internationally renowned researchers and consultants Ian C. MacMillan and Raphael Amit. Alumni are a large part of the WEP network. They provide guidance and expertise through outreach activities for student direction.

Another resource you can explore is to join a trek—scouting opportunities for potential jobs in a variety of industries around the world. A group from Wharton travels together to information sessions with different companies. These are intended to lead to summer internships and possibly full-time jobs after graduation. Rory Conway talks about one of his treks. "Over spring break [March 2009], I went on the Korea trek. One of the students was friends with the Korean president's son. We went to the Blue House, the president's residence, for afternoon tea and discussed the global economy. President Lee Myung-bak shared his opinions and preparations for the upcoming [April 2009] G20 summit in London. There is a trek to Israel coming up and the students are supposed to meet President [Shimon Peres]. The co-production (or energy), talent, and connections of the students here really drives the Wharton experience."

CAREER CHECK: WHARTON MBA EMPLOYMENT BY JOB FUNCTION

- Finance/Accounting: 55%
- Consulting: 28%
- Marketing/Sales: 7%
- General Management: 6%
- Other: 4%

"Career Services has been doing a lot of reaching out and beating of the bushes with employers," says Conway. In addition, "With the economy being down a bit, a lot of my colleagues are pursuing entrepreneurial opportunities and teaming up together." He explains, "The school has brought in a number of speakers who are talking about how now is a good time to start a company and how many good new companies emerge from recessions."

"Wharton did a tremendous job of preparing me for re-entering the business world," relates Henning. "I absolutely use what I learned in my life today. In addition, on more than one occasion, I have referred back to my notes and textbooks, too." As with most endeavors in life, Wharton is what you make of it. "The more engaged you are with your classmates, the more you will get out of business school."

ALUMNI ACTUALS

MBA alumni worldwide: 38,000+

Business school alumni networking site: www.whartonconnect.com/

Current MBA students have access to the alumni database.

Match Made in Heaven: Is the Wharton Business School Right for You?

You are an ideal student if you

- Want to learn through a variety of approaches that include case studies, team-based projects, Leadership Ventures, and technology-enabled simulations.
- Wish to work in collaborative groups with a prime educational focus on "innovation," and look forward to being part of a student body with substantial diversity of international students.
- Seek to develop your leadership skills you can use in a global arena.
- Want to be part of an evolutionary process where new course offerings reflect the shifting realm of real-world business.

University of Southern California Marshall School of Business

Popovich Hall Room 308
630 Childs Way
Los Angeles, CA 90089

Phone: 213.740.7846
E-mail: marshallmba@marshall.usc.edu
Web site: http://www.marshall.usc.edu/mbaadmissions/

Dean: James G. Ellis
Associate Dean, MBA Programs: Cherie Scricca

"At Marshall, we strive to imbue our students with a learning experience that uniquely prepares them to lead and thrive in the most challenging of environments while maintaining a commitment to integrity and the community. As such, we value the potential of every student, and we are here to support their loftiest dreams and career aspirations." —Dean Ellis

Quick Facts

MBA PROGRAMS

Full-time MBA
Part-time MBA
Executive MBA
GEMBA (Shanghai)
IBEAR MBA

FULL-TIME MBA SNAPSHOT

Total enrollment: 446
Class of 2010: 219
Length of program: 21 months
Campus location: Los Angeles, CA
Program commences in August
Pre-term orientation required, some activities optional

APPLICATION NOTES

Requirements: Four-year bachelor degree; transcripts; GMAT; TOEFL; four essays; resume; recommendations; application; GRE not accepted
Letters of recommendation: 2–3

GMAT: Required
Number of applicants: 2,076
Admittance rate: 23%

CLASS OF 2010 PROFILE

Male: 70% Female: 30%
Minority Americans: 30%
International: 34%
Average age: 28
Combined average years of work experience: 5.2 years
GMAT score range (20th–80th): 640–740
GMAT score average: 692
GPA average: 3.3

ACADEMIC BACKGROUND OF INCOMING STUDENTS

Business: 26%
Computer Sciences: 8%
Economics: 14%
Engineering/Science: 27%
Humanities: 25%

The Art and Science of Business

Academic excellence, innovative research, and cutting-edge business theory are the hallmarks of the USC Marshall School of Business. The oldest AACSB-accredited school of business in Southern California, the school was established in 1920, and in 1997 it was renamed for Gordon S. Marshall in honor of his $35 million contribution. A member of USC's class of 1946, he founded Marshall Industries in 1954, which became one of the nation's largest distribution companies of electronic components and production supplies. As chairman of Marshall Industries, he has experienced firsthand the impact of technological change on business and the necessity of a first-class business education to anticipate those changes. Thus, he is also a major shareholder in Amistar Corporation (now Amistar Automation, Inc.), another innovative company that specializes in automatic and semiautomatic equipment for assembling electronic components.

On campus at Marshall.

Today, more than 5,000 undergraduate, graduate, professional, and executive-education students attend the five schools of USC Marshall at the main campus in Los Angeles and at the satellite campuses located in Irvine or San Diego, California. Along with its southern California location, USC Marshall possesses a strong regional reputation, programs based on real-world global business, and the benefits inherent to a prestigious university. The school draws on the rich resources of the USC academic system and shares its history of producing top-of-the-line scholars who not only learn the technical side of business, but its human side as well. USC's MBA program is flexible and innovative, offering many joint degree programs and options for students to attend the program on a full- or part-time basis. USC Marshall also operates a Global MBA program with Jiao Tong University in Shanghai, China.

Why Marshall?

The USC Marshall School of Business reigns on the cutting edge of global diversity and curriculum, consistently ranking high on the world's top MBA program lists. USC has the largest alumni population of any university in the United States and members are often referred to as the "Trojan Family Network." Alexander Capello, class of 1977 and founder of Capello Group Inc., calls the Trojan Family close-knit. "You're a member in good standing until you breech the trust, and nobody does that." Marshall takes care of its students.

Because a third of incoming students are international, there is a one-week orientation especially for new U.S. arrivals before the general all-student orientation. Current MBA candidates introduce the ways of Americans and work in information on Marshall's classroom environment and academic expectations amidst the orientation's fun events. After that, first-year students arrive on campus for their introduction to the program, followed by second-year students—most of whom they will meet when classes begin.

One area in which USC Marshall excels is conferences. Take the Asia Pacific Business Outlook Conference, 22 years old and counting. For businesses of medium size or smaller, this is a premium annual event that introduces entrepreneurs to Asian companies to share information about the current economic rules and realities. Marshall partners with the U.S. Department of Commerce to facilitate idea sharing among experts and attendees. The 2009 two-day event, with 300 participants, is an indicator of how vital this conference has become to understanding business in the Pacific Rim.

The Global Mobility Roundtable (GMR) Conference has been held every year since 2002 and is an international event organized through USC's Institute for Communication Technology Management. Researchers and industry members come together with experts in policy and decision making to network and exchange the latest findings. In 2009 the GMR was held in Cairo, Egypt in conjunction with the American University of Cairo's International Executive Education Institute.

In addition to its strength in conferences, Marshall has strong academic programs—especially in accounting and finance. Marshall is a recognized Chartered Financial Analyst (CFA) Program Partner institution. CFA Program Partners offer degree programs that cover at least 70 percent of the CFA Program Candidate Body of Knowledge, the CFA Institute of ethical and professional standards, and other requirements. Recognition as a CFA Program Partner signals to potential students, employers, and the marketplace that the university curriculum is closely tied to professional practice and is well-suited to preparing students to sit for the three levels of CFA examinations. "USC is proud to join a select group of universities around the world to be recognized by [the] CFA Institute as providing students with a solid grounding in the concepts and principles, including strong ethical and professional standards, required to become CFA charter holders," says Larry Harris, director of the Center for Investment Studies at Marshall.

Marshall's ongoing development of instruction includes mobile wireless computer labs and electronic communication. For example, "Marshall TV" is the school's moniker on YouTube.com, where anyone can view conversations with recent USC Marshall authors, receive an insider's view of student life, or check out some of the recent research results. As of Spring 2009, Marshall is also revamping its international exchange program for the MBA program to include not only many of its current partner schools but expanding the international opportunities available through partnerships in countries not previously available.

FUN FACTS

- Life's a beach: It's a common misconception that USC students practically live at the beach. Not with Marshall's rigorous MBA program! Most of the time is spent with classmates in study sessions, although many students live in area beach communities.

- On-duty U.S. military personnel stationed worldwide now have the opportunity to study free via the Internet to become Chartered Financial Analysts at USC Marshall. The program began in January 2009.

- Paul Orfalea, class of 1971, founder of Kinko's, is a self-proclaimed "terrible reader" because of dyslexia and can't fix a copier to save his life.

- Professor S. Mark Young brings narcissistic celebrity behavior under scrutiny in the MBA classroom.

Course Offerings

Seven academic departments make up USC Marshall's MBA program: Accounting, Finance and Business Economics, Information and Operations Management, Marketing, Management and Organization, Management Communication, and Entrepreneurship. Each department is not an entity unto itself and is purposefully multidisciplinary, drawing from USC's masters program and the university's arts and sciences program.

The MBA's first year is designed to maximize the fundamental tools and functional knowledge that every leader in business must have to make decisions. The second year allows you to draw on 108 available electives that interest you and your career aspirations. Both years balance theory and practice that give Marshall students scholarship and practical experiences that create today's global business leaders. Electives recently added include Ethics and Social Issues in Business and Leadership and Executive Development.

The collaborative nature of the course offerings helps teach decision making and the social responsibility that goes along with the ethics of business and sustainable development. It's not just about making a profit anymore, today and tomorrow's new brand of business leaders look with an eye to future generations and keeping our planet and the businesses therein healthy and sustainable on every level. USC Marshall brings your MBA to life through apprenticeships, internships, and other pertinent business experiences such as alumni affiliations. The courses bridge theory and teamwork to create a unique learning experience.

All full-time MBA candidates are required to participate in an international experience, during which you and your classmates work on business problems facing real companies. In your second year, you undertake your project with PRIME—Pacific Rim International Management Education. PRIME consists of lectures related to a country's economics, businesses, international trade, and corporate culture. After you have gained an understanding of these dynamics, you work with your team on a project assigned to you that explores a global strategy in a specific industry. After the lectures and team-project conclusion, you travel to the country about which you have become acquainted for some experiential learning exercises. For a week, you can put your knowledge to work by aiding in a real corporation quandary and presenting your team's finding to the chief company officers. By the time you return home, you have developed a new perspective through this international immersion in business.

An unusual option is the Marshall MBA.PM (Professional and Managers), a flexible three- to five-year degree with a choice of locations. You can attend either at the main Los Angeles campus or at the new Orange County Center in Irvine, California. The program is similar to the full-time MBA in that it requires a year of core courses, including a semester of macroeconomics. The MBA.PM is a rare program, however, because it requires an international component, the PM.GLOBE—a week-long session in Shanghai or Beijing, China; Delhi or Bangalore, India; Kyoto or Tokyo, Japan; Seoul, Korea; Singapore; or Bangkok, Thailand. After that, you take courses with a schedule that is best for you in the evenings after work. Professors, facilities, computer labs, and study rooms are all of the highest quality at both campuses.

For mid-level managers with a decade of work experience, Marshall offers the IBEAR International Business Education and Research—which graduated its 30th class of students in 2008. When the program began, "international" had quite a different meaning than it does today. Because the world of business has expanded to include so many countries, one of the highlights of the intensive one year of education is the final 17 weeks of team-focused research. Your class is divided into groups of five students each. Each group is destined to visit a different country.

IBEAR mixes the international attributes of more than 50 students each year with the broad-view expertise of its international faculty. This combination forms a close-knit family of global citizens who are conversant in multicultural, multi-approach business best practices.

Because of its innovative, entrepreneurial, research, and international academic focuses, the number of centers on campus is exceptional. The Center for Effective Organizations, for one, conducts the survey "Leadership Pulse" every quarter. The results include opinions from almost 4,000 business leaders in the United States from an array of various industry groups.

Unique among research centers is the Center for Global Innovation. Through the partnership of Marshall, the University of Minnesota, Imperial College London, and Cambridge University, the center carries out its research to identify why and how companies and countries undertake innovations. No other business school conducts this level of research on a global scale.

For MBA candidates, the Experiential Learning Center (ELC) will become part of your life at Marshall. The ELC makes use of its geographic location among the prominent Southern California industries of entertainment, biotech, health science, multimedia, and aerospace to engage students in hands-on, real-world learning. Along with meeting local business executives, attending conferences, mastering another language, supporting club activities, and meeting with your classmates, you spend half your time somehow involved with ELC. The collective nature of problem solving at the center in the condensed atmosphere of a research lab allows you to learn at advanced speed the up-to-the-minute problem-solving required in today's world.

RESEARCH CENTERS

Center for Effective Organizations

Center for International Business Education and Research

Center for Investment Studies

Center for Management Communication

Center for Technology Commercialization

Center for Global Innovation

Center for Global Logistics and Supply Chain

Experiential Learning Center

Global Branding Center

Greif Center for Entrepreneurial Studies

Initiative and Referendum Institute

Institute for Communication Technology Management

Lusk Center for Real Estate

What Marshall Professors Teach

Globalization is the future of business, and Marshall recognizes that teaching students to be global leaders is key not only to the business school experience but to their professional lives after the students leave school. So the faculty strives to define the theory and practice of the business administration program by bridging state-of-the-art research with real-world learner-centric experiences and a curriculum guided by the "knowledge creators" of the Marshall research faculty.

"Marshall staff makes sure that all students have the opportunity to get to know each other prior to beginning the first semester of business school. They set up an online networking website, various social activities, and an amazing admit weekend and orientation experience. Through these tools, students are able to truly connect before school begins," says Leann Sarkisian, class of 2010. Marshall's teaching and research faculty are world-class. One example is Tom O'Malia, director of the Greif Center, who is widely recognized as one of the country's top professors in entrepreneurship. The Greif Center is the oldest integrated entrepreneurship program in the United States. And because up-and-coming entrepreneurs gravitate toward programs emphasizing feasibility studies and local business community interaction, students flock to Marshall. For first-year students, professors team teach core courses to reveal the connections among subjects vital to a business education.

Professors at Marshall make a lasting impression on their students. After you have adjusted to the rigorous expectations of your Marshall MBA education, you will remember most the business experts who taught you. A few of these are Management Professor Lucy Lee, Finance and Business Economics Professors Henry Cheeseman and Thomas Gilligan, Accounting Professor Mark DeFond, and Management and Organization Professors Arvind Bhambri and Thomas Cummings. They are recognized not only for the depth of knowledge they bring to their topics but also for their teaching abilities. To have such professors teach students at USC is a great opportunity.

FACULTY FACTS

Total full-time faculty employed by the b-school: 198

Permanent/tenured faculty: 73

Adjunct or visiting faculty: 2

Tenured faculty who are women: 10

Tenured faculty who are underrepresented minorities: 11

Tenured international faculty: 19

SAMPLING OF NOTABLE PROFESSORS

- Yehuda Bassock: Sportswear company owner; award-winning professor of information and operations management
- Warren Bennis: Leadership expert called the "dean of leadership gurus"
- Dave Logan: Best-selling co-author, with Steve Zaffron, of *Three Laws of Performance: Rewriting the Future of Your Organization and Your Life*

- Zoe-Vonna Palmrose: Named one of *Treasury and Risk* magazine's 100 Most Influential People in Finance; named the American Accounting Association's 2008 Presidential Scholar
- Robyn Walker: Clinical management communication expert; editor of the *Journal of Business Communication*
- S. Mark Young: Specialist in the psychology of celebrity and pop culture, author or co-author of many books including, with Drew Pinksy, *The Mirror Effect: How Celebrity Narcissism Is Seducing America*

CONCENTRATIONS AND SPECIALIZATIONS OFFERED IN FULL-TIME MBA PROGRAM

Accounting	Healthcare Advisory Services
Business of Creative Industries	Information Services
Business of Entertainment	Management and Organization
Business of Education	Marketing
Entrepreneurship	Operations Management
Entrepreneurship and Operations	Technology Development and E-business
Finance and Business Economics	

JOINT DEGREES AND DUAL DEGREES

MBA/JD	Master of Business Taxation Working Professionals
MBA/MD	
MBA/MA (Arts)	Master of Medical Management
MBA (Accounting)	Master of Science in Business Administration (for holders of previous MBA only)
Master of Business Taxation	

What Admissions Is All About

Mind your p's and q's. Dot your i's and cross your t's. One of the most common mistakes is the cut-and-paste method that tells the admissions staff that you may have lacked attention to detail and thought with the application. Tell your story through your essays and during your interview. Admissions committee members want to feel that they know you. And be sure to read the instructions thoroughly. Give what's asked for and no more. For example, Admissions requires two letters of recommendation, not six. Marshall wants outside-of-the-box thinkers and leaders, but also people who can follow directives.

Director of Full-Time Admissions Keith Vaughn shares, "There are no minimum requirements to be admitted to Marshall. However, admittance is highly competitive and our student body is diverse on every level, professionally and personally. Students working on careers in the entertainment industry, for instance, are strong additions to the class of 2010. Our students are entrepreneurial and passionate about their future and highly motivated."

There are five main MBA programs, all with their own admissions processes. All programs interview by invitation only, and 97 percent of admitted applicants are interviewed, so the interview is very important. The majority of interviews are held on one or two "super Saturdays," during which alumni come in to assist the admissions staff with the 70 to 100 interviews each of those days.

For Marshall's dual degree programs, applicants must be admitted through both degree applicant processes to be considered.

Full-time MBAs receiving financial aid through school: 80%

Institutional (merit-based and need-based) scholarships: 103

Full-tuition scholarships school awarded for academic year: 41

Financially Aided

Costs for the MBA programs vary with the program. Despite the worldwide economic downturn, Marshall maintains a "pretty decent" budget for scholarships. There are a number of merit-based fellowships available. The Admissions Committee offers awards based on a range of criteria including academic merit, work experience, leadership experience, and value that the applicant may add to the MBA experience.

Something to keep in mind, Marshall does not offer scholarships or fellowships for any students in the MBA fully employed programs (including the MBA.PM program). For full-time MBA applicants, scholarships are based on merit and awarded to the top 25 percent of the incoming class.

FULL-TIME MBA PROGRAM (TOTAL DIRECT COSTS)

Resident: $85,750

Nonresident: $138,000

International: $138,000

What Marshall Students Know

As a first-year student, you learn the value of making sure your brain works at 8 a.m., because you take core courses that early. Time does fly by, however, and the next thing you know, you are eating lunch with your classmates while you go over class notes. Alternatively, you could be attending a lunchtime meeting or career events. Leann Sarkisian, class of 2010, says, "Marshall is unique in that it offers prime networking opportunities, which are extremely important in business school and career development. People that attend Marshall are not Trojans for their business school years, but they are truly Trojans for life. Marshall alumni are excited and willing to help out students and alumni." She adds, "Whenever visitors come to Marshall, they comment on the number of students sitting in the courtyard or common spaces and studying together. Students at Marshall use studying spaces to work together, which makes studying a much more enjoyable experience."

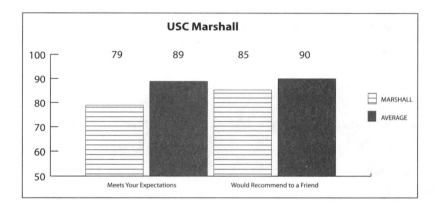

Your afternoon schedule consists of more classes, studying, research and writing, or team time. Evenings are slated for student clubs and events, which are vital to your experiential learning experience at Marshall. While you apply your b-school skills, you can indulge in your interests and help the world at the same time. For instance, for students who want to have a great education in community-based social responsibility, the Good Neighbor program is the place to find it. Continually expanding, the program has been active for more than 13 years and serves more school kids with afterschool programs than ever before. Do you want to learn about neighborhood health wellness? You can get on board the mobile dental clinic bus that travels to the public for oral health checkups and care. Do you want to teach kids a sport? USC Marshall students serve as coaches in tennis, swimming, baseball, volleyball, golf, martial arts—you name it. How about science? If you are out of touch with your inner scientist, find the fun again while you mentor curious young people through the trials and errors of everyday science exploration. Or you can tap your "rock god" alter ego and champion the Thornton Guitar masters-in-the-making as they sing and learn guitar riffs.

If you want to test your leadership chops, a great way to do it is through the MBA Leadership Challenge. Sure, you can go head to head in the classroom when you are defending your point of view, but can you keep up with a U.S. Marine? The partnership between the Marshall Military Veterans

Association and the U.S. Marine Corps involves two days of training exercises, teamwork, problem solving, and strategy decisions under fast-changing military situations. Since the challenge was established in 2004, these leadership exercises have trained students to think on their feet, protect their team, handle pressure, and resolve predicaments—all vital skills for top managers. Joseph Hernandez, who is the program coordinator for Marshall's full-time MBA program, has seen an increase in participation by 30 percent since the course's creation.

In addition to social responsibility and leadership, you will find many venues in which to test your competitiveness. USC's MBA chapter of Net Impact sponsored the second annual AlterEnergy forum, a panel discussion about challenges facing the energy industry. Net Impact is an international nonprofit organization with the mission of making a positive impact on society. This is accomplished through growing leaders who use business to improve the world. After you have served humanity at large, you will be ready to relax at the MBA mixer, an event held every Thursday evening.

On to your second year: Compared with your first year of frenetic learning, Year Two will feel more like a normal job. You select your courses, work with your mentors and team members, research and write during non-class hours, and focus on your future. After having spent the previous summer in an internship, you are so sophisticated about the ways of the business world that you are ready to tackle whatever comes your way.

CAREER CHECK: MARSHALL MBA EMPLOYMENT BY JOB FUNCTION

- Marketing/Sales: 32%
- Finance/Accounting: 31%
- Consulting: 18%
- Human Resources: 3%
- Operations/Logistics: 3%
- General Management: 1%
- Management Information Systems (MIS): 1%
- Other: 11%

What's Next? Your Career

For any career information you may need, the staff at the Keenan MBA Career Resource Center (CRC) has loads of job ideas for you to explore. Providing you the best career resources is the goal of the CRC's Executive Director Peter Giulioni and the Keenan Center staff. Marshall places many graduates in leading firms, and in return, alums turn to their alma mater when looking for highly qualified candidates to fill their open positions. Typically Marshall hosts more than 100 company recruiters on campus every year.

Students meet with employment representatives through career management programs such as the Alumni Mentor Program and student club events. In addition, the CRC holds Industry Institutes— seminars detailing careers in a particular industry. Each Institute is an all-day event and is a popular information exchange opportunity for MBA candidates and their future employers.

ALUMNI ACTUALS

MBA alumni worldwide: 22,476

Business school alumni networking site: http://www.marshall.usc.edu/alumni

Current MBA students have access to the alumni database.

One of USC Marshall's well-known strengths lies in its amazing, active alumni association with its involvement with prospective and current students. There are more than 22,000 alumni living all over the globe, and their commitment and enthusiasm for the world's future leaders shows not only in their financial support to the school, but in their participatory support through mentoring and allowing students to pick their brains for whatever helpful information they can offer. USC Marshall hosts annual networking days, alumni portals and chapters, access to lifelong e-mail, career resources, and many other privileges as part of being a Trojan.

In 2009, USC Marshall held its first MBA reunion weekend. Although some alums had been away for decades, the MBAs did what MBAs do best—connect with friends and former classmates, network and share business tips, and mix education with fun. The weekend brought together alums from far-flung locations around the world and prompted many participants' reaction of "Why didn't we do this before?" No doubt this first reunion event won't be the last.

Match Made in Heaven: Is USC Marshall School of Business Right for You?

You are an ideal student if you

- Can capitalize on the diversity and culture of the USC Marshall community with a view toward forming global partnerships and skills.
- Seek business skills to address local, regional, or international finance and marketing to become a multidimensional corporate citizen.
- Require a world-class faculty and opportunities to develop your entrepreneurial and innovation skills in one of the nation's most entrepreneurial regions.
- Value the impact of a broad and influential alumni association and look forward to supporting those that follow you just as you are supported.

University of Texas at Austin McCombs School of Business

1 University Station, B6000
Austin, TX 78712

Phone: 512.471.5921
E-mail: texasmba@mccombs.utexas.edu
Web site: http://mba.mccombs.utexas.edu

Dean: Thomas W. Gilligan
Senior Associate Dean: Janet Dukerich, Academic Affairs
Associate Dean for Graduate Programs: Eric Hirst

"Our faculty, combined with some of the best students in the world, make for some of the best academic programming one can possibly imagine." —Dean Gilligan

Quick Facts

MBA PROGRAMS

Full-time MBA
Part-time MBA: Texas Evening MBA (evening program locations in Austin, Houston, and Dallas/Ft. Worth)
Executive MBA (weekend program; locations in Austin and Mexico City)

FULL-TIME MBA SNAPSHOT

Total enrollment: 520
Class of 2010: 264
Length of program: 21 months
Campus: Austin, Texas
Program commences in August
Pre-term orientation attendance required

APPLICATION NOTES

Requirements: Four-year U.S. bachelor's degree or equivalent; at least two years of full-time work experience; GMAT score; transcript; three essays; resume; GRE not accepted
Letters of recommendation: 2
Interview: By invitation only
Number of applicants: 1,929
Admittance rate: 27%

CLASS OF 2010 PROFILE

Male 69%, Female 31%
Minority Americans: 11%
International: 24%
Average age: 28
Average years of work experience: 5 years
GMAT score range (20th–80th percentile): 620–730
GMAT score average: 681
Average GPA: 3.4

ACADEMIC BACKGROUND OF INCOMING STUDENTS

Business: 31%
Economics: 15%
Liberal Arts: 14%
Technical: 35%
Other: 5%

An Original, Yesterday and Today

Austin, Texas, has undergone a tremendous amount of growth, transformation, and revitalization over the course of its history. The town founded at the same location in the 1830s was named Waterloo. The Texas Congress selected Waterloo as the site of the state capital (when Texas became a state) and renamed it Austin in honor of Stephen Fuller Austin, an early leader in the battle for state independence.

Austinites tend to fall to the political left, and this leads them to support local and independent business with deep dedication, despite the collection of national firms located around the city. A point of pride for the city-dwellers is their eccentricity. In fact, a popular motto is "Keep Austin Weird." Austin's official motto is "The Live Music Capital of the World." It backs up this claim by hosting more live music venues than any other city.

The University of Texas at Austin was founded in 1883. The School of Business was established in 1922, although the first MBA degree was conferred in 1920. In its first year of operation, the school graduated 45 students, including seven women. The school quickly evolved, offering courses in a variety of disciplines. In response to the high levels of applications received in 1924, the school raised its standards to curb growth.

On campus at McCombs.

Three hundred and thirty-eight miles northwest of Austin, Billy Joe ("Red") McCombs was born in Spur, Texas, in 1927. When he was a teenager, his family moved 500 miles south to Corpus Christi. He joined the army at age 19 and served for two years. Afterward, he enrolled in business school and law school at the University of Texas. By 1952 at age 25, he had advanced from a job selling cars to owning his first dealership (later to evolve into a dealership conglomerate) and owning his first sports team (baseball's Corpus Christi Clippers). By the time he and his wife Charline moved 145 miles north to San Antonio in the late 1950s, McCombs had established his key qualities for building a successful business: exceptional passion for the business, personal integrity, consistent work ethic, accurate analysis of opportunities, superior commitment to excellence, and never forgetting the needs of the customer.

Meanwhile, advancements at UT Austin were happening as well. The graduate school of business became a separate school in 1964, and the MBA program itself transferred into its own space in 1976. Red McCombs, who had been involved in hundreds of business and sports ventures, donated $50 million to his alma mater in 2000, and thus the University of Texas at Austin School of Business was renamed the Red McCombs School of Business in his honor.

Why McCombs?

Key to the success of McCombs graduates are the four key pillars the program is built around. First, is the academic foundation, through which MBAs not only learn the basics, but also study in special fields. Second is enhancing leadership skills. Thirty-five percent of the McCombs experience is geared toward creating conditions of direct contact between students and industry. The third pillar is creating community, through the cohort system, team projects, study groups, and an offering of professional and social student organizations. The Career Services office is dedicated to helping students establish their fourth pillar: identifying and executing a successful life and career plan.

A highly emphasized facet of the McCombs MBA experience is the PLUS program, which allows students an opportunity to utilize their knowledge for real-world problem solving, giving them experience and showing the initiative that recruiters look for. The PLUS program is unique in both being innovative among b-schools, and creating a broad exposure to human as well as business knowledge.

The city sometimes called "Silicon Hills" has plenty of room to spare for other industries to evolve. Currently, much of the industrial growth around Austin is in pharmaceuticals and biotechnology. Interested in retail and sustainability? Whole Foods, a Fortune 500 firm, is headquartered here. Whatever industry you are interested in, you are sure to find a broad array of opportunities to connect to and learn from the businesses surrounding the McCombs campus. The strength of the graduates from McCombs has not gone unnoticed by local corporations, and the administration has cultivated ongoing relationships with many of these, so you will find it easy to make connections between your education and the living, breathing corporate world.

From the beginning, school administrators have recognized the skills of the School of Business students and have encouraged them to develop these skills to their highest potential. Students at McCombs have traditionally been given leeway to be innovative in creating and establishing business practices and competitions. Some examples of these are the Moot Corp, a new venture competition that is the longest-running one nationwide; the MBA Investment Fund, which was the first such fund to be established solely for the purpose of allowing students to learn how to run a mutual fund hands-on; and the Internet Economy Indicator, created via collaboration between Cisco and McCombs students. Austin is a city that has always embraced creativity, and this has been imbued into the university, as well.

Having an array of opportunities to take your classroom education and practical skills abroad is another key benefit to getting your education at McCombs. The school recognizes the importance of understanding global issues and offers these international opportunities to better prepare MBAs to be effective leaders, wherever in the world they are, to work ethically and responsibly within the global context, and to think strategically in any international arena.

FUN FACTS

- Fun and cultural events include the O. Henry pun-off, Eeyore's Birthday Party, Spamarama, Carnaval, Pecan Street Festival, and the Austin City Limits Music Festival.

- At night, artificial "moonlight" highlights sections of Austin. This lighting system dates back to the late 19th century and consists of lamps radiating out from 150-foot towers. Only 17 of the original 31 Moonlight Towers remain in operation.

- Austin was voted the Number 1 College Town by the Travel Channel and the Greenest City in America by MSN. *Travel & Leisure* magazine ranks Austin Number 2 for cities with the "best people." Maybe because the citizens spend a lot of time getting noticed. According to demographers, Austin residents read and contribute to more blogs than any other U.S. metropolis's population.

- This natural event is one that Austinites are proud of, and it contributes to the ideal of keeping Austin weird: the nightly bat watch that takes place from April through October.

There is even a bat-watching boat cruise, where riders can get a premium view of the bat antics.

- Filmmakers like Austin so much, it is the second most popular city in the country for making films.

Course Offerings

At the beginning of the program, students are organized into cohorts—groups of about 70 students, with whom they will be taking all the basic classes. Project teams of about five students are formed within these cohorts. Students are required to follow the core curriculum, which is a group of ten courses to give them a base of fundamentals and to develop their competencies in general management. The essentials transmitted through these core courses include business ethics; teamwork and leadership skills; effective written and oral communications; presentation skills; cross-functional problem solving; and the ability to manage change, risk, human resources, and diversity. The courses are completed across the first three semesters, and students can begin taking elective courses in their first spring semester, to allow customization of their degree. Choosing a concentration is not required, but the school offers so much leeway in creating a highly customized degree, students would do well to create their own. Many students create a personally customized concentration based on their own skills and interests, as well as perceptions of what employers want. Courses taught at the school are market-driven, allowing students to get an education in areas that are relevant now.

Unique to McCombs is a program called PLUS, which strives to connect students to the business world through a constantly evolving series of micro-consulting projects, services, and workshops. Through the program, MBA students are exposed to a select group of communication and executive coaches who work with students to create impactful messages. The micro-consulting projects connect students to organizations that interest them. Industry experts present seminars that supplement the knowledge gained in the classroom.

Global exposure is the aim of McCombs's other offerings—international exchange programs and Global Connections Study Tours. MBA candidates may spend a semester abroad at one of more than 20 prestigious schools worldwide. Global Connections Study Tours are three-credit courses taken during the spring semester that culminate in a two-week-long business trip abroad. That means that an MBA degree from McCombs gives you a variety of options to choose from to broaden your understanding of the business world locally and abroad, with practical, real-world experience to boot!

McCombs Exchange Programs

Australian Graduate School of Management (AGSM): Sydney, Australia	China Europe International Business School (CEIBS): Shanghai, China

---

Chinese University of Hong Kong (CUHK): Hong Kong, China

Copenhagen Business School: Copenhagen, Denmark

ESADE Business School: Barcelona, Spain

Escuela de Administración de Negocios para Graduados (ESAN): Lima, Perú

Fundação Getúlio Bargas: São Paulo, Brazil

HEC School of Management: Paris, France

Helsinki School of Economics: Helsinki, Finland

INCAE Business School: Alajuela, Costa Rica

Indian Institute of Managment: Ahmedabad, India

Instituto de Altos Estudios Empresariales (IAE): Buenos Aires, Argentina

Instituto Tecnológico y de Estudios Superiores de Monterrey (ITESM-EGADE): Monterrey, Mexico

Koç University: Istanbul, Turkey

Manchester Business School: Manchester, United Kingdom

McGill University Montreal: Québec, Canada

Melbourne Business School: Melbourne, Australia

National University of Singapore: Singapore

Pontificia Universidad Católica de Chile: Santiago, Chile

Rotterdam School of Management: Rotterdam, The Netherlands

Stockholm School of Economics: Stockholm, Sweden

University of St. Gallen: St. Gallen, Switzerland

Warwick Business School: Coventry, United Kingdom

Wits Business School: Johannesburg, South Africa

What McCombs Professors Teach

Professors at McCombs teach management education, and students will acquire book knowledge, a practical understanding of business concepts, and the soft skills recruiters seek.

The faculty at McCombs is among the most productive in the nation. Although this indicates that many of your professors will be researching and publishing, they place the teaching experience first. On the upside, MBA students here get to harvest this knowledge almost as quickly as it is researched, and will be exposed to more theories and perspectives than the average MBA student, greatly enhancing their exposure to many aspects of the business world. McCombs graduates are recruited by local corporations, and the closeness to these corporations allows many partnering opportunities between them and the school, giving students hands-on experience. McCombs is all about turning out a well-rounded MBA who is ready to hit the ground running at whatever organization he or she joins.

FACULTY FACTS

Full-time faculty employed by the
b-school: 162

Adjunct or visiting faculty: 6

Permanent/tenured professors: 87

Tenured faculty who are women: 18

Tenured faculty who are underrepresented
minorities: 15

SAMPLING OF NOTABLE PROFESSORS

- Anant Balkrishnan: Associate editor for *Operations Research, Management Science, and Networks*; Best Paper Award, INFORMS (2002); Transportation Science Best Dissertation Prize, Operations Research Society of America (1985); Zannetos Thesis Prize, MIT (1985); Outstanding MBA Teaching Award, Salgo Noren (1988)
- Pamela Haunschild: Best Paper Award, Academy of Management; Fulbright Viterbo Distinguished Chair in Corporate Governance; Award for Research Excellence, McCombs School (2004–2005); Rockefeller Grant (2006)
- George Huber: Author of *The Necessary Nature of Future Firms*; Fellow of the Academy of Management; Fellow of the Decision Sciences Institute; MOC Scholar
- Vijay Mahajan: Maynard Award, *Journal of Marketing* (1990); Charles Coolidge Parlin Marketing Research Award (1997); Marketing Research Special Interest Group Gilbert Churchill Award, AMA (1999); in 2000, the AMA created the Vijay Mahajan Award for Career Contributions to Marketing Strategy in his honor
- Andrew Whinston: Co-author or co-editor of 28 books and more than 350 articles; editor-in-chief of *Decision Support Systems*; board member of most major Information Systems research journals; Leo Award recipient for a lifetime of exceptional achievement in information systems

CONCENTRATIONS AND SPECIALIZATIONS OFFERED IN FULL-TIME MBA PROGRAM

Brand Management	Management
Corporate Finance	Marketing
Customer Insight	Operations Management
Energy Finance	Private Equity Finance
Entrepreneurship	Real Estate Finance
Finance	Risk Management
Global Business	Social Enterprise
Information Management	Strategic Marketing
Investment Management	

JOINT DEGREES AND DUAL DEGREES

JD/MBA

MBA/MA (Asian Studies; Latin American
    Studies; Middle Eastern Studies; Russian,
    Eastern European, and Eurasian Studies)

MBA/MA (Communication)

MBA/MA (Nursing)

MBA/MA (Public Affairs)

MBA/MS (Manufacturing and Decision
    Systems Engineering)

What Admissions Is All About

Since the inception of the School of Business, admissions selectivity has evolved several times. Entrance to McCombs is highly selective, and the criteria used to evaluate applicants are both quantitative and qualitative.

The admissions committee first evaluates candidates on their potential to lead, succeed academically, and grow professionally. Particular attention is paid to personal essays, work history, goals for after the program, undergraduate academic record, recommendations, extracurricular activities, honors and achievements, and test scores.

Your motivation and character are important and need to be demonstrated through your community, public, or military service; travel experiences; hobbies; special abilities; and any honors and recognition achieved. Director of Admissions Tina Mabley advises, "The most important thing for applicants to do when looking at McCombs is to think about their story. We look for students to be very aware of where they've been, what skills they've developed up to this point, where they are trying to go and how an MBA fits into that set of goals. They need a coherent and understandable application that shows they really know themselves."

Having limited work experience also will not preclude your acceptance if you qualify via one of the two following special considerations: Jump Start and McCombs Scholars. Both programs are for undergraduate seniors who qualify academically but lack the work experience. If you receive an offer from a participating company to sponsor you in a full-time or internship position for three years, you are eligible for admission. Upon getting sponsored, the student will be admitted to the program. To be admitted immediately after completing your undergraduate degree, you need to show extremely strong academic performance, proven leadership, and a strong likelihood for success in business. Although the application process is the same as for standard applicants, applicants are advised to highlight and demonstrate the criteria listed.

Applications are reviewed chronologically. This means none will be grouped into rounds, but in the order in which they were received. Interviews are conducted on an invitation-only basis at any point during the admissions process. Typically, you will be notified within a few weeks after you interview whether you have been accepted. Occasionally, notifications are made as long as two months later.

The deadline is a suggested date but is not an absolute deadline. McCombs encourages applicants to submit their applications earlier rather than later, but it is highly preferable to submit a strong application later in the season than a weak one at the beginning. McCombs continues to accept applications until admissions committee members believe the incoming class is full, so you may be accepted even if you submit your application after the published deadline.

Full-time MBAs receiving financial aid through school: 64%

Institutional (merit-based) scholarships: 151

Assistantships: 23

Full-tuition scholarships school awarded for academic year: 18

Financially Aided

Financial aid is a necessity for most full-time students these days. From the time you submit your application, you are automatically considered for recruiting scholarships—no extra paperwork required. In addition to qualifying for federal and state loans, first-year students are offered loans through McCombs. This does require extra paperwork to be submitted to the Office of Student Financial Services. Unlike many programs, at McCombs you will be notified of your admission before you are apprised of any scholarship offering. Financial awards are not part of your acceptance package but are decided within a week or two.

Whereas students are not required to file the FAFSA before submitting an application for the school loans, the financial aid office advises that students "start smart" by filling out a FAFSA application. The priority deadline for filing the FAFSA is March 31, the same as the recommended deadline for applying for the school loans. There are other avenues for financing your education, including fellowships for double-degree programs, current MBA student loans, teaching assistantships, and research assistant positions. For minority students, there are merit-based scholarships, as well as tuition assistance for Mexican students who can demonstrate need.

In determining need, the Office of Student Financial Services first awards eligible students with grants, then work-study, and loans are considered last.

Full-Time MBA Program (Total Direct Costs)

In-state: $80,800

Out-of-state: $113,400

International: $113,400

Part-time MBA program costs: Evening, $83,800; Weekend, $88,500

TEMBA (Texas EMBA) program costs: $75,000

What McCombs Students Know

Applicants are able to tell right away that McCombs is a people school, finding the administration there to be more responsive and supportive than many others. Other students find the people skills personified in their professors. Michael Leins, class of 2009, declares, "Having the dean of the graduate school, Dean Hirst, as our accounting professor says something good about the priorities of this program. Despite having many other obligations, he displays a passion for teaching his subject matter, which he imparts upon his students. I think his commitment to understanding the faculty-student connection firsthand and drawing upon that in his leadership of the rest of the faculty greatly improves our academic experience." The importance of a personalized education is also evident to students, who find themselves collaborating in a team environment, not only with other students but also with professors and administrators. This environment fosters a strong network that ensures students' success.

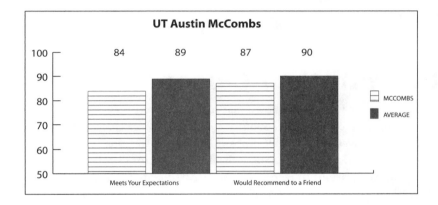

McCombs students know that they will have opportunities to develop their business skills via real application. Tony Laurel, class of 2009, says, "The consulting practicum was a rewarding experience because my team was able to use classroom experiences to create real-world business solutions for a local venture capital company. In the end, we used our experiences to create a product launch strategy for a new chemical technology—I would have never imagined this was possible before business school!"

Participating in the international exchange program provides students with opportunities to enhance their resumes to stand out from the rest. Taking the time to study business in other areas of the world and incorporating this into a project with real-world applications makes for a solid bonus to getting to travel as part of your studies. Some students report that these experiences have helped them snag highly sought-after internships and jobs.

McCombs's close ties to the business community of Austin provide students with many opportunities to thoroughly investigate their chosen career path: "Getting to interact on a daily basis with venture capital and private equity firms has taught me volumes about the industry and been one of the highlights of my time at McCombs," reports Ron Zboril, class of 2009. Incoming students are advised to use their time at McCombs to discover their passion and investigate how to transform that passion into their profession. By building a plan to achieve their definition of success and taking action to make that plan a reality, McCombs graduates can display the value of their business school education. With the support of your fellow students, faculty, and the administration at McCombs, you should be well on your way to achieving your goals.

CAREER CHECK: McCOMBS MBA EMPLOYMENT BY JOB FUNCTION

- Finance/Accounting: 40%
- Consulting: 23%
- Marketing/Sales: 17%
- General Management: 14%
- Operations/Logistics: 4%
- Other: 2%

What's Next? Your Career

If you could meet recruiters from well-known, national employers for internships or full-time employment, wouldn't you feel confident about your success? More than 130 select hiring firms work with the Career Services office at McCombs. These are in addition to the many vibrant, young companies dotting the Austin landscape. Stacey Rudnick, director of MBA Career Services, is responsible for encouraging corporations to recruit Texas MBA students, "Our primary goal is to facilitate productive interactions between recruiters and students." These interactions can take place because the school maintains relationships with companies, actively expands the alumni network, and adds new corporate relationships. This work allows the career services department to provide a plethora of employment opportunities to students, as well as a network that can be used in the future.

These employers are well aware of the quality of students graduating from McCombs and actively seek to add them to their ranks. Hiring companies have noted that McCombs graduates hold many key positions within their companies and have seen leadership exemplified in these employees, encouraging them to keep returning to this ever-improving group. Typically by January or February, exiting students have jobs lined up. In the current job market, which has seen a downturn in hiring, McCombs's MBA Career Services office has worked proactively to partner with nonprofit and government agencies that are seeking to hire top-quality MBAs. In the current economic climate, McCombs has sought to be proactive by giving presentations on industries not typically considered by MBA graduates, in an effort to give students information on other sectors they may be interested in searching for employment. This action shows the level of support McCombs offers to its students, to ensure their future.

ALUMNI ACTUALS

MBA alumni worldwide: 16,800+

Business school alumni networking site: http://www.mccombs.utexas.edu/alumni/mma/info/exchange/2008/chapter2.asp

Current MBA students have access to the alumni database.

The Texas MBA network is strong, and many alumni report a deep level of satisfaction with their education, as well as their personal and professional development. The unique challenges posed by the rigorous curriculum and professors at McCombs have been described as rewarding and are credited with giving students opportunities to expand their personal creativity and self-confidence. Some have found that attending McCombs has assisted them in revitalizing their career, gaining knowledge and experience in new industries that has allowed them to transition seamlessly from one industry into another. The leadership and networking skills acquired at McCombs also assist in this transition and renewal.

The experience of attending McCombs extends past graduation. Alums report that the opportunities to connect with alumni while they were still students helped them develop their understanding of the industries they chose to study. After graduation, they have found themselves in a tight-knit community in which the members look out for one another in a way that other schools can't brag about. Even in international travels, far from the Austin area, alums may find themselves talking with a McCombs alum in the seat next to them. Many say connections lead to career success, and this is one of the key things a McCombs graduate will take with him or her. Alumni feel a sense of reward, as all students have the opportunity to create and implant a unique idea to leave behind, if they desire. Students have been the driving force behind launching several prominent competitions and financial institutions that are nationally recognized, such as the McCombs REIT Fund, which was established by five MBA students and two professors. In the future McCombs students will continue to operate this fund, providing another arena for real-life experience. Students have a range of opportunities available to participate in, and, should they recognize an area lacking, they will find the support needed from their professors and the administration to bring their ideas to life. Returning to campus always recaptures that sense of the personalized experience, when alums report that they always find themselves feeling warmly welcomed and energized by meeting current students. It is a feeling of returning home.

Match Made in Heaven: Is the McCombs School of Business for you?

You are an ideal student if you

- Expect a complete, all-around education in which you are fully engaged with your peers, professors, and administration.
- Want the choice to personalize your MBA experience for a particular industry or market as well as receive a global education.
- Strive to be current in business practices and applications, and seek a variety of opportunities to apply your classroom education to practical problems.
- Enjoy being part of a vibrant, widespread network that you can continue to tap into after graduation.

University of Virginia Darden Graduate School of Business Administration

100 Darden Blvd.
Charlottesville, VA 22903

Phone: 434.924.7281
E-mail: darden@virginia.edu
Web site: www.darden.virginia.edu/html/programs.aspx

Dean: Robert F. Bruner
Associate Dean, MBA Program. Robert Carraway
Director, MBA for Executives: Barbara Millar

"The classroom must balance freedom of expression with the kind of respectful discourse that actually moves us toward deeper insight, mastery, and truth…. The kind of self-discipline that enables tough and tender discourse is one big contribution of the movement toward diversity and inclusiveness: Through it we learn the kind of mutual respect that helps the community move toward a common goal." —Dean Bruner

Quick Facts

MBA PROGRAMS

Full-time MBA
Executive MBA
International MBA

FULL-TIME MBA SNAPSHOT

Total enrollment: 651
Class of 2010: 333
Length of program: 21 months
Campus location: Charlottesville, VA
Program commences in August
Pre-term orientation attendance not required but highly recommended

APPLICATION NOTES

Requirements: GMAT scores; TOEFL scores (if applicable); resume; essays; self-reported transcripts; application; and Honor Code agreement; GRE not accepted

(continued)

(continued)

Letters of recommendation: 2
Interview: By invitation only
Number of applicants: 2,762
Admittance rate: 25%

CLASS OF 2010 PROFILE

Male 71%, Female 29%
Minority Americans: 15%
International: 30%
Average age: 28
Average years of work experience: 4 years
GMAT score range (20th–80th percentile): 650–740
GMAT score average: 700
GPA average: 3.35

ACADEMIC BACKGROUND OF INCOMING STUDENTS

Business: 24%
Economics: 15%
Engineering/Math/Sciences: 34%
Humanities: 23%
Other: 4%

History, Community, and the World

Charlottesville, Virginia, is a picturesque town situated within the foothills of the Blue Ridge Mountains in historic Albemarle County. The area has a population of approximately 120,000. Those who call Charlottesville home have the best of all worlds: The city is about an hour and a half south of the nation's capital of Washington, D.C., and a little more than an hour's drive west of Richmond. Beachgoers need only travel three hours to the east to breathe in the surf. All this, and the nearest ski resort is less than 50 miles away. The area is easily accessible and is serviced by major commuter airlines, bus lines, and AMTRAK rail. Founded in 1954, the Darden business school is named for Colgate Whitehead Darden, Jr., a former Virginia governor and congressman, as well as a past president of the University of Virginia.

Today Darden's campus, called "the Grounds," boasts a community of learners where respect, camaraderie, and ethics are prized above all else. Students are fortunate to be a part of a strong network of supportive peers, faculty, staff, and alumni. To maintain these strong bonds, Darden hosts a number of organizations, events, and activities to encourage fellowship among the Darden family.

On the Grounds at Darden.

A tradition stretching back 50 years to the school's founding, First Coffee is a daily event that is exemplary of the school's rich community spirit. Every morning, without fail, students, faculty, staff, and any visitors on campus meet in the PepsiCo Forum to socialize over a cup of coffee or tea. This is an informal assemblage, occasionally punctuated by special announcements, award presentations, and performances by Darden's *a capella* group, the Cold Call Chorus. It is just another way that Darden maintains strong ties within the campus community.

Darden's classrooms fully engage students in every aspect of learning. Darden utilizes a case study method paired with its unique Four-Step learning process. Students are challenged to gain a full understanding of real-world business situations. Students learn to work well under pressure, and arrive in class primed to think, decide, and act. They master the very skills that are requisite of today's most successful business leaders.

Why Darden?

Darden's mission is to improve society by developing principled leaders for the world of practical affairs. To achieve this noble goal, the school takes an approach to learning that is both rigorous and collaborative in nature. This approach encourages and guides students to make informed decisions that take into consideration all aspects of global enterprise. In so doing, the Darden faculty strive to create within their students a knowledge base that will help them to succeed not only as students, but as managers and thought leaders within their respective corporations upon graduation. The school seeks to accomplish this while fostering enduring relationships that motivate and sustain organizations, and help them to grow.

The Darden experience fosters a diverse community that broadens understanding and elevates performance. To this end, about one-third of Darden's student body is composed of international students who hail from a plethora of countries and cultures. Their presence lends a global perspective to class discussions. Darden furthers global understanding for all students by offering courses and case studies that address world business issues, employing a number of international faculty members, and offering exchange programs with top MBA programs around the world. One of the leadership residencies is held in Beijing, China. Darden graduates are equipped to be responsible, effective, and action-oriented leaders in any field, in any country.

Darden is also a perfect fit for those who have served our country. Darden expects all students to adhere to a strict honor code, one that tolerates no exceptions. Military personnel exemplify this standard and bring a solid experiential practice to whichever incoming class they join. The school recognizes the valuable skill set that America's finest possess. Darden has always been committed to recruiting our military men and women into the MBA program and working with them to sharpen and refine the leadership skills they obtained while in the Armed Forces. Darden's Military Consortium works hard to actively recruit and support those who have served in the military into Darden's MBA program.

For this elite group, there exists a competitive advantage in the business world. After all, the men and women who serve in the Armed Forces are not strangers to hard work, self-discipline, responsibility, and integrity—core ideals at Darden. Add to this a strong sense of leadership, and the ability to analyze situations quickly and make decisions, and Darden becomes more than a good place to launch your business career. It becomes a perfect match, and recruiters know it. For those who have been on active duty within the past three years prior to applying for Darden's MBA program, the application fee is waived.

FUN FACTS

- Charlottesville was rated the best place to live in the USA in the book *Cities Ranked and Rated* based on 10 categories including economy and jobs, cost of living, climate, education, health and health care, crime, transportation, leisure, arts and culture, and overall quality of life.

- The University of Virginia is the only university in the world to make the United Nations World Heritage List, which includes the Great Wall of China, the Grand Canyon, the Statue of Liberty, and the Taj Mahal.

- Charlottesville was the home of three presidents. A visit to the city affords you the opportunity to tour James Monroe's Ash Lawn–Highland, Thomas Jefferson's Monticello, and James Madison's Montpelier.

Course Offerings

One of Darden's trademarks is its integrated curriculum. The Darden faculty carefully coordinate the 10 required first-year courses for its students. These courses give students a firm foundation upon which to build in the second year, when business projects and electives take the integrated curriculum in a new direction. With the help of elective courses, Darden students can structure and refine their coursework to suit their personal and professional interests and needs. Darden's curriculum has five components: leadership residencies, core courses (such as Basics of Business, Competing and Collaborating, and Ethics), electives, action learning, and professional development.

Darden's signature approach to the case study method is presented through the Four-Step process. Your learning team, composed of five or six classmates, receives a case for you to evaluate. Once you have broken down its components into problems to solve, alternatives to consider, possible decisions, and probable course of action, you are ready for the next step. This is a (no doubt spirited) discussion debating the pros and cons of each of the components. You analyze and deliberate every aspect of the case until your team develops workable ideas for a solution. On to the next step: During class discussion, all teams explain to the professor what they regard as the important considerations. After all students have shared their opinions, the professor compares what has been discussed to successful management practices. This step ensures that you will learn the finer points of how business decisions are made, despite what information you may or may not have at your disposal. And finally, step four is when you examine why your team chose the direction it did. What went right, what went wrong, and what new direction might you consider for the next case?

Moving from this intensely focused classroom practice, Darden students also have the opportunity to participate in the broadly enriching Global Business Experience (GBE). For one to two weeks, you travel to a country (other than your own) and study economic, cultural, political, and business-related issues. You will return to campus with a greater understanding of the challenges in various markets.

Recent GBEs have taken place in Buenos Aires, Argentina; Manama, Bahrain; Sao Paulo, Brazil; Beijing, China; Shanghai, China; New Delhi, India; Hyderabad, India; Mexico City, Mexico; Barcelona, Spain; and Stockholm, Sweden.

RESEARCH CENTERS

Batten Institute for Entrepreneurship and Innovation

Business Roundtable Institute for Corporate Ethics

Darden-Curry Partnership for Education Curriculum

Olsson Center for Business Ethics

Tayloe Murphy International Center for Global Business

What Darden Professors Teach

Since its founding more than a half-century ago, Darden has been blazing the trail for others to follow when it comes to innovative teaching and learning methods. A prime example of this would be its use of the case method of instruction. The case method is the core of the business school's MBA programs. What better way to prepare for life in the business world than to examine real businesses and the very real issues facing them? Professors introduce major business challenges for students to analyze through lively exchange in class and informal discussion groups. The programs are taught by Darden faculty who are experts in their specialty areas and are skilled in addressing key issues in case discussions. Students work to identify the successes, failures, and challenges facing business leaders in some of the world's most renowned companies and organizations. Rarely does any one case have a single solution; thus, the case method seeks to challenge students to look at real problems head on and make decisions to affect the outcome—just as their counterparts do.

Most business problems involve several disciplines or areas of expertise. For example, a case taught in Accounting class may also include issues covered in Ethics or Operations classes. This integrated approach allows students to approach issues from different perspectives. As Peter Rodriquez, associate professor of Business Administration and associate dean for International Affairs explains, "The art of doing a case is in part taking a specific example and capturing from it what's really relevant, what's really universal. In looking at that, we can catch a glimmer of what happens every single day in the business world."

FACULTY FACTS

Full-time faculty employed by the b-school: 63

Adjunct or visiting faculty: 31

Permanent/tenured professors: 47

Tenured faculty who are women: 9

Tenured faculty who are underrepresented minorities: 8

SAMPLING OF NOTABLE PROFESSORS

- Robert F. Bruner: Specialist in several areas of business administration, including innovation, mergers, acquisitions, financial crises, investment in emerging markets, technology transfer, and corporate finance
- Edward D. Hess: Attorney; strategy consultant; investment specialist; author of five books, including *The Successful Family Business* and *The Road to Organic Growth*
- Ronald T. Wilcox: Former economist for the U.S. Securities and Exchange Commission; researcher focusing on marketing financial services and its relationship with public policy; author of *Whatever Happened to Thrift? Why Americans Don't Save and What to Do About It*
- Patricia H. Werhane: Leader in the field of business ethics; founder and a former editor-in-chief of *Business Ethics Quarterly*, a founding member and former president of the Society for Business Ethics

---

CONCENTRATIONS AND SPECIALIZATIONS OFFERED IN FULL-TIME MBA PROGRAM

General Management only

JOINT DEGREES AND DUAL DEGREES

MBA/JD

MBA/MA (East Asian Studies)

MBA/MA (Government or Foreign Affairs)

MBA/ME (Engineering)

MBA/MS (Science)

MBA/MSN (Nursing)

MBA/PhD

What Admissions Is All About

Darden's MBA program sets itself apart from other MBA programs by its use of the case method. With this method, students are challenged to develop their full leadership potential and grow. The case method requires full commitment and participation on the part of the student, so the most successful candidates for admission are those deemed to be a good match for this approach to learning.

Candidates are evaluated in three areas when being considered for admission to Darden: academics, professional experience, and personal qualities and characteristics. As far as academics, the most successful candidates are those who exhibit superior academic ability and intellect, as well as a proficiency in the English language. While GMAT scores are required, Darden does not have a minimum GMAT score requirement. Says Director of Admissions Sara Neher, "It's important, but it is only one element of the process. We're looking for you to be able to demonstrate quantitative ability, and you can do that through your GMAT, GPA, or through your work experience."

With regard to professional experience, the ideal Darden candidate is innovative and creative, demonstrating the potential for action-based leadership in a number of practical ways within the business industry. Applicants to Darden's MBA program have an average of 4 years of full-time work experience, although the range is anywhere from 0 to 10 years. Successful candidates are able to demonstrate strength in Darden's criteria regardless of the number of years of their work experience.

The admissions committee strives for a good understanding of candidates on a personal level. The ideal candidates are well rounded, having had a number of enriching life experiences, and employ a strong work ethic, integrity, and a sense of maturity and self-awareness. The committee also likes to see candidates with a demonstrated interest in community service and those who are motivated self-starters. Factors such as international exposure, diversity, and culture/gender sensitivity are also taken into consideration. Many of these factors are explored in depth during the required 45-minute blind interview.

In the interview, potential candidates are screened not only by the school's professionals, but also by students. Jamala Massenburg, class of 2009, serves on Darden's admissions committee and participates actively in the interviewing of Darden candidates. She says that among the things she looks

---

for in a candidate are self-confidence and leadership potential—traits that will complement the case method learning experience. "Candidates must be comfortable with sharing their ideas, and at times, agreeing to disagree with others. A community of learners with mutual respect and mutual trust of each other is what makes the case method so successful. We learn to respect each other's points of view, and see a more global perspective. As a student, you have to be willing to speak up and contribute, willing to lead and to stretch beyond your comfort zone."

Full-time MBAs receiving financial aid through school: 88%

Institutional (merit-based) scholarships: 90

Full-tuition scholarships school awarded for academic year: 37

Financially Aided

Darden remains dedicated to helping its students find the financial aid necessary to obtain their MBA. The school firmly believes that financial obligations should not be the primary consideration or concern for those who have chosen Darden. Rather, it is the goal of the financial aid department that those students in attendance spend their time focusing on the Darden experience. To that end, financial aid is widely available.

Applying for financial assistance is a process that occurs in two phases. Incoming students must apply to the federal government and University of Virginia's Student Financial Services Office for federal loan consideration. International students have access to several merit-based scholarships as well as third-party loans. All options are presented to students through the financial aid office.

FULL-TIME MBA PROGRAM (TOTAL DIRECT COSTS)

In-state: $60,500

Out-of-state: $65,500

International: $72,500

EMBA program costs: $109,000 inclusive

What Darden Students Know

Prepare to stretch to meet your full potential, Bill Gray, class of 2009, advises potential applicants. "There is no such thing as sitting passively in this program. It is an 8 a.m. to 9 p.m. program of things going back to back." He acknowledges that the case method approach to learning isn't for everyone but instead seems to better suit dynamic learners who prize hands-on learning.

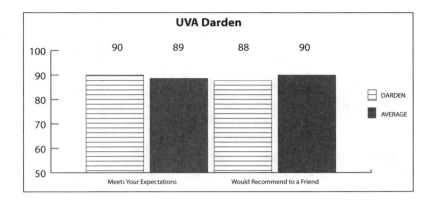

For sports enthusiasts, intramural sports provide a great way to relax while engaging in exercise and fun! Intramural sports are available widely through the University of Virginia. Popular sports include, but are certainly not limited to, football, volleyball, floor hockey, basketball, and softball. The Darden Cup Competition is open to both students and faculty. It consists of a series of intramural events during which Darden sponsors City League soccer and volleyball teams. Come spring, Darden plays host to teams from other leading business schools in the United States at the Darden Invitational Softball tournament.

About 25 percent of incoming students each year relocate to the Charlottesville area with their families. Darden aims to provide continuous support and services for them to make the transition to Darden life smooth for all. One pivotal resource for families remains the Darden Partners Association (DPA), and its efforts to help spouses, children, and other family members adjust to their life in Charlottesville are much appreciated. Regular meetings and activities sponsored by the DPA throughout the year allow family members the chance to make new friends and explore the Charlottesville area. Other services provided by the DPA include career assistance, volunteer opportunities, kids' activities, and continuing education opportunities. With the help of the DPA, students' extended families can make the transition to a new life in a new place almost seamlessly.

Just as the Darden experience is unique, no less can be said for its community approach to student life. One of the most noteworthy distinctions Darden claims is its strong, supportive community. The school's small class size and emphasis on communication and teamwork lend themselves to the creation of a body of people who are close-knit but diverse, and who all share the same vision and mission.

Among the students, faculty, and staff exist a camaraderie and mutual respect that you cannot miss. Holding to the belief in community, Darden encourages further fellowship and socializing through its hosting of several organizations, events, and other bonding activities for its faculty, staff, students, and visitors. Lifelong friendships are cultivated here.

This heavy support is a major drawing point for many students. Bill Gray was particularly impressed with the family and community themes Darden interweaves into its learning experience. For Gray, class size and the case study method used by the school were just what he was looking for. He also valued the level of interaction among faculty and students. "The professors don't just sit and lecture.

They have a true open door policy, and they strive to challenge you and prepare you for the world you are going out into. They prepare you for long-term, lifelong success."

For Jamala Massenburg, Darden's case method of study was the main draw. Massenburg had attended the University of Virginia as an undergraduate and earned a degree in engineering. She already knew that she liked Charlottesville; it offered the advantages of city life without the distractions and the noise and bustle. What she wanted was a program that would push her to grow and strengthen her skill set as far as being an effective communicator. When Massenburg visited classes and saw the case method approach in action, she was sold. "The teachers ask leading and provocative questions to facilitate instruction, and to make sure that you gain the perspectives that you are meant to get from the examples used. I felt that this type of class participation and dialogue would give me the opportunities to grow to my potential in ways that a traditional lecture environment would not. And the smaller, close-knit environment provides more chances to bond. Here, we spend time together both in class and out. We're like family."

Whatever the possible drawbacks, the closeness is worth it, Massenburg assures would-be applicants. "Even when we disagree, it's respectfully. Differences in opinion are opportunities to discuss, not fuss. We learn to work through it." She feels that Darden has prepared her for the workforce in ways that go beyond the classroom. Darden, with its global approach to learning, has given her a wider perspective on business issues and invaluable leadership skills. "I am more comfortable working in the foreground and being assertive. I think the skills bring more value to my career as a whole, and my ability to contribute to a corporation's overall success." Massenburg lined up her postgraduate job with DS Consulting in Boston. The job marries both her engineering expertise and her business acumen. And she feels strongly that the opportunity would not have been possible without Darden.

CAREER CHECK: DARDEN MBA EMPLOYMENT BY JOB FUNCTION

- Finance/Accounting: 44%
- General Management: 21%
- Consulting: 20%
- Information Systems: 6%

What's Next? Your Career

Darden's Career Development Center (CDC) is frequently ranked among the best programs in the United States. The CDC helps Darden students to take ownership of their job search, both while at Darden and afterward. The CDC offers a variety of programs and resources to help students target and secure the careers that match their individual preferences and goals. Darden acknowledges that its students' goals extend beyond an academic degree. For many students, the focus is on finding just the right job to launch a successful MBA career. Director Everette Fortner has stated that Darden aims to ensure its graduates are well prepared to embark on a rewarding long-term career path. To that end, the CDC emphasizes career exploration, self-assessment, long-term career planning, and networking skills. In addition, students are taught to master career search skills and strategies.

Darden's CDC places a strong focus on student success, as well as on creating and maintaining a positive relationship with employers of all business industries. The career team works closely with those companies that recruit students, striving to make sure the process is as smooth and worry-free as possible. Along with faculty, administration, corporate representatives, and students, the CDC forges new relationships with recruiting companies, while maintaining strong ties with existing partners.

The CDC helps manage the more technical aspects of the job hunt with the aid of an intranet system. The system allows students to use any on-Grounds computer or an online portal to research companies, find contacts, search and apply for employment, register for on-Grounds company presentations and interviews, and perform a host of other tasks.

Darden's CDC is outfitted with a suite of private interview rooms that are employed for Darden's on-Grounds interviews. These interviews are the primary hiring method employed by many partnering companies. Participants screen students based on their resumes or other criteria and invite students to interview for positions with their companies. Students not invited to interview with a company may still secure an interview slot using a bidding system accessible through the CDC intranet.

On-Grounds recruiting is an integral part of many Darden students' search for a career. Still, the majority of Darden students seek out those companies that recruit outside Darden. The CDC also offers resources to aid this part of the search and provides ongoing support during this important time. Darden students have been extremely successful in securing employment, even in fields that do not typically employ MBAs.

The Darden Networking Partnership is an online directory of nearly 2,000 Darden alumni who have volunteered to help other Darden grads with the search for a career. Networking partners broaden students' networking capabilities by sharing their own contacts, providing leads, and helping to pave the way to a new career. Darden second-year students can also log on to the University of Virginia's Career Assistance Network, a database of almost 20,000 alumni partners who have volunteered to offer students and graduates career-search guidance and information.

The top priority among Darden faculty, staff, and administration is the professional success of Darden students. Darden creates leaders who are sharp, motivated, passionate, and committed. Recruiters recognize this and continue to hire and promote Darden students to fill roles in a variety of industries at ever-higher levels of responsibility.

ALUMNI ACTUALS

MBA alumni worldwide: 7,500+

Business school alumni networking site: www.darden.virginia.edu/html/acs-content.aspx

Current MBA students have access to the alumni database.

Don't worry that your involvement with Darden may end upon graduation. Darden is very committed to maintaining strong ties with its alumni. Darden Alumni Relations and Alumni Career Services are committed to ensuring your lifelong involvement in the Darden School. To that end, Darden hosts several reunions, facilitates networking among alums, helps to set up and maintain alumni chapters, and hosts numerous events for alumni around the world. Every effort is made to help Darden alumni stay in touch and connected with the Business School—and each other.

All alumni are granted access to Darden's database of graduates. Through Alumni Relations, grads can find out what happened to that colleague from class, find employment opportunities or share them, volunteer at Darden, and stay in the loop with Darden happenings.

Alumni Career Services (ACS) seeks to provide all Darden School alumni with lifelong career advice and assistance. ACS provides counseling services to alumni to help them identify and create career goals and objectives, and provides resources via intranet to help alumni tap into the job market to seek and secure employment. All counseling and associated services are free to any graduate of the Darden MBA, Ph.D., and MBA for Executives programs. Whether you are in transition or ready to make a career change, ACS aims to help.

Match Made in Heaven: Is the Darden Graduate School of Business Administration Right for You?

You are an ideal student if you

- Wish to hone your leadership, quantitative abilities, and communication skills.
- Expect the highest ethical standards taught in the classroom and required of all students.
- Desire to be a part of a friendly local community and learn in an atmosphere where family and community themes are part of Darden's learning experience.
- Want to learn about business from a global perspective using 100 percent case method.

Vanderbilt University Owen Graduate School of Management

401 21st Avenue South
Nashville, TN 37203

Phone: 615.322.6469, 800.288.6936
E-mail: admissions@owen.vanderbilt.edu
Web site: www.owen.vanderbilt.edu

Dean: Jim Bradford
Associate Dean, Healthcare MBA Program: Jon Lehman

"In the past few years, we have augmented an already stellar faculty and launched important new programs, building an academic infrastructure that will serve the school for years to come." —Dean Bradford

Quick Facts

MBA Programs

Full-time MBA
Health Care MBA
Executive MBA

Full-Time MBA Snapshot

Total enrollment: 382
Class of 2010: 176
Length of program: 22 months
Campus: Nashville, TN
Program commences in August
Pre-term orientation attendance required

Application Notes

Requirements: Professional experience not required but highly recommended (average work experience is five years); a four-year bachelor's degree or equivalent; GMAT score; application; essays; recommendations; GRE not accepted
Letters of recommendation: 2
Interview: By invitation only

(continued)

(continued)

Number of applicants: 986
Admittance rate: 36%

CLASS OF 2010 PROFILE

Male 75%, Female 25%
Minority Americans: 14%
International: 23%
Average age: 28
Married/Partnered, Single: 23%, 77%
Average years of work experience: 4.6 years
GMAT range (20th–80th percentile): 580–730
GMAT average: 656
GPA average: 3.3

ACADEMIC BACKGROUND OF INCOMING STUDENTS

Business: 32%
Computer Science: 3%
Economics: 18%
Engineering: 13%
Humanities: 10%
Law: 1%
Science: 4%
Social Science: 10%
Other: 9%

Mid-South Meets World

Cornelius Vanderbilt, whose nickname was Commodore, made his fortune in shipping. "Commodore" Cornelius Vanderbilt's only major philanthropic act proved to have an enduring legacy. Persuaded to build a Southern university by his wife's cousin, Vanderbilt endowed and built the school bearing his name with a gift of $1 million in 1873. The man who convinced Vanderbilt to make the gift, Methodist Bishop Holland N. McTyeire, selected the site for the university in Nashville, Tennessee. Buildings on the original campus date to its founding. The original Owen Graduate School of Management was opened in a former funeral home in 1969. Today the school is located a mile and a half southwest of downtown Nashville on the 330-acre campus, which resembles a park. The school is home to more than 300 tree and shrub varieties and was designated a national arboretum in 1988. The Peabody section of campus has been a registered National Historic Landmark since 1966.

Scenes from Owen.

Since its inception more than 135 years ago, Vanderbilt University has grown an international reputation for excellence. Its undergraduate students can choose from a wide variety of programs in the liberal arts and sciences, including engineering, music, education, and human development, as well as many graduate and professional degrees.

Thanks to its well-earned reputation, the university attracts top students from throughout the United States and around the world. Graduates have gone on to careers in Congress, courts at every level, the highest echelons of the business world, the medical community, the world of literary and performance arts, and even professional athletics.

Why Owen?

Vanderbilt University's Owen Graduate School of Management was founded in 1969 and named after Ralph Owen and his wife, Lulu Hampton Owen. Ralph Owen graduated from Vanderbilt in 1928 and started his own company—Equitable Securities—two years later. When his company merged with American Express, he served as American Express's president and then chairman. In 1976 Ralph and Lulu bequeathed $33.5 million to the Owen Graduate School of Management. In total, the Owen family contributed more than $62 million to create and fund the school.

With Nashville's mild climate and 11 colleges and universities, Owen is situated in one of the best locations of all MBA programs. It is no secret that Nashville is aptly nicknamed Music City, USA. However, music is only one of its many assets. With a southern charm and urban sophistication, a low cost of living and a high quality of life, Nashville has received a wave of accolades in the media, including being named the Number 1 Smartest Place to Live by *Kiplinger's Personal Finance* and the Number 1 Hottest City for Business Relocation and Expansion by *Expansion Management*. Nashville's economy is diverse, including industries such as education, health care, hospitality, entertainment, transportation, retail, and construction. Nashville is home to 15 publicly traded health care companies, the largest health care cluster in the nation. Many companies have chosen Nashville as their corporate headquarters, including Nissan North America, Louisiana Pacific, HCA, and CVS Caremark.

Owen is dedicated to continual transformation as it seeks to offer the best possible intellectual and personal preparation in a world of constant change. To that end, the school focuses on developing student leadership, community involvement, problem-solving expertise, and teamwork. To achieve this, it emphasizes meaningful immersion in real business situations. To develop a global perspective, Owen's curriculum includes travel, and its classes are composed of a diverse student body. A chief educational goal is to build interaction among students, faculty, business leaders, and alumni so that students are exposed to the most up-to-date and relevant information available.

The Health Care MBA is an example. The evolving curriculum helps shape the future of the industry as Owen pursues its vision of offering the nation's premiere health care MBA program. This unique confluence of resources brings together the business acumen of the Owen faculty, the cutting-edge knowledge and wealth of experience of the Vanderbilt University Medical Center—one of the nation's most respected hospitals—and the advantages of a city recognized as a true hub of the health care field. Owen takes full advantage of the region's medical facilities, a day-to-day process that brings the classroom work to life.

FUN FACTS

- Vanderbilt's intercollegiate athletic mascot is "Mr. C," named for the naval officer rank of commodore. Mr. C is present at all Vanderbilt games dressed in his 1800s naval uniform, cutlass, and mutton chops.
- The Bicentennial Oak, which dates back to the American Revolution, calls the campus of Vanderbilt home.
- Vanderbilt is the second largest private employer in the state of Tennessee with a staff of more than 21,500 employees and more than 2,800 full-time faculty members.
- Three Vanderbilt alumni and four current or former faculty members of Vanderbilt have been bestowed with the Nobel Prize in their respective fields of expertise.

Course Offerings

The MBA curriculum is composed of "modules" or "mods" of four types: the core, specializations, concentrations, and emphases. Students are based on campus for two years and complete eight mods. Each mod is seven weeks long, and there are two per semester. You must complete four semesters for graduation. Twenty-two credit hours are earned in required core courses. Twelve credit hours are dedicated to one concentration with another 12 hours outside your concentration area. You can have either one or two concentrations.

The seven-week mod system gives you a fast start by allowing you to take courses in your chosen career path as early as spring of your first year. Over the duration of the program, you have the freedom to take electives within your specialty. And Owen continues to expand course offerings. The second-year Capstone Project gives you the chance to put together real-world projects that integrate every aspect of your MBA instruction. A recent update of the MBA curriculum includes an early emphasis on financial and quantitative elements, a move that helps students maximize preparation for recruiting visits.

Depending on your type of career, you can devote 20 credit hours of coursework to a specialization. Specializations include experiential courses with professionals in each industry. You have choices of Brand Management, Corporate Finance, Health Care, Human and Organizational Performance, Investment Management, or Operations Management. "Owen has certainly equipped me with the finance background that will help me be successful in a career in wealth management," imparts Amanda Pullins, class of 2009. Pullins's areas of focus are Finance and Marketing. "Beyond that, however," she continues, "interacting with its incredible students and supportive alumni network has helped solidify my networking skills, which are just as crucial as knowing the intricacies of accounting. I also thought I knew how to multitask from my previous jobs but balancing work, life and everything in between during the first year has made me confident that I will never be overwhelmed with too many demands again."

For an emphasis, you spend eight credit hours learning about Entrepreneurship, Environmental Management, International Studies, or Real Estate. Emphases offer yet another way for you to hone your knowledge in ways that will further your future career.

In addition, Owen has an extensive student exchange program, one of the strongest in the nation. Kristina Entcheva, class of 2009, learned about Owen and came "for its finance courses and the class sizes. I am an exchange student from Vienna, Austria, and at my school [Wirtschaftsuniversität Wien], there are 25,000 students with classes up to 600 people, so the small class sizes here attracted me. And I also find being here very culturally enriching."

OWEN PARTNER SCHOOLS

Bocconi University: Milan, Italy

ESSEC Business School: Cergy-Pontoise, France

European Business School (EBS): Oestrich-Winkel, Germany

ESADE Business School: Barcelona, Spain

Fudan University: Shanghai, China

Guanghua School of Management, Peking University: Beijing, China

Hong Kong University of Science and Technology: Hong Kong, China

INCAE: Alajuela, Costa Rica

International University of Japan: Niigata, Japan

Manchester Business School: Manchester, England

Melbourne Business School: Melbourne, Australia

National University of Singapore: Singapore

Norwegian School of Economics and Business Administration: Bergen, Norway

Otto Beisheim Graduate School of Management: Koblenz, Germany

Pontificia Universidad Católica de Chile: Santiago, Chile

Rotterdam School of Management: Rotterdam, The Netherlands

(continued)

(continued)

Universidade de São Paulo: São Paulo, Brazil

University of Karlsruhe: Karlsruhe, Germany

Vienna University of Economics and Business Administration (Wirtschaftsuniversität Wien): Vienna, Austria

Wits Business School: Johannesburg, South Africa

What Owen Professors Teach

With a student/faculty ratio of 10 to 1, students and professors are able to develop close and enduring relationships. Students are able to take advantage of Owen's impressive array of expertise among its faculty. For example, Bill Christie, a professor of management, conducted research that led to sweeping reform of NASDAQ trading practices. Christie is also professor of law and a faculty director for the EMBA program. Bill Frist, M.D., is a former U.S. Senate majority leader and a transplant surgeon. At Owen, Frist created a unique class that combines business students with fourth-year medical students to examine financing, quality, and delivery of health care. Dawn Iacobucci, a professor in marketing, is renowned for her expertise on networks, as well as customer satisfaction and service marketing. She is deeply involved in quantitative psychological research and serves as associate dean for faculty development.

Faculty Facts

Full-time faculty employed by the b-school: 52

Adjunct or visiting faculty: 37

Permanent/tenured professors: 34

Tenured faculty who are women: 4

Tenured faculty who are underrepresented minorities: 0

Tenured international faculty: 5

Sampling of Notable Professors

- J. Dewey Daane: Former Federal Reserve Board member; represented the United States as one of the two U.S. deputies of the Group of Ten
- Luke Froeb: Leading antitrust expert; former director of the Bureau of Economics at the Federal Trade Commission
- David Owens: Developing a holistic and innovative approach to the university's strategic planning disciplines for health care reform
- James Shore: Co-founder of Net Impact; noted authority on socially conscious entrepreneurship
- Hans Stoll: Researcher who revolutionized the field of financial derivatives and market microstructure

- Robert Whaley: Research and industry innovator who developed the Market Volatility Index, the NASDAQ Market Volatility Index, and the Buy Write Monthly Index (BXM) for the Chicago Board Options Exchange

---

CONCENTRATIONS AND SPECIALIZATIONS OFFERED IN FULL-TIME MBA PROGRAM

Accounting	International Business
Brand Management	Investment Management
Corporate Finance	Marketing
Entrepreneurship	Operations Management
Finance	Real Estate
General Management	Strategy
Health Care Administration	Technology
Human Resource Management	

JOINT DEGREES AND DUAL DEGREES

MBA/JD	MBA/MSN (Nursing)
MBA/MD	MBA/PhD (Medicine)
MBA/MALAS (Latin American Studies)	MBA/PhD (Engineering)
MBA/MDIV (Divinity)	

What Admissions Is All About

The class of 2010 showed the largest and strongest field of prospective students in Owen's history. The number of applicants increased by 30 percent with Owen admitting 36 percent of candidates. While test scores are important, Owen also seeks intangibles such as leadership, communication, and engagement—qualities that make for exceptional students and business leaders. Owen aims to bring in the best possible students with an eye to global diversity and balance. There are currently 30 countries represented in the Owen student body.

Manan Singh, class of 2010 and Operations Club president, shares, "I really like the small classes and interaction with exchange students. The faculty is very involved with the career paths of the students, giving advice and professional experience. For example, my management professor has met with me, told me what books to read for my area of interest and helped me. Even the alums are involved with the current students … and share their recent experiences."

Director of Admissions John Roeder offers advice and tips for those applying to the program. "We are looking for candidates who have strong work experience. It is not the quantity of years of work experience that we are looking for, rather the quality. We are looking at how a candidate has impacted their organization and whether they showed progression or increased responsibility within their roles and positions. When you apply, aim to help us understand the nature of your work, the level of challenge, supervision, and progression of responsibility. We will evaluate your ability to achieve results. You can also show your leadership abilities through extracurricular activities. The GMAT score is an important part of the application but is something that is looked at in conjunction with work experience and academic background."

At Owen, the right fit is important—and that is most often assessed in the interview process. The interview is a significant aspect of your application. How you interview for admittance to Owen, Admissions has found, is also a great indicator of how you might interview in front of a corporate recruiter. Those who have more work experience have an edge in the interview process because they have more areas from which to demonstrate leadership, teamwork, and other extremely important attributes. Interviews and essays are the vehicles through which you share your story by giving examples of personal and professional experiences, clarify your record of achievement, and demonstrate your interpersonal and communication skills and focus.

John Roeder adds, "To enhance the educational experience of all students at Owen, we seek to increase diversity in the student body. We host a Diversity Symposium and a Women's Symposium to help candidates learn about student life, challenges facing minorities in business, and Vanderbilt's commitment to diversity."

Full-time MBAs receiving financial aid through school: 78%

Institutional (merit-based) scholarships: 102

Assistantships: varies

Full-tuition scholarships awarded for academic year: 12

Financially Aided

Vanderbilt Owen has an outstanding number and variety of scholarships for its students. The average award is around half the yearly tuition and continues into the second year based on certain levels of academic achievement. Among the plentiful merit-based scholarships is the Dean's Scholarship. Awarded to a handful of incoming students, this full-tuition scholarship is conferred for exceptional personal commitment to positive change, a wealth of experience, and a range of leadership characteristics. To ensure equal representation in the MBA program, Diversity Scholarships are awarded to students based on European or Latin American citizenship. Additionally, Latin American students may receive the Martin S. Geisel Memorial Scholarship. American minority applicants and/or women are also eligible for Diversity Scholarships.

First-year women are eligible for the merit-based Amy Jorgensen Scholarship. Merit-based funding is also awarded through the Edna B. Morris and John A. Morris Scholarships for students who show leadership potential in the investment field. For students in marketing, there is the Douglas W. Binns Memorial Scholarship. For students in entrepreneurship, there is the Ralph Owen Jr. Scholarship, the Oehmig Scholarship, and the William Walker Scholarship. If you are studying finance, you may be eligible to receive the Wigginton Memorial Scholarship. If you are studying international finance in particular, you are eligible for the Tse-Liang Soong Scholarship.

From the general to the refined to the amazingly specific, Owen offers some scholarships that fit only a small portion of incoming students. For example, if you are from Mississippi and possess learning disabilities, you are eligible for the Victor and Gayle Maver Scholarship. If you are a home-state student from Tennessee, you may be considered for the Henry D. Jamison Scholarship.

The scholarships mentioned here are not all the possibilities. Staff at the Office for Student Financial Aid counsel students on scholarships as well as loans, work options, and personal savings contributions.

Full-Time MBA Program (Total Direct Costs)

In-state: $80,384

Out-of-state: $80,334

International: $80,645

What Owen Students Know

Owen's Leadership Development Program in full swing. Its goal is to provide an exclusive, innovative, and transformative experience to all Owen students and centers around best-in-class leadership development typically reserved for senior managers at Fortune 500 companies. The program includes the Hogan Leadership Assessment suite, team applications, and intensive, professional-level coaching for all students. There are opportunities to dive deeper into leadership development during the second year of the program. Past experiences have included a military leadership immersion, which students described as "awe-inspiring" and "life-altering." This option, called Leadership in Action, tests your abilities under stress while accompanying Aviation Regiment soldiers training at nearby Fort Campbell. Second-year students also have the opportunity to demonstrate real-world leadership by finding, contracting, designing, and running projects for area companies and organizations.

Owen students have the opportunity to participate in and lead unique clubs such as the Vanderbilt Culinary Society, Entrepreneurship Association, Owen Black Student's Association, Cork and Barrel Club, TVA Investment Challenge, Media and Entertainment Association, Owen Armed Forces Club, Latin Business Association, and many more.

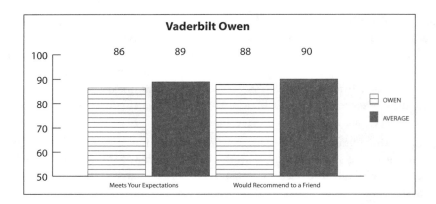

One MBA candidate specializing in Finance and Strategy, class of 2009 student Alexander Olsen, relates his leadership experience. "Between all of the organizations and clubs in the school and the opportunities to work both with Vanderbilt and the community I have had plenty of opportunities to lead. The faculty and staff at Owen have the pulse of the community and bring in great companies to sponsor student-led projects, as well as networking students with opportunities elsewhere.... Owen has let me go as far as I can with several projects that I have undertaken and has always given the tools and support to succeed."

Aaron Brown, class of 2010, shares, "This summer I will be working in Private Wealth Management for Morgan Stanley, splitting time between the New York, Houston and Dallas offices. It is completely different from both my previous work experience and what I anticipated doing when I entered business school. At Owen, I was able to quickly gain exposure to opportunities in industries and job functions that I had never before considered, and I feel as if my internship is the perfect fit to help me launch a new career. I intend to contribute to the organization's success by providing a fresh perspective, a willingness to learn and a strong desire to succeed."

Paras Agarwal is an MBA candidate with a concentration in Strategy and Operations. A member of the class of 2009, he is also the Consulting Club president. Regarding his choice of Owen for grad school, he relates, "A part of my career vision is the optimization of my present abilities. Acquiring an MBA was a step in this direction. It challenged me to step out and develop new and latent abilities, to grow both as a professional and as a person. In order to achieve this goal it was important that I pursue an MBA from a business school where the quality and quantum of challenges endeavor to bring about this growth."

The breadth and depth of service by Owen students, apparent in those initiatives, led the school to be awarded the 2008 Team MBA Award for Outstanding Community Service, a prestigious honor bestowed by the Graduate Management Admissions Council, the leading advocate and resource for quality graduate schools around the world. Owen students demonstrated the caliber of their academic accomplishments with recent first-place wins at the Rolanette and Berdon Lawrence Finance Case Competition at the Freeman School of Business (Tulane) and the Global Supply Chain Management MBA Case Competition (Purdue), and a second-place finish at the Venture Capital Investment Competition held at the Wharton School of Business.

The 2007–2008 academic year saw student accomplishment of national and international scope. Students launched or continued initiatives that bettered the school, the community, and the world. Examples of Owen student-led initiatives are prolific. OwenBloggers.com attracts readers from around the world with its honest assessments of the joys and challenges of the Owen life. Owen Voices pairs domestic and international students to boost class unity while benefiting the community. The Women's Business Association hosted the first-ever Networking Conference at Vanderbilt, extending communication, networking, and opportunity nationwide. Project Pyramid takes on a number of initiatives in its continuing fight to eliminate global poverty, recently including a trip to Bangladesh that featured an inspiring visit with Nobel laureate and Vanderbilt alumnus Dr. Muhammad Yunus. The Project Pyramid Case Competition offered a cash award for the best business solution to a real-life poverty problem. Net Impact, one of the largest and most successful gatherings in Vanderbilt history, brought together 1,800 graduate business students, faculty, and administrators from business schools around the globe, as well as corporate and nonprofit professionals, to explore corporate social responsibility with speakers, panels, workshops, and a career fair. The event brought wider attention both to the drive for social responsibility in business and to Owen.

What's Next? Your Career

Vanderbilt has a dedicated alumni career services function that provides services to graduating students until the time they retire. Services include career coaching, resume reviews, and an online job posting system. Director of the Career Management Center (CMC) Joyce Rothenberg states, "The Owen Career Management Center takes pride in providing you with service above and beyond expectations. Our goal is to get to know you personally, and to work diligently to support you as you choose and follow your career path."

Owen offers a highly personal approach to career management, ensuring that students receive individual attention and access to the knowledge, resources, and guidance required to accomplish career goals. The CMC is staffed by professionals from the business world—most with their own advanced business degrees—who provide students with career consultation. Additionally, the CMC provides educational, networking, and interviewing opportunities. As the central nervous system for both full-time and internship employment, the CMC provides a variety of services to students and recruiters to help the two come together in mutually beneficial ways. Career assistance activities for students include one-on-one and small group advising, resume and cover letter reviews, tools and guidance for developing career vision and strategy, career skills workshops, mock interviews, peer coaching, industry seminars, functional training programs, online student resume books, information sessions, on-campus recruiting events and interviews, off-campus career events, job postings, and Wall Street Week.

CAREER CHECK: OWEN EMPLOYMENT BY JOB FUNCTION

- Finance/Accounting: 35%
- Marketing/Sales: 23%

(continued)

(continued)

- Consulting: 17%
- General Management: 15%
- Operations/Production: 6%
- Human Resources: 2%

Owen's alumni network stretches from coast to coast and around the globe, so that mentors and connections exist for students regardless of chosen career path. It's made up of people who carry the school's unique spirit of support and camaraderie with them wherever they go. Vanderbilt MBAs are global business leaders, executives, and entrepreneurs. Owen students will find that they are more than willing to share their advice and experience on career options and opportunities.

Owen Connect (www.owenconnect.com) is an online community for communication, networking, contribution, and involvement with Owen alumni. The site allows alumni to view, add, and access information pertaining to classes, career resources, and fellow graduates. Current MBA students also have access to the alumni database that allows users to build contacts and stay on top of current and upcoming Owen events.

ALUMNI ACTUALS

MBA alumni worldwide: 7,600+

Business school alumni networking site: www.owen.vanderbilt.edu/vanderbilt/Community/alumni/

Current MBA students have access to the alumni database.

Match Made in Heaven: Is the Owen Graduate School of Business Right for You?

You are an ideal student if you

- Understand that leadership development, market-focused curricula, and real-world projects will bring your professional endeavors to new heights.
- Are particularly interested in the finance and health care industries.
- Find a small class size and a collegial, supportive community appealing and want to be rigorously challenged in the classroom.
- Are passionate about making a difference in the community, your chosen profession, and the world.

Yale University
Yale School of Management

135 Prospect Street
P.O. Box 208200
New Haven, CT 06520-8200

Phone: 203.432.5635
E-mail: mba.admissions@yale.edu
Web site: http://mba.yale.edu/MBA/

Dean: Sharon M. Oster
Deputy Dean: Stanley J. Garstka

"We need leaders who are not just pursuing narrow, specialized interests, but rather engaging with each other to find solutions. We expect Yale SOM [School of Management] graduates, as they rise in the world, to fulfill that role." —Dean Oster

Quick Facts

MBA PROGRAMS

Full-time MBA
Executive MBA focusing on Healthcare Leadership
Accelerated MBA/JD (Yale SOM-Yale Law School) plus other joint degree programs with professional schools and graduate departments at Yale

FULL-TIME MBA SNAPSHOT

Total enrollment: 386
Class of 2010: 193
Length of program: 21 months
Campus location: New Haven, Connecticut
Program commences in September
Pre-term orientation attendance required

APPLICATION NOTES

Requirements: application; transcripts; recommendations; GMAT scores; work experience; essays; GRE not accepted
Letters of recommendation: 2
Interview: By invitation only
Number of applicants: 3,051
Admittance rate: 14%

(continued)

(continued)

CLASS OF 2010 PROFILE

Male 66%, Female 34%
Minority Americans: 20%
International: 28%
Average age: 28
Average years of work experience: 5.4 years
GMAT score average: 718
GMAT score range (20th–80th percentile): 670–760
GPA average: 3.5

ACADEMIC BACKGROUND OF INCOMING STUDENTS

Business: 19%
Computer Science: 3%
Economics: 18%
Engineering: 16%
Humanities: 19%
Law: 1%
Math: 3%
Social Science: 15%
Science: 6%

An Extensive History, a Bright Future

Yale's roots extend back to the 1640s, when colonial clergymen led an effort to establish a college in New Haven to preserve the tradition of European liberal education in the New World. This vision was fulfilled in 1701 when the charter was granted for a school "wherein Youth may be instructed in the Arts and Sciences [and] through the blessing of Almighty God may be fitted for Publick employment both in Church and Civil State." The original name was the Collegiate School. In 1718, the school was renamed Yale College in gratitude to the Welsh merchant Elihu Yale, who had donated the proceeds from the sale of nine bales of goods together with 417 books and a portrait of King George I. Yale's "Old Campus" is an original section of the school with the oldest building dating back to 1752. This building, Connecticut Hall, is considered a national historic landmark. Other buildings on the "Old Campus" include Durfee Hall, Welch Hall, and Lanman-Wright Hall, all of which still house freshmen today.

Yale College spent the next 100 years expanding. The college—and later the university—can claim a number of "firsts," and among them are first planned college campus, first college with a mascot, and first college daily newspaper. The Yale School of Medicine was chartered in 1810. Next came the Divinity School in 1822, the Law School in 1824, and the Graduate School of Arts and Sciences in 1847 (which awarded the first doctorate degree in the United States in 1861). More schools were added: Art in 1869, Music in 1894, Forestry and Environmental Studies in 1900, Nursing in 1923, Drama in 1955, Architecture in 1972, and Management in 1974.

On campus at Yale.

Yale has one foot in history and another in current events. In the spring of 2009, the Millstein Center for Corporate Governance and Performance released guidelines to "boost transparency among institutional investors and the proxy voting services that advise them on relations with corporations." The center also proposed the first industry-wide code of professional conduct for proxy services as a means of increasing transparency and policing conflicts of interest within the industry. Practices highlighted in the code include a ban on a vote advisor performing consulting work for any company on which it provides voting recommendations or ratings.

Millstein Center will serve as a leading global resource for testing, challenging, and advancing the premise that corporations should and can serve society. The center pursues its mission by convening events; sponsoring empirical research; generating policy briefing; building market capacity by developing training, databases, and institutions; teaching; and engaging in student interaction.

Why Yale SOM?

The mission of the Yale School of Management (SOM) is to educate leaders for business and society. Yale embodies this mission through its distinctive integrated MBA curriculum, through the equally distinctive model of leadership developed in its students, and through its unique vision. Yale SOM graduates are expected to become broadly engaged, inspiring leaders who own and solve hard problems that matter.

Kimberly Yerino, a student ambassador, relates that Yale's philosophy is "'educating leaders for business and society.' As a student, I have seen this mission manifest in the course work and cases we do, in the way students treat one another and the kind of opportunities that are made available to us." For example, Yerino notes an early experience as an MBA candidate. "During our school orientation, we were introduced to the concept of values-driven leadership. The Leadership Development

Program [LDP] provides the space and encouragement for us to explore those personal values and the source of those values. For me, that source was Judeo-Christianity. Even though SOM is in no way a religious school, the LDP created a comfortable environment for me to engage who I am, what I believe, and the impact I want those beliefs to have on my career." She explains, "Ethical considerations are upheld throughout the cases that we study. In a financial crisis such as the one in which we find ourselves today, it is especially critical for leaders to be rooted in a sense of morals that brings purpose to their lives beyond the acquisition of financial gain." Yerino says, "Throughout the school, I am surrounded by people who not only want to be managers, but who want their lives to mean something. It is personally exciting for me to learn in a rigorous academic environment that is preparing me for not only personal success, but making a difference in business and society."

Today, the most significant and important managerial problems are defined by many functions and industries, including financial markets, globalization, climate change, corporate governance, health care, education, development, and entrepreneurial activity, among others. The critical concerns in today's world economy require a broader perspective and a deeper sensitivity to the ways in which market forces can be brought to bear not just to create and sustain wealth, but also to address and alleviate some of the most vexing societal problems. Far from being exclusive to one another, wealth generation and social benefit can go hand in hand. Yale's dual focus on business and society creates leaders who fundamentally understand this essential synergy, and who are uniquely suited for success and positive impact in every sector, in any field, anywhere in the world.

Historically, Yale has been dedicated to finding new approaches, ideas, and solutions to some of the most multifaceted, integrated management problems of the time. The integrated MBA curriculum reaches across all national, cultural, academic, or organizational boundaries. Students learn to be accountable leaders, putting into practice their values, sense of purpose, passion and fair play, as well as their honesty and creativity into each management decision. David Bledin, class of 2009, concurs. "When I was considering MBA schools, I wanted to find a place that wasn't just a breeding ground for the next generation of i-bankers and management consultants, since I'd had experience in both of those industries and ruled them out. I looked at Yale and liked the small class size, the quirkiness, and the emphasis on ethics and values … it seemed the type of place that didn't just crank out the archetypal MBA grad who is reviled by most everybody else."

Yale SOM embraces innovative, multidisciplinary, team approaches to learning, bringing in the "real world" from the first day. Management is not an entity isolated to itself; it lends itself to every level of input. Yale MBA students embody that spirit of invention and collaboration.

"We know the solutions to these complex problems can best be achieved when you bring together people who know about finance, who know about macroeconomics, who know about leadership, who know about politics, and who know about organizations," says Dean Sharon Oster.

The New Haven community is a wonderful place to call home. The city's diversity is apparent in its neighborhoods, which range from quiet residential blocks to lively downtown streets. Its population combines the socioeconomic mix of a New England city with that of a global university. New Haven has been home to Yale University for nearly three centuries. As a center for business and a mecca for the arts, New Haven is recognized as a city of innovation, culture, and prosperity. Approximately 20 square miles with nearly 130,000 residents, New Haven is conveniently located between Boston and

New York. Yale President Richard C. Levin, a 30-year resident of New Haven notes that the town is "large enough to be interesting, yet small enough to be friendly."

Yale School of Management is wireless, and you can pop open your laptop anywhere on campus and check your e-mail or the Yale blogs.

FUN FACTS

- No more Bladderball! Bladderball is a Yale-originated game similar to rugby and was originally played using an inflated animal bladder. The tradition, which began in 1954, ended in 1982 owing to dangerous antics and injury.
- Yale and Secret Societies: CNN's Anderson Cooper, class of 1989, majored in political science and was a member of the Yale secret society, Manuscript. Fifteen juniors are inducted to Yale's best-known secret society, Skull and Bones, every year. Two famous "Bonesmen" are John Kerry, class of 1965, and George W. Bush, class of 1968.
- Indra Nooyi, class of 1980, CEO of PepsiCo, worked the graveyard shift as dorm receptionist while a student at Yale because the job paid 50 cents more per hour than the day shift.

Course Offerings

Yale SOM introduced a new era in MBA education in 2006. The school wholly redesigned its first-year core curriculum by replacing courses in the traditional disciplines, such as finance, accounting and marketing, with courses called "Organizational Perspectives," which are organized from the viewpoints of the constituencies a manager must engage and lead to maximize value within an organization. This approach provides the frameworks and concepts of MBA education in a richer, more relevant context—and is responsive to the demands of contemporary business.

Admissions Director Bruce DelMonico describes the advent of the curriculum. "The senior faculty voted unanimously to adopt it in March 2006 and worked very hard over the summer to implement it. It rolled out in September 2006, which was an amazing achievement. The basic thrust of the new core curriculum is that management education had lost touch with the way business is practiced today. In the past, MBA graduates would have a relatively stable, straightforward job with the same company for a number of years and would work their way up vertically within the organization. Today, people's careers are much more fluid, much more dynamic, and even if they are staying in the same organization, they tend to jump around in terms of their responsibilities. As they work their way up in the organization, they have to bring in a very broad perspective and be very multidisciplinary in how they approach things."

Conversely, DelMonico continues, "The new core curriculum is meant to reflect this business reality and to train MBA students to succeed in today's business environment. For example, instead of a Finance course, there is a course on the Investor; instead of a traditional Marketing course, there is a course on the Customer. The heart of the core curriculum is a series of eight of these new multi-disciplinary courses, called Organizational Perspectives. These courses are structured around the organizational roles a manager must engage in order to solve problems. The idea is that this focus on organizational role, instead of disciplinary topic, creates a richer context for students to learn the concepts they need to succeed as managers."

Introduced in 2009, the Accelerated Integrated JD/MBA program allows students to earn both degrees in three years and does not include a summer session. For students with a special interest in business law, graduates with the degree will be prepared for careers as managers and entrepreneurs not only for business companies, but also for nonprofit organizations. A more traditional four-year JD/MBA program remains available.

RESEARCH CENTERS

Center for Business and the Environment

International Center for Finance

Millstein Center for Corporate Governance and Performance

Program on Social Enterprise

Yale Center for Customer Insights

What Admissions Is All About

Bruce DelMonico shares, "The main thing is be yourself in your application. Authenticity is key. A lot of times we will get applicants and it's clear that they're telling us what they think we want to hear. We don't want them to tell us what they think we're looking for. We want them to be authentic about who they are, what they want to do, and what their passions and interests are. The main piece of advice I tend to give applicants who ask how they can positively affect their application is to really pay attention to their essays. That's the one place in which you can speak directly to us and tell us about yourself. You've already taken your GMAT. Your GPA is what it is. The essays are the one thing you have real control over, so pay attention to them and make sure that they are coherent, concise, on-topic, and well-written. It's amazing how far a well-written essay will go."

Admittance is competitive. Something to think about: If you are invited to interview, go. Thirty-two percent of applicants were interviewed and every admitted candidate was interviewed. Yale has announced plans to increase the student body for the 2009–2010 academic year to up to 220 (approximately the size of the class before 2006–2007), assuming that the exceptional quality of the pool holds. The school will go back to four smaller cohorts rather than the three larger cohorts established in the 2006–2007 year.

It is important to note that the Leadership in Healthcare MBA for Executives has its own separate admissions process. Some of the requirements include seven or more years of work experience and current experience working full time in a management or executive position in health care.

FACULTY FACTS

Full-time faculty employed by the b-school: 62

Adjunct or visiting faculty: 26

Permanent/tenured professors: 20

Tenured faculty who are women: 10

Tenured faculty who are underrepresented minorities: n/a

Tenured international faculty: 27

SAMPLING OF NOTABLE PROFESSORS

- James N. Baron: Author of many human resources books; won the 2003 Accenture Award for making "the most important contribution to improving the practice of management"
- Ravi Dhar: Marketing expert; serves as director of the Center for Customer Insights at the Yale SOM; has written more than 40 articles; serves on many editorial boards of leading marketing journals
- Andrew Metrick: Leading finance scholar; researcher in economics, private equity, corporate governance, and other subjects; author of *Venture Capital and the Finance of Innovation*
- Jeffrey A. Sonnenfeld: Founder and president of the Chief Executive Leadership Institute; corporate consultant; author of many published works; named one of the most 10 influential business school professors

---

CONCENTRATIONS AND SPECIALIZATIONS OFFERED IN FULL-TIME MBA PROGRAM

Leadership in Healthcare MBA for Executives

JOINT DEGREES AND DUAL DEGREES

MBA/JD

MBA/MEM or MF (Environment or Forestry)

MBA/MD

MBA/MFA (Drama)

MBA/MDIV or MAR (Divinity or Religion)

MBA/MARCH (Architecture)

MBA/MPH (Public Health)

MBA/MA (in International Relations or Russian and East European Studies)

MBA/PhD

What Yale SOM Professors Teach

Yale SOM professors talk to each other. They know what you are learning in your other classes and reinforce that learning by mentioning key concepts. Students agree that is one of the best ways to keep you on your toes. The new integrated MBA curriculum seamlessly draws on an interdisciplinary perspective to provide students with an "everything comes together" approach to learning from the basic skills to leadership and making the tough decisions.

Paul Holzer, class of 2009, finds that "the size of the school makes relationship building with faculty incredibly easy; and, for those of us trying to start a business, being able to seek the counsel of experts among the faculty is a huge resource. I can literally make an appointment with whichever member of faculty I choose and solicit their help on what is most important to me."

Yale's curriculum underwent a significant overhaul in 2006. Numerous electives have been added to the curriculum. A sampling of these electives include: Faith and Globalization, Understanding Global Financial Centers, Healthcare Operations, Venture Capital, and the Finance of Innovation and Business Process Reengineering.

Each professor approaches a course by integrating the key principles of business organization. A multitude of components drive the direction and success of any given company (including people, economic environment, business culture, and overarching business practices), and professors vary their teaching methods course by course to impart these principles. Teaching methods include the case study, lecture, experiential learning, and team projects. Often the raw case method works best. The "raw case," introduced in 2006, is the school's description for an online, multimedia case. Each case also takes into account videotaped interviews, online deal documents, analysts' reports, and web-based newspaper articles.

Financially Aided

All full-time MBAs apply for financial aid through the dedicated financial aid office of the SOM. Twenty-two percent received aid through the school. Be mindful that there is an annual recommended budget for residents of the MBA program to help you plan your expenses. The SOM has 36 named scholarships based on academic merit. All applicants are considered for those merit-based scholarships. No separate application is required. Recipients are notified at the same time that they are admitted.

Specific to the school is the Silver Scholars, a program for students to come to Yale SOM directly after college. Additionally, Yale was the first school to launch an Internship Fund; it is now three decades old. The money is used to help provide salaries for students of the School of Management and is raised primarily through the efforts of current students.

In April 2008, the Consortium for Graduate Study in Management began recruiting prospective MBA students for Yale SOM, with the first class to graduate in the spring of 2011. Yale joins 13 other top business schools in the Consortium to promote diversity and inclusion in American business and award merit-based, full-tuition fellowships.

Yale also supports a loan forgiveness program for alumni working in the nonprofit or public sectors. Eligible alumni can receive full reimbursement for their annual debt repayment on need-based loans. Other alumni who qualify can receive partial loan forgiveness.

Full-time MBAs receiving financial aid through school: 22%

Institutional (merit-based) scholarships: 36

Assistantships: n/a

Full-tuition scholarships school awarded for academic year: 10

FULL-TIME MBA PROGRAM (TOTAL DIRECT COSTS)

In-state: $93,098

Out-of-state: $93,098

International: $93,098

Other programs: dependent on the curriculum plan established for each student

What Yale SOM Students Know

"Here's the amazing thing about SOM," explains Easy Office founder Jeff Russell, class of 2009. "My wife and I decided to see if a handful of students would help us with the work of getting the idea off the ground; and we were able to recruit about 20 fellow first-years—that's 10 percent of the class. Basically, the workload for them was like another class. And they got no credit for it. Nothing. So it was just to help me out and, in turn, help out the idea. Former Dean Podolny, Dean Oster, and Professor Brewer all coached us on the project and provided feedback, and really helped us through the process. At the end of the project, Amy Karson [class of 2008] approached me about getting more involved. Now we're essentially partners—she's handling sales in the Northeast. After graduation I'm moving to Boise to run operations and as a bonus, there are over 250 environmental nonprofits nearby in the Yellowstone region. And they're all small. And they need help. And we're happy to provide it."

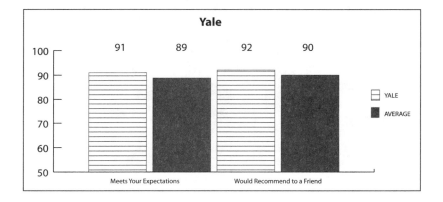

Paul Holzer researched top MBA programs extensively. "Yale seemed like the only place where instead of just the 'Net Impact' club caring about having an impact on society, the entire school cared about leadership and impacting society. People like me who strive to effect change on a really large scale feel so lucky to be part of this community."

John Eng, class of 2009, was bitten by the business bug and chose not to follow family into medicine. The Career Development Office steered him into the direction of a Sears summer internship where he utilized what he learned from his core curriculum right away. "I got to spend some time with several executives; every two days I had a meeting with the Chief Marketing Officer; I had regular meetings with the head of Innovation," Eng recalls. "Everything I saw confirmed just how relevant the curriculum is to what managers face every day. It's amazing how something that can seem so different in the abstract is really so practical when you put it into action."

Joseph Wright Alsop Memorial Scholarship recipient Roberto Jimenez, class of 2009, is determined to help people in developing nations climb out of poverty. He envisions safeguarding the developing world as well as the environment by working in the energy sector. "Clean, affordable supplies of energy are fundamental to development. I'll be working in the Future Fuels and CO2 group at Shell. I considered working for a small renewable energy company, but the more I thought about it, the more I saw how important it is for global companies such as Shell to get seriously involved in renewable energy. To have any real impact, you need scale. A company with global reach and real market muscle can have a huge impact."

Jeff Russell loves helping people and business become more efficient. As an engineer, efficiency was second nature to him. After traveling all over the world, he noticed that "people really needed help." So he started the Momentum Group, which takes "business professionals overseas to help entrepreneurs and aid groups get up and running, set up a website, or learn to run more efficiently." He believes that a person can make money and do good in the world. After deciding to pursue his MBA, Russell came to the conclusion that the greatest good that he could do for the greatest number of people was to help give them the tools to make their lives better by providing back-office services to small and medium nonprofits so that they could focus on their mission-related work. He utilized the School of Management to help him.

What's Next? Your Career

Yale SOM graduates enjoy full immersion into the marketplace from day one in fields such as consulting, finance, and marketing, which made up 87 percent of the class of 2008's postgraduate employment. The remaining 13 percent were sprinkled within the fields of general management, HR, MIS, general operations, and nonprofits.

CAREER CHECK: YALE MBA EMPLOYMENT BY JOB FUNCTION

- Finance: 40%
- Consulting: 25%
- General Management: 21%
- Marketing: 10%
- Human Resources: 2%
- Information Technology (MIS): 1%
- Operations: 1%

Yale SOM alumni are among the most loyal in the country. Each graduating class is small, and as a result, connections are deep. The Class of 2009 set a new record of school support through a 100 percent participation in the class gift. The current national economic challenge was a deciding factor for many because grads realized their participation meant more this year than in other years.

Students and alumni who spearheaded the fundraising can point to the power of the Yale SOM education as the backbone of the effort. After all, the new grads had spent the last two years learning (among other skills) how to add value to an organization. In this case the organization is the school itself, and the value added is financial support for future students.

ALUMNI ACTUALS

MBA alumni worldwide: 5,600+

Business school alumni networking site: http://mba.yale.edu/alumni/

Current MBA students have access to the alumni database.

Match Made in Heaven: Is the Yale School of Management Right for You?

You are an ideal student if you

- Have a clear purpose, possess deep passion for your business future, and are accountable to yourself and your classmates to grow throughout your educational experience.
- Want access and conversations with your professors who are experts in their fields.
- Learn well through integrated curriculum that views business through a multitude of personnel and organizational positions.
- Want to develop values-based leadership and the ability to resolve difficult challenges in an evolving business climate.

Indian School of Business (ISB)

Gachibowli
Hyderabad, Andhra Pradesh, India 500 032

Phone: +91 40 2300 7000
E-mail: pgpadmissions@isb.edu
Web site: www.isb.edu/pgp/

Dean: Ajit Rangnekar
Associate Dean: Kavil Ramchandran
Associate Dean of Academic Programs: Dishan Kamdar
Associate Dean and Chief Executive, Mohali Campus: Savita Mahajan

"At ISB, it has been our constant endeavor to encourage entrepreneurial initiatives by our students as well as equip them to be an integral part of the global business community. This initiative would be another step in this direction." —Dean Rangnekar

Quick Facts

MBA PROGRAMS

Executive education
Full-time postgraduate program in Management
Post-doctoral program

FULL-TIME MBA SNAPSHOT

Total enrollment: 976
Class of 2010: 569
Length of program: 12 months
Campus: Hyderabad, India
Program commences in April
Pre-term orientation attendance required

APPLICATION NOTES

Requirements: Bachelor's degree; GMAT score; preferably two years of full-time work experience; three application essays; GRE accepted
Letters of recommendation: 2
Interview: By invitation only
Number of applicants: 5,000
Admittance rate: 9%

CLASS OF 2010 PROFILE

Male 76%, Female 24%
Minority Americans: 1%
International: 4%
Average age: 27
Married or Partnered, Single: 27%, 73%
Combined average years of work experience: 5 years
GMAT score range (20th–80th percentile): 690–740
GMAT score average: 715
Average GPA: At least 3.5 by U.S. standards

ACADEMIC BACKGROUND OF INCOMING STUDENTS

Accounts/Financing: 20%
Business: 6%
Economics: 4%
Engineering: 56%
Medicine: 3%
Sciences: 6%
Other: 5%

An Indian B-school Enters the International Arena

After the economic liberalization of India in 1991, what India Inc. needed was a business school that would represent India and its corporate leaders at the international level. The ever-changing world of business necessitates training young leaders to understand the finer nuances of transitional economies. Another important consideration was developing innovative academic programs that were not only world class but also affordable.

ISB is located in Hyderabad, the tropical-climate state capital and most populous city in Andhra Pradesh. With a population of nearly seven million residents, Hyderabad is similar in size to Mumbai, Delhi, Chennai, and Kolkata. The city, known for its rich history, culture, and architecture, is often referred to as the meeting point of North and South India.

Scenes from ISB.

ISB was founded by Anil Ambani, Rahul Bajaj, Adi Godrej, and Rajat Gupta. Initially, the founders had three cities in mind for the site of the school. However, Chief Minister Chandrababu Naidu asked them to consider Hyderabad. He invited them to tour Hyderabad and view the 250-acre site he had set aside as a possible location. Once an agreement with the government of Andhra Pradesh cleared the way for setting up ISB, the founders' decision to build in Hyderabad subsequently changed the town into the modern hub of information technology, ITES, and biotechnology that it is today.

The Kellogg School of Management and the Wharton School synergized their strengths with ISB and became its academic associates. Prior to the launch of the first postgraduate program (PGP) in 2001, London Business School became the third academic associate. ISB now plans to open its second campus in Mohali, Punjab, by 2012.

Why ISB?

Within seven years of inception, ISB has emerged as a worldwide leader in management education. The first incoming class was composed of 128 students. In 2008, 220 attended. Part of this growth can be attributed to ISB's five Centers of Excellence, with each center focusing on issues pertaining to developing markets. The centers partner with industry and provide a vibrant research environment at the school. One of the well-regarded research institutes is the Center for Global Logistics and Manufacturing Strategies (GLAMS). It serves as a research partner and collaborator with government and leading industrial institutions. GLAMS researchers analyze and design techniques and networks in logistics, supply chain management, retail in emerging markets, and rural business, among other areas.

The full-time course at ISB is a one-year program. "Everybody is a star in their own right even before coming to ISB, but once here they are even greater stars, and superstars and shooting stars and what not," declares Nalin Kant Srivastava, class of 2009. "Most of the students deciding to join ISB come here to save that precious one year, which might be hard to spare once you are working. At ISB everything is done at double speed, as it is two years of rigorous course condensed into a year's course. The process is so intense that out of the total 440 people, you will get to know around 100-odd in the first week and then it is up to you as to what relationships you develop, what effort you make to learn more about the rest, and how quickly you accomplish it."

Students work on projects in groups with four or five classmates, and the groups change frequently so that you interact with as many of your peers as possible. Every incoming class has students from as many professions as possible and includes military personnel, attorneys, and international business students, including MBA candidates from the United States. The diversity of classmates allows for a rounded approach to situations and provides an immensely important and rewarding learning experience by sharing thought processes.

The campus of ISB provides its students with world-class facilities. The nucleus of the campus, the Academic Center, boasts an impressive library, lecture theater, computer centers, meeting rooms, and an auditorium. The campus is Wi-Fi enabled, ensuring connectivity in every space a student may use. In addition, all the classrooms are fitted with state-of-the-art conferencing equipment. As a demonstration of the high regard these facilities have generated, ISB served as host for the National Summit of the Association of Indian Management Schools Organizers in August 2009.

FUN FACTS

- Be sure to visit Lumbini Park to view the charming musical fountains, which are usually played in the evenings. The Public Gardens is a beautiful sprawling green garden where you can relax peacefully and visit the heritage buildings, which are symbols of the cultural and political heritage of Hyderabad. In Sanjeevaiah Park, you can find some rare species of roses that are a beautiful sight.

- Raymond's Tomb is situated in Saroornagar, 10 kilometers east of Hyderabad's city center. People from all over the city pay respect on the anniversary of the late army general's death by lighting incense sticks near the tomb.

- From Hindi love stories to international comedies, the movie industry centered in Hyderabad has spawned a second industry of consumers. The city attracts more buyers than anywhere in the country who purchase such items as football jerseys, ice-cream machines, designer pens, and keychains.

Course Offerings

Because the course curriculum is developed jointly by Kellogg, Wharton, LBS, and ISB, you receive a judicious blend of insights from East and West, offering you a coherent understanding of the developed and developing economies of the world. Every year the curriculum is upgraded to keep in sync with changing paradigms of the business world.

The postgraduate program (PGP) commences with a weeklong pre-term orientation course conducted by the students of the previous incoming class. This course allows MBA candidates to understand in detail what lies ahead and how ISB differs from two-year programs. Students are then better prepared to break the mold of their previous life and embrace the life at ISB. The Indian School of Business is all about ideas. It is student friendly, and while professors are available and supportive, they expect your primary comprehension of the concepts to come through group study. You can participate in various boards and groups as a leader in training. In this role, you are encouraged to move your ideas forward in a constructive way and see them through to the implementation stage.

The program at ISB consists of eight terms of six weeks each. The first four terms cover core subjects and are compulsory. The second four terms are elective. It is during these elective terms that students may opt for an international exchange program for either one or two terms. Your choices of destination include more than 30 top-ranked programs from around the world in Australia, Canada, China, France, Germany, Israel, Italy, Korea, the Netherlands, Pakistan, Singapore, Spain, South Africa, Taiwan, the United Kingdom, and the United States.

Development of soft skills is an important value of the school. The Leadership Development Program helps you fine-tune your communication and leadership skills. Industry partners present students with a current consulting problem. You work with your group as consultants to companies. Nothing is simulated. Every student interacts with real professionals from industry and works with them on real problems.

Any student can add one or two specializations. In addition, you can enroll in two additional electives, which are outside a specialization. More than 70 electives are offered that combine into six concentrations. They include Analytical Finance, Entrepreneurship, Information Technology Management, Operations Management, Strategic Marketing, and Strategy and Leadership.

ISB Partner Schools

Bocconi University, SDA, Italy

Cheung Kong Graduate School of Business, China

China Europe International Business School, Shanghai, China

Darden School of Business, University of Virginia

Duke University, Fuqua, North Carolina

Erasmus University, Rotterdam, the Netherlands

ESADE Business School, Spain

HEC School of Management, France

Hong Kong University of Science and Technology, School of Business and Management, Hong Kong

IE Business School, Spain

IESE Business School, University of Navarra, Spain

KAIST Graduate School of Business, Korea

Lahore University of Management Sciences, Pakistan

National Chengchi University College of Commerce, Taiwan

National University of Singapore, Singapore

Northwestern University, Kellogg, Illinois

Queen's School of Business, Queen's University, Canada

Tel Aviv University Recanati, Israel

Thunderbird School of Global Management, California

Tsinghua University, School of Economics and Management, China

Tuck School of Business, Dartmouth College, Hanover, New Hampshire

Tufts University, Fletcher, Medford, Massachusetts

University of California Berkeley Haas, California

University of Cape Town Graduate School of Business, South Africa

University of Cambridge, Judge, England

University of Melbourne, Australia

University of North Carolina, Kenan-Flagler, Chapel Hill, North Carolina

University of Toronto, Rotman, Canada

WHU, Otto Beisheim Graduate School of Management, Germany

York University, Schulich, Canada

What ISB Professors Teach

ISB has access to high-quality professors on a global scale. Around 100 visit every year. This number is in addition to the 30 or so permanent ISB faculty members. The institute approaches highly proven teachers and researchers that the management has identified after thorough research. All are best in their league in their subjects. Visiting faculty from Wharton, Kellogg, London Business School, Cornell, Chicago, Duke, and UCLA are among them. As the school is gaining international recognition, research scholars from around the world come to ISB on long-term sabbaticals. Rajat Gupta, Senior Partner Worldwide, McKinsey and Company; Ajit Dangi, Organization of Pharmaceutical Producers of India (OPPI); and C Rangarajan, chairman of the 12th Finance Commission, India, are some examples.

Kavil Ramchandran, professor and an associate dean of ISB, explains that ISB faculty try to instill certain principles in students. "One part is that we try to fill in leadership skills with the students. Another is that they should learn an international orientation. The mental build up should be a global build up rather than Indian. This is achieved by the presence of visiting faculty who bring a lot of international exposure into the classrooms. The third part is entrepreneurship, which is a very important part of the curriculum here. We encourage students to become entrepreneurs and provide them with mentorship to enable them."

And as far as focus of the curriculum is concerned, Professor N. Viswanadham is of the view that "we want to make them the leaders, so there are three things required for that. One is that they should have the skills—communications skills, listening skills, leading skills, ability to lead skills, etc. Then they need to have knowledge in [a] number of areas—maybe marketing, maybe finance, maybe statistics, or even HR. Students need to have the mental framework and the attitude to take that subject up. The curriculum is focused on imparting these skills."

ISB professors constantly upgrade their skills and the research projects in which they take part. They attend conferences and publish research together. Most faculty members hold doctorate degrees. A large number of visitors who come to ISB are from industry, and they impart their own experiences in the classrooms. Ramachandran further adds, "We do not have anything similar to the summer internships but … we have enough things to cover for that."

FACULTY FACTS

Full-time faculty employed by the b-school: 42

Adjunct or visiting faculty: 105

Permanent/tenured professors: 30

Tenured faculty who are women: 4

Tenured faculty who are underrepresented minorities: N/A

SAMPLING OF NOTABLE PROFESSORS

- Sanjay Kallapur: Well-regarded professor of economics; editor of *The Accounting Review*
- Kavil Ramachandran: Expert in entrepreneurship and strategic management; associate dean of Academic Programs; holds a multitude of strategic advisory roles, including Confederation of Indian Industry and the Committee of the Securities and Exchange Board of India
- Rajesh Chakrabarti: Well-established researcher and author of the book *The Financial Sector in India—Emerging Issues*; co-author of *The Asian Manager's Handbook of E-Commerce*; columnist for the *Financial Express of India*
- Sumit Agarwal: Co-author of *Household Credit Usage: Personal Debt and Mortgage*; consultant for the Bank of Uganda and the World Bank
- Shamika Ravi: Professor of economics; awarded with prestigious grants from the Ford Foundation and Open Society Institute

CONCENTRATIONS AND SPECIALIZATIONS OFFERED IN FULL-TIME MBA PROGRAM

Analytical Finance

Entrepreneurship

Information Technology Management

Operations Management

Strategic Marketing

Strategy and Leadership

JOINT DEGREES AND DUAL DEGREES

Not applicable

What Admissions Is All About

The application process differs for candidates with Indian passports and those with non-Indian passports. For the non-Indian passport holder, the application process starts in June every year and goes on until the following January. International students need to have valid GMAT scores to be considered. V. K. Menon, senior director of Admissions and Financial Aid says, "The cut-off scores for the GMAT are raised every year. In 2008–2009, it was 713." And starting with the 2009–2010 school year, ISB's incoming class size is expanding to 560 students.

ISB looks for an excellent academic record, with a minimum two years of work experience, good communication skills, and solid application essays. Menon also points out, "We need two or a maximum of three recommendation letters. Under no circumstances are these to come from family, friends, or subordinates. It may ruin the chances of your getting selected." Also, keep in mind that your application is reviewed by Kellogg's admissions staff as well as at ISB. If selected for the interview, the b-school conducts telephone interviews for international students, which is the most important aspect of the interview process. During February, an offer is made to selected candidates, and students have a 15-day period to confirm their acceptance.

Having diversity in ethnicity and work backgrounds is important at ISB. Menon points out, "Our aim is to have around a third of the class comprised of international students. It may take us a little time to get there but we are going in the right direction. For example, right now we have about 20 percent of the class that do not have Indian passports including the students of the NRIs as well as purely non-Indians. There are also students who may have one parent who is Indian. And there are a few people from Malaysia. One class of 2010 student is from Pakistan."

The sole aim of students entering ISB is to advance their careers without slowing down their pace, which may occur by joining a two-year MBA program. International exposure and the chance to work with some of the best people in industry are truly thought changing. When people such as Bill Gates or Michael Dell come to ISB, recruiters definitely cannot stay away.

V. K. Menon explains, "ISB seeks demonstrated initiative and leadership potential, consistently good academic performance, strong communication skills, team playing, and other contributing participative learning skills in prospective applicants."

Full-time MBAs receiving financial aid through school: 100

Institutional (merit-based) scholarships: 11

Assistantships: N/A

Full-tuition scholarships school awarded for academic year: 100

Financially Aided

ISB, along with Association Internationale des Étudiants en Sciences Économiques et Commerciales (AIESEC), offers three international students scholarships covering 75 percent of expenses incurred during the entire program. Selected students need to submit a scholarship essay to AIESEC to be considered. ISB also has the International Diversity Scholarship Program, which finances two or three students every year, all expenses covered. A third option for financial aid for international students is to approach the International Education Finance Corporation, which offers full financial assistance to deserving students. Many other scholarships are available.

Companies such as Citigroup, HSBC, Novartis, Cognizant, and Sierra Atlantic offer limited scholarships, but only Indian students are eligible for such scholarships. Fee structure is the same for all the students. The school awards institutional grants and corporate-sponsored scholarship assistance in addition to facilitating long-term, low-interest loans through financing sources. Statistics show that nearly 30 percent of students receive scholarships from various organizations, and the rest manage to obtain educational loans.

New in 2009 is the Nurture India Scholarships initiative, which pays two years of a student's education loans. The initiative aims to motivate and support its graduates who are keen to start entrepreneurial ventures or work with organizations in the development sector (social ventures and NGOs). ISB supported five graduates in 2009. Eligible to apply are those who have accepted employment in social ventures (microfinance, NGOs, grassroots-level development institutions, and others) or those who are in the process of rolling out their own ventures immediately after graduation.

FULL-TIME MBA PROGRAM (TOTAL DIRECT COSTS)

In-country: $39,500 USD

International: $39,500 USD

What ISB Students Know

Jacob Kanadhil, class of 2009, states, "At ISB we have a lot of professional clubs such as the marketing club, real estate club, etc. So there is a lot of interaction and exchange that happens through clubs. We also have access to alumni who come once in a while and spend time with us and they too connect with us through these clubs." Apart from this, ISB hosts many conferences, and the biggest names across the world take part. Additionally, the library at ISB is simply world class. And because the campus is wireless, there is no need to go to a computer lab.

Students have direct access to all the resident and visiting faculty of the school. Kanadhil believes the best time to interact with professors is when they come to their on-campus parties.

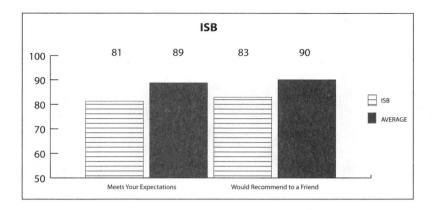

There are plenty of open spaces on campus used for group study—for instance, the atrium. This space with open sides has the library and other facilities on its top. It is one of the common places for most students to study because there is a cafeteria nearby, which even professors frequent.

Nalin Kant Srivastava describes a typical day. "Well, I wake up after four or five hours of sleep (at max) and then run between classes, grabbing food whenever I can, grappling with assignments and projects. The day vanishes amidst all this. However, sometimes we make up during the weekends." Students at ISB find that 24 hours seems like less here because of the competition to succeed— some of the toughest in the world—so time flies as students try to complete all the program's requirements.

Immediately after the pre-term orientation, an alum is assigned as a mentor to every student, which helps you tackle the fast-paced life at ISB. This becomes apparent from Kanadhil's view that "what really freaks people out here is the work pressure and it is tough to be able to survive." In regard to Kanadhil's experience with mentors, he continues, "Actually, there is a lot of formal and informal exchange of information that happens here. But [your mentor] can tell you, don't worry, things like these happen all the time and this will pass. While working on a project also, students can seek guidance of their mentor as he might have a better idea of the outside world. We also use alums to send across our resumes and visit them for mock interviews."

Most of the students are of the view that ISB not only prepares you for a future career, but also enables you to think fast, think on your feet, and work with the best in terms of the competition. "In this way," Kanadhil adds, "the program prepares you for the real world. And given that we all come from the industry background, this makes it all the more relevant for us."

CAREER CHECK: ISB MBA EMPLOYMENT BY JOB FUNCTION

- Information Systems/Technology: 23%
- Operations/Production: 19%
- Finance/Accounting: 15%
- Marketing/Sales: 14%
- General Management: 8%
- Consulting: 4%

What's Next? Your Career

ISB was founded by executives of some of the Fortune 500 companies, which is a primary reason why students from ISB are so sought after. More than 80 percent of the ISB students made career shifts during the placement season. This indicates the avenues an education at ISB opens up for graduates. Out of 657 offers made to 442 students in 2008, 111 were from international companies (33 from the United Kingdom and Europe, 27 from the United States). Nearly 40 percent of the offers were made from IT and Telecom sectors, followed by consulting with 21 percent.

Because ISB is one of the top schools among more than 1,000 in India, graduates are treated on par with those from top American business schools. Many grads have received senior management positions with titles such as COO, VP of International Marketing, Head of Marketing, International Country Manager Designate, and others from leading domestic and international companies. And as the data show, changing industries and functions is easy for ISBians.

ALUMNI ACTUALS

MBA alumni worldwide: 2,000+

Business school alumni networking site: isbalumni.isb.edu/isbalumni/alumni/

Current MBA students have access to the alumni database.

Once onboard, students are immediately connected to the alumni network of ISB, which spans across 25 countries worldwide. Alumni Relations officers enable past and present students to access resources for organizing events and reunions. As an alum, you are part of a lifelong e-mail forwarding facility that helps you network with other alumni.

There are plenty of opportunities during the program to develop networking skills with alumni, professors, visiting faculty, and renowned people who lecture at regular intervals. Also, any big industry figure could be invited to ISB at any given point of time. Even after graduation, there are plenty of opportunities to network. Alumni are grouped into chapters according to the location where they work. For instance, managers in Hyderabad form a part of the Hyderabad chapter, Delhi people form the Delhi chapter, and so on. Also included are international chapters, such as in Singapore.

Vikas Garg, class of 2008, works in a management consultancy firm. He says, "ISB's networking has helped in many ways. There are so many ISB pass outs [graduates] who are investment bankers or into PE firms and are just a phone call away from me because of the kind of network we have." Mangesh Venkatraman, class of 2008, is pleased with the way things have turned out for him after ISB. He opines, "I do not think there is really a need to change anything about ISB. Almost everything is at your disposal to learn at the school, and if not, and one wants to learn, things are laid down to enable that kind of learning. So most of the time, the learning is more than what one could have expected. It depends upon how well you use all those resources. I myself have seen the most disciplined of institutions, and I know for a fact that ISB is even a league higher in that category."

Match Made in Heaven: Is the Indian School of Business Right for You?

You are an ideal student if you

- Would like to keep your career moving forward by participating in a one-year intense program.
- Want to change your industry or career path while working with some of the greatest minds in the world.
- Seek to develop your leadership and management skills with an international orientation.
- Are ready to work building your vision and make an impact in the changing economic arena.

INSEAD Business School
Institut Européen d'Administration des Affaires

Boulevard de Constance
77305 Fontainebleau, France

Phone: +33 01 60 72 40 05
E-mail: mba.info@insead.edu
Web site: www.insead.edu/mba

Asia Campus
1 Ayer Rajah Avenue
Singapore 138676

Phone: +65 6799 5990
E-mail: mba.info@insead.edu
Web site: www.insead.edu/mba

Dean: J. Frank Brown
Dean of the MBA Program: Jake Cohen

"Today's organizations need leaders with the knowledge and sensitivity to operate anywhere in the world. This is why business turns to INSEAD—to develop the next generation of transcultural leaders." —Dean Brown

Quick Facts

MBA PROGRAMS

Full-time MBA
Part-time Executive, Accelerated

FULL-TIME MBA SNAPSHOT

Total enrollment: 480
Class of 2010: 300 (Fontainebleau), 180 (Singapore)
Length of program: 10 months (fall accelerated program), 12 months (winter program)
Campus locations: Fontainebleau, France, and Buona Vista, Singapore
Program commences in late August and early January

APPLICATION NOTES

Requirements: Profile; job description; fluency in English plus one additional language; five essays; statement of integrity; photograph; application; transcripts; GMAT; GRE not accepted
Letters of recommendation: 2
Interview: By invitation only

CLASS OF 2010 PROFILE

Male 71%, Female 29%
North Americans: 14%
International: 90%
Average age: 29
Married or Partnered, Single: 25%, 75%
Combined average years of work experience: 5.25 years
GMAT score average: 700
GMAT score range (20th–80th percentile): 650–750
GPA Average: N/A
Pre-term orientation attendance not required

ACADEMIC BACKGROUND OF INCOMING STUDENTS

Arts: 5%
Business/Administration: 23%
Economics: 12%
Engineering: 35%
Law/Political Sciences: 8%
Other: 8%
Sciences: 9%

Old World Meets Whole World

The town of Fontainebleau is a picturesque French town steeped in history and named after the fresh water spring that gave rise to it. There are a surrounding forest and castle that are well known not just among INSEAD students, but worldwide. With around 15 million visitors a year, the forest is one of France's major tourist and leisure activity attractions. It is particularly known for its unique rock formations and soft white sand and has been described as simply "the best bouldering area in Europe if not the world."

Scenes from INSEAD's campuses.

INSEAD's European campus in Fontainebleau was founded in 1957. It provides the best in on-campus facilities for students, faculty, and staff with 23 auditoria and 6 classrooms that can seat more than 2,150 people. In addition, the Fontainebleau campus provides many specialized group work areas situated all around the campus. The campus also boasts a fully equipped gym facility, campus bookstore, postal and courier services, a licensed bar, and a self-service restaurant that offers a wide variety of worldwide cuisine. The campus provides so many amenities that it's like a village that students never need to leave. It is a self-sustaining community.

Why INSEAD?

With two fully integrated campuses in Europe and Asia and more than 70 different nationalities in the classroom, it is hard to think of another business school that offers such a multicultural experience. The goal of the accelerated 10-month curriculum is to develop successful, thoughtful leaders and entrepreneurs who create value for their organizations and communities. Alumni often say that their year at INSEAD was a life-changing one.

In addition to the two campuses in France and Singapore, INSEAD has an exchange program with the Wharton School of Business at the University of Pennsylvania. In September 2007, INSEAD also inaugurated its Centre for Executive Education and Research in Abu Dhabi. Attracted by Abu Dhabi's international outlook and vibrant business community, this helped to confirm the INSEAD vision as "The Business School for the World."

INSEAD's Executive MBA program offers both company-specific and open enrollment programs. The four open enrollment executive programs in 2008–2009 include Negotiation Dynamics, Achieving Outstanding Performance, Mastering Alternative Investments, and Learning to Lead. The school also offers one of three modules for the International Executive Program in Abu Dhabi, with the other modules in Fontainebleau and Singapore.

Opened in October 2007, the New York City office of INSEAD is intended to foster relationships with its extensive alumni base in the United States while strengthening the INSEAD brand stateside. The school also hopes to develop new corporate relationships as well as to promote its MBA and EMBA programs in the United States.

The INSEAD MBA seeks to prepare its students to become leaders who can work effectively in any culture anywhere on the globe. Since 1959, when INSEAD pioneered the one-year MBA program, the school has continued to challenge convention and maintain an innovative, cutting-edge program. The curriculum prepares participants for a career in international business by reliance on group work and looking closely at international markets and settings. INSEAD encourages teamwork during the entire program through the sharing of knowledge and experience.

This is the MBA program for you if you are looking for a place that promotes diversity, intensity, quality, and lifelong bonds between classmates and alumni. The cultural diversity of faculty and participants and the spectrum of activities on both campuses make INSEAD a unique learning environment.

Across Europe and World Renowned

INSEAD plans to build one of the largest and most diverse entrepreneurship faculties in the world. Already, its Entrepreneurship and Family Enterprise Department has nine full-time, tenure-track professors as well as five affiliate professors, two jointly appointed tenure-track professors, and nine adjunct professors.

There are several student clubs on campus that focus on entrepreneurship, including the INSTEAD Entrepreneurship Club and the INSTEAD Private Equity Club. The Singapore campus also features the newly built Rudolf and Valeria Maag International Center for Entrepreneurship, whose mission includes worldwide outreach and support of alumni.

One of INSEAD's most noted events is the annual Leadership Summit, held on both campuses since 2007. International leaders in business, government, academia, nongovernment organizations and media join together to address current global issues. In light of the current worldwide economic challenges, the April 2009 summit focused on what rules and regulations are necessary for financial market stability.

FUN FACTS

- INSEAD's European campus is home to 275 trees, including the Tree of Liberty, a gingko biloba that was planted in 1989 to commemorate the bicentennial of the French Revolution. INSEAD also participates in reforesting the surrounding Forêt de Fountainebleau.

- Fontainebleau is considered the equestrian capital of France, with a long tradition in the equestrian arts. The area boasts two race tracks: the Hippodrome Grand Parquet and the Hippodrome de la Solle.

- Many students studying in Fontainebleau share off-campus houses with their peers. It has become a tradition for these student houses to host one another at large dinner parties.

- Fontainebleau is a popular destination for boulder climbers. More than two dozen boulders are climbed by amateurs and experts every year.

Course Offerings

The MBA curriculum is designed to prepare participants for a career in international business. The first few terms are based on a structured series of 13 core classes, including accounting, finance, statistics, strategy, marketing, operations management, and organizational behavior. Other courses focus on the business environment. The later part of the program can be adapted to each student's needs or interests with a minimum of 10 electives, creating a mix of topics that will support individual educational and professional goals.

During the core curriculum of study, students are required to work in study groups of five to six people in which no more than two students of the same nationality may be represented. Groups are not predetermined for elective courses, but INSEAD's focus on group work and peer-to-peer learning is emphasized.

The course load is strenuous, with students covering nearly 80 percent of the two-year program of other schools' coursework with little downtime. Therefore, the days can be very long, but despite the intensity of the curriculum, students still find the time and energy to participate in activities outside the classroom.

RESEARCH CENTERS

Asia Pacific Institute of Finance

Blue Ocean Strategy Institute

Center for Advanced Learning Technologies

Center for Decision Making and Risk Analysis

Center for Executive Education and Research (Abu Dhabi)

Center for Global Research and Education (with Wharton School)

Center for Human Resources in Asia

eLab INSEAD

Global Leadership Center

Rudolf and Valeria Maag International Center for Entrepreneurship

Social Innovation Center

Social Science Research Center

Wendel International Center for Family Enterprise

What INSEAD Professors Teach

INSEAD's faculty is a diverse one, with 137 resident professors from 35 different countries. The faculty includes the world's leading researchers in management and produce cutting-edge work in all major academic areas. They are also experts at passing on their skills. At INSEAD, there is a great emphasis on the faculty's ability to work beyond the classroom and inspire research. To further develop INSEAD's international appeal, the school has a faculty exchange program with the Wharton School of Business, along with dedicated centers carrying out research in Abu Dhabi, India, and Israel.

Whereas some MBA programs adhere to a single, uniform teaching method, there is no preferred teaching method at INSEAD. This provides students with the unique experience of being exposed to a wide variety of teaching styles, including case studies, computer simulations, and role-playing exercises.

For Professor Patrick Turner, who specializes in teaching entrepreneurship, what he tries to instill most in his students is a "tolerance of cultural differences and the ability to operate in multicultural contexts." In terms of the real-world connection between the coursework and the students' careers, Turner says, "The most popular course I teach is a sort of 'reality show' that is a very faithful reflection of a real business situation." In terms of INSEAD's future, Turner believes that the MBA program is heading "toward a much greater variety of imaginative and groundbreaking learning experiences, on a worldwide scale." Turner really enjoys "the diversity of background, age, and outlook with my colleagues. INSEAD has to have one of the most diverse faculty bodies in the world."

FACULTY FACTS

Full-time faculty employed by both campuses: 512

Full-time faculty employed on the Fontainebleau campus: 137

Adjunct or visiting faculty: 84

Permanent/tenured professors: 67

Tenured faculty who are women: 3

Tenured faculty who are underrepresented minorities: N/A

SAMPLING OF NOTABLE PROFESSORS

- Robert U. Ayres: Pioneer in material flows and transformations (industrial ecology or industrial metabolism); co-author with Benjamin Warr of *The Economic Growth Engine: How Energy and Work Drive Material Prosperity*

- Jean Dermine: Esteemed researcher on such topics as asset and liability management, and European financial markets; author of *Asset and Liability Management: A Guide to Value Creation and Risk Control*

- W. Chan Kim and Renée Mauborgne: Co-authors of *Blue Ocean Strategy: How to Create Uncontested Market Space and Make Competition Irrelevant*

- Bruce Kogut: Prominent scholar; author of *Knowledge, Options, and Institutions*

- Manfred Kets de Vries: Celebrated academic and recent recipient of the International Leadership Association's Lifetime Achievement Award

- Luk Van Wassenhove: Globally recognized expert in operations and supply chain management; author of several teaching case studies such as "Fighting the Flu: Tamiflu Stockpiling: A Pandemic Preparedness Policy"

CONCENTRATIONS AND SPECIALIZATIONS OFFERED IN FULL-TIME MBA PROGRAM

Accounting and Control

Asian Business and Comparative
  Management

Decision Sciences

Economics and Political Science

Entrepreneurship and Family Enterprise

Finance

Marketing

Strategy

Technology and Operations Management

JOINT DEGREES AND DUAL DEGREES

Executive MBA (Tsinghua-INSEAD)

What Admissions Is All About

INSEAD states that it is looking for students who seek "intellectual curiosity coupled with a desire to learn and stretch yourself in a rigorous academic program, as well as personal qualities to contribute to the many activities of the school."

It seems like a daunting mandate but the admissions committee does an excellent job in terms of selecting a mix of cultures and backgrounds from its applicants. In turn, the MBA program is intensive, rigorous, and challenging. All applicants must have a bachelor's degree or equivalent from a recognized college or university (although in exceptional circumstances, they waive this requirement for otherwise outstanding candidates with substantial professional experience). Although many applicants do possess advanced degrees, this is not compulsory for admissions. The committee looks at the applicant's academic background and considers the competitiveness of the academic institution each applicant attended, as well as his or her academic performance.

INSEAD seeks out applicants who can demonstrate their potential as leaders, and professional experience is assessed. Participants in the current class have an average of nearly six years of work experience. Younger applicants who can demonstrate exceptional maturity and outstanding leadership through their professional and personal experiences will also be considered.

As for the actual application process itself, according to Carol Diarte Edwards, director of admissions, "There are many elements to the application process (essays, recommendations, GMAT, TOEFL for non English speakers, interviews, and so on) and they are all important." Being a good student is not enough, as she adds, "Candidates need to prove themselves on all dimensions. We evaluate the overall picture, and we do not weigh one element more heavily than another." The INSEAD MBA attracts applicants with cross-cultural sensitivity and an international outlook. Fluent English is a prerequisite at INSEAD, and you must also prove that you have practical knowledge of at least one other language.

Diarte Edwards explains that the four key factors that differentiate INSEAD's MBA programs are "diversity, intensity, quality, and the lifelong bonds formed between classmates and alumni."

If you are looking to pursue an international career, this is definitely the place for you. The MBA program had made one recent change. Says Diarte Edwards, "We are opening a new section on the Singapore campus. We have had two sections of 80 students each in Singapore, but as of September 2009, there are three sections of 60 students each." She adds, "We have no quotas, but thanks to the tremendous diversity in our applicant pool, we rarely see more than 10 percent of one particular nationality in the class." She also notes that, "We offer Forte scholarships for women, and attend Forte events. We are very keen to promote access to management education for women."

INSEAD students have varied career goals. Diarte Edwards notes, "Our graduates go on to work for more than 200 different organizations in 55 different countries. Most of our students are looking to make some sort of career change, and nearly 90 percent of them do change—either function, sector, geography, or on more than one of these dimensions." She emphasizes that, "INSEAD has the advantage of having the MBA program running in parallel across two campuses on two continents. The Fontainebleau campus is in the heart of one of Europe's largest and most beautiful forests, not far from Paris—a city that needs no introduction! The Singapore campus, on the other hand, is in an intensely urban environment, at the heart of Southeast Asia. This, as well as the exchange with Wharton, enables students to experience very different geographical and cultural environments during their year."

Full-time MBAs receiving financial aid through school: 20%

Institutional (merit-based and need-based) scholarships: varies

Assistantships: varies

Full-tuition scholarships school awarded for academic year: not available

Financially Aided

INSEAD offers an amazing diversity of scholarships. More than 50 are available to students and are disseminated based on merit, need, student field of study, and country. And new scholarships are still joining the list. Among the newest are the Borsen/Danish Council scholarship, Greek Friends scholarships, Spain Council scholarships, and Swedish Council scholarships. You can obtain details of these and others on the school's Web site and determine your eligibility.

Of course, financing your MBA includes loans and personal savings. Be sure to prepare a budget for yourself and seek advice from the school's financial aid officers as soon as you plan to attend either campus of INSEAD.

> ## FULL-TIME MBA PROGRAM (TOTAL DIRECT COSTS)
>
> In-country: $70,000 USD
>
> International: $70,000
>
> Part-time Executive program cost: $114,000

What INSEAD Students Know

Current MBA students talk about the attraction of the INSEAD MBA program. Says one student, "I saw INSEAD as unique in that no one nationality makes up more than 10 percent of its students. In addition, it is the school that pioneered the one-year MBA, and I believe INSEAD still does it better than anyone else. Additionally, I really hit it off with the students and alumni I met. INSEAD students seem to have a broader perspective on business, the world, and life than the students at other MBA programs." Maiya Shur, class of 2009, adds, "After living in Boston for the last 10 years, I started thinking about needing a change. A friend happened to tell me about an INSEAD event and it quickly got me thinking about the program. The location, name recognition, and emphasis on recruitment of female MBAs all helped me make my decision."

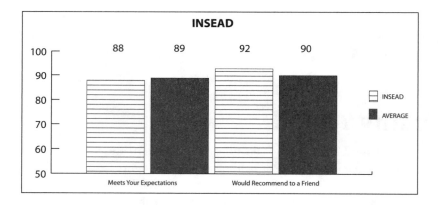

For another class of 2009 student, when it came time to decide on enrolling in INSEAD, it was not difficult. He says, "I thought INSEAD opens up the broadest range of opportunities for its MBA graduates. Its alumni network spans the globe unlike any other graduate school program; it is strong in all the primary areas of business. I am not 100 percent sure what I want to do after the program, so what was important to me was that the program would maximize my career opportunities. INSEAD does this unlike any other MBA program."

As alluring as the European campus is, there can also be some drawbacks. Says Shur, "While Fontainebleau is certainly beautiful, I arrived here in January in the middle of winter! Maybe it was not the best time to start here. While there is a two-language prerequisite, French was not one of my languages, so that was definitely a challenge. I guess I have to say that I feel a bit homesick." However, she does add that, "I came here with the goal of working internationally, so INSEAD has worked out well in that sense."

Concerning the orientation program, one current student says, "There were many presentations to help us get settled, but the most memorable experience was Outward Bound, where my study group ventured into the snowy, freezing forest for a whole day together. We climbed rocks, played games, and really got to know each other."

INSEAD is one of the first management schools to dip a toe into the online economy instead of merely studying it. With the creation of Second Life—a three-dimensional alternative universe complete with its own currency—INSEAD is gearing up to use this program on a regular basis. "The purpose is to do everything we already do but better," says Miklos Sarvary, associate professor of Marketing and manager of the International Centre for Learning Innovation at INSEAD. In addition to Second Life, MBA student clubs are popular with the student body. Indevor, one of these clubs, was founded in 1993. It serves as a forum for those interested in social, environmental, and ethical issues, often bridging the gap between business and the social sector.

INSEAD MBAs have also created the Green INSEAD Week (held on the European campus in March and on the Asian campus in April). The week is supported by the INSTEAD Social Innovation Centre and welcomes distinguished speakers from across industries to discuss the global effects, implications, and needs of the environment. The week also provides INSEAD students and staff an opportunity to showcase their contributions to a greener campus and their overall dedication to the cause through information tables, social gatherings, and local community involvement. Both campuses promote the use of public transportation with shuttle buses within campus and to rapid transit stations. The Asia campus also offers free showers for anyone cycling to campus.

In terms of the INSEAD philosophy, most students agree that it's about challenges. Says a current student, "Here it is about providing students with infinite opportunities—whatever you want, you just have to go out and grab it. The experience is overwhelming and at times ridiculous in its intensity, but I think it is in these intense times that people learn the most about themselves and their peers." Shur adds that, "I think that in order to succeed here, a lot of it comes from you internally, you have to be prepared to challenge yourself. INSEAD has been great in that it has definitely challenged my thinking."

For academic and career support, students often turn to one another. One student explains that "We connect through casual interaction on campus, through our study groups, through our career-oriented student clubs. Also, during the period before exams, we get together at the library and help each other with the material."

Students form strong bonds not only with one another, but also with faculty. According to a class of 2009 MBA candidate, "The teaching faculty is very open during class and available outside class when you need them. The teaching here has been excellent so far; professors are able to take abstract theories and show us how we can use them in our lives and our jobs." He continues, "None of our teachers are nerds like my professors in college were. These people are extremely knowledgeable about what we students are trying to accomplish in life, and they do what they can to help us. The environment here is not about testing us or teaching for the sake of teaching—the focus is on learning, and in particular on learning the deep, important things that affect people's lives and careers. The career services department is very helpful as well. Each student has two free consultations with a career coach; resume workshops and one-on-one reviews; and a plethora of self-examination tools to help us figure out what we want to do and why."

Another member of the class of 2010 sums up by saying, "I think one thing I've learned here is that there's no 'right' or 'wrong' path for me—careers are about exploration, and I no longer feel pressure to get the 'perfect job' after graduation. My plan now is to try different things in different stages of my future life, as my needs and preferences will change as I grow and mature."

What's Next? Your Career

INSEAD is recognized by companies worldwide as a key source for individuals with proven academic excellence and strong managerial potential. The MBA Career Services team connects companies with INSEAD MBA graduates and guides MBA participants in developing their employment-seeking strategy. Diarte Edwards find that, "INSEAD's offering is unique—no other school offers the same combination of a top quality, one year program, access to such a diverse and international student body and alumni community, and a springboard to such a diverse range of outstanding career opportunities."

CAREER CHECK: INSEAD MBA EMPLOYMENT BY JOB FUNCTION

- Consulting: 46%
- Finance/Accounting: 21%
- Marketing/Sales: 13%
- General Management: 10%
- Operations/Logistics: 2%
- Other: 8%

Sandra Schwarzer, director of Career Services at INSEAD, notes, "The job market, just like business, is becoming more and more globalized. Through INSEAD's curriculum, MBA and EMBA students are equipped with the tools to navigate in this global economy. INSEAD students learn first-hand through their group work where the German engineer, the British consultant, the American banker, the Chinese regulator, and the Chilean marketer experience how to lead in a multicultural environment. Career Services adapts its curriculum to the current job market—we offer multiple workshops on job search strategies, networking, competency based interviewing, social networking Web sites and how to use them during the job search, and working with executive search firms."

Internships opportunities and subsequent work offers are extremely crucial for MBA students. According to Schwarzer, "INSEAD students have a multitude of options for their summer internship— whether it is the more traditional Summer Associates Program in Investment Banking, or the more unusual social impact projects or entrepreneurial ventures."

The alumni network at INSEAD also aids current students seeking out career advice and networking opportunities. Adds Schwarzer, "In a sense, you never leave INSEAD. As your MBA comes to an end, your life as an INSEAD alumnus or alumna begins. Throughout the unique and intense experience of the INSEAD MBA, students form strong and lasting friendships with their fellow participants. They become members of a diverse alumni network of around 37,200 members worldwide, 19,000 of which are MBA alumni! Alumni usually return on campus to recruit new talent for their organizations or participate as speakers in the classroom. Many coach students through interview processes or invite students to visit their companies during career treks."

Alumni Actuals

MBA alumni worldwide: 17,800+

Business school alumni networking site: www.insead.edu/alumni

Current MBA students have access to the alumni database.

An alum who works in the nonprofit sector concludes, "My MBA experience absolutely exceeded my expectations. I met some truly amazing students who impressed me in many different ways with their personalities and intellect. I grew very much personally as I became more curious about the world, braver as a person, and more confident of my ability to express my opinion and lead. While there were some very intense study times, I was also able to live a life full of new experiences abroad, get to know what life is like on three different continents, and find out more about who I am and what I want in life."

Another alum who is now a consultant says, "INSEAD is amazing, but not for the faint-hearted. It is extremely intense. But, if you are prepared to put everything into it, the rewards are worth it."

Today, INSEAD alumni live and work in more than 150 countries, creating powerful and resourceful international networks. A majority of alumni are members of the INSTEAD Alumni Association with its 40 national alumni associations, and they return for their alumni reunions on campus. For Elizabeth Hendricks, class of 1992, "Prior to INSEAD, I had very few networking opportunities. Since the MBA, INSEAD opened up the doors for me to a very vast network of alumni." Hendricks really values "the international perspective INSEAD afforded me. It has given me a more broad perspective and made me more aware of cultural differences. INSEAD really placed a strong emphasis on networking at all levels, which has helped me to this day!"

Match Made in Heaven: Is INSEAD Business School Right for You?

You are an ideal INSEAD student if you

- Are excited about courses that stimulate an intense learning environment that includes brainstorming with classmates and meeting short deadlines.

- Expect a program that encourages a diverse student makeup, intense and high-quality learning, and the establishment of lifelong bonds between classmates and alumni.

- Desire the confidence and skills necessary to ask tough questions and question traditional business practices, and are looking to challenge your philosophy.

- Seek a program with campuses in both Europe and Asia that furthers your language capabilities and provides unusual career opportunities.

London Business School

Regent's Park
London NW1 4SA, United Kingdom

Phone: (+44) 020 7000 7000
E-mail: mbainfo@london.edu
Web site: www.london.edu/mba.html

Dean: Sir Andrew Likierman
Deputy Dean of Programs: Julian Birkinshaw

"London Business School enjoys an enviable reputation for academic excellence and continues to attract many of the world's best talents—both to its faculty and staff and to its degree and executive education programs. The school's vision is to be the preeminent global business school." —Dean Likierman

Quick Facts

MBA PROGRAMS

Full-time MBA
EMBA Global (LBS–Columbia–Hong Kong University)
Dubai-London Executive MBA

FULL-TIME MBA SNAPSHOT

Total enrollment: 635
Class of 2010: 320
Length of program: 15–21 months, depending on the track
Campus location: Regent's Park, London
Program commences in August
Pre-term orientation attendance required

APPLICATION NOTES

Requirements: Application form; application essays; curriculum vitae/resume; official transcript GMAT score; GRE not accepted
Letters of recommendation: 2
Interview: By invitation only
Number of applicants: 2,365
Admittance rate: 14%

(continued)

(continued)

Youth Transforms into Global Visionary

Nestled in a quiet, fashionable part of Central London, London Business School's location has always been a distinct advantage. Perched on the edge of Regent's Park, one of the most beautiful royal parks in England, the school also benefits from its base in one of the most dynamic and impressive cities in the world.

The strategic position is, of course, a real selling point and it's not hard to see why. London brims full of different nationalities, cuisines, and cultures, which lends it a vibrancy and uniqueness that's hard to match. London feels like a mirror to the world, and the School's truly global nature can be easily witnessed from faculty to the classroom, and from its alumni to its corporate partners.

Scenes from London Business School.

London Business School's top-class rankings are particularly impressive when one considers its relative youth. Founded in 1964, the school started life as the London Graduate School with just two professors. By 1970, it had secured its present location, which was opened by Queen Elizabeth II. One of the first programs was the Sloan Fellowship aimed at senior executives who have strategic experience in business. Since then the School has expanded, and in the past decade has added new programs including the Executive MBA Global in 2001, the Dubai-London Executive degree in 2007, and the EMBA Global Asia in 2008.

In March 2009, LBS hosted the Global Leadership Summit. This event was last held at LBS in 2007 and brought together world leaders to debate current pressing issues. Business, government, financial, and corporate leaders joined with LBS administrators, faculty, students, and alumni. The first Global Leadership Summit was originated by the school and held in 2003. Expanding its role as a business thought leader, in April 2009, LBS partnered with Google and Telegraph.co.uk to create *Survival of the Fastest*. This is a YouTube channel Web site for pertinent and immediate commentary by respected business leaders to share their insights on the rapid evolution of business management. Faculty at LBS frequently are called upon to share their expertise about current practices and controversies.

Why LBS?

Choosing a quality MBA brand that is recognized and respected in the corporate world has to be top of the list for any prospective MBA student. The London Business School brand stands above the international business school competition.

"Global" is perhaps top of the watchword list for faculty, alumni, and students alike when asked to describe the school and its approach to learning. You only need to walk through the hallways and courtyards to appreciate its global nature. Students from the United Kingdom make up around 10 percent of the student body, and the rest of the students reflect regions throughout the world, with North American students comprising 23 percent. The school also has more than 140 faculty members from more than 30 countries and has a presence in London, New York, Hong Kong, and Dubai. Its overall community of 28,000 alumni provides a wealth of knowledge, business experience, and worldwide networking opportunities. The global advantage has a practical benefit according to Mary Ferreira, senior marketing manager for the full-time MBA program. "Graduates must be able to work in a multi-cultural team anywhere in the world and London Business School's global culture lays the foundations. We want students to broaden their horizons and go beyond London and gain truly international exposure."

Flexibility is also an important selling point of the school. MBA students have different needs and requirements, so a one-size-fits-all approach will not suit everyone. The curriculum supports individual development needs through greater choice and flexibility. By offering three separate exit points to choose from—15, 18, or 21 months—you can tailor a course to suit your own changing priorities and needs. One of the real strengths of the school is the understanding that there is no such thing as a typical student. Students are drawn from a diverse range of professional environments, from prospective entrepreneurs seeking to perfect their business idea to people who want to change careers to those who wish to climb higher up the corporate ladder. London Business School understands that the reasons for undertaking an MBA are varied, and the individual needs and outcomes are equally so.

All universities and business schools highlight the importance of the academic community. Here, it takes on a whole new significance. Indeed, it's of critical importance to the culture and experience of London Business School. A quick glance through the school's list of clubs speaks volumes about the commitment and support students give toward making the most of their learning experience. More than 100 student clubs are scattered throughout professional interests, nationalities, regions, and social clubs. You could find yourself organizing the Marketing Club; getting to know about the culture and business environment in Brazil, Africa, or India; or taking up a new sport such as judo, squash, or shooting.

The opportunities to lead and organize student events are huge. Peruse some of the events and you realize that many reflect the main pillars of global business: The Asia Business Forum, Global Energy Summit, and Silicon Valley Trek. The Global Leadership Summit is a flagship event at the school that held its sixth meeting in June 2009. Attending were some of the leading corporate executives from banking and finance as well as media, LBS faculty, and alumni. The focal point was an exchange of ideas to emerge from the worldwide economic downturn with new initiatives for long-term business trade.

LBS also specializes in niche events, including The Art Investment Conference or The Boutique Consulting Conference, not to mention the multitude of social activities including the Summer Ball, Caribbean Sailing Trip, and Sundowners—a weekly sponsored event with staff, students, and alumni.

FUN FACTS

- London is the scheduled location of the 2012 Summer Olympic Games, making it the first city in the world to host the Summer Olympics three times.
- The first subway in the world was the London Underground (which is also known as the "Tube"). It was built in 1863.
- London is one of the three command centers for the world economy, the others being New York City and Tokyo.

Course Offerings

At the core of a student's first year is the Global Leadership Assessment for Managers (GLAM). The course expands your vision and scope at the outset of your term by bridging the gap between understanding new countries and cultures. It also enables you to lead teams around the globe. The remainder of the first year concentrates on developing core knowledge and skills. As you would expect from an MBA program so focused on global opportunities, learning a second language takes center stage for first-year students. You are enrolled automatically in the MBA Language Program and are expected to achieve competency in a second language by graduation. Your first-year offerings have an impressive range. More established courses such as Management Accounting and Marketing mix with the groundbreaking Discovering Entrepreneurial Opportunities course to build a solid learning foundation for the first year.

After the summer break, you start into your second and final year. The flexibility of the courses really comes into its own. You can choose from a wide and varied offering. You have the power to take electives over the full term or opt for the Block Week format where you complete one elective within a short time. Finally, students can participate in The Shadowing Project. In this hugely important and engaging elective, second-year students source and shadow a senior manager for a week. The manager, in turn, gives an appraisal report, which is then graded by the LBS faculty.

Like MIT Sloan and Stanford GSB, London Business School offers the Sloan Fellowship Program, an 11-month curriculum for mid-career executives who average a decade of professional experience. The program's goal is for students to attain effective and successful leadership skills and earn a Masters of Science in Leadership and Strategy.

In October 2008, LBS added a new institute to fund private equity research. Jeremy Coller, who heads one of the United Kingdom's largest private equity firms, Coller Capital, donated $10 million (USD) from Coller's family foundation. LBS's private equity program is already one of the biggest in the field, and its private equity club has the most members of all the school's professional clubs. Professor Eli Talmor serves as the first chairman. The Coller Institute of Private Equity expand LBS's current program by adding MBA electives and executive education courses.

In May 2009, the Executive MBA expanded beyond London-Dubai or EMBA Global with Columbia School of Business cooperative education. Now students can choose the EMBA Global Asia, which offers a joint degree from LBS, Columbia School of Business, *and* Hong Kong University. In August 2009, LBS launched its new Master in Management degree aimed at students who have less than one year of workplace experience. The 11-month degree covers all functional areas of business through lectures, workshops, case studies, and projects. In many ways this degree resembles the full-time MBA's first-year program.

LBS PARTNER SCHOOLS

China Europe International Business School (CEIBS)

Columbia Business School

Hong Kong University

Indian School of Business (ISB)

CONCENTRATIONS AND SPECIALIZATIONS OFFERED IN FULL-TIME MBA PROGRAM

Entrepreneurship

Finance

International Business

Manufacturing and Technology
Management

Marketing

Strategy

JOINT DEGREES AND DUAL DEGREES

London-Dubai EMBA

EMBA Global Finance or Marketing

RESEARCH CENTERS AND INSTITUTES

Aditya Birla India Center

Center for Corporate Governance

Center for Women in Business

Coller Institute of Private Equity

Energy Markets Group

Family Business Research Initiative

Foundation and Endowment Asset
Management

Global Entrepreneurship Monitor

Hedge Fund Center

Institute of Technology

What LBS Professors Teach

For Professor of Strategic and International Management and Deputy Dean Julian Birkinshaw, the school's academic experience is heavily influenced by its global outlook and close links to the city of London. "The links with real-world practice are very close and real." LBS uses its location in one of the most powerful and dynamic business centers in the world to its full advantage. Visits from leading business figures from the city are ingrained in the faculty teaching and student learning experience. "Being in the heart of a big city enables us to draw from the vast practical experience in the business world." Birkinshaw adds, "London is the best location in the world for studying the trends and changes underway in business right now. Hundreds of major companies have their global headquarters within a 30-minute taxi journey of the school, and this allows me to bring my research and consultancy work directly into the classroom."

Naturally, the school is very proud of its own culture. Rather than molding students to fit a set corporate culture, the emphasis at LBS is on widening the students' skill set. "Softer skills, personal skills, and problem solving are all important parts of the student learning experience," says Birkinshaw. Whereas the approach in many business schools results in turning out a steady stream of "oven-ready" graduates, LBS seeks to refine its students' abilities and characteristics. For the faculty, "strategic agility" is now a vitally important skill. With businesses having to manage faster change and make tougher choices about the future—and sometimes survival—of their organizations, it's imperative that they manage that change most effectively.

In addition to learning problem-solving and workplace skills, student experience is also enriched by the quality of the school's research. In the latest Research Evaluation Exercise, a key quality indicator for third-level education institutions in the United Kingdom, LBS scored highly. Professor Birkinshaw points out that high-quality research with an international focus is a defining factor in the school's overall capability. Cutting-edge research helps students, faculty, and corporate partners to gain access to the latest business developments.

Entrepreneurship courses are among the most prized by students year after year. Successful company leaders give talks at the school as well as partner with LBS professors to write case studies based on entrepreneur business they have experienced. In addition, students receive classroom benefits of research conducted at the world-renowned Global Entrepreneurship Monitor (GEM). In conjunction with Babson College, this center houses one of the largest concentrations of research activities in the entrepreneurship field. In 2009, the co-founders of The Lonely Planet publishing house donated around $4 million (USD) to establish the Tony and Maureen Wheeler Chair in Entrepreneurship at LBS, furthering the objectives of the school's commitment to the field.

FACULTY FACTS

Full-time faculty employed by the b-school: 97

Adjunct or visiting faculty: 44

Permanent/tenured professors: 50

Tenured faculty who are women: 6

Tenured faculty who are underrepresented minorities: 0

Tenured international faculty: 37

SAMPLING OF NOTABLE PROFESSORS

- Rob Goffee: Specialist in entrepreneurship, business formation and growth, and managerial careers; author of seven books including *Entrepreneurship in Europe*, *Women in Charge*, *Reluctant Managers*, and *Corporate Realities*

- Lynda Gratton: Leading authority on women in business; recently ranked second in *HR* magazine's Top 100 Most Influential Thinkers

- Nirmalya Kumar: Author of *Global Marketing*; noted marketing authority; director of the Centre for Marketing; co-director of Aditya V. Birla India Centre

- Costas Markides: Well-known authority on strategic and international management; author of *Strategy, Innovation, and Change: Challenges for Management*

- Richard Portes: Leading expert on international financial stability and European bond markets, among other subjects; senior editor and co-chairman of the Board of Economic policy; writes extensively on international currencies, financial stability, and globalization

What Admissions Is All About

Only one in seven applicants is accepted into the London Business School, and the criteria are based on more than grades alone. The 2007–2008 season was the busiest year on record for full-time MBA admissions. If you want to navigate the admissions process successfully, you should concentrate on your personal profile and carefully set out what you can bring to the program. Assistant Director for the MBA program David Simpson comments, "Candidates need to stand out from the crowd. We want to hear about you and hear some stories through the essay, why you want to take an MBA, and tell us what you believe you can contribute towards the school." Just as the strength of "community" is stressed throughout the school as a whole, its impact is also critical to the admissions process. So the admissions staff is really looking for how students will benefit and contribute to the community both during and after their studies.

The admissions process can be broken down into two stages: application and interview. With your initial application, you need to send your resume, employment details, and essays. "It's important that you tell us about past experiences and track record," says Simpson, who also stresses the value of using personal and professional stories to highlight each student's background and suitability in the essays. The next stage is the interview, and it is here that students can really shine. The interviews take place all over the world supported by the extensive global network of alumni. Here, the alumni find out more about the prospective students' professional background, their work experience, what makes them tick, and their working style.

> Full-time MBAs receiving financial aid through school: 23%
>
> Institutional (merit-based and need-based) scholarships: 11
>
> Assistantships: varies
>
> Full-tuition scholarships school awarded for academic year: 5

Financially Aided

"Most of the students raise funding from a combination of sources, including bank loans, savings, scholarships, and grants from their companies," says Ani Gregorian, officer in Financial Aid. However, the main source for prospective students is the bank loan. London Business School has a special arrangement with HSBC. Typically, students who apply for a loan then top it off with savings.

Many U.S. students have traditionally taken U.S. loans in the form of Federal Stafford loans and MBA private loans. However, in today's rapidly changing fiscal environment, Ani Gregorian relates, "A lot more U.S. students are applying for the United Kingdom HSBC loan as the U.S. bank loans tend to be tied to higher interest rates." For the bank loan, the criteria are still similar in the UK, so make sure you have good account conduct and can show you are a trustworthy, suitable candidate with a strong need for financing. There are also scholarships available for prospective students who qualify. These are calculated on merit and are viewed by the MBA program officers who take into account GMAT scores, admission essays, and academic merit when assessing applications.

FULL-TIME MBA PROGRAM (TOTAL DIRECT COSTS)

In-country: $73,315 USD

International: $73,315

EMBA program costs: $61,120

What London Business School Students Know

First impressions really count, maintains Helen Pearce, class of 2009. The warmth displayed by prospective students mixed with the staff engagement at the orientation weekend persuaded her that London Business School was right for her. The school organizes the Admits Weekend for students to get to know future classmates and sample the school life. "It was very well organized and I think it convinced a few people to send in their acceptances as there were a number of undecided students," Pearce says. "It's a great chance for meeting and bonding with fellow students and it meant orientation week wasn't daunting so you could have lots of fun and laughter before settling into term."

Community bonding was only one of the many factors that attracted Pearce to LBS. Location and flexibility were both paramount in choosing the school above all others. "I wanted to be in the center of a really vibrant city. But I also wanted to keep my options open regarding the program duration. The 15- to 21-month program allows me to take advantage of additional time should I need it." For prospective MBA students, the value attached to the school brand can be a deciding factor. For Pearce, the London Business School brand ensured it came to the top of her short list. "It's so important to go to a school that people will recognize when you are applying for jobs afterwards; employers really need to know that it's a good school in order to give you the chance of getting the job you want. Of course, it's only a foot in the door and it won't guarantee anything, but it all helps!"

Nicholas Harvey, class of 2009, was originally attracted to London Business School by its global outlook and vibrant city location. For him, the Career Services department gives an outstanding service and acts as a vitally important resource for all students. "They are fantastic ... not only arranging for top recruiters to come to our campus for networking/recruiting opportunities, but they also conduct valuable training sessions such as industry specific mock interviews, cover letter surgery sessions, resume review sessions, and networking tutorials."

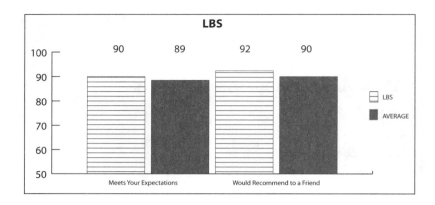

What's Next? Your Career

Career training lies at the heart of the School's MBA program. Investing in a gold standard Careers Service delivering real career results for its students has become a priority for London Business School.

The school has traditionally cultivated close links with major recruiters. From banking giants such as Credit Suisse and HSBC, to leading consulting firms including Booz Allen Hamiliton and Bain and Company, through to innovative tech companies such as Google, LBS makes the best of its close links with companies. "We foster very close links with our corporate partners and really include them in the program," says Claire Hewitson, senior manager with Marketing and Communications, Career Services. "The result is a refined and practical learning experience that our students don't necessarily get in the academic world. Benefits of networking and interview preparation really go a long way in helping the students prepare for their next step on the career ladder." Indeed, this may explain the success its students have in accessing permanent recruitment offers.

The corporate partnership approach also encourages students to get seriously involved in improving their career prospects. The school hosts its own Corporate Partner Week during the first week of the semester. The week is made as interactive and interesting as possible, and it even includes a corporate "speed dating" evening. "We really encourage our students to get involved with clubs to help them build up contacts," says Hewitson, who believes strongly in providing a variety of practical opportunities for students seeking to learn more about potential employers. "Through company treks and tours to destinations worldwide, we make sure our students can physically look inside the company environment and speak to senior staff. It's an important part of the learning process and the career process. In 2007, 97 percent of our graduates received full-time job offers within three months of graduation."

And how will the career progression fare in the uncertainties of a severe global recession? Hewitson maintains, "We really encourage students to widen their scope during this time. They should look at areas outside of what are maybe traditional preferences." For the years ahead, MBA graduates will have to scan a wider horizon than finance and management consulting and look toward the new emerging opportunities in more innovative areas.

For Thomas Kingombekock, class of 2008, the London Business School MBA opens up a world that would have been inaccessible before his graduation. "I wouldn't have been able to pursue the level or quality of companies and jobs that I have, if I hadn't shown up at their door backed by the 'quality' stamp of an admired institution such as LBS." The power of the brand helps graduates stand apart from its competitors—a point reinforced by both alumni and employers. With current employers now facing an unprecedented choice of MBA graduates from various institutions, it is reassuring for students that their degree is held in such high regard.

Mention the benefits of a London Business School MBA to alumni and the words "networking power" arise time and time again. Alumni talk freely about how they can access the school network so easily and the impact their global community has on their career progression. One reason for the close links between alumni is the sense of community and cohesion that the school fosters so well. "The school does a lot of alumni networking events as well. I now have a ready made global community that I can draw upon if I need to, including being part of alumni clubs and emails that present new opportunities all the time," says Kingombekock.

Match Made in Heaven: Is the London Business School Right for You?

You are an ideal student if you

- Expect your MBA degree to prepare you for a truly global career and want to have the opportunity for an excellent education in marketing and entrepreneurship.
- Work well as part of an exciting and close-knit student community.
- Want to gain real practical experience from serious business leaders.
- Seek an international school setting that will provide you with an international career path.

University of Navarra IESE Business School

Barcelona campus
Avenida Pearson, 21
08034 Barcelona, Spain

Phone: (+34) 93.253.4200
E-mail: mbainfo@iese.edu
Web site: www.iese.edu

Madrid campus
Camino del Cerro del Águila, 3
28023 Madrid, Spain

Phone: (+34) 91.211.3000
E-mail: mbainfo@iese.edu
Web site: www.iese.edu

Germany campus
Pacellistr, 4
80333 Munich, Germany

Phone: (+49) 89.2420.9790
E-mail: germany@iese.edu
Web site: www.iese.edu

Dean: Jordi Canals
Madrid Dean: José Toribio

"At IESE, we seek to transmit a spirit of service, placing a special emphasis on human, ethical, and social aspects of business management." —Dean Canals

Quick Facts

MBA PROGRAMS

Full-time MBA
Executive MBA
Global Executive MBA

FULL-TIME MBA SNAPSHOT

Total enrollment: 458
Class of 2010: 215
Length of program: 19 months

Campus: Barcelona, Spain
Program commences in October
Pre-term orientation attendance required

APPLICATION NOTES

Requirements: Professional experience not required but highly recommended; a four-year
  bachelor's degree or equivalent; transcript; essays; references; resume; GRE not accepted
Letters of recommendation: 2
Interview: By invitation only
Number of applicants: 1,530
Admittance rate: 17%

CLASS OF 2010 PROFILE

Male 71%, Female 29%
International: 80%
Average age: 27
Married or Partnered, Single: 10%, 90%
Average years of work experience: 4 years
GMAT score average: 676
GMAT range (20th–80th percentile): 620–730

ACADEMIC BACKGROUND OF INCOMING STUDENTS

Business Administration: 24%
Economics: 16%
Engineering: 34%
Humanities: 6%
Political Science and Law: 8%
Sciences: 12%

A Pioneer in Europe's Higher Education

IESE stands for the "Instituto de Estudios Superiores de la Empresa" in Spanish and "Institute of Higher Business Studies" or "International Graduate School of Management" in English. The framework for the creation of IESE Business School was laid down by Professor Antonio Valero in 1957. A former textile engineer, Valero formed the school and served as its first director. The school launched its MBA program in 1964 under the guidance of an advisory committee set up between Harvard Business School and IESE. It became the first two-year MBA program in Europe and the first bilingual program in the world, drawing students from all over the globe.

IESE opened its Madrid campus in 1974 to meet the high demand for executive education in the Spanish capital. In 1980, IESE began offering the world's premier bilingual (Spanish-English) MBA program. And in 1993, the school pioneered the concept of joint-venture executive education.

On campus at IESE.

Initially, the school offered an array of executive education programs for managers at a time when the concept of executive education was scarcely known outside the United States. Establishing these programs, aimed mainly at experienced business leaders, constituted a landmark in the history of executive education in Europe. Since then, more than 30,000 people have taken part in such programs.

INTERNATIONAL EXCHANGE PROGRAMS WITH IESE

Columbia Business School, New York

Cornell University, Johnson, New York

China Europe International Business School, Shanghai

Dartmouth University, Tuck, Hanover, New Hampshire

Duke University, Fuqua School of Business, North Carolina

Erasmus University, Rotterdam, The Netherlands

HEC School of Management, Paris

IAE, Instituto de Altos Estudios Empresariales, University of Australia and Argentina

IPADE, Institute Panamerican de Alta Direccion de Empresa, Mexico

Indian School of Business, Hyberadad, India

London Business School, England

Massachusetts Institute of Technology, Sloan, New York

New York University, Stern

Northwestern University, Kellogg, Illinois

University of California, Berkeley, Haas

University of California, Los Angeles, Anderson

University of Chicago Booth, Illinois

University of Melbourne Business School, Australia

University of Michigan, Ross, Ann Arbor

University of North Carolina, Kenan-Flagler, Chapel Hill

University of Pennsylvania, Wharton, Philadelphia

University of Virginia, Darden, Charlottesville

Yale School of Management, New Haven, Connecticut

Why IESE?

IESE Business School believes that the development and well-being of people should be the cornerstone of all management practices. The school is committed to developing leaders who have a positive, deep, and lasting effect on people, firms, and society. IESE accomplishes this through professionalism, integrity, and spirit of service. Only by placing priority on the people who work for and are affected by company activities can organizations prosper and benefit society in the long term. Above all, companies are communities of people who work better in an atmosphere of trust. IESE teaches leadership development based on the pillars of human and ethical values, international character, transformational impact, and knowledge development.

This emphasis extends to whatever programs in which the school is involved. Students and faculty see each other often in and out of class for conversation and consultation. Many students as well as graduates from IESE are especially impressed with the friendly atmosphere and count it highly as a reason to attend the school. Because of the small size of each incoming class, the experience often is like living in a new family.

Truly Global Education

IESE began forging joint programs with a number of top U.S. business schools to offer open enrollment and customized programs in response to a rapidly globalizing environment. In 2000, IESE launched its Global Executive MBA, featuring modular residential sessions in Barcelona; Silicon Valley, California; and Shanghai, China; as well as state-of-the-art distance learning technology. IESE today offers its Executive MBA program in Madrid in addition to a host of in-company programs.

Each year, 60 IESE MBA students are selected on a competitive basis and spend the first semester of their second year at one of IESE's partner schools. The chance to supplement their MBA program in Barcelona with a semester at a top business school in another country provides an additional challenge as well as valuable academic and networking opportunities.

In terms of diversity, IESE cannot be topped. Among the 215 full-time MBA students, 80 percent are international, representing 48 countries. The number of Indian-born applicants has significantly increased in the past few years (from one student in 2003 to 15 students in 2008) and about 19 percent of the student body hails from Asia. To add to this already-impressive class profile, IESE students speak an average of three different languages.

FUN FACTS

- In January 2007, IESE expanded its Barcelona campus with a new, state-of-the-art building just up the road from the main campus. The King and Queen of Spain presided over the ceremony. The building has stunning views, wireless Internet throughout, and a special auditorium for conferences.

- The Barcelona campus is situated in the Pedrables section of town, one of the best residential districts in the city. It is easily accessible from the airport, and just as easy to get to the city center using public transport.

- Barcelona lies in the province of Catalunya. Catalan is spoken in addition to Spanish, and the city is known for its stunning architecture, particularly the buildings of Antoni Gaudí.

- Woody Allen filmed his recent movie *Vicky Cristina Barcelona* in and around Barcelona.

Course Offerings

The first year of the MBA program is divided into three sections, each comprising 70 students. The sections are equal in all aspects, except one section will have classes in Spanish and English while the other two have classes in English. In the third term of the first year, students have the option to change sections. This allows for integration of all students during the first year. During the second year of the program, students choose elective courses, thus interacting with all students.

Keeping in mind that Barcelona is an international locale, non-Spanish students are thoroughly prepped in a pre-MBA, intensive Business Spanish course. The objective is to help develop the students' linguistic capabilities. Other pre-term courses include basic quantitative methods in business and an introductory financial accounting course. All these courses are held in September prior to the start of the regular fall term to ensure that all students are well equipped to handle their first year workload.

However, students who arrive with a sufficient level of Spanish can commence bilingual study in their first year by joining the Bilingual Section. In the Bilingual Section, 50 percent of classes are taught in Spanish. Students must show a fluent or excellent proficiency level to be admitted to this section. During the Admissions Process interview, candidates will be able to speak to admissions representatives regarding their section preference. The Admissions Committee reserves the right to assign students to a specific section, although student preference will be largely taken into account.

What IESE Professors Teach

IESE faculty members believe in the value of leading by example and that management education should be centered around people: how to deal effectively with people, how to create a context for professional and personal development, how to create powerful teams, and how to develop and sustain trust in personal relationships. The ethical and moral values the school draws from have their roots in social and human progress not only in Europe but in many other regions of the world.

The faculty is composed of multicultural, multilingual, and internationally acclaimed experts who research on current business issues. Moreover, they are successful businesspeople themselves, many with their own consulting firms operating in the real world of international business. With a student/faculty ratio of 4 to 1, students and professors are able to develop close and enduring relationships. Professors have open-door policies to encourage students to come to their offices to talk about their classes, assignments, career goals, and personal challenges. Using the case method, students start with individual preparation and then work in teams to analyze, discuss, and propose solutions to hundreds of different business problems drawn from real-life scenarios. This means that students learn to make business decisions and take action by thinking, arguing, and defending their interpretations and recommendations against a multitude of equally plausible solutions.

For Antonio Dávila, professor of Accounting and Control and Entrepreneurship and the director of the Ph.D. program at IESE, what distinguishes the IESE experience from its peers is that "it's a smaller group with a focus on general management and on growing people with the diverse set of skills that they need to be excellent managers." Jan Simon, instructor of Financial Management, agrees with this assessment. "In general, being a smaller school, we are able to be closer to our students than in the average MBA program."

As two of IESE's favorite professors, both work hard to instill a sense of work ethic, technical skills, and organizational ability. Both are active in continuing education themselves by participating in various academic courses and conferences in and out of IESE. For students who go into investment banking, Simon sees the real-world connection between his coursework and the students' future careers. Along with coursework, he focuses on preparing his students via mock interviews and through working under pressure. Dávila focuses his students by "teaching them how to interpret profitability at different levels of an organization."

Neither faculty member differentiates in his teaching style between male and female students. In fact, Simon explains, "I try to avoid using gender specific terminology. To make any distinction between these groups is unfair and unnecessary."

FACULTY FACTS

Full-time faculty employed by the b-school: 97

Adjunct or visiting faculty: 46

Permanent/tenured professors: 66

Tenured faculty who are women: 12

Tenured faculty who are underrepresented minorities: 12

SAMPLING OF NOTABLE PROFESSORS

- Antonio Argandoña: IESE Chair of Corporate Social Responsibility and Corporate Governance; finalist for the Faculty Pioneer Awards given by the European Academy of Business in Society (EABIS) and the Aspen Institute in 2006

(continued)

(continued)

- Pankaj Ghemawat: One of the world's leading international strategy specialists; co-edited with Joan Enric Ricart and Africa Ariño the book *Creating Value Through International Strategy*; co-edited with Bruno Cassiman a special issue of *Management Science* on strategic dynamics
- Lluis Renart: Expert case writer; has written more than 100 cases that are used at U.S., French, and Spanish b-schools, among others
- Josep María Rosanas: Specialist in cost accounting systems, management control systems, economics of organization, and management and organization theory
- Thomas Wedell-Wedellsborg: Specialist in innovation and creative methodologies

---

CONCENTRATIONS AND SPECIALIZATIONS OFFERED IN FULL-TIME MBA PROGRAM

General Management only

JOINT DEGREES AND DUAL DEGREES

None

What Admissions Is All About

"Admissions compares all good people; therefore it is not enough to tell us you are great. You need to demonstrate to us what makes you different, by unique achievements in and out of the classroom. We are looking for those future CEOs, top managers, and leaders," says Javier Muñoz, director of MBA Admissions. Are you up for the challenge? If you are looking for a business school with a world-renowned reputation and strong ties, look no further. Muñoz adds, "IESE utilizes teaching through the case method, and there is a strong emphasis on general management with an ethical perspective."

Admissions can be described as a three-step process: the informative interview, the process interview, and finally, the admissions committee review. In addition, some candidates may be invited to participate in an Assessment Day, which is designed to gain more information about candidates and typically consists of a group of candidates spending an entire day with the admissions team. Assessment Day, held in several cities, is not a mandatory step in the admissions process, and most candidates will receive their final decision from the admissions committee without having to participate in an Assessment Day. However, Muñoz still sees the Assessment Day as a crucial step in the admissions process. "I would highly recommend taking part in an Assessment Day if possible," he says. "It's a good way for potential candidates to get a feel for the team and vice versa. Sometimes (as in particular with the case of India) we can use an Assessment Day to differentiate stellar candidates. Again, using India as an example, we found all the candidates to be so highly qualified and the field to be so extremely competitive that we had to improve our admissions process by use of the Assessment Day."

While the acceptance rate has reached 32 percent in some years, there is a waitlist system in place. "The waitlist depends on each year," notes Muñoz. "It usually runs large and there is an admitted waiting list [for candidates who will join either the current class or the next available] and a regular waiting list [for candidates who may need a stronger application]. Again, the numbers vary from year to year, depending on accepted candidates and the rest of the applicant pool."

The admissions team at IESE is thorough, basing their decisions on 17 unique parameters and eight different components. A new feature added to this year's MBA program is the Young Talent Program. "In our quest to work with the world's best students, we created the Young Talent Program," says Muñoz. "The program basically provides graduates with a two-year work placement with some of the world's leading companies and grants them pre-admission into the IESE MBA program." Students with exemplary academic records and extracurricular achievements are encouraged to apply in their junior or senior year of undergraduate study.

Gaining admission into the IESE MBA can be extremely competitive and highly rewarding. According to Muñoz, "We are not just looking at your academic record and career achievements. We are looking for potential students that also share the IESE mission—to attract the best we must bring up the best."

Financially Aided

The IESE Global Loan is available to all accepted candidates for the full-time MBA program. The loan is offered through Banco Sabadell, a private Spanish bank that provides all admitted students up to 100 percent coverage of the tuition fees without a co-signer nor guarantee.

Other alternatives are corporate sponsorship, scholarship, and financial aid for both native Spaniards and international students. Corporate sponsorship is dependent on the company for which you work and whether or not it will cover the cost of your MBA.

IESE scholarship applications should be completed and submitted within the MBA application form to the Admissions Department (organizations should not be approached directly). Recipients are informed of any award as soon as the Scholarships Committee decides. All other scholarship applications are processed by the sponsoring organization or corporation and are not associated with school aid.

Financial aid is an additional responsibility handled by the admissions department. While exploring financing options for the MBA, Anna Lee and Jaume Nuñez, associate directors in MBA admissions, agree that some companies will underwrite MBA expenses, but the process varies company to company, with the contract typically being negotiated between the student and his or her company. "It is also important to mention that fee structures have never and will never vary based on a student's age, gender or nationality," says Lee.

Also, while 55 percent to 70 percent of IESE students receive financial aid, they are not obligated to fulfill any teaching requirements that may come attached with the financial aid. Typically, 24 out of 35 students receive U.S.-based financial aid.

With regard to the sometimes-complicated issues of visas, do not worry because IESE has it covered. "We help students with visas on an individual basis," says Jaume Nuñez. "In the instance where a student might be facing problems due to visas that must be extended to family, or when their process needs to be expedited in order for them to be in Spain by the beginning of class, we can help."

FULL-TIME MBA PROGRAM (TOTAL DIRECT COSTS)

Full-time program: $91,013 USD

Part-time program: $76,000

Global Executive MBA: $111,000

Full-time MBAs receiving financial aid: 68%

Institutional (merit-based) scholarships: 20–30

Assistantships: varies

What IESE Students Know

When applying to MBA programs, candidates need to consider why they really want to invest both financially and emotionally into two years of intense study. U.S. citizen Vanessa Meyers explains that one of the main attractions to IESE was "the steepness of the cultural-learning curve. I felt that if I went to business school in the U.S., I would basically be in classes with people who would think more or less just as I did." She adds, "I felt that IESE offered the experience of real diversity—not just in terms of location and country but in the way they think, motivate, and collaborate."

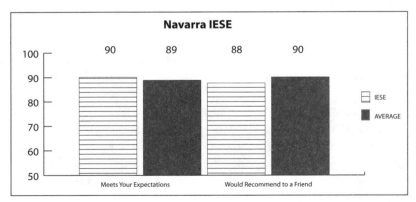

Victor Garcia of Spain, however, had different objectives in mind. "I wanted to be 100 percent immersed in case method classes. After spending six years at university studying a double degree, I knew I wanted something different in terms of the way my classes were taught; I wanted something practical. The decision was easy."

Both students were highly motivated by the international factor, the potential to expand their networking circles, and the ability to explore work opportunities in Barcelona and the rest of Europe. In particular, Meyers adds, "On a positive note, being in Spain where the majority of the students don't speak the language fluently and are out of their element forces students to bond together. I think the location is a huge factor increasing the strong, family-like community that exists at IESE. Additionally, living in a different country and speaking another language for me enhances the MBA experience by adding a whole other layer of learning outside the classroom."

Even though Victor Garcia (a Spanish native with prior financial knowledge and consulting work-experience) had to attend the pre-term courses, he still found that "the practical way the courses are shown was totally new to me. Furthermore, the most important thing was the fact that I could get to know my new friends and classmates and get used to the new environment."

Both Meyers and Victor Garcia found that the enforced first-year study teams did help with their ability to work in teams and roll with the punches. Teamwork also teaches students to develop effective interpersonal communication skills, which come in handy in the workplace. Says Garcia, "I knew the MBA was a really intense program. However, I was not expecting to know everyone that well. I used to hear from alumni about the 'IESE family.' It is now a concept I totally understand and could share with them."

With respect to the overall IESE philosophy, both have found it to be very value-driven, emphasizing hard work but also enjoy time away from classes. Meyers adds, "I think that the IESE philosophy is a bit break-you-down to then build-you-up. What I've seen is that students respond to this treatment in different ways. For some it's great, for others it's overbearing. For me, I've appreciated the challenge of interacting with IESE as an institution, trying to forge relationships, earn respect, gain influence within such an environment. It's another part of the IESE experience."

The fact that the IESE campus is not sprawling but compact adds positives and negatives. Garcia found that "I use the study and social spaces every day. I enjoy spending time at IESE and I really feel I have made the right choice in terms of fit of the school I got into." Conversely, Meyers says, "Students do use the library a lot. I personally do not because at the end of a full day of classes I prefer to get off campus to study and change environments."

Career support is readily available but varies from student to student. Garcia found everything he needed from the career team, while Meyers had more of a struggle since she wants to live outside Spain in the long term. Says Garcia, "Since almost the first day, I have been in contact with recruiters. Consulting and banking are the first to come to school but many other companies are active as well. This is a great opportunity to better understand where my options are after the MBA."

Both students also had the chance to intern at companies while at IESE, on opposite ends of the spectrum—Garcia working at the Bridgespan Group (a nonprofit organization) and Meyers at MUJI (a Japanese retailer with international operations).

What's Next? Your Career

The Career Services department at IESE is made up of an eight-person team that oversees relationships and recruiting within the various business sectors. In addition to providing career advice and support for postgraduation, the Career Services department is also active in helping students find corporate internships between their first and second year of the MBA. "The corporate internship's objective, from a student perspective, is to apply knowledge learned during the MBA; to assess the culture and work environment of a company and to serve as a stepping stone towards obtaining a full-time position," says Amelia Salerno, associate director of Career Services. She goes onto add, "Although the corporate internship is not compulsory, 90 percent of our students take advantage of this opportunity."

The corporate internships are typically global in scope, covering a variety of sectors. Almost 80 percent of IESE's students obtain their internship through the assistance of MBA Career Services. The projects typically last from about 8 to 12 weeks, coinciding with summer break.

Career services relies greatly on strong relationships developed over the years with leading corporations. The department organizes different events throughout the academic year to help them identify the right student profiles. Adds Salerno, "Our main event is the Career Forum, organized in late October, that attracts companies to campus to carry out presentations, interview second-year students for full-time positions, and participate in the Career Fair."

During a recent Career Forum, IESE had more than 50 companies participate including Citigroup, Santander, McKinsey, Bain and Company, and Du Pont to name a few. Salerno finds that "companies are particularly drawn to the international character and mindset of our students. Eighty percent of our students are international, and the program specifically prepares them to lead in today's global business environment." By graduation, "around 85 percent of the class has been extended an offer by a company or has already accepted a job."

CAREER CHECK: IESE MBA EMPLOYMENT BY JOB FUNCTION

- Finance: 36%
- Consulting: 31%
- Consumer and Retail: 7%
- Real Estate and Construction: 4%
- High Tech: 2%
- Other: 20%

IESE's Alumni Association has brought together executives and managers who, after having participated in one of the school's core programs, seek to strengthen their ties with the school. The IESE Alumni Association came into being in 1959, thanks to the graduates of the first executive education program (PADE-I-59). These alumni sought to create a group to keep alumni updated on new concepts; allow them to share experiences through continuing education; keep them closely connected to their school, its professors, and their classmates; and allow them to actively participate in IESE's development.

However, opportunities extend beyond the student years, as noted by graduate Mar Guinot, class of 2000. "Being an IESE MBA alumnus, you have access to other alumni that have participated in several IESE courses such as EMBA, executive programs, etc. The IESE spirit draws alumni together, helping each other network in the professional field. Working at A. T. Kearney, a management consultancy, I have contacted alumni to get specific knowledge of an industry when preparing a project, and always have received willingness to help." From the perspective of IESE graduate Emily Kunze, class of 2000, the networking opportunities as an MBA student were excellent. She says, "While I was at IESE, there were many career forums, and the department did an excellent job of bringing in a variety of employers. I was also at IESE during the Internet boom height and I think it was a good time for everyone."

Both have found their MBAs to be excellent in terms of contacts, reputation (particularly in European-based companies), and with adding to their skill set. For Kunze, "The first-year classes were extraordinary. [Now] I can't experience anything without wanting to analyze the cash flow or understand how it makes money. All business experiences I see as potential case studies. IESE gave me tools that allow me to 'always be thinking' and enriched my overall intellectual potential."

Guinot concurs on the use of the case study method, saying, "Being an economist, the MBA curriculum was more or less what I had expected, but what was great was the use of the case method in class; that really exceeded my expectations as a student. The way of learning and interacting with other students in class, and how the different lectures were more interactive helped you learn much more from your colleagues than in a normal lecture class."

As members of the alumni network, both are extremely satisfied with their MBA experience and happy to give back to the current student body. Kunze recommends that MBA students take advantage of the faculty. "The professors were accessible and I usually advise current students to use this access to professors as much as they can while they are students because it is much more difficult to keep in touch or develop relationships after one has left IESE."

ALUMNI ACTUALS

MBA alumni worldwide: 31,800+

Business school alumni networking site: www.iese.edu/en/OurCommunity/Alumninew/Home/Home.asp

Current MBA students have access to the alumni database.

Match Made in Heaven: Is the IESE School of Business Right for You?

You are an ideal student if you

- Work well in a close-knit community among both students and faculty and a campus central to many European cities.
- Are keen on learning primarily through the case study method and developing a broad general management perspective.
- Want a learning environment focused on core human and ethical values.
- Expect to develop international experience in a bilingual program as well as gain access to international networks.

University of Toronto Joseph L. Rotman School of Management

105 St. George Street
Toronto, Ontario
Canada M5S 3E6

Phone: 416.978.3499
E-mail: mba@rotman.utoronto.ca
Web site: www.rotman.utoronto.ca/mba

Dean: Roger L. Martin
Associate Dean and Executive Director: Richard C. Powers

"Formulaic approaches to problem solving are increasingly ineffective. Success in today's environment does not result from emulating others but from using organizational assets to build unique models, products, and experiences." —Dean Martin

Quick Facts

MBA Programs

Full-time MBA
Part-time MBA (morning program, evening program)
Executive MBA
Omnium Global Executive MBA (Rotman-University of St. Gallen)

Full-Time MBA Snapshot

Total enrollment: 537
Class of 2010: 262
Length of program: 20 months
Campus: Toronto, Ontario
Program commences in September
Pre-term orientation attendance required

Application Notes

Requirements: Full-time work experience with a record of accomplishment in employment; recognized undergraduate degree; essays; GMAT; GRE not accepted
Letters of recommendation: 2

(continued)

(continued)

Number of applicants: 1,103
Admittance rate: 46%

CLASS OF 2010 PROFILE

Male 71%, Female 29%
North Americans: 58%
International: 44%
Average age: 28
Combined average years of work experience: 4 years
GMAT score range (20th–80th percentile): 580–730
GMAT average: 653
GPA average: 3.4

ACADEMIC BACKGROUND OF INCOMING STUDENTS

Engineering: 39%
Life Sciences: 6%
Math/Computer Science: 6.5%
Social Sciences/Humanities: 15%
Other: 4%

At the Intersection of Commerce and Growth

The land on which the city of Toronto now stands was first claimed by French fur traders in 1615. Subsequently, they competed—for the next 145 years—with arriving British traders for control of the crucially situated region. When under British dominion from 1760 on, the original settlement changed from a military border command center during the Revolutionary War to a planned town by the harbor. The small town became the capital of Upper Canada with centralized government. The expanding population consequently created a city, and was officially named Toronto in 1834. In 1867, Toronto was designated the capital of the new Ontario province.

The Rotman School of Business has a long and illustrious history dating back to 1902 when the University of Toronto began offering undergraduate courses in management. The school introduced its Master of Commerce degree in 1938 and the Faculty of Management degree in 1971. Soon, the program's growth required a new home. Thanks to the support of the Rotman family, the school officially became the Joseph L. Rotman School of Management after the University matched their $15 million gift in 1997. To date, Rotman has donated $36 million to the school.

On campus at Rotman.

A Toronto native, Joseph Rotman, Canadian businessman and entrepreneur, received his Master of Commerce (MCom) degree from the University of Toronto in 1960. He continues to champion society's advancement as demonstrated by his appointment to the Canada Counsel for the Art in 2008. Rotman states, "I see my appointment as a unique opportunity to apply my skills and experience to something I care deeply about—keeping Canada at the forefront of cultural development. A half-century of public investment in the arts has helped make Canada a world leader on the artistic front, but few Canadians fully appreciate what arts and culture contribute to society, and how much more could be accomplished with additional investment." Rotman was inducted into the Canadian Business Hall of Fame in 2009.

Why Rotman?

Roger L. Martin became dean of the Rotman School of Management in 1998 and brought about a new era for the school. In 2000, he oversaw the advent of Integrative Thinking and a new model of business education for this century. Since then, Rotman has experienced great advancement, with a $50 million expansion housing the new Martin Prosperity Institute. The Jeffrey Skoll BASc/MBA program was created to join engineering undergrads with courses leading to an MBA.

The school is on the verge of an enormous upgrade. Classrooms with wireless networks will be incorporated into the new building to open in 2011. This initiative is funded by a five-year fundraising campaign for the $200 million expansion. The addition comprises not only the physical building but future support for Rotman's impressive depth of faculty and overall student graduate program. The government of Ontario alone is contributing $50 million, and other government funds have been committed for the effort. This is the largest business school fundraising campaign in Canadian history. The school is expected to double in size over the next few years.

Dean Roger Martin implemented the focus on integrative thinking skills to enable students to think like successful business leaders instead of spending much of their time on the fundamentals of business operations. In fact, through financial investments from Marcel Desautels, Canadian Credit Management Foundation's president, the Center for Integrative Thinking was established in 2000 and expanded in 2008 for the sole purpose of developing "a new way of thinking" for the business community.

Toronto is Canada's financial, commercial, and cultural capital. Students have access to business leaders who drop by regularly for presentations and events, and outstanding speakers are common. Toronto is consistently rated as one of the best cities in the world to live and has a reputation as a clean and safe metropolitan area.

The Rotman School is a home away from home for its students and the design is both functional and comfortable. Technologically equipped classrooms are just the tip of the iceberg. The true technological masterpiece is the Financial Research and Trading Lab, a state-of-the-art trading floor where students have access to a wide variety of financial analysis software packages and data sets and advanced computer hardware. The Trading Lab gives students the opportunity to experience the global financial community in a real-time setting. This hands-on approach better prepares students for the fast pace and competitiveness of the financial world. The Rotman Interactive Trader software (RIT) is an authentic simulation of a stock exchange. Users transact financial securities with each other in real time. RIT allows students to experience various trading options, including equities, fixed income, options, and futures.

In addition, the Toronto Public Library is home to the largest library system in Canada and the second most visited in the world (after Hong Kong's). On the University of Toronto campus, the Business Information Center is the library specifically for Rotman school students, and it has one of the latest electronic infrastructures. This includes Bloomberg and Reuters terminals—computer systems for finance and international marketing students. Robarts Library is named after former Ontario Premier John Robarts. It is the third largest academic library system in North America. The two largest are Harvard and Yale.

Rotman students have the opportunity to participate in the MBA International Exchange Program, which offers students full-term exchanges at 19 leading universities worldwide. Also, full-term international study tours are offered to second-year students that include visits to international businesses and also cultural and tourist activities, giving participants an intimate view of the economy and market they are visiting. Among the recent locations, students visited Africa, China, India, and Latin America.

FUN FACTS

- In 2008, Toronto's film industry made around $800 million. Past films with scenes at the University of Toronto include *Police Academy* (1984), *Urban Legend* (1994), *Tommy Boy* (1995), *Good Will Hunting* (1997), *Skulls* (2000), and *Mean Girls* (2004).

- Toronto's Yonge Street was created in 1796 and is often cited as the longest street in the world at 1,178 miles (1,896 kilometers). This would be true if some of its sections (Highway 11, York Regional Road 1, York Regional Road 51, and Simcoe County Road 4) were called Yonge Street. One end of the motorway starts on the edge of Lake Ontario, and the other end finishes beyond Lake Superior.

- Bay Street—Canada's equivalent to America's Wall Street—has three new buildings called the Murano (North and South) and the Burano. The Burano is a 48-story condominium complex. The Murano North, across the street, is a 36-story condominium complex. The Murano South, also across the street, has 43 stories. "Murano" and "Burano" share their names with two islands near Venice, Italy.

- Meetings are where managers do their most important work, according to Professor Minhea Moldoveanu, who estimates that you will attend some 40,000 in your career. If you make 10 significant contributions per meeting, over the course of your career, you will make 400,000 meaningful speech acts.

Course Offerings

Before beginning the rigors of the full-time MBA program, students are offered a pre-MBA session, which features refresher courses in Accounting, Finance, and Quantitative Methods. Professional skills workshops are available as well as orientation for international students. This is not the same as Orientation, which is a one-day Rotman school acclimation and a three-day event conducted mainly by second-year MBA candidates. In fact, the incoming class stays at a summer camp facility for three days of fun, fun, fun, and a bit of academic challenge, just to get your mind both relaxed and ready for the first-year program.

Your first year is similar to other MBA programs—a grounding in Financial Accounting, Organizational Management, Managerial Economics, Statistics, and the like. However, while you are mastering Negotiations, Strategy, Operations Management, Leadership, and so on, you are also learning Integrative Thinking. Along with the core curriculum, you have Foundations of Integrative Thinking and an Integrative Thinking Practicum.

The second year offers more than 80 electives to choose from and several majors, each with its own set of recommended courses. By the end of this year, you will have completed 10 electives from seven areas of focus (Accounting; Business Economics; Finance; Organizational Behavior and Human Resource Management; Marketing; Operations Management, Management Science and Statistics; and Strategic Management). In addition, Integrative Thinking maintains its ubiquitous presence.

And what is Integrative Thinking again? It is creative problem solving, step by step, to reach a decision that is uniquely suited to the issue at hand. "Salience," the first step, involves identifying what factors are important in your decision-making process. "Causality" is the second step and focuses on how these factors relate to each other. "Architecture" is step three, during which you use all your information to form possible models to address the issue. And last, step four, "Resolution," brings to bear the previous reasoning to reach a decision. The idea for a final decision, however, incorporates everything you have brought together—all variables—and creates a multidimensional, multifactored, multifaceted conclusion instead of eliminating variables to determine the right direction.

RESEARCH CENTERS

AIC Institute for Corporate Citizenship

Business Information Center

Capital Markets Institute

Center for Finance

Center for Management

Clarkson Center for Business Ethics and Board Effectiveness

Innovation in Accounting Education

Institute for International Business

International Center for Pension Institute for International Business

Marcel Desautels Center for Integrative Thinking

Teaching Effectiveness Center

What Admissions Is All About

Executive Director of Rotman's Corporate Connections Center Jeff Muzzerall says Rotman is different from other programs by how it moves beyond the fundamentals. "Our curriculum takes the core foundation of a traditional MBA (i.e., Finance, Marketing, Accounting, Economics, Statistics, Operations, Leadership) and seamlessly weaves the principles of Integrated Thinking and Business Design with real-time business events in order to enable our student to integrate and apply cutting edge theory and management practice to a constantly evolving business environment."

Admissions officers at Rotman advise you to take the opportunity to write your essays to tell your own story, who you are, where you want to be, and why. "Don't spend too much time trying to be who you think we want you to be. Be yourself," advises Cheryl Millington, director of MBA Recruitment and Admissions. Rotman's admissions department is looking for the next generation of great leaders. "We're an energetic school and we like to see our energy reflected in our students," she adds. Each part of an applicant is considered important to your overall fit with the school. Life experience, professional experience, school experience, and personal characteristics create a unique person who will become a management innovator at Rotman.

Potential applicants have the opportunity for building and class tours, to meet with student ambassadors (for international candidates, ambassadors are accessible by e-mail), and to meet the admissions team at recruitment events. Be sure to take advantage of as many of these activities as you can to understand the program first hand.

Full-time MBAs receiving financial aid through school: 75%

Institutional (merit-based and need-based) scholarships: 40

Assistantships: varies

Full-tuition scholarships school awarded for academic year: 5

Financially Aided

Each year the Rotman School grants approximately $4.2 million in entrance scholarships, fellowships, and awards. Scholarships are available and are based on merit, work experience, GMAT scores, essays ... the same criteria for admissions to the school. Some private companies also offer full or partial scholarships. Students in the full-time MBA program are eligible for a slew of scholarships with merit- and need-based (combined) requirements. For example, various financial support is directed specifically for students from Canada, Argentina, Australia, Colombia, Hong Kong, Indonesia, Japan, Korea, Romania, and Thailand. In 2008, in partnership with the Graduate Student Endowment Fund, two new scholarships were added. The Birch Hill Equity Partners Award is awarded to a Canadian student in the two-year MBA program. The George C. Vilim Scholarship in Effective Management is for MBA students who exhibit outstanding achievements in strategic management studies.

Scotiabank Interest-Subsidized Tuition and Laptop Loans are available, as are government loans. Federal loans for U.S. students include the Stafford, Perkins, and Federal Family Education Loan Program. Other options to finance your education are also available and can be part of your overall plan. Rotman's financial officers can coordinate a funding package with you.

FULL-TIME MBA PROGRAM (TOTAL DIRECT COSTS)

In-country: $64,550 USD

International: $81,225 USD

Part-time program cost: $66,650 USD (in-country); $86,955 USD (international)

Omnium GEMBA program cost: $76,130 USD

What Rotman Professors Teach

The key words again are Integrative Thinking. In addition to a core curriculum, Rotman courses focus on thinking outside the box, how to take calculated risks, and how to choose one best decision among many. Associate Dean Richard Powers explains, "Our graduate students are taught by some of the top academics in the world. As a result, they have a very strong academic base to work from. A significant portion of our graduating class is international students who bring a broad range of skills and interests to perspective employers. Many speak several languages, which makes them prime candidates for international postings." In comparison to many top programs, he continues, "Our students are better prepared to excel in today's changing business environment." They are taught by professors of great business renown and are introduced to other influential luminaries who visit often for conferences, seminars, and speaker's series. One class of 2009 student notes, "When I was considering grad schools, I found that Rotman was the best in finance in North America. Rotman faculty come from London Business School, Harvard Business School, and Tuck School of Business."

The Rotman School of Management has the most international faculty, 67 percent, of all top MBA programs worldwide.

Powers adds, "I teach Ethics to the first-year MBA students, and I would suggest that one of the most important concepts that we try to instill in our students is integrity. A focus throughout our MBA program is leadership and that requires intelligent, fair, and compassionate decision-making. Many of our courses require teamwork and again, this is an important aspect of any business environment. Acting ethically and responsibly may be catch phrases in today's business schools, but the concepts are treated very seriously here at the Rotman School."

One example of the high level of responsibility that Rotman professors maintain came from the Premier of Ontario, Dalton McGuinty. In 2008, he called upon Dean Martin and Professor Florida to study Ontario's global economic and workforce competitiveness. Richard Florida is highly recognized for his expertise in economic competitiveness, demographic trends, and cultural and technological innovation. After forming a research team, they studied these issues and provided Premier McGuinty with recommendations on how Ontario can prosper as a province and affect worldwide economic growth.

Faculty Facts

Full-time faculty employed by the b-school: 126

Adjunct or visiting faculty: 19

Permanent/tenured professors: 100

Tenured faculty who are women: 24

Tenured international faculty: 84

Sampling of Notable Professors

- John Hull: Globally recognized expert in risk management; voted as the academic "who has made the biggest contribution to the derivatives industry in the last five years" at the 2006 Global Derivatives Conference in Paris

- Anita McGahon: Senior associate at Harvard University's Institute for Strategy and Competitiveness; named by *CIO* magazine as one of five international experts on the strategic use of technology

- Joanne Oxley: Exceptional teacher and prolific researcher in organizational and performance of strategic alliances and joint ventures; member of the oldest and largest scholarly management association in the world, the Academy of Management

- Maria Rotundo: Pioneer in the areas of job performance evaluation, employee retention, leadership, and labor market skills-wage relationships

- Brian Silverman: Leading expert in strategic management; highly recognized worldwide for work involving the conjunction of strategy and economics

- Dilip Soman: World-renowned researcher in behavioral economics and marketing; winner of the Society for Consumer Psychology's Early Career Award in 2004

CONCENTRATIONS AND SPECIALIZATIONS OFFERED TO FULL-TIME MBA STUDENTS

Brand Management

Consulting

Entrepreneurship

Finance

Financial Engineering

Funds Management

Global Management

Healthcare Administration and Management

Human Resources Management

International Business

Investment Banking

Risk Management

JOINT DEGREES AND DUAL DEGREES

MBA/JD

MBA/BASc (Behavioral Science)

Collaborative Programs in Asia-Pacific Studies and Environmental Studies

What Rotman Students Know

For a student moving from New York City to Toronto, location was extremely important in Laurin Mayer's business school decision. "The opportunities are greater in this area and the location also made it easier to be connected to industry professionals," says Mayer. "The faculty is accessible, providing extra help whenever needed and the facilities are world-class." She adds, "The school is wireless, allowing students to work in any part of the building, which is vital when they spend as much time working on group projects and research as Rotman students do. Students have summer internships in their chosen field where their skills are utilized fully and they can gain work experience."

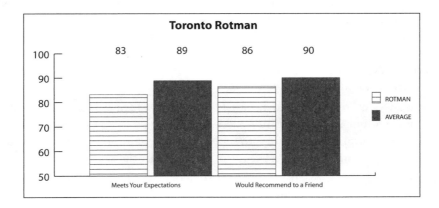

One of Mayer's classmates also touts the school's location. He expounds, "Toronto is a great financial and business city, and provides a lot of networking opportunities, international culture, and ways to meet different industry people." He adds that his pre-term orientation experience was "full of fun. We met with international students from more than 40 cultures, had lots of competition, met with alumni and second years, and had lunch with professors and university staff. The dean talked about the plans for a new building and upcoming events."

He continues, "Rotman's school philosophy is about integrative thinking—finding new solutions rather than choosing from existing options. This idea is well known but people find it somewhat difficult to swallow because of the difficulty in the implementation of the proposed solution."

Margi Moscoe, class of 2009, chose Rotman because of its "strong academic reputation, the international opportunities (such as study tours and exchanges), and its top faculty." She also points out the appeal of Dean Roger Martin's high profile and his innovative concepts. "Integrative Thinking and Business Design is at the forefront of business education." Moscoe was able to prepare for the two-year MBA program before starting her first class. "Orientation was a great way to get to know my fellow classmates in an informal setting, and Pre-term helped prepare me for the academics, especially Accounting and Finance courses."

What's Next? Your Career

Networking opportunities are plentiful before graduation and increase exponentially after graduation. Lifelong friendships are formed and alumni events are organized regularly. Fellow students, mentors, and faculty make Rotman a valuable experience as graduates re-enter the workforce and for years afterward. Rotman's Corporate Connections Center (CCC) is available to help with resume preparation, self-marketing, networking, and career coaching. Alumni receive lifelong support through the CCC and keep a job posting board as well as other resources to help as graduates progress in their chosen fields.

Jeff Muzzerall explains how the center supports students. "Our Career Center continuously collects data from our students in order to align their career aspirations with the most desirable companies globally. We then capitalize on the power of our alumni, faculty and career networks to make warm introductions and personalized requests to recruiters to gauge recruiting needs, identify fit and post their job opportunities to our students and alumni. We offer our recruiters highly specialized and personalized service at no expense."

Muzzerall continues, "Our recruiting partners tell us that our value premise is hard to beat. Our students bring outstanding analytical ability, excel at teamwork, have a can-do attitude. They are as highly attuned to the complexities required to succeed in multi-cultural, multi-national matrix organizations as small and medium enterprises requiring entrepreneurial savvy."

Associate Dean Powers comments, "It is important to understand that while the MBA designation indicates a certain level of attainment in the business education world, the programs at each school are quite different. The Rotman Program is holistic in its approach. While engaged in a demanding academic curriculum, our students benefit from additional opportunities for international study, case competitions, presentation skills and teamwork—all directed to provide the essential tools required by recruiters in their search for talent. In many respects we are judged by the product that we put onto the street. That said, recruiters continue to look to the Rotman School in their search for talent."

CAREER CHECK: ROTMAN MBA EMPLOYMENT BY JOB FUNCTION

- Finance/Accounting: 43%
- Consulting: 26%
- Financial (other): 12%
- Marketing: 10%
- General Management: 6%
- Human Resources: 1%
- Operations/Logistics: 1%
- Other: 1%

Mitchell Radowitz, class of 2000, chose Rotman for several reasons. "I was looking for an urban school with a good reputation. I liked that at the time it had a small class size—120 students in two sections. Also, Rotman is well connected to the business community and the prospect of getting work seemed much greater." Radowitz adds, "Dean Roger Martin was new that year and had great goals for the school, which was also very appealing."

Regarding his educational experience, Radowitz expounds, "When I was a student, the philosophy of Rotman was just transforming into what the school is today with its focus on Integrative Thinking. I am a true believer that having that philosophy woven into the curriculum helped me become a better employee and later a better manager. Rotman taught me to step back and assess situations before jumping to conclusions, resulting in better business and life decisions. I didn't take the traditional finance or consulting route that most students back in 2000 took once graduating. I went into industry and took the Rotman philosophies to each company I worked at. I think it helped me navigate my career along the way and led me to where I am today. I still use these skills as the base and I've added to them over the years with my different experiences."

Before graduating, Radowitz discovered the benefit of knowing Rotman alumni. "Another major way the school helped me was to teach me the importance of networking. The group of individuals I met while at Rotman will always be a resource for me and as the alumni representative for my class, I realized that all alumni are equally available to me or any Rotman graduate."

If Radowitz were to start over, he would have changed one factor: "I would have done a Law MBA. I have no regrets in choosing Rotman. I would do it again if I had the choice. What I value most from those two years are the amazing people I met. I have remained close to a group of people from there who are very good friends of mine today. The school experience also enabled me to venture out onto a career path that I never would have thought possible before moving to Toronto. While I believe I went to Rotman with a good head on my shoulders and common sense, the MBA program and the school helped me hone those skills and gave me a tool box filled with new concepts and insights that

I have been able to transfer into my jobs. I don't take things at face value and am always looking for creative ways to add value and improve efficiencies."

Coming from a family business in Montreal," Radowitz explains, "I never thought that other careers existed for me. The decision to go to Rotman put me on a path that I never would have been able to experience. I always knew we lived in this emerging global economy. Rotman allowed me to see the opportunities that were available to us if we chose to go that route. I expected to go to school, get a degree, and go back to Montreal and work. I got an eye-opening experience that put me on a path with many twists and turns, and I am having a great time navigating it and looking forward to my next challenge. All of this is possible because I chose to do my MBA at Rotman."

ALUMNI ACTUALS

MBA alumni worldwide: 11,000+

Business school alumni networking site: www.alumni.utoronto.ca/rotman

Current MBA students have access to the alumni database.

Chokks Natarajan, class of 2007, shares what he most valued about his graduate education. He reflects that it was "the course content, interaction with other students, practical application of concepts I learned in class, and, of course, the network of other MBA colleagues." He continues, "My MBA gave me a lot of soft skills along with the business coursework. I have achieved my goal of starting a post MBA career with a consulting firm." Natarajan now works at one of the largest information technology, management consulting, outsourcing, and professional services companies in the world. He explains that his employers "value my personal and communication skills, presentation ability, client readiness—all skills I learned because of my MBA." In addition, he discovered, among other things, the "importance of listening to other viewpoints, embracing diversity of thoughts and ideas, and analyzing the situation from all perspectives before coming to a conclusion" have aided his career advancement.

As an alum, Natarajan encourages current and future students to learn skills necessary to balance classroom learning and searching for postgraduate jobs through the on-campus recruiting process. He also suggests furthering their education on how to recruit future workplace staff, manage that staff, and retain good employees, all of which are essential in the work world.

Match Made in Heaven: Is the Rotman School of Management Right for You?

You are an ideal student if you

- Want to understand how to use opposing models to find solutions best suited to evolving business problems and issues.
- Have the potential to build on success you have already achieved in your field.
- Are interested in a balanced program that utilizes multiple teaching methods and venues.
- Seek a transformational learning experience, which prepares you for the complex, evolving business world.

University of Western Ontario Richard Ivey School of Business

1151 Richmond St. North
London, Ontario
Canada N6A 3K7

Phone: 519.661.3212
E-mail: mba@ivey.ca
Web site: www.ivey.uwo.ca/mba

Asia Campus
Hong Kong Convention and Exhibition Center
Phase 1, 5/F, 1
Harbour Road, Wanchai, Hong Kong

Phone: 852 2808 4488
E-mail: mba@ivey.ca
Web site: www.ivey.uwo.ca/mba

Dean: Carol Stephenson
Director, MBA Program: Rick Robertson

"To develop business leaders who think globally, act strategically and contribute to the societies in which they operate is the goal of the Ivey School of Business." —Dean Stephenson

Quick Facts

MBA PROGRAMS

Full-time MBA
Executive MBA
Executive MBA, Hong Kong
Accelerated MBA

FULL-TIME MBA SNAPSHOT

Total enrollment: 288
Class of 2010: 144
Length of program: 12 months
Campus location: London, Ontario
Program commences in May
Pre-term orientation attendance required

APPLICATION NOTES

Requirements: History of full-time employment; resume; recommendation letters; official transcripts; GMAT score; three to five essays; English proficiency score if applicable; GRE not accepted

Letters of recommendation: 2 or 3

Interview: By invitation only

Number of applicants: figure not released by school

Admittance rate: 30%–35%

CLASS OF 2010 PROFILE

Male 75%, Female 25%

Average age: 29

Average years of work experience: 4.5 years

GMAT score average: 650

GMAT score range (20th–80th percentile): 580–770

GPA average: 3.0

ACADEMIC BACKGROUND OF INCOMING STUDENTS

Arts: 10%

Business: 27%

Computer Science: 5%

Engineering: 33%

Law: 10%

Science: 11%

Other: 4%

A Canadian First, Now a Canadian Leader

London is a city in Southwestern Ontario, Canada, along the Quebec City–Windsor Corridor with a metropolitan area population of around 450,000. Known as the "forest city" because travelers had to pass through forest to reach it, London is in lower Middlesex County and approximately halfway between Toronto, Ontario, and Detroit, Michigan. The business school is named after Richard G. Ivey, a successful lawyer, businessman, and philanthropist. In 1948, Ivey became the first chairman of the Advisory Committee, which was critical in helping the school establish itself as a separate faculty and as the first national school of business.

Ivey also helped to lead the fund drive that made possible the building on campus. His interests extended beyond just building, though, and he financed the first Canadian MBA program, the first

---

Management Training Course, and the first doctorate program in Business. Ivey also generously donated to the school's Research Fund as well as to the continuing Plan for Excellence, which placed Western's Business School in a leadership position in Canada.

Scenes from Ivey.

Today, the University of Western Ontario's Richard Ivey School of Business is widely regarded as the prototypical case study school. Not only does the school base its educational approach on the case study method, but it is the world's largest producer of Asian business case studies and second largest overall in the world, next to Harvard Business School, for all other case studies. In 2006, the school expanded its pedagogical approach, combining case study with what it calls Cross-Enterprise Business Issues (CEBI), designed to emphasize the ways in which the fundamental areas of business come together in the real world. This approach teaches you the skills to recognize, understand, and act upon issues involving globalization, competition, productivity, and innovation. Many CEBI courses are team taught to promote learning across subject areas as well as to understand interdependent business functions.

Why Ivey?

Ivey helped pioneer the Cross-Enterprise Leadership approach to teaching and research. In addition, two in five of the school's 20,000 graduates carry the title of Chair, President, CEO, Vice Chair, Vice President, or Managing Director/Partner of their companies. Ivey has earned an international reputation for its teaching and research excellence and the high caliber of its students and faculty. And it was the first North American business school to open a permanent campus in Hong Kong.

Ivey seeks to create future leaders, and class of 2009 student Pat Giles has found that the school's philosophy "is more than a buzz term; it's the foundation for the academic experience at Ivey. It's about analyzing cases in a multi-disciplinary fashion, as opposed to viewing issues in silos or in isolation. Cross-Enterprise Leadership produces leaders who think outside traditional boundaries to solve business issues that span across numerous disciplines."

FUN FACTS

- London, Canada, and the surrounding area are collectively known as Southwestern Ontario. The cities of Toronto, Windsor, Detroit, Cleveland, and Buffalo are all within a 200-kilometer (125-mile) radius.
- Ivey Business School is home to *Ivey Business Journal*, Canada's leading magazine of business thought and management practice, as well as the prestigious *International Transactions in Operational Research*.
- London, Ontario, has a sister city (also known as a twin town): Nanjing, China.

Course Offerings

The core of the program focuses on three elements of Cross-Enterprise Leadership: thinking, acting, and leading. The first element focuses on understanding management and business thinking. Ivey wants to challenge the way future managers think about business. The second element focuses on action. A critical element before a manager can act is for him or her to understand the "anatomy" of an enterprise. There are a number of business processes, and by understanding these processes, managers can better understand how enterprises operate to create value. With this understanding, they can focus on how they should make decisions and operate at a Cross-Enterprise level. The third element focuses on leadership, gaining a Cross-Enterprise orientation and dealing with Cross-Enterprise issues. Once Ivey has broadened the way future managers think and provided a foundation of how businesses work, students will be ready to deal with issues by focusing on action and leadership, not merely "thinking" or understanding.

In terms of the international market, Career Services Director Sharon Irwin-Foulon says, "There are international study options for our students including the LEADER project, the China Teaching Project and the China Study trip, giving students the opportunity to immerse themselves in these international markets and learn about global issues and business practices. In addition, the GLOBE module in the MBA curriculum uses cases based on the most current and up-to-date global business issues; students learn to analyze and make decisions within a GLO-bal Business Environment (GLOBE)."

Admissions Director Niki Healey shares, "Our one-year program is the only one of its kind in Canada. This case-based method acts as a 'flight simulator' for students to analyze, communicate, and make decisions on real-world business issues in a risk-free environment. The Ivey MBA is designed to develop leaders and arm Ivey graduates for career success with an approach to learning that teaches students how to think strategically about issues that affect an organization as a whole—not just in functional areas. This prepares them to be leaders and managers who can think, act, and lead across a whole organization."

RESEARCH CENTERS

Asian Management Institute

Building Sustainable Value

Center for International Business Studies

Cheng Yu Tung Management Institute

Driving Growth Through
  Entrepreneurship and Innovation

Engaging Emerging Markets

ING Leadership Center

Institute for Entrepreneurship

Ivey Center for Health Innovation and
  Leadership (ICHIL), to come

Ivey Purchasing Managers Index

Lawrence Center

Leading Cross-Enterprise

Spencer Leadership Center

What Ivey Professors Teach

Ivey faculty members are world leaders in developmental research; they have made significant contributions toward global and national business practices. Finance Professor Jim Hatch notes, "Ivey has a heavy focus on the case method, which results in very active classroom contribution and a dynamic learning environment.... The success of this learning environment relies on admitting students with significant business experience." Hatch adds, "There is an extensive use of student study groups, so teamwork is an especially important piece of Ivey's MBA program."

Strategic Management Professor Mary Crossan explains, "I develop cases and have co-authored a strategy textbook designed to ensure that what we do in the classroom prepares the students for their future careers. Everything we do has that aim in mind. For example, I will have them apply the concepts of strategy to the strategy of a business they have been in, or are in, to identify gaps and an action plan to close them."

For each case, students step into the shoes of the decision maker (the CEO, CFO, Board Director, and so on) and solve the problem. Professors facilitate discussion, and as a class, students come up with solutions utilizing the tools that have been taught. Says Hatch, "Although students learn basic theories and frameworks as well as typical MBA tools, this is all taught within the environment likely to be faced by the practicing manager. Our method of instruction places the onus of learning on the students. We believe this reflects the real world in the sense that they will have to become used to lifelong learning in order to grow and develop after graduation."

Crossan remarks, "Unlike many business schools, literally decades of careful hiring have built a culture at Ivey where faculty believe that they can deliver more together than they can separately. Our profession tends to reward individual scholarship, and ours is a group of unique individuals who are inspired by the vision to truly make a difference. One needs a passion for both teaching and research, and a group of us continue to innovate to ensure that what we offer and how we do it continues to equip students for the leadership challenges they will face." Further, "We really try to prepare our students with deep insight into complex business issues, the capacity to deal with uncertainty and complexity, the confidence to excel, and a willingness and capability to express their ideas." She notes that this education applies to all future managers. "We go well beyond male and female learners since we are also dealing with multi-cultural differences, disciplinary differences, and learning style differences. Since we encourage diversity, we must also be mindful and capable of managing it."

Hatch notes, "We provide students with the core skills and knowledge to obtain a job, but more importantly we provide them with a platform for lifelong learning. We also concentrate on the ability to lead (from the top and the bottom) and an ability to address complexity through our cross-enterprise approach to education." And what he enjoys most about his colleagues is that, "We have a very strong culture of teamwork. We are all focused on teaching excellence within a teacher/scholar framework. We are all committed to a management point of view."

Faculty Facts

Full-time faculty employed by the b-school: 77

Adjunct or visiting faculty: 4

Permanent/tenured professors: 51

Tenured faculty who are women: 8

Tenured faculty who are underrepresented minorities: 21

Sampling of Notable Professors

- George Athanassakos: Accomplished and highly regarded scholar, currently serving on the Editorial Board of the *Canadian Investment Review*, *European Research Studies Journal*, and *Multinational Finance Journal*
- Pratima Bansal: Honored as Faculty Pioneer for Academic Leadership by the Aspen Institute Center for Business Education
- Jane Howell: Maintains the prestigious position of J. Allyn Taylor and Arthur H. Mingay Chair in Leadership and is a well-known expert on the topics of leadership and followership
- Robert Klassen: Received the 2008 Page Prize for Environment Sustainability Curriculum with his innovative course "Managing for Sustainability Development"; currently serves on the Editorial Review Board for the *Journal of Operations Management*
- Simon C. Parker: Noteworthy contributor to the study of entrepreneurship and renowned author of the book *The Economics of Entrepreneurship*

Concentrations and Specializations Offered in Full-Time MBA Program

Consulting

Corporate Strategy and Leadership

Entrepreneurship

Finance

Health Sector Management

Information Systems

(continued)

(continued)

International Management

Investment Banking

Marketing

Operations

Organizational Behavior

JOINT DEGREES AND DUAL DEGREES

Not applicable

What Admissions Is All About

The Ivey MBA Program is designed to develop leaders, and the Admissions department seeks prospective applicants who can contribute to and benefit from the Ivey experience. Leadership accomplishments, a strong commitment to achievement, diverse life experiences, and the desire for team-based learning are all valued in candidates. The case-based environment at Ivey is both engaging and challenging, and candidates should demonstrate the ability to succeed in a collaborative and highly interactive environment.

Niki Healey says, "Once an application is complete, it is reviewed by the admissions coordinator on our Recruiting and Admissions team. If the application looks strong, the candidate will be invited to interview with a member of our Admissions team. If the candidate is successful in this interview, he or she may be invited to interview with a member of our Career Management team. Once the interviews are completed, the entire file will be reviewed by our Admissions Committee and a final decision is made regarding an offer of admission." And while there has been an increase in the percentage of highly qualified Indian-born students applying to Ivey, both within the international population and as Canadian citizens, the selectivity for admissions into the full-time program is typically 30 to 35 percent.

According to Healey, many prospective MBAs look to Ivey because of "the case-method approach to learning, the student experience, the alumni network, and the Career Management department. The case-method approach puts students in the shoes of real decision makers dealing with real-world business issues. This provides a dynamic and action-oriented style of learning that prepares students to be leaders who can think strategically, act decisively, communicate persuasively, manage complexity, and maximize team potential."

Additionally, she notes, "The student experience both inside and outside of the classroom is second to none at Ivey. The diversity in the classroom and team-learning environment create a dynamic culture where students rely and depend on each other to maximize their experience during an intense one-year of learning. This creates a tight-knit classroom environment that spills over into social activities outside of the classroom. Not only are there countless ways for students to get involved in various clubs and organizations within the school, but the 'we're all in this together' attitude also creates a strong social circle outside of student activities, where life-long friendships are formed."

For Ivey undergraduates looking to transition into the MBA, "Ivey offers an Accelerated MBA program for those with an undergraduate degree from Ivey. However, these applicants must meet the same rigorous admissions criteria required from those who are applying for the full-time, one-year MBA—including a minimum two years of full-time work experience."

Healey points out, "Despite having minimum application criteria, we really don't have ideal applicants to the Ivey Program. We have ideal graduates."

Full-time MBAs receiving financial aid through school: 42%

Institutional (merit-based) scholarships: 110

Assistantships: none

Full-tuition scholarships school awarded for academic year: 1 to 5

Financially Aided

The cost of the program coupled with the absence of income is a significant commitment and, in turn, Ivey is committed to providing financial aid commensurate with the financial burden. Students may be asked to provide a financial guarantee statement confirming that they have sufficient funds to cover their living expenses and tuition while studying at Ivey.

Loans and grants are made available through the Canada Student Loan Program and Provincial Student Loan Programs to residents of Canada to help pay for students' education depending on need. The assistance through OSAP is available to citizens of Canada or landed immigrants who are residents of Ontario. In addition, Ivey has developed the MBA Loan Program in partnership with several Canadian banks to create attractive loan packages for Ivey candidates.

FULL-TIME MBA PROGRAM (TOTAL DIRECT COSTS)

In-state: $65,411 USD

Out-of-state: $75,227 USD

International: $75,227 USD

EMBA program costs: $75,858 USD

What Ivey Students Know

Ivey MBA classes are diverse, and students are committed to an intense year of study. Says Pat Giles, "When selecting prospective MBA programs, for me Ivey stood out from other business schools because of its overall reputation, its one-year program, and its case study teaching method." Giles adds,

"I didn't want an MBA from just any business school; I wanted an Ivey MBA. Ivey had everything I was looking for: a great location, an outstanding faculty, a renowned academic reputation, a lower opportunity cost due to the one-year program, and a proven track record in producing exceptional alumni."

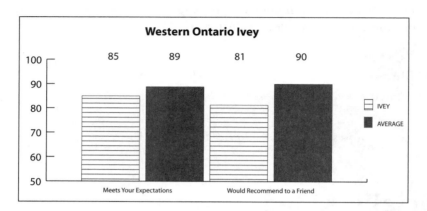

For Adwoa Mould-Mograbi, class of 2009, the location of Ivey was just as important. "Ivey is located in London, Ontario, a mid-sized city with a vibrant and active social scene. It is small enough to create a community, big enough to offer a full experience during the 12-month program, and close enough to Toronto for job interviews. The best parts are the affordable housing and living expenses, which reduce the financial burden on students." In terms of the pre-term/orientation experience, Giles found the "two-week Preparatory Knowledge Program (PKP), an excellent academic overview of the core skills required to begin the MBA program. It was a very useful course, especially for students who had been out of school for some time." Adds Mould-Mograbi, "The orientation experience included both formal and informal activities. The Ivey MBA Association, a student-run organization, sets up incoming students with an Ivey 'buddy,' a current student who is available to us to answer questions and help us get settled. This informal access gave us an opportunity to attend a number of events to get comfortable and acquainted with the school as quickly as possible."

Since the program is intensive, the relationships with the faculty are important and Giles finds that, "The faculty at Ivey is incredibly approachable and available. The level of engagement with students is very high, especially since the case study method promotes a great deal of communication with professors. Many students have found faculty members to be excellent mentors who collaborate with them on academic projects, business ventures, and personal undertakings." And in terms of networking and career services, he adds, "Since Ivey is a 12-month program, there is no formalized internship program. That said, there are plenty of opportunities for exposure with companies through Ivey's alumni partnership program."

Both students utilize the study and social spaces at Ivey quite frequently. Says Mould-Mograbi, "We have a private location that is fully networked and has 24-hour access for classrooms and study rooms. Also there is free parking, printing, a gym, and a diner. It is set up like a private club that provides a comfortable space for studying individually and in teams and the many extras (free coffee, tea, newspapers, friendly staff, free shuttle to the main campus) make it a one-of-a-kind experience." Additionally, "It's impossible to obtain an MBA from Ivey without growing as a person. Every experience is a learning experience and Ivey provides access to guest speakers, study trips, conferences, events, seminars and competitions that have introduced me to new ideas and new ways of thinking. The Ivey experience is intense as we grow in knowledge and ability but also in our perspective about how we can influence change in a positive way as a business leader. I have developed incredible self-confidence during this MBA journey and an unshakable belief in my own ability to build, manage, and lead a successful and thriving business enterprise."

Giles comments, "I never expected to learn so much from my peers; their experiences, knowledge, and insight have been invaluable to my experience at Ivey."

What's Next? Your Career

The Ivey Career Management department has a good reputation for responsive client service built on an ability to suggest tailored options that work for individual MBAs throughout the process. For Sharon Irwin-Foulon, "Real-world business experience is critical to get the most out of and contribute to a case study learning environment. Ivey acts as a 'flight simulator' for dealing with real-world business issues. This is an applied degree that has students in 'meetings' every day, contributing ideas and experiences to learn and build credibility and confidence in your leadership skill set."

Ivey maintains connections with both the local and national business communities. Iwin-Foulon maintains that, "All of the faculty, staff and students at the school are deeply involved in various initiatives in and around the city. This includes participating in pro-bono consulting projects, not for profit boards, and student initiatives such as Community Action Day … and Ivey Career Management has relationships with firms and organizations all over Canada who come to Ivey to recruit. In addition, Dean Carol Stephenson is very involved in various boards and initiatives on both a national and international scale. She currently serves on several boards for top Canadian companies and on important government committees."

The school attracts recruiters through initiatives such as Ivey's Relationship Management and Get Connected Week. Also, says Irwin-Foulon, "Our Corporate Development team consistently works to reach out, bring on board, and build relationships with new recruiting organizations who can benefit from the talent of Ivey grads." Just as important is the Alumni Partnership Program. "The student/alumni relationship is a very important one at Ivey, and a big part of the Ivey culture—there is a close camaraderie between Ivey students and alums, and they certainly rely on each other," says Irwin-Foulon. "It is incredibly rare that an alum would ever turn down an ask or invitation to meet a current student for coffee, or a quick phone call. Get Connected week is another formal way in which our students and alumni have the chance to connect, in addition to other CM programs that are related to coaching and prep into specific organizations. We also have many alumni guest speakers throughout the year."

CAREER CHECK: IVEY MBA EMPLOYMENT BY JOB FUNCTION

- Consulting: 37%
- Finance/Accounting: 24%
- Marketing/Sales: 15%
- General Management: 8%
- Operations/Production: 6%
- Other: 10%

ALUMNI ACTUALS

MBA alumni worldwide: 10,500+

Business school alumni networking site: www.ivey.ca/alumni/portal/

Current MBA students have access to the alumni database.

Ivey is the only Canadian business school with North American, European, and Asian Advisory Boards, 15 alumni ambassador chapters, and an Alumni Partnership Program designed to connect students with alumni who can help make a difference in their careers. One in four Ivey alumni is a senior executive in a company that spans every industry and every continent around the world. Through the Ivey Alumni Partnership Program, students partner with alumni, who in turn share career and business advice. The partnership allows students and alumni to network with new contacts—people who can provide career information that can lead to new career opportunities.

For Jon Saunders, class of 2007, "the networking environment that the Ivey Career Management department fosters is one that is relaxed and safe. Reaching out to alumni is made easier, and as a result, your network grows considerably as a student, and further as an alumnus. Through my networking experience at Ivey, not one alum ever refused to speak with me. Now that I am an alumnus, I take my responsibility seriously. Ivey's alumni network is powerful and grows stronger each year with a new wave of enthusiastic graduates. The focus on giving back ensures a welcoming community to those prospective students about to join."

Saunders believes that, "The experience I gained at Ivey exceeded my expectations. From an education perspective, the faculty members and industry visitors were world class. The highlight was when the Alumni Advisory Board participated in one of our classes. Canadian and International CEOs who are normally on TV were now sitting beside us, debating the price and feasibility of an international acquisition opportunity. It was incredibly powerful and beyond my imagination."

For Linda Liem, class of 2008, her Ivey MBA proved beneficial to her in that "employers tell me they value my hard work ethic and my ability to make valuable business connections.... I graduated in one of the worst economic times, and I was able to develop some amazing job leads. I eventually landed a position at a great firm. I did not expect to get the level of career coaching that I received from career management. It was more than a few mock interviews. I was able to call anyone at anytime and ask for advice on any job lead I had. Career Management helped guide me through every initial outreach, informational meeting, and interview, and provided me with insightful advice that I will take with me throughout my career."

Match Made in Heaven: Is the Ivey School of Business Right for You?

You are an ideal student if you

- Wish to approach business management using the concept of Cross-Enterprise Leadership of thinking, acting, and leading.
- Expect intellectual challenge through team learning, as well as understand how to be the solution, not the problem regardless of the situation.
- Want to be involved in a strong MBA alumni network with contacts worldwide.
- Seek to develop a high degree of confidence that will allow you to work with anyone.

ABOUT THE
ACCOMPANYING CD-ROM

Minimum system requirements for the accompanying CD-ROM: Pentium 4 2.0 GHz with 1 MB RAM, Internet Explorer 6.0 or Mozilla Firefox 1.6 or higher or Mac equivalent with high-speed Internet connection.

When you open your CD-ROM, you will be prompted to register on the AdmissionsConsultants Web site. Enter a valid e-mail address to receive your password. If you lose your password, you can request it again on the Web site. Within topmba.admissionsconsultants.com, you can create your own business school rankings. You can also compare the 31 schools across any school selection criteria if you wish to zero in on one or two key variables.

As you use the Web site, remember that your preferences reflect you and no one else. Your best fit depends on what learning environment is most compatible with you and what educational program you need to advance your career. While anyone can decide these things for you, you are attending the school. Only you are forging your career path. As an illustration of the importance of this concept, say you like to golf, and golf courses are important to you. Now let's say your friend is a hiker who prefers spending time on trails in forests. You both enjoy the outdoors. You both may describe your environments as "relaxing" or "exciting" or even "perfect." Are you and your friend describing the same place? No. Only one is relaxing, exciting, or perfect for you. The same is true for your MBA program.

This Web site is an excellent tool for introspection on what's really important to you. Essentially, the rankings are a weighted average formula. Begin your exploration by assigning percentages to what is most important to you. You may discover that your total percentages do not add up to 100. Perhaps your highest-rated factors are more important you thought. Conversely, if you go through the exercise and find that your total percentages exceed 100 percent (don't worry, the algorithm won't allow that to happen), you may have found more factors to include and then discovered the need to go back and adjust the weights of each category. Consider this rankings tool to be a taste of what awaits you in b-school, where you will learn how to quantify nearly everything to ensure that decisions are made optimally and objectively.

The selection tool allows you to exclude schools based on their geographic region, policy for accepting the GRE and GMAT, and program length. Only the 31 schools profiled in this book are included in the Web site database. Be aware that the more specific your requirements, the fewer schools that will come up in your results. If you receive fewer results than you would like, go back and reduce specificity (in other words, reduce your number of exclusion parameters).

B-school selection is a very serious matter and shouldn't be rushed. It's way too costly in terms of time and money. The difference between experiencing a good education and a life-altering one will make the time you spend now worth the effort. Additionally, it could help you accelerate your career because, as stated earlier, your chances of admission will be strongest where your fit is best.

The Web site uses AdmissionsConsultants' surveys, conversations with current students and alumni, visits to the campuses, and other primary and secondary research to assign values to most of the business school selection criteria. The data was then normalized by rescaling the top score, or scores in the event of a tie, to 100.

In addition to the database values, some of the categories are quite subjective. These are the preferred geographic region, campus setting, teaching method, graduating class size, specific versus general nature of the curriculum, and cooperative versus competitive study body. Rank your preferred geographic region, campus setting, and teaching method so that the highest preference is given a score of 100. For example, if you give your most preferred school setting a value of 60 and a 5 percent weighting in your school ranking (which is a weighted average), it would carry as much weight as another factor that had a 100 score to which you assigned a 3 percent weight. The other variables in the model are fact based (preferred graduating class size, specific versus general nature of the curriculum, and competitive versus cooperative student body), and you need only to enter your preferred value. The calculation will then rank the schools based on how close they come to your preferred point on the spectrum.

For a general category about which you are indifferent or have no opinion, assign it a weight of 0 percent. Fill in the "Other" category for any additional criterion you may find important to you. (You will have to provide that value for all of the selected schools.) "Other" can mean anything ranging from the practical (access to bus transportation) to the esoteric (number of Brazilian jiu jitsu dojos within a five-mile radius of campus).

Rankings appear in the book for "meets your expectations" and "would recommend to a friend" that do not appear in the rankings customization tool on the Web site. Because of the highly subjective nature of these metrics, they were not appropriate for the rankings algorithm. Instead, the algorithm allows you to determine more specific criteria for selecting a school (recruitability by region, curriculum strengths, and so on) that are only implicitly calculated within the two rankings that are exclusive to the book. This is also why you will see no perfect 100 scores in the school profile graphs; they use the raw data and don't need to be normalized.

Best of luck in your pursuit of a world-class business education!

Software Licensing Agreement

This is a legal agreement between you, the end user, and JIST Publishing, regarding your use of the *Top MBA Programs: Finding the Best Business School for You* CD-ROM and Web site subscription ("Software"). By using the Software, you agree to be bound by the terms of this agreement.

1. **Grant of License.** JIST hereby grants to you (an individual) the revocable, personal, non-exclusive, and nontransferable right to use the Software on one computer solely for your personal and non-commercial use. Sharing this Software with other individuals, or allowing other individuals to view the contents of this Software, is in violation of this license. You may not make the Software available on a network or in any way provide the Software to multiple users.

2. **Copyright.** The Software is owned by JIST and protected by United States and international copyright law. You may not remove or conceal any proprietary notices, labels, or marks from the Software.

3. **Restrictions on Use.** You may not, and you may not permit others to copy (other than one backup copy), distribute, publicly display, transmit, sell, rent, lease, or otherwise exploit the Software.

4. **Term of Agreement.** The term of this Agreement begins upon initial use of this Software and shall terminate 3 years from the date of purchase.

5. LIMITED WARRANTY

(A) FOR A PERIOD OF 30 DAYS FROM THE DATE OF PURCHASE, THE CD-ROM THAT CONTAINS THIS SOFTWARE IS WARRANTED TO BE FREE FROM DEFECTS IN MATERIAL AND WORKMANSHIP. IF THE MEDIA IS DEFECTIVE OR FAULTY IN WORKMANSHIP, YOU MAY RETURN THE MEDIA TO JIST WITH A WRITTEN DESCRIPTION OF THE DEFECT, AND JIST WILL REPLACE THE MEDIA WITHOUT CHARGE OR MAKE THE CONTENT AVAILABLE TO YOU ON-LINE. REPLACEMENT OF THE MEDIA IS YOUR SOLE AND EXCLUSIVE REMEDY AND JIST'S SOLE LIABILITY.

(B) EXCEPT FOR EXPRESS PROVISIONS IN PARAGRAPH (A), THE SOFTWARE AND ACCOMPANYING WRITTEN MATERIALS ARE PROVIDED ON AN "AS IS" BASIS, WITHOUT ANY WARRANTIES OF ANY KIND, INCLUDING, BUT NOT LIMITED TO, ANY IMPLIED WARRANTIES OF MERCHANTABILITY OR FITNESS FOR ANY PARTICULAR PURPOSE. NO ORAL OR WRITTEN INFORMATION OR ADVICE GIVEN BY JIST, ITS DEALERS, DISTRIBUTORS, AGENTS OR EMPLOYEES, SHALL CREATE A WARRANTY, OR IN ANY WAY INCREASE THE SCOPE OF THIS WARRANTY, AND YOU MAY NOT RELY ON ANY SUCH INFORMATION OR ADVICE. JIST DOES NOT WARRANT, GUARANTEE, OR MAKE ANY REPRESENTATIONS REGARDING THE USE OR THE RESULTS OF USE, OF THE SOFTWARE OR WRITTEN MATERIALS IN TERMS OF CORRECTNESS, ACCURACY, RELIABILITY, CURRENTNESS, OR OTHERWISE, AND THE ENTIRE RISK AS TO THE RESULTS AND PERFORMANCE OF THE SOFTWARE IS ASSUMED BY YOU. IF THE SOFTWARE OR WRITTEN MATERIALS ARE DEFECTIVE, YOU, AND NOT JIST OR ITS DEALERS, DISTRIBUTORS, AGENTS, OR EMPLOYEES, ASSUME THE ENTIRE COST OF ALL NECESSARY SERVICING, REPAIR, OR CORRECTION OTHER THAN EXPRESSLY DESCRIBED ABOVE.

(C) NEITHER JIST NOR ANYONE ELSE WHO HAS BEEN INVOLVED IN THE CREATION, PRODUCTION, OR DELIVERY OF THIS PRODUCT SHALL BE LIABLE FOR ANY DIRECT, INDIRECT, CONSEQUENTIAL, OR INCIDENTAL DAMAGES (INCLUDING DAMAGES FOR LOSS OF BUSINESS PROFITS, BUSINESS INTERRUPTION, LOSS OF BUSINESS INFORMATION, AND THE LIKE) ARISING OUT OF THE USE OR INABILITY TO USE SUCH PRODUCT OR RELATED TO THIS AGREEMENT, EVEN IF JIST HAS BEEN ADVISED OF THE POSSIBILITY OF SUCH DAMAGES. JIST SHALL NOT BE LIABLE TO YOU FOR ANY INDIRECT, SPECIAL, INCIDENTAL, OR CONSEQUENTIAL DAMAGES OR LOST PROFITS ARISING OUT OF OR RELATED TO THIS AGREEMENT OR YOUR USE OF THE SOFTWARE AND/OR THE RELATED DOCUMENTATION, EVEN IF JIST HAS BEEN ADVISED OF THE POSSIBILITY OF SUCH DAMAGES. IN NO EVENT SHALL JIST'S LIABILITY HEREUNDER, IF ANY, EXCEED THE PURCHASE PRICE PAID BY YOU FOR THE SOFTWARE AND BOOK.

6. **General.** This Agreement and any dispute under it will be governed by the laws of the State of Indiana and the United States of America, without regard to their conflict of laws principles. Both parties consent to the exclusive jurisdiction and venue of the federal and state courts in the county of Marion and the state of Indiana. This Agreement constitutes the entire agreement between you and JIST with respect to its subject matter, and supersedes other communication, advertisement, or understanding with respect to the Software. This Agreement may not be amended or modified except in a writing executed by both parties. If any provision of this Agreement is held invalid or unenforceable, the remainder shall continue in full force and effect. All provisions of this Agreement relating to disclaimers of warranties, limitation of liability, remedies, or damages, and JIST's ownership of the Software survive termination.

ACKNOWLEDGMENT

BY USING THE SOFTWARE, YOU ACKNOWLEDGE THAT YOU HAVE READ AND UNDERSTAND THE FOREGOING AND THAT YOU AGREE TO BE BOUND BY ITS TERMS AND CONDITIONS. YOU ALSO AGREE THAT THIS AGREEMENT IS THE COMPLETE AND EXCLUSIVE STATEMENT OF AGREEMENT BETWEEN THE PARTIES AND SUPERSEDES ALL PROPOSED OR PRIOR AGREEMENTS, ORAL OR WRITTEN, AND ANY OTHER COMMUNICATIONS BETWEEN THE PARTIES RELATING TO THE LICENSE DESCRIBED HEREIN.

INDEX

A

AACSB (Association to Advance Collegiate Schools of Business International), 8, 20

Abdelal, Rawi E., 184

academic requirements, determining fit, 25

acceptance letters
  admission etiquette, 73
  multiple acceptances, deciding among, 68–70

acceptance rates to schools, 12

accreditation, 8, 20

adjustment to business school environment. *See* transition to business school environment

admission etiquette, 73

admissions
  Anderson School of Management, 273–274
  Booth School of Business, 286–287
  Columbia Business School, 114
  Darden Graduate School of Business Administration, 373–374
  Fuqua School of Business, 149–150
  Goizueta Business School, 161–162
  Haas School of Business, 261–262
  Harvard Business School, 185–186
  IESE Business School, 444–445
  Indian School of Business, 409
  INSEAD Business School, 420–421
  Ivey School of Business, 470–471
  Johnson Graduate School of Management, 126–127
  Kelley School of Business, 198
  Kellogg School of Management, 236
  Kenan-Flagler Business School, 324
  London Business School, 434
  Marshall School of Business, 349–350
  McCombs School of Business, 361–362
  McDonough School of Business, 172–173
  Owen Graduate School of Management, 385–386
  Ross School of Business, 312
  Rotman School of Management, 456
  Sloan School of Management, 210
  Smith School of Business, 300
  Stanford Graduate School of Business, 249–250
  Stern School of Business, 222
  Tepper School of Business, 101
  Tuck School of Business, 138–139
  Wharton School of Business, 336–337
  Yale School of Management, 396

Agarwal, Ritu, 299

Agarwal, Sumit, 408

Ahaju, Guatam, 310

Alfred P. Sloan School of Management. *See* Sloan School of Management (MIT)

Almeida, Paul, 171

alternative transcripts, 39–40

Altman, Edward, 221

alumni resources
  Anderson School of Management, 277
  Booth School of Business, 291

Columbia Business School, 118–119

Darden Graduate School of Business Administration, 377–378

Fuqua School of Business, 153

Goizueta Business School, 165

Haas School of Business, 266

Harvard Business School, 189

IESE Business School, 448–449

Indian School of Business, 412–413

INSEAD Business School, 425

Ivey School of Business, 474

Johnson Graduate School of Management, 130

Kelley School of Business, 201

Kellogg School of Management, 241

Kenan-Flagler Business School, 327–328

London Business School, 437

Marshall School of Business, 353

McCombs School of Business, 365

McDonough School of Business, 177

networking tips for career development, 87–89

Owen Graduate School of Management, 390

Ross School of Business, 315–316

Rotman School of Management, 461–462

Sloan School of Management, 213

Smith School of Business, 303

Stanford Graduate School of Business, 253–254

Stern School of Business, 225–227

Tepper School of Business, 105

Tuck School of Business, 142

Wharton School of Business, 340

Yale School of Management, 401

AMBA (Association of MBAs), 20

Anderson School of Management (UCLA), 267–278

  admissions, 273–274

  alumni, role of, 277

  background, 268–269

  career services, 276–277

  class size, 14

  coursework, 271

  faculty, 272–273

  financial aid, 274–275

  fit, determining, 278

  geographic location, 22, 268–269

  quick facts, 267–268

  reasons for attending, 270–271

  student opinions, 275–276

  teaching style, 21

Andreasen, Alan R., 171

Andrews, Jonlee, 197

applications process

  backup plans, 65

  completion of, 58

  deadlines, 42–50

    determining, 44

    preparing for, 43

    timeline for meeting, 45–50

  essay writing. *See* essay writing

  final decisions

    admission etiquette, 73

    deciding among multiple acceptances, 68–70

    deferrals, 71–72

    receiving, 66, 68

    rejection letters, 72–73

    waitlist process, 70–71

  interviews. *See* interviews

monitoring after submission, 60–61

positioning yourself, 41

reapplication, assessing, 73

recommendations, 40–41

test scores

improving, 37–38

preparing for, 33–35

timing for pursuing MBA, 30–33

transcripts, 38

alternative transcripts, 39–40

when to request, 48

undergraduate school, effect of, 35–37

waiting after submission, 59–60

Argandona, Antonia, 443

Ariely, Dan, 149, 209

assertiveness in networking, 89

Association of MBAs (AMBA), 20

Association to Advance Collegiate Schools of Business International (AACSB), 8, 20

Athanassakos, George, 469

Ayres, Robert U., 419

B

backup plans for applications process, 65

Balachandran, Bala, 235

Balkrishnan, Anant, 360

Ball, Michael, 299

Bansal, Pratima, 469

Baron, James N., 397

Barth, Mary, 249

Bassock, Yehuda, 348

Bennis, Warren, 348

Berkeley. *See* Haas School of Business (University of California at Berkeley)

Bernardo, Anthony, 272

Bhattacharya, Utpal, 197

Bhide, Amarnath, 113

Bies, Robert J., 171

big-city schools, list of, 22

Biggadike, E. Ralph, 113

blind interviews, 63

blue-chip experience in MBA admissions policies, 15–16

Bodin, Lawrence, 299

Booth School of Business (University of Chicago), 7, 279–291

admissions, 286–287

alumni, role of, 291

background, 280–281

career services, 289–291

class size, 14

coursework, 283–284

faculty, 284–286

financial aid, 287–288

fit, determining, 291

geographic location, 22, 280–281

international study opportunities, 282–283

quick facts, 279–280

reasons for attending, 281–282

student opinions, 288–289

Borenstein, Severin, 260

"brand" school degrees, 8–9

Brandenburger, Adam, 221

Bruner, Robert F., 372

business schools (b-schools). *See* MBA schools

business simulation teaching style, 21

C

Capelli, Peter, 335

career development

    extracurricular activities, 85–86

    international study opportunities, 86

    networking tips, 87–89

    patience in, 89

    role of career services in, 87

career research during transition to business school environment, 80

career services

    Anderson School of Management, 276–277

    Booth School of Business, 289–291

    Columbia Business School, 117–119

    Darden Graduate School of Business Administration, 376–378

    determining fit, 24

    Fuqua School of Business, 152–153

    Goizueta Business School, 164–165

    Haas School of Business, 265

    Harvard Business School, 188–189

    IESE Business School, 447–449

    Indian School of Business, 412–413

    INSEAD Business School, 424–425

    Ivey School of Business, 473–475

    Johnson Graduate School of Management, 129–131

    Kelley School of Business, 200–202

    Kellogg School of Management, 240–241

    Kenan-Flagler Business School, 326–328

    London Business School, 436–437

    Marshall School of Business, 352–353

    McCombs School of Business, 364–365

    McDonough School of Business, 175–177

    Owen Graduate School of Management, 389–390

    role in career development, 87

    Ross School of Business, 314–316

    Rotman School of Management, 460–462

    Sloan School of Management, 212–214

    Smith School of Business, 303–304

    Stanford Graduate School of Business, 253–254

    Stern School of Business, 225–227

    Tepper School of Business, 104–105

    Tuck School of Business, 141–142

    Wharton School of Business, 339–340

    Yale School of Management, 400–401

Carnegie Mellon University. *See* Tepper School of Business (Carnegie Mellon University)

Carrington Cox, John, 209

case studies, importance of fit, 15–17

case study teaching style, 21

cell phones in classroom, rules for, 84

Chakrabarti, Rajesh, 408

Chatman, Jennifer, 260

cheating, avoiding, 84

Chicago, University of. *See* Booth School of Business (University of Chicago)

classroom test preparation, 34

Cochrane, John, 285

Cockrun, William, 273

cold calls, 83

collaboration

    at Smith School of Business, 295

    value of, 9, 85

Columbia Business School, 1, 107–119

    admissions, 114

    alumni, role of, 118–119

background, 108–109

career services, 117–119

class size, 14

coursework, 110–112

faculty, 112–114

financial aid, 115

fit, determining, 119

geographic location, 22, 108–109

international study opportunities, 110

quick facts, 107–108

reasons for attending, 109

student opinions, 116–117

computer skills, preparation for coursework, 81

concentrations

Anderson School of Management, 273

Booth School of Business, 286

Columbia Business School, 113

Darden Graduate School of Business
Administration, 373

Fuqua School of Business, 148

Goizueta Business School, 161

Haas School of Business, 260–261

Harvard Business School, 185

IESE Business School, 444

Indian School of Business, 408

INSEAD Business School, 420

Ivey School of Business, 469–470

Johnson Graduate School of Management, 126

Kelley School of Business, 198

Kellogg School of Management, 235

Kenan-Flagler Business School, 322

London Business School, 432

Marshall School of Business, 349

McCombs School of Business, 360

McDonough School of Business, 172

Owen Graduate School of Management, 385

Ross School of Business, 310

Rotman School of Management, 459

Sloan School of Management, 209

Smith School of Business, 299

Stanford Graduate School of Business, 248

Stern School of Business, 221

Tepper School of Business, 100

Tuck School of Business, 138

Wharton School of Business, 335

Yale School of Management, 397

concise writing, importance of, 57

convenience considerations, value of MBA, 9–10

Corbett, Charles, 273

Cornell University. *See* Johnson Graduate School
of Management (Cornell University)

cost. *See* tuition cost

coursework

Anderson School of Management, 271

Booth School of Business, 283–284

Columbia Business School, 110–112

Darden Graduate School of Business
Administration, 370–371

Fuqua School of Business, 147–148

Goizueta Business School, 158–159

Haas School of Business, 259

Harvard Business School, 182

IESE Business School, 442

Indian School of Business, 405–407

INSEAD Business School, 418

Ivey School of Business, 467

Johnson Graduate School of Management, 124

Kelley School of Business, 195–196

Kellogg School of Management, 231–232

Kenan-Flagler Business School, 321–322

London Business School, 430–432

Marshall School of Business, 346–347

McCombs School of Business, 358–359

McDonough School of Business, 169–170

Owen Graduate School of Management, 382–384

preparing for, 81

Ross School of Business, 308–309

Rotman School of Management, 455

Sloan School of Management, 206–207

Smith School of Business, 296–297

Stanford Graduate School of Business, 247–248

Stern School of Business, 219

Tepper School of Business, 99–100

Tuck School of Business, 136

Wharton School of Business, 333

Yale School of Management, 395–396

credit reports, 46–47

cultural diversity. *See* international study opportunities

curriculum, determining fit, 23

Czinkota, Michael R., 171

D

Daane, J. Dewey, 384

Damodaran, Aswath, 221

Darden Graduate School of Business Administration (University of Virginia), 1, 367–378

admissions, 373–374

alumni, role of, 377–378

background, 368–369

career services, 376–378

class size, 14

coursework, 370–371

faculty, 371–372

financial aid, 374

fit, determining, 378

geographic location, 23, 368–369

quick facts, 367–368

reasons for attending, 369–370

student opinions, 374–376

teaching style, 21

Dartmouth College. *See* Tuck School of Business (Dartmouth College)

deadlines for applications process, 42–50

determining, 44

preparing for, 43

timeline for meeting, 45–50

decision-making in applications process. *See* final decisions

Dees, J. Gregory, 149

deferrals, 71–72

Dermine, Jean, 419

Dhar, Ravi, 397

Dichev, Ilia, 310

distance-learning MBA programs, 10

draft stage of essay writing, 54–55

dropping out of MBA schools, reasons for, 44

dual degrees

Anderson School of Management, 273

Booth School of Business, 286

Columbia Business School, 114

Darden Graduate School of Business Administration, 373

Fuqua School of Business, 148

Goizueta Business School, 161

Haas School of Business, 261

Harvard Business School, 185

IESE Business School, 444

Indian School of Business, 408

INSEAD Business School, 420

Ivey School of Business, 470

Johnson Graduate School of Management, 126

joint degrees versus, 10

Kelley School of Business, 198

Kellogg School of Management, 235

Kenan-Flagler Business School, 322

London Business School, 432

Marshall School of Business, 349

McCombs School of Business, 361

McDonough School of Business, 172

Owen Graduate School of Management, 385

Ross School of Business, 310–311

Rotman School of Management, 459

Sloan School of Management, 209

Smith School of Business, 299

Stanford Graduate School of Business, 248

Stern School of Business, 222

Tepper School of Business, 100

Tuck School of Business, 138

Wharton School of Business, 336

Yale School of Management, 397

Duke University. *See* Fuqua School of Business (Duke University)

E

editing essays, 56–57

Edmondson, Amy C., 184

Edmondson Bell, Ella L. J., 137

Emory University. *See* Goizueta Business School (Emory University)

Engle, Robert, 221

English language proficiency tests, 25–26

EQUIS (European Quality Improvement System), 20

essay writing, 51–58

draft stage, 54–55

grammar and spelling, 56–57

humor in, 54

optional essays, 57

planning, 51–52

types of questions, 52

what to include, 29, 52–54

when to start, 45, 49

wow factor, 55

European Quality Improvement System (EQUIS), 20

exchange programs. *See also* international study opportunities

at IESE Business School, 440–441

at McCombs School of Business, 358–359

extracurricular activities

for career development, 85–86

determining fit, 23–24

F

faculty

Anderson School of Management, 272–273

Booth School of Business, 284–286

Columbia Business School, 112–114

Darden Graduate School of Business Administration, 371–372

determining fit, 23

Fuqua School of Business, 148–149

Goizueta Business School, 159–160

Haas School of Business, 259–260

Harvard Business School, 183–184

IESE Business School, 442–444

Indian School of Business, 407–408

INSEAD Business School, 418–419

Ivey School of Business, 468–469

Johnson Graduate School of Management, 124–125

Kelley School of Business, 196–197

Kellogg School of Management, 233–235

Kenan-Flagler Business School, 322–323

London Business School, 432–433

Marshall School of Business, 348–349

McCombs School of Business, 359–360

McDonough School of Business, 170–172

Owen Graduate School of Management, 384–385

Ross School of Business, 309–311

Rotman School of Management, 457–458

Sloan School of Management, 208–209

Smith School of Business, 297–299

Stanford Graduate School of Business, 248–249

Stern School of Business, 220–221

Tepper School of Business, 102–103

Tuck School of Business, 136–138

Wharton School of Business, 334–335

Yale School of Management, 397–398

Fader, Peter, 335

FAFSA (Free Application for Federal Student Aid), 47

Fama, Eugene, 286

final decisions

admission etiquette, 73

deferrals, 71–72

multiple acceptances, deciding among, 68–70

receiving, 66, 68

rejection letters, 72–73

waitlist process, 70–71

financial aid, 46–47

Anderson School of Management, 274–275

Booth School of Business, 287–288

Columbia Business School, 115

Darden Graduate School of Business Administration, 374

Fuqua School of Business, 150

Goizueta Business School, 162–163

Haas School of Business, 262–263

Harvard Business School, 186–187

IESE Business School, 445–446

Indian School of Business, 409–410

INSEAD Business School, 421–422

Ivey School of Business, 471

Johnson Graduate School of Management, 127–128

Kelley School of Business, 198–199

Kellogg School of Management, 236–237

Kenan-Flagler Business School, 325

London Business School, 434–435

Marshall School of Business, 350

McCombs School of Business, 362

McDonough School of Business, 173–174

Owen Graduate School of Management, 386–387

Ross School of Business, 312–313

Rotman School of Management, 456–457

Sloan School of Management, 210–211

Smith School of Business, 300–301

Stanford Graduate School of Business, 250–251

Stern School of Business, 222–223

Tepper School of Business, 101–102

Tuck School of Business, 139–140

Wharton School of Business, 337–338

Yale School of Management, 398–399

financial aspects of transition to business school, 77–78

fit, 1–2, 11–17

at Anderson School of Management, 278

at Booth School of Business, 291

case study, 15–17

at Columbia Business School, 119

at Darden Graduate School of Business Administration, 378

determining, 18–26

accreditation, 20

personal priorities, 19

rankings, 19–20

school profiles, 21–24

school requirements, 25–26

teaching styles, 21

at Fuqua School of Business, 154

at Goizueta Business School, 165

at Haas School of Business, 266

at Harvard Business School, 190

at IESE Business School, 450

importance of, 13–15

at Indian School of Business, 413

at INSEAD Business School, 426

at Ivey School of Business, 475

at Johnson Graduate School of Management, 131

at Kelley School of Business, 202

at Kellogg School of Management, 242

at Kenan-Flagler Business School, 328

at London Business School, 437

at Marshall School of Business, 353

at McCombs School of Business, 366

at McDonough School of Business, 177

at Owen Graduate School of Management, 390

at Ross School of Business, 317

at Rotman School of Management, 463

at Sloan School of Management, 214

at Smith School of Business, 304

at Stanford Graduate School of Business, 254

at Stern School of Business, 227

at Tepper School of Business, 106

at Tuck School of Business, 142

at Wharton School of Business, 341

at Yale School of Management, 401

for-profit schools versus not-for-profit schools, 7–8

Forbes, Kristin J., 209

Frank, Howard, 299

Frank, Robert H., 125

Free Application for Federal Student Aid (FAFSA), 47

Froeb, Luke, 384

Fu, Michael, 299

Fuqua School of Business (Duke University), 143–154

admissions, 149–150

alumni, role of, 153

background, 144–145

career services, 152–153

class size, 14

coursework, 147–148

faculty, 148–149

financial aid, 150

fit, determining, 154

geographic location, 22, 144–145

quick facts, 143–144

reasons for attending, 145–147

student opinions, 150–151

G

Galloway, Scott, 221

Gass, Saul, 299

Georgetown University. *See* McDonough School of Business (Georgetown University)

Ghemawat, Pankaj, 444

global studies. *See* international study opportunities

GMAT

improving, 37–38

preparing for, 33–35

Goffee, Rob, 433

Goizueta Business School (Emory University), 155–165

admissions, 161–162

alumni, role of, 165

background, 156–157

career services, 164–165

class size, 13

coursework, 158–159

faculty, 159–160

financial aid, 162–163

fit, determining, 165

geographic location, 22, 156–157

quick facts, 155–156

reasons for attending, 157–158

student opinions, 163–164

Golden, Bruce, 299

Goodfriend, Marvin, 103

Govindarajan, Vijay, 138

GPA

improving, 37–38

transcripts and, 38

Graduate School of Business (GSB). *See* Stanford Graduate School of Business

grammar, checking in essays, 56–57

Gratton, Lynda, 433

GRE, preparing for, 33–35

Green, Rick, 103

Greenwald, Bruce, 113

GSB (Graduate School of Business). *See* Stanford Graduate School of Business

H

Haas School of Business (University of California at Berkeley), 255–266

admissions, 261–262

alumni, role of, 266

background, 256–257

career services, 265

class size, 14

coursework, 259

faculty, 259–260

financial aid, 262–263

fit, determining, 266

geographic location, 23, 256–257

quick facts, 255–256

reasons for attending, 257–258

student opinions, 263–264

Hamada, Robert, 7

Harrigan, Kathryn, 113

Harrington, John Richard, 209

Harvard Business School, 1, 178–190

acceptance rates to, 12

admissions, 185–186

alumni, role of, 189

background, 179–180

career services, 188–189

class size, 14

Cornell University, comparison with, 11

coursework, 182

faculty, 183–184

financial aid, 186–187

fit, determining, 190

geographic location, 22, 179–180

leadership qualities wanted, 16

quick facts, 178–179

reasons for attending, 180–182

student opinions, 187–188

teaching style, 21

Harvey, Campbell, 149

Haunschild, Pamela, 360

Hennessy, Julie, 235

Hess, Edward D., 372

Ho, Teck, 260

Hofmann, David A., 323

housing, arranging for, 78–80

Howell, Jane, 469

Huber, George, 360

Hull, John, 458

humor in essays, 54

I

IELTS (International English Language Testing System), 25

IESE Business School (University of Navarra), 438–450

admissions, 444–445

alumni, role of, 448–449

background, 439–440

career services, 447–449

class size, 14

coursework, 442

faculty, 442–444

financial aid, 445–446

fit, determining, 450

geographic location, 22, 439–440

quick facts, 438–439

reasons for attending, 441–442

student opinions, 446–447

teaching style, 21

incidental influences, effect on decision-making, 25

Indian School of Business (ISB), 402–413

admissions, 409

alumni, role of, 412–413

background, 403–404

career services, 412–413

class size, 14

coursework, 405–407

faculty, 407–408

financial aid, 409–410

fit, determining, 413

geographic location, 22, 403–404

quick facts, 402–403

reasons for attending, 404–405

student opinions, 410–411

Indiana University. *See* Kelley School of Business (Indiana University)

informed interviews, 63

INSEAD Business School, 414–426

admissions, 420–421

alumni, role of, 425

background, 415–416

career services, 424–425

class size, 14

coursework, 418

faculty, 418–419

financial aid, 421–422

fit, determining, 426

geographic location, 22–23, 415–416

quick facts, 414–415

reasons for attending, 416–417

student opinions, 422–424

institutes. *See* research centers

institutional accreditation, 20

International English Language Testing System (IELTS), 25

international students, visa applications, 66

international study opportunities. *See also* exchange programs; IESE Business School (University of Navarra); Indian School of Business (ISB); INSEAD Business School; Ivey School of Business (University of Western Ontario); London Business School; Rotman School of Management (University of Toronto)

at Booth School of Business, 282–283

for career development, 86

at Columbia Business School, 110

at Sloan School of Management, 207–208

at Smith School of Business, 296

at Tepper School of Business, 98–99

interviews

avoiding common mistakes, 64–65

blind interviews, 63

informed interviews, 63

invitations for, 61

preparing for, 62–64

scheduling, 49

stress interviews, 62

invitations for interviews, 61

ISB. *See* Indian School of Business (ISB)

Ivey School of Business (University of Western Ontario), 464–475

admissions, 470–471

alumni, role of, 474

background, 465–466

career services, 473–475

class size, 13

coursework, 467

faculty, 468–469

financial aid, 471

fit, determining, 475

geographic location, 23, 465–466

quick facts, 464–465

reasons for attending, 466–467

student opinions, 471–473

teaching style, 21

Ivy League schools, effect on applications process, 36

J

Jacoby, Sanford, 273

Jarrow, Robert, 125

Johnson Graduate School of Management (Cornell University), 120–131

admissions, 126–127

alumni, role of, 130

background, 121–123

career services, 129–131

class size, 14

coursework, 124

faculty, 124–125

financial aid, 127–128

fit, determining, 131

geographic location, 23, 121–123

Harvard Business School, comparison with, 11

quick facts, 120–121

reasons for attending, 123–124

student opinions, 128–129

Johnson, James H., 323

Johnson, M. Eric, 137

joint degrees

Anderson School of Management, 273

Booth School of Business, 286

Columbia Business School, 114

Darden Graduate School of Business Administration, 373

dual degrees versus, 10

Fuqua School of Business, 148

Goizueta Business School, 161

Haas School of Business, 261

Harvard Business School, 185

IESE Business School, 444

Indian School of Business, 408

INSEAD Business School, 420

Ivey School of Business, 470

Johnson Graduate School of Management, 126

Kelley School of Business, 198

Kellogg School of Management, 235

Kenan-Flagler Business School, 322

London Business School, 432

Marshall School of Business, 349

McCombs School of Business, 361

McDonough School of Business, 172

Owen Graduate School of Management, 385

Ross School of Business, 310–311

Rotman School of Management, 459

Sloan School of Management, 209

Smith School of Business, 299

Stanford Graduate School of Business, 248

Stern School of Business, 222

Tepper School of Business, 100

Tuck School of Business, 138

Wharton School of Business, 336

Yale School of Management, 397

Joseph L. Rotman School of Management. *See* Rotman School of Management (University of Toronto)

K

Kallapur, Sanjay, 408

Kanter, Rosabeth M., 184

Katz, Michael, 260

Kazanjian, Robert K., 160

Keller, Kevin Lane, 137

Kelley School of Business (Indiana University), 191–202

admissions, 198

alumni, role of, 201

background, 192–193

career services, 200–202

class size, 14

coursework, 195–196

faculty, 196–197

financial aid, 198–199

fit, determining, 202

geographic location, 23, 192–193

interview requirements, 61

quick facts, 191–192

reasons for attending, 193–195

student opinions, 199–200

teaching style, 21

Kellogg School of Management (Northwestern University), 1, 228–242
  acceptance rates to, 12
  admissions, 236
  alumni, role of, 241
  background, 229–230
  career services, 240–241
  class size, 14
  coursework, 231–232
  faculty, 233–235
  financial aid, 236–237
  fit, determining, 242
  geographic location, 23, 229–230
  quick facts, 228–229
  reasons for attending, 230–231
  student opinions, 238–239
  undergraduate school representation, 36
Kenan-Flagler Business School (University of North Carolina at Chapel Hill), 318–328
  admissions, 324
  alumni, role of, 327–328
  background, 319–320
  career services, 326–328
  class size, 14
  coursework, 321–322
  faculty, 322–323
  financial aid, 325
  fit, determining, 328
  geographic location, 23, 319–320
  quick facts, 318–319
  reasons for attending, 320–321
  student opinions, 325–326
Kets de Vries, Manfred, 419
Kim, W. Chan, 419
Klassen, Robert, 469

Kogut, Bruce, 419
Kotler, Philip, 235
Kumar, Nirmalya, 433
Kuratko, Donald F., 197
Kyle, Albert "Pete", 299

L

Lave, Lester, 103
LBS. *See* London Business School
Leamer, Edward, 273
leaving workplace, 76–77
lecture teaching style, 21
Lee, Hau, 249
Leland, Hayne, 260
Leonard N. Stern School of Business. *See* Stern School of Business (New York University)
Lichtenburg, Frank, 113
loans for financial aid, 47
Logan, Dave, 348
London Business School, 427–437
  admissions, 434
  alumni, role of, 437
  background, 428–429
  career services, 436–437
  class size, 14
  coursework, 430–432
  faculty, 432–433
  financial aid, 434–435
  fit, determining, 437
  geographic location, 22, 428–429
  quick facts, 427–428
  reasons for attending, 429–430
  student opinions, 435–436
London, Ted, 310

M

Macher, Jeffrey T., 172

Mahajan, Vijay, 360

majors. *See* concentrations; specializations

Markides, Costas, 433

Marshall School of Business (University of Southern California), 342–353

    admissions, 349–350

    alumni, role of, 353

    background, 343–344

    career services, 352–353

    class size, 14

    coursework, 346–347

    faculty, 348–349

    financial aid, 350

    fit, determining, 353

    geographic location, 22, 343–344

    quick facts, 342–343

    reasons for attending, 344–345

    student opinions, 351–352

Maryland, University of. *See* Smith School of Business (University of Maryland)

Massachusetts Institute of Technology (MIT). *See* Sloan School of Management (MIT)

Mauborgne, Renee, 419

MBA degree, value of, 6–10

    accreditation, 8

    "brand" school degrees, 8–9

    collaboration and teamwork, 9

    convenience considerations, 9–10

    for-profit versus not-for-profit schools, 7–8

    return on investment, 31–32

MBA schools

    acceptance rates to, 12

    class sizes, 13–14

    dropping out of, 44

    fit. *See* fit

    researching, 24

McCombs School of Business (University of Texas at Austin), 354–366

    admissions, 361–362

    alumni, role of, 365

    background, 355–356

    career services, 364–365

    class size, 14

    coursework, 358–359

    faculty, 359–360

    financial aid, 362

    fit, determining, 366

    geographic location, 22, 355–356

    quick facts, 354–355

    reasons for attending, 356–358

    student opinions, 363–364

McDonough School of Business (Georgetown University), 166–177

    admissions, 172–173

    alumni, role of, 177

    background, 167–168

    career services, 175–177

    class size, 14

    coursework, 169–170

    faculty, 170–172

    financial aid, 173–174

    fit, determining, 177

    geographic location, 22, 167–168

    quick facts, 166–167

    reasons for attending, 168–169

    student opinions, 174–175

McGahon, Anita, 458

Meltzer, Allan, 103

Metrick, Andrew, 397

Michigan, University of. *See* Ross School of Business (University of Michigan)

mid-size city schools, list of, 22

mid-tier MBA programs, value of, 9

MIT (Massachusetts Institute of Technology). *See* Sloan School of Management (MIT)

Mitchell, Olivia, 335

Mitchell, Will, 149

monitoring applications after submission, 60–61

Moore, Jeffrey H., 249

Morgan, John, 260

Morici, Peter, 299

multiple acceptances, deciding among, 68–70

Murphy, Kevin, 286

N

Navarra, University of. *See* IESE Business School (University of Navarra)

Nelson, Mark W., 125

networking tips for career development, 87–89

New York University. *See* Stern School of Business (New York University)

North Carolina, University of. *See* Kenan-Flagler Business School (University of North Carolina at Chapel Hill)

Northwestern University. *See* Kellogg School of Management (Northwestern University)

not-for-profit schools versus for-profit schools, 7–8

O

O'Hara, Maureen, 125

online application accounts, 48–49

online MBA programs versus not-for-profit schools, 7–8

opinions. *See* student opinions about school

optional essays, 57

organization skills, 83–85

out-of-the-way schools, list of, 23

Owen Graduate School of Management (Vanderbilt University), 379–390

admissions, 385–386

alumni, role of, 390

background, 380–381

career services, 389–390

class size, 13

coursework, 382–384

faculty, 384–385

financial aid, 386–387

fit, determining, 390

geographic location, 22, 380–381

quick facts, 379–380

reasons for attending, 381–382

student opinions, 387–389

teaching style, 21

Owens, David, 384

Oxley, Joanne, 458

P

Palepu, Krishna G., 184

Palmrose, Zoe-Vonna, 349

Parker, Simon C., 469

part-time MBA programs, 9

partner schools

at Columbia Business School, 111

at Indian School of Business, 406–407

at London Business School, 431

at Owen Graduate School of Management, 383–384

partnerships. *See* research centers

Patell, James, 249

patience in networking, 89

Pedler, Mike, 310

peer recommendations, 49

Pennsylvania, University of. *See* Wharton School of Business (University of Pennsylvania)

personal fit. *See* fit

Pfeffer, Jeffrey, 249

Porter, Michael E., 184

Portes, Richard, 433

Powell, Stephen, 138

Prahalad, C. K., 310

priorities, determining fit, 19

proofreading essays, 56–57

Puri, Manju, 149

Q–R

quantitative skills, preparation for coursework, 81

Ramachandran, Kavil, 408

rankings, determining fit, 19–20

Rao, Vithala R., 125

Ravi, Shamika, 408

reapplication, assessing, 73

Rebelo, Sergio, 235

recommendations

in applications process, 40–41

when to start, 47, 49

rejection letters, 72–73

rejections with encouragement to reapply, 72

Renart, Lluis, 444

research centers

Anderson School of Management, 271

Columbia Business School, 112

Darden Graduate School of Business Administration, 371

Fuqua School of Business, 148

Harvard Business School, 183

INSEAD Business School, 418

Ivey School of Business, 467

Kelley School of Business, 196

Kellogg School of Management, 232

Kenan-Flagler Business School, 322

London Business School, 432

Marshall School of Business, 347

McDonough School of Business, 170

Ross School of Business, 310–311

Rotman School of Management, 456

Stern School of Business, 220

Tepper School of Business, 98

Tuck School of Business, 137

Wharton School of Business, 333

Yale School of Management, 396

researching

business schools, 24

careers, during transition to business school environment, 80

return on investment of MBA degree, 31–32

Richard Ivey School of Business. *See* Ivey School of Business (University of Western Ontario)

Robert E. McDonough School of Business. *See* McDonough School of Business (Georgetown University)

Robert H. Smith School of Business. *See* Smith School of Business (University of Maryland)

Rosanas, Josep Maria, 444

Rosensweig, Jeffrey A., 160

Ross School of Business (University of Michigan), 1, 305–317

   admissions, 312

   alumni, role of, 315–316

   background, 306–307

   career services, 314–316

   class size, 14

   coursework, 308–309

   faculty, 309–311

   financial aid, 312–313

   fit, determining, 317

   geographic location, 23, 306–307

   quick facts, 305–306

   reasons for attending, 307–308

   student opinions, 313–314

Rotman School of Management (University of Toronto), 451–463

   admissions, 456

   alumni, role of, 461–462

   background, 452–453

   career services, 460–462

   class size, 14

   coursework, 455

   faculty, 457–458

   financial aid, 456–457

   fit, determining, 463

   geographic location, 22, 452–453

   quick facts, 451–452

   reasons for attending, 453–455

   student opinions, 459–460

   teaching style, 21

Rotundo, Maria, 458

Roubini, Nouriel, 221

Rubinstein, Mark, 260

Rugman, Alan M., 197

Rust, Roland, 299

S

salary differences for MBA with/without work experience, 31–32

sample essays, whether to read, 53

Sange, Peter, 209

S.C. Johnson Graduate School of Management. *See* Johnson Graduate School of Management (Cornell University)

scheduling interviews, 49

Schipper, Katherine, 149

school profiles, determining fit, 21–24

school rankings, determining fit, 19–20

school requirements, determining fit, 25–26

school selectivity, 2

Schrager, James, 285

self-study test preparation, 34

Shackelford, Douglas A., 323

Shanken, Jay, 160

Shore, James, 384

Siegel, Jeremy, 335

Silverman, Brian, 458

Sloan School of Management (MIT), 203–214

   admissions, 210

   alumni, role of, 213

   background, 204–205

   career services, 212–214

   class size, 14

   coursework, 206–207

   faculty, 208–209

   financial aid, 210–211

   fit, determining, 214

   geographic location, 22, 204–205

international study opportunities, 207–208

peer recommendations, 40

quick facts, 203–204

reasons for attending, 205–206

student opinions, 211–212

small-town schools, list of, 23

Smith School of Business (University of Maryland), 292–304

  admissions, 300

  alumni, role of, 303

  background, 293–294

  career services, 303–304

  class size, 13

  collaboration and hands-on learning, 295

  coursework, 296–297

  faculty, 297–299

  financial aid, 300–301

  fit, determining, 304

  geographic location, 23, 293–294

  international study opportunities, 296

  quick facts, 292–293

  reasons for attending, 294–295

  student opinions, 301–302

social aspects of transition to business school, 77–78

Soman, Dilip, 458

Sonnenfeld, Jeffrey A., 397

Sood, Ashish, 160

Southern California, University of. *See* Marshall School of Business (University of Southern California)

specializations

  Anderson School of Management, 273

  Booth School of Business, 286

  Columbia Business School, 113

  Darden Graduate School of Business Administration, 373

  Goizueta Business School, 161

  Haas School of Business, 260–261

  Harvard Business School, 185

  IESE Business School, 444

  Indian School of Business, 408

  INSEAD Business School, 420

  Ivey School of Business, 469–470

  Johnson Graduate School of Management, 126

  Kelley School of Business, 198

  Kellogg School of Management, 235

  Kenan-Flagler Business School, 322

  London Business School, 432

  Marshall School of Business, 349

  McCombs School of Business, 360

  Owen Graduate School of Management, 385

  Ross School of Business, 310

  Rotman School of Management, 459

  Sloan School of Management, 209

  Smith School of Business, 299

  Stanford Graduate School of Business, 248

  Stern School of Business, 221

  Tepper School of Business, 100

  Tuck School of Business, 138

  Wharton School of Business, 335

  Yale School of Management, 397

specialized accreditation, 20

spelling, checking in essays, 56–57

Spiro, Rosann L., 197

standardized test scores. *See* test scores

Stanford Graduate School of Business, 1, 243–254

  acceptance rates to, 12

  admissions, 249–250

alumni, role of, 253–254

background, 244–245

career services, 253–254

class size, 14

coursework, 247–248

faculty, 248–249

financial aid, 250–251

fit, determining, 254

geographic location, 22, 244–245

intellectual qualities wanted, 16

quick facts, 243–244

reasons for attending, 245–247

student opinions, 251–252

undergraduate school representation, 36

Stanford University. *See* Stanford Graduate School of Business

Stephen M. Ross School of Business. *See* Ross School of Business (University of Michigan)

Stern School of Business (New York University), 215–227

admissions, 222

alumni, role of, 225–227

background, 216–217

career services, 225–227

class size, 14

coursework, 219

faculty, 220–221

financial aid, 222–223

fit, determining, 227

geographic location, 22, 216–217

quick facts, 215–216

reasons for attending, 217–218

student opinions, 223–224

teaching style, 21

Stoll, Hans, 384

stress interviews, 62

Stuart, Toby E., 184

student loans, 47

student opinions about school

Anderson School of Management, 275–276

Booth School of Business, 288–289

Columbia Business School, 116–117

Darden Graduate School of Business Administration, 374–376

Fuqua School of Business, 150–151

Goizueta Business School, 163–164

Haas School of Business, 263–264

Harvard Business School, 187–188

IESE Business School, 446–447

Indian School of Business, 410–411

INSEAD Business School, 422–424

Ivey School of Business, 471–473

Johnson Graduate School of Management, 128–129

Kelley School of Business, 199–200

Kellogg School of Management, 238–239

Kenan-Flagler Business School, 325–326

London Business School, 435–436

Marshall School of Business, 351–352

McCombs School of Business, 363–364

McDonough School of Business, 174–175

Owen Graduate School of Management, 387–389

Ross School of Business, 313–314

Rotman School of Management, 459–460

Sloan School of Management, 211–212

Smith School of Business, 301–302

Stanford Graduate School of Business, 251–252

Stern School of Business, 223–224

Tepper School of Business, 103–104

Tuck School of Business, 140–141

Wharton School of Business, 338–339

Yale School of Management, 399–400

student profiles, determining fit, 24

Studer-Ellis, Erich, 299

Swaminathan, Jayashankar M., 323

T

teaching styles, determining fit, 21

team project teaching style, 21

teamwork. *See* collaboration

technology in classroom, rules for, 84

Teece, David, 260

Tepper School of Business (Carnegie Mellon University), 95–106

    admissions, 101

    alumni, role of, 105

    background, 96–97

    career services, 104–105

    class size, 14

    coursework, 99–100

    faculty, 102–103

    financial aid, 101–102

    fit, determining, 106

    geographic location, 22, 96–97

    international study opportunities, 98–99

    quick facts, 95–96

    reasons for attending, 97–98

    student opinions, 103–104

    teaching style, 21

Test of English as a Foreign Language (TOEFL), 25

Test of English for International Communication (TOEIC), 25–26

test scores

    improving, 37–38

    preparing for, 33–35

Texas, University of. *See* McCombs School of Business (University of Texas at Austin)

time management, 83–85

timeline for meeting application deadlines, 45–50

timing for pursuing MBA, 30–33

TOEFL (Test of English as a Foreign Language), 25

TOEIC (Test of English for International Communication), 25–26

top-tier MBA programs, value of, 8–9

Toronto, University of. *See* Rotman School of Management (University of Toronto)

town schools, list of, 23

Towry, Kristy, 160

transcripts, 38

    alternative transcripts, 39–40

    when to request, 48

transition to business school environment

    career research during, 80

    financial and social aspects, 77–78

    housing and transportation, 78–80

    leaving workplace, 76–77

    preparation for coursework, 81

    time management, 83–85

transportation, arranging for, 78–80

Tuck School of Business (Dartmouth College), 132–142

    admissions, 138–139

    alumni, role of, 142

    background, 133–134

    career services, 141–142

class size, 14

coursework, 136

faculty, 136–138

financial aid, 139–140

fit, determining, 142

geographic location, 23, 133–134

interview requirements, 61

quick facts, 132–133

reasons for attending, 134–135

student opinions, 140–141

teaching style, 21

undergraduate school representation, 36

tuition cost

Anderson School of Management, 275

Booth School of Business, 287–288

Columbia Business School, 115

Darden Graduate School of Business Administration, 374

Fuqua School of Business, 150

Goizueta Business School, 163

Haas School of Business, 263

Harvard Business School, 187

IESE Business School, 446

Indian School of Business, 410

INSEAD Business School, 422

Ivey School of Business, 471

Johnson Graduate School of Management, 128

Kelley School of Business, 199

Kellogg School of Management, 237

Kenan-Flagler Business School, 325

London Business School, 435

Marshall School of Business, 350

McCombs School of Business, 362

McDonough School of Business, 174

Owen Graduate School of Management, 387

Ross School of Business, 313

Rotman School of Management, 457

Sloan School of Management, 211

Smith School of Business, 301

Stanford Graduate School of Business, 251

Stern School of Business, 223

Tepper School of Business, 102

Tuck School of Business, 140

Wharton School of Business, 338

Yale School of Management, 399

tutors for test preparation, 34

U

UCLA (University of California at Los Angeles). *See* Anderson School of Management (UCLA)

Ulrich, Dave, 310

undergraduate school, effect on applications process, 35–37

University of California at Berkeley. *See* Haas School of Business (University of California at Berkeley)

University of California at Los Angeles (UCLA). *See* Anderson School of Management (UCLA)

University of Chicago. *See* Booth School of Business (University of Chicago)

University of Maryland. *See* Smith School of Business (University of Maryland)

University of Michigan. *See* Ross School of Business (University of Michigan)

University of Navarra. *See* IESE Business School (University of Navarra)

University of North Carolina at Chapel Hill. *See* Kenan-Flagler Business School (University of North Carolina at Chapel Hill)

University of Pennsylvania. *See* Wharton School of Business (University of Pennsylvania)

University of Southern California. *See* Marshall School of Business (University of Southern California)

University of Texas at Austin. *See* McCombs School of Business (University of Texas at Austin)

University of Toronto. *See* Rotman School of Management (University of Toronto)

University of Virginia. *See* Darden Graduate School of Business Administration (University of Virginia)

University of Western Ontario. *See* Ivey School of Business (University of Western Ontario)

Useem, Michael, 335

Uzzi, Brian, 235

V

value of MBA, 6–10
    accreditation, 8
    "brand" school degrees, 8–9
    collaboration and teamwork, 9
    convenience considerations, 9–10
    for-profit versus not-for-profit schools, 7–8
    return on investment, 31–32

Van Wassenhove, Luk, 419

Vanderbilt University. *See* Owen Graduate School of Management (Vanderbilt University)

Vincent, Linda, 235

Virginia, University of. *See* Darden Graduate School of Business Administration (University of Virginia)

visa applications, 66

visiting schools
    after acceptance, 68–70
    during applications process, 48

W

waiting process after submitting applications, 59–60

waitlist process, 70–71

Walker, Robyn, 349

Walter A. Haas School of Business. *See* Haas School of Business (University of California at Berkeley)

Wedell-Wedellsborg, Thomas, 444

Weingart, Laurie, 103

Welch, Jack, 209

Wellington, Sheila, 221

Werhane, Patricia H., 372

Western Ontario, University of. *See* Ivey School of Business (University of Western Ontario)

Whaley, Robert, 385

Whang, Seungjin, 249

Wharton School of Business (University of Pennsylvania), 329–341
    acceptance rates to, 12
    admissions, 336–337
    alumni, role of, 340
    background, 330–331
    career services, 339–340
    class size, 14
    coursework, 333
    faculty, 334–335
    financial aid, 337–338
    fit, determining, 341
    geographic location, 22, 330–331
    quick facts, 329–330
    reasons for attending, 331–332
    student opinions, 338–339
    well-rounded qualities wanted, 16

Whinston, Andrew, 360

Wilcox, Ronald T., 372

work experience

    deferrals to obtain, 72

    effect on salary expectations, 31–32

    importance in applications process, 30–31

workplace, leaving on good terms, 76–77

wow factor in essay writing, 55

X–Z

Yale School of Management (SOM), 391–401

    admissions, 396

    alumni, role of, 401

    background, 392–393

    career services, 400–401

    class size, 13

    coursework, 395–396

    faculty, 397–398

    financial aid, 398–399

    fit, determining, 401

    geographic location, 22, 392–393

    quick facts, 391–392

    reasons for attending, 393–395

    student opinions, 399–400

Young, S. Mark, 349

Zeithaml, Valarie, 323

Zettelmeyer, Florian, 260

Zimjewski, Mark, 285